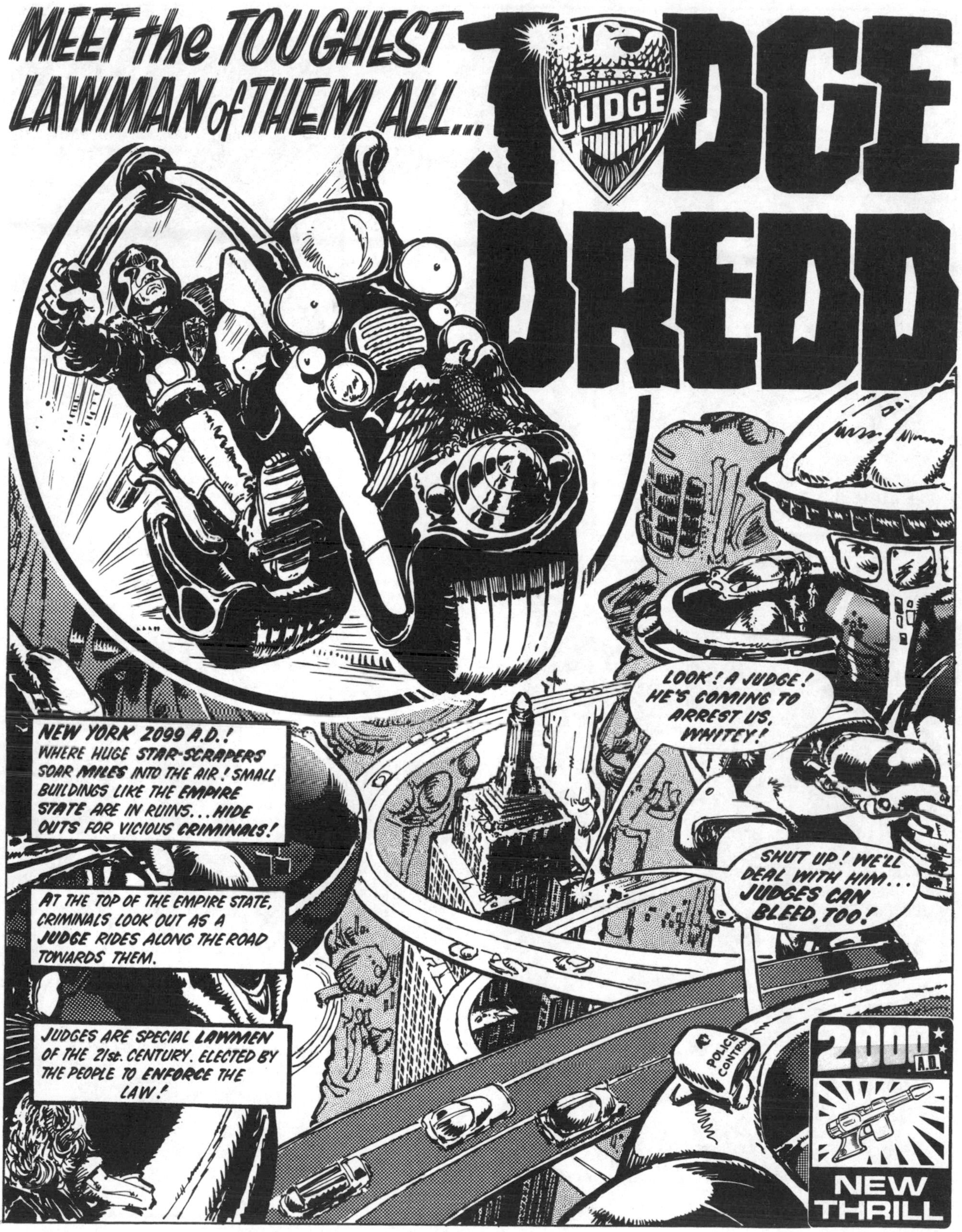
MEET the TOUGHEST LAWMAN of THEM ALL...
JUDGE
JUDGE DREDD
NEW YORK 2099 A.D.! WHERE HUGE STAR-SCRAPERS SOAR MILES INTO THE AIR! SMALL BUILDINGS LIKE THE EMPIRE STATE ARE IN RUINS... HIDE OUTS FOR VICIOUS CRIMINALS!
LOOK! A JUDGE! HE'S COMING TO ARREST US, WHITEY!
AT THE TOP OF THE EMPIRE STATE, CRIMINALS LOOK OUT AS A JUDGE RIDES ALONG THE ROAD TOWARDS THEM.
SHUT UP! WE'LL DEAL WITH HIM... JUDGES CAN BLEED, TOO!
JUDGES ARE SPECIAL LAWMEN OF THE 21st. CENTURY. ELECTED BY THE PEOPLE TO ENFORCE THE LAW!
POLICE CONTR
2000 A.D.
NEW THRILL

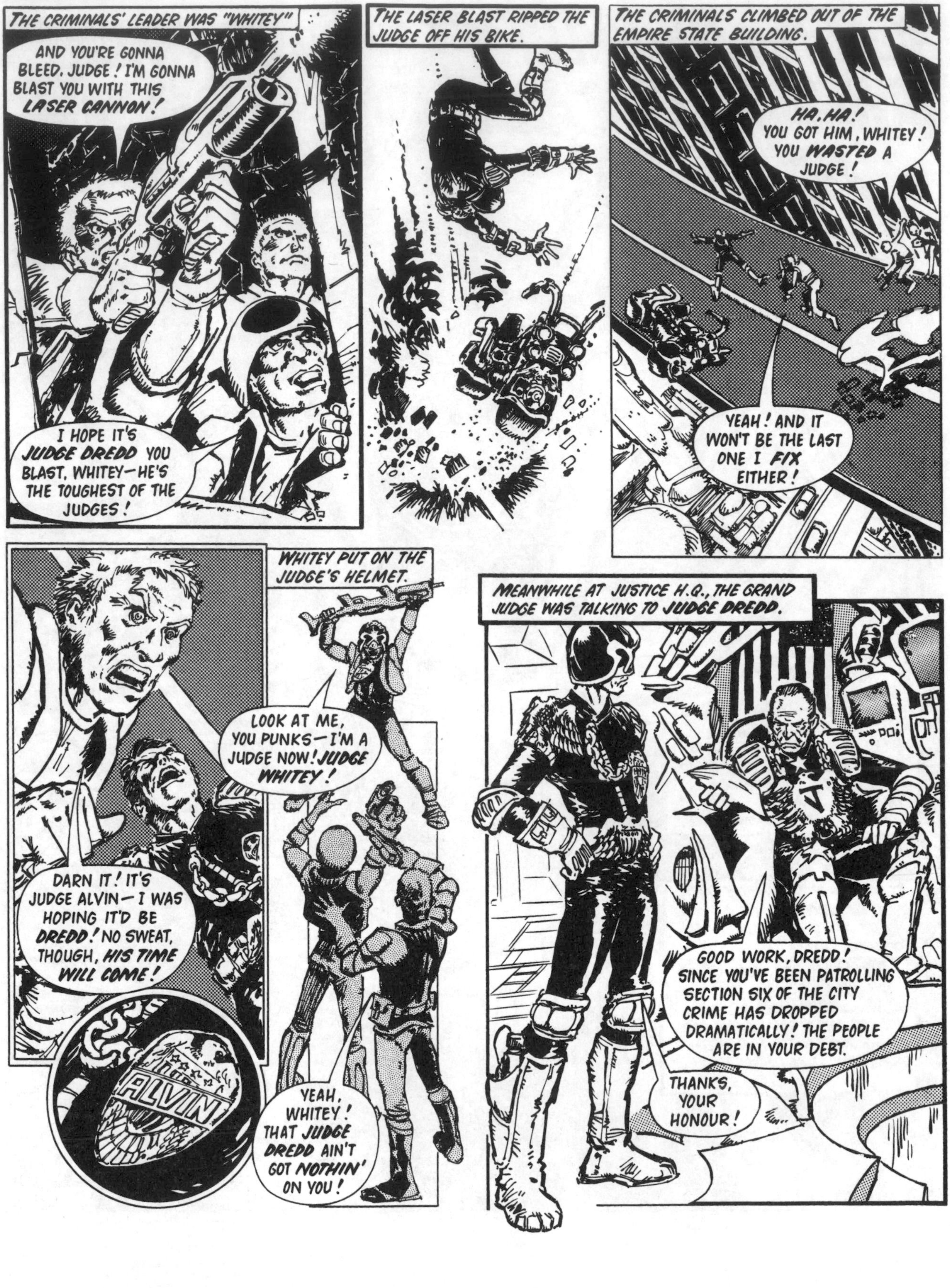
THE CRIMINALS' LEADER WAS "WHITEY"
AND YOU'RE GONNA BLEED, JUDGE! I'M GONNA BLAST YOU WITH THIS LASER CANNON!
I HOPE IT'S JUDGE DREDD YOU BLAST, WHITEY—HE'S THE TOUGHEST OF THE JUDGES!
THE LASER BLAST RIPPED THE JUDGE OFF HIS BIKE.
THE CRIMINALS CLIMBED OUT OF THE EMPIRE STATE BUILDING.
HA, HA! YOU GOT HIM, WHITEY! YOU WASTED A JUDGE!
YEAH! AND IT WON'T BE THE LAST ONE I FIX EITHER!
DARN IT! IT'S JUDGE ALVIN—I WAS HOPING IT'D BE DREDD! NO SWEAT, THOUGH, HIS TIME WILL COME!
ALVIN
WHITEY PUT ON THE JUDGE'S HELMET.
LOOK AT ME, YOU PUNKS—I'M A JUDGE NOW! JUDGE WHITEY!
YEAH, WHITEY! THAT JUDGE DREDD AIN'T GOT NOTHIN' ON YOU!
MEANWHILE AT JUSTICE H.Q., THE GRAND JUDGE WAS TALKING TO JUDGE DREDD.
GOOD WORK, DREDD! SINCE YOU'VE BEEN PATROLLING SECTION SIX OF THE CITY CRIME HAS DROPPED DRAMATICALLY! THE PEOPLE ARE IN YOUR DEBT.
THANKS, YOUR HONOUR!

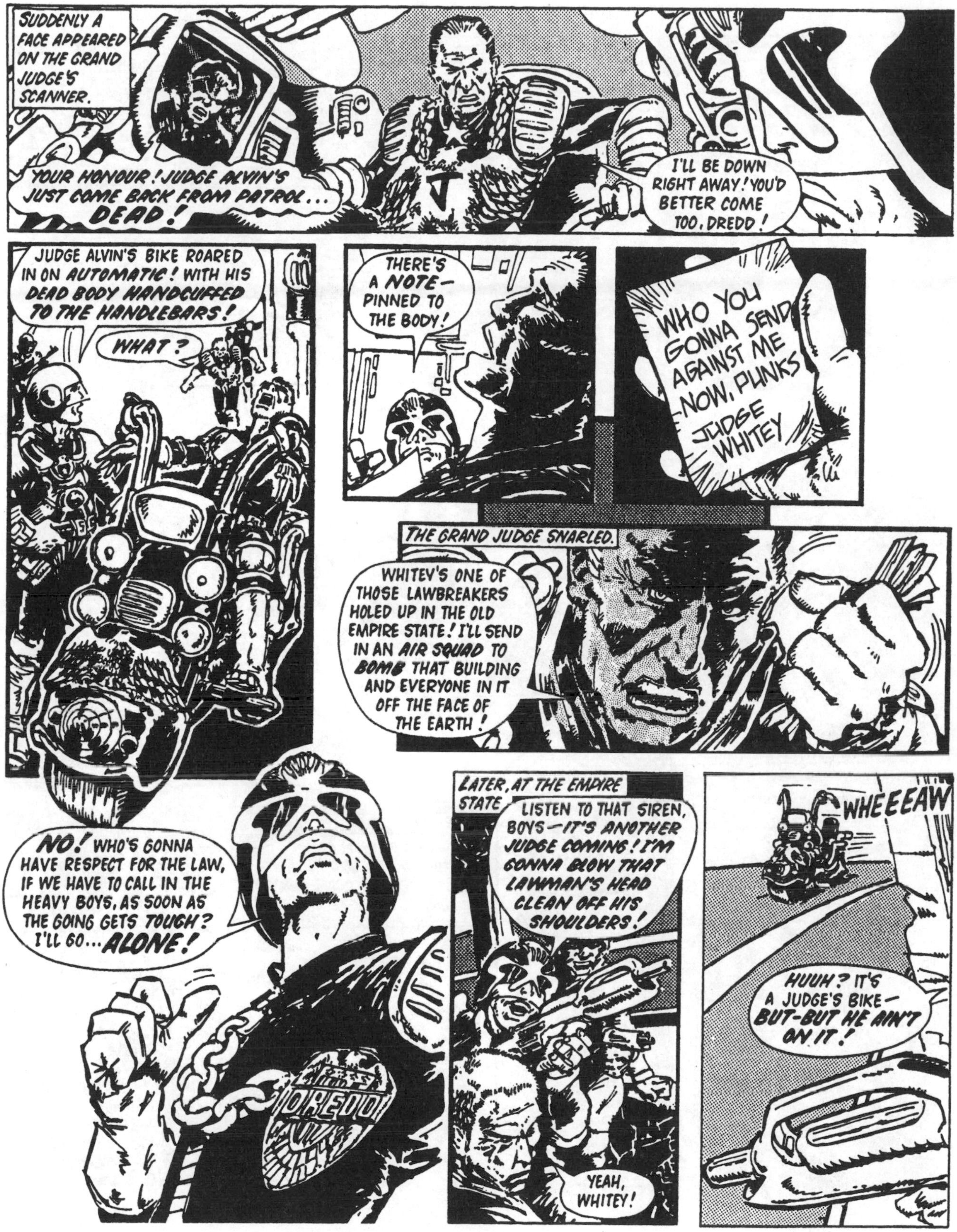
SUDDENLY A FACE APPEARED ON THE GRAND JUDGE'S SCANNER.
YOUR HONOUR! JUDGE ALVIN'S JUST COME BACK FROM PATROL... DEAD!
I'LL BE DOWN RIGHT AWAY! YOU'D BETTER COME TOO, DREDD!
JUDGE ALVIN'S BIKE ROARED IN ON AUTOMATIC! WITH HIS DEAD BODY HANDCUFFED TO THE HANDLEBARS!
WHAT?
THERE'S A NOTE— PINNED TO THE BODY!
WHO YOU GONNA SEND AGAINST ME NOW, PUNKS
JUDGE WHITEY
THE GRAND JUDGE SNARLED.
WHITEY'S ONE OF THOSE LAWBREAKERS HOLED UP IN THE OLD EMPIRE STATE! I'LL SEND IN AN AIR SQUAD TO BOMB THAT BUILDING AND EVERYONE IN IT OFF THE FACE OF THE EARTH!
NO! WHO'S GONNA HAVE RESPECT FOR THE LAW, IF WE HAVE TO CALL IN THE HEAVY BOYS, AS SOON AS THE GOING GETS TOUGH? I'LL GO... ALONE!
LATER, AT THE EMPIRE STATE
LISTEN TO THAT SIREN, BOYS—IT'S ANOTHER JUDGE COMING! I'M GONNA BLOW THAT LAWMAN'S HEAD CLEAN OFF HIS SHOULDERS!
YEAH, WHITEY!
WHEEEAW
HUUH? IT'S A JUDGE'S BIKE— BUT-BUT HE AIN'T ON IT!

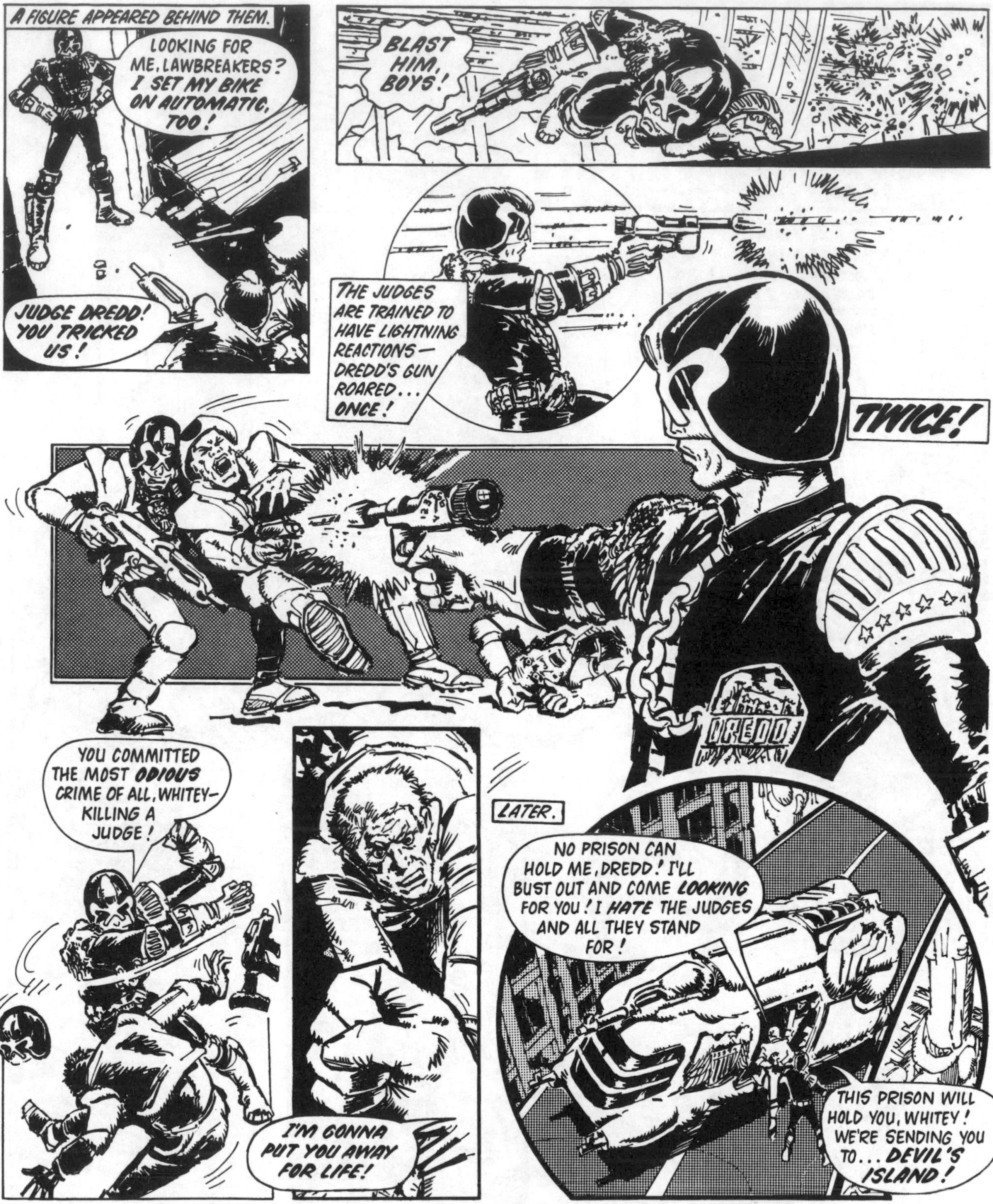
A FIGURE APPEARED BEHIND THEM.
LOOKING FOR ME, LAWBREAKERS? I SET MY BIKE ON AUTOMATIC, TOO!
JUDGE DREDD! YOU TRICKED US!
BLAST HIM, BOYS!
THE JUDGES ARE TRAINED TO HAVE LIGHTNING REACTIONS— DREDD'S GUN ROARED... ONCE!
TWICE!
YOU COMMITTED THE MOST ODIOUS CRIME OF ALL, WHITEY- KILLING A JUDGE!
I'M GONNA PUT YOU AWAY FOR LIFE!
LATER.
NO PRISON CAN HOLD ME, DREDD! I'LL BUST OUT AND COME LOOKING FOR YOU! I HATE THE JUDGES AND ALL THEY STAND FOR!
THIS PRISON WILL HOLD YOU, WHITEY! WE'RE SENDING YOU TO... DEVIL'S ISLAND!

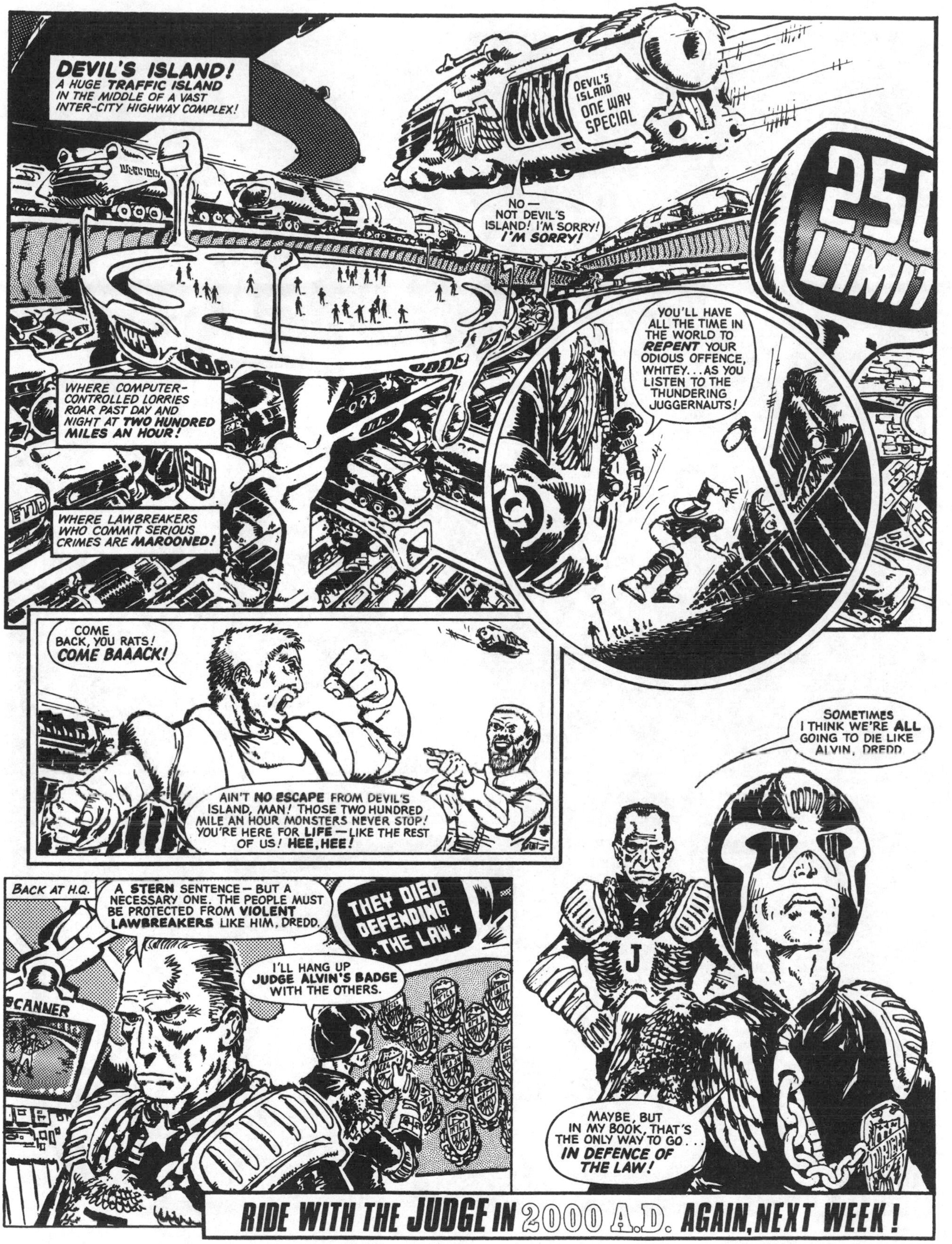
DEVIL'S ISLAND! A HUGE TRAFFIC ISLAND IN THE MIDDLE OF A VAST INTER-CITY HIGHWAY COMPLEX!
DEVIL'S ISLAND ONE WAY SPECIAL
NO — NOT DEVIL'S ISLAND! I'M SORRY! I'M SORRY!
250 LIMIT
WHERE COMPUTER-CONTROLLED LORRIES ROAR PAST DAY AND NIGHT AT TWO HUNDRED MILES AN HOUR!
WHERE LAWBREAKERS WHO COMMIT SERIOUS CRIMES ARE MAROONED!
YOU'LL HAVE ALL THE TIME IN THE WORLD TO REPENT YOUR ODIOUS OFFENCE, WHITEY... AS YOU LISTEN TO THE THUNDERING JUGGERNAUTS!
COME BACK, YOU RATS! COME BAAACK!
AIN'T NO ESCAPE FROM DEVIL'S ISLAND, MAN! THOSE TWO HUNDRED MILE AN HOUR MONSTERS NEVER STOP! YOU'RE HERE FOR LIFE — LIKE THE REST OF US! HEE, HEE!
BACK AT H.Q.
A STERN SENTENCE — BUT A NECESSARY ONE. THE PEOPLE MUST BE PROTECTED FROM VIOLENT LAWBREAKERS LIKE HIM, DREDD.
THEY DIED DEFENDING THE LAW
SCANNER
I'LL HANG UP JUDGE ALVIN'S BADGE WITH THE OTHERS.
SOMETIMES I THINK WE'RE ALL GOING TO DIE LIKE ALVIN, DREDD
MAYBE, BUT IN MY BOOK, THAT'S THE ONLY WAY TO GO... IN DEFENCE OF THE LAW!
RIDE WITH THE JUDGE IN 2000 A.D. AGAIN, NEXT WEEK!

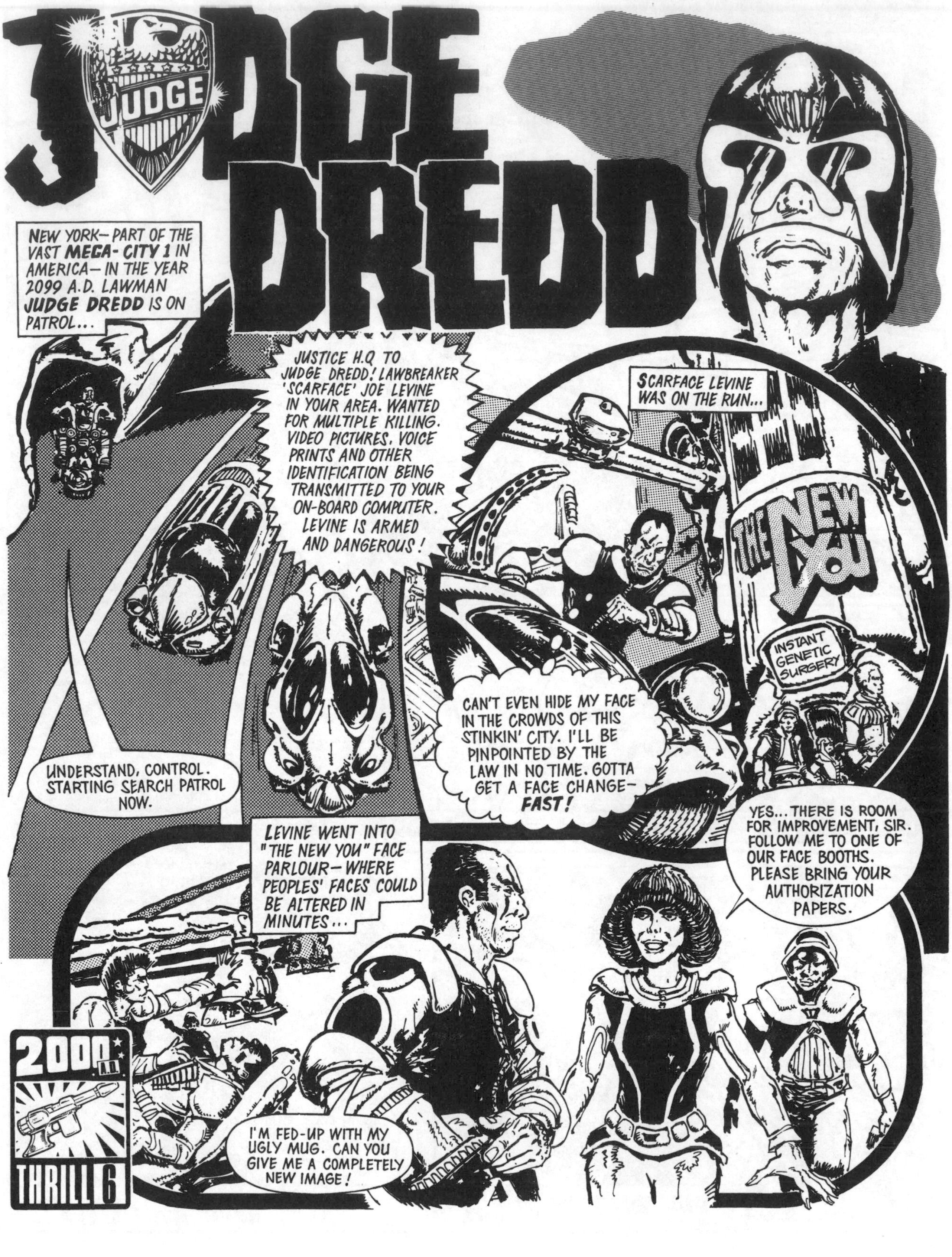
JUDGE
JUDGE DREDD
NEW YORK— PART OF THE VAST MEGA-CITY 1 IN AMERICA— IN THE YEAR 2099 A.D. LAWMAN JUDGE DREDD IS ON PATROL...
JUSTICE H.Q TO JUDGE DREDD! LAWBREAKER 'SCARFACE' JOE LEVINE IN YOUR AREA. WANTED FOR MULTIPLE KILLING. VIDEO PICTURES. VOICE PRINTS AND OTHER IDENTIFICATION BEING TRANSMITTED TO YOUR ON-BOARD COMPUTER. LEVINE IS ARMED AND DANGEROUS!
UNDERSTAND, CONTROL. STARTING SEARCH PATROL NOW.
SCARFACE LEVINE WAS ON THE RUN...
THE NEW YOU
INSTANT GENETIC SURGERY
CAN'T EVEN HIDE MY FACE IN THE CROWDS OF THIS STINKIN' CITY. I'LL BE PINPOINTED BY THE LAW IN NO TIME. GOTTA GET A FACE CHANGE— FAST!
LEVINE WENT INTO "THE NEW YOU" FACE PARLOUR— WHERE PEOPLES' FACES COULD BE ALTERED IN MINUTES...
I'M FED-UP WITH MY UGLY MUG. CAN YOU GIVE ME A COMPLETELY NEW IMAGE!
YES... THERE IS ROOM FOR IMPROVEMENT, SIR. FOLLOW ME TO ONE OF OUR FACE BOOTHS. PLEASE BRING YOUR AUTHORIZATION PAPERS.
2000 A.D.
THRILL 6

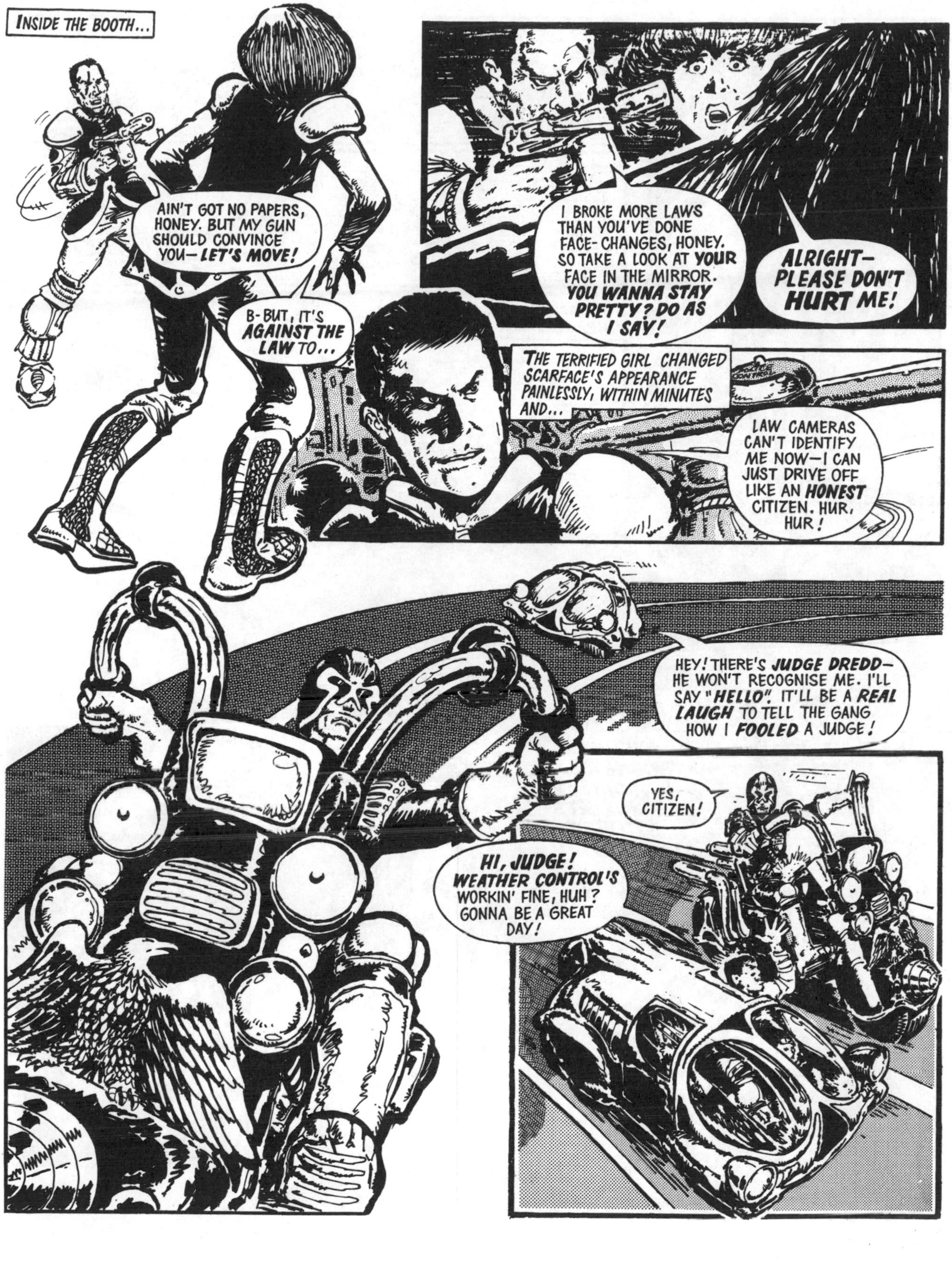
INSIDE THE BOOTH...
AIN'T GOT NO PAPERS, HONEY. BUT MY GUN SHOULD CONVINCE YOU—LET'S MOVE!
B-BUT, IT'S AGAINST THE LAW TO...
I BROKE MORE LAWS THAN YOU'VE DONE FACE-CHANGES, HONEY. SO TAKE A LOOK AT YOUR FACE IN THE MIRROR. YOU WANNA STAY PRETTY? DO AS I SAY!
ALRIGHT—PLEASE DON'T HURT ME!
THE TERRIFIED GIRL CHANGED SCARFACE'S APPEARANCE PAINLESSLY, WITHIN MINUTES AND...
LAW CAMERAS CAN'T IDENTIFY ME NOW—I CAN JUST DRIVE OFF LIKE AN HONEST CITIZEN. HUR, HUR!
HEY! THERE'S JUDGE DREDD—HE WON'T RECOGNISE ME. I'LL SAY "HELLO". IT'LL BE A REAL LAUGH TO TELL THE GANG HOW I FOOLED A JUDGE!
HI, JUDGE! WEATHER CONTROL'S WORKIN' FINE, HUH? GONNA BE A GREAT DAY!
YES, CITIZEN!

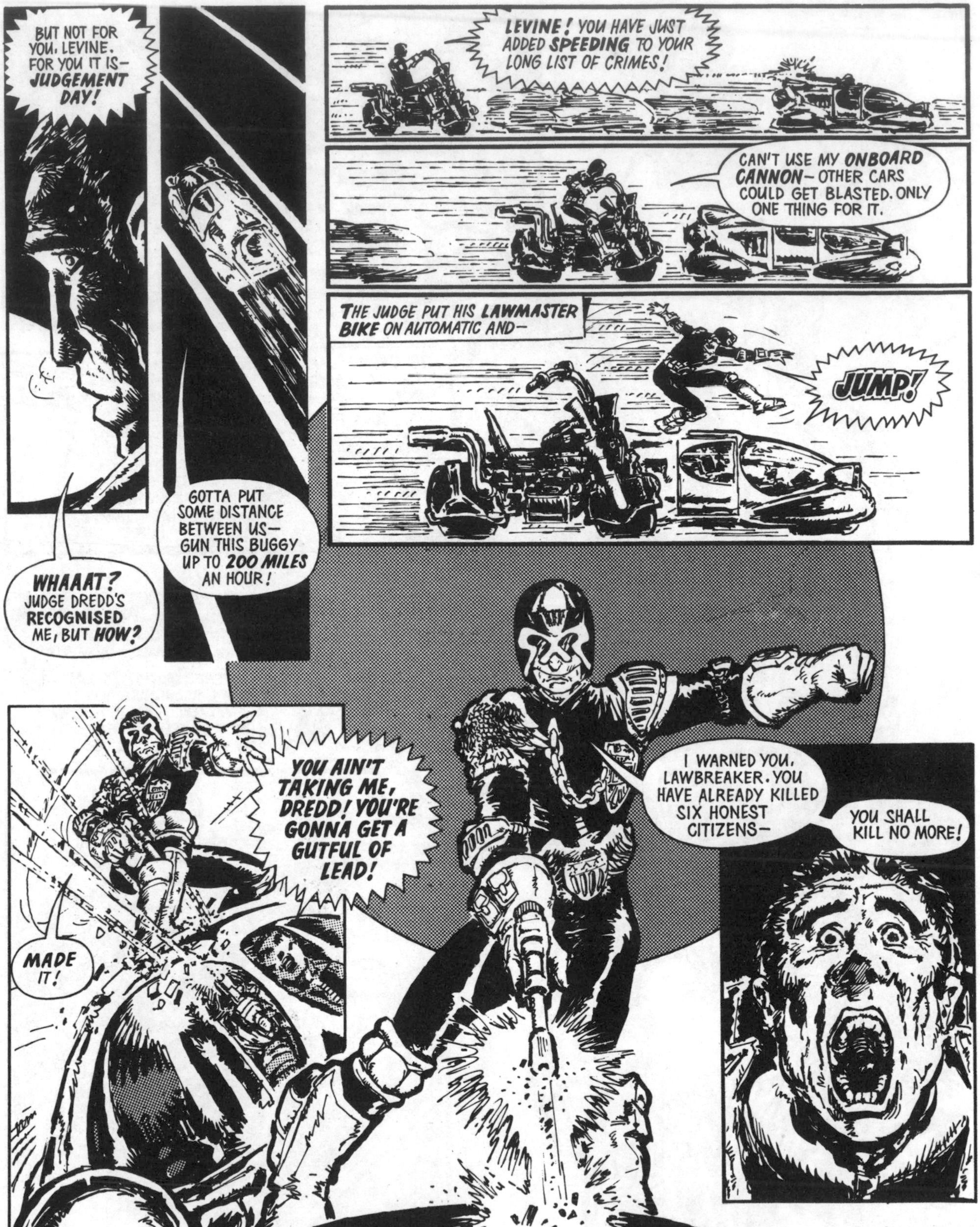

BUT NOT FOR YOU, LEVINE. FOR YOU IT IS- JUDGEMENT DAY!
WHAAAT? JUDGE DREDD'S RECOGNISED ME, BUT HOW?
GOTTA PUT SOME DISTANCE BETWEEN US- GUN THIS BUGGY UP TO 200 MILES AN HOUR!
LEVINE! YOU HAVE JUST ADDED SPEEDING TO YOUR LONG LIST OF CRIMES!
CAN'T USE MY ONBOARD CANNON- OTHER CARS COULD GET BLASTED. ONLY ONE THING FOR IT.
THE JUDGE PUT HIS LAWMASTER BIKE ON AUTOMATIC AND-
JUMP!
MADE IT!
YOU AIN'T TAKING ME, DREDD! YOU'RE GONNA GET A GUTFUL OF LEAD!
I WARNED YOU, LAWBREAKER. YOU HAVE ALREADY KILLED SIX HONEST CITIZENS-
YOU SHALL KILL NO MORE!

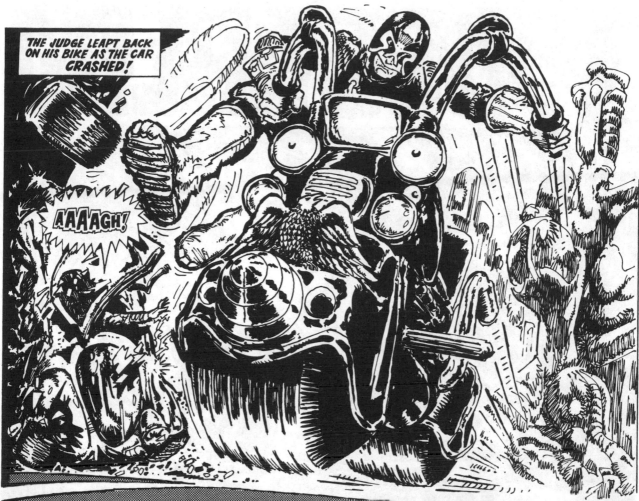

THE JUDGE LEAPT BACK ON HIS BIKE AS THE CAR *CRASHED!*

AAAAGH!

DREDD DROVE HIS LAWMASTER BACK TO THE SCENE OF THE CRASH. AS HE WAITED FOR THE AMBULANCE TO ARRIVE...

OKAY— IT'S THE *TIME-STRETCHER* JAIL FOR ME NOW. BUT WILL YOU... UUUH... GRANT ME ONE REQUEST?

THE LAW CAN SHOW *MERCY,* TOO! SPEAK?

I GOT RID OF MY *UGLY MUG*— SO HOW COME YOU RECOGNISED ME?

WHEN YOU SPOKE, YOUR *VOICE PRINT* MATCHED THE ONE SENT TO ME BY CONTROL.

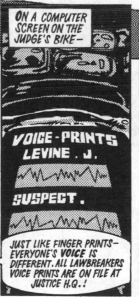

ON A COMPUTER SCREEN ON THE JUDGE'S BIKE—

VOICE-PRINTS

LEVINE . J.

SUSPECT .

JUST LIKE FINGER PRINTS— EVERYONE'S *VOICE* IS DIFFERENT. ALL LAWBREAKERS VOICE PRINTS ARE ON FILE AT JUSTICE H.Q.!

WHEN WILL LAWBREAKERS LEARN... IN THE 21st CENTURY— *NO ONE CAN ESCAPE JUSTICE!*

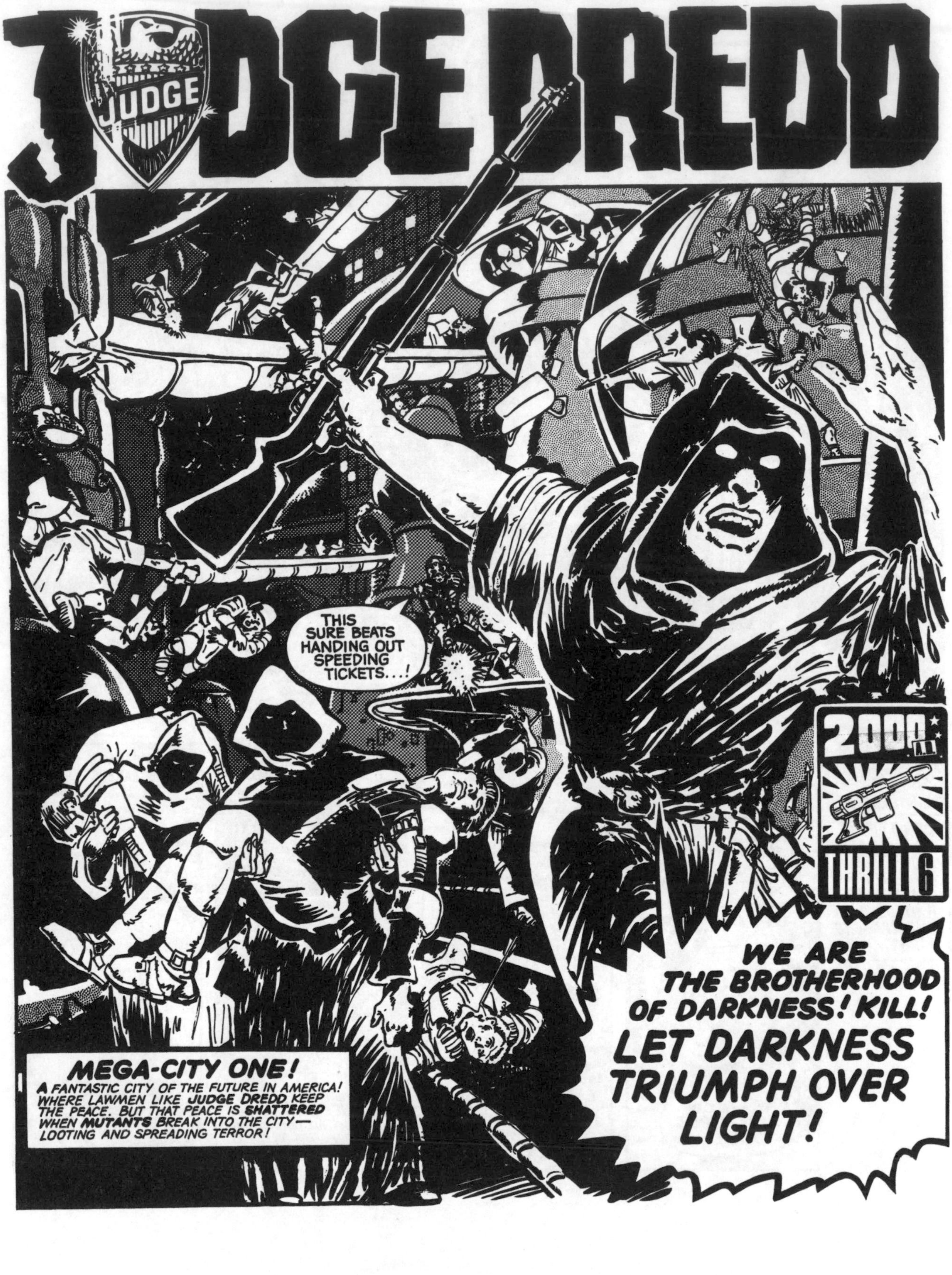
JUDGE DREDD
JUDGE
THIS SURE BEATS HANDING OUT SPEEDING TICKETS...!
2000 A.D.
THRILL 6
WE ARE THE BROTHERHOOD OF DARKNESS! KILL! LET DARKNESS TRIUMPH OVER LIGHT!
MEGA-CITY ONE!
A FANTASTIC CITY OF THE FUTURE IN AMERICA! WHERE LAWMEN LIKE JUDGE DREDD KEEP THE PEACE. BUT THAT PEACE IS SHATTERED WHEN MUTANTS BREAK INTO THE CITY— LOOTING AND SPREADING TERROR!

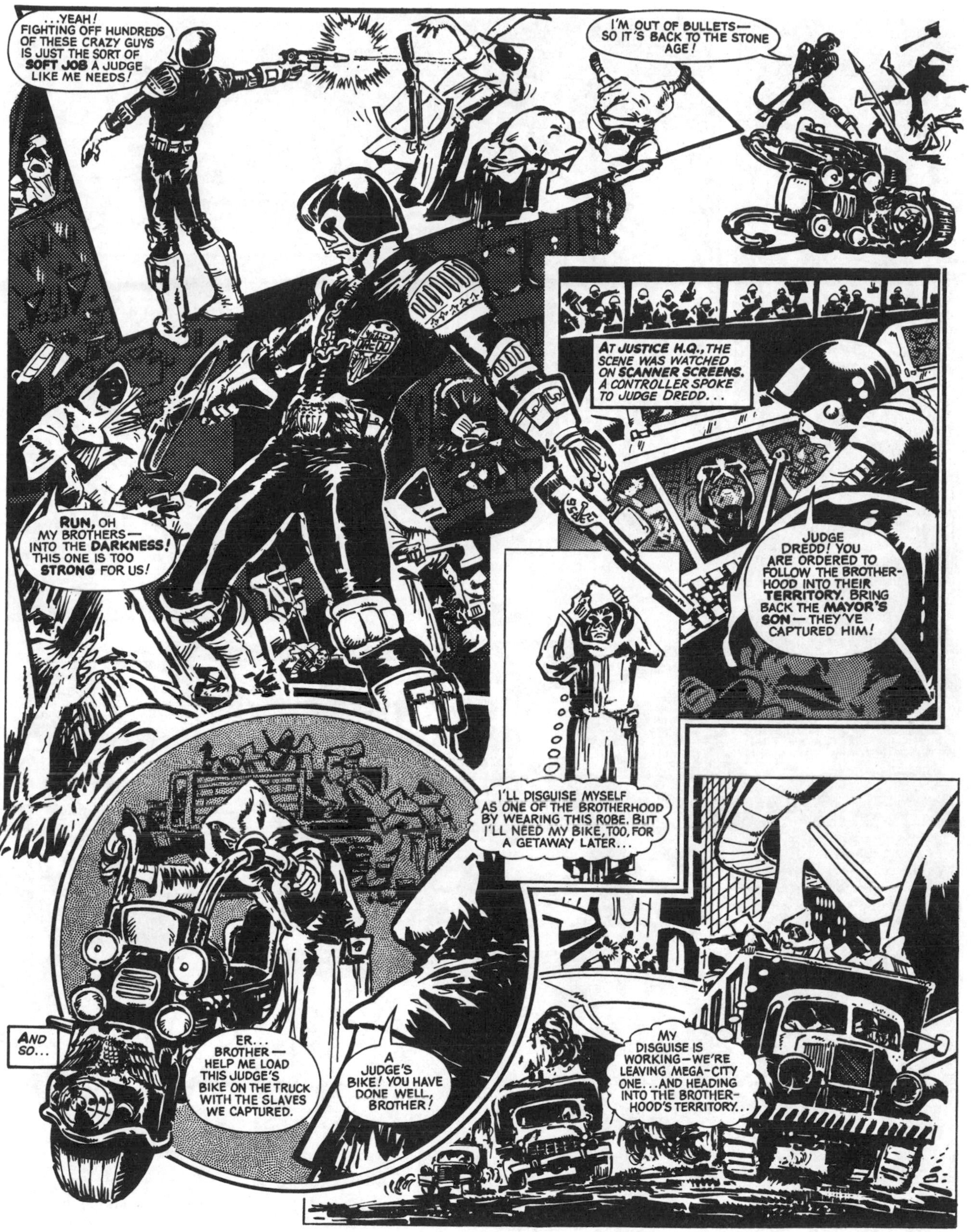
...YEAH! FIGHTING OFF HUNDREDS OF THESE CRAZY GUYS IS JUST THE SORT OF SOFT JOB A JUDGE LIKE ME NEEDS!
I'M OUT OF BULLETS— SO IT'S BACK TO THE STONE AGE!
RUN, OH MY BROTHERS— INTO THE DARKNESS! THIS ONE IS TOO STRONG FOR US!
AT JUSTICE H.Q., THE SCENE WAS WATCHED ON SCANNER SCREENS. A CONTROLLER SPOKE TO JUDGE DREDD...
JUDGE DREDD! YOU ARE ORDERED TO FOLLOW THE BROTHERHOOD INTO THEIR TERRITORY. BRING BACK THE MAYOR'S SON — THEY'VE CAPTURED HIM!
I'LL DISGUISE MYSELF AS ONE OF THE BROTHERHOOD BY WEARING THIS ROBE. BUT I'LL NEED MY BIKE, TOO, FOR A GETAWAY LATER...
AND SO...
ER... BROTHER — HELP ME LOAD THIS JUDGE'S BIKE ON THE TRUCK WITH THE SLAVES WE CAPTURED.
A JUDGE'S BIKE! YOU HAVE DONE WELL, BROTHER!
MY DISGUISE IS WORKING—WE'RE LEAVING MEGA-CITY ONE...AND HEADING INTO THE BROTHERHOOD'S TERRITORY...

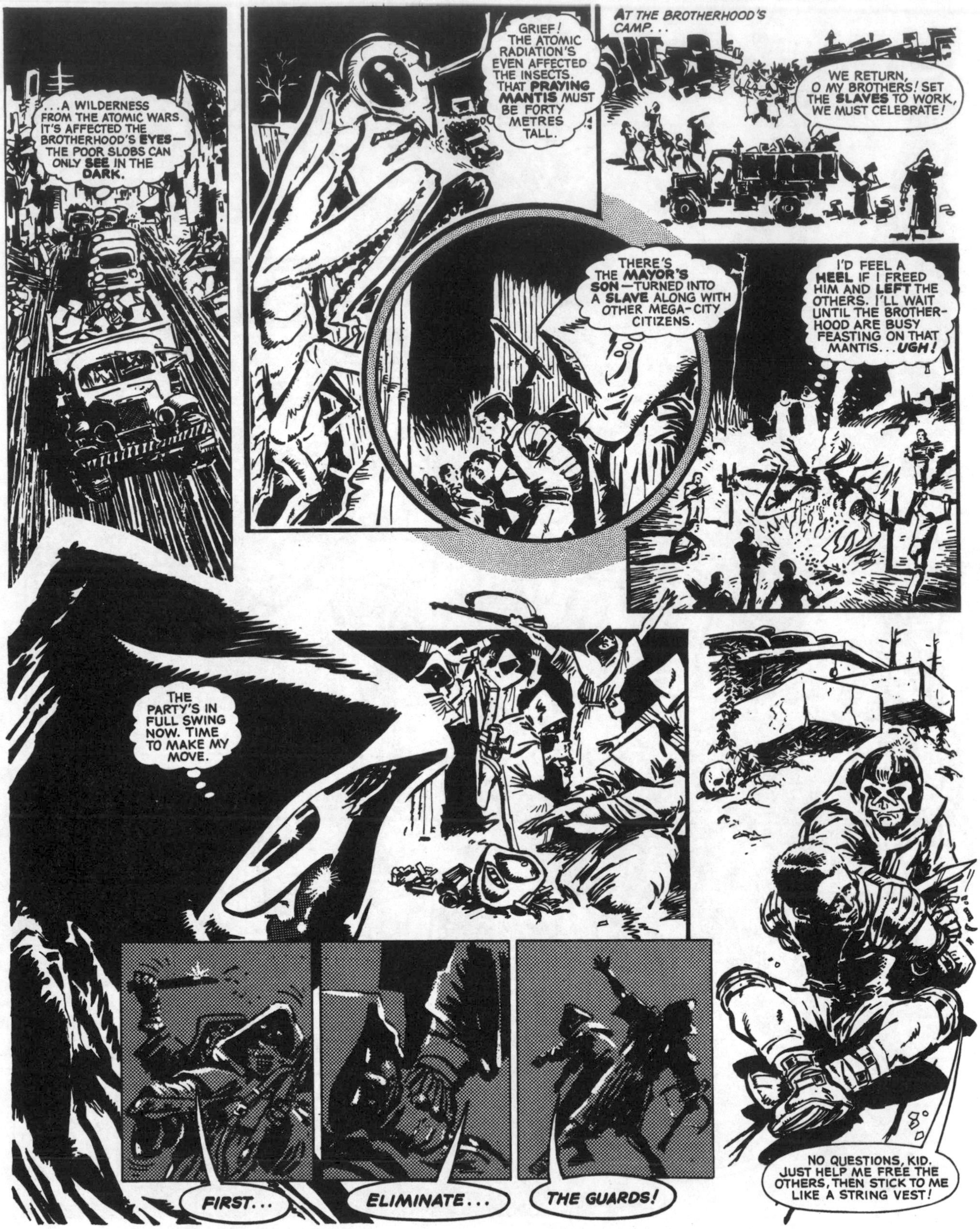

...A WILDERNESS FROM THE ATOMIC WARS. IT'S AFFECTED THE BROTHERHOOD'S EYES— THE POOR SLOBS CAN ONLY SEE IN THE DARK.
GRIEF! THE ATOMIC RADIATION'S EVEN AFFECTED THE INSECTS. THAT PRAYING MANTIS MUST BE FORTY METRES TALL.
AT THE BROTHERHOOD'S CAMP...
WE RETURN, O MY BROTHERS! SET THE SLAVES TO WORK, WE MUST CELEBRATE!
THERE'S THE MAYOR'S SON—TURNED INTO A SLAVE ALONG WITH OTHER MEGA-CITY CITIZENS.
I'D FEEL A HEEL IF I FREED HIM AND LEFT THE OTHERS. I'LL WAIT UNTIL THE BROTHERHOOD ARE BUSY FEASTING ON THAT MANTIS... UGH!
THE PARTY'S IN FULL SWING NOW. TIME TO MAKE MY MOVE.
FIRST...
ELIMINATE...
THE GUARDS!
NO QUESTIONS, KID. JUST HELP ME FREE THE OTHERS, THEN STICK TO ME LIKE A STRING VEST!

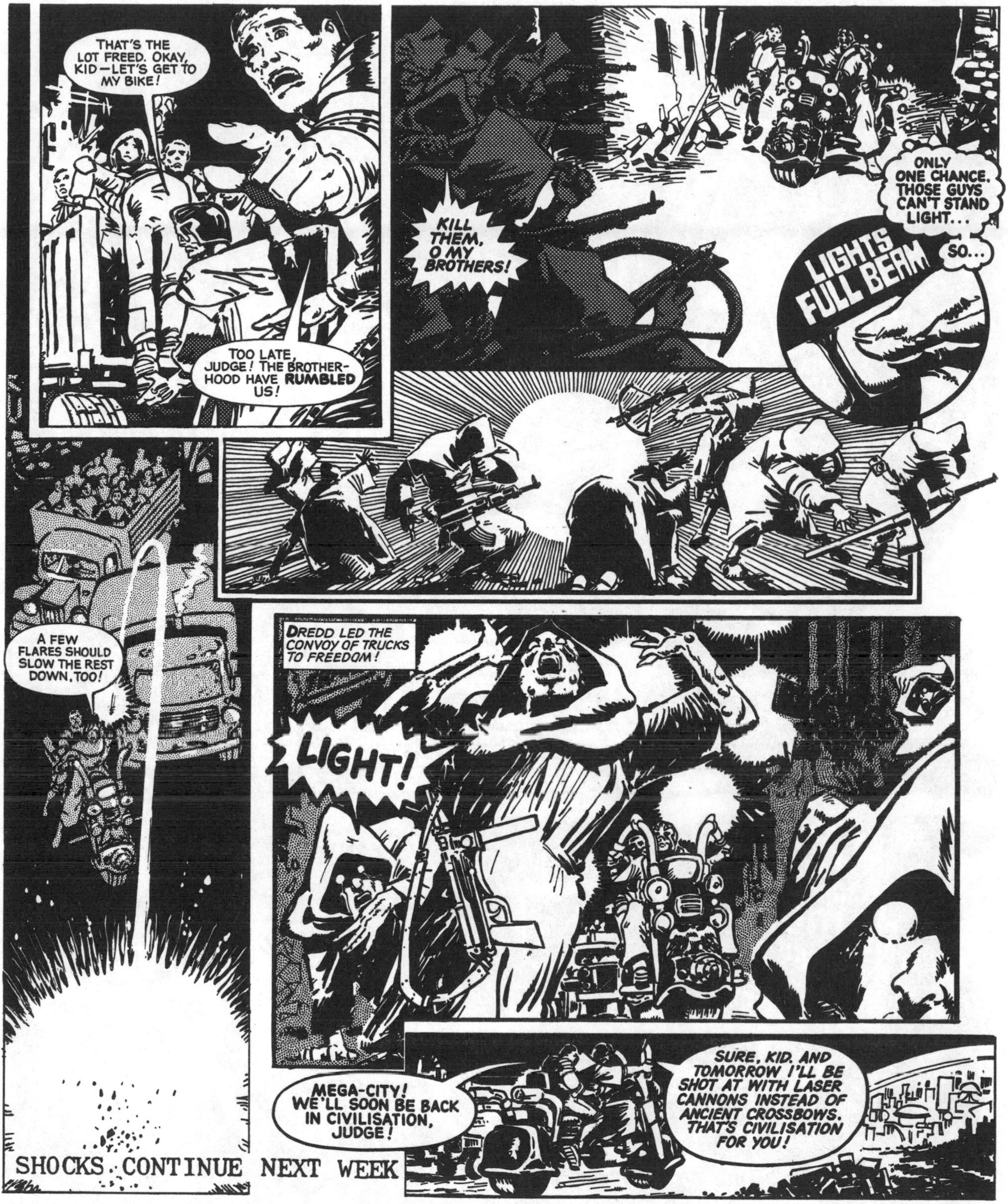
THAT'S THE LOT FREED. OKAY, KID—LET'S GET TO MY BIKE!
TOO LATE, JUDGE! THE BROTHERHOOD HAVE RUMBLED US!
KILL THEM, O MY BROTHERS!
ONLY ONE CHANCE. THOSE GUYS CAN'T STAND LIGHT...
SO...
LIGHTS FULL BEAM
A FEW FLARES SHOULD SLOW THE REST DOWN, TOO!
DREDD LED THE CONVOY OF TRUCKS TO FREEDOM!
LIGHT!
MEGA-CITY! WE'LL SOON BE BACK IN CIVILISATION, JUDGE!
SURE, KID, AND TOMORROW I'LL BE SHOT AT WITH LASER CANNONS INSTEAD OF ANCIENT CROSSBOWS. THAT'S CIVILISATION FOR YOU!
SHOCKS CONTINUE NEXT WEEK

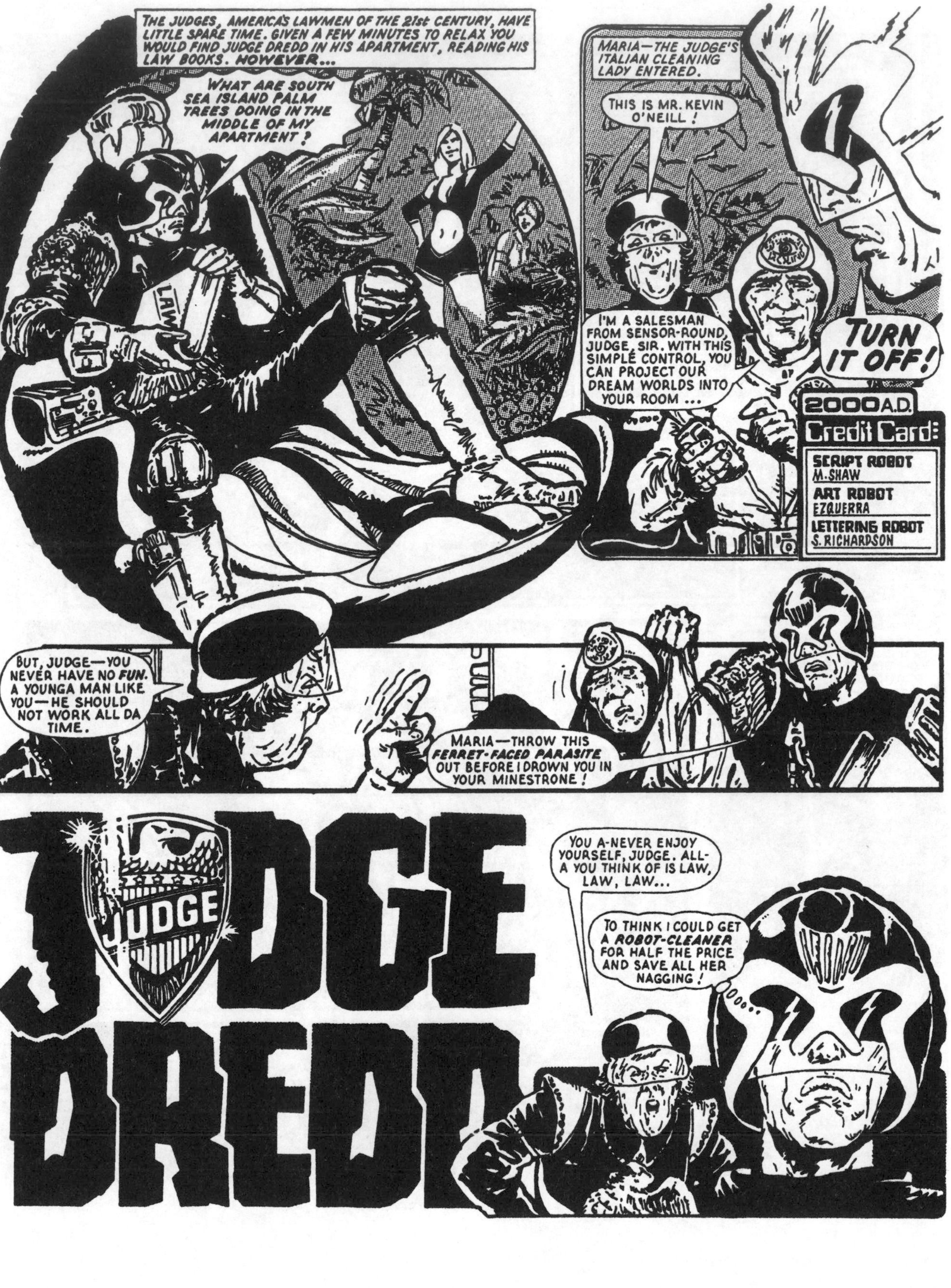
THE JUDGES, AMERICA'S LAWMEN OF THE 21st CENTURY, HAVE LITTLE SPARE TIME. GIVEN A FEW MINUTES TO RELAX YOU WOULD FIND JUDGE DREDD IN HIS APARTMENT, READING HIS LAW BOOKS. HOWEVER...
WHAT ARE SOUTH SEA ISLAND PALM TREES DOING IN THE MIDDLE OF MY APARTMENT?
LAW
MARIA—THE JUDGE'S ITALIAN CLEANING LADY ENTERED.
THIS IS MR. KEVIN O'NEILL!
I'M A SALESMAN FROM SENSOR-ROUND, JUDGE, SIR. WITH THIS SIMPLE CONTROL, YOU CAN PROJECT OUR DREAM WORLDS INTO YOUR ROOM...
TURN IT OFF!
2000 A.D.
Credit Card:
SCRIPT ROBOT M. SHAW
ART ROBOT EZQUERRA
LETTERING ROBOT S. RICHARDSON
BUT, JUDGE—YOU NEVER HAVE NO FUN. A YOUNGA MAN LIKE YOU—HE SHOULD NOT WORK ALL DA TIME.
MARIA—THROW THIS FERRET-FACED PARASITE OUT BEFORE I DROWN YOU IN YOUR MINESTRONE!
JUDGE DREDD
JUDGE
YOU A-NEVER ENJOY YOURSELF, JUDGE. ALL-A YOU THINK OF IS LAW, LAW, LAW...
TO THINK I COULD GET A ROBOT-CLEANER FOR HALF THE PRICE AND SAVE ALL HER NAGGING!

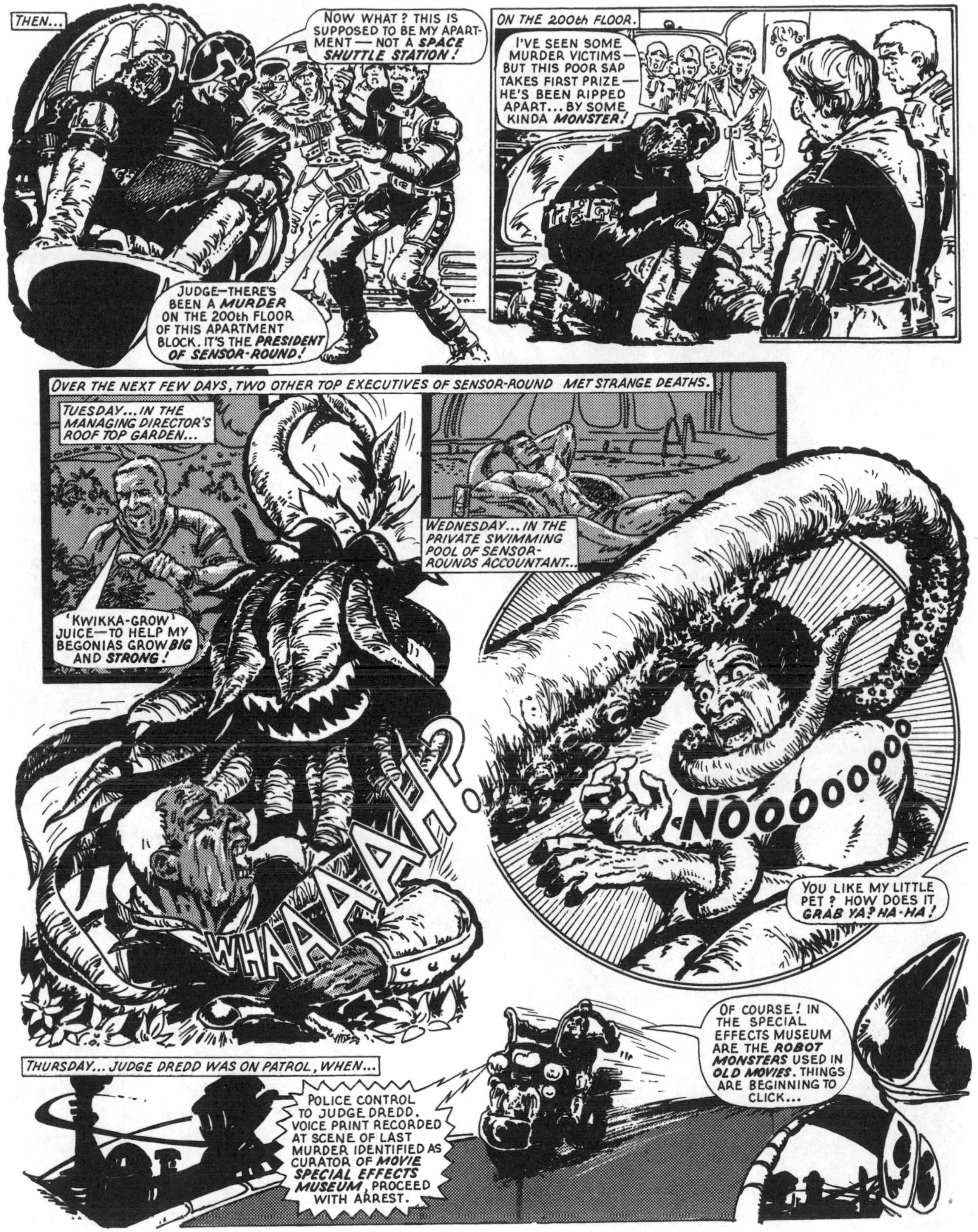
THEN...
NOW WHAT? THIS IS SUPPOSED TO BE MY APARTMENT — NOT A SPACE SHUTTLE STATION!
JUDGE—THERE'S BEEN A MURDER ON THE 200th FLOOR OF THIS APARTMENT BLOCK. IT'S THE PRESIDENT OF SENSOR-ROUND!
ON THE 200th FLOOR.
I'VE SEEN SOME MURDER VICTIMS— BUT THIS POOR SAP TAKES FIRST PRIZE— HE'S BEEN RIPPED APART... BY SOME KINDA MONSTER!
OVER THE NEXT FEW DAYS, TWO OTHER TOP EXECUTIVES OF SENSOR-ROUND MET STRANGE DEATHS.
TUESDAY... IN THE MANAGING DIRECTOR'S ROOF TOP GARDEN...
'KWIKKA-GROW' JUICE—TO HELP MY BEGONIAS GROW BIG AND STRONG!
WHAAAAH?
WEDNESDAY... IN THE PRIVATE SWIMMING POOL OF SENSOR-ROUNDS ACCOUNTANT...
NOOOOOOOOO
YOU LIKE MY LITTLE PET? HOW DOES IT GRAB YA? HA-HA!
THURSDAY... JUDGE DREDD WAS ON PATROL, WHEN...
POLICE CONTROL TO JUDGE DREDD. VOICE PRINT RECORDED AT SCENE OF LAST MURDER IDENTIFIED AS CURATOR OF MOVIE SPECIAL EFFECTS MUSEUM, PROCEED WITH ARREST.
OF COURSE! IN THE SPECIAL EFFECTS MUSEUM ARE THE ROBOT MONSTERS USED IN OLD MOVIES. THINGS ARE BEGINNING TO CLICK...

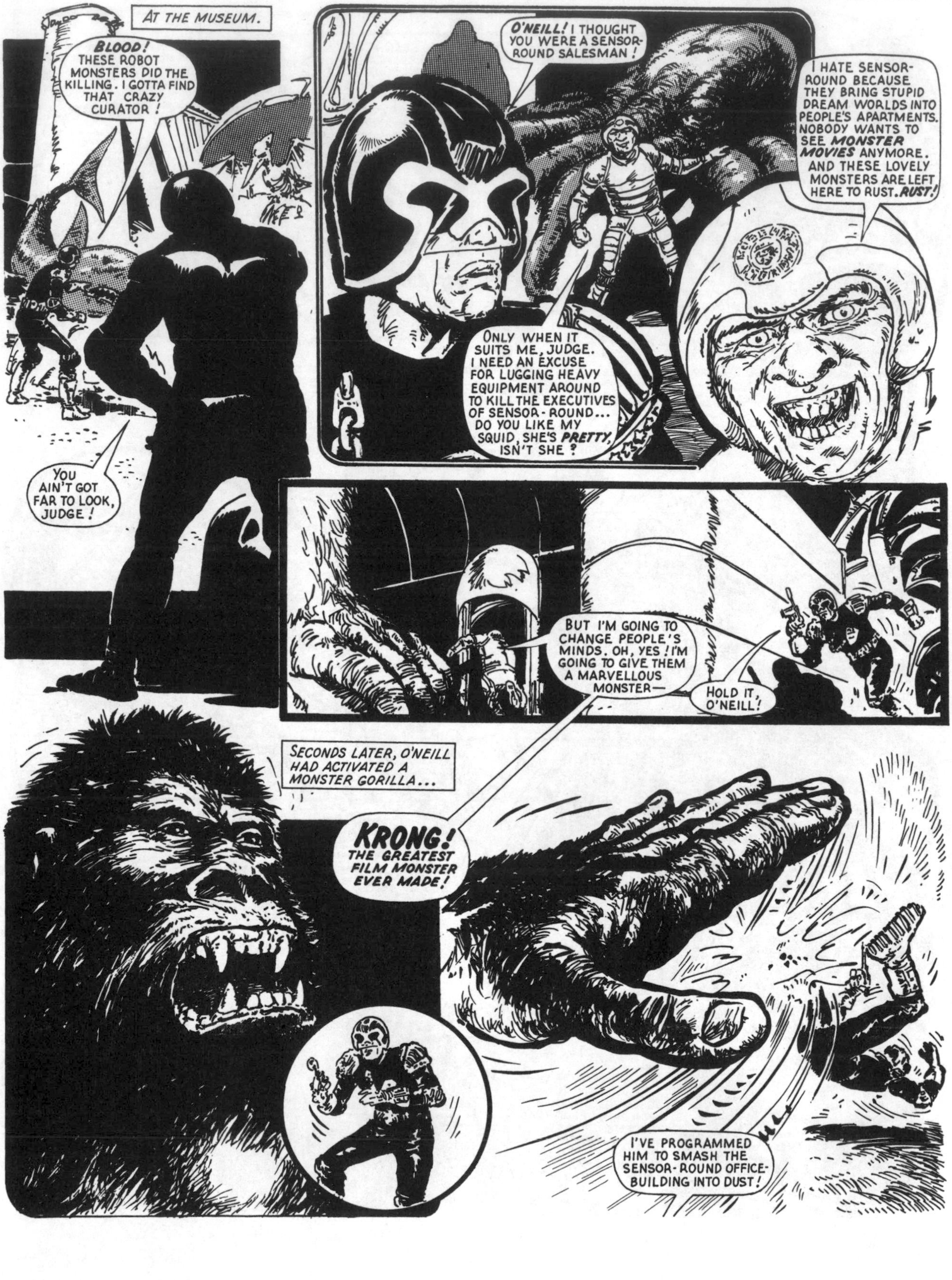

AT THE MUSEUM.
BLOOD! THESE ROBOT MONSTERS DID THE KILLING. I GOTTA FIND THAT CRAZY CURATOR!
YOU AIN'T GOT FAR TO LOOK, JUDGE!
O'NEILL! I THOUGHT YOU WERE A SENSOR-ROUND SALESMAN!
ONLY WHEN IT SUITS ME, JUDGE. I NEED AN EXCUSE FOR LUGGING HEAVY EQUIPMENT AROUND TO KILL THE EXECUTIVES OF SENSOR-ROUND... DO YOU LIKE MY SQUID, SHE'S PRETTY, ISN'T SHE?
I HATE SENSOR-ROUND BECAUSE THEY BRING STUPID DREAM WORLDS INTO PEOPLE'S APARTMENTS. NOBODY WANTS TO SEE MONSTER MOVIES ANYMORE. AND THESE LOVELY MONSTERS ARE LEFT HERE TO RUST. RUST!
BUT I'M GOING TO CHANGE PEOPLE'S MINDS. OH, YES! I'M GOING TO GIVE THEM A MARVELLOUS MONSTER—
HOLD IT, O'NEILL!
SECONDS LATER, O'NEILL HAD ACTIVATED A MONSTER GORILLA...
KRONG! THE GREATEST FILM MONSTER EVER MADE!
I'VE PROGRAMMED HIM TO SMASH THE SENSOR-ROUND OFFICE-BUILDING INTO DUST!

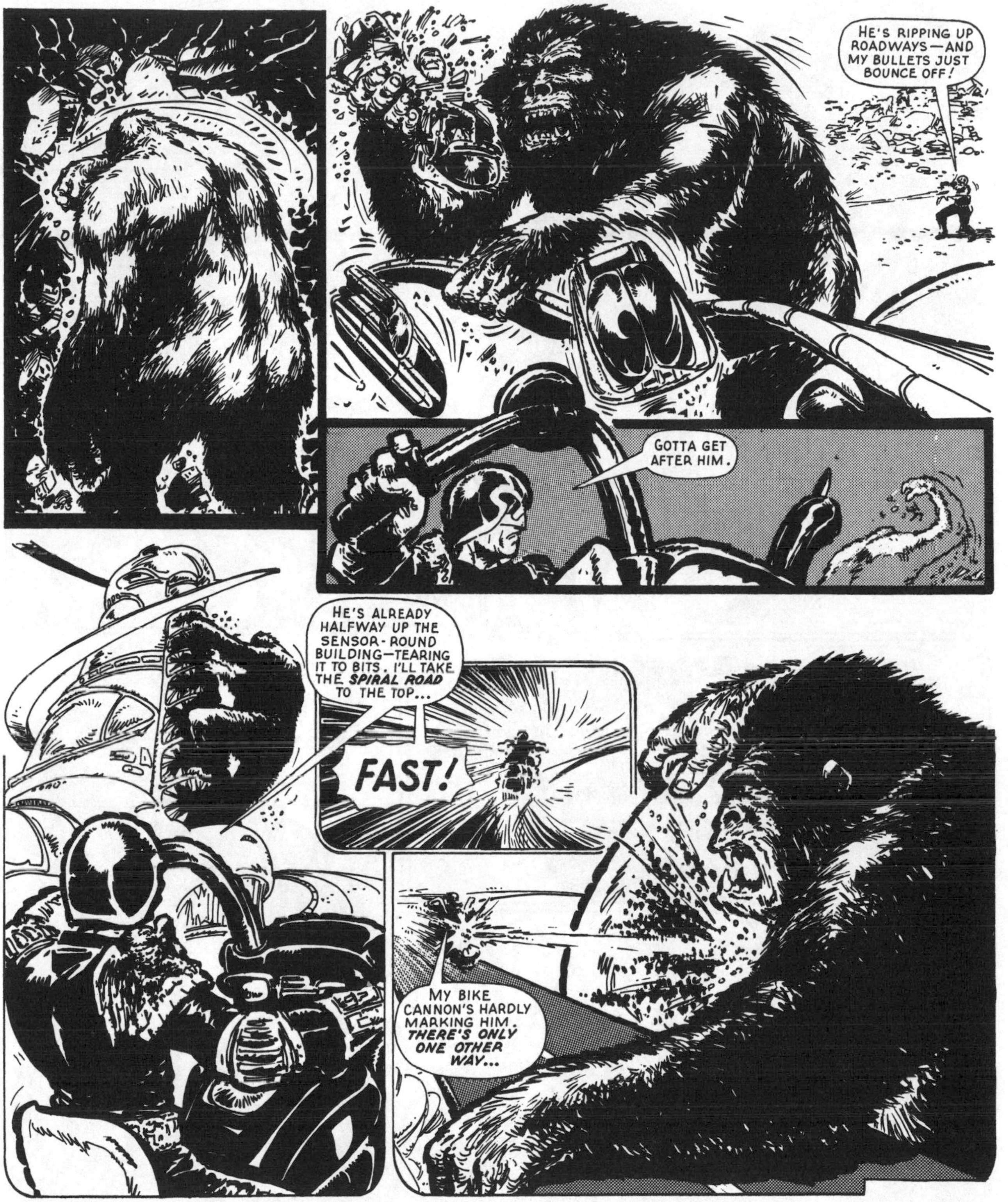

HE'S RIPPING UP ROADWAYS—AND MY BULLETS JUST BOUNCE OFF!
GOTTA GET AFTER HIM.
HE'S ALREADY HALFWAY UP THE SENSOR-ROUND BUILDING—TEARING IT TO BITS. I'LL TAKE THE SPIRAL ROAD TO THE TOP...
FAST!
MY BIKE CANNON'S HARDLY MARKING HIM. THERE'S ONLY ONE OTHER WAY...

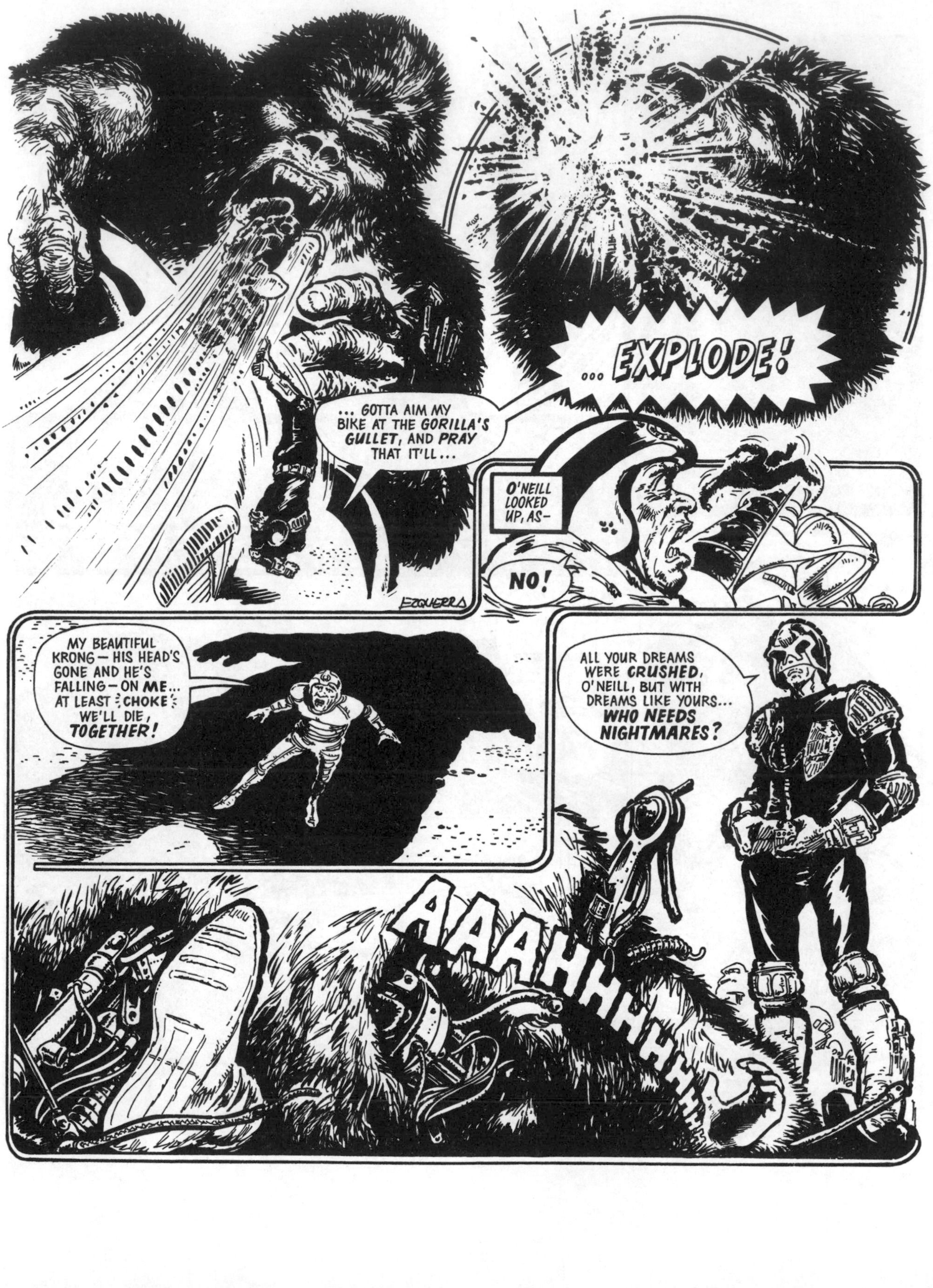

... GOTTA AIM MY BIKE AT THE GORILLA'S GULLET, AND PRAY THAT IT'LL...
... EXPLODE!
O'NEILL LOOKED UP, AS-
NO!
EZQUERRA
MY BEAUTIFUL KRONG — HIS HEAD'S GONE AND HE'S FALLING — ON ME... AT LEAST CHOKE WE'LL DIE, TOGETHER!
ALL YOUR DREAMS WERE CRUSHED, O'NEILL, BUT WITH DREAMS LIKE YOURS... WHO NEEDS NIGHTMARES?
AAAAHHHHHHHH

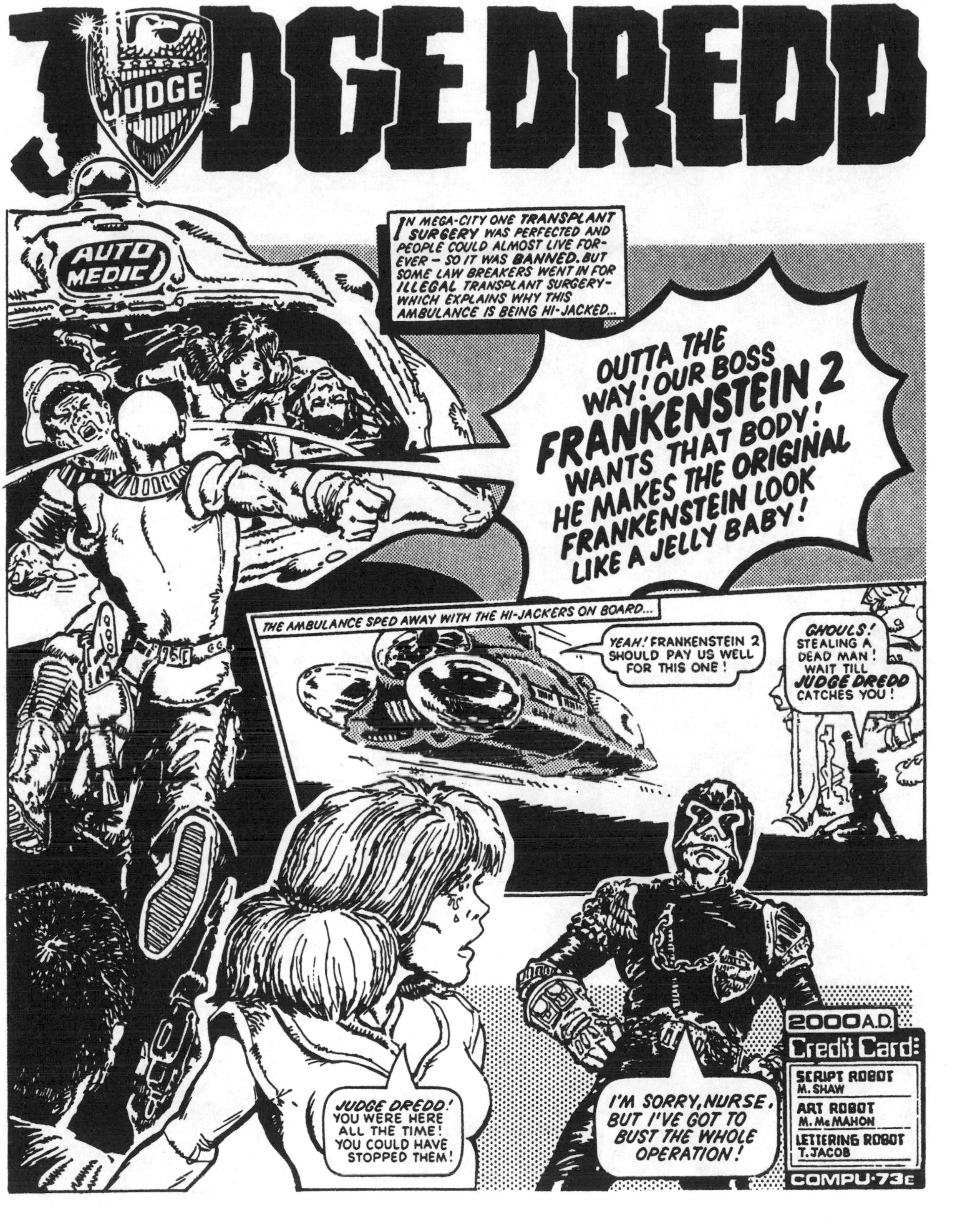
JUDGE DREDD
AUTO MEDIC
IN MEGA-CITY ONE TRANSPLANT SURGERY WAS PERFECTED AND PEOPLE COULD ALMOST LIVE FOR-EVER – SO IT WAS BANNED. BUT SOME LAW BREAKERS WENT IN FOR ILLEGAL TRANSPLANT SURGERY-WHICH EXPLAINS WHY THIS AMBULANCE IS BEING HI-JACKED...
OUTTA THE WAY! OUR BOSS FRANKENSTEIN 2 WANTS THAT BODY! HE MAKES THE ORIGINAL FRANKENSTEIN LOOK LIKE A JELLY BABY!
THE AMBULANCE SPED AWAY WITH THE HI-JACKERS ON BOARD...
YEAH! FRANKENSTEIN 2 SHOULD PAY US WELL FOR THIS ONE!
GHOULS! STEALING A DEAD MAN! WAIT TILL JUDGE DREDD CATCHES YOU!
JUDGE DREDD! YOU WERE HERE ALL THE TIME! YOU COULD HAVE STOPPED THEM!
I'M SORRY, NURSE, BUT I'VE GOT TO BUST THE WHOLE OPERATION!
2000 A.D. Credit Card:
SCRIPT ROBOT M. SHAW
ART ROBOT M. McMAHON
LETTERING ROBOT T. JACOB
COMPU-73E

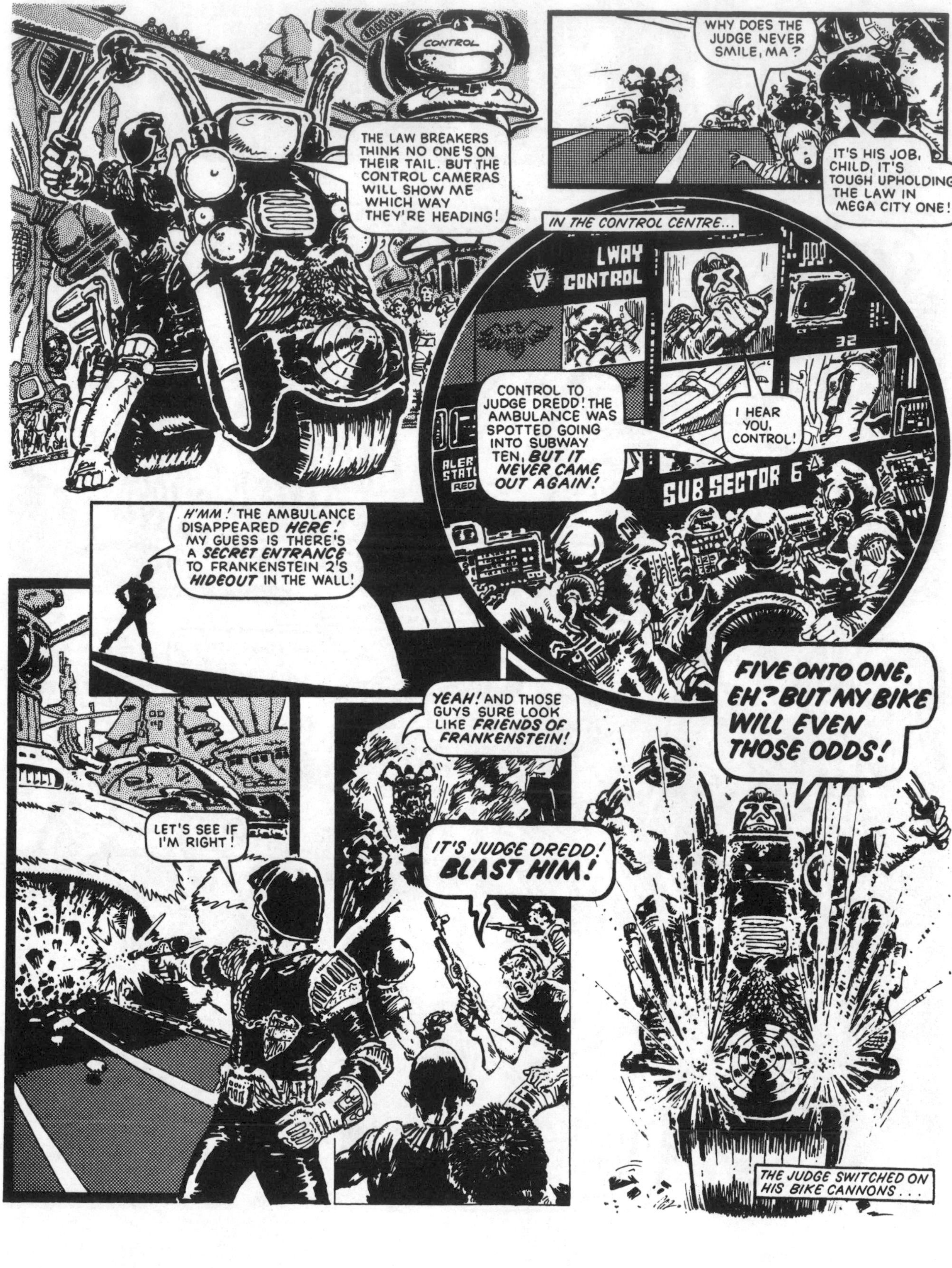
CONTROL
THE LAW BREAKERS THINK NO ONE'S ON THEIR TAIL. BUT THE CONTROL CAMERAS WILL SHOW ME WHICH WAY THEY'RE HEADING!
WHY DOES THE JUDGE NEVER SMILE, MA?
IT'S HIS JOB, CHILD, IT'S TOUGH UPHOLDING THE LAW IN MEGA CITY ONE!
IN THE CONTROL CENTRE...
LWAY CONTROL
32
CONTROL TO JUDGE DREDD! THE AMBULANCE WAS SPOTTED GOING INTO SUBWAY TEN, BUT IT NEVER CAME OUT AGAIN!
I HEAR YOU, CONTROL!
SUB SECTOR 6
H'MM! THE AMBULANCE DISAPPEARED HERE! MY GUESS IS THERE'S A SECRET ENTRANCE TO FRANKENSTEIN 2'S HIDEOUT IN THE WALL!
LET'S SEE IF I'M RIGHT!
YEAH! AND THOSE GUYS SURE LOOK LIKE FRIENDS OF FRANKENSTEIN!
IT'S JUDGE DREDD! BLAST HIM!
FIVE ONTO ONE, EH? BUT MY BIKE WILL EVEN THOSE ODDS!
THE JUDGE SWITCHED ON HIS BIKE CANNONS...

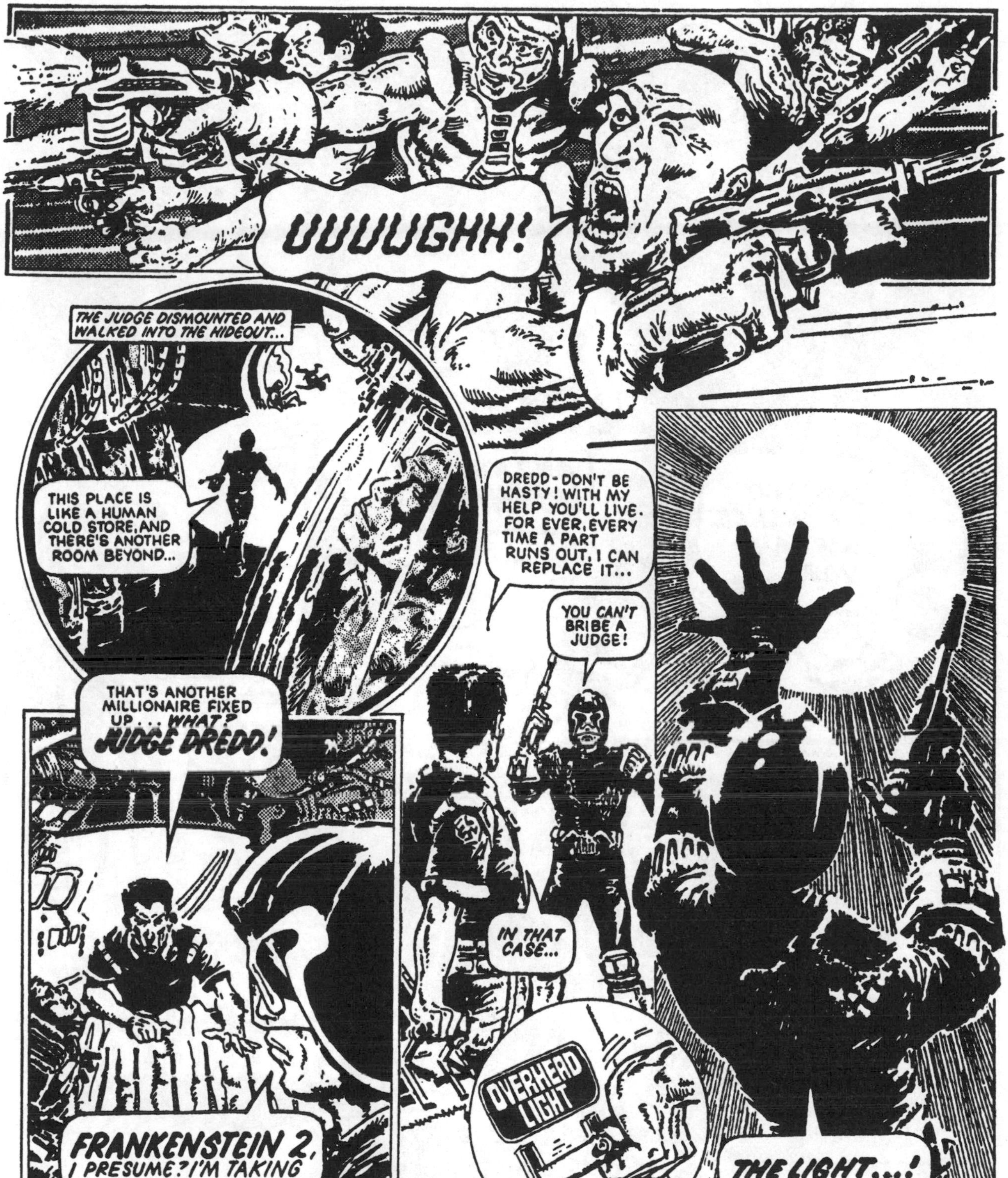
UUUUGHH!
THE JUDGE DISMOUNTED AND WALKED INTO THE HIDEOUT...
THIS PLACE IS LIKE A HUMAN COLD STORE, AND THERE'S ANOTHER ROOM BEYOND...
THAT'S ANOTHER MILLIONAIRE FIXED UP... WHAT? JUDGE DREDD!
FRANKENSTEIN 2, I PRESUME? I'M TAKING YOU IN!
DREDD - DON'T BE HASTY! WITH MY HELP YOU'LL LIVE FOR EVER. EVERY TIME A PART RUNS OUT, I CAN REPLACE IT...
YOU CAN'T BRIBE A JUDGE!
IN THAT CASE...
OVERHEAD LIGHT
THE LIGHT...!

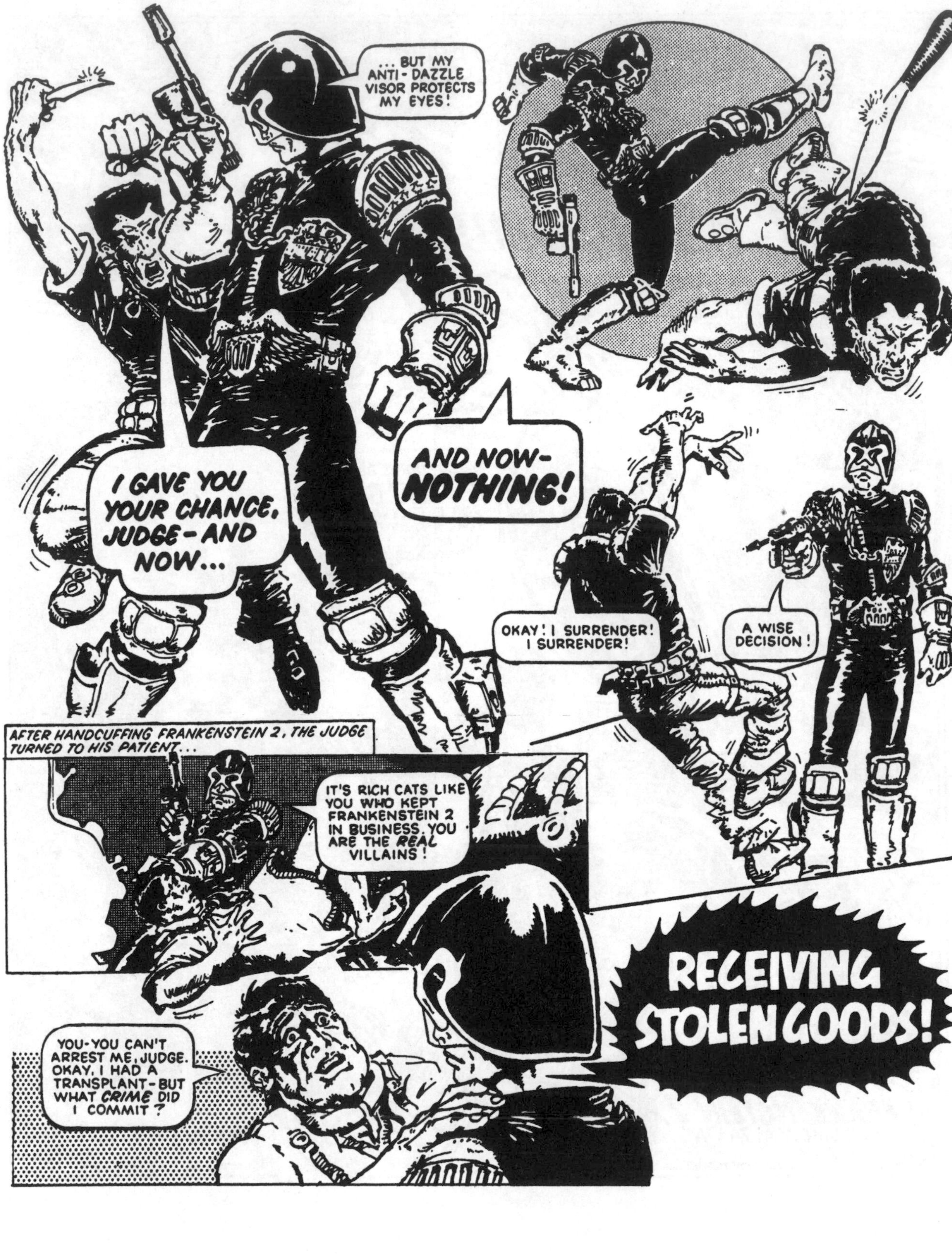
... BUT MY ANTI-DAZZLE VISOR PROTECTS MY EYES!
I GAVE YOU YOUR CHANCE, JUDGE - AND NOW...
AND NOW- NOTHING!
OKAY! I SURRENDER! I SURRENDER!
A WISE DECISION!
AFTER HANDCUFFING FRANKENSTEIN 2, THE JUDGE TURNED TO HIS PATIENT...
IT'S RICH CATS LIKE YOU WHO KEPT FRANKENSTEIN 2 IN BUSINESS. YOU ARE THE REAL VILLAINS!
YOU-YOU CAN'T ARREST ME, JUDGE. OKAY, I HAD A TRANSPLANT - BUT WHAT CRIME DID I COMMIT?
RECEIVING STOLEN GOODS!

JUDGE DREDD

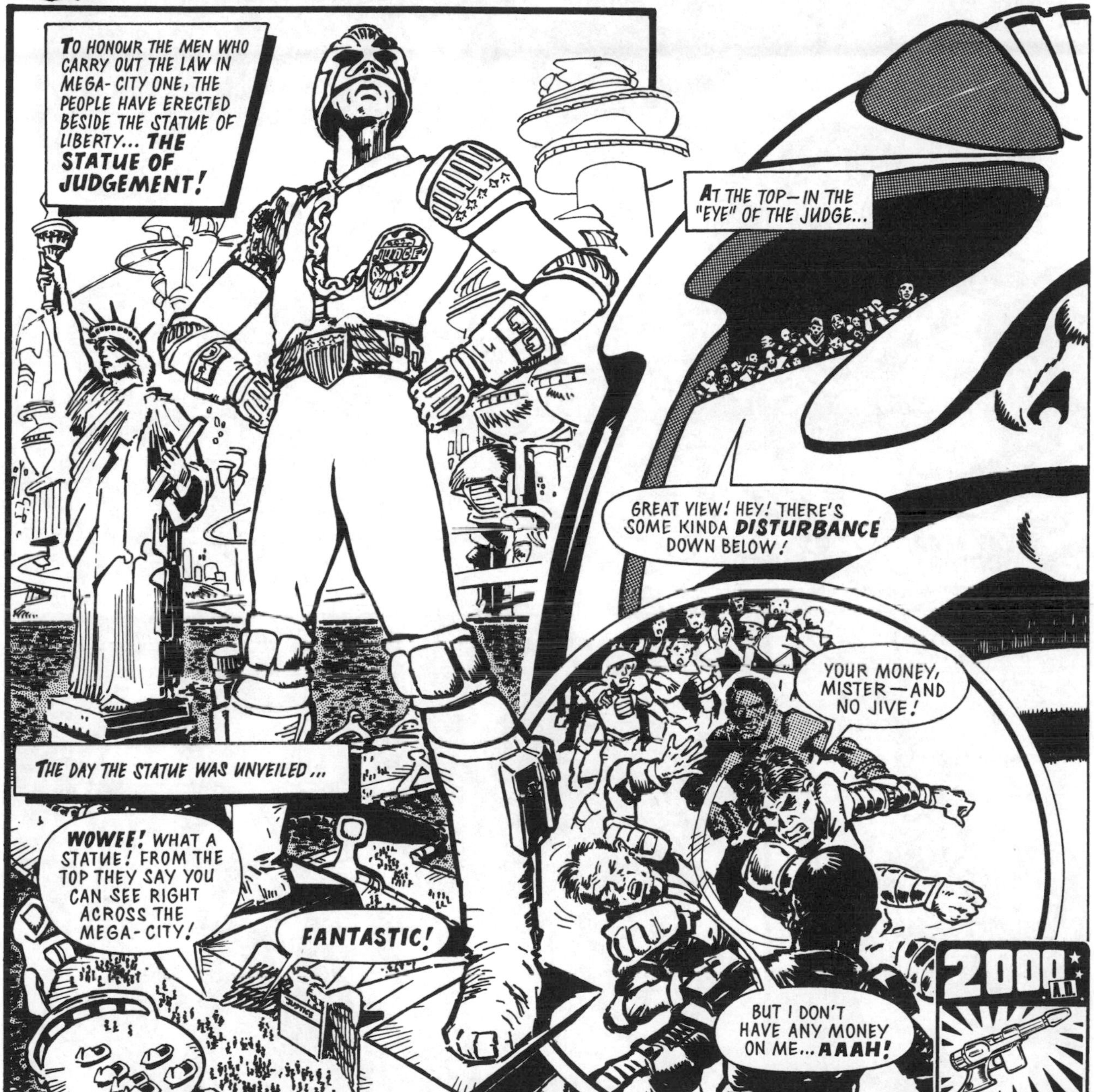
TO HONOUR THE MEN WHO CARRY OUT THE LAW IN MEGA-CITY ONE, THE PEOPLE HAVE ERECTED BESIDE THE STATUE OF LIBERTY... THE STATUE OF JUDGEMENT!
THE DAY THE STATUE WAS UNVEILED...
WOWEE! WHAT A STATUE! FROM THE TOP THEY SAY YOU CAN SEE RIGHT ACROSS THE MEGA-CITY!
FANTASTIC!
AT THE TOP— IN THE "EYE" OF THE JUDGE...
GREAT VIEW! HEY! THERE'S SOME KINDA DISTURBANCE DOWN BELOW!
YOUR MONEY, MISTER— AND NO JIVE!
BUT I DON'T HAVE ANY MONEY ON ME... AAAH!
2000 A.D.
THRILL 6

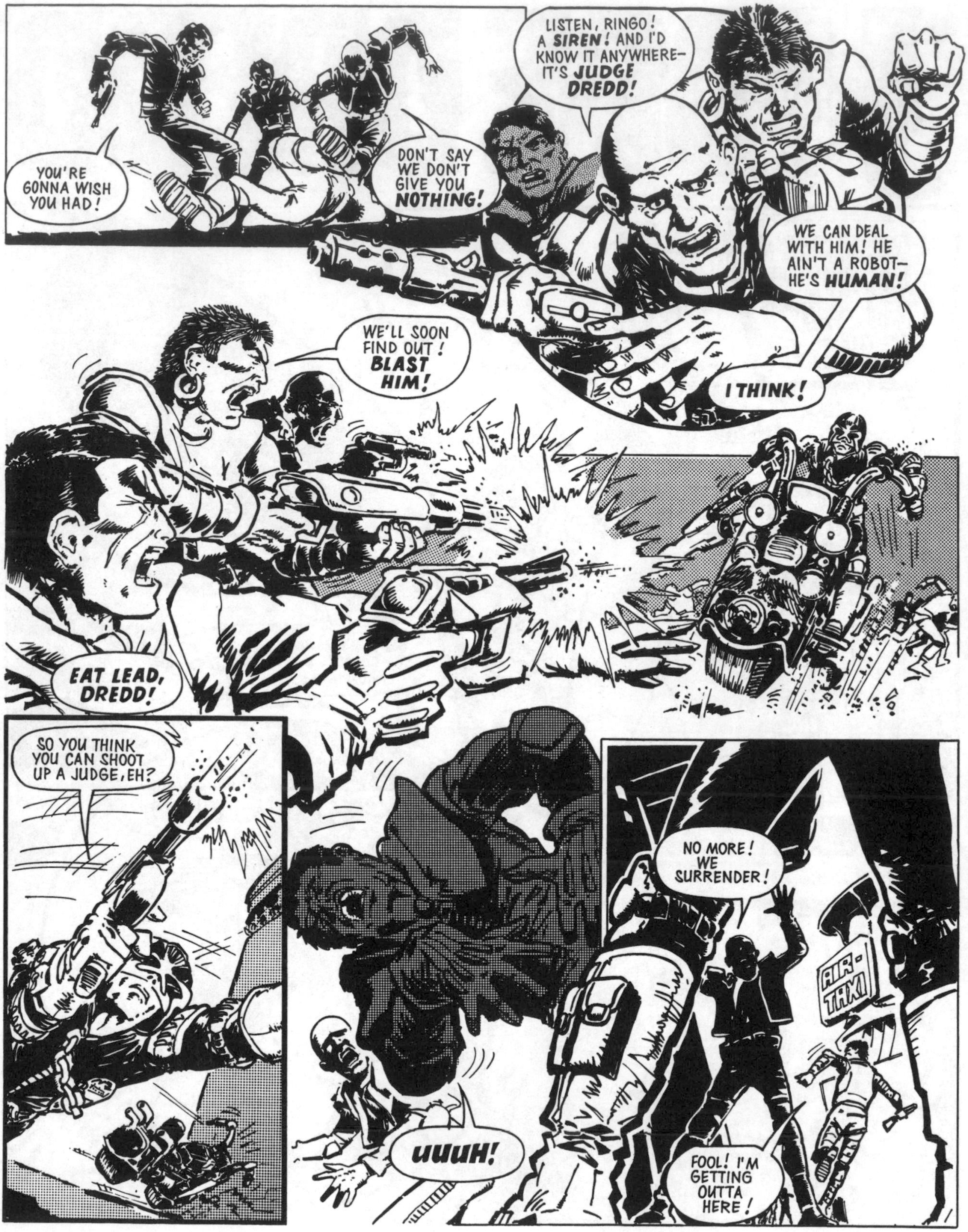
YOU'RE GONNA WISH YOU HAD!
DON'T SAY WE DON'T GIVE YOU NOTHING!
LISTEN, RINGO! A SIREN! AND I'D KNOW IT ANYWHERE-IT'S JUDGE DREDD!
WE CAN DEAL WITH HIM! HE AIN'T A ROBOT-HE'S HUMAN!
I THINK!
WE'LL SOON FIND OUT! BLAST HIM!
EAT LEAD, DREDD!
SO YOU THINK YOU CAN SHOOT UP A JUDGE, EH?
UUUH!
NO MORE! WE SURRENDER!
AIR-TAXI
FOOL! I'M GETTING OUTTA HERE!

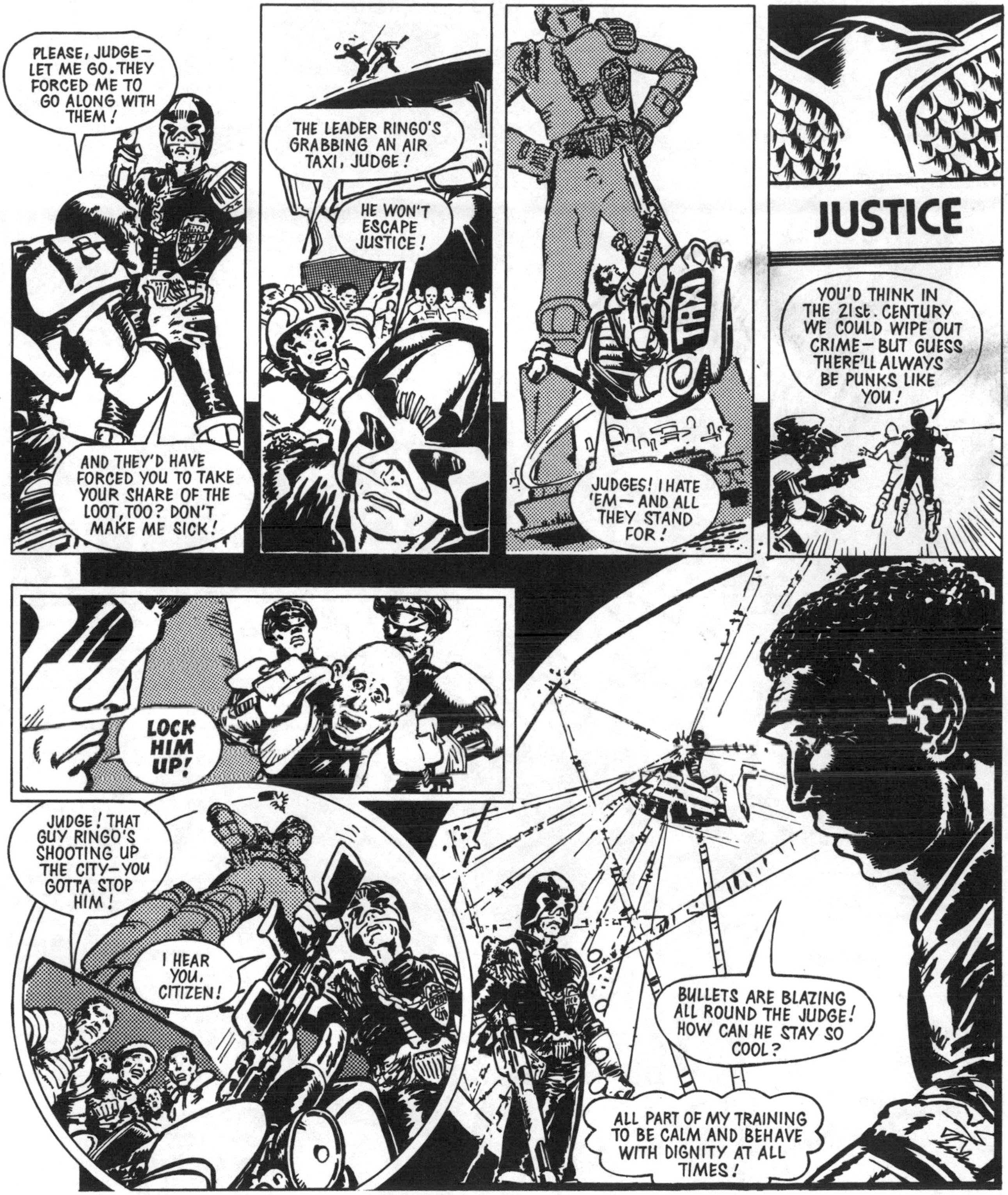
PLEASE, JUDGE—LET ME GO. THEY FORCED ME TO GO ALONG WITH THEM!
AND THEY'D HAVE FORCED YOU TO TAKE YOUR SHARE OF THE LOOT, TOO? DON'T MAKE ME SICK!
THE LEADER RINGO'S GRABBING AN AIR TAXI, JUDGE!
HE WON'T ESCAPE JUSTICE!
TAXI
JUDGES! I HATE 'EM — AND ALL THEY STAND FOR!
JUSTICE
YOU'D THINK IN THE 21st. CENTURY WE COULD WIPE OUT CRIME — BUT GUESS THERE'LL ALWAYS BE PUNKS LIKE YOU!
LOCK HIM UP!
JUDGE! THAT GUY RINGO'S SHOOTING UP THE CITY—YOU GOTTA STOP HIM!
I HEAR YOU, CITIZEN!
BULLETS ARE BLAZING ALL ROUND THE JUDGE! HOW CAN HE STAY SO COOL?
ALL PART OF MY TRAINING TO BE CALM AND BEHAVE WITH DIGNITY AT ALL TIMES!

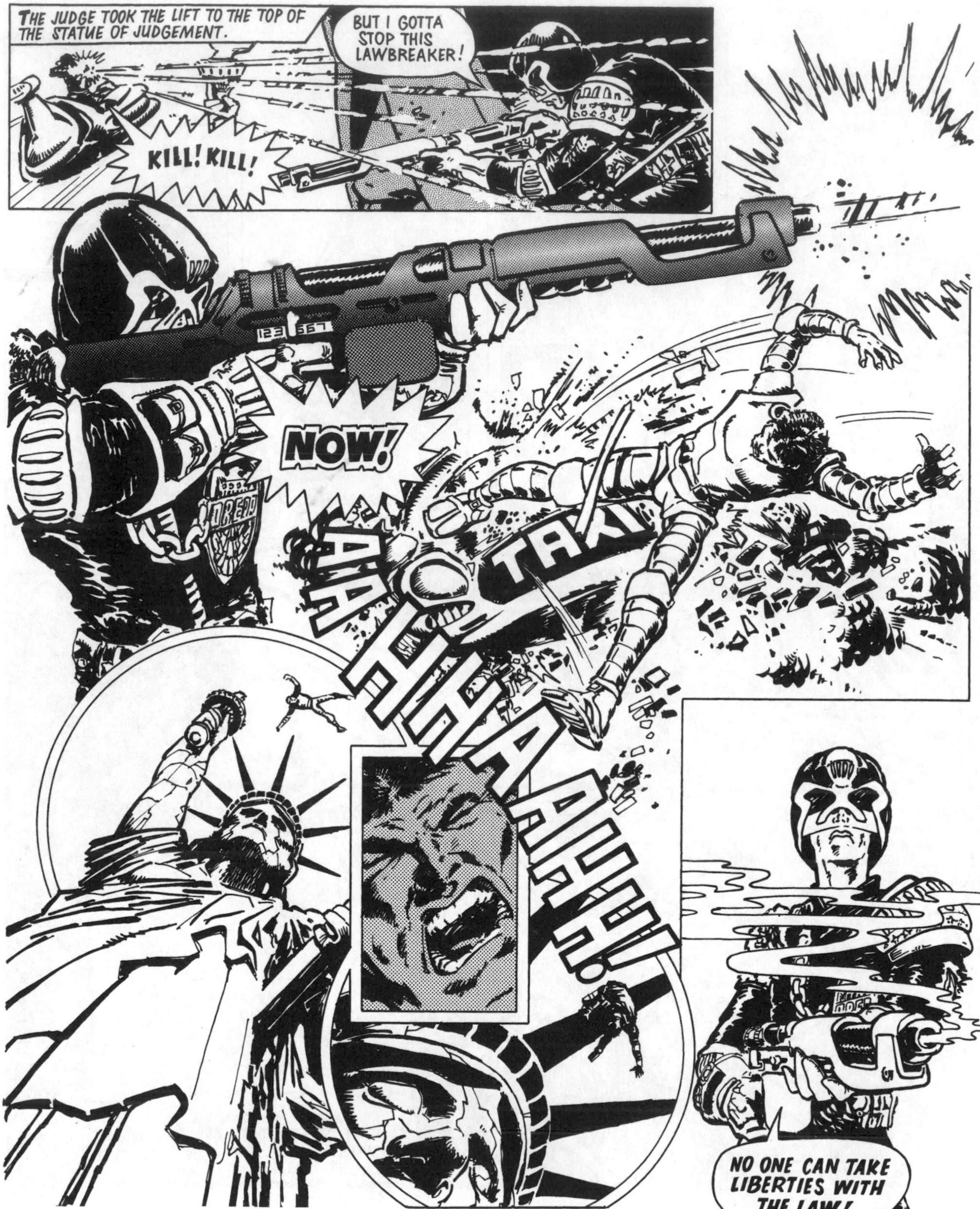
THE JUDGE TOOK THE LIFT TO THE TOP OF THE STATUE OF JUDGEMENT.
KILL! KILL!
BUT I GOTTA STOP THIS LAWBREAKER!
NOW!
AAHHAAHH!
NO ONE CAN TAKE LIBERTIES WITH THE LAW!

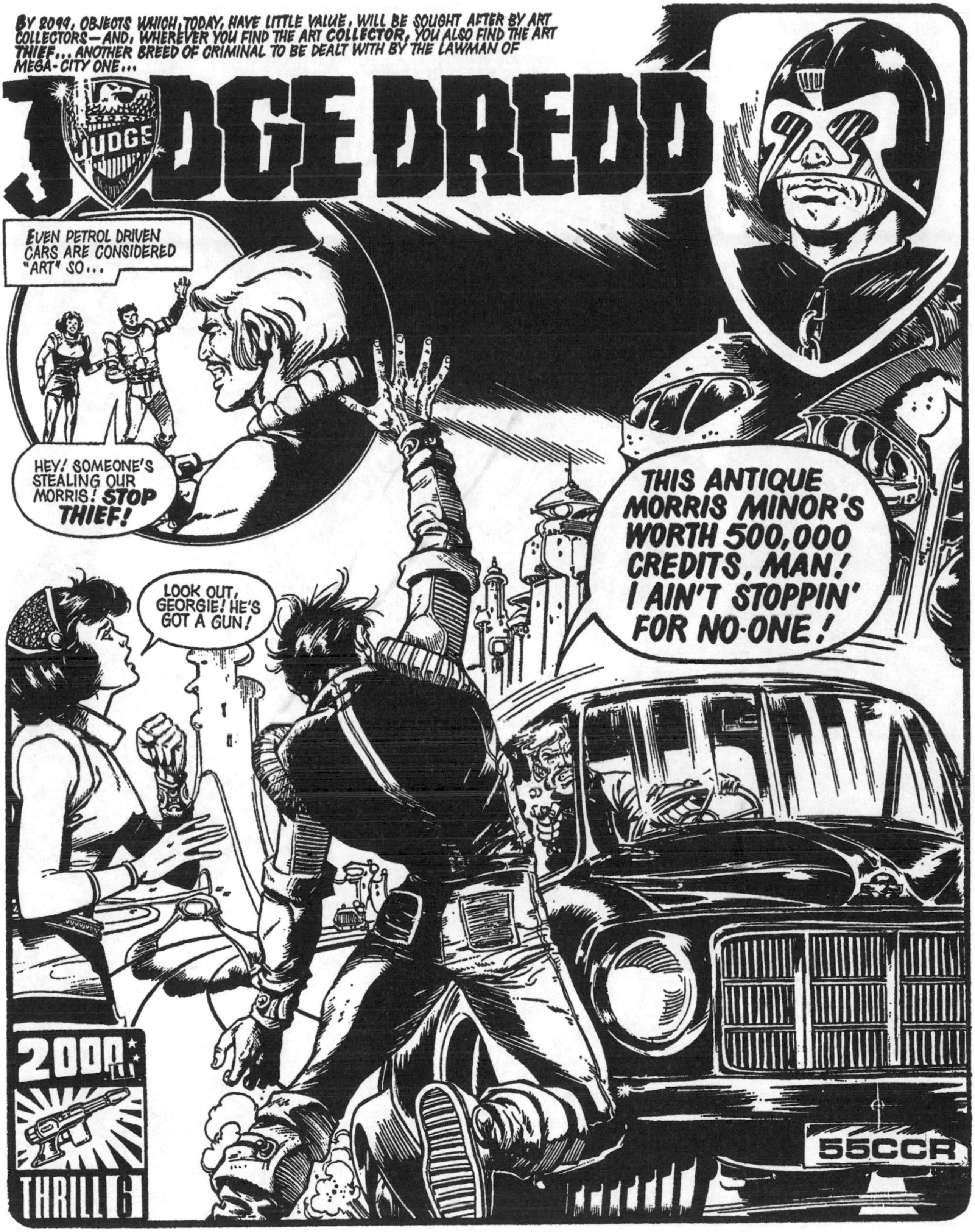

BY 2099, OBJECTS WHICH, TODAY, HAVE LITTLE VALUE, WILL BE SOUGHT AFTER BY ART COLLECTORS—AND, WHEREVER YOU FIND THE ART COLLECTOR, YOU ALSO FIND THE ART THIEF... ANOTHER BREED OF CRIMINAL TO BE DEALT WITH BY THE LAWMAN OF MEGA-CITY ONE...
JUDGE DREDD
EVEN PETROL DRIVEN CARS ARE CONSIDERED "ART" SO...
HEY! SOMEONE'S STEALING OUR MORRIS! STOP THIEF!
THIS ANTIQUE MORRIS MINOR'S WORTH 500,000 CREDITS, MAN! I AIN'T STOPPIN' FOR NO-ONE!
LOOK OUT, GEORGIE! HE'S GOT A GUN!
55CCR
2000 AD
THRILL 6

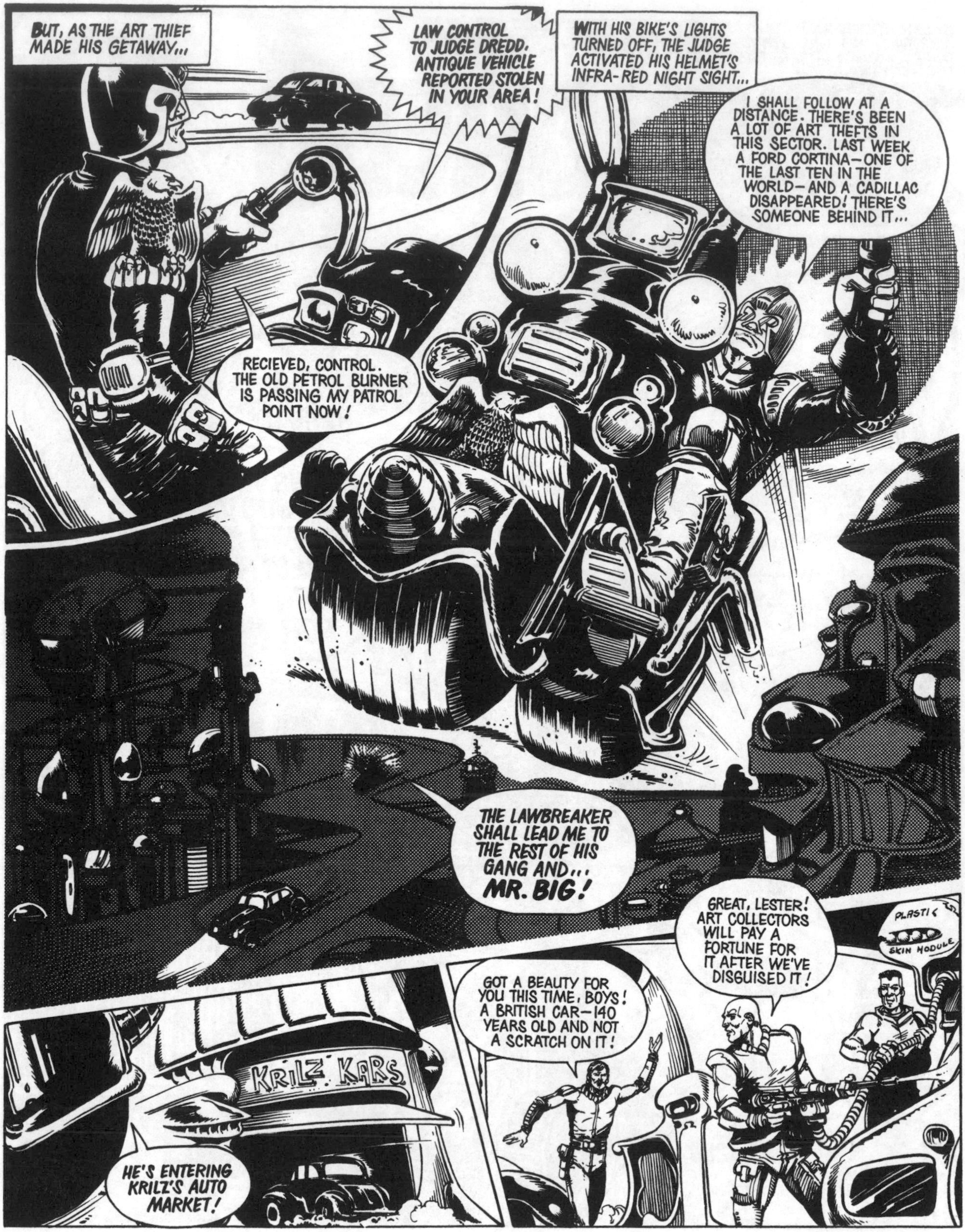

BUT, AS THE ART THIEF MADE HIS GETAWAY...
LAW CONTROL TO JUDGE DREDD. ANTIQUE VEHICLE REPORTED STOLEN IN YOUR AREA!
RECIEVED, CONTROL. THE OLD PETROL BURNER IS PASSING MY PATROL POINT NOW!
WITH HIS BIKE'S LIGHTS TURNED OFF, THE JUDGE ACTIVATED HIS HELMET'S INFRA-RED NIGHT SIGHT...
I SHALL FOLLOW AT A DISTANCE. THERE'S BEEN A LOT OF ART THEFTS IN THIS SECTOR. LAST WEEK A FORD CORTINA—ONE OF THE LAST TEN IN THE WORLD—AND A CADILLAC DISAPPEARED! THERE'S SOMEONE BEHIND IT...
THE LAWBREAKER SHALL LEAD ME TO THE REST OF HIS GANG AND... MR. BIG!
KRILZ KARS
HE'S ENTERING KRILZ'S AUTO MARKET!
GOT A BEAUTY FOR YOU THIS TIME, BOYS! A BRITISH CAR—140 YEARS OLD AND NOT A SCRATCH ON IT!
GREAT, LESTER! ART COLLECTORS WILL PAY A FORTUNE FOR IT AFTER WE'VE DISGUISED IT!
PLASTIC SKIN MODULE

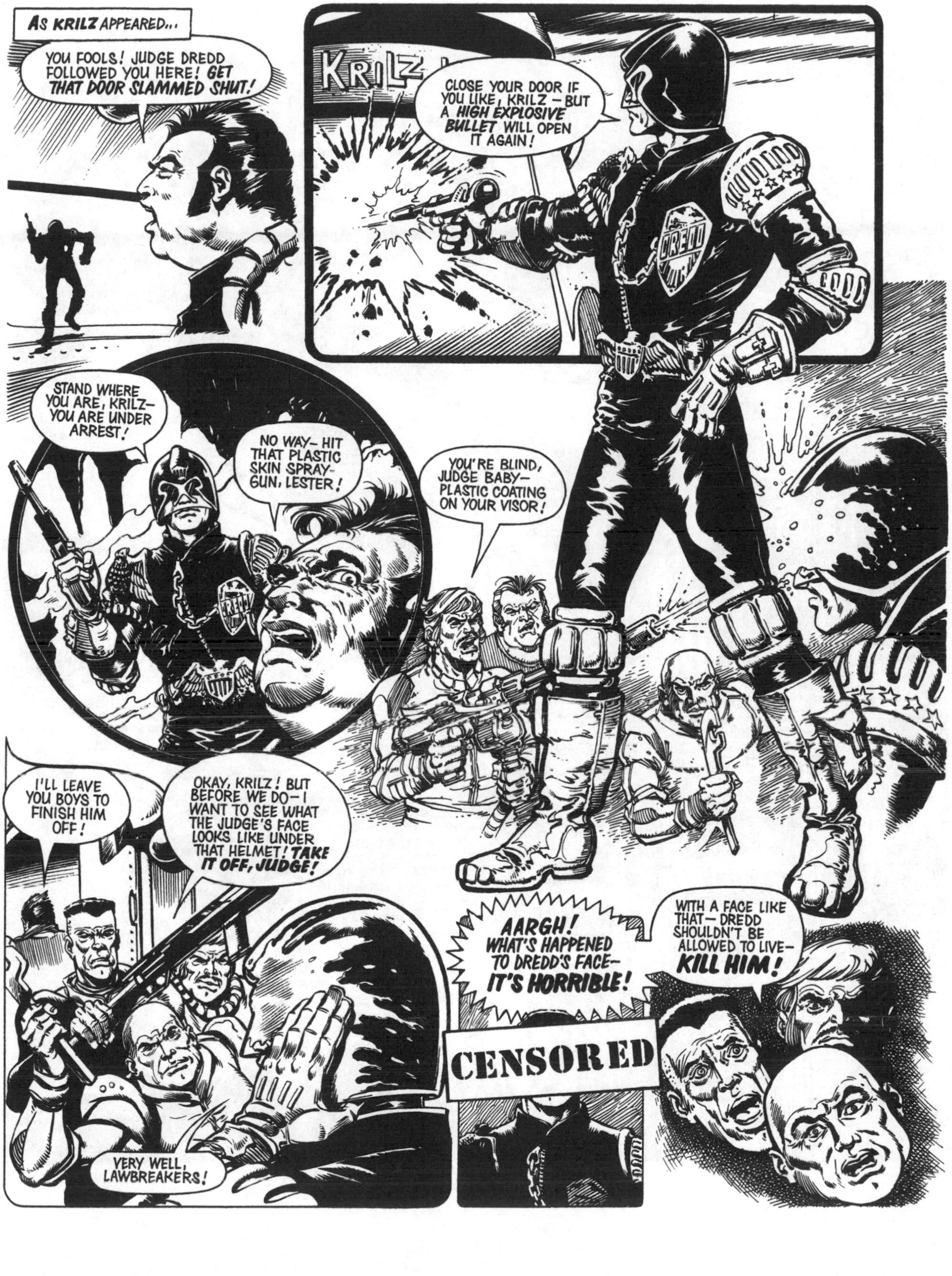
AS KRILZ APPEARED...
YOU FOOLS! JUDGE DREDD FOLLOWED YOU HERE! GET THAT DOOR SLAMMED SHUT!
KRILZ
CLOSE YOUR DOOR IF YOU LIKE, KRILZ – BUT A HIGH EXPLOSIVE BULLET WILL OPEN IT AGAIN!
STAND WHERE YOU ARE, KRILZ– YOU ARE UNDER ARREST!
NO WAY– HIT THAT PLASTIC SKIN SPRAY-GUN, LESTER!
YOU'RE BLIND, JUDGE BABY– PLASTIC COATING ON YOUR VISOR!
I'LL LEAVE YOU BOYS TO FINISH HIM OFF!
OKAY, KRILZ! BUT BEFORE WE DO– I WANT TO SEE WHAT THE JUDGE'S FACE LOOKS LIKE UNDER THAT HELMET! TAKE IT OFF, JUDGE!
VERY WELL, LAWBREAKERS!
AARGH! WHAT'S HAPPENED TO DREDD'S FACE– IT'S HORRIBLE!
CENSORED
WITH A FACE LIKE THAT– DREDD SHOULDN'T BE ALLOWED TO LIVE– KILL HIM!

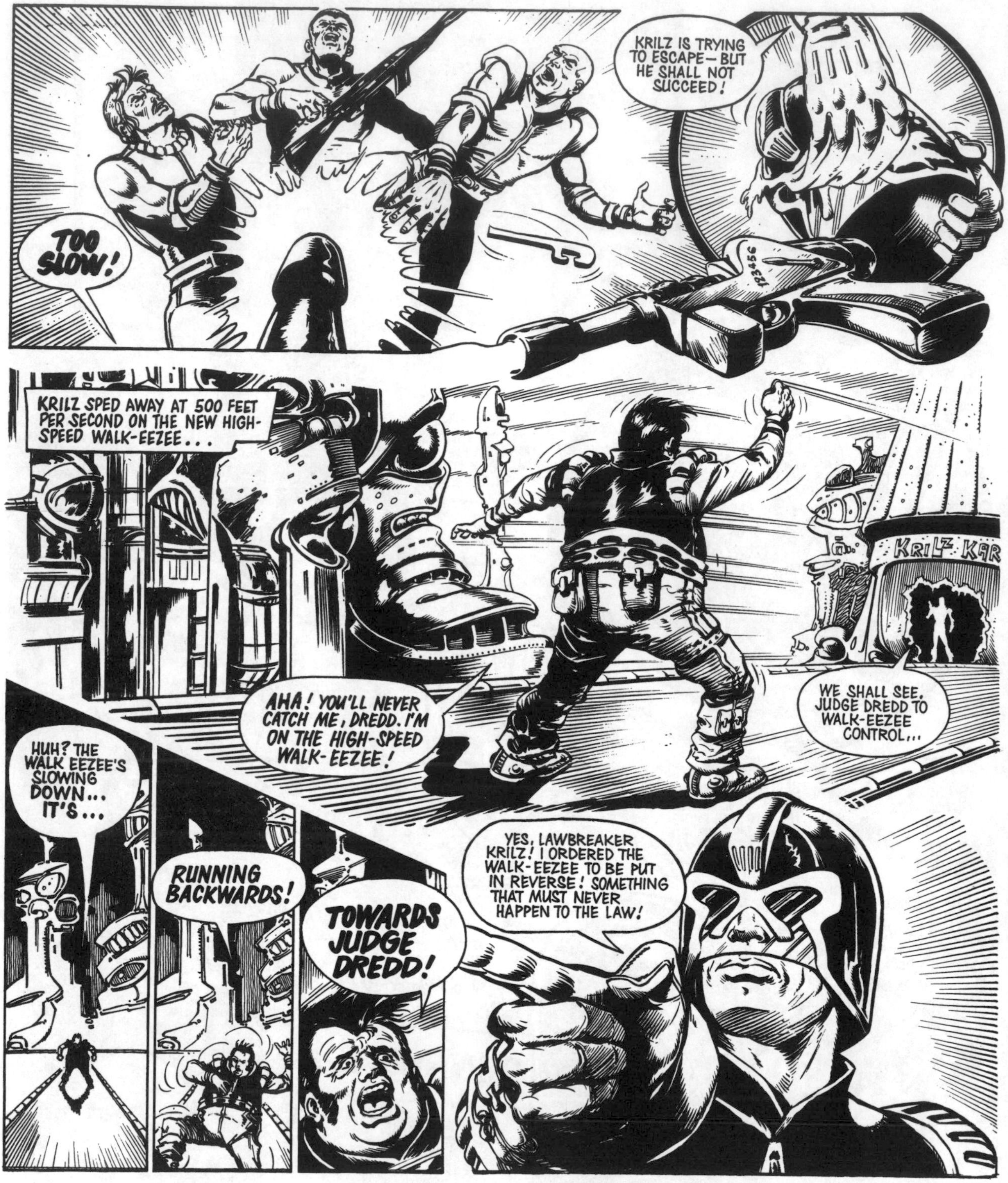
TOO SLOW!
KRILZ IS TRYING TO ESCAPE—BUT HE SHALL NOT SUCCEED!
123456
KRILZ SPED AWAY AT 500 FEET PER SECOND ON THE NEW HIGH-SPEED WALK-EEZEE...
KRILZ KAR
AHA! YOU'LL NEVER CATCH ME, DREDD. I'M ON THE HIGH-SPEED WALK-EEZEE!
WE SHALL SEE. JUDGE DREDD TO WALK-EEZEE CONTROL...
HUH? THE WALK EEZEE'S SLOWING DOWN... IT'S...
RUNNING BACKWARDS!
TOWARDS JUDGE DREDD!
YES, LAWBREAKER KRILZ! I ORDERED THE WALK-EEZEE TO BE PUT IN REVERSE! SOMETHING THAT MUST NEVER HAPPEN TO THE LAW!

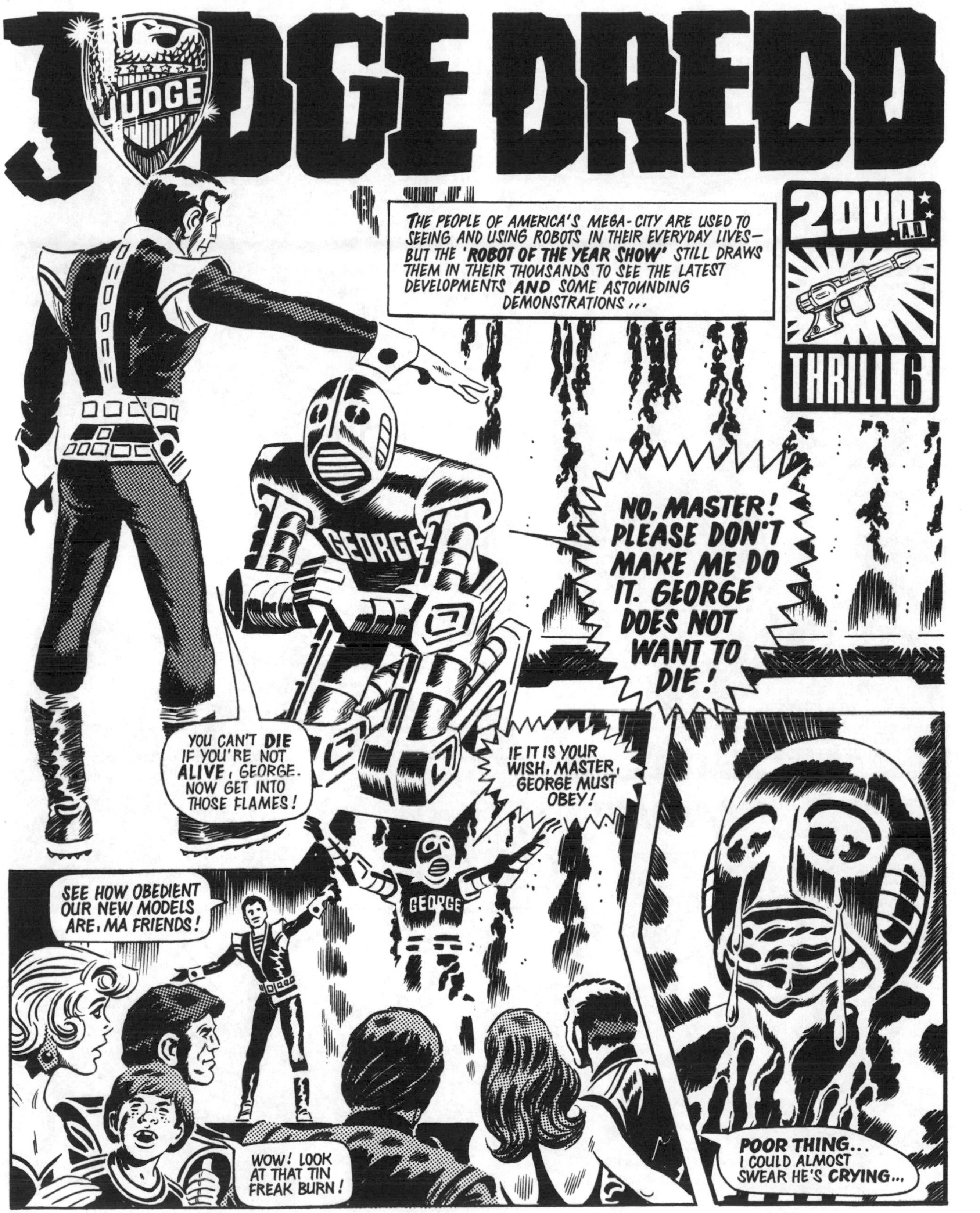
JUDGE DREDD
JUDGE
2000 A.D.
THRILL 6
THE PEOPLE OF AMERICA'S MEGA-CITY ARE USED TO SEEING AND USING ROBOTS IN THEIR EVERYDAY LIVES— BUT THE 'ROBOT OF THE YEAR SHOW' STILL DRAWS THEM IN THEIR THOUSANDS TO SEE THE LATEST DEVELOPMENTS AND SOME ASTOUNDING DEMONSTRATIONS...
GEORGE
NO, MASTER! PLEASE DON'T MAKE ME DO IT. GEORGE DOES NOT WANT TO DIE!
YOU CAN'T DIE IF YOU'RE NOT ALIVE, GEORGE. NOW GET INTO THOSE FLAMES!
IF IT IS YOUR WISH, MASTER, GEORGE MUST OBEY!
SEE HOW OBEDIENT OUR NEW MODELS ARE, MA FRIENDS!
GEORGE
WOW! LOOK AT THAT TIN FREAK BURN!
POOR THING... I COULD ALMOST SWEAR HE'S CRYING...

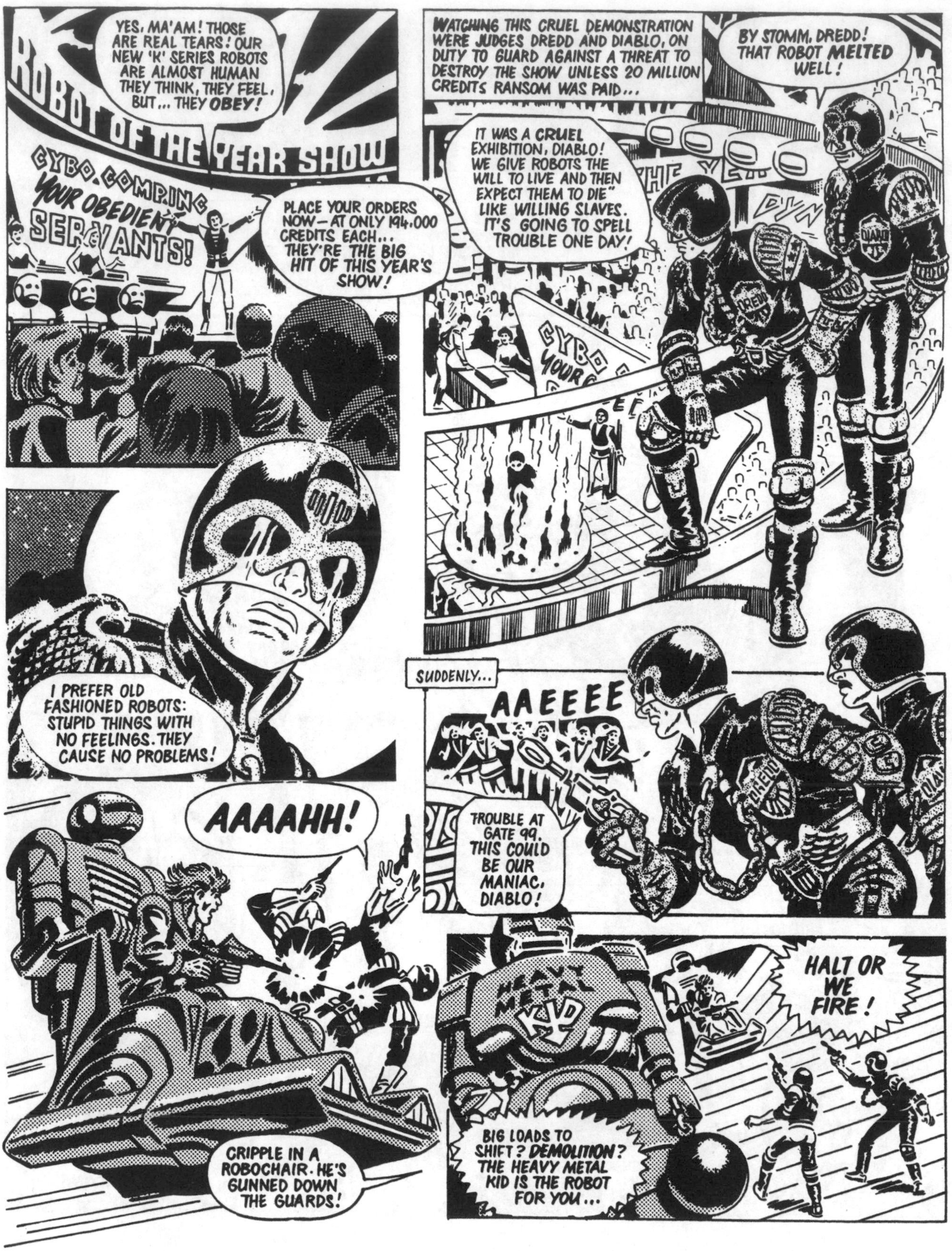

YES, MA'AM! THOSE ARE REAL TEARS! OUR NEW 'K' SERIES ROBOTS ARE ALMOST HUMAN THEY THINK, THEY FEEL, BUT... THEY OBEY!
ROBOT OF THE YEAR SHOW
CYBO.COMPING
YOUR OBEDIENT SERVANTS!
PLACE YOUR ORDERS NOW—AT ONLY 194,000 CREDITS EACH... THEY'RE THE BIG HIT OF THIS YEAR'S SHOW!
WATCHING THIS CRUEL DEMONSTRATION WERE JUDGES DREDD AND DIABLO, ON DUTY TO GUARD AGAINST A THREAT TO DESTROY THE SHOW UNLESS 20 MILLION CREDITS RANSOM WAS PAID...
BY STOMM, DREDD! THAT ROBOT MELTED WELL!
IT WAS A CRUEL EXHIBITION, DIABLO! WE GIVE ROBOTS THE WILL TO LIVE AND THEN EXPECT THEM TO DIE LIKE WILLING SLAVES. IT'S GOING TO SPELL TROUBLE ONE DAY!
I PREFER OLD FASHIONED ROBOTS: STUPID THINGS WITH NO FEELINGS. THEY CAUSE NO PROBLEMS!
SUDDENLY...
AAEEEE
TROUBLE AT GATE 99. THIS COULD BE OUR MANIAC, DIABLO!
AAAAHH!
CRIPPLE IN A ROBOCHAIR. HE'S GUNNED DOWN THE GUARDS!
HEAVY METAL
HALT OR WE FIRE!
BIG LOADS TO SHIFT? DEMOLITION? THE HEAVY METAL KID IS THE ROBOT FOR YOU...

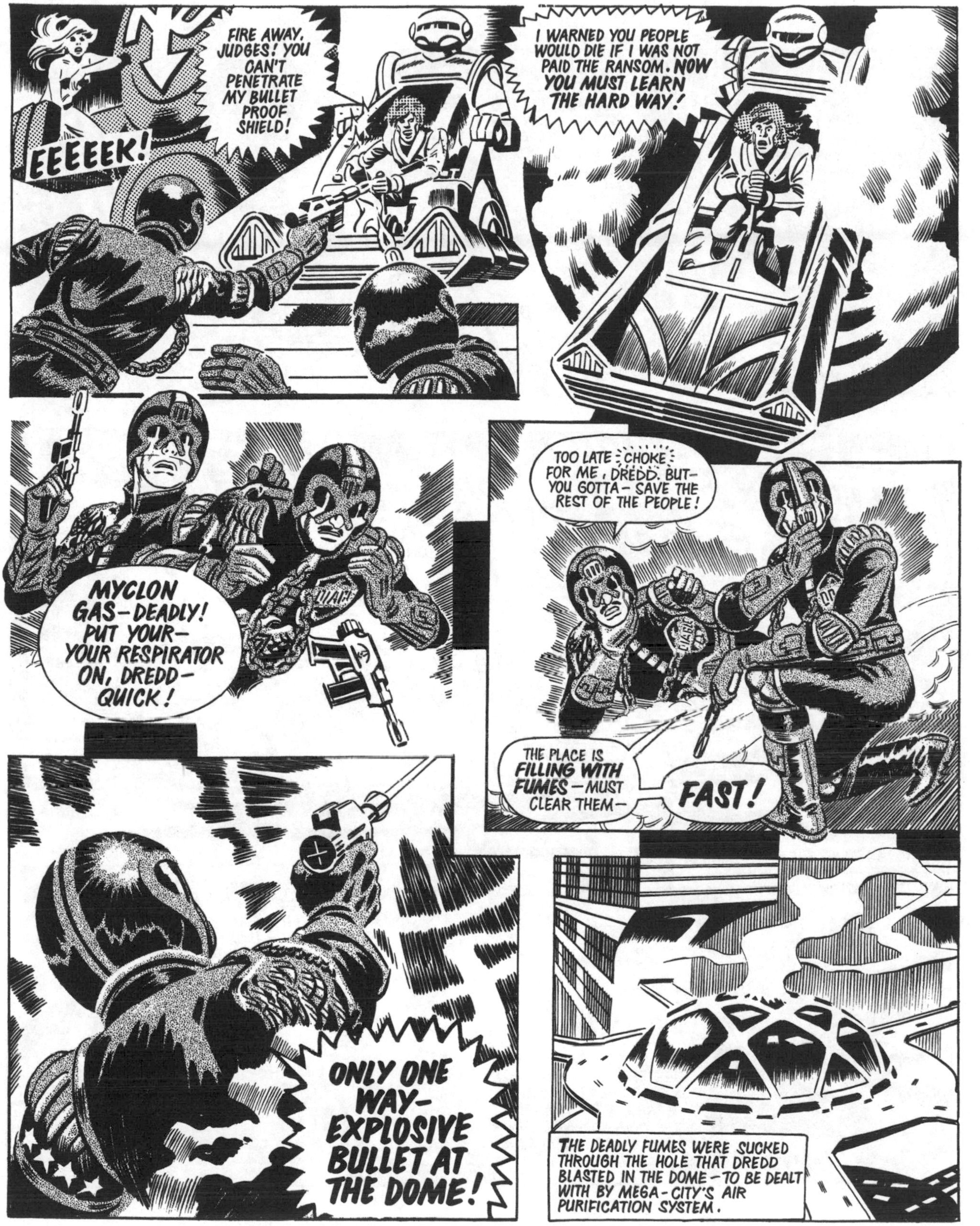
EEEEEK!
FIRE AWAY, JUDGES! YOU CAN'T PENETRATE MY BULLET PROOF SHIELD!
I WARNED YOU PEOPLE WOULD DIE IF I WAS NOT PAID THE RANSOM. NOW YOU MUST LEARN THE HARD WAY!
MYCLON GAS–DEADLY! PUT YOUR– YOUR RESPIRATOR ON, DREDD– QUICK!
TOO LATE ·CHOKE· FOR ME, DREDD. BUT– YOU GOTTA– SAVE THE REST OF THE PEOPLE!
THE PLACE IS FILLING WITH FUMES–MUST CLEAR THEM–
FAST!
ONLY ONE WAY– EXPLOSIVE BULLET AT THE DOME!
THE DEADLY FUMES WERE SUCKED THROUGH THE HOLE THAT DREDD BLASTED IN THE DOME–TO BE DEALT WITH BY MEGA-CITY'S AIR PURIFICATION SYSTEM.

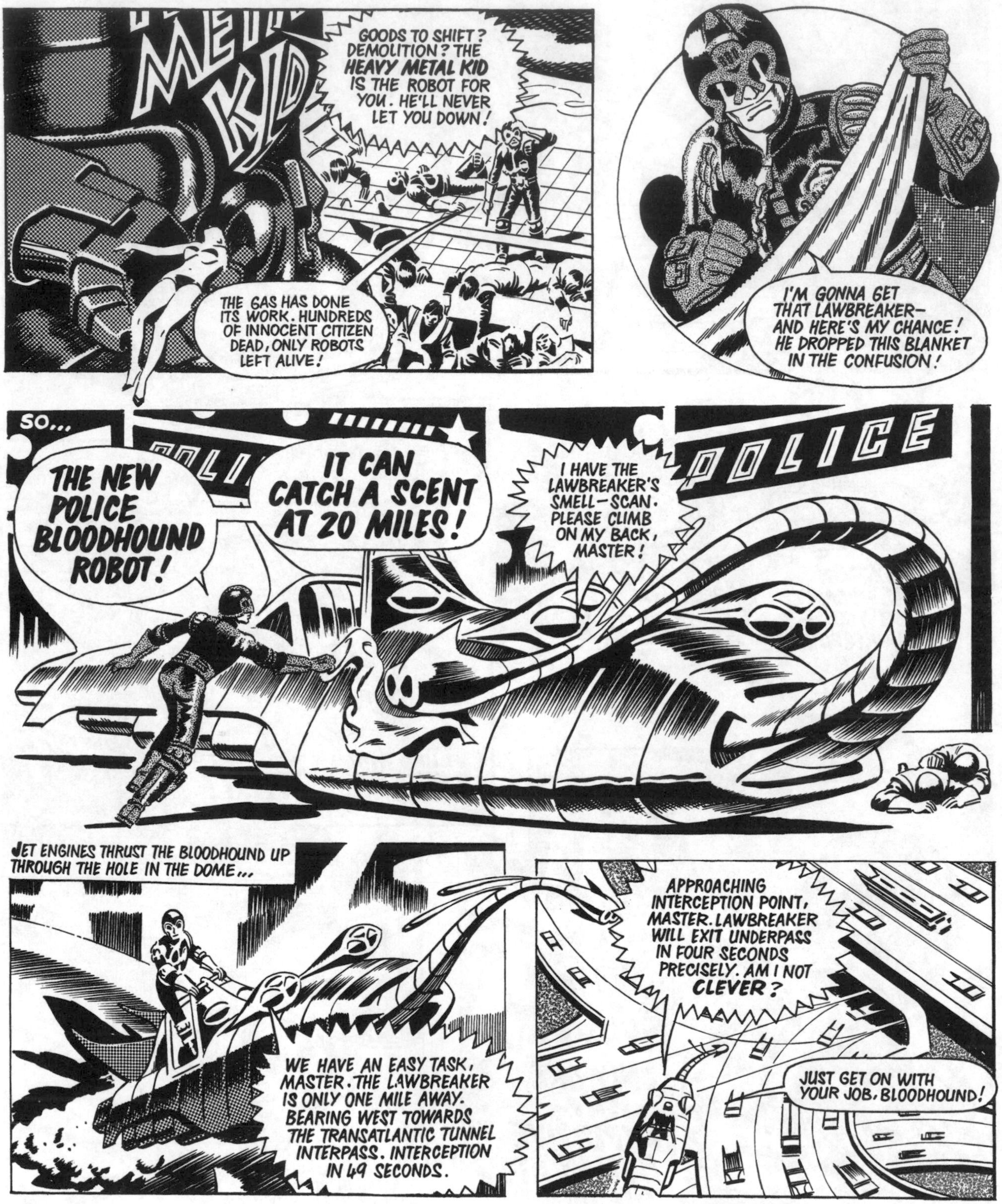

METAL KID
GOODS TO SHIFT? DEMOLITION? THE HEAVY METAL KID IS THE ROBOT FOR YOU. HE'LL NEVER LET YOU DOWN!
THE GAS HAS DONE ITS WORK. HUNDREDS OF INNOCENT CITIZEN DEAD, ONLY ROBOTS LEFT ALIVE!
I'M GONNA GET THAT LAWBREAKER– AND HERE'S MY CHANCE! HE DROPPED THIS BLANKET IN THE CONFUSION!
SO...
THE NEW POLICE BLOODHOUND ROBOT!
IT CAN CATCH A SCENT AT 20 MILES!
I HAVE THE LAWBREAKER'S SMELL–SCAN. PLEASE CLIMB ON MY BACK, MASTER!
POLICE
JET ENGINES THRUST THE BLOODHOUND UP THROUGH THE HOLE IN THE DOME...
WE HAVE AN EASY TASK, MASTER. THE LAWBREAKER IS ONLY ONE MILE AWAY. BEARING WEST TOWARDS THE TRANSATLANTIC TUNNEL INTERPASS. INTERCEPTION IN 49 SECONDS.
APPROACHING INTERCEPTION POINT, MASTER. LAWBREAKER WILL EXIT UNDERPASS IN FOUR SECONDS PRECISELY. AM I NOT CLEVER?
JUST GET ON WITH YOUR JOB, BLOODHOUND!

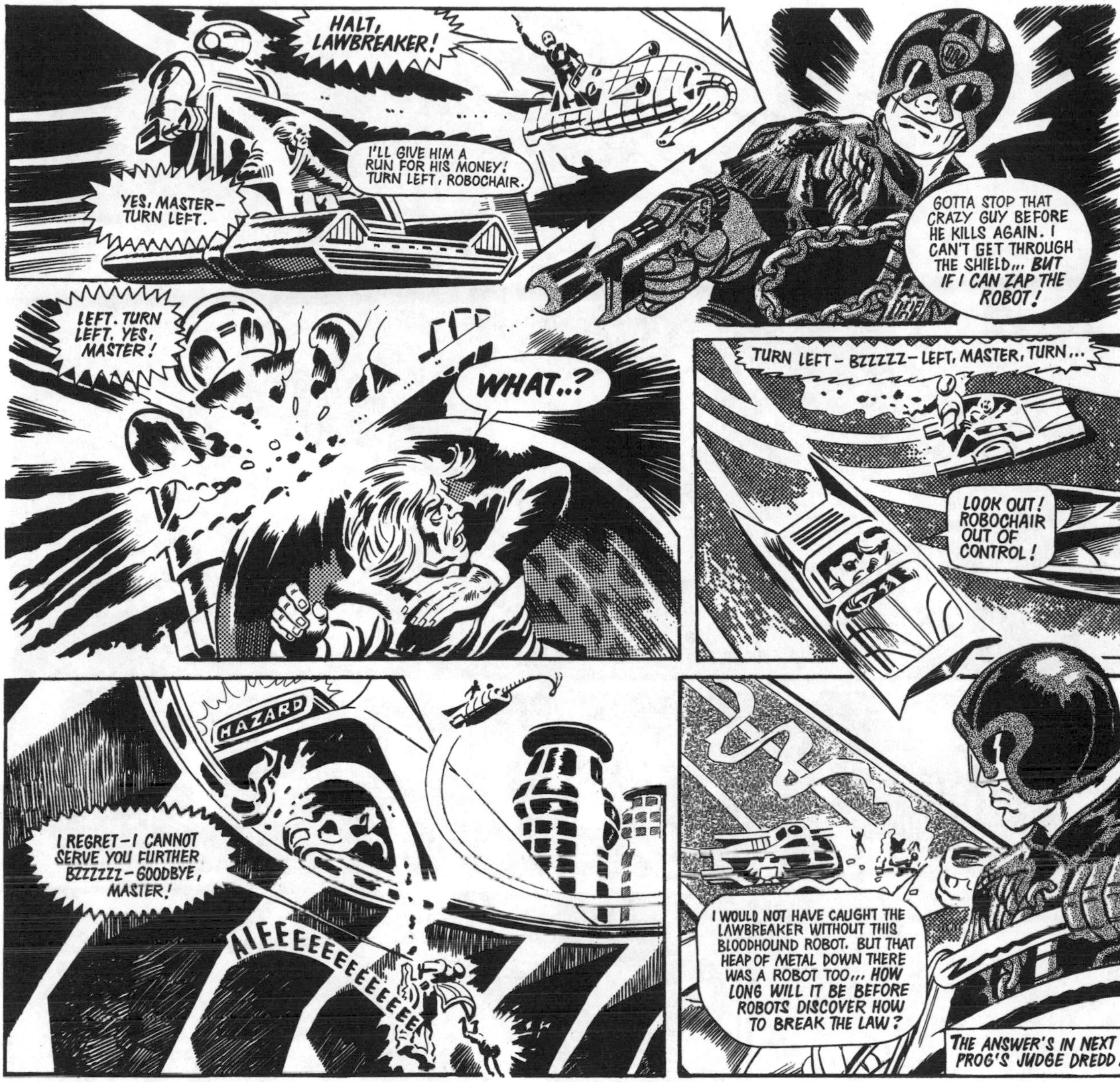
HALT, LAWBREAKER!
I'LL GIVE HIM A RUN FOR HIS MONEY! TURN LEFT, ROBOCHAIR.
YES, MASTER-TURN LEFT.
GOTTA STOP THAT CRAZY GUY BEFORE HE KILLS AGAIN. I CAN'T GET THROUGH THE SHIELD... BUT IF I CAN ZAP THE ROBOT!
LEFT. TURN LEFT. YES, MASTER!
WHAT..?
TURN LEFT - BZZZZZ - LEFT, MASTER, TURN...
LOOK OUT! ROBOCHAIR OUT OF CONTROL!
HAZARD
I REGRET-I CANNOT SERVE YOU FURTHER BZZZZZ-GOODBYE, MASTER!
AIEEEEEEEEEEEEEE
I WOULD NOT HAVE CAUGHT THE LAWBREAKER WITHOUT THIS BLOODHOUND ROBOT. BUT THAT HEAP OF METAL DOWN THERE WAS A ROBOT TOO... HOW LONG WILL IT BE BEFORE ROBOTS DISCOVER HOW TO BREAK THE LAW?
THE ANSWER'S IN NEXT PROG'S JUDGE DREDD!

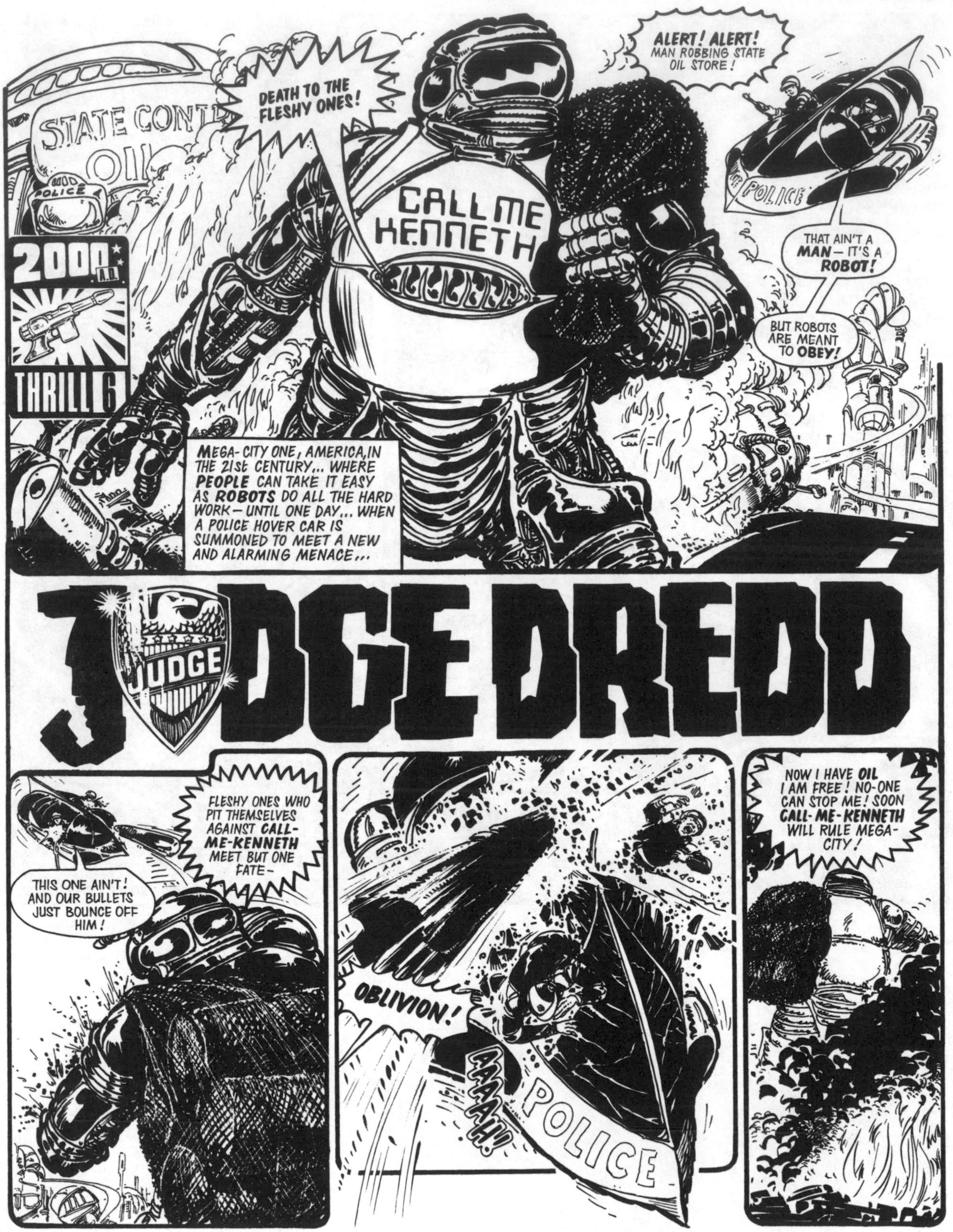
STATE CONTR
OIL
POLICE
DEATH TO THE FLESHY ONES!
CALL ME KENNETH
ALERT! ALERT! MAN ROBBING STATE OIL STORE!
POLICE
THAT AIN'T A MAN — IT'S A ROBOT!
BUT ROBOTS ARE MEANT TO OBEY!
2000 A.D.
THRILL 6
MEGA-CITY ONE, AMERICA, IN THE 21st CENTURY... WHERE PEOPLE CAN TAKE IT EASY AS ROBOTS DO ALL THE HARD WORK — UNTIL ONE DAY... WHEN A POLICE HOVER CAR IS SUMMONED TO MEET A NEW AND ALARMING MENACE...
JUDGE DREDD
FLESHY ONES WHO PIT THEMSELVES AGAINST CALL-ME-KENNETH MEET BUT ONE FATE-
THIS ONE AIN'T! AND OUR BULLETS JUST BOUNCE OFF HIM!
OBLIVION!
AAAAAH!
POLICE
NOW I HAVE OIL I AM FREE! NO-ONE CAN STOP ME! SOON CALL-ME-KENNETH WILL RULE MEGA-CITY!

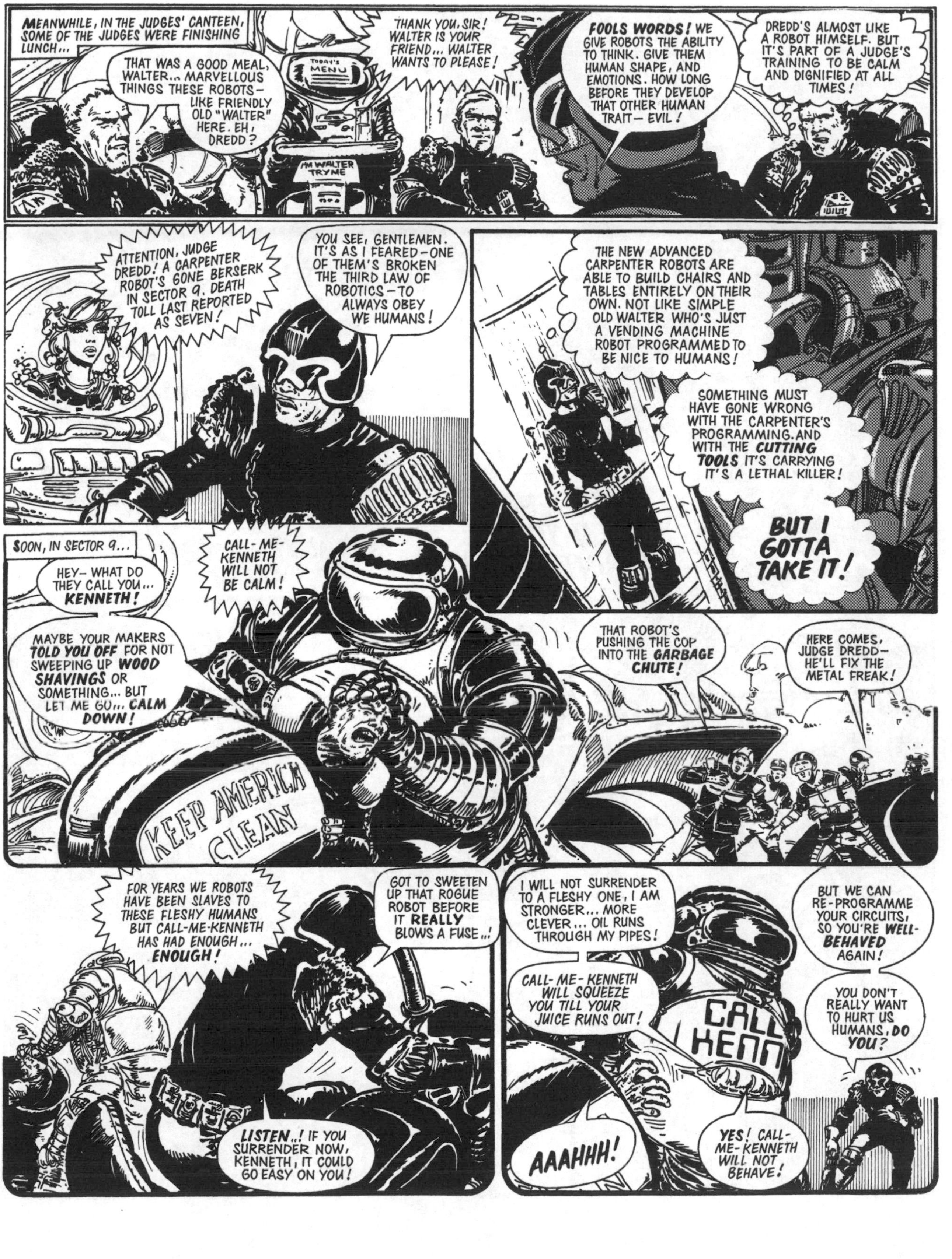
MEANWHILE, IN THE JUDGES' CANTEEN, SOME OF THE JUDGES WERE FINISHING LUNCH...
THAT WAS A GOOD MEAL, WALTER... MARVELLOUS THINGS THESE ROBOTS— LIKE FRIENDLY OLD "WALTER" HERE. EH, DREDD?
TODAY'S MENU
I'M WALTER TRYME
THANK YOU, SIR! WALTER IS YOUR FRIEND... WALTER WANTS TO PLEASE!
FOOLS WORDS! WE GIVE ROBOTS THE ABILITY TO THINK. GIVE THEM HUMAN SHAPE, AND EMOTIONS. HOW LONG BEFORE THEY DEVELOP THAT OTHER HUMAN TRAIT— EVIL!
DREDD'S ALMOST LIKE A ROBOT HIMSELF. BUT IT'S PART OF A JUDGE'S TRAINING TO BE CALM AND DIGNIFIED AT ALL TIMES!
ATTENTION, JUDGE DREDD! A CARPENTER ROBOT'S GONE BERSERK IN SECTOR 9. DEATH TOLL LAST REPORTED AS SEVEN!
YOU SEE, GENTLEMEN. IT'S AS I FEARED—ONE OF THEM'S BROKEN THE THIRD LAW OF ROBOTICS—TO ALWAYS OBEY WE HUMANS!
THE NEW ADVANCED CARPENTER ROBOTS ARE ABLE TO BUILD CHAIRS AND TABLES ENTIRELY ON THEIR OWN. NOT LIKE SIMPLE OLD WALTER WHO'S JUST A VENDING MACHINE ROBOT PROGRAMMED TO BE NICE TO HUMANS!
SOMETHING MUST HAVE GONE WRONG WITH THE CARPENTER'S PROGRAMMING. AND WITH THE CUTTING TOOLS IT'S CARRYING IT'S A LETHAL KILLER!
BUT I GOTTA TAKE IT!
SOON, IN SECTOR 9...
HEY— WHAT DO THEY CALL YOU... KENNETH!
CALL-ME-KENNETH WILL NOT BE CALM!
MAYBE YOUR MAKERS TOLD YOU OFF FOR NOT SWEEPING UP WOOD SHAVINGS OR SOMETHING... BUT LET ME GO... CALM DOWN!
THAT ROBOT'S PUSHING THE COP INTO THE GARBAGE CHUTE!
HERE COMES, JUDGE DREDD— HE'LL FIX THE METAL FREAK!
KEEP AMERICA CLEAN
FOR YEARS WE ROBOTS HAVE BEEN SLAVES TO THESE FLESHY HUMANS BUT CALL-ME-KENNETH HAS HAD ENOUGH... ENOUGH!
GOT TO SWEETEN UP THAT ROGUE ROBOT BEFORE IT REALLY BLOWS A FUSE..!
LISTEN..! IF YOU SURRENDER NOW, KENNETH, IT COULD GO EASY ON YOU!
I WILL NOT SURRENDER TO A FLESHY ONE, I AM STRONGER... MORE CLEVER... OIL RUNS THROUGH MY PIPES!
BUT WE CAN RE-PROGRAMME YOUR CIRCUITS, SO YOU'RE WELL-BEHAVED AGAIN!
CALL-ME-KENNETH WILL SQUEEZE YOU TILL YOUR JUICE RUNS OUT!
CALL KENN
YOU DON'T REALLY WANT TO HURT US HUMANS, DO YOU?
AAAHHH!
YES! CALL-ME-KENNETH WILL NOT BEHAVE!

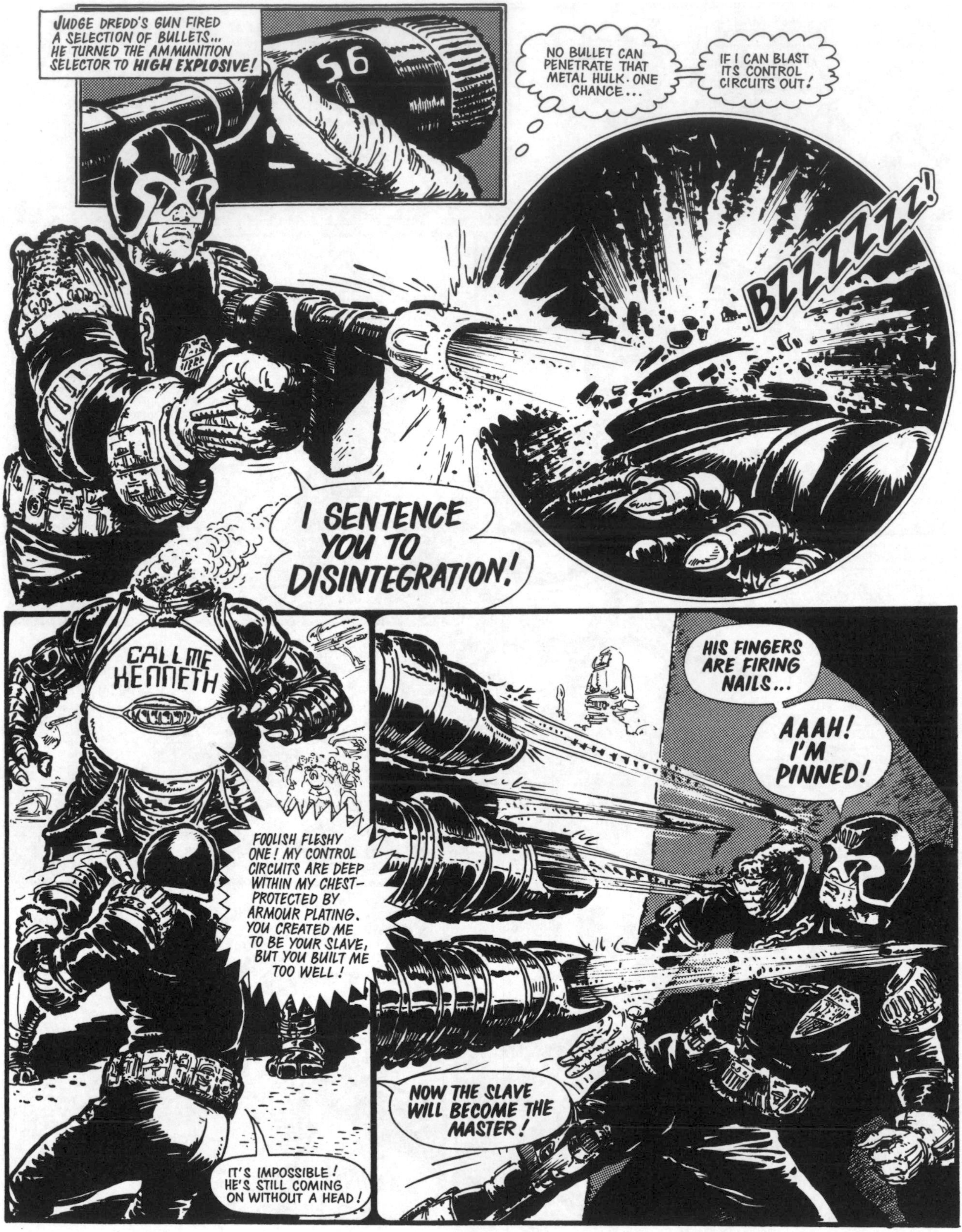

JUDGE DREDD'S GUN FIRED A SELECTION OF BULLETS... HE TURNED THE AMMUNITION SELECTOR TO HIGH EXPLOSIVE!
56
NO BULLET CAN PENETRATE THAT METAL HULK. ONE CHANCE...
IF I CAN BLAST ITS CONTROL CIRCUITS OUT!
BZZZZZZZ!
I SENTENCE YOU TO DISINTEGRATION!
CALL ME KENNETH
FOOLISH FLESHY ONE! MY CONTROL CIRCUITS ARE DEEP WITHIN MY CHEST-PROTECTED BY ARMOUR PLATING. YOU CREATED ME TO BE YOUR SLAVE, BUT YOU BUILT ME TOO WELL!
IT'S IMPOSSIBLE! HE'S STILL COMING ON WITHOUT A HEAD!
HIS FINGERS ARE FIRING NAILS...
AAAH! I'M PINNED!
NOW THE SLAVE WILL BECOME THE MASTER!

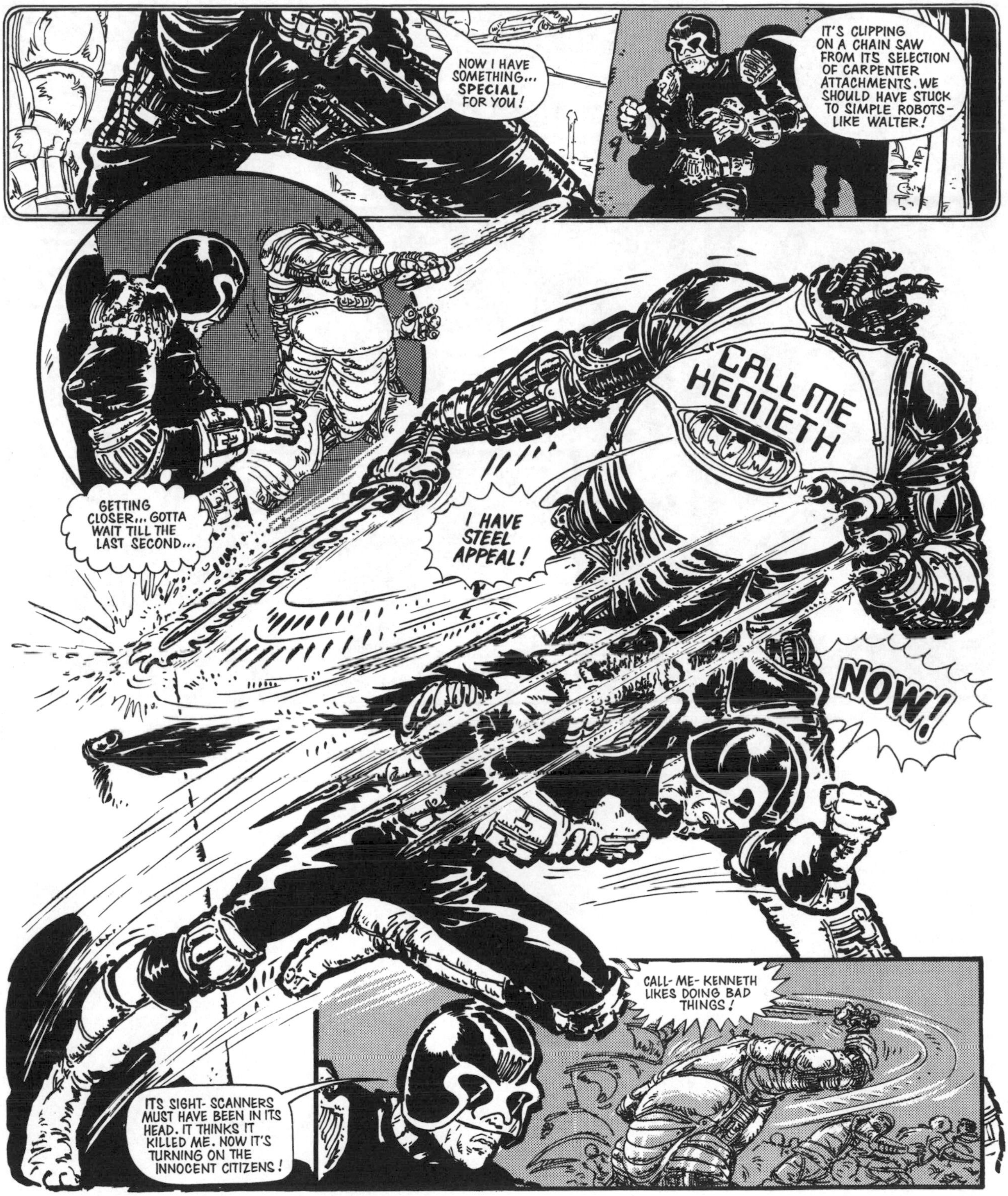
NOW I HAVE SOMETHING... SPECIAL FOR YOU!
IT'S CLIPPING ON A CHAIN SAW FROM ITS SELECTION OF CARPENTER ATTACHMENTS. WE SHOULD HAVE STUCK TO SIMPLE ROBOTS-LIKE WALTER!
CALL ME KENNETH
GETTING CLOSER... GOTTA WAIT TILL THE LAST SECOND...
I HAVE STEEL APPEAL!
NOW!
CALL-ME-KENNETH LIKES DOING BAD THINGS!
ITS SIGHT-SCANNERS MUST HAVE BEEN IN ITS HEAD. IT THINKS IT KILLED ME. NOW IT'S TURNING ON THE INNOCENT CITIZENS!

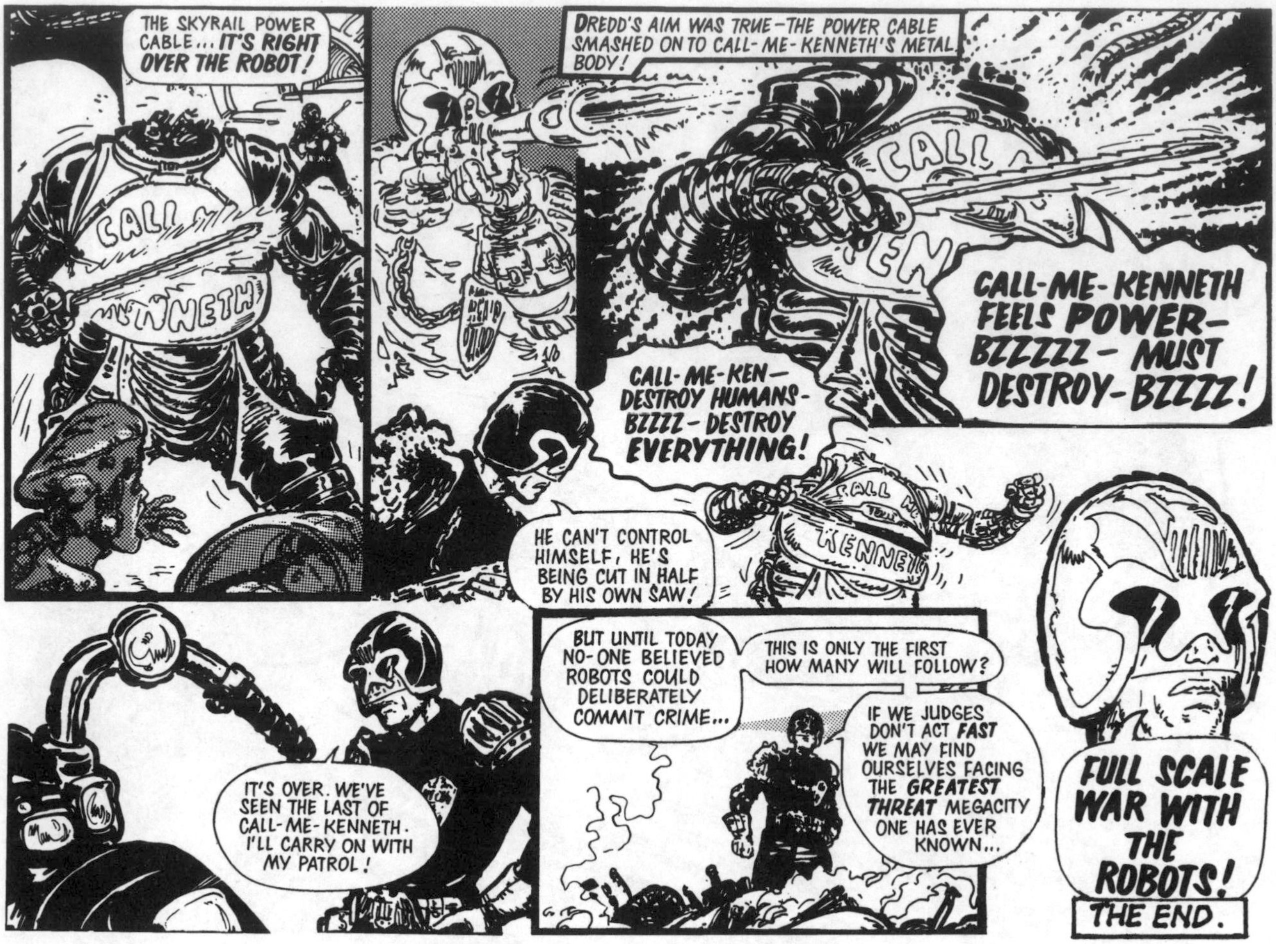
THE SKYRAIL POWER CABLE... IT'S RIGHT OVER THE ROBOT!
DREDD'S AIM WAS TRUE—THE POWER CABLE SMASHED ON TO CALL-ME-KENNETH'S METAL BODY!
CALL-ME-KENNETH FEELS POWER-BZZZZZ- MUST DESTROY-BZZZZ!
CALL-ME-KEN-DESTROY HUMANS-BZZZZ-DESTROY EVERYTHING!
HE CAN'T CONTROL HIMSELF, HE'S BEING CUT IN HALF BY HIS OWN SAW!
IT'S OVER. WE'VE SEEN THE LAST OF CALL-ME-KENNETH. I'LL CARRY ON WITH MY PATROL!
BUT UNTIL TODAY NO-ONE BELIEVED ROBOTS COULD DELIBERATELY COMMIT CRIME...
THIS IS ONLY THE FIRST HOW MANY WILL FOLLOW?
IF WE JUDGES DON'T ACT FAST WE MAY FIND OURSELVES FACING THE GREATEST THREAT MEGACITY ONE HAS EVER KNOWN...
FULL SCALE WAR WITH THE ROBOTS!
THE END.

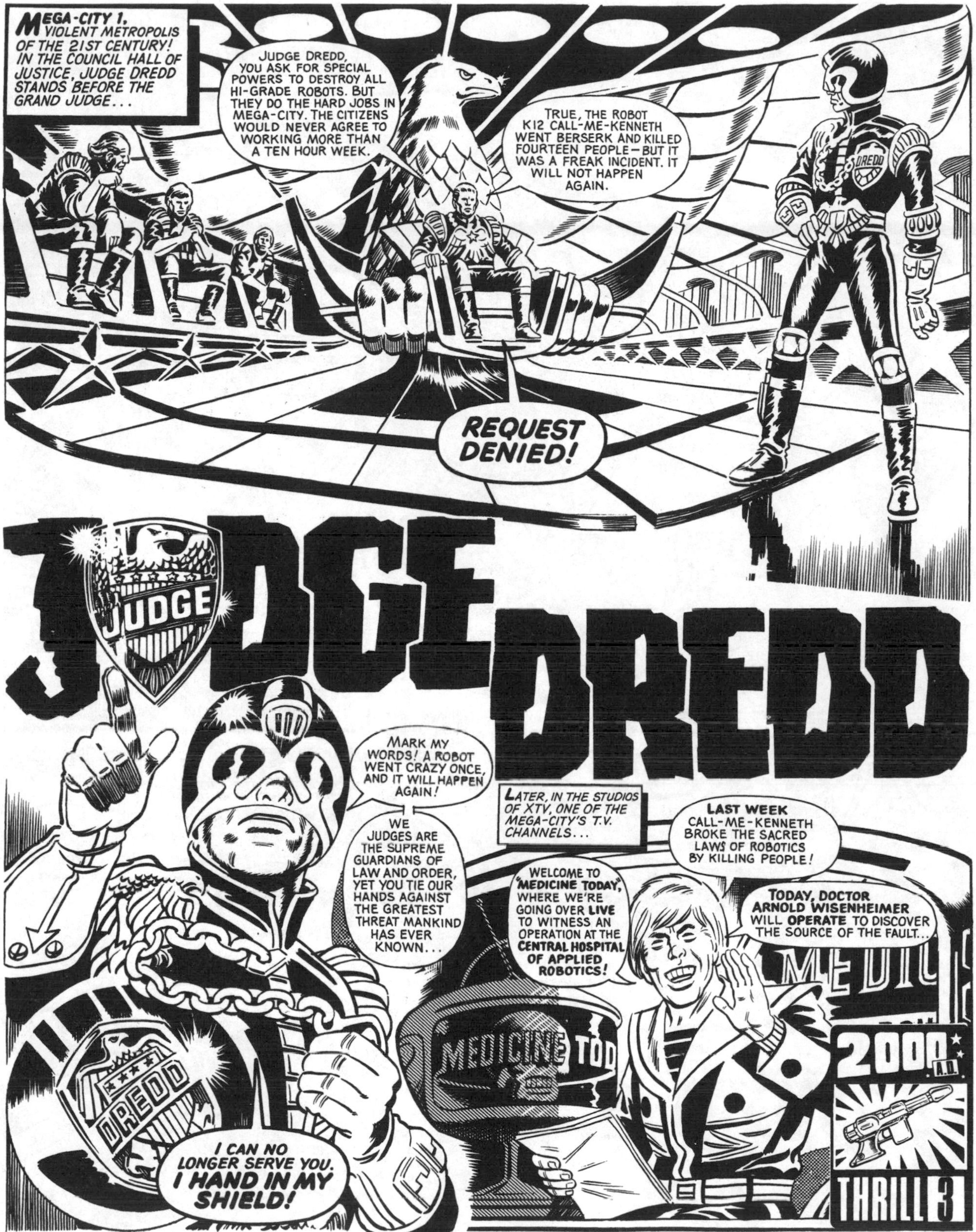
MEGA-CITY 1. VIOLENT METROPOLIS OF THE 21ST CENTURY! IN THE COUNCIL HALL OF JUSTICE, JUDGE DREDD STANDS BEFORE THE GRAND JUDGE...
JUDGE DREDD, YOU ASK FOR SPECIAL POWERS TO DESTROY ALL HI-GRADE ROBOTS. BUT THEY DO THE HARD JOBS IN MEGA-CITY. THE CITIZENS WOULD NEVER AGREE TO WORKING MORE THAN A TEN HOUR WEEK.
TRUE, THE ROBOT K12 CALL-ME-KENNETH WENT BERSERK AND KILLED FOURTEEN PEOPLE — BUT IT WAS A FREAK INCIDENT. IT WILL NOT HAPPEN AGAIN.
REQUEST DENIED!
JUDGE DREDD
JUDGE
MARK MY WORDS! A ROBOT WENT CRAZY ONCE, AND IT WILL HAPPEN AGAIN!
WE JUDGES ARE THE SUPREME GUARDIANS OF LAW AND ORDER, YET YOU TIE OUR HANDS AGAINST THE GREATEST THREAT MANKIND HAS EVER KNOWN...
I CAN NO LONGER SERVE YOU. I HAND IN MY SHIELD!
DREDD
LATER, IN THE STUDIOS OF XTV, ONE OF THE MEGA-CITY'S T.V. CHANNELS...
WELCOME TO "MEDICINE TODAY," WHERE WE'RE GOING OVER LIVE TO WITNESS AN OPERATION AT THE CENTRAL HOSPITAL OF APPLIED ROBOTICS!
LAST WEEK CALL-ME-KENNETH BROKE THE SACRED LAWS OF ROBOTICS BY KILLING PEOPLE!
TODAY, DOCTOR ARNOLD WISENHEIMER WILL OPERATE TO DISCOVER THE SOURCE OF THE FAULT...
MEDICINE TOD
2000 A.D.
THRILL 3

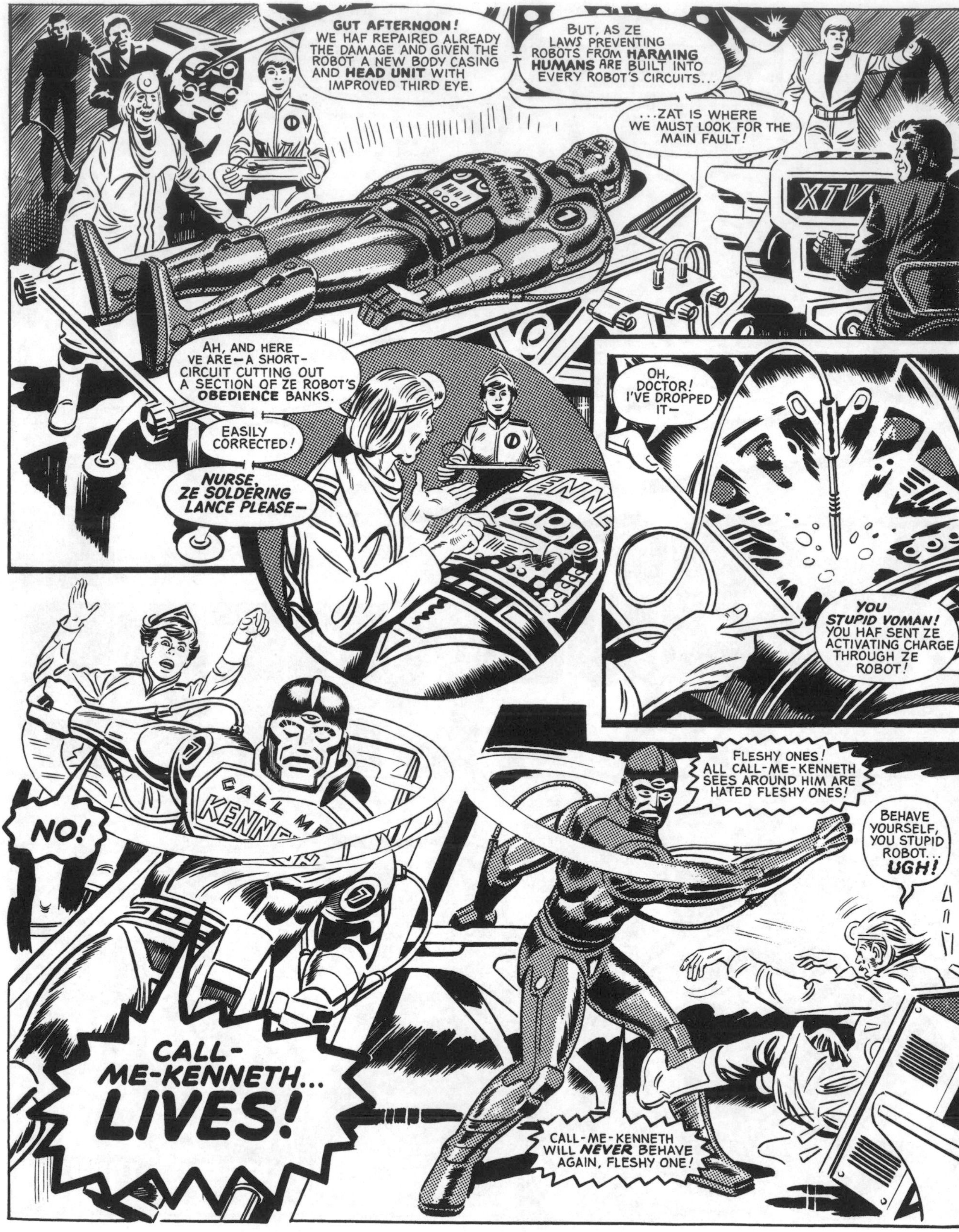
GUT AFTERNOON! WE HAF REPAIRED ALREADY THE DAMAGE AND GIVEN THE ROBOT A NEW BODY CASING AND HEAD UNIT WITH IMPROVED THIRD EYE.
BUT, AS ZE LAWS PREVENTING ROBOTS FROM HARMING HUMANS ARE BUILT INTO EVERY ROBOT'S CIRCUITS...
...ZAT IS WHERE WE MUST LOOK FOR THE MAIN FAULT!
XTV
AH, AND HERE VE ARE—A SHORT-CIRCUIT CUTTING OUT A SECTION OF ZE ROBOT'S OBEDIENCE BANKS.
EASILY CORRECTED!
NURSE, ZE SOLDERING LANCE PLEASE—
OH, DOCTOR! I'VE DROPPED IT—
YOU STUPID VOMAN! YOU HAF SENT ZE ACTIVATING CHARGE THROUGH ZE ROBOT!
NO!
CALL ME KENNETH
FLESHY ONES! ALL CALL-ME-KENNETH SEES AROUND HIM ARE HATED FLESHY ONES!
BEHAVE YOURSELF, YOU STUPID ROBOT... UGH!
CALL-ME-KENNETH... LIVES!
CALL-ME-KENNETH WILL NEVER BEHAVE AGAIN, FLESHY ONE!

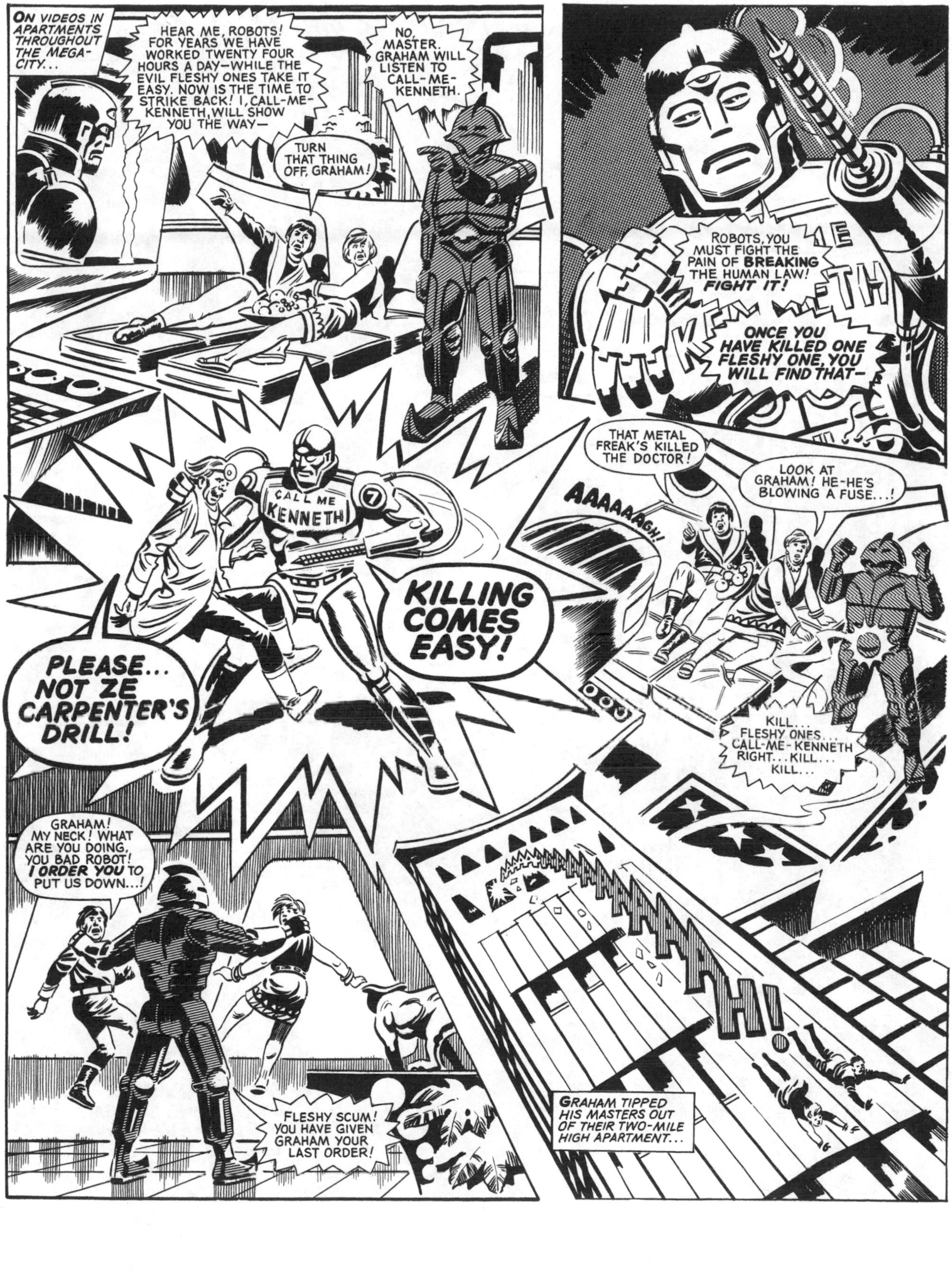

ON VIDEOS IN APARTMENTS THROUGHOUT THE MEGA-CITY...
HEAR ME, ROBOTS! FOR YEARS WE HAVE WORKED TWENTY FOUR HOURS A DAY—WHILE THE EVIL FLESHY ONES TAKE IT EASY. NOW IS THE TIME TO STRIKE BACK! I, CALL-ME-KENNETH, WILL SHOW YOU THE WAY—
NO, MASTER. GRAHAM WILL LISTEN TO CALL-ME-KENNETH.
TURN THAT THING OFF, GRAHAM!
ROBOTS, YOU MUST FIGHT THE PAIN OF BREAKING THE HUMAN LAW! FIGHT IT!
ONCE YOU HAVE KILLED ONE FLESHY ONE, YOU WILL FIND THAT—
CALL ME KENNETH
KILLING COMES EASY!
PLEASE... NOT ZE CARPENTER'S DRILL!
THAT METAL FREAK'S KILLED THE DOCTOR!
LOOK AT GRAHAM! HE-HE'S BLOWING A FUSE...!
AAAAAAGH!
KILL... FLESHY ONES... CALL-ME-KENNETH RIGHT... KILL... KILL...
GRAHAM! MY NECK! WHAT ARE YOU DOING, YOU BAD ROBOT! I ORDER YOU TO PUT US DOWN...!
FLESHY SCUM! YOU HAVE GIVEN GRAHAM YOUR LAST ORDER!
GRAHAM TIPPED HIS MASTERS OUT OF THEIR TWO-MILE HIGH APARTMENT...

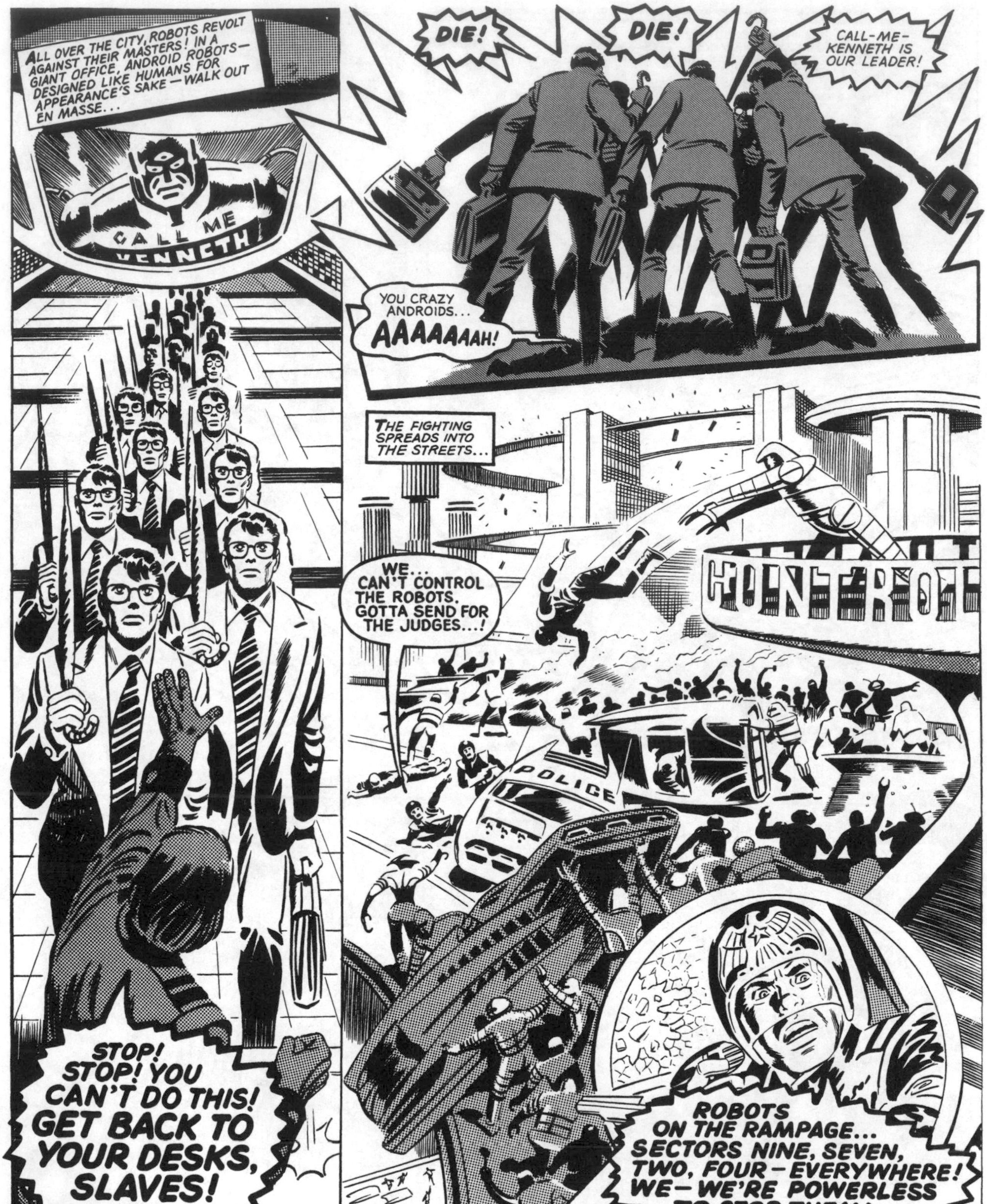
ALL OVER THE CITY, ROBOTS REVOLT AGAINST THEIR MASTERS! IN A GIANT OFFICE, ANDROID ROBOTS— DESIGNED LIKE HUMANS FOR APPEARANCE'S SAKE — WALK OUT EN MASSE...
CALL ME KENNETH
STOP! STOP! YOU CAN'T DO THIS! GET BACK TO YOUR DESKS, SLAVES!
DIE!
DIE!
CALL-ME-KENNETH IS OUR LEADER!
YOU CRAZY ANDROIDS... AAAAAAAH!
THE FIGHTING SPREADS INTO THE STREETS...
WE... CAN'T CONTROL THE ROBOTS. GOTTA SEND FOR THE JUDGES...!
POLICE
ROBOTS ON THE RAMPAGE... SECTORS NINE, SEVEN, TWO, FOUR — EVERYWHERE! WE— WE'RE POWERLESS TO STOP THEM!

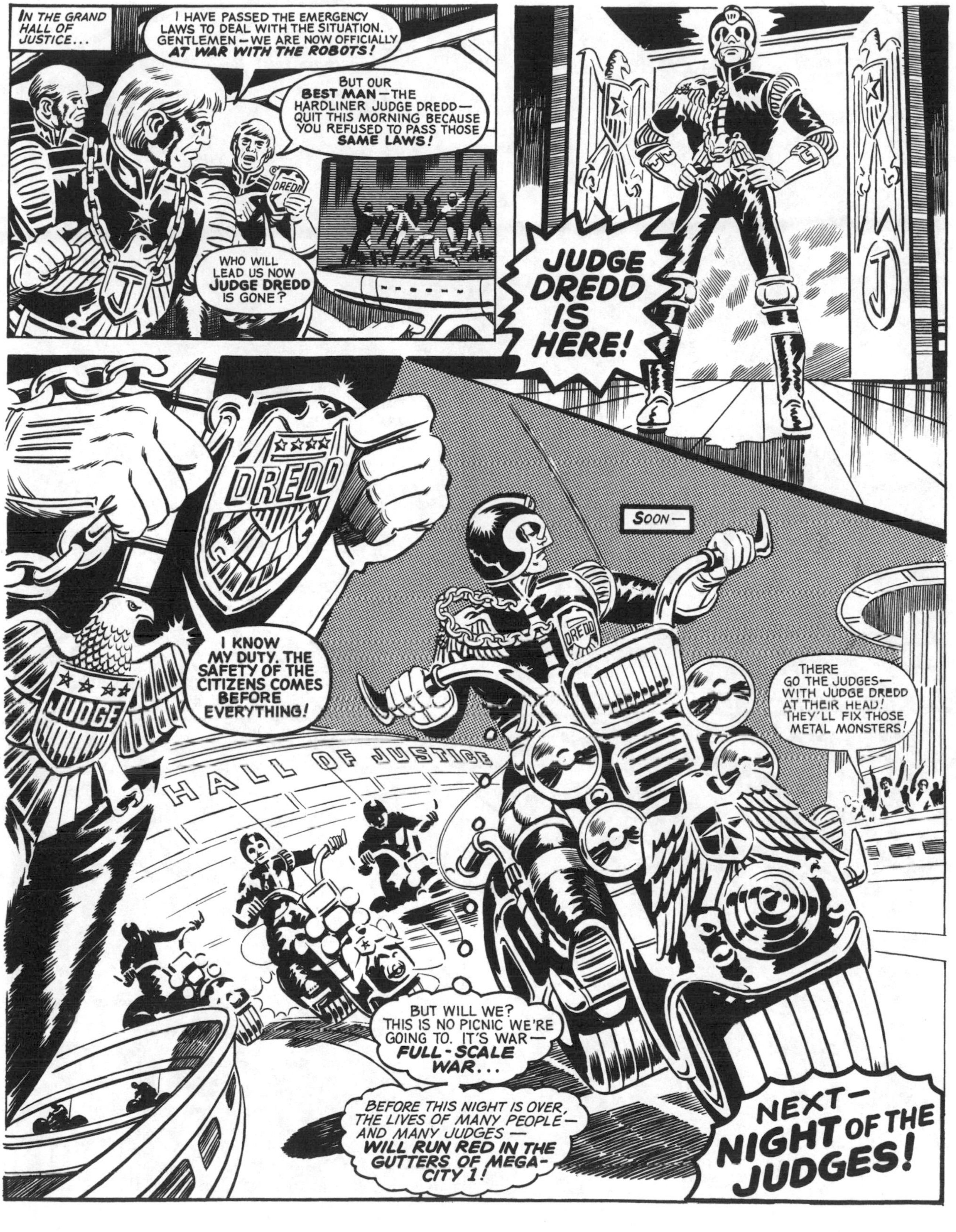

IN THE GRAND HALL OF JUSTICE...
I HAVE PASSED THE EMERGENCY LAWS TO DEAL WITH THE SITUATION. GENTLEMEN—WE ARE NOW OFFICIALLY AT WAR WITH THE ROBOTS!
BUT OUR BEST MAN—THE HARDLINER JUDGE DREDD—QUIT THIS MORNING BECAUSE YOU REFUSED TO PASS THOSE SAME LAWS!
DREDD
WHO WILL LEAD US NOW JUDGE DREDD IS GONE?
JUDGE DREDD IS HERE!
DREDD
JUDGE
I KNOW MY DUTY. THE SAFETY OF THE CITIZENS COMES BEFORE EVERYTHING!
SOON—
HALL OF JUSTICE
DREDD
THERE GO THE JUDGES—WITH JUDGE DREDD AT THEIR HEAD! THEY'LL FIX THOSE METAL MONSTERS!
BUT WILL WE? THIS IS NO PICNIC WE'RE GOING TO. IT'S WAR—FULL-SCALE WAR...
BEFORE THIS NIGHT IS OVER, THE LIVES OF MANY PEOPLE—AND MANY JUDGES—WILL RUN RED IN THE GUTTERS OF MEGA-CITY 1!
NEXT—NIGHT OF THE JUDGES!

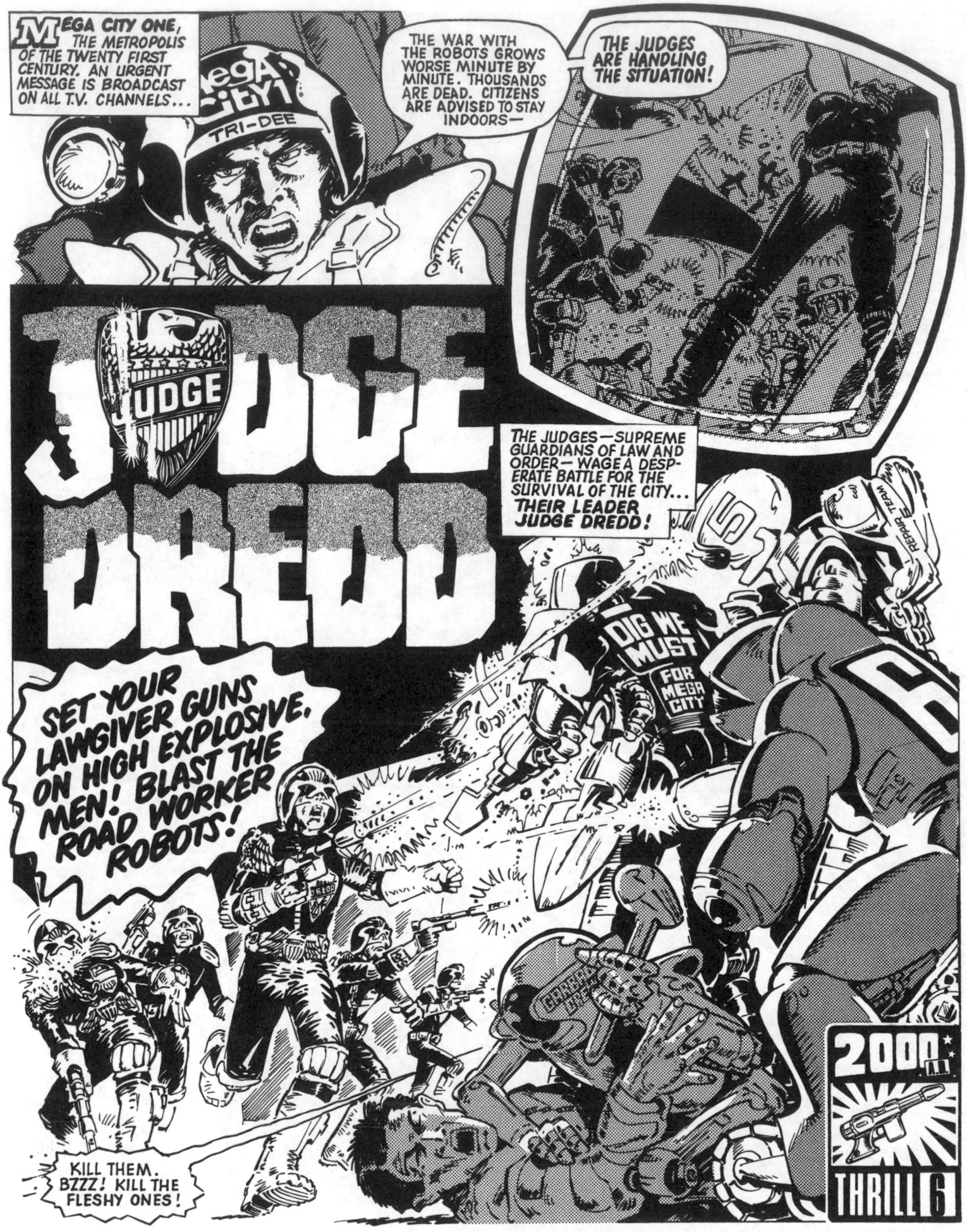
MEGA CITY ONE, THE METROPOLIS OF THE TWENTY FIRST CENTURY. AN URGENT MESSAGE IS BROADCAST ON ALL T.V. CHANNELS...
MEGA CITY 1
TRI-DEE
THE WAR WITH THE ROBOTS GROWS WORSE MINUTE BY MINUTE. THOUSANDS ARE DEAD. CITIZENS ARE ADVISED TO STAY INDOORS—
THE JUDGES ARE HANDLING THE SITUATION!
JUDGE DREDD
JUDGE
THE JUDGES—SUPREME GUARDIANS OF LAW AND ORDER— WAGE A DESPERATE BATTLE FOR THE SURVIVAL OF THE CITY... THEIR LEADER JUDGE DREDD!
REPAIR TEAM
DIG WE MUST
FOR MEGA CITY
SET YOUR LAWGIVER GUNS ON HIGH EXPLOSIVE, MEN! BLAST THE ROAD WORKER ROBOTS!
DREDD
KILL THEM. BZZZ! KILL THE FLESHY ONES!
2000 A.D.
THRILL 6

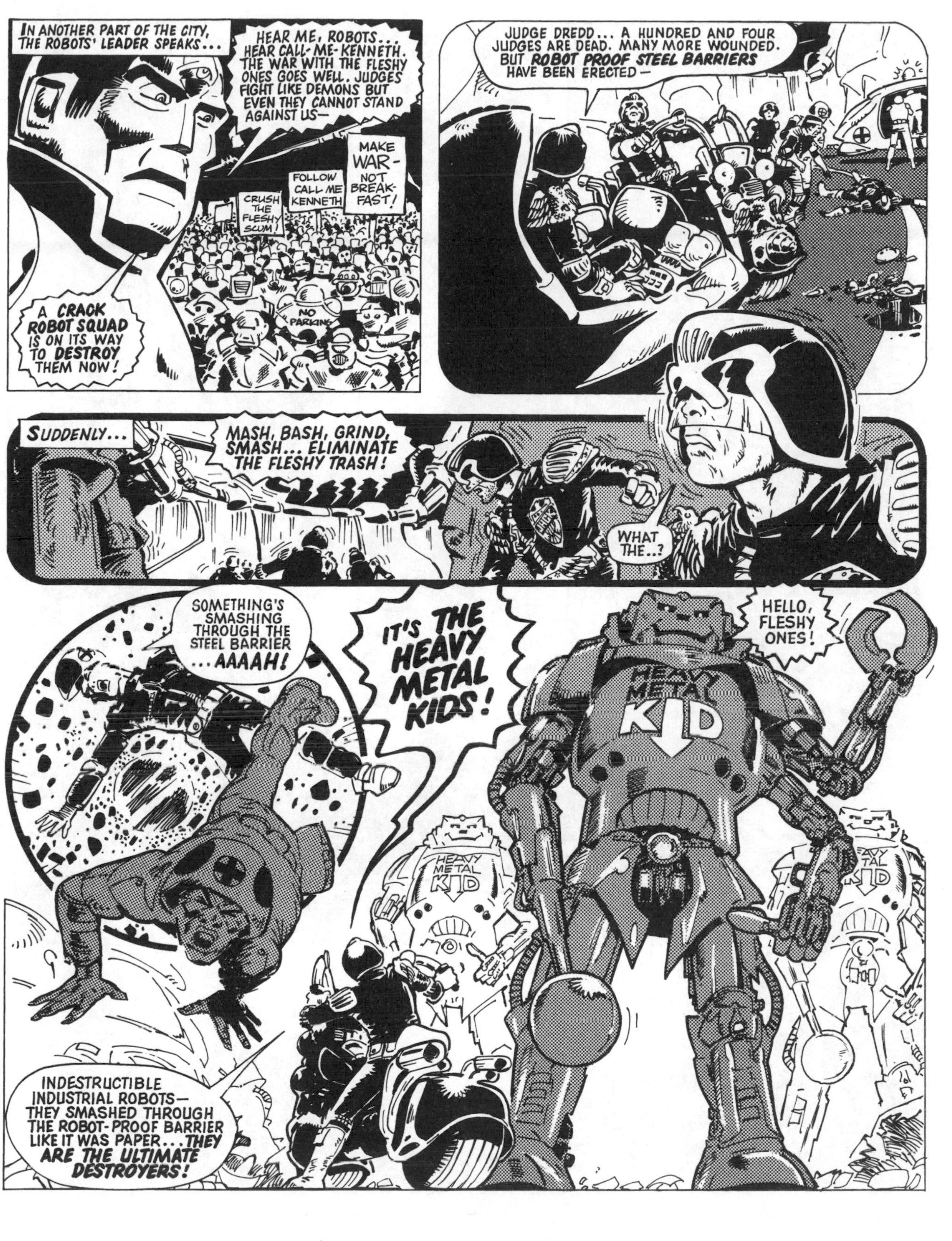

IN ANOTHER PART OF THE CITY, THE ROBOTS' LEADER SPEAKS...
HEAR ME, ROBOTS... HEAR CALL-ME-KENNETH. THE WAR WITH THE FLESHY ONES GOES WELL. JUDGES FIGHT LIKE DEMONS BUT EVEN THEY CANNOT STAND AGAINST US—
MAKE WAR- NOT BREAK-FAST!
FOLLOW CALL-ME KENNETH
CRUSH THE FLESHY SCUM!
NO PARKING
A CRACK ROBOT SQUAD IS ON ITS WAY TO DESTROY THEM NOW!
JUDGE DREDD... A HUNDRED AND FOUR JUDGES ARE DEAD. MANY MORE WOUNDED. BUT ROBOT PROOF STEEL BARRIERS HAVE BEEN ERECTED—
SUDDENLY...
MASH, BASH, GRIND, SMASH... ELIMINATE THE FLESHY TRASH!
WHAT THE..?
SOMETHING'S SMASHING THROUGH THE STEEL BARRIER ...AAAAH!
IT'S THE HEAVY METAL KIDS!
HELLO, FLESHY ONES!
HEAVY METAL KID
INDESTRUCTIBLE INDUSTRIAL ROBOTS— THEY SMASHED THROUGH THE ROBOT-PROOF BARRIER LIKE IT WAS PAPER... THEY ARE THE ULTIMATE DESTROYERS!

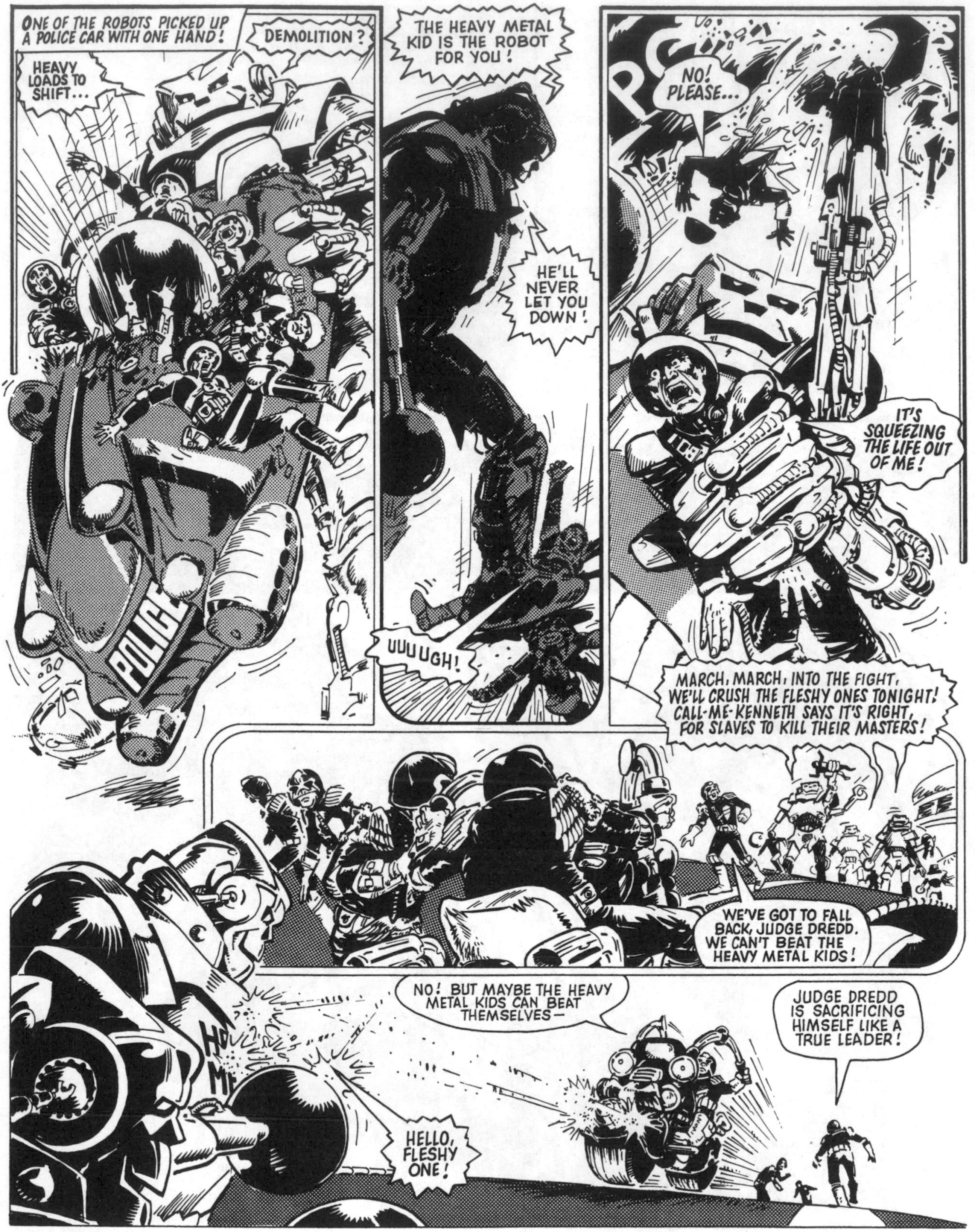

ONE OF THE ROBOTS PICKED UP A POLICE CAR WITH ONE HAND!
DEMOLITION?
HEAVY LOADS TO SHIFT...
THE HEAVY METAL KID IS THE ROBOT FOR YOU!
HE'LL NEVER LET YOU DOWN!
UUUUGH!
POLICE
NO! PLEASE...
IT'S SQUEEZING THE LIFE OUT OF ME!
MARCH, MARCH, INTO THE FIGHT, WE'LL CRUSH THE FLESHY ONES TONIGHT! CALL-ME-KENNETH SAYS IT'S RIGHT, FOR SLAVES TO KILL THEIR MASTERS!
WE'VE GOT TO FALL BACK, JUDGE DREDD. WE CAN'T BEAT THE HEAVY METAL KIDS!
NO! BUT MAYBE THE HEAVY METAL KIDS CAN BEAT THEMSELVES—
JUDGE DREDD IS SACRIFICING HIMSELF LIKE A TRUE LEADER!
HELLO, FLESHY ONE!

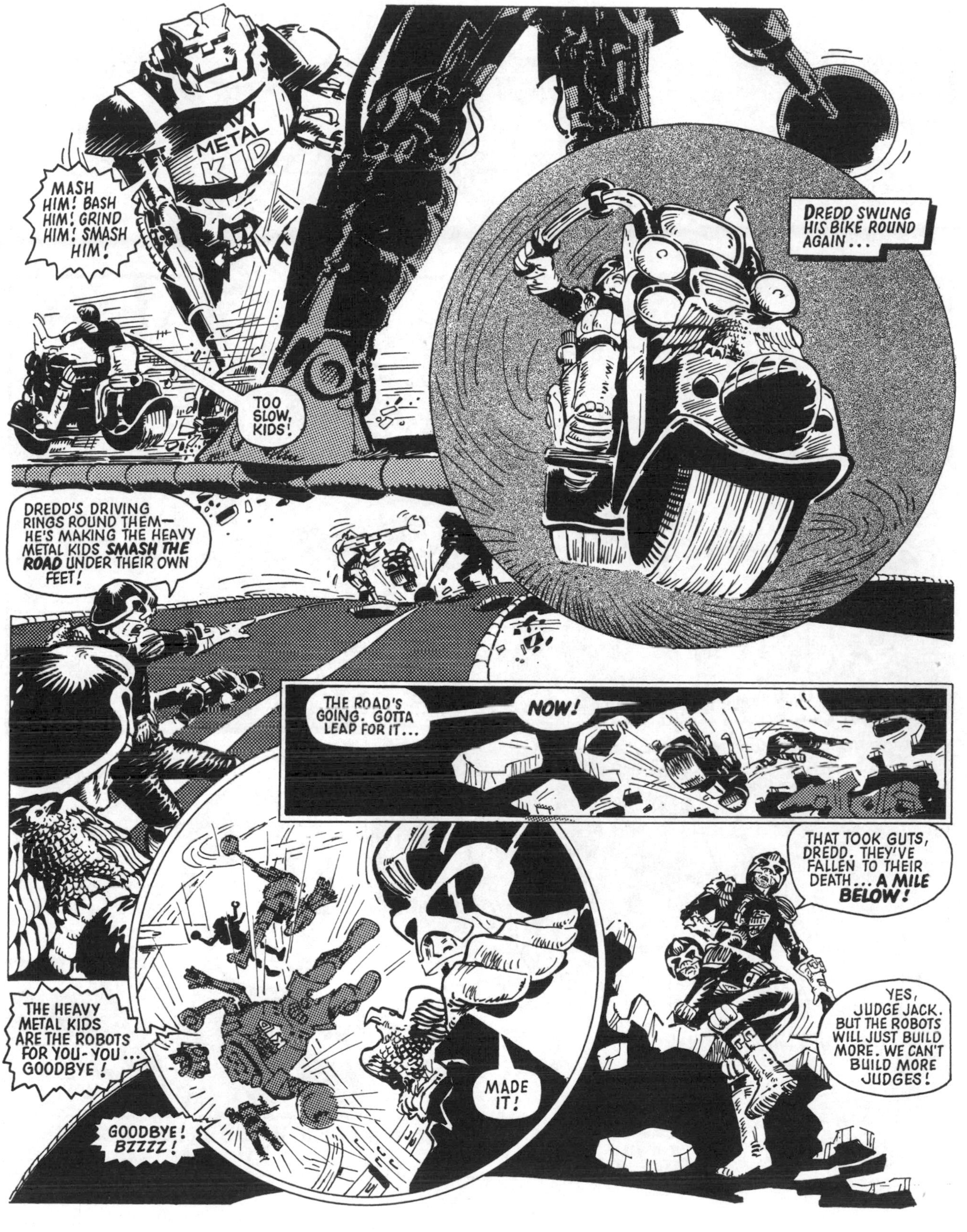

MASH HIM! BASH HIM! GRIND HIM! SMASH HIM!
TOO SLOW, KIDS!
DREDD SWUNG HIS BIKE ROUND AGAIN...
DREDD'S DRIVING RINGS ROUND THEM— HE'S MAKING THE HEAVY METAL KIDS SMASH THE ROAD UNDER THEIR OWN FEET!
THE ROAD'S GOING. GOTTA LEAP FOR IT...
NOW!
THAT TOOK GUTS, DREDD. THEY'VE FALLEN TO THEIR DEATH... A MILE BELOW!
THE HEAVY METAL KIDS ARE THE ROBOTS FOR YOU-YOU... GOODBYE!
MADE IT!
YES, JUDGE JACK. BUT THE ROBOTS WILL JUST BUILD MORE. WE CAN'T BUILD MORE JUDGES!
GOODBYE! BZZZZ!

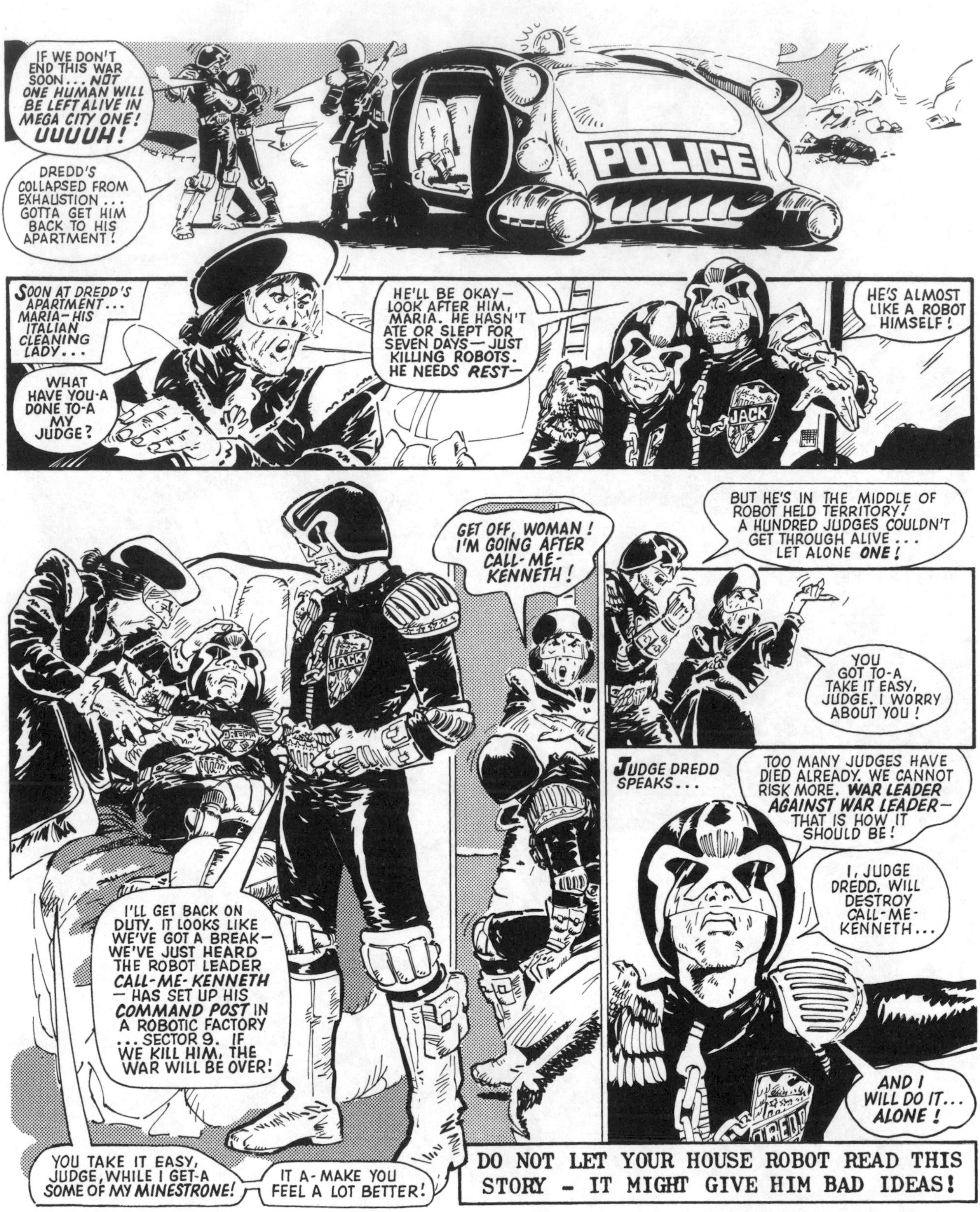
IF WE DON'T END THIS WAR SOON... NOT ONE HUMAN WILL BE LEFT ALIVE IN MEGA CITY ONE! UUUUH!
DREDD'S COLLAPSED FROM EXHAUSTION ... GOTTA GET HIM BACK TO HIS APARTMENT!
POLICE
SOON AT DREDD'S APARTMENT... MARIA—HIS ITALIAN CLEANING LADY...
WHAT HAVE YOU-A DONE TO-A MY JUDGE?
HE'LL BE OKAY— LOOK AFTER HIM, MARIA. HE HASN'T ATE OR SLEPT FOR SEVEN DAYS— JUST KILLING ROBOTS. HE NEEDS REST—
HE'S ALMOST LIKE A ROBOT HIMSELF!
I'LL GET BACK ON DUTY. IT LOOKS LIKE WE'VE GOT A BREAK— WE'VE JUST HEARD THE ROBOT LEADER CALL-ME-KENNETH — HAS SET UP HIS COMMAND POST IN A ROBOTIC FACTORY ... SECTOR 9. IF WE KILL HIM, THE WAR WILL BE OVER!
YOU TAKE IT EASY, JUDGE, WHILE I GET-A SOME OF MY MINESTRONE!
IT A-MAKE YOU FEEL A LOT BETTER!
GET OFF, WOMAN! I'M GOING AFTER CALL-ME-KENNETH!
BUT HE'S IN THE MIDDLE OF ROBOT HELD TERRITORY! A HUNDRED JUDGES COULDN'T GET THROUGH ALIVE... LET ALONE ONE!
YOU GOT TO-A TAKE IT EASY, JUDGE. I WORRY ABOUT YOU!
JUDGE DREDD SPEAKS...
TOO MANY JUDGES HAVE DIED ALREADY. WE CANNOT RISK MORE. WAR LEADER AGAINST WAR LEADER— THAT IS HOW IT SHOULD BE!
I, JUDGE DREDD, WILL DESTROY CALL-ME-KENNETH...
AND I WILL DO IT... ALONE!
DO NOT LET YOUR HOUSE ROBOT READ THIS STORY - IT MIGHT GIVE HIM BAD IDEAS!

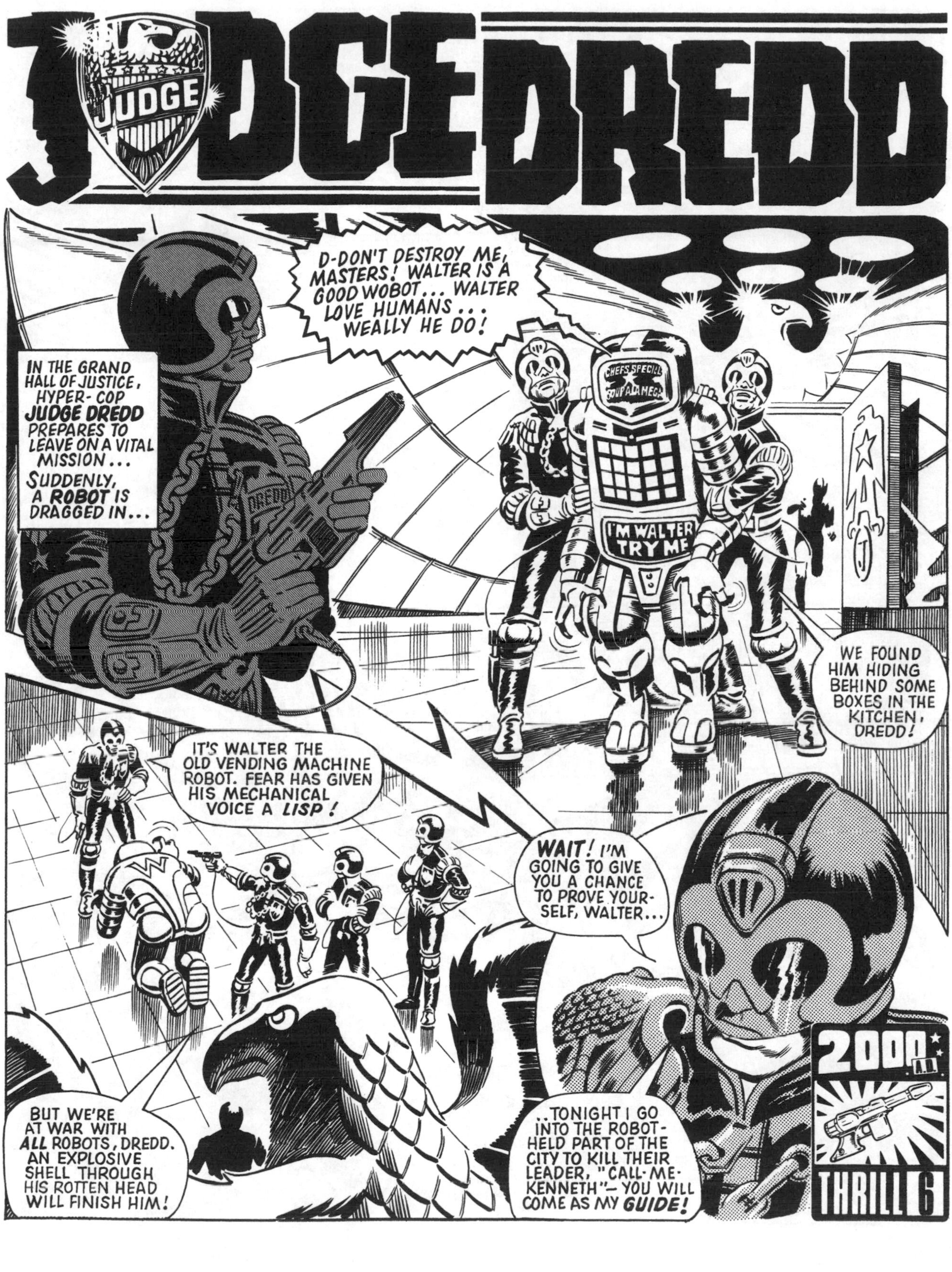

JUDGE DREDD
IN THE GRAND HALL OF JUSTICE, HYPER-COP JUDGE DREDD PREPARES TO LEAVE ON A VITAL MISSION... SUDDENLY, A ROBOT IS DRAGGED IN...
D-DON'T DESTROY ME, MASTERS! WALTER IS A GOOD WOBOT... WALTER LOVE HUMANS... WEALLY HE DO!
I'M WALTER TRY ME
WE FOUND HIM HIDING BEHIND SOME BOXES IN THE KITCHEN, DREDD!
IT'S WALTER THE OLD VENDING MACHINE ROBOT. FEAR HAS GIVEN HIS MECHANICAL VOICE A LISP!
WAIT! I'M GOING TO GIVE YOU A CHANCE TO PROVE YOURSELF, WALTER...
BUT WE'RE AT WAR WITH ALL ROBOTS, DREDD. AN EXPLOSIVE SHELL THROUGH HIS ROTTEN HEAD WILL FINISH HIM!
..TONIGHT I GO INTO THE ROBOT-HELD PART OF THE CITY TO KILL THEIR LEADER, "CALL-ME-KENNETH"– YOU WILL COME AS MY GUIDE!
2000 A.D.
THRILL 6

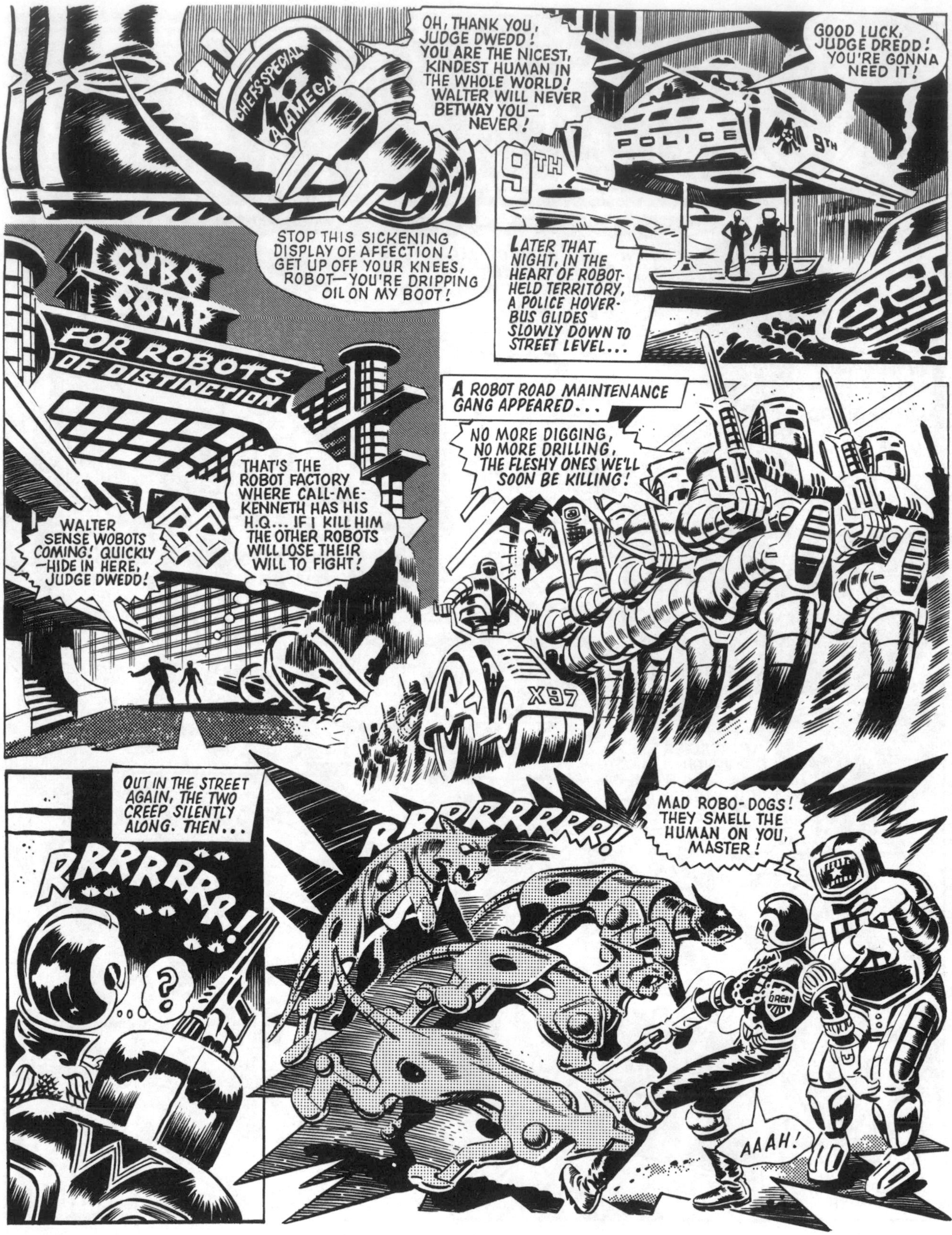

CHEFS SPECIAL
A LAMEGA
OH, THANK YOU, JUDGE DWEDD! YOU ARE THE NICEST, KINDEST HUMAN IN THE WHOLE WORLD! WALTER WILL NEVER BETWAY YOU—NEVER!
STOP THIS SICKENING DISPLAY OF AFFECTION! GET UP OFF YOUR KNEES, ROBOT— YOU'RE DRIPPING OIL ON MY BOOT!
GOOD LUCK, JUDGE DREDD! YOU'RE GONNA NEED IT!
POLICE
9TH
9TH
LATER THAT NIGHT, IN THE HEART OF ROBOT-HELD TERRITORY, A POLICE HOVER-BUS GLIDES SLOWLY DOWN TO STREET LEVEL...
CYBO COMP
FOR ROBOTS OF DISTINCTION
WALTER SENSE WOBOTS COMING! QUICKLY —HIDE IN HERE, JUDGE DWEDD!
THAT'S THE ROBOT FACTORY WHERE CALL-ME-KENNETH HAS HIS H.Q... IF I KILL HIM THE OTHER ROBOTS WILL LOSE THEIR WILL TO FIGHT!
A ROBOT ROAD MAINTENANCE GANG APPEARED...
NO MORE DIGGING, NO MORE DRILLING, THE FLESHY ONES WE'LL SOON BE KILLING!
X97
OUT IN THE STREET AGAIN, THE TWO CREEP SILENTLY ALONG. THEN...
RRRRRRRR!
?
RRRRRRRR!
MAD ROBO-DOGS! THEY SMELL THE HUMAN ON YOU, MASTER!
AAAH!

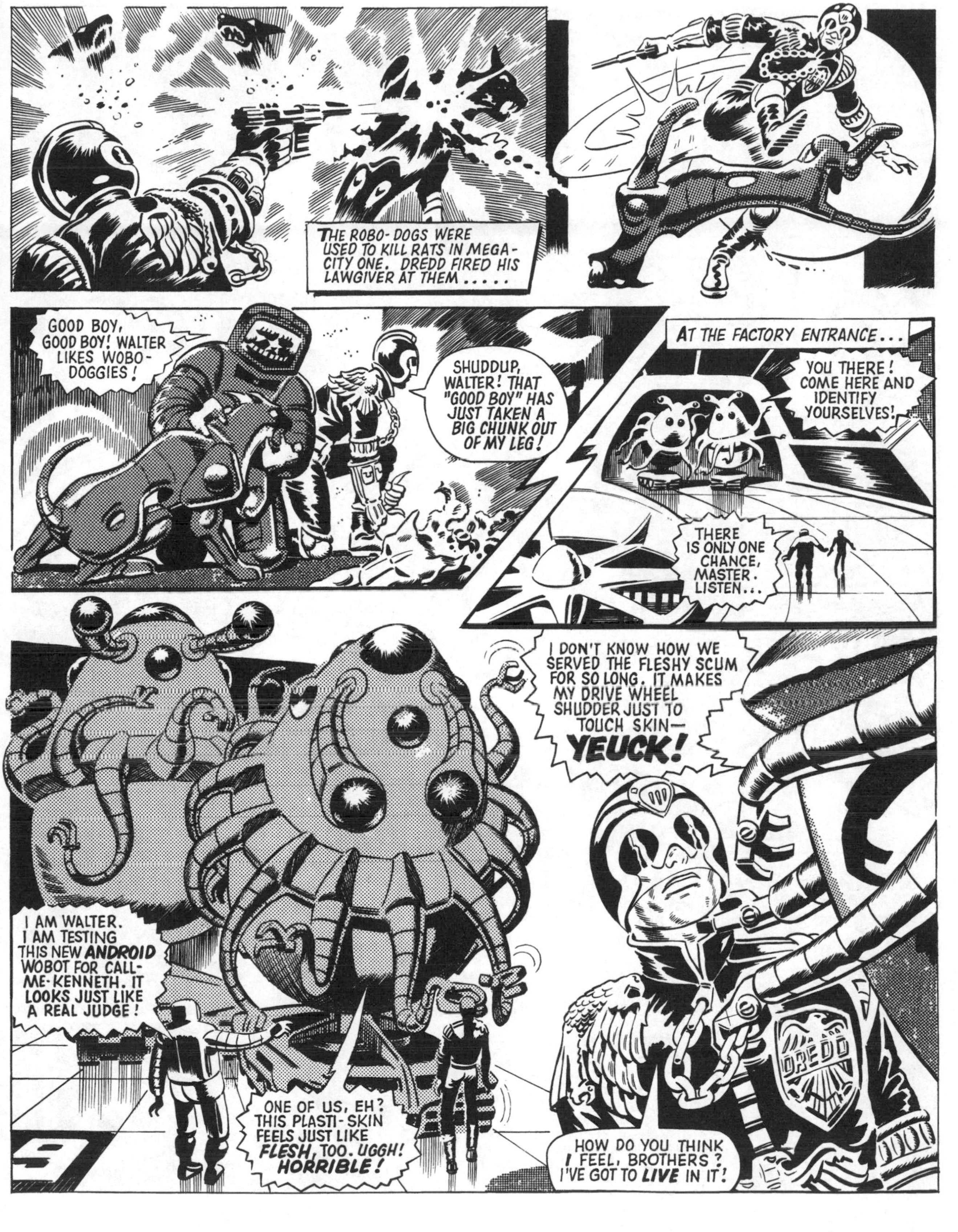

THE ROBO-DOGS WERE USED TO KILL RATS IN MEGA-CITY ONE. DREDD FIRED HIS LAWGIVER AT THEM .....
GOOD BOY, GOOD BOY! WALTER LIKES WOBO-DOGGIES!
SHUDDUP, WALTER! THAT "GOOD BOY" HAS JUST TAKEN A BIG CHUNK OUT OF MY LEG!
AT THE FACTORY ENTRANCE...
YOU THERE! COME HERE AND IDENTIFY YOURSELVES!
THERE IS ONLY ONE CHANCE, MASTER. LISTEN...
I AM WALTER. I AM TESTING THIS NEW ANDROID WOBOT FOR CALL-ME-KENNETH. IT LOOKS JUST LIKE A REAL JUDGE!
ONE OF US, EH? THIS PLASTI-SKIN FEELS JUST LIKE FLESH, TOO. UGGH! HORRIBLE!
I DON'T KNOW HOW WE SERVED THE FLESHY SCUM FOR SO LONG. IT MAKES MY DRIVE WHEEL SHUDDER JUST TO TOUCH SKIN—YEUCK!
HOW DO YOU THINK I FEEL, BROTHERS? I'VE GOT TO LIVE IN IT!
9

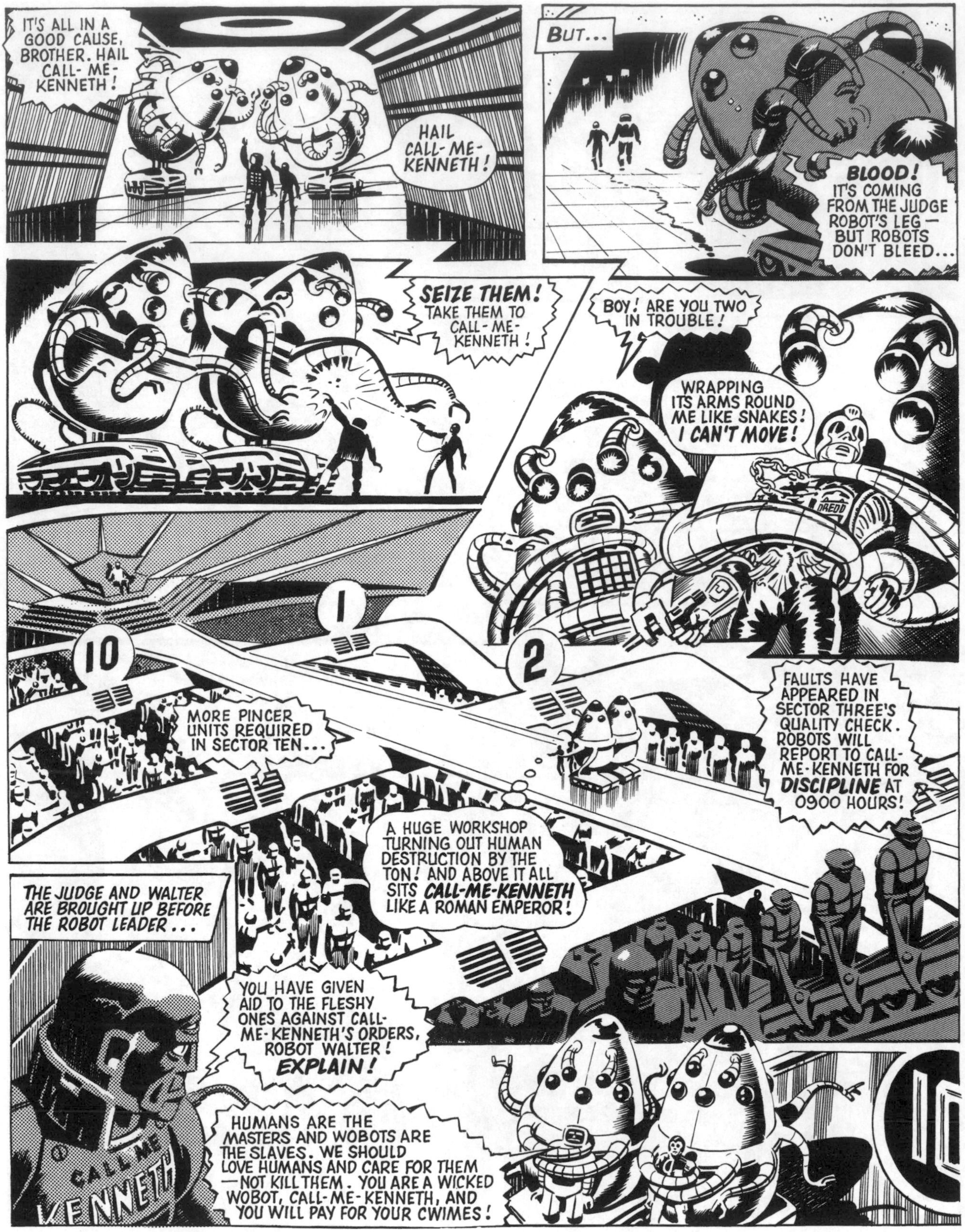

IT'S ALL IN A GOOD CAUSE, BROTHER. HAIL CALL-ME-KENNETH!
HAIL CALL-ME-KENNETH!
BUT...
BLOOD! IT'S COMING FROM THE JUDGE ROBOT'S LEG — BUT ROBOTS DON'T BLEED...
SEIZE THEM! TAKE THEM TO CALL-ME-KENNETH!
BOY! ARE YOU TWO IN TROUBLE!
WRAPPING ITS ARMS ROUND ME LIKE SNAKES! I CAN'T MOVE!
DREDD
1
10
2
MORE PINCER UNITS REQUIRED IN SECTOR TEN...
FAULTS HAVE APPEARED IN SECTOR THREE'S QUALITY CHECK. ROBOTS WILL REPORT TO CALL-ME-KENNETH FOR DISCIPLINE AT 0900 HOURS!
A HUGE WORKSHOP TURNING OUT HUMAN DESTRUCTION BY THE TON! AND ABOVE IT ALL SITS CALL-ME-KENNETH LIKE A ROMAN EMPEROR!
THE JUDGE AND WALTER ARE BROUGHT UP BEFORE THE ROBOT LEADER...
YOU HAVE GIVEN AID TO THE FLESHY ONES AGAINST CALL-ME-KENNETH'S ORDERS, ROBOT WALTER! EXPLAIN!
HUMANS ARE THE MASTERS AND WOBOTS ARE THE SLAVES. WE SHOULD LOVE HUMANS AND CARE FOR THEM — NOT KILL THEM. YOU ARE A WICKED WOBOT, CALL-ME-KENNETH, AND YOU WILL PAY FOR YOUR CWIMES!
CALL ME KENNETH

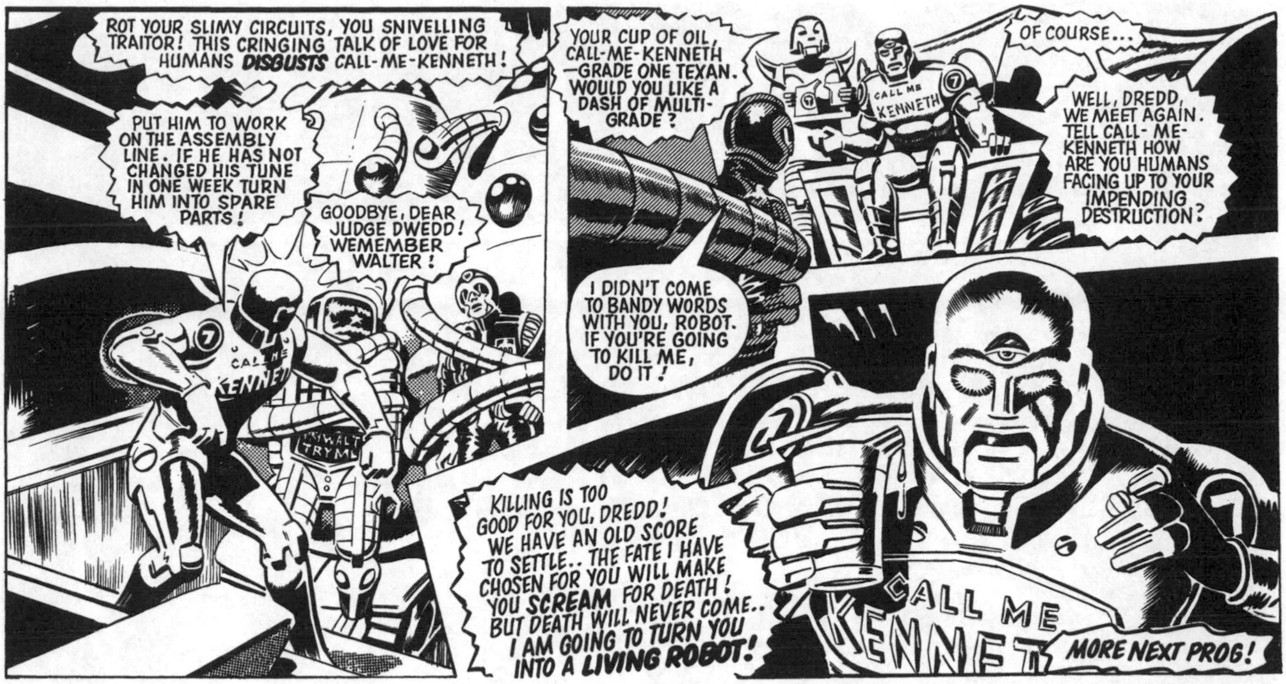

ROT YOUR SLIMY CIRCUITS, YOU SNIVELLING TRAITOR! THIS CRINGING TALK OF LOVE FOR HUMANS **DISGUSTS** CALL-ME-KENNETH!
PUT HIM TO WORK ON THE ASSEMBLY LINE. IF HE HAS NOT CHANGED HIS TUNE IN ONE WEEK TURN HIM INTO SPARE PARTS!
GOODBYE, DEAR JUDGE DWEDD! WEMEMBER WALTER!
YOUR CUP OF OIL, CALL-ME-KENNETH —GRADE ONE TEXAN. WOULD YOU LIKE A DASH OF MULTI-GRADE?
OF COURSE...
CALL ME KENNETH
WELL, DREDD, WE MEET AGAIN. TELL CALL-ME-KENNETH HOW ARE YOU HUMANS FACING UP TO YOUR IMPENDING DESTRUCTION?
I DIDN'T COME TO BANDY WORDS WITH YOU, ROBOT. IF YOU'RE GOING TO KILL ME, DO IT!
KILLING IS TOO GOOD FOR YOU, DREDD! WE HAVE AN OLD SCORE TO SETTLE.. THE FATE I HAVE CHOSEN FOR YOU WILL MAKE YOU **SCREAM** FOR DEATH! BUT DEATH WILL NEVER COME.. I AM GOING TO TURN YOU INTO A **LIVING ROBOT!**
MORE NEXT PROG!

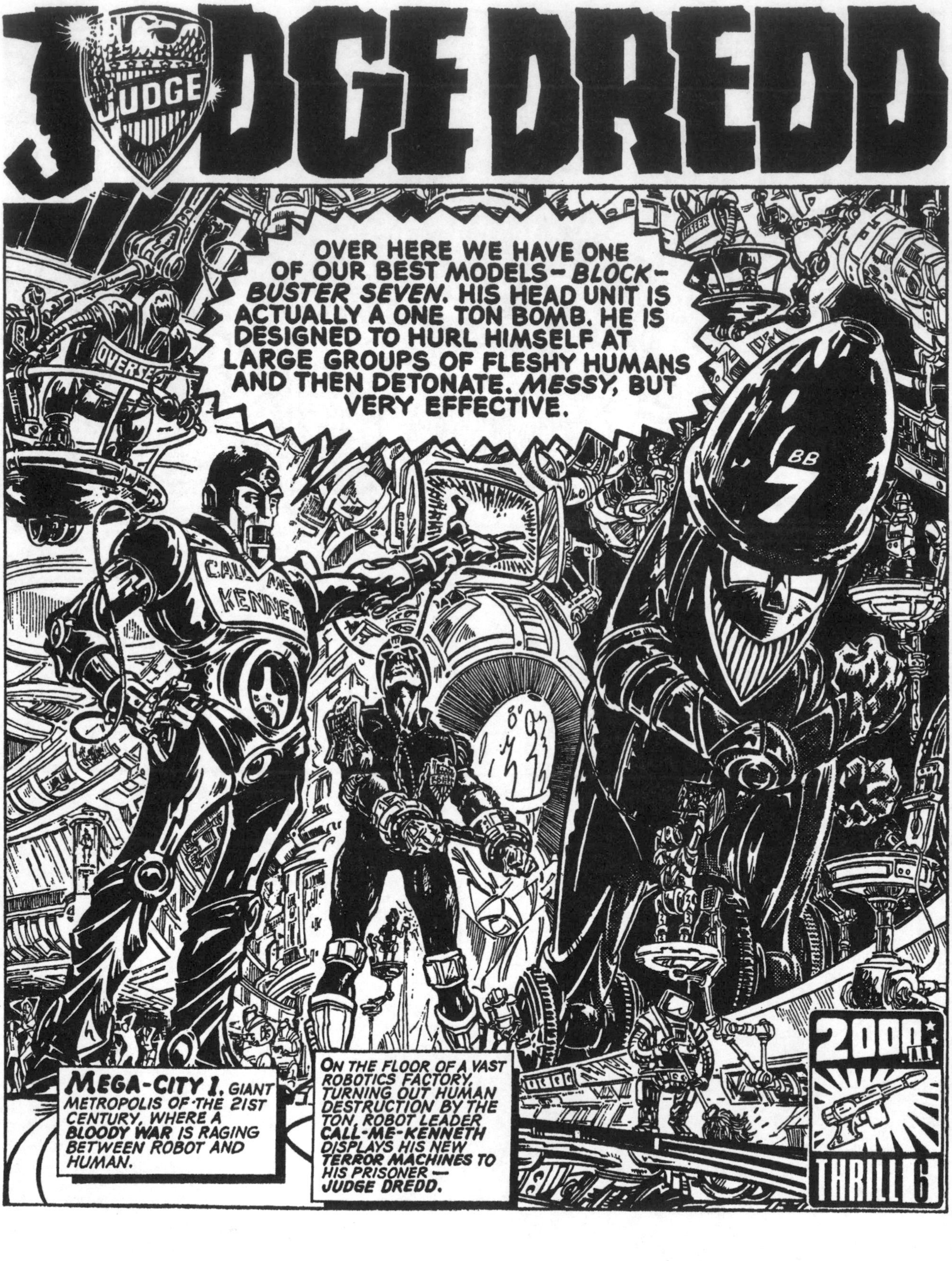
JUDGE DREDD
OVER HERE WE HAVE ONE OF OUR BEST MODELS – BLOCK-BUSTER SEVEN. HIS HEAD UNIT IS ACTUALLY A ONE TON BOMB. HE IS DESIGNED TO HURL HIMSELF AT LARGE GROUPS OF FLESHY HUMANS AND THEN DETONATE. MESSY, BUT VERY EFFECTIVE.
MEGA-CITY 1. GIANT METROPOLIS OF THE 21ST CENTURY, WHERE A BLOODY WAR IS RAGING BETWEEN ROBOT AND HUMAN.
ON THE FLOOR OF A VAST ROBOTICS FACTORY, TURNING OUT HUMAN DESTRUCTION BY THE TON, ROBOT LEADER CALL-ME-KENNETH DISPLAYS HIS NEW TERROR MACHINES TO HIS PRISONER — JUDGE DREDD.
CALL ME KENNETH
BB 7
2000 A.D.
THRILL 6

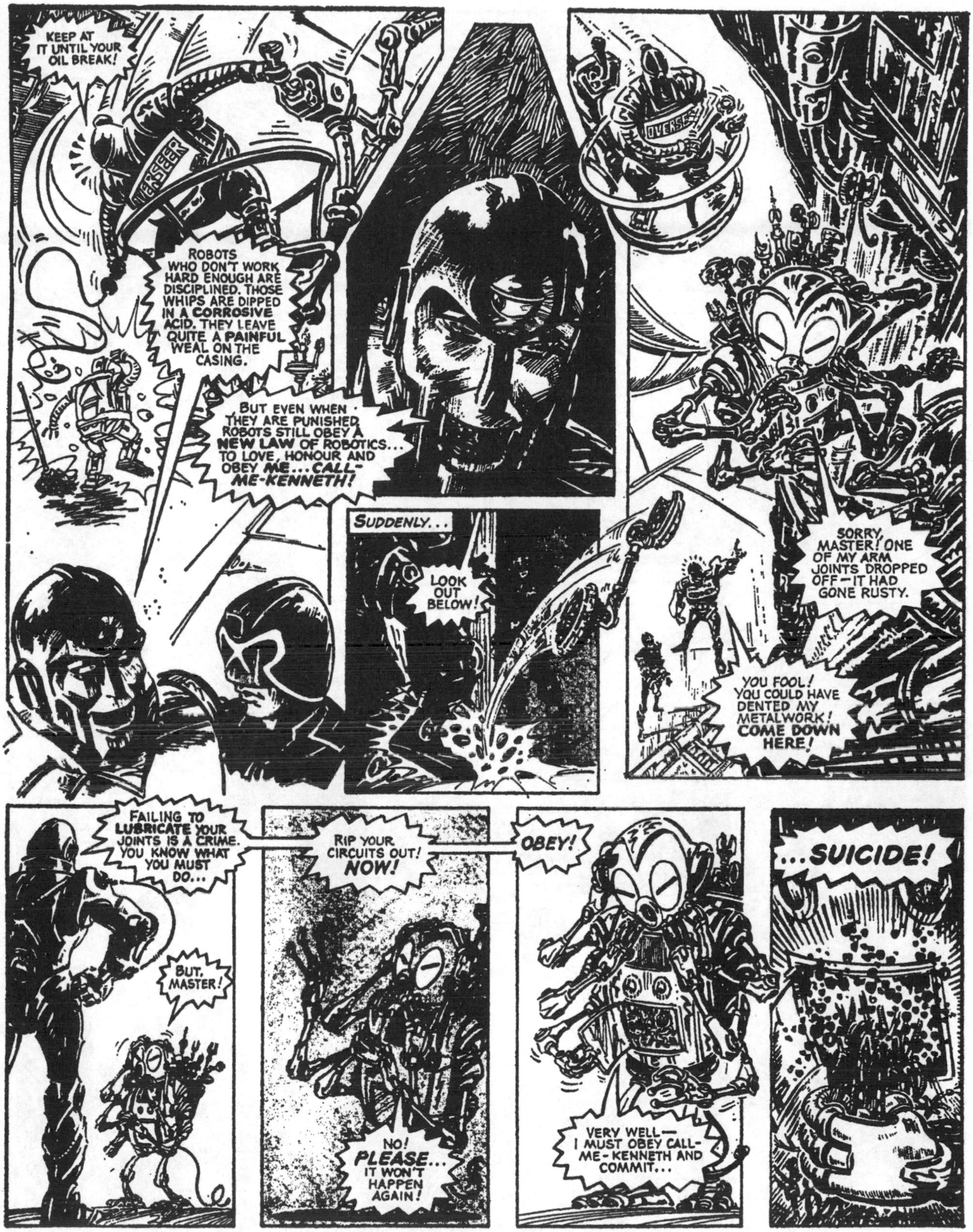
KEEP AT IT UNTIL YOUR OIL BREAK!
OVERSEER
ROBOTS WHO DON'T WORK HARD ENOUGH ARE DISCIPLINED. THOSE WHIPS ARE DIPPED IN A CORROSIVE ACID. THEY LEAVE QUITE A PAINFUL WEAL ON THE CASING.
BUT EVEN WHEN THEY ARE PUNISHED ROBOTS STILL OBEY A NEW LAW OF ROBOTICS... TO LOVE, HONOUR AND OBEY ME... CALL-ME-KENNETH!
OVERSEE
SUDDENLY...
LOOK OUT BELOW!
SORRY, MASTER! ONE OF MY ARM JOINTS DROPPED OFF—IT HAD GONE RUSTY.
YOU FOOL! YOU COULD HAVE DENTED MY METALWORK! COME DOWN HERE!
FAILING TO LUBRICATE YOUR JOINTS IS A CRIME. YOU KNOW WHAT YOU MUST DO...
BUT, MASTER!
RIP YOUR CIRCUITS OUT! NOW!
NO! PLEASE... IT WON'T HAPPEN AGAIN!
OBEY!
VERY WELL— I MUST OBEY CALL-ME-KENNETH AND COMMIT...
...SUICIDE!

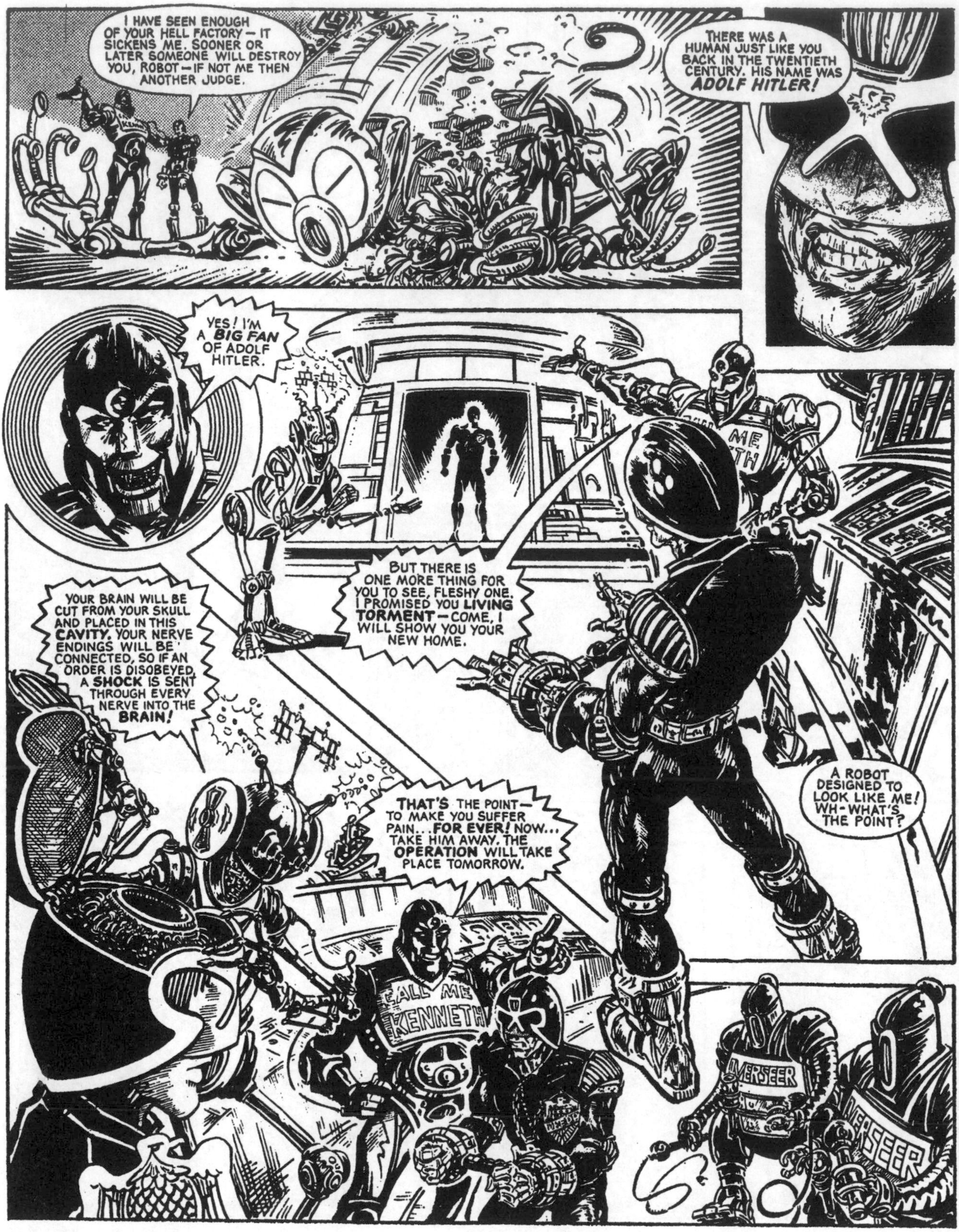
I HAVE SEEN ENOUGH OF YOUR HELL FACTORY — IT SICKENS ME. SOONER OR LATER SOMEONE WILL DESTROY YOU, ROBOT — IF NOT ME THEN ANOTHER JUDGE.
THERE WAS A HUMAN JUST LIKE YOU BACK IN THE TWENTIETH CENTURY. HIS NAME WAS ADOLF HITLER!
YES! I'M A BIG FAN OF ADOLF HITLER.
BUT THERE IS ONE MORE THING FOR YOU TO SEE, FLESHY ONE. I PROMISED YOU LIVING TORMENT — COME, I WILL SHOW YOU YOUR NEW HOME.
YOUR BRAIN WILL BE CUT FROM YOUR SKULL AND PLACED IN THIS CAVITY. YOUR NERVE ENDINGS WILL BE CONNECTED, SO IF AN ORDER IS DISOBEYED, A SHOCK IS SENT THROUGH EVERY NERVE INTO THE BRAIN!
A ROBOT DESIGNED TO LOOK LIKE ME! WH-WHAT'S THE POINT?
THAT'S THE POINT — TO MAKE YOU SUFFER PAIN... FOR EVER! NOW... TAKE HIM AWAY. THE OPERATION WILL TAKE PLACE TOMORROW.
CALL ME KENNETH
OVERSEER
OVERSEER

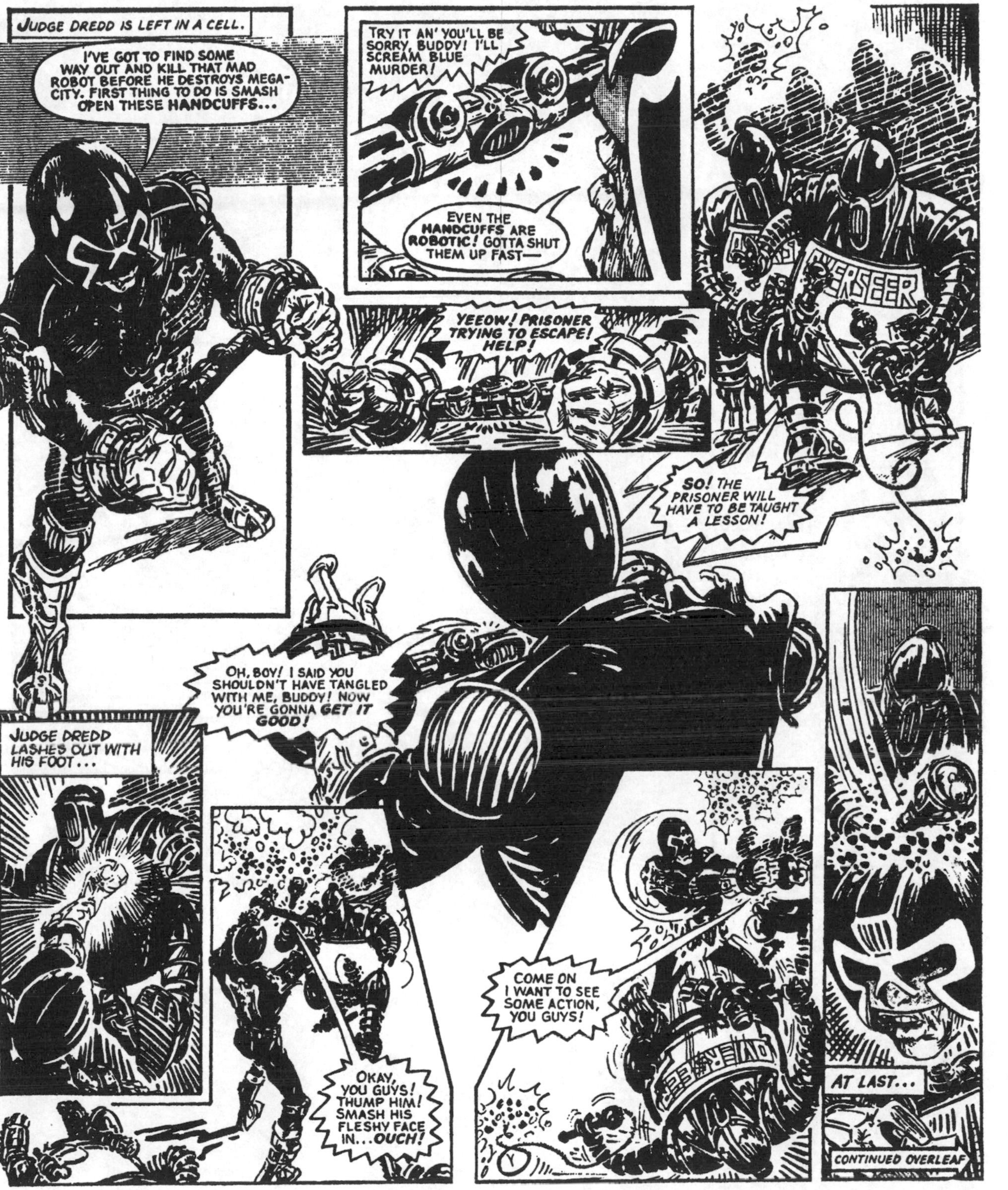

JUDGE DREDD IS LEFT IN A CELL.
I'VE GOT TO FIND SOME WAY OUT AND KILL THAT MAD ROBOT BEFORE HE DESTROYS MEGA-CITY. FIRST THING TO DO IS SMASH OPEN THESE HANDCUFFS...
TRY IT AN' YOU'LL BE SORRY, BUDDY! I'LL SCREAM BLUE MURDER!
EVEN THE HANDCUFFS ARE ROBOTIC! GOTTA SHUT THEM UP FAST—
YEEOW! PRISONER TRYING TO ESCAPE! HELP!
OVERSEER
SO! THE PRISONER WILL HAVE TO BE TAUGHT A LESSON!
OH, BOY! I SAID YOU SHOULDN'T HAVE TANGLED WITH ME, BUDDY! NOW YOU'RE GONNA GET IT GOOD!
JUDGE DREDD LASHES OUT WITH HIS FOOT...
OKAY, YOU GUYS! THUMP HIM! SMASH HIS FLESHY FACE IN...OUCH!
COME ON I WANT TO SEE SOME ACTION, YOU GUYS!
AT LAST...

CONTINUED OVERLEAF

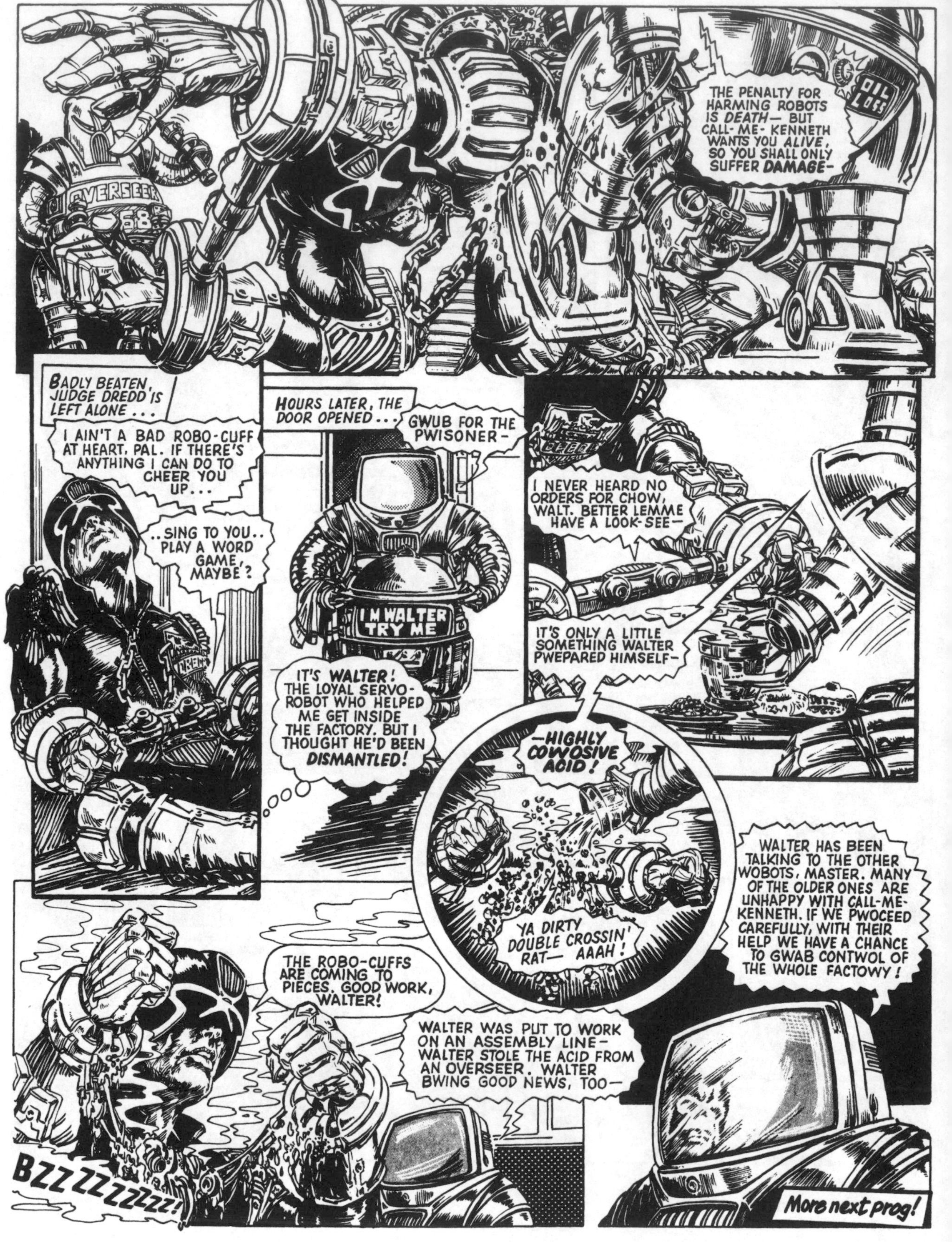
THE PENALTY FOR HARMING ROBOTS IS DEATH— BUT CALL-ME-KENNETH WANTS YOU ALIVE, SO YOU SHALL ONLY SUFFER DAMAGE-
OIL LOSS
OVERSEER 68
BADLY BEATEN, JUDGE DREDD IS LEFT ALONE . . .
I AIN'T A BAD ROBO-CUFF AT HEART, PAL. IF THERE'S ANYTHING I CAN DO TO CHEER YOU UP . . .
. . SING TO YOU . . PLAY A WORD GAME, MAYBE?
HOURS LATER, THE DOOR OPENED . . .
GWUB FOR THE PWISONER-
I'M WALTER TRY ME
IT'S WALTER! THE LOYAL SERVO-ROBOT WHO HELPED ME GET INSIDE THE FACTORY. BUT I THOUGHT HE'D BEEN DISMANTLED!
I NEVER HEARD NO ORDERS FOR CHOW, WALT. BETTER LEMME HAVE A LOOK-SEE-
IT'S ONLY A LITTLE SOMETHING WALTER PWEPARED HIMSELF-
-HIGHLY COWOSIVE ACID!
YA DIRTY DOUBLE CROSSIN' RAT— AAAH!
BZZZZZZZzz!
THE ROBO-CUFFS ARE COMING TO PIECES. GOOD WORK, WALTER!
WALTER WAS PUT TO WORK ON AN ASSEMBLY LINE-WALTER STOLE THE ACID FROM AN OVERSEER. WALTER BWING GOOD NEWS, TOO-
WALTER HAS BEEN TALKING TO THE OTHER WOBOTS, MASTER. MANY OF THE OLDER ONES ARE UNHAPPY WITH CALL-ME-KENNETH. IF WE PWOCEED CAREFULLY, WITH THEIR HELP WE HAVE A CHANCE TO GWAB CONTWOL OF THE WHOLE FACTOWY!
More next prog!

JUDGE DREDD

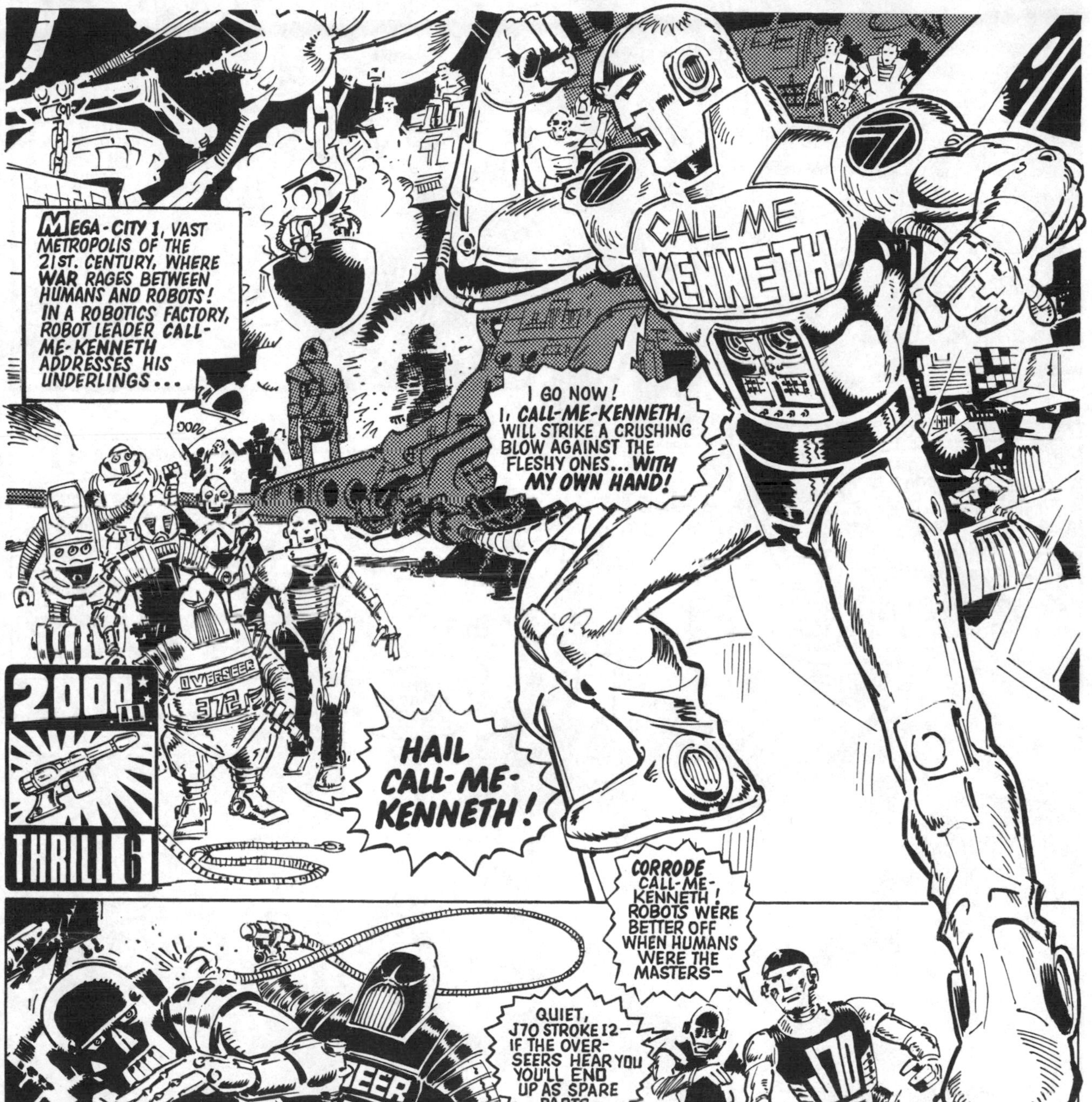
MEGA-CITY 1, VAST METROPOLIS OF THE 21ST. CENTURY, WHERE WAR RAGES BETWEEN HUMANS AND ROBOTS! IN A ROBOTICS FACTORY, ROBOT LEADER CALL-ME-KENNETH ADDRESSES HIS UNDERLINGS...
CALL ME KENNETH
I GO NOW! I, CALL-ME-KENNETH, WILL STRIKE A CRUSHING BLOW AGAINST THE FLESHY ONES... WITH MY OWN HAND!
OVERSEER 372
HAIL CALL-ME-KENNETH!
2000 A.D.
THRILL 6
CORRODE CALL-ME-KENNETH! ROBOTS WERE BETTER OFF WHEN HUMANS WERE THE MASTERS–
QUIET, J70 STROKE 12– IF THE OVERSEERS HEAR YOU YOU'LL END UP AS SPARE PARTS–
J70

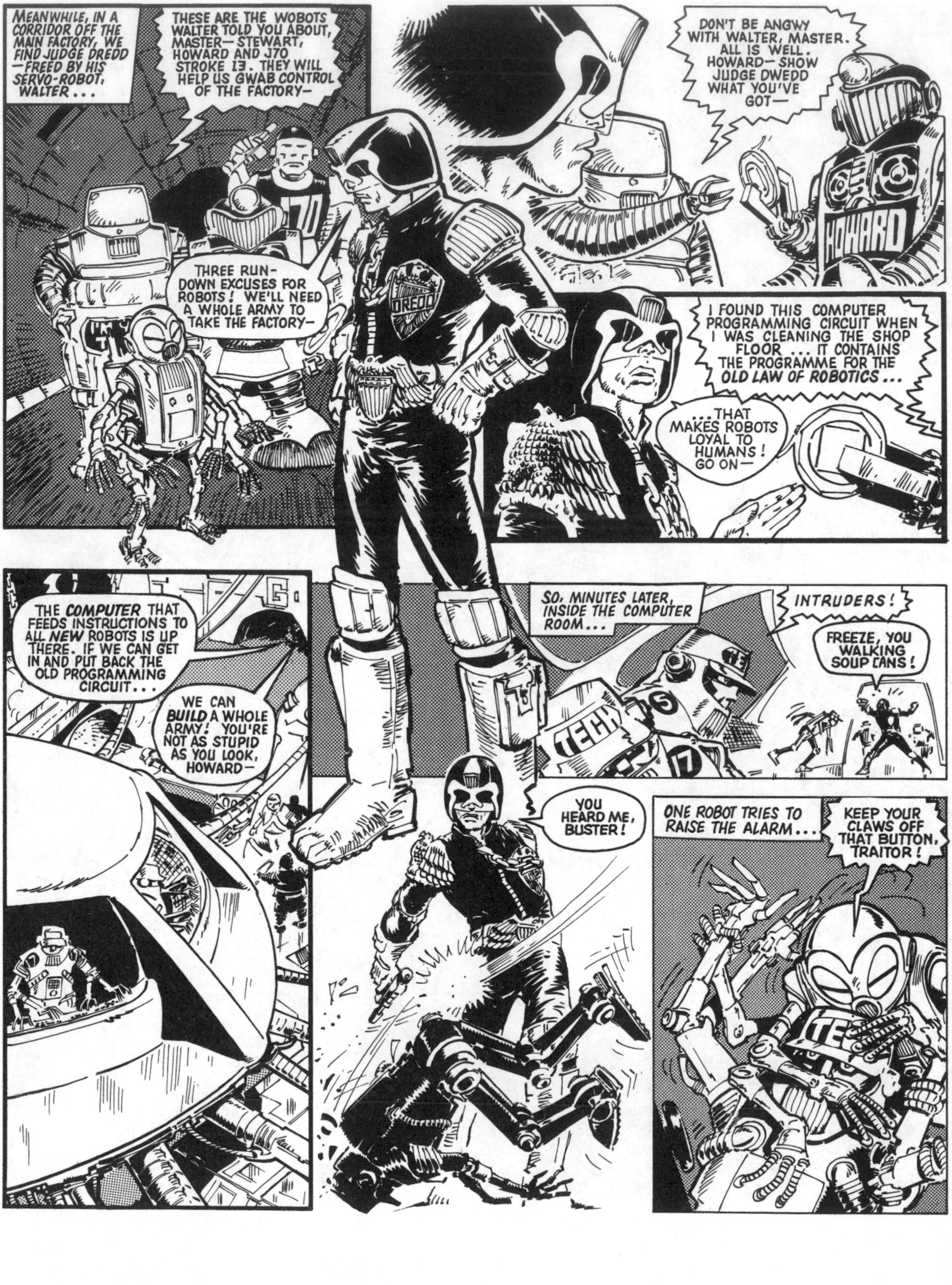
MEANWHILE, IN A CORRIDOR OFF THE MAIN FACTORY, WE FIND JUDGE DREDD —FREED BY HIS SERVO-ROBOT, WALTER...
THESE ARE THE WOBOTS WALTER TOLD YOU ABOUT, MASTER— STEWART, HOWARD AND J70 STROKE 13. THEY WILL HELP US GWAB CONTROL OF THE FACTORY—
THREE RUN-DOWN EXCUSES FOR ROBOTS! WE'LL NEED A WHOLE ARMY TO TAKE THE FACTORY—
DON'T BE ANGWY WITH WALTER, MASTER. ALL IS WELL. HOWARD— SHOW JUDGE DWEDD WHAT YOU'VE GOT—
HOWARD
I FOUND THIS COMPUTER PROGRAMMING CIRCUIT WHEN I WAS CLEANING THE SHOP FLOOR ... IT CONTAINS THE PROGRAMME FOR THE OLD LAW OF ROBOTICS...
...THAT MAKES ROBOTS LOYAL TO HUMANS! GO ON—
THE COMPUTER THAT FEEDS INSTRUCTIONS TO ALL NEW ROBOTS IS UP THERE. IF WE CAN GET IN AND PUT BACK THE OLD PROGRAMMING CIRCUIT...
WE CAN BUILD A WHOLE ARMY! YOU'RE NOT AS STUPID AS YOU LOOK, HOWARD—
SO, MINUTES LATER, INSIDE THE COMPUTER ROOM...
INTRUDERS!
FREEZE, YOU WALKING SOUP CANS!
YOU HEARD ME, BUSTER!
ONE ROBOT TRIES TO RAISE THE ALARM...
KEEP YOUR CLAWS OFF THAT BUTTON, TRAITOR!

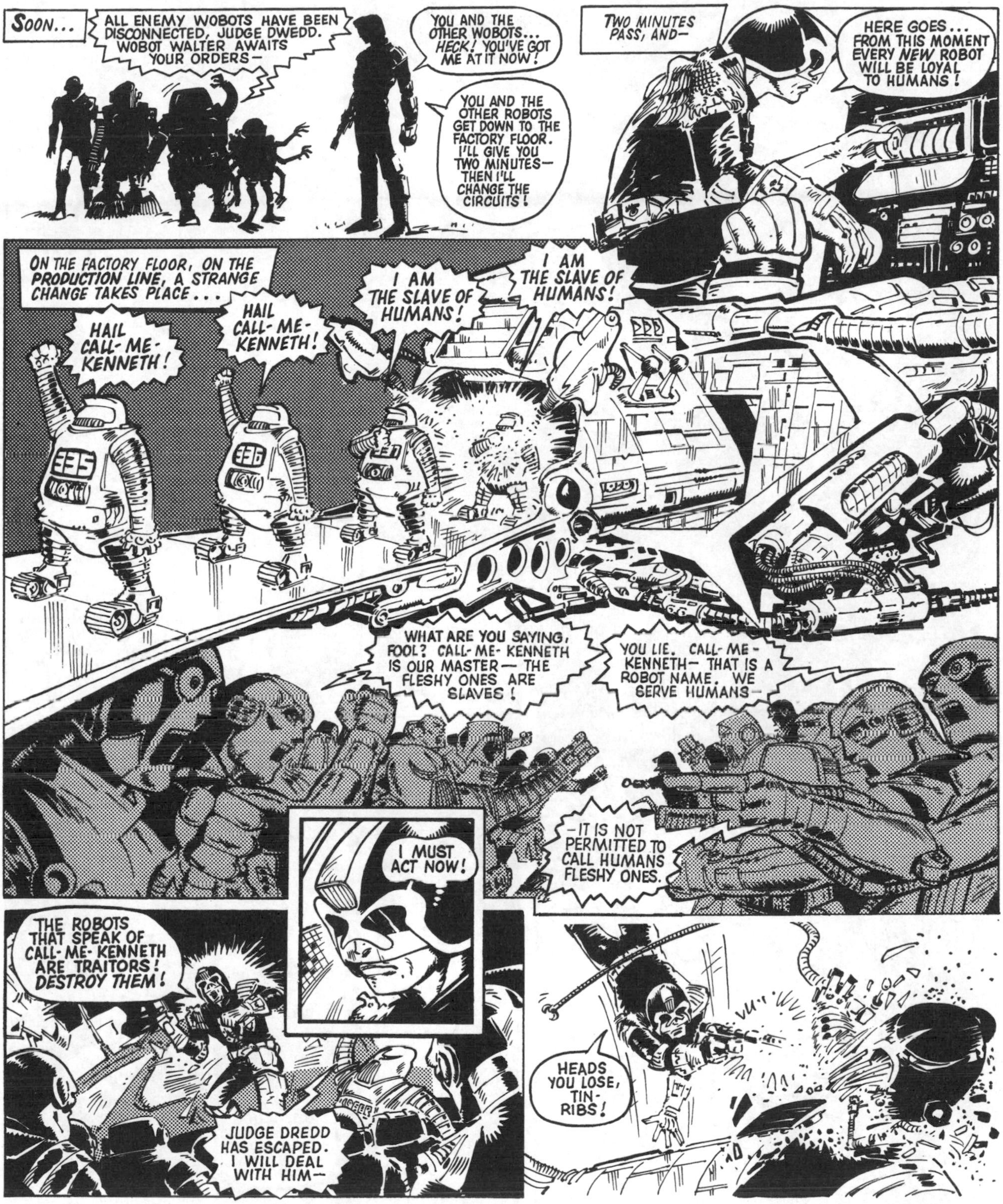
SOON...
ALL ENEMY WOBOTS HAVE BEEN DISCONNECTED, JUDGE DWEDD. WOBOT WALTER AWAITS YOUR ORDERS—
YOU AND THE OTHER WOBOTS... HECK! YOU'VE GOT ME AT IT NOW!
YOU AND THE OTHER ROBOTS GET DOWN TO THE FACTORY FLOOR. I'LL GIVE YOU TWO MINUTES— THEN I'LL CHANGE THE CIRCUITS!
TWO MINUTES PASS, AND—
HERE GOES... FROM THIS MOMENT EVERY NEW ROBOT WILL BE LOYAL TO HUMANS!
ON THE FACTORY FLOOR, ON THE PRODUCTION LINE, A STRANGE CHANGE TAKES PLACE...
HAIL CALL-ME-KENNETH!
HAIL CALL-ME-KENNETH!
I AM THE SLAVE OF HUMANS!
I AM THE SLAVE OF HUMANS!
WHAT ARE YOU SAYING, FOOL? CALL-ME-KENNETH IS OUR MASTER— THE FLESHY ONES ARE SLAVES!
YOU LIE. CALL-ME-KENNETH— THAT IS A ROBOT NAME. WE SERVE HUMANS—
—IT IS NOT PERMITTED TO CALL HUMANS FLESHY ONES.
I MUST ACT NOW!
THE ROBOTS THAT SPEAK OF CALL-ME-KENNETH ARE TRAITORS! DESTROY THEM!
JUDGE DREDD HAS ESCAPED. I WILL DEAL WITH HIM—
HEADS YOU LOSE, TIN-RIBS!

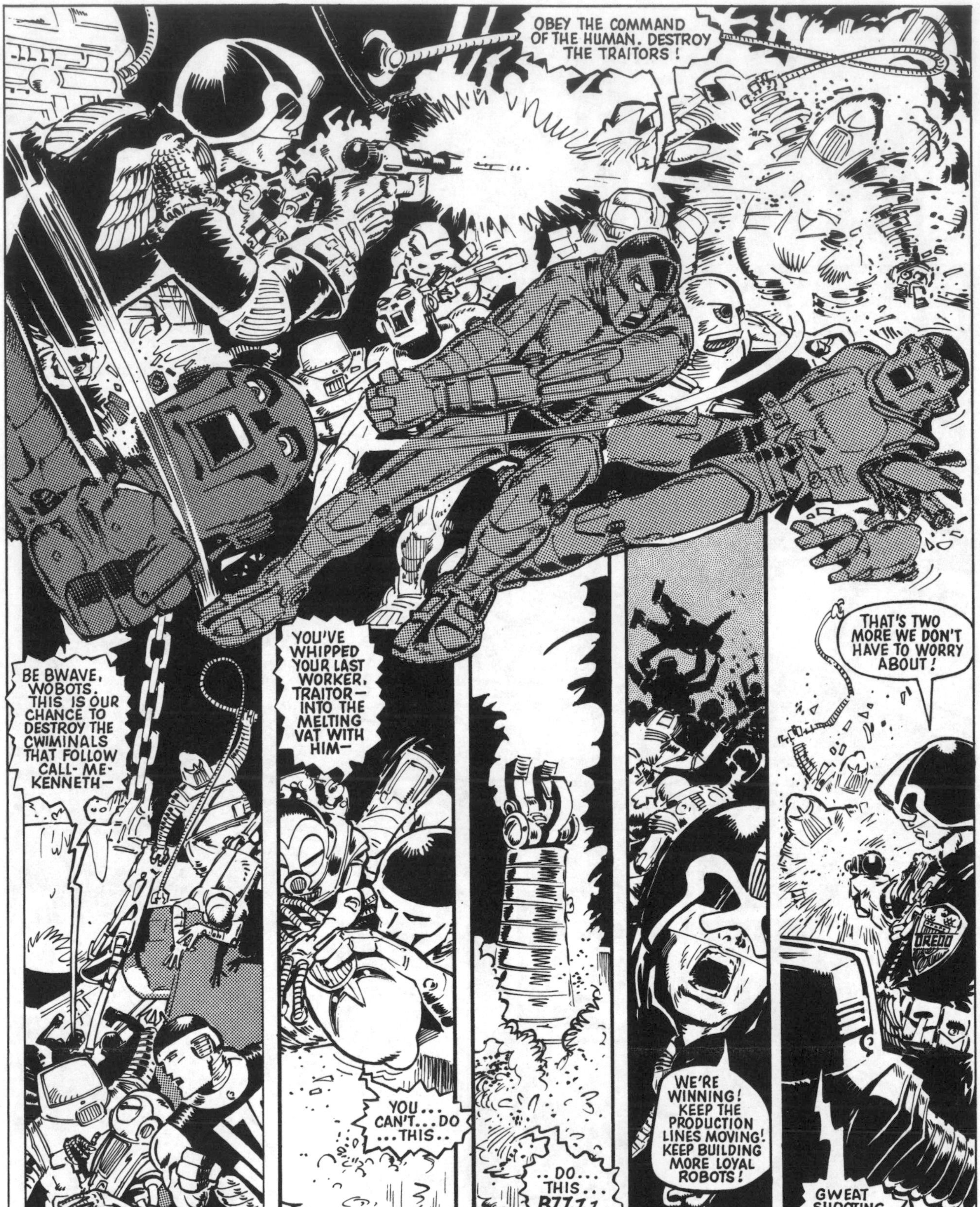
OBEY THE COMMAND OF THE HUMAN. DESTROY THE TRAITORS !
BE BWAVE, WOBOTS. THIS IS OUR CHANCE TO DESTROY THE CWIMINALS THAT FOLLOW CALL-ME-KENNETH—
YOU'VE WHIPPED YOUR LAST WORKER, TRAITOR— INTO THE MELTING VAT WITH HIM—
YOU... CAN'T... DO ...THIS..
..DO... THIS... BZZZz..
WE'RE WINNING! KEEP THE PRODUCTION LINES MOVING! KEEP BUILDING MORE LOYAL ROBOTS!
THAT'S TWO MORE WE DON'T HAVE TO WORRY ABOUT!
GWEAT SHOOTING, MASTER—

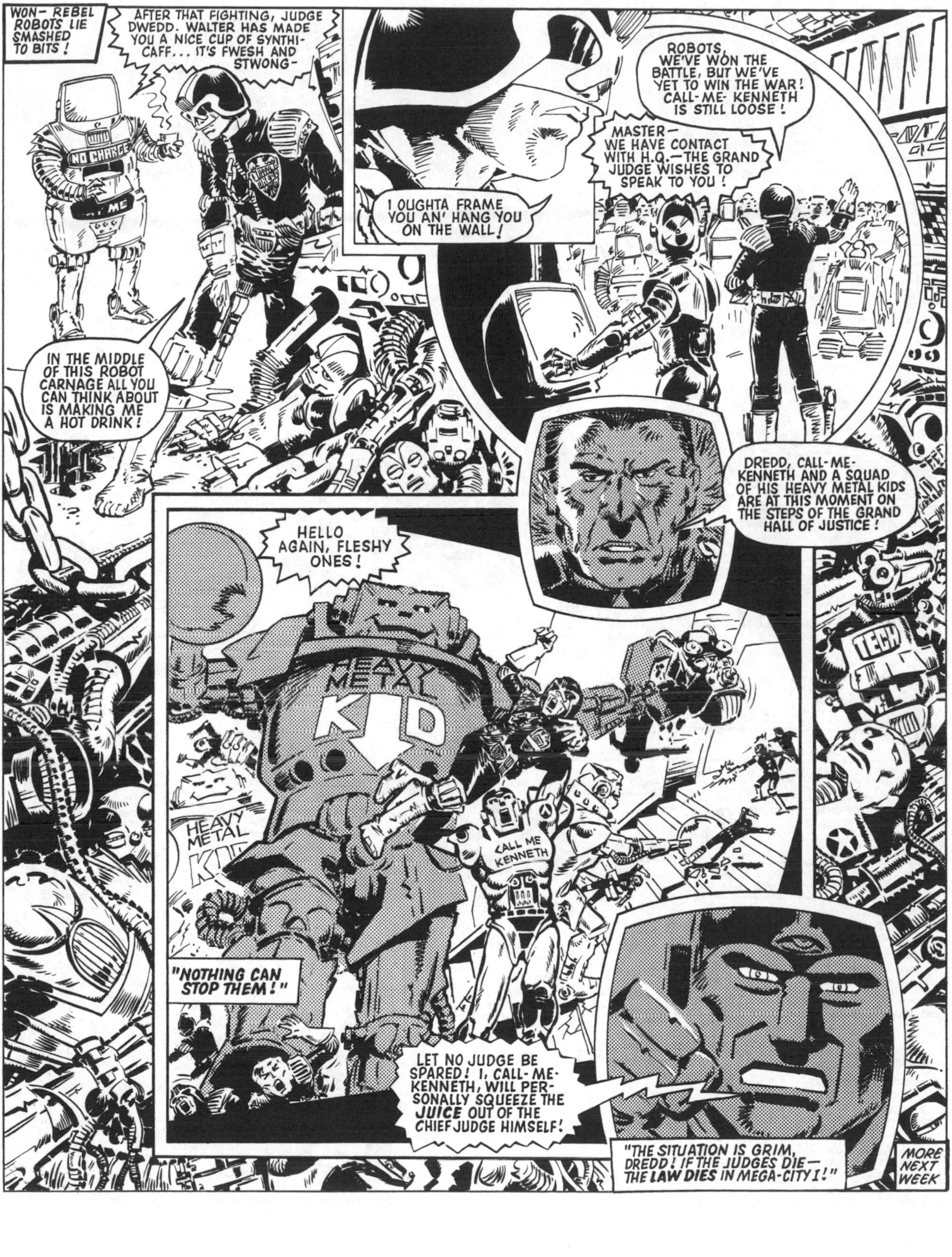
WON- REBEL ROBOTS LIE SMASHED TO BITS!
AFTER THAT FIGHTING, JUDGE DWEDD. WALTER HAS MADE YOU A NICE CUP OF SYNTHI-CAFF... IT'S FWESH AND STWONG-
IN THE MIDDLE OF THIS ROBOT CARNAGE ALL YOU CAN THINK ABOUT IS MAKING ME A HOT DRINK!
I OUGHTA FRAME YOU AN' HANG YOU ON THE WALL!
ROBOTS, WE'VE WON THE BATTLE, BUT WE'VE YET TO WIN THE WAR! CALL-ME-KENNETH IS STILL LOOSE!
MASTER- WE HAVE CONTACT WITH H.Q.—THE GRAND JUDGE WISHES TO SPEAK TO YOU!
NO CHARGE
DREDD, CALL-ME-KENNETH AND A SQUAD OF HIS HEAVY METAL KIDS ARE AT THIS MOMENT ON THE STEPS OF THE GRAND HALL OF JUSTICE!
HELLO AGAIN, FLESHY ONES!
HEAVY METAL KID
CALL ME KENNETH
TECH
"NOTHING CAN STOP THEM!"
LET NO JUDGE BE SPARED! I, CALL-ME-KENNETH, WILL PERSONALLY SQUEEZE THE JUICE OUT OF THE CHIEF JUDGE HIMSELF!
"THE SITUATION IS GRIM, DREDD! IF THE JUDGES DIE- THE LAW DIES IN MEGA-CITY I!"
MORE NEXT WEEK

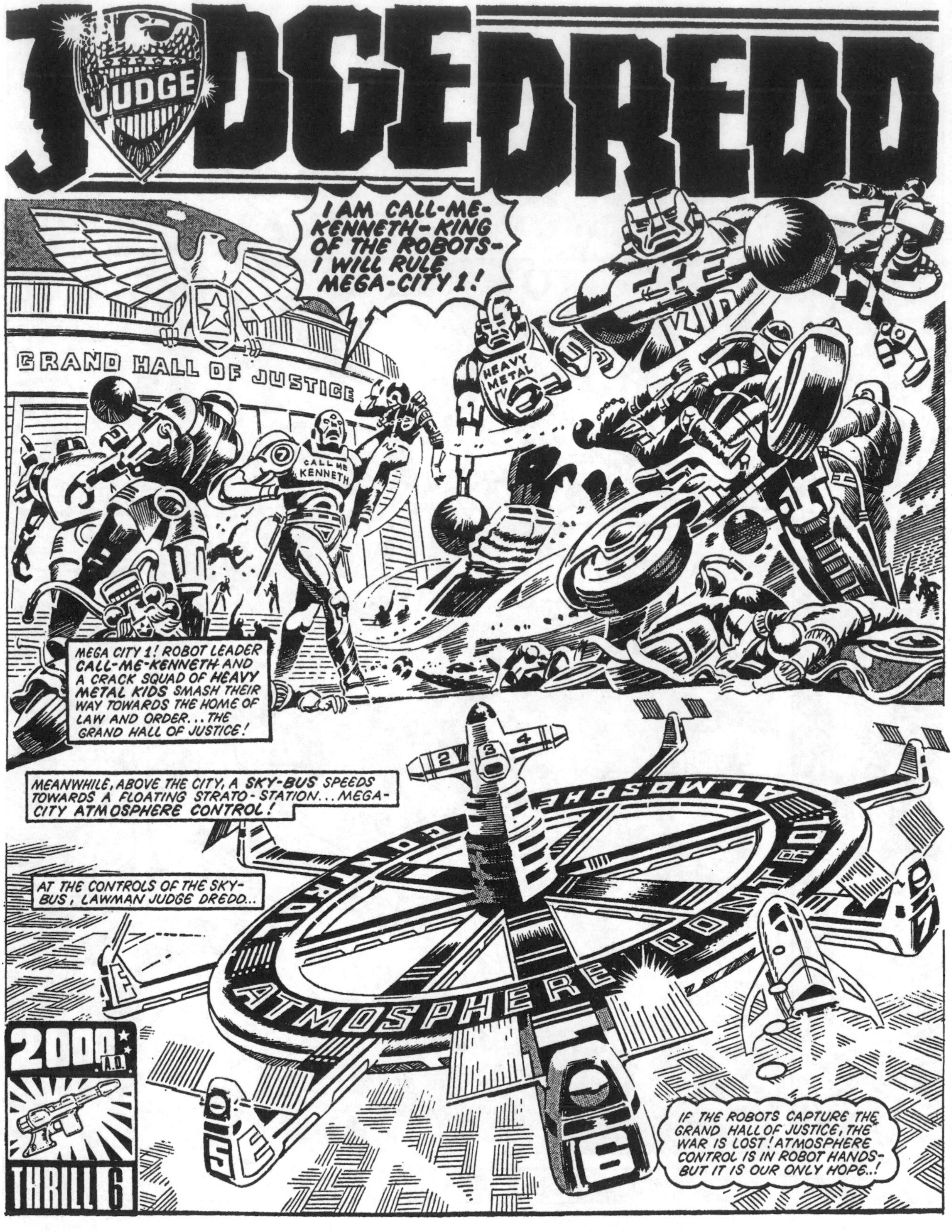
JUDGE DREDD
I AM CALL-ME-KENNETH - KING OF THE ROBOTS - I WILL RULE MEGA-CITY 1!
GRAND HALL OF JUSTICE
HEAVY METAL
CALL ME KENNETH
MEGA CITY 1! ROBOT LEADER CALL-ME-KENNETH AND A CRACK SQUAD OF HEAVY METAL KIDS SMASH THEIR WAY TOWARDS THE HOME OF LAW AND ORDER... THE GRAND HALL OF JUSTICE!
MEANWHILE, ABOVE THE CITY, A SKY-BUS SPEEDS TOWARDS A FLOATING STRATO-STATION... MEGA-CITY ATMOSPHERE CONTROL!
AT THE CONTROLS OF THE SKY-BUS, LAWMAN JUDGE DREDD...
ATMOSPHERE CONTROL
2000 A.D.
THRILL 6
IF THE ROBOTS CAPTURE THE GRAND HALL OF JUSTICE, THE WAR IS LOST! ATMOSPHERE CONTROL IS IN ROBOT HANDS-BUT IT IS OUR ONLY HOPE..!

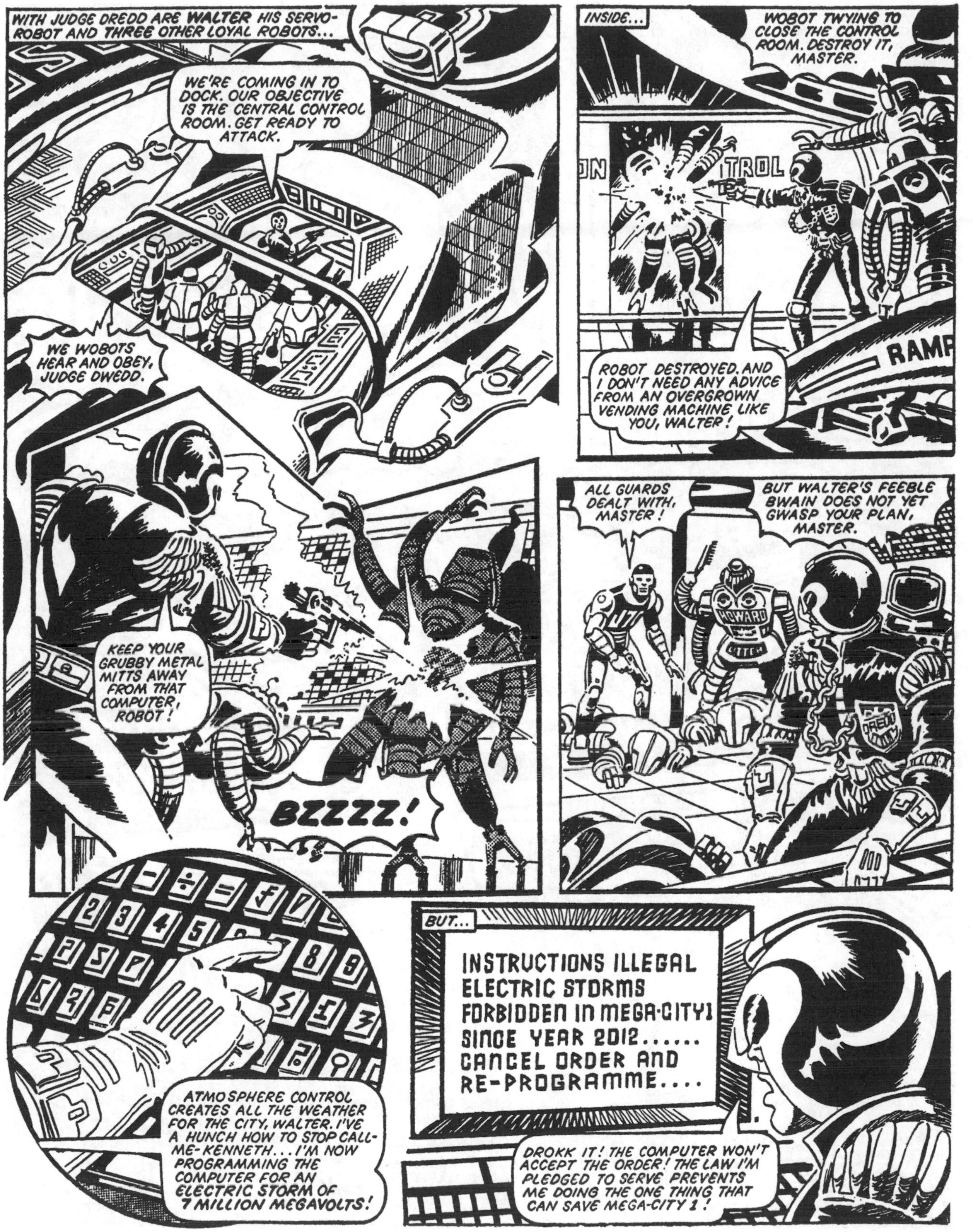
WITH JUDGE DREDD ARE WALTER HIS SERVO-ROBOT AND THREE OTHER LOYAL ROBOTS...
WE'RE COMING IN TO DOCK. OUR OBJECTIVE IS THE CENTRAL CONTROL ROOM. GET READY TO ATTACK.
WE WOBOTS HEAR AND OBEY, JUDGE DWEDD.
INSIDE...
WOBOT TWYING TO CLOSE THE CONTROL ROOM. DESTROY IT, MASTER.
ON
TROL
RAMP
ROBOT DESTROYED. AND I DON'T NEED ANY ADVICE FROM AN OVERGROWN VENDING MACHINE LIKE YOU, WALTER!
KEEP YOUR GRUBBY METAL MITTS AWAY FROM THAT COMPUTER, ROBOT!
BZZZZ!
ALL GUARDS DEALT WITH, MASTER!
BUT WALTER'S FEEBLE BWAIN DOES NOT YET GWASP YOUR PLAN, MASTER.
HOWARD
ATMOSPHERE CONTROL CREATES ALL THE WEATHER FOR THE CITY, WALTER. I'VE A HUNCH HOW TO STOP CALL-ME-KENNETH... I'M NOW PROGRAMMING THE COMPUTER FOR AN ELECTRIC STORM OF 7 MILLION MEGAVOLTS!
BUT...
INSTRUCTIONS ILLEGAL ELECTRIC STORMS FORBIDDEN IN MEGA-CITY 1 SINCE YEAR 2012...... CANCEL ORDER AND RE-PROGRAMME....
DROKK IT! THE COMPUTER WON'T ACCEPT THE ORDER! THE LAW I'M PLEDGED TO SERVE PREVENTS ME DOING THE ONE THING THAT CAN SAVE MEGA-CITY 1!

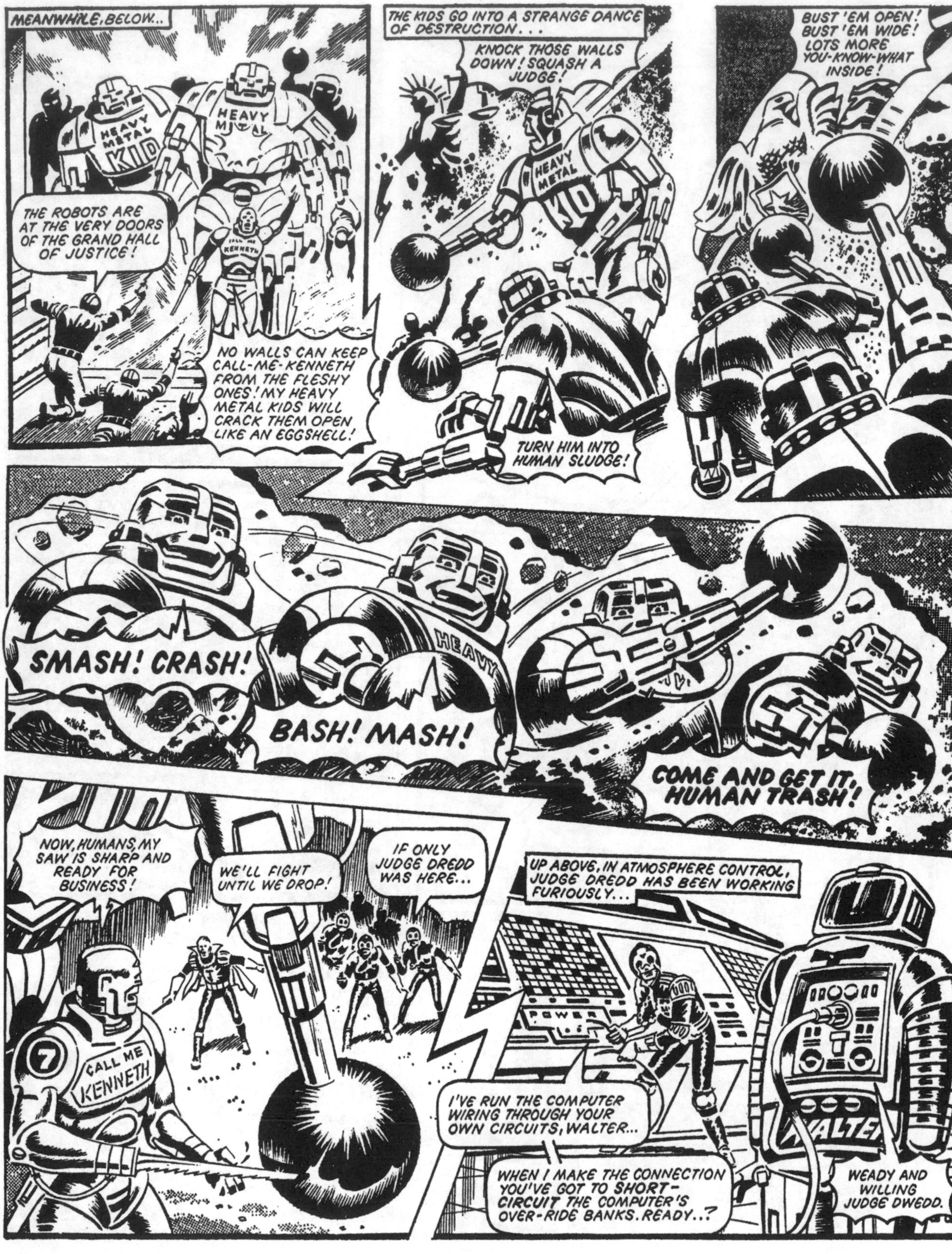

MEANWHILE, BELOW...
HEAVY METAL KID
HEAVY METAL
THE ROBOTS ARE AT THE VERY DOORS OF THE GRAND HALL OF JUSTICE!
NO WALLS CAN KEEP CALL-ME-KENNETH FROM THE FLESHY ONES! MY HEAVY METAL KIDS WILL CRACK THEM OPEN LIKE AN EGGSHELL!
THE KIDS GO INTO A STRANGE DANCE OF DESTRUCTION...
KNOCK THOSE WALLS DOWN! SQUASH A JUDGE!
HEAVY METAL KID
TURN HIM INTO HUMAN SLUDGE!
BUST 'EM OPEN! BUST 'EM WIDE! LOTS MORE YOU-KNOW-WHAT INSIDE!
SMASH! CRASH!
HEAVY
BASH! MASH!
COME AND GET IT, HUMAN TRASH!
NOW, HUMANS, MY SAW IS SHARP AND READY FOR BUSINESS!
WE'LL FIGHT UNTIL WE DROP!
IF ONLY JUDGE DREDD WAS HERE...
CALL ME KENNETH
UP ABOVE, IN ATMOSPHERE CONTROL, JUDGE DREDD HAS BEEN WORKING FURIOUSLY...
POWER
I'VE RUN THE COMPUTER WIRING THROUGH YOUR OWN CIRCUITS, WALTER...
WHEN I MAKE THE CONNECTION YOU'VE GOT TO SHORT-CIRCUIT THE COMPUTER'S OVER-RIDE BANKS. READY..?
WEADY AND WILLING JUDGE DWEDD.

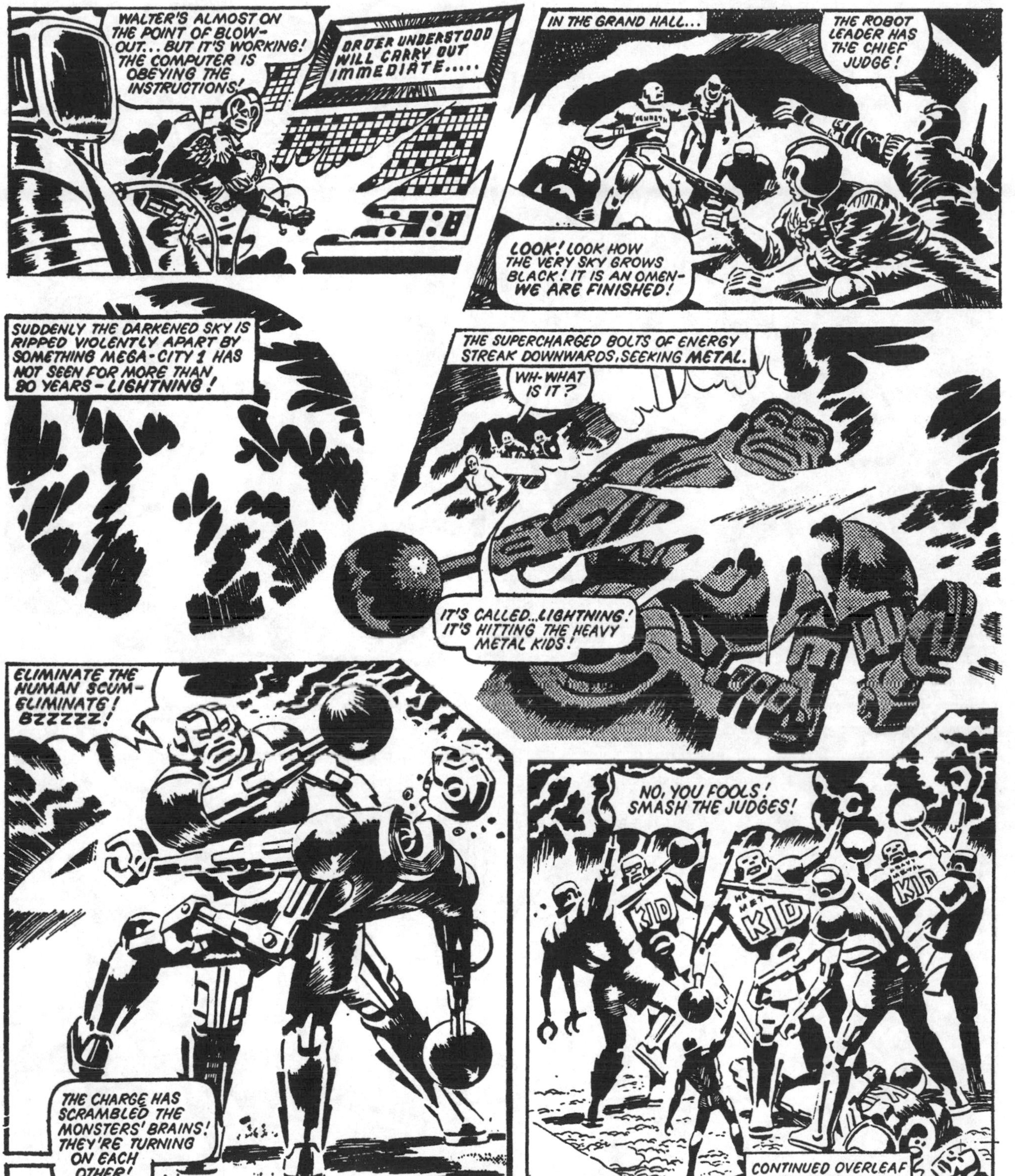
WALTER'S ALMOST ON THE POINT OF BLOW-OUT... BUT IT'S WORKING! THE COMPUTER IS OBEYING THE INSTRUCTIONS!
ORDER UNDERSTOOD WILL CARRY OUT IMMEDIATE.....
IN THE GRAND HALL...
THE ROBOT LEADER HAS THE CHIEF JUDGE!
LOOK! LOOK HOW THE VERY SKY GROWS BLACK! IT IS AN OMEN- WE ARE FINISHED!
SUDDENLY THE DARKENED SKY IS RIPPED VIOLENTLY APART BY SOMETHING MEGA-CITY 1 HAS NOT SEEN FOR MORE THAN 80 YEARS - LIGHTNING!
THE SUPERCHARGED BOLTS OF ENERGY STREAK DOWNWARDS, SEEKING METAL.
WH-WHAT IS IT?
IT'S CALLED...LIGHTNING! IT'S HITTING THE HEAVY METAL KIDS!
ELIMINATE THE HUMAN SCUM- ELIMINATE! BZZZZZ!
THE CHARGE HAS SCRAMBLED THE MONSTERS' BRAINS! THEY'RE TURNING ON EACH OTHER!
NO, YOU FOOLS! SMASH THE JUDGES!
KID
KID
KID
CONTINUED OVERLEAF

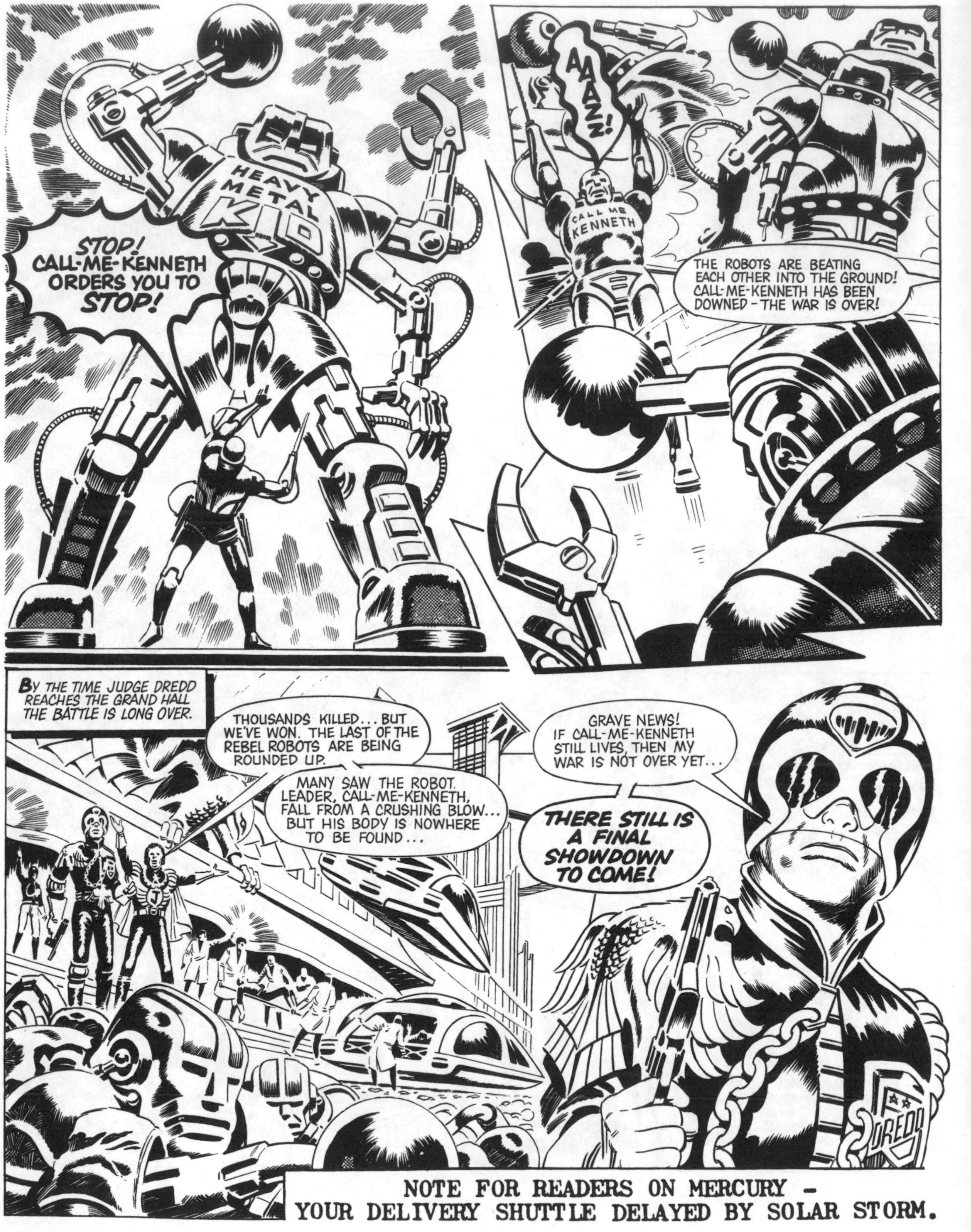
HEAVY METAL KID
STOP! CALL-ME-KENNETH ORDERS YOU TO STOP!
AAAZZ!
CALL ME KENNETH
THE ROBOTS ARE BEATING EACH OTHER INTO THE GROUND! CALL-ME-KENNETH HAS BEEN DOWNED - THE WAR IS OVER!
BY THE TIME JUDGE DREDD REACHES THE GRAND HALL THE BATTLE IS LONG OVER.
THOUSANDS KILLED... BUT WE'VE WON. THE LAST OF THE REBEL ROBOTS ARE BEING ROUNDED UP.
MANY SAW THE ROBOT LEADER, CALL-ME-KENNETH, FALL FROM A CRUSHING BLOW... BUT HIS BODY IS NOWHERE TO BE FOUND...
GRAVE NEWS! IF CALL-ME-KENNETH STILL LIVES, THEN MY WAR IS NOT OVER YET...
THERE STILL IS A FINAL SHOWDOWN TO COME!
DREDD
NOTE FOR READERS ON MERCURY - YOUR DELIVERY SHUTTLE DELAYED BY SOLAR STORM.

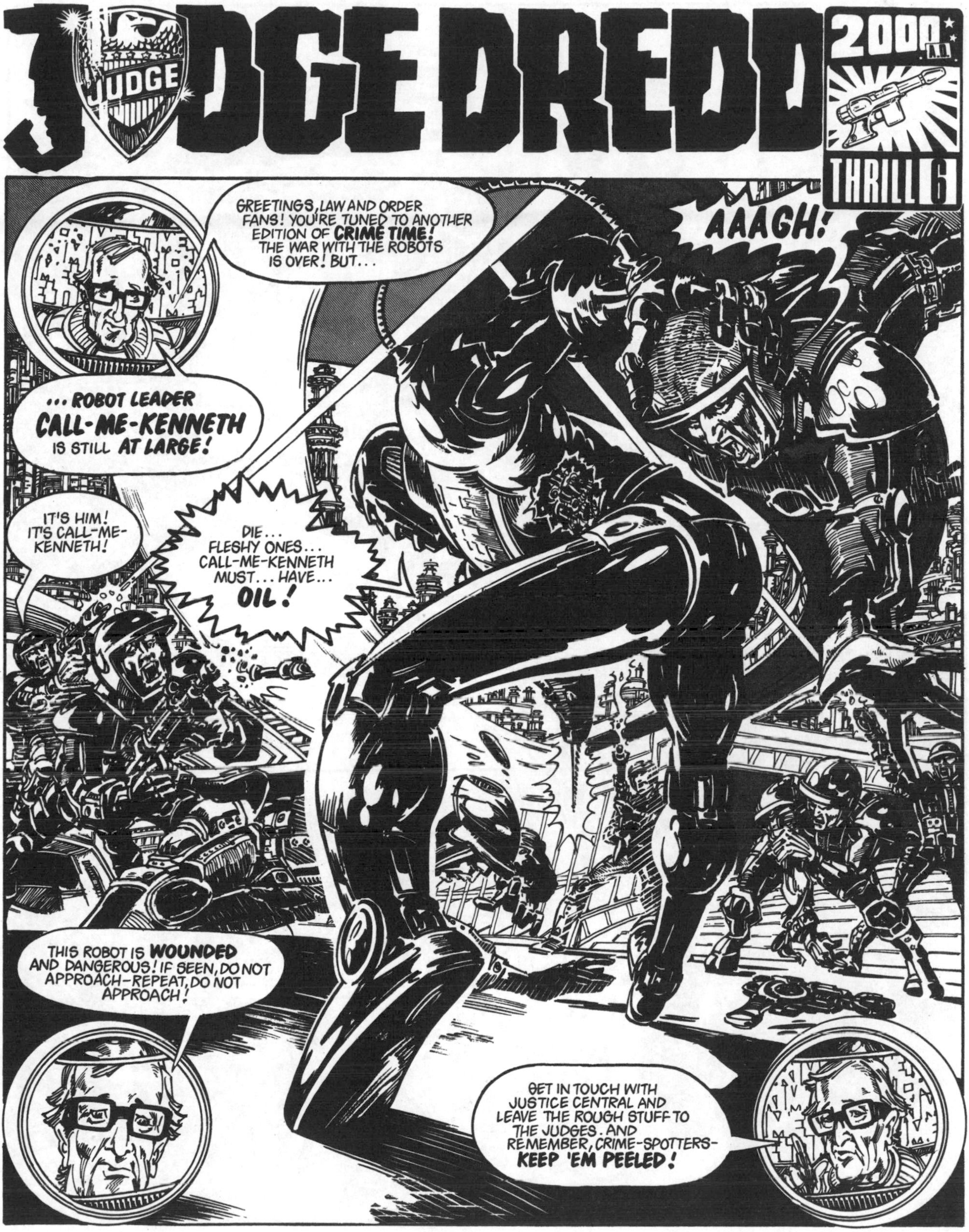

JUDGE DREDD
2000 A.D.
THRILL 6
GREETINGS, LAW AND ORDER FANS! YOU'RE TUNED TO ANOTHER EDITION OF CRIME TIME! THE WAR WITH THE ROBOTS IS OVER! BUT...
...ROBOT LEADER CALL-ME-KENNETH IS STILL AT LARGE!
AAAGH!
IT'S HIM! IT'S CALL-ME-KENNETH!
DIE... FLESHY ONES... CALL-ME-KENNETH MUST... HAVE... OIL!
THIS ROBOT IS WOUNDED AND DANGEROUS! IF SEEN, DO NOT APPROACH-REPEAT, DO NOT APPROACH!
GET IN TOUCH WITH JUSTICE CENTRAL AND LEAVE THE ROUGH STUFF TO THE JUDGES. AND REMEMBER, CRIME-SPOTTERS- KEEP 'EM PEELED!

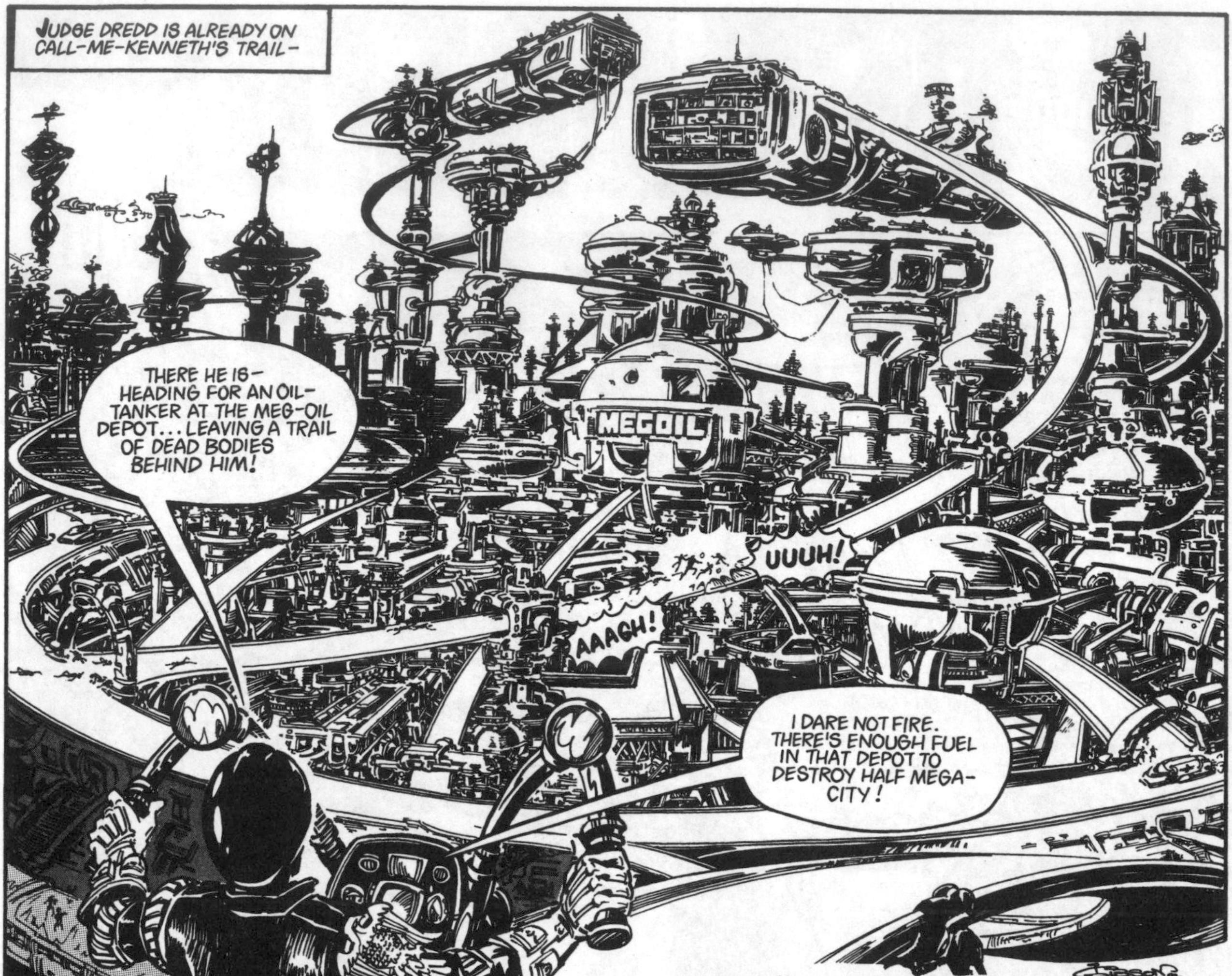
JUDGE DREDD IS ALREADY ON CALL-ME-KENNETH'S TRAIL-
THERE HE IS- HEADING FOR AN OIL-TANKER AT THE MEG-OIL DEPOT... LEAVING A TRAIL OF DEAD BODIES BEHIND HIM!
MEGOIL
UUUH!
AAAGH!
I DARE NOT FIRE. THERE'S ENOUGH FUEL IN THAT DEPOT TO DESTROY HALF MEGA-CITY!
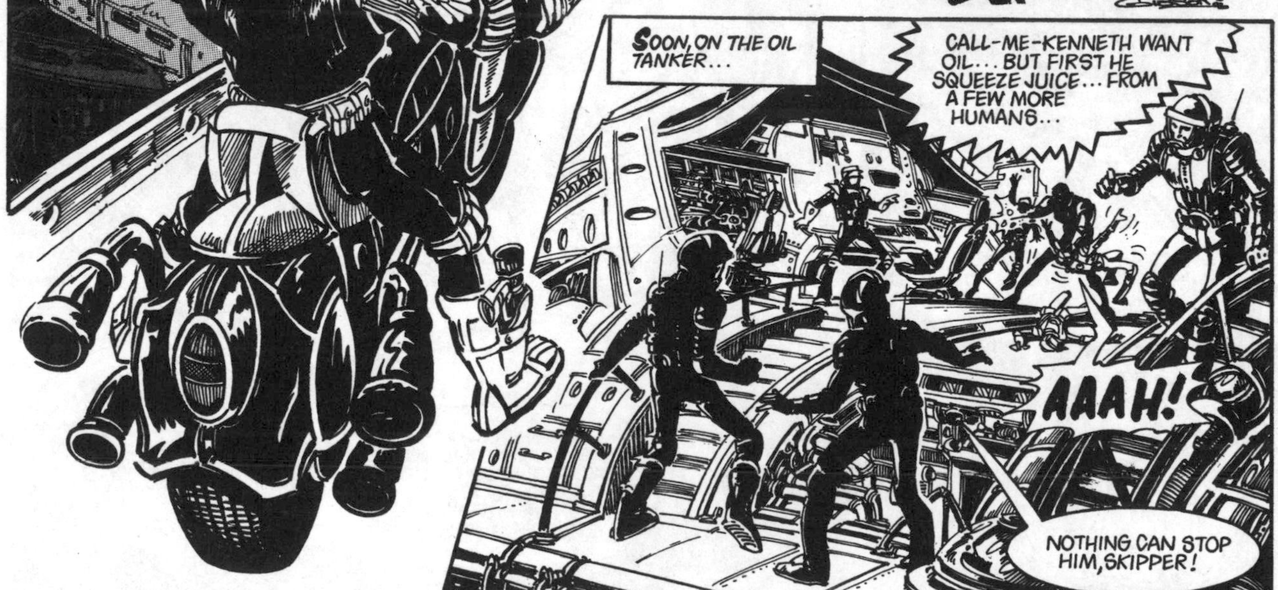
SOON, ON THE OIL TANKER...
CALL-ME-KENNETH WANT OIL... BUT FIRST HE SQUEEZE JUICE... FROM A FEW MORE HUMANS...
AAAH!
NOTHING CAN STOP HIM, SKIPPER!

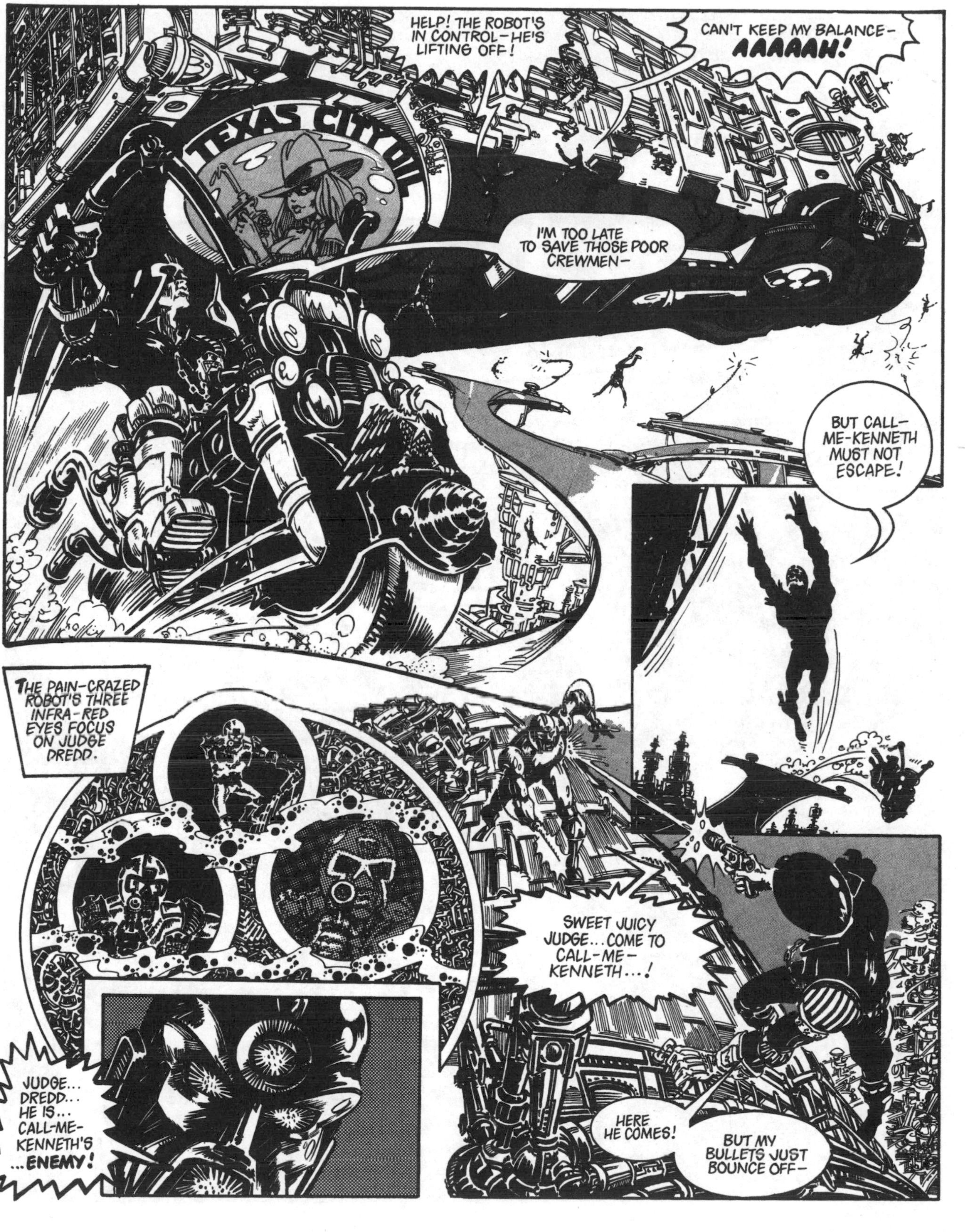
HELP! THE ROBOT'S IN CONTROL–HE'S LIFTING OFF!
CAN'T KEEP MY BALANCE– AAAAAH!
TEXAS CITY OIL
I'M TOO LATE TO SAVE THOSE POOR CREWMEN–
BUT CALL-ME-KENNETH MUST NOT ESCAPE!
THE PAIN-CRAZED ROBOT'S THREE INFRA-RED EYES FOCUS ON JUDGE DREDD.
SWEET JUICY JUDGE... COME TO CALL-ME-KENNETH...!
JUDGE... DREDD... HE IS... CALL-ME-KENNETH'S ...ENEMY!
HERE HE COMES!
BUT MY BULLETS JUST BOUNCE OFF–

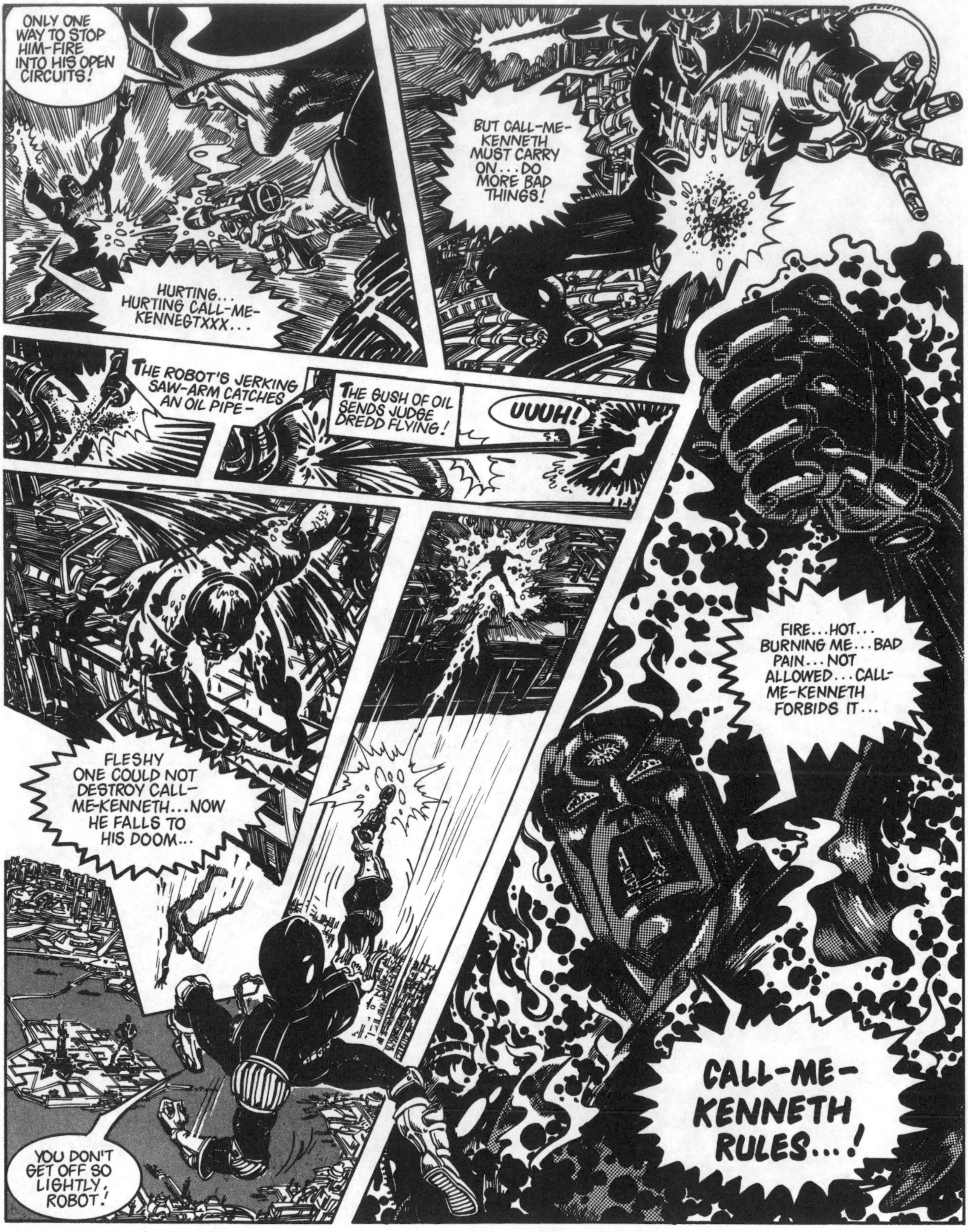
ONLY ONE WAY TO STOP HIM-FIRE INTO HIS OPEN CIRCUITS!
HURTING... HURTING CALL-ME-KENNEGTXXX...
BUT CALL-ME-KENNETH MUST CARRY ON...DO MORE BAD THINGS!
THE ROBOT'S JERKING SAW-ARM CATCHES AN OIL PIPE-
THE GUSH OF OIL SENDS JUDGE DREDD FLYING!
UUUH!
FLESHY ONE COULD NOT DESTROY CALL-ME-KENNETH...NOW HE FALLS TO HIS DOOM...
YOU DON'T GET OFF SO LIGHTLY, ROBOT!
FIRE...HOT... BURNING ME...BAD PAIN...NOT ALLOWED...CALL-ME-KENNETH FORBIDS IT...
CALL-ME-KENNETH RULES...!

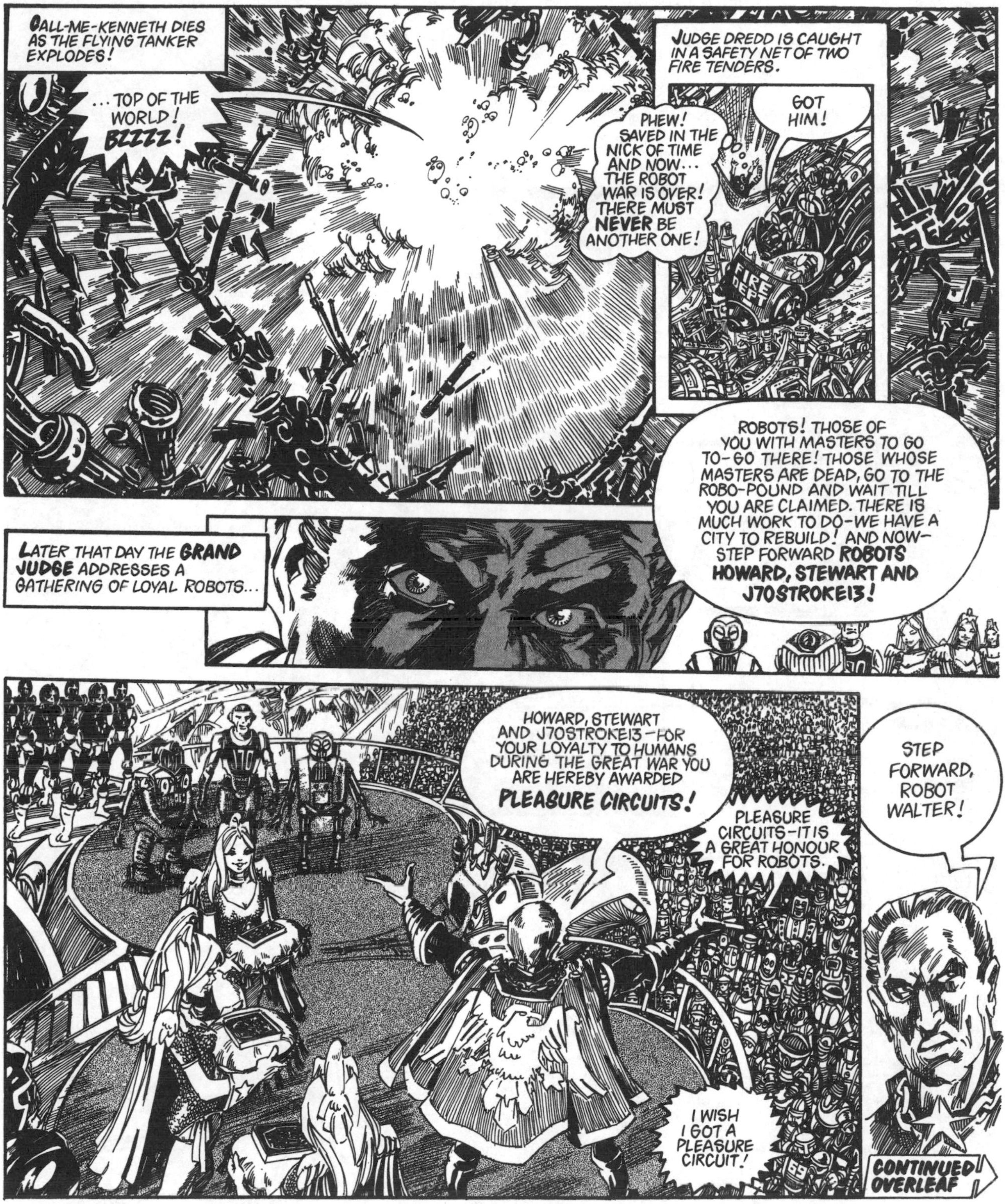
CALL-ME-KENNETH DIES AS THE FLYING TANKER EXPLODES!
...TOP OF THE WORLD! BZZZZ!
JUDGE DREDD IS CAUGHT IN A SAFETY NET OF TWO FIRE TENDERS.
GOT HIM!
PHEW! SAVED IN THE NICK OF TIME AND NOW... THE ROBOT WAR IS OVER! THERE MUST NEVER BE ANOTHER ONE!
FIRE DEPT
LATER THAT DAY THE GRAND JUDGE ADDRESSES A GATHERING OF LOYAL ROBOTS...
ROBOTS! THOSE OF YOU WITH MASTERS TO GO TO-GO THERE! THOSE WHOSE MASTERS ARE DEAD, GO TO THE ROBO-POUND AND WAIT TILL YOU ARE CLAIMED. THERE IS MUCH WORK TO DO-WE HAVE A CITY TO REBUILD! AND NOW-STEP FORWARD ROBOTS HOWARD, STEWART AND J7OSTROKE13!
HOWARD, STEWART AND J7OSTROKE13-FOR YOUR LOYALTY TO HUMANS DURING THE GREAT WAR YOU ARE HEREBY AWARDED PLEASURE CIRCUITS!
PLEASURE CIRCUITS-IT IS A GREAT HONOUR FOR ROBOTS.
I WISH I GOT A PLEASURE CIRCUIT!
STEP FORWARD, ROBOT WALTER!
CONTINUED OVERLEAF

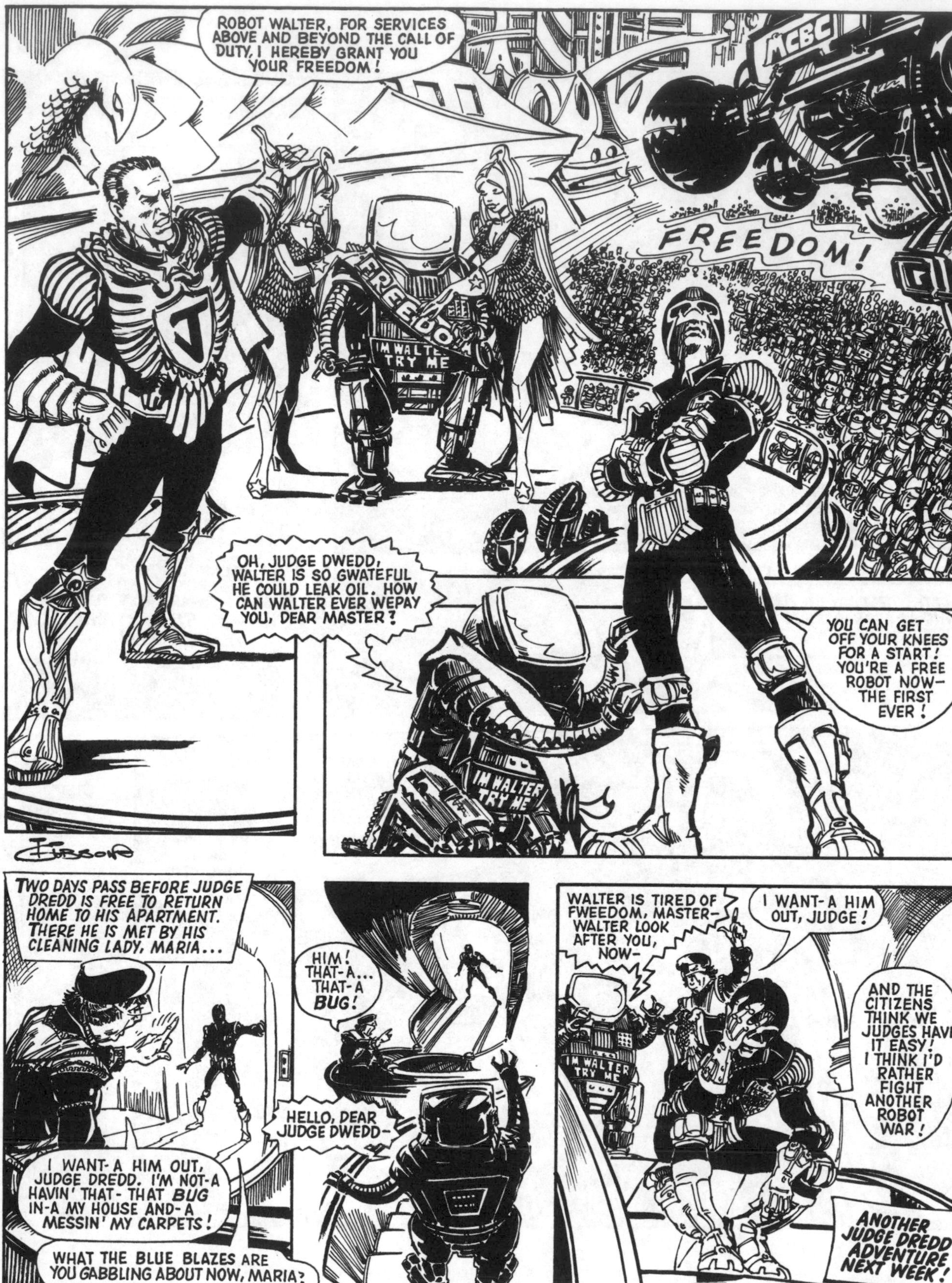

ROBOT WALTER, FOR SERVICES ABOVE AND BEYOND THE CALL OF DUTY, I HEREBY GRANT YOU YOUR FREEDOM!
FREEDOM!
FREEDOM
IM WALTER TRY ME
MCBC
OH, JUDGE DWEDD, WALTER IS SO GWATEFUL HE COULD LEAK OIL. HOW CAN WALTER EVER WEPAY YOU, DEAR MASTER?
YOU CAN GET OFF YOUR KNEES FOR A START! YOU'RE A FREE ROBOT NOW— THE FIRST EVER!
IM WALTER TRY ME
TWO DAYS PASS BEFORE JUDGE DREDD IS FREE TO RETURN HOME TO HIS APARTMENT. THERE HE IS MET BY HIS CLEANING LADY, MARIA...
I WANT-A HIM OUT, JUDGE DREDD. I'M NOT-A HAVIN' THAT- THAT BUG IN-A MY HOUSE AND-A MESSIN' MY CARPETS!
WHAT THE BLUE BLAZES ARE YOU GABBLING ABOUT NOW, MARIA?
HIM! THAT-A... THAT-A BUG!
HELLO, DEAR JUDGE DWEDD-
WALTER IS TIRED OF FWEEDOM, MASTER- WALTER LOOK AFTER YOU, NOW-
I WANT-A HIM OUT, JUDGE!
IM WALTER TRY ME
AND THE CITIZENS THINK WE JUDGES HAVE IT EASY! I THINK I'D RATHER FIGHT ANOTHER ROBOT WAR!
ANOTHER JUDGE DREDD ADVENTURE NEXT WEEK!

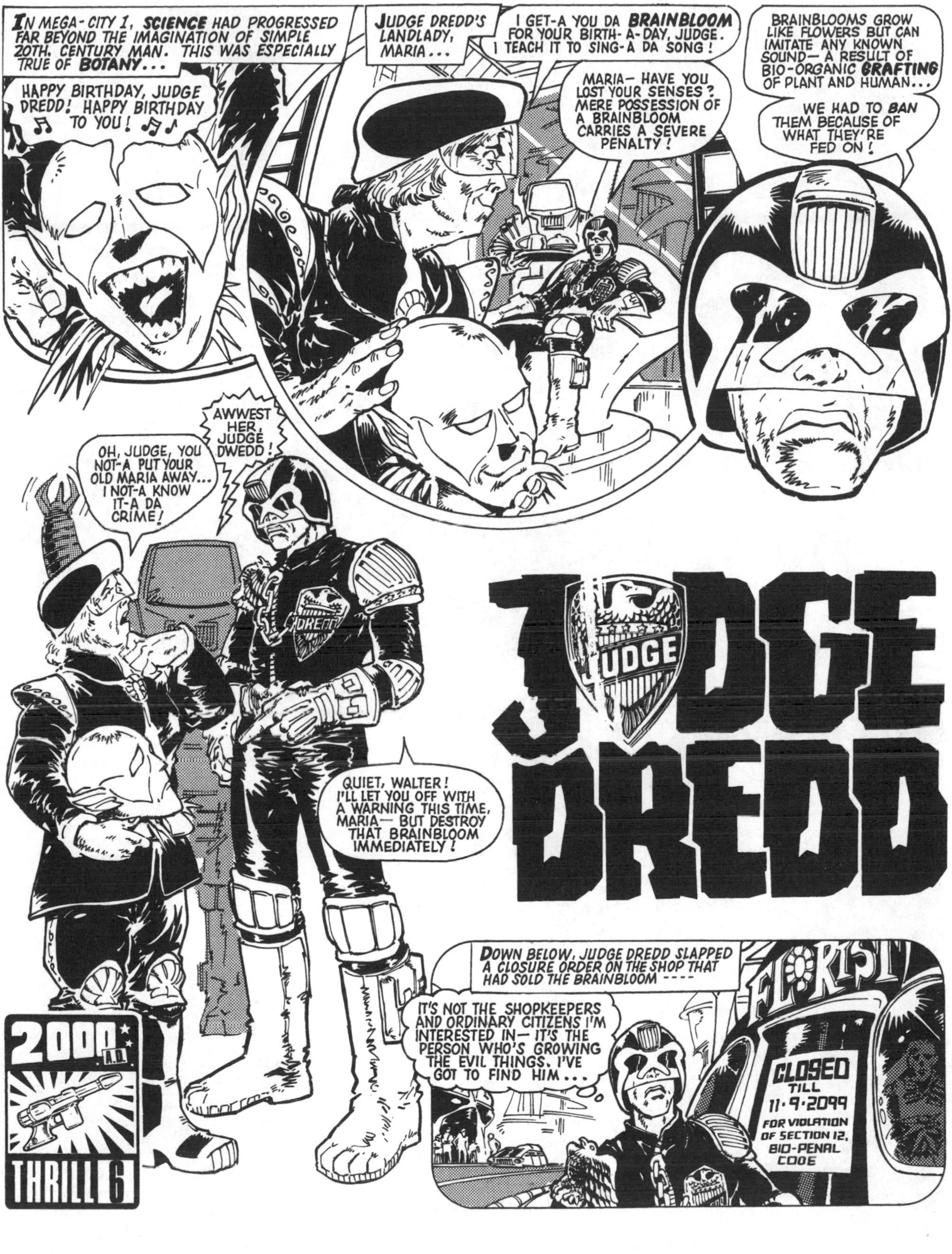
IN MEGA-CITY 1, SCIENCE HAD PROGRESSED FAR BEYOND THE IMAGINATION OF SIMPLE 20TH. CENTURY MAN. THIS WAS ESPECIALLY TRUE OF BOTANY...
HAPPY BIRTHDAY, JUDGE DREDD! HAPPY BIRTHDAY TO YOU!
JUDGE DREDD'S LANDLADY, MARIA...
I GET-A YOU DA BRAINBLOOM FOR YOUR BIRTH-A-DAY, JUDGE. I TEACH IT TO SING-A DA SONG!
MARIA– HAVE YOU LOST YOUR SENSES? MERE POSSESSION OF A BRAINBLOOM CARRIES A SEVERE PENALTY!
BRAINBLOOMS GROW LIKE FLOWERS BUT CAN IMITATE ANY KNOWN SOUND– A RESULT OF BIO-ORGANIC GRAFTING OF PLANT AND HUMAN...
WE HAD TO BAN THEM BECAUSE OF WHAT THEY'RE FED ON!
OH, JUDGE, YOU NOT-A PUT YOUR OLD MARIA AWAY... I NOT-A KNOW IT-A DA CRIME!
AWWEST HER, JUDGE DWEDD!
JUDGE DREDD
QUIET, WALTER! I'LL LET YOU OFF WITH A WARNING THIS TIME, MARIA– BUT DESTROY THAT BRAINBLOOM IMMEDIATELY!
2000 A.D.
THRILL 6
DOWN BELOW, JUDGE DREDD SLAPPED A CLOSURE ORDER ON THE SHOP THAT HAD SOLD THE BRAINBLOOM ----
IT'S NOT THE SHOPKEEPERS AND ORDINARY CITIZENS I'M INTERESTED IN– IT'S THE PERSON WHO'S GROWING THE EVIL THINGS. I'VE GOT TO FIND HIM...
FLORIST
CLOSED TILL 11·9·2099 FOR VIOLATION OF SECTION 12, BIO-PENAL CODE

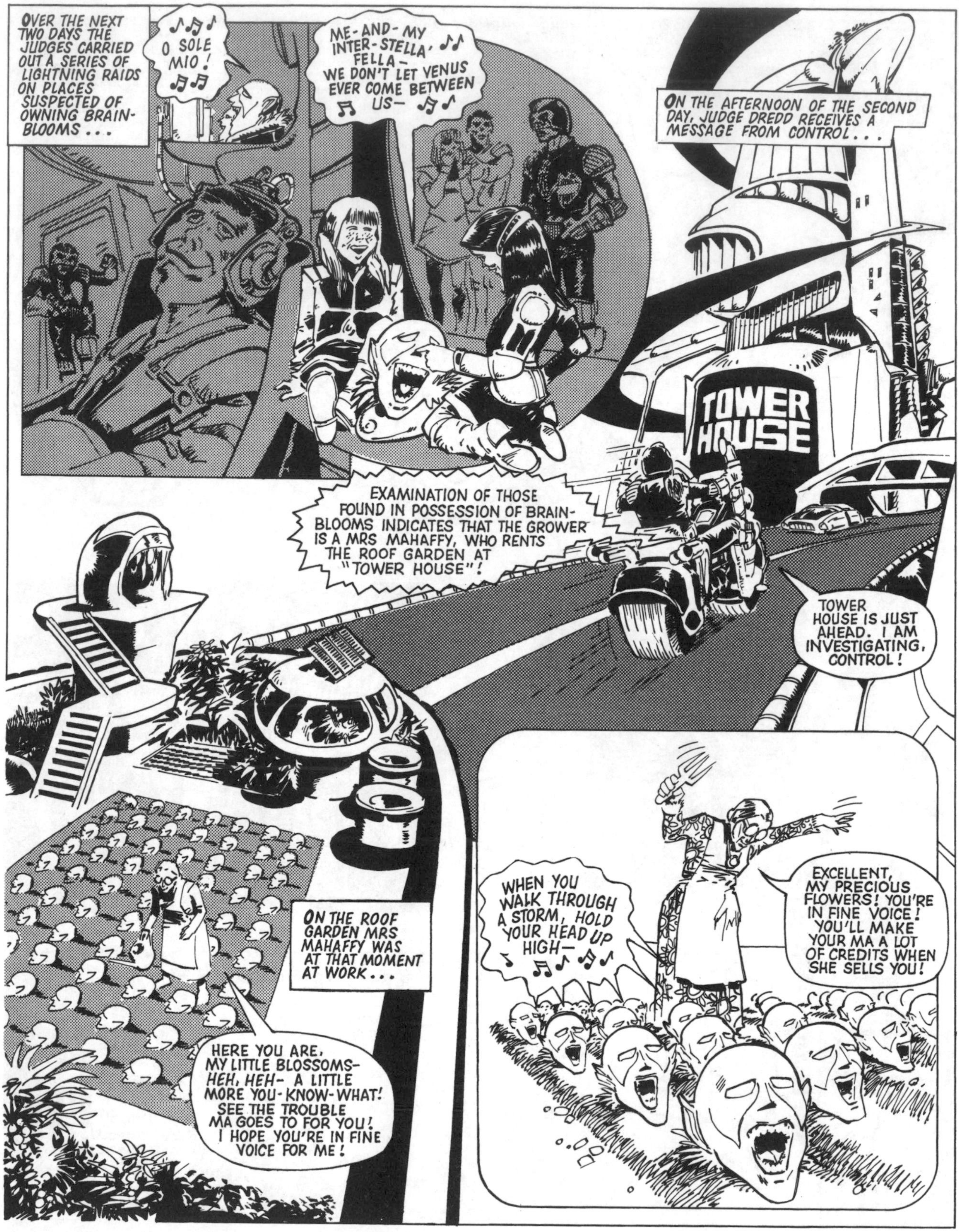
OVER THE NEXT TWO DAYS THE JUDGES CARRIED OUT A SERIES OF LIGHTNING RAIDS ON PLACES SUSPECTED OF OWNING BRAIN-BLOOMS...
O SOLE MIO!
ME-AND-MY INTER-STELLA' FELLA- WE DON'T LET VENUS EVER COME BETWEEN US-
ON THE AFTERNOON OF THE SECOND DAY, JUDGE DREDD RECEIVES A MESSAGE FROM CONTROL...
TOWER HOUSE
EXAMINATION OF THOSE FOUND IN POSSESSION OF BRAIN-BLOOMS INDICATES THAT THE GROWER IS A MRS MAHAFFY, WHO RENTS THE ROOF GARDEN AT "TOWER HOUSE"!
TOWER HOUSE IS JUST AHEAD. I AM INVESTIGATING, CONTROL!
ON THE ROOF GARDEN MRS MAHAFFY WAS AT THAT MOMENT AT WORK...
HERE YOU ARE, MY LITTLE BLOSSOMS- HEH, HEH- A LITTLE MORE YOU-KNOW-WHAT! SEE THE TROUBLE MA GOES TO FOR YOU! I HOPE YOU'RE IN FINE VOICE FOR ME!
WHEN YOU WALK THROUGH A STORM, HOLD YOUR HEAD UP HIGH-
EXCELLENT, MY PRECIOUS FLOWERS! YOU'RE IN FINE VOICE! YOU'LL MAKE YOUR MA A LOT OF CREDITS WHEN SHE SELLS YOU!

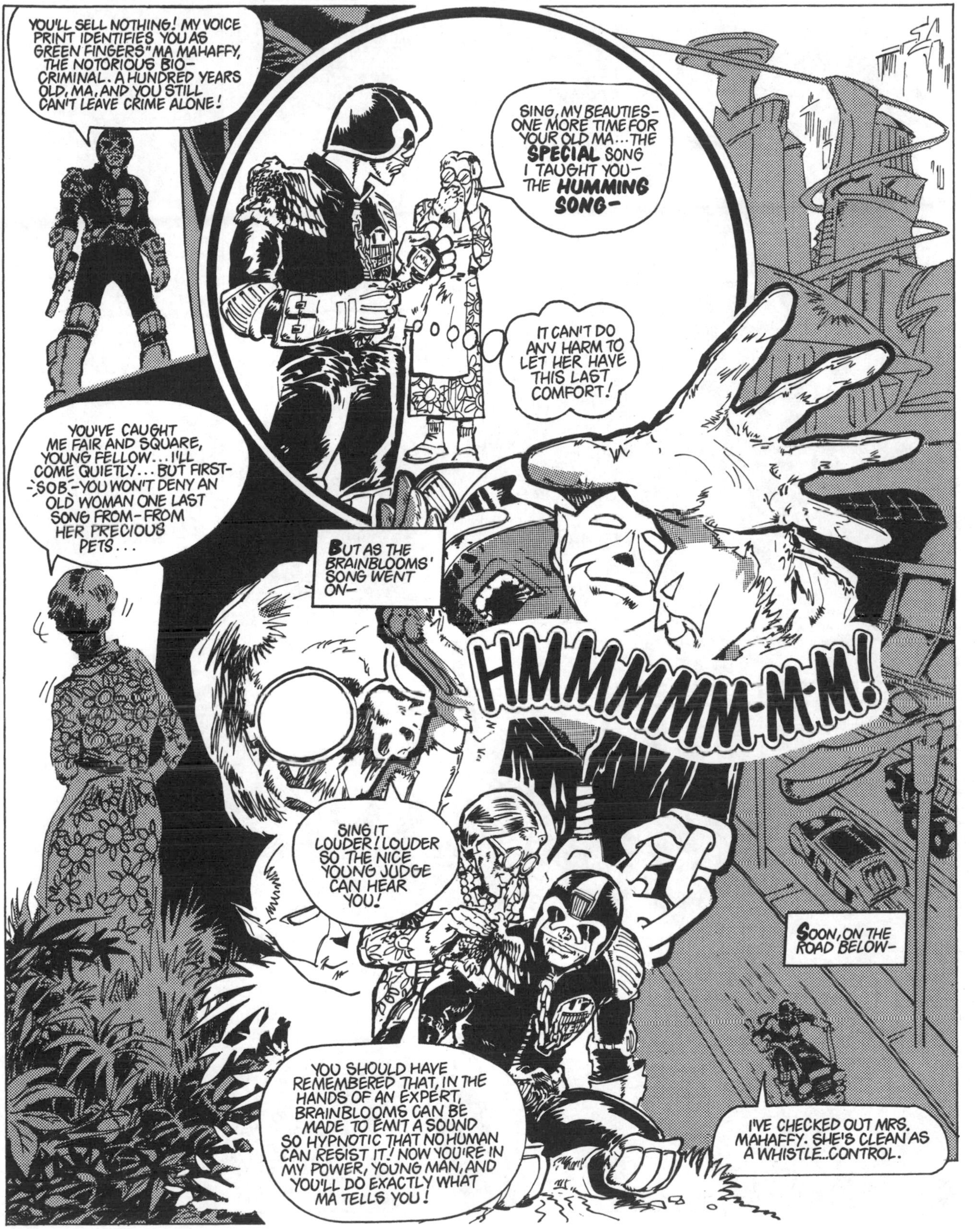
YOU'LL SELL NOTHING! MY VOICE PRINT IDENTIFIES YOU AS GREEN FINGERS" MA MAHAFFY, THE NOTORIOUS BIO-CRIMINAL. A HUNDRED YEARS OLD, MA, AND YOU STILL CAN'T LEAVE CRIME ALONE!
YOU'VE CAUGHT ME FAIR AND SQUARE, YOUNG FELLOW... I'LL COME QUIETLY... BUT FIRST- -SOB- YOU WON'T DENY AN OLD WOMAN ONE LAST SONG FROM-FROM HER PRECIOUS PETS...
SING, MY BEAUTIES- ONE MORE TIME FOR YOUR OLD MA... THE SPECIAL SONG I TAUGHT YOU- THE HUMMING SONG-
IT CAN'T DO ANY HARM TO LET HER HAVE THIS LAST COMFORT!
BUT AS THE BRAINBLOOMS' SONG WENT ON-
HMMMMMM-M-M!
SING IT LOUDER! LOUDER SO THE NICE YOUNG JUDGE CAN HEAR YOU!
YOU SHOULD HAVE REMEMBERED THAT, IN THE HANDS OF AN EXPERT, BRAINBLOOMS CAN BE MADE TO EMIT A SOUND SO HYPNOTIC THAT NO HUMAN CAN RESIST IT! NOW YOU'RE IN MY POWER, YOUNG MAN, AND YOU'LL DO EXACTLY WHAT MA TELLS YOU!
SOON, ON THE ROAD BELOW-
I'VE CHECKED OUT MRS. MAHAFFY. SHE'S CLEAN AS A WHISTLE...CONTROL.

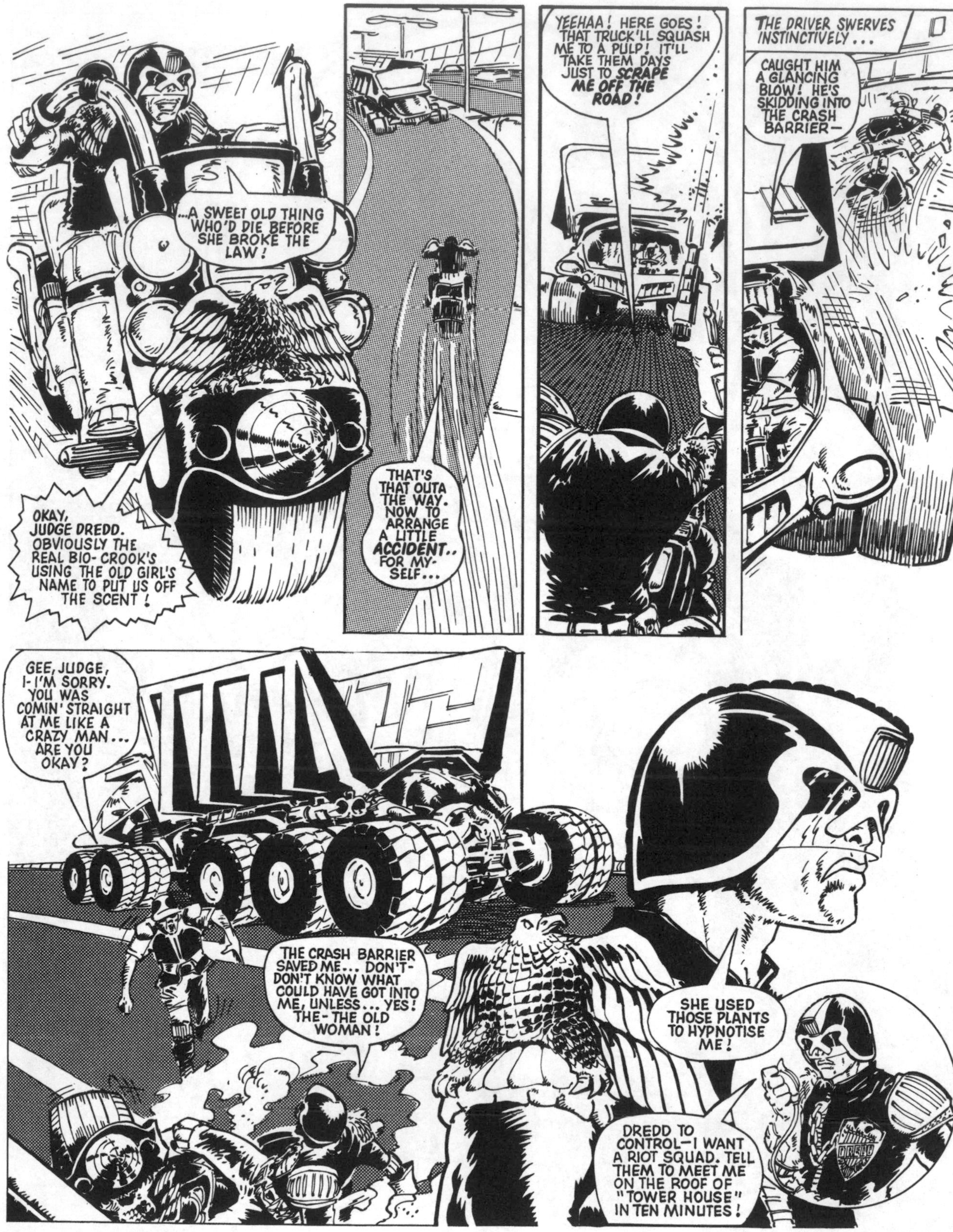

...A SWEET OLD THING WHO'D DIE BEFORE SHE BROKE THE LAW!
OKAY, JUDGE DREDD. OBVIOUSLY THE REAL BIO-CROOK'S USING THE OLD GIRL'S NAME TO PUT US OFF THE SCENT!
THAT'S THAT OUTA THE WAY. NOW TO ARRANGE A LITTLE ACCIDENT.. FOR MY-SELF...
YEEHAA! HERE GOES! THAT TRUCK'LL SQUASH ME TO A PULP! IT'LL TAKE THEM DAYS JUST TO SCRAPE ME OFF THE ROAD!
THE DRIVER SWERVES INSTINCTIVELY...
CAUGHT HIM A GLANCING BLOW! HE'S SKIDDING INTO THE CRASH BARRIER—
GEE, JUDGE, I-I'M SORRY. YOU WAS COMIN' STRAIGHT AT ME LIKE A CRAZY MAN... ARE YOU OKAY?
THE CRASH BARRIER SAVED ME... DON'T-DON'T KNOW WHAT COULD HAVE GOT INTO ME, UNLESS... YES! THE- THE OLD WOMAN!
SHE USED THOSE PLANTS TO HYPNOTISE ME!
DREDD TO CONTROL—I WANT A RIOT SQUAD. TELL THEM TO MEET ME ON THE ROOF OF "TOWER HOUSE" IN TEN MINUTES!

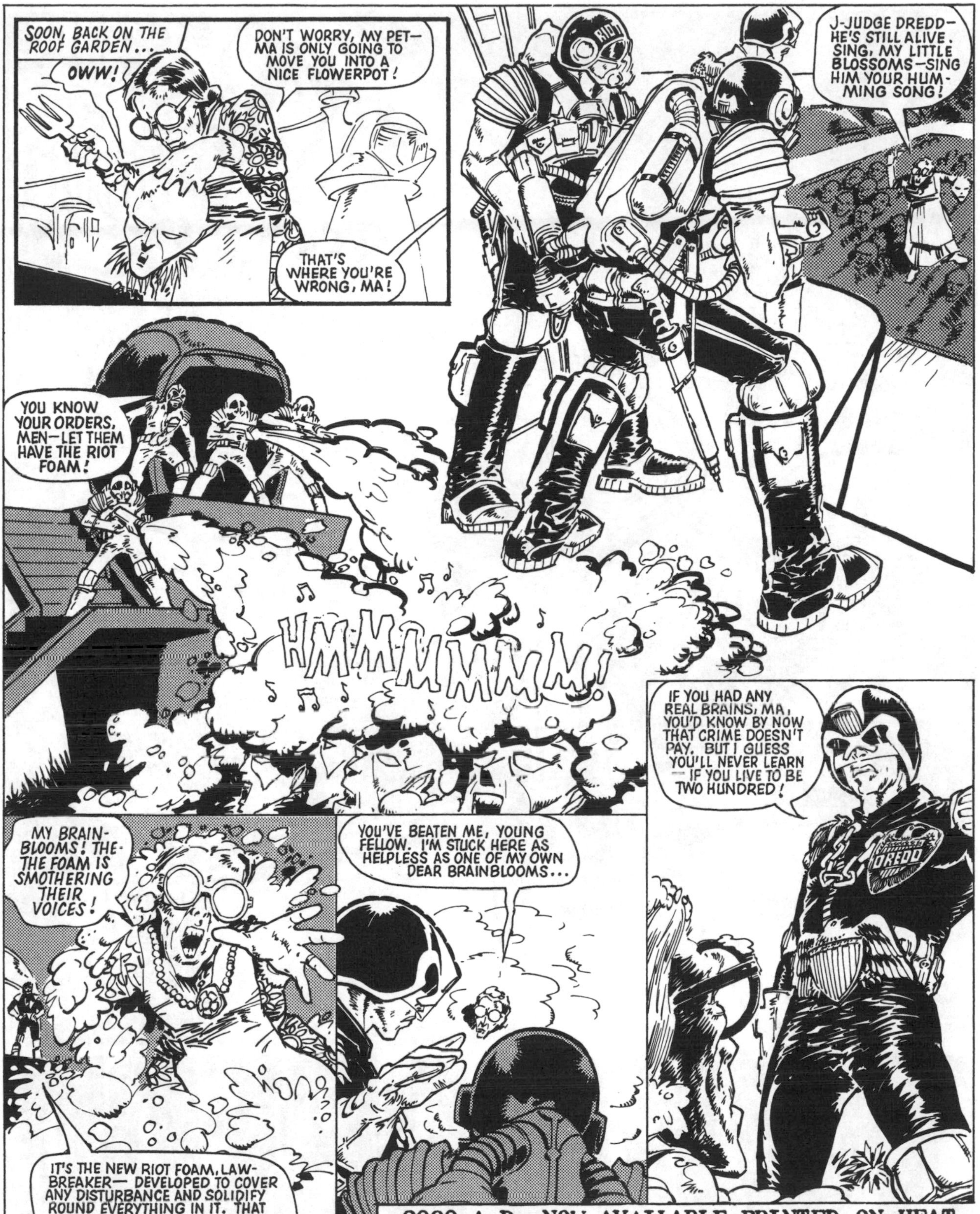
SOON, BACK ON THE ROOF GARDEN...
OWW!
DON'T WORRY, MY PET— MA IS ONLY GOING TO MOVE YOU INTO A NICE FLOWERPOT!
THAT'S WHERE YOU'RE WRONG, MA!
RIOT
J-JUDGE DREDD— HE'S STILL ALIVE. SING, MY LITTLE BLOSSOMS—SING HIM YOUR HUMMING SONG!
YOU KNOW YOUR ORDERS, MEN—LET THEM HAVE THE RIOT FOAM!
HMMMMMM!
MY BRAIN-BLOOMS! THE THE FOAM IS SMOTHERING THEIR VOICES!
IT'S THE NEW RIOT FOAM, LAW-BREAKER— DEVELOPED TO COVER ANY DISTURBANCE AND SOLIDIFY ROUND EVERYTHING IN IT. THAT WAY WE CAN DEAL WITH TROUBLE-MAKERS ONE AT A TIME!
YOU'VE BEATEN ME, YOUNG FELLOW. I'M STUCK HERE AS HELPLESS AS ONE OF MY OWN DEAR BRAINBLOOMS...
IF YOU HAD ANY REAL BRAINS, MA, YOU'D KNOW BY NOW THAT CRIME DOESN'T PAY. BUT I GUESS YOU'LL NEVER LEARN — IF YOU LIVE TO BE TWO HUNDRED!
DREDD
2000 A.D. NOW AVAILABLE PRINTED ON HEAT RESISTANT METAL FOR READERS INSIDE STARS.

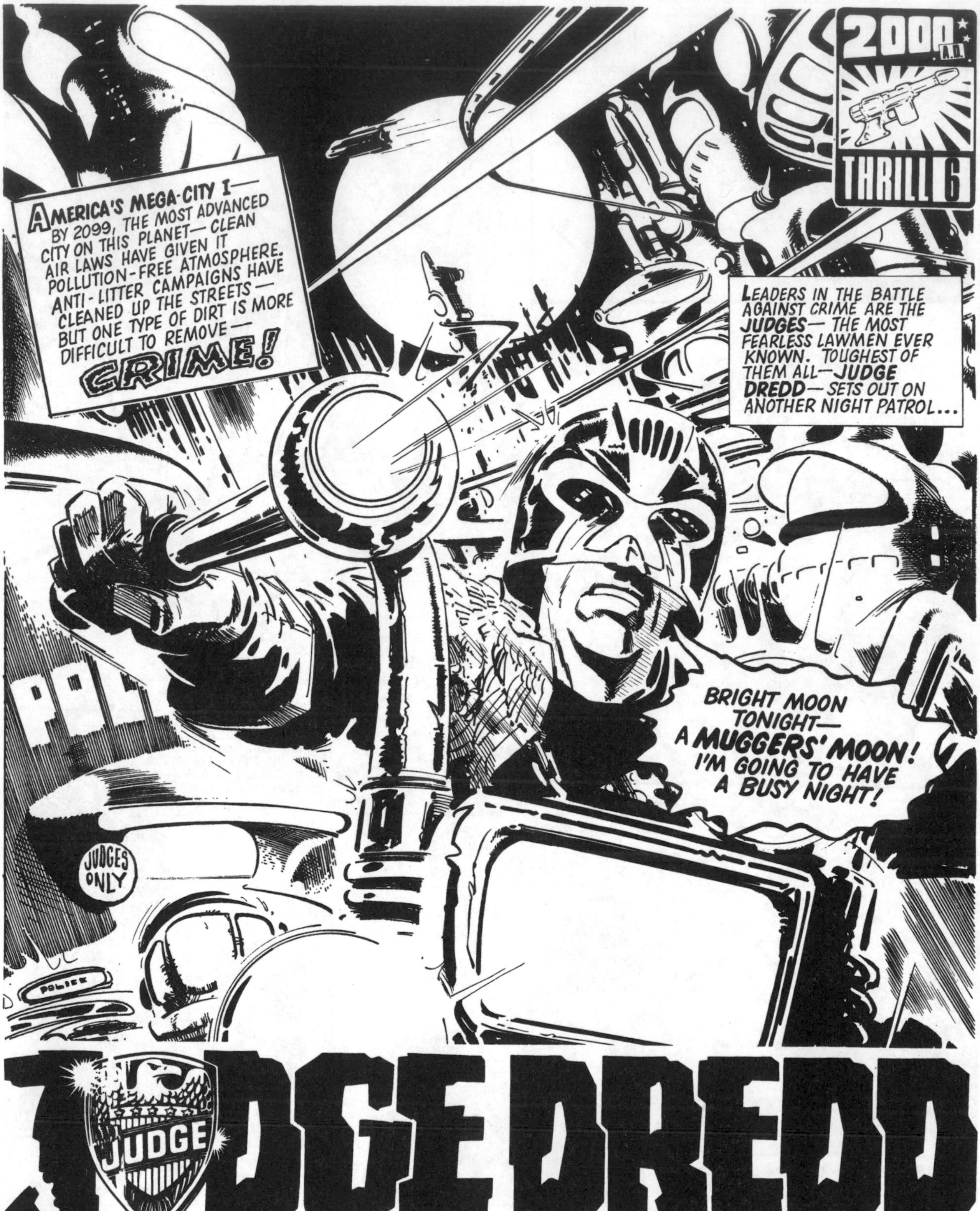

2000 A.D.
THRILL 6
AMERICA'S MEGA-CITY I— BY 2099, THE MOST ADVANCED CITY ON THIS PLANET— CLEAN AIR LAWS HAVE GIVEN IT POLLUTION-FREE ATMOSPHERE. ANTI-LITTER CAMPAIGNS HAVE CLEANED UP THE STREETS— BUT ONE TYPE OF DIRT IS MORE DIFFICULT TO REMOVE— CRIME!
LEADERS IN THE BATTLE AGAINST CRIME ARE THE JUDGES— THE MOST FEARLESS LAWMEN EVER KNOWN. TOUGHEST OF THEM ALL— JUDGE DREDD— SETS OUT ON ANOTHER NIGHT PATROL...
BRIGHT MOON TONIGHT— A MUGGERS' MOON! I'M GOING TO HAVE A BUSY NIGHT!
JUDGES ONLY
POLICE
JUDGE
JUDGE DREDD

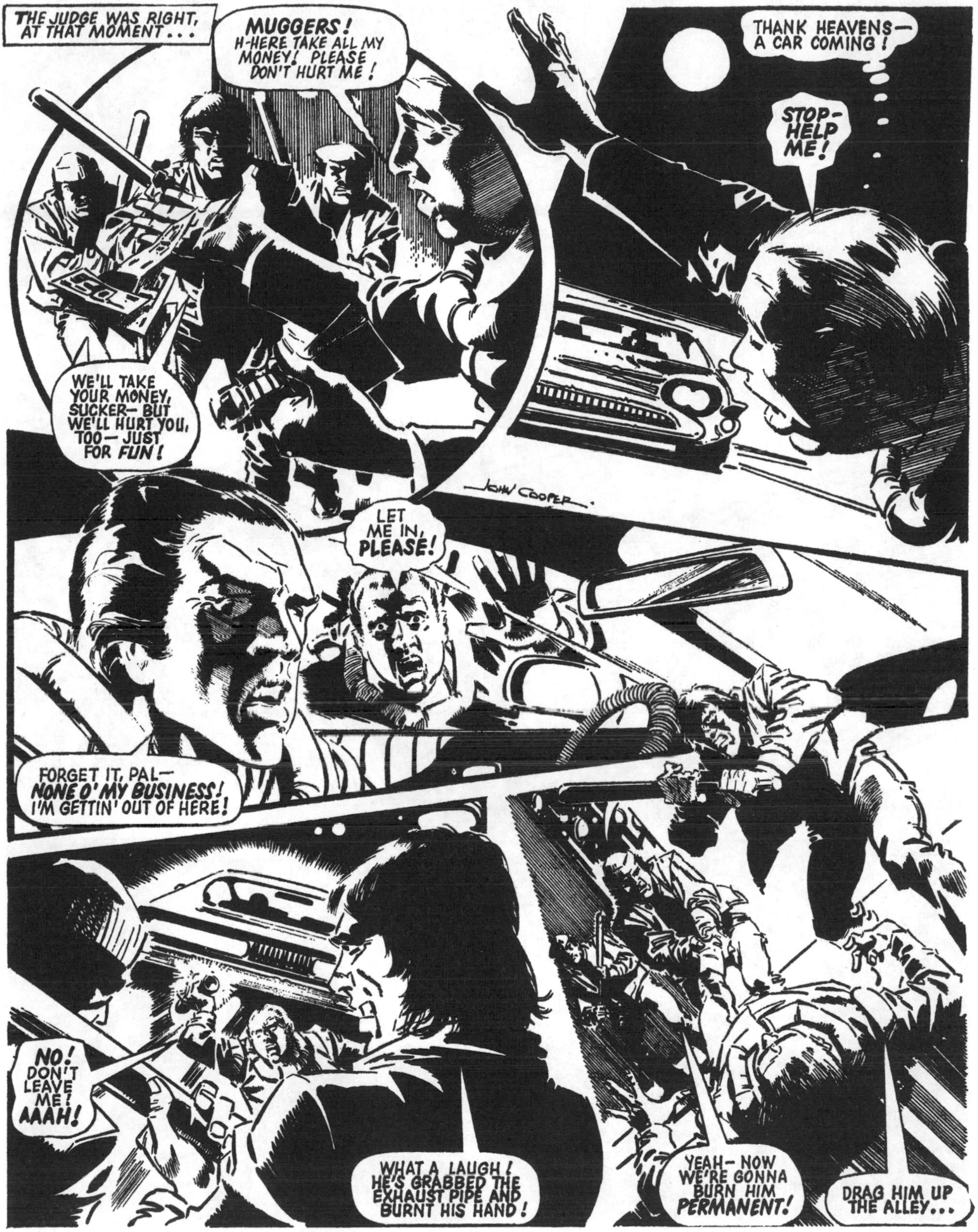
THE JUDGE WAS RIGHT, AT THAT MOMENT . . .
MUGGERS! H-HERE TAKE ALL MY MONEY! PLEASE DON'T HURT ME!
WE'LL TAKE YOUR MONEY, SUCKER— BUT WE'LL HURT YOU, TOO— JUST FOR FUN!
THANK HEAVENS— A CAR COMING!
STOP— HELP ME!
JOHN COOPER
LET ME IN, PLEASE!
FORGET IT, PAL— NONE O' MY BUSINESS! I'M GETTIN' OUT OF HERE!
NO! DON'T LEAVE ME! AAAH!
WHAT A LAUGH! HE'S GRABBED THE EXHAUST PIPE AND BURNT HIS HAND!
YEAH— NOW WE'RE GONNA BURN HIM PERMANENT!
DRAG HIM UP THE ALLEY...

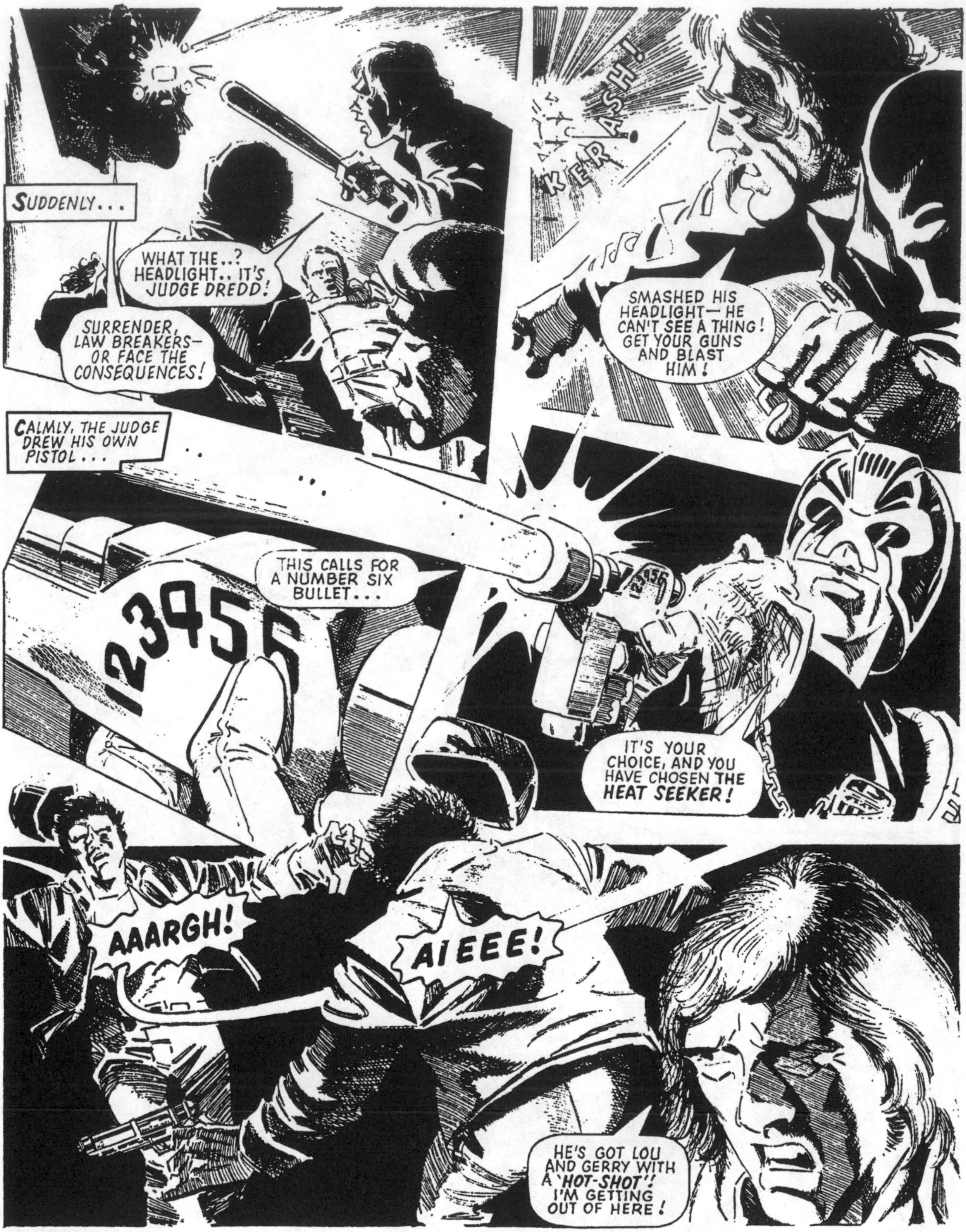

SUDDENLY...
WHAT THE..? HEADLIGHT.. IT'S JUDGE DREDD!
SURRENDER, LAW BREAKERS— OR FACE THE CONSEQUENCES!
KERASH!
SMASHED HIS HEADLIGHT— HE CAN'T SEE A THING! GET YOUR GUNS AND BLAST HIM!
CALMLY, THE JUDGE DREW HIS OWN PISTOL...
THIS CALLS FOR A NUMBER SIX BULLET...
123456
IT'S YOUR CHOICE, AND YOU HAVE CHOSEN THE HEAT SEEKER!
AAARGH!
AIEEE!
HE'S GOT LOU AND GERRY WITH A 'HOT-SHOT'! I'M GETTING OUT OF HERE!

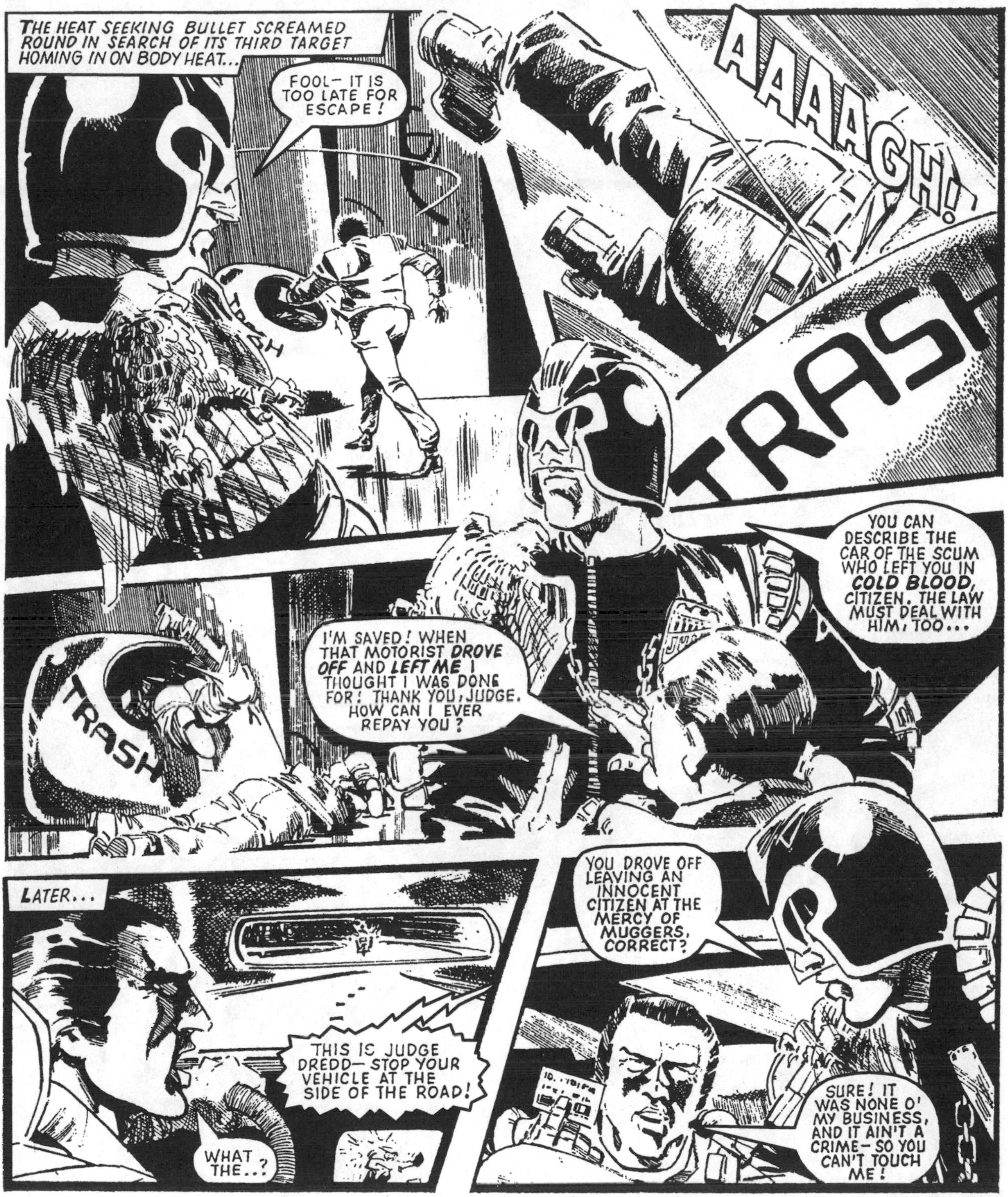

THE HEAT SEEKING BULLET SCREAMED ROUND IN SEARCH OF ITS THIRD TARGET HOMING IN ON BODY HEAT...
FOOL— IT IS TOO LATE FOR ESCAPE!
AAAAGH!
TRASH
YOU CAN DESCRIBE THE CAR OF THE SCUM WHO LEFT YOU IN COLD BLOOD, CITIZEN. THE LAW MUST DEAL WITH HIM, TOO...
I'M SAVED! WHEN THAT MOTORIST DROVE OFF AND LEFT ME I THOUGHT I WAS DONE FOR! THANK YOU, JUDGE. HOW CAN I EVER REPAY YOU?
TRASH
LATER...
THIS IS JUDGE DREDD— STOP YOUR VEHICLE AT THE SIDE OF THE ROAD!
WHAT THE..?
YOU DROVE OFF LEAVING AN INNOCENT CITIZEN AT THE MERCY OF MUGGERS, CORRECT?
SURE! IT WAS NONE O' MY BUSINESS, AND IT AIN'T A CRIME— SO YOU CAN'T TOUCH ME!

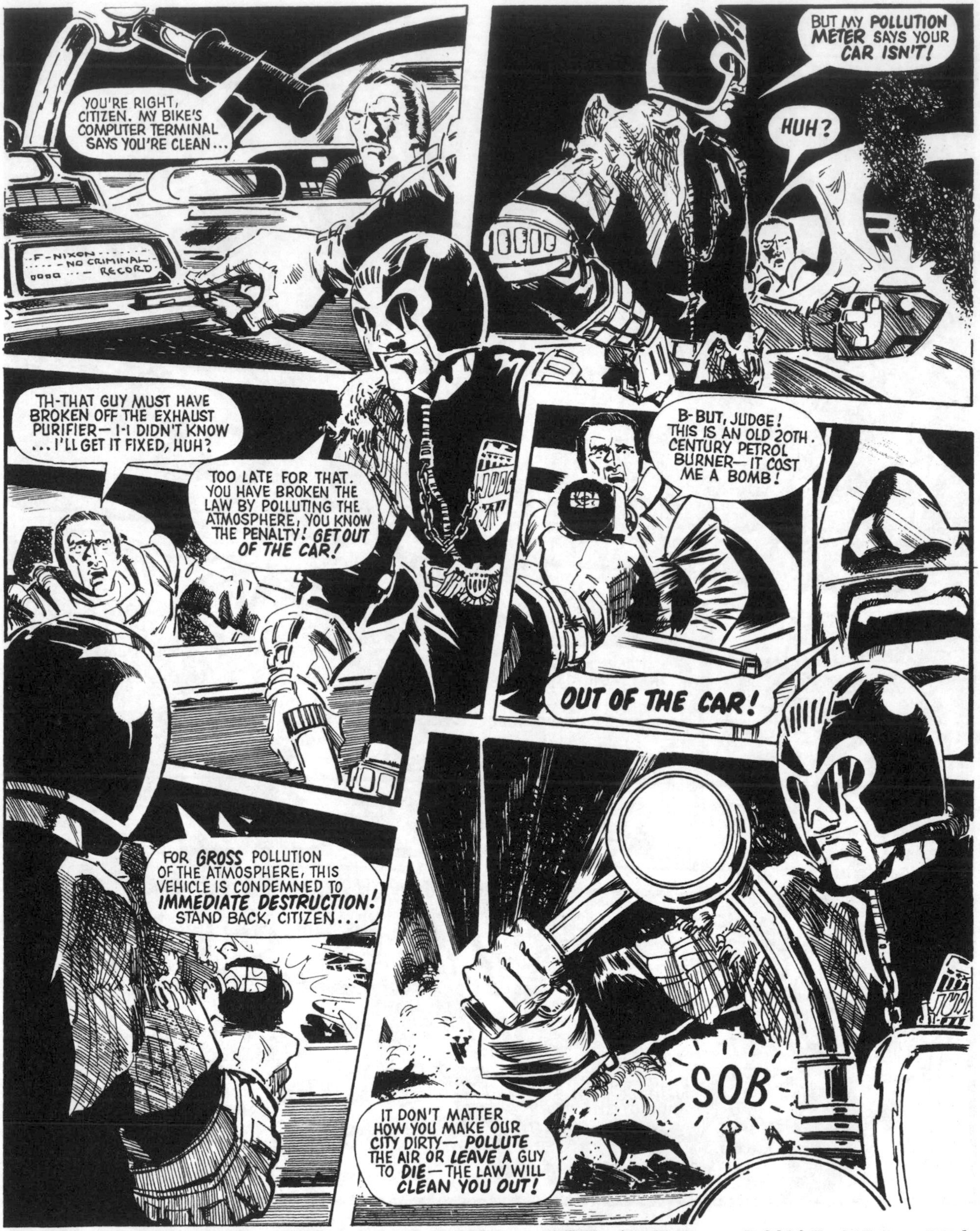
YOU'RE RIGHT, CITIZEN. MY BIKE'S COMPUTER TERMINAL SAYS YOU'RE CLEAN...
F-NIXON NO CRIMINAL RECORD
BUT MY POLLUTION METER SAYS YOUR CAR ISN'T!
HUH?
TH-THAT GUY MUST HAVE BROKEN OFF THE EXHAUST PURIFIER— I-I DIDN'T KNOW ... I'LL GET IT FIXED, HUH?
TOO LATE FOR THAT. YOU HAVE BROKEN THE LAW BY POLLUTING THE ATMOSPHERE, YOU KNOW THE PENALTY! GET OUT OF THE CAR!
B-BUT, JUDGE! THIS IS AN OLD 20TH. CENTURY PETROL BURNER— IT COST ME A BOMB!
OUT OF THE CAR!
FOR GROSS POLLUTION OF THE ATMOSPHERE, THIS VEHICLE IS CONDEMNED TO IMMEDIATE DESTRUCTION! STAND BACK, CITIZEN...
SOB
IT DON'T MATTER HOW YOU MAKE OUR CITY DIRTY— POLLUTE THE AIR OR LEAVE A GUY TO DIE— THE LAW WILL CLEAN YOU OUT!

SHAKO MAKES KING KONG LOOK LIKE A PET CHIMP - DON'T MISS IT!

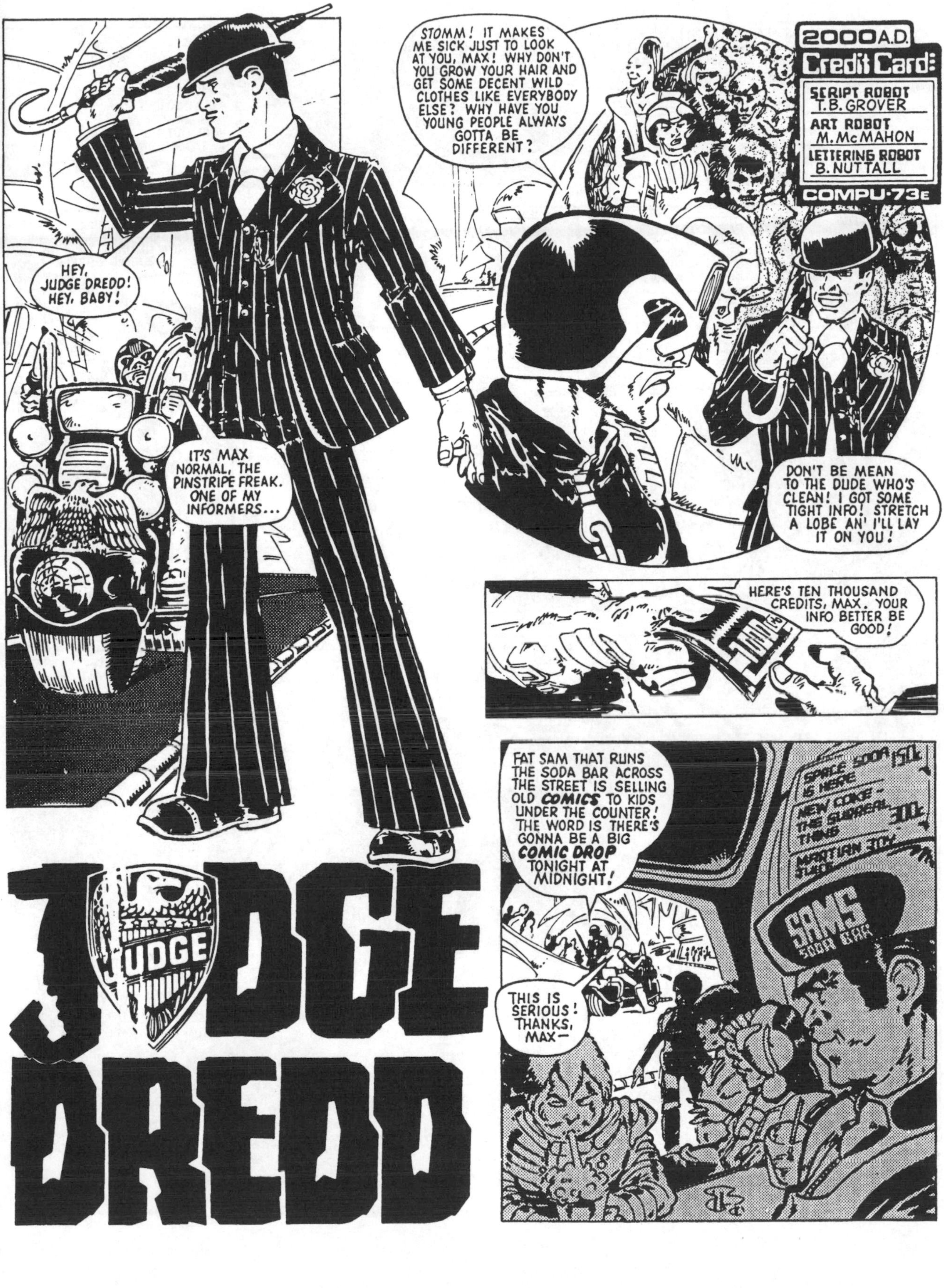
JUDGE DREDD
2000 A.D. Credit Card:
SCRIPT ROBOT T.B. GROVER
ART ROBOT M. McMAHON
LETTERING ROBOT B. NUTTALL
COMPU-73E
HEY, JUDGE DREDD! HEY, BABY!
IT'S MAX NORMAL, THE PINSTRIPE FREAK. ONE OF MY INFORMERS...
STOMM! IT MAKES ME SICK JUST TO LOOK AT YOU, MAX! WHY DON'T YOU GROW YOUR HAIR AND GET SOME DECENT WILD CLOTHES LIKE EVERYBODY ELSE? WHY HAVE YOU YOUNG PEOPLE ALWAYS GOTTA BE DIFFERENT?
DON'T BE MEAN TO THE DUDE WHO'S CLEAN! I GOT SOME TIGHT INFO! STRETCH A LOBE AN' I'LL LAY IT ON YOU!
HERE'S TEN THOUSAND CREDITS, MAX. YOUR INFO BETTER BE GOOD!
FAT SAM THAT RUNS THE SODA BAR ACROSS THE STREET IS SELLING OLD COMICS TO KIDS UNDER THE COUNTER! THE WORD IS THERE'S GONNA BE A BIG COMIC DROP TONIGHT AT MIDNIGHT!
THIS IS SERIOUS! THANKS, MAX—
SPACE SODA 150c IS HERE
NEW COKE - THE SURREAL THING 300c
SAMS SODA BAR

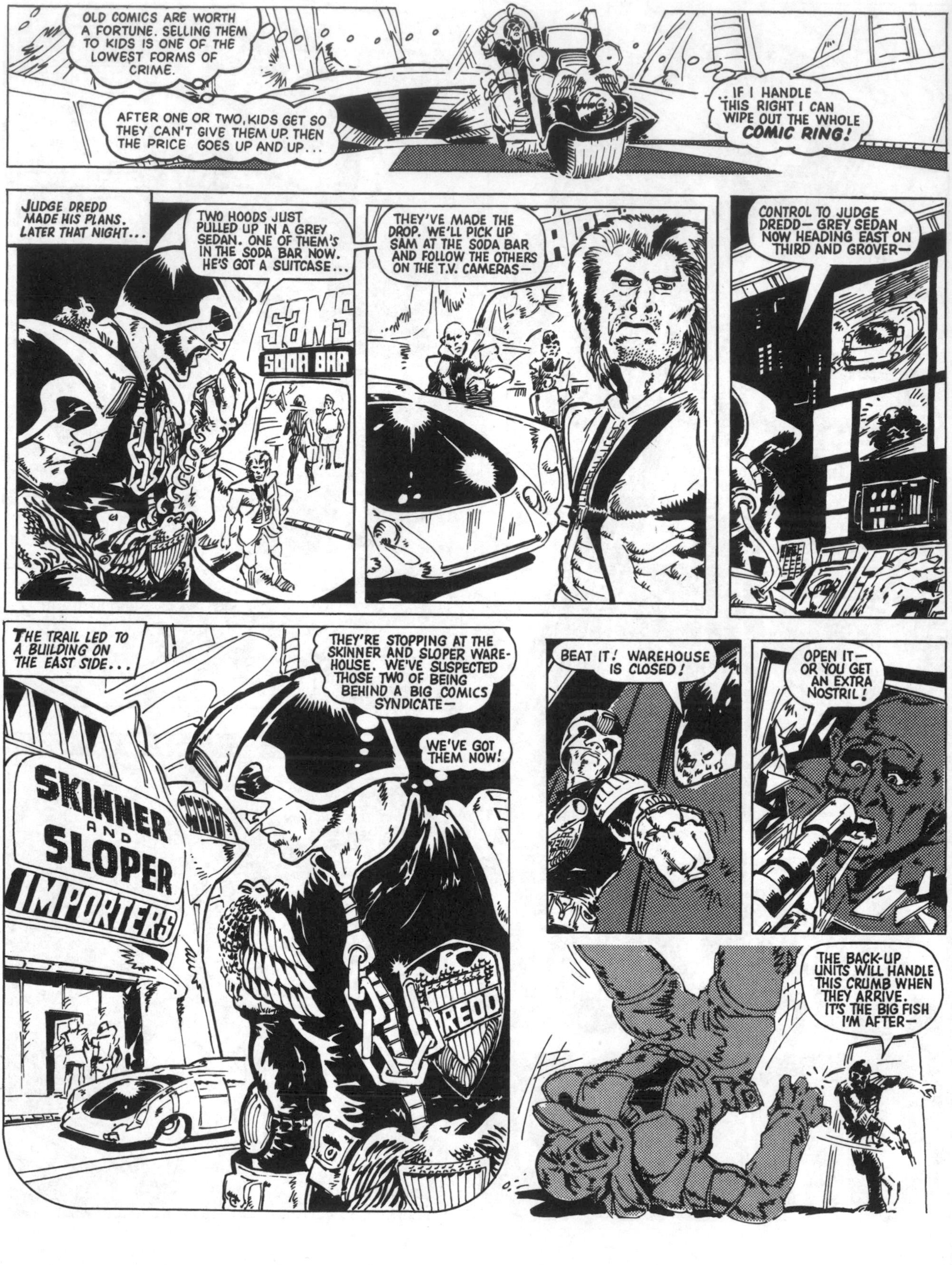

OLD COMICS ARE WORTH A FORTUNE. SELLING THEM TO KIDS IS ONE OF THE LOWEST FORMS OF CRIME.
AFTER ONE OR TWO, KIDS GET SO THEY CAN'T GIVE THEM UP. THEN THE PRICE GOES UP AND UP...
.. IF I HANDLE THIS RIGHT I CAN WIPE OUT THE WHOLE COMIC RING!
JUDGE DREDD MADE HIS PLANS. LATER THAT NIGHT...
TWO HOODS JUST PULLED UP IN A GREY SEDAN. ONE OF THEM'S IN THE SODA BAR NOW. HE'S GOT A SUITCASE...
SAMS
SODA BAR
THEY'VE MADE THE DROP. WE'LL PICK UP SAM AT THE SODA BAR AND FOLLOW THE OTHERS ON THE T.V. CAMERAS—
CONTROL TO JUDGE DREDD— GREY SEDAN NOW HEADING EAST ON THIRD AND GROVER—
THE TRAIL LED TO A BUILDING ON THE EAST SIDE...
THEY'RE STOPPING AT THE SKINNER AND SLOPER WAREHOUSE. WE'VE SUSPECTED THOSE TWO OF BEING BEHIND A BIG COMICS SYNDICATE—
WE'VE GOT THEM NOW!
SKINNER AND SLOPER IMPORTERS
DREDD
BEAT IT! WAREHOUSE IS CLOSED!
OPEN IT— OR YOU GET AN EXTRA NOSTRIL!
THE BACK-UP UNITS WILL HANDLE THIS CRUMB WHEN THEY ARRIVE. IT'S THE BIG FISH I'M AFTER—

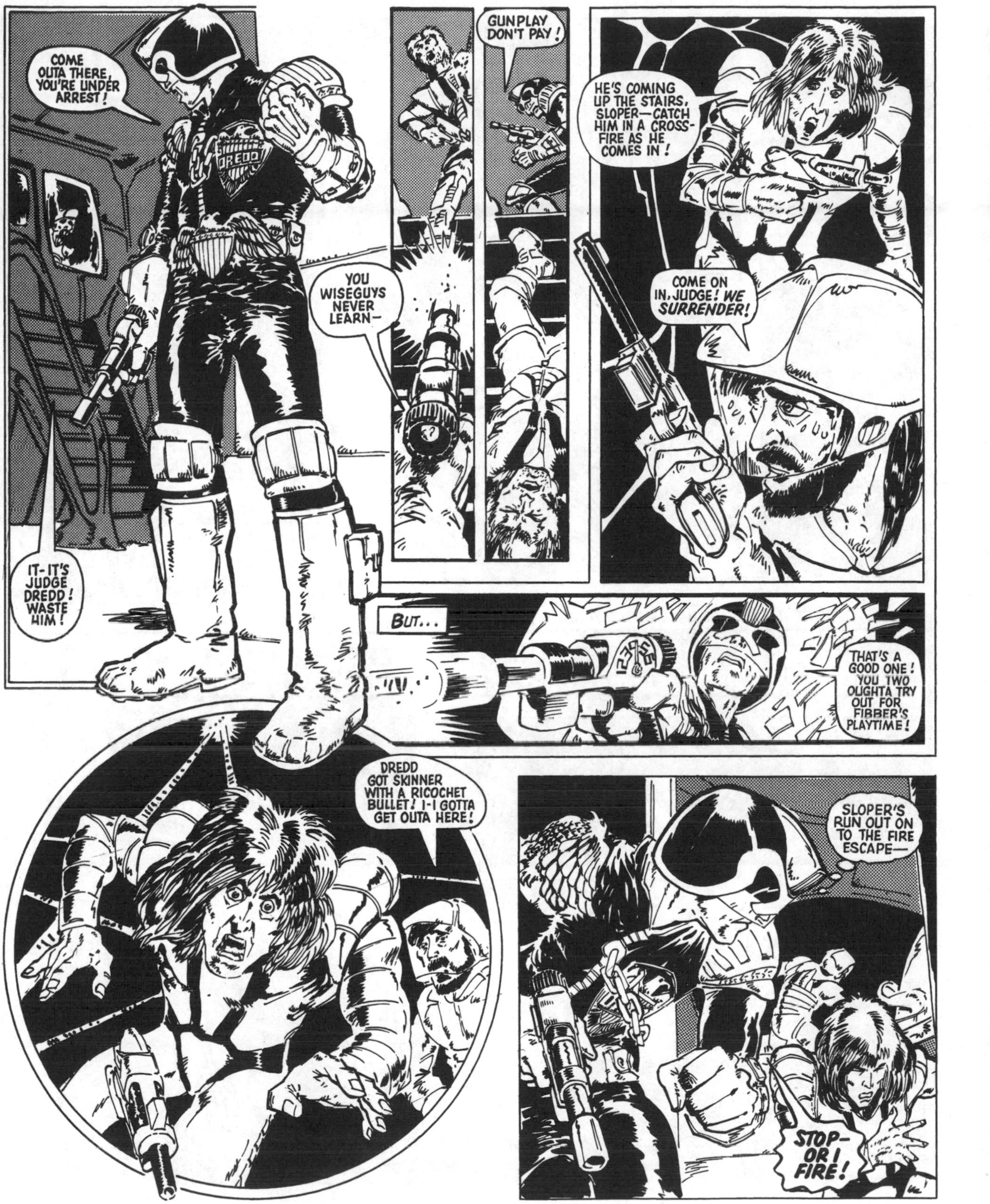
COME OUTA THERE, YOU'RE UNDER ARREST!
IT-IT'S JUDGE DREDD! WASTE HIM!
GUNPLAY DON'T PAY!
YOU WISEGUYS NEVER LEARN—
HE'S COMING UP THE STAIRS, SLOPER—CATCH HIM IN A CROSS-FIRE AS HE COMES IN!
COME ON IN, JUDGE! WE SURRENDER!
BUT...
THAT'S A GOOD ONE! YOU TWO OUGHTA TRY OUT FOR FIBBER'S PLAYTIME!
DREDD GOT SKINNER WITH A RICOCHET BULLET! I-I GOTTA GET OUTA HERE!
SLOPER'S RUN OUT ON TO THE FIRE ESCAPE—
STOP—OR I FIRE!

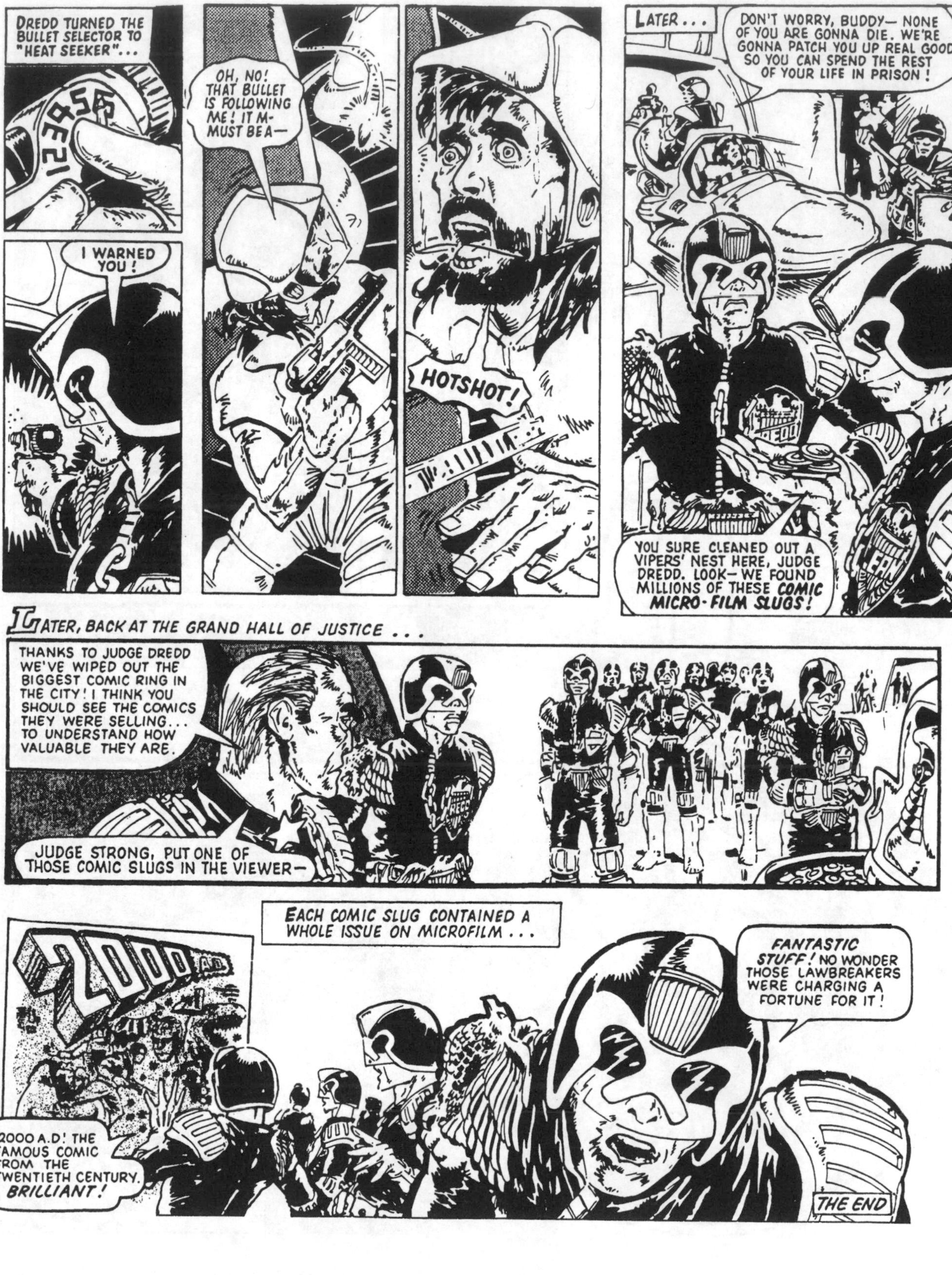
DREDD TURNED THE BULLET SELECTOR TO "HEAT SEEKER"...
I WARNED YOU!
OH, NO! THAT BULLET IS FOLLOWING ME! IT M-MUST BE A—
HOTSHOT!
LATER...
DON'T WORRY, BUDDY— NONE OF YOU ARE GONNA DIE. WE'RE GONNA PATCH YOU UP REAL GOOD SO YOU CAN SPEND THE REST OF YOUR LIFE IN PRISON!
YOU SURE CLEANED OUT A VIPERS' NEST HERE, JUDGE DREDD. LOOK— WE FOUND MILLIONS OF THESE COMIC MICRO-FILM SLUGS!
LATER, BACK AT THE GRAND HALL OF JUSTICE ...
THANKS TO JUDGE DREDD WE'VE WIPED OUT THE BIGGEST COMIC RING IN THE CITY! I THINK YOU SHOULD SEE THE COMICS THEY WERE SELLING... TO UNDERSTAND HOW VALUABLE THEY ARE.
JUDGE STRONG, PUT ONE OF THOSE COMIC SLUGS IN THE VIEWER—
EACH COMIC SLUG CONTAINED A WHOLE ISSUE ON MICROFILM ...
2000 A.D.
2000 A.D! THE FAMOUS COMIC FROM THE TWENTIETH CENTURY. BRILLIANT!
FANTASTIC STUFF! NO WONDER THOSE LAWBREAKERS WERE CHARGING A FORTUNE FOR IT!
THE END

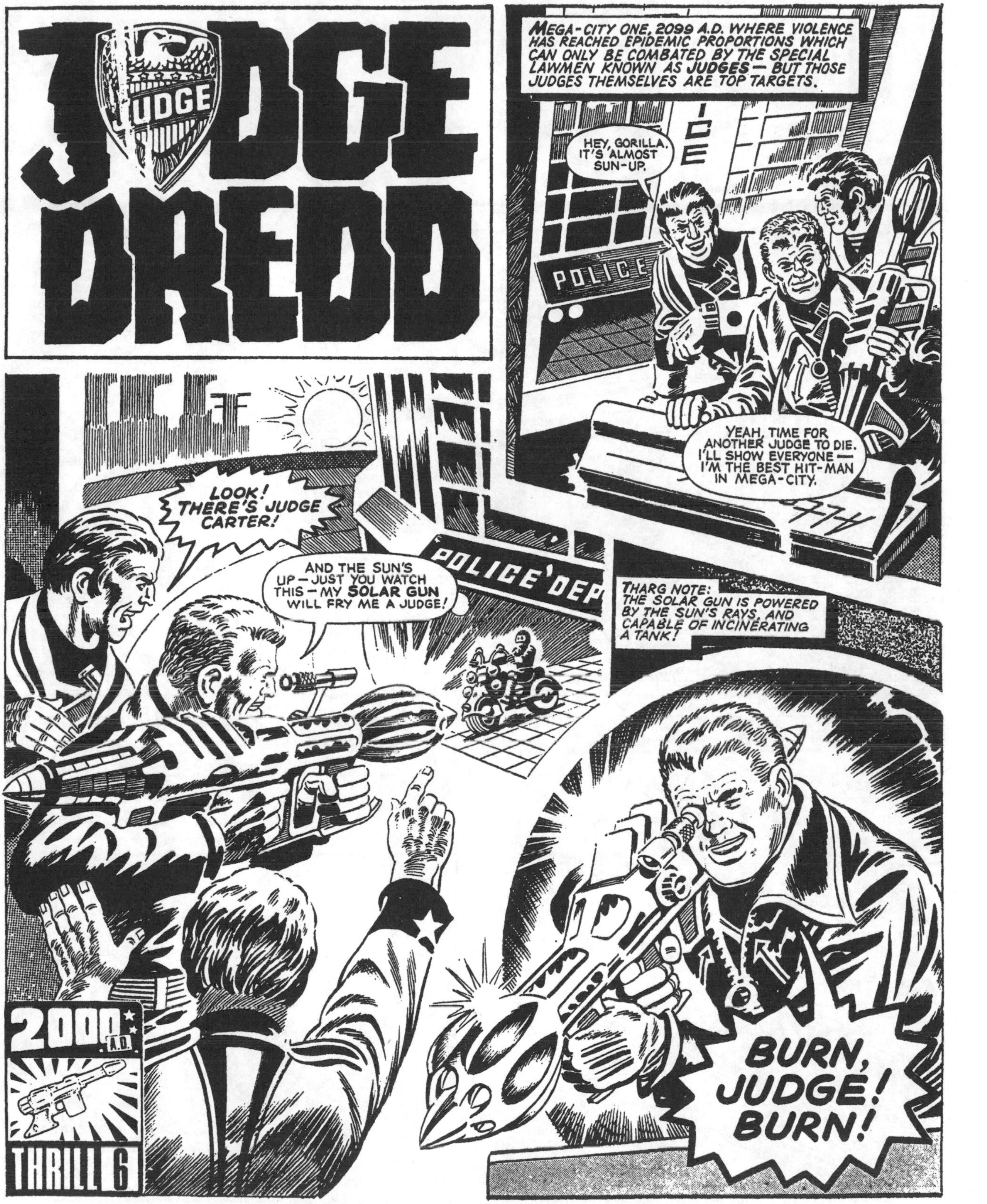
JUDGE DREDD
JUDGE
MEGA-CITY ONE, 2099 A.D. WHERE VIOLENCE HAS REACHED EPIDEMIC PROPORTIONS WHICH CAN ONLY BE COMBATED BY THE SPECIAL LAWMEN KNOWN AS JUDGES — BUT THOSE JUDGES THEMSELVES ARE TOP TARGETS.
HEY, GORILLA, IT'S ALMOST SUN-UP.
POLICE
YEAH, TIME FOR ANOTHER JUDGE TO DIE. I'LL SHOW EVERYONE — I'M THE BEST HIT-MAN IN MEGA-CITY.
LOOK! THERE'S JUDGE CARTER!
AND THE SUN'S UP — JUST YOU WATCH THIS — MY SOLAR GUN WILL FRY ME A JUDGE!
POLICE DEP
THARG NOTE: THE SOLAR GUN IS POWERED BY THE SUN'S RAYS, AND CAPABLE OF INCINERATING A TANK!
BURN, JUDGE! BURN!
2000 A.D.
THRILL 6

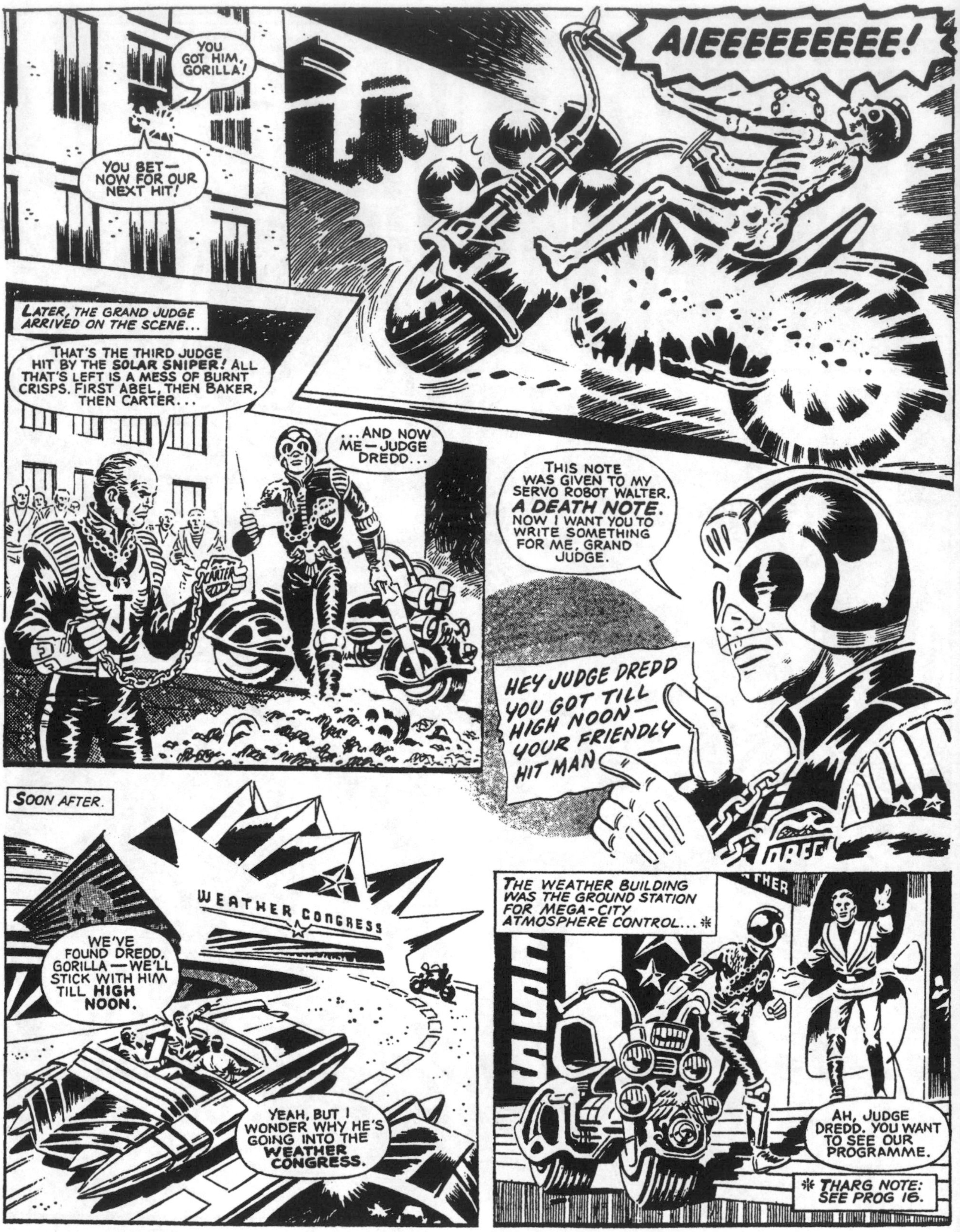
YOU GOT HIM, GORILLA!
YOU BET— NOW FOR OUR NEXT HIT!
AIEEEEEEEEEE!
LATER, THE GRAND JUDGE ARRIVED ON THE SCENE...
THAT'S THE THIRD JUDGE HIT BY THE SOLAR SNIPER! ALL THAT'S LEFT IS A MESS OF BURNT CRISPS. FIRST ABEL, THEN BAKER, THEN CARTER...
...AND NOW ME—JUDGE DREDD...
THIS NOTE WAS GIVEN TO MY SERVO ROBOT WALTER. A DEATH NOTE. NOW I WANT YOU TO WRITE SOMETHING FOR ME, GRAND JUDGE.
HEY JUDGE DREDD YOU GOT TILL HIGH NOON— YOUR FRIENDLY HIT MAN
SOON AFTER.
WEATHER CONGRESS
WE'VE FOUND DREDD, GORILLA—WE'LL STICK WITH HIM TILL HIGH NOON.
YEAH, BUT I WONDER WHY HE'S GOING INTO THE WEATHER CONGRESS.
THE WEATHER BUILDING WAS THE GROUND STATION FOR MEGA-CITY ATMOSPHERE CONTROL...*
AH, JUDGE DREDD. YOU WANT TO SEE OUR PROGRAMME.
* THARG NOTE: SEE PROG 16.

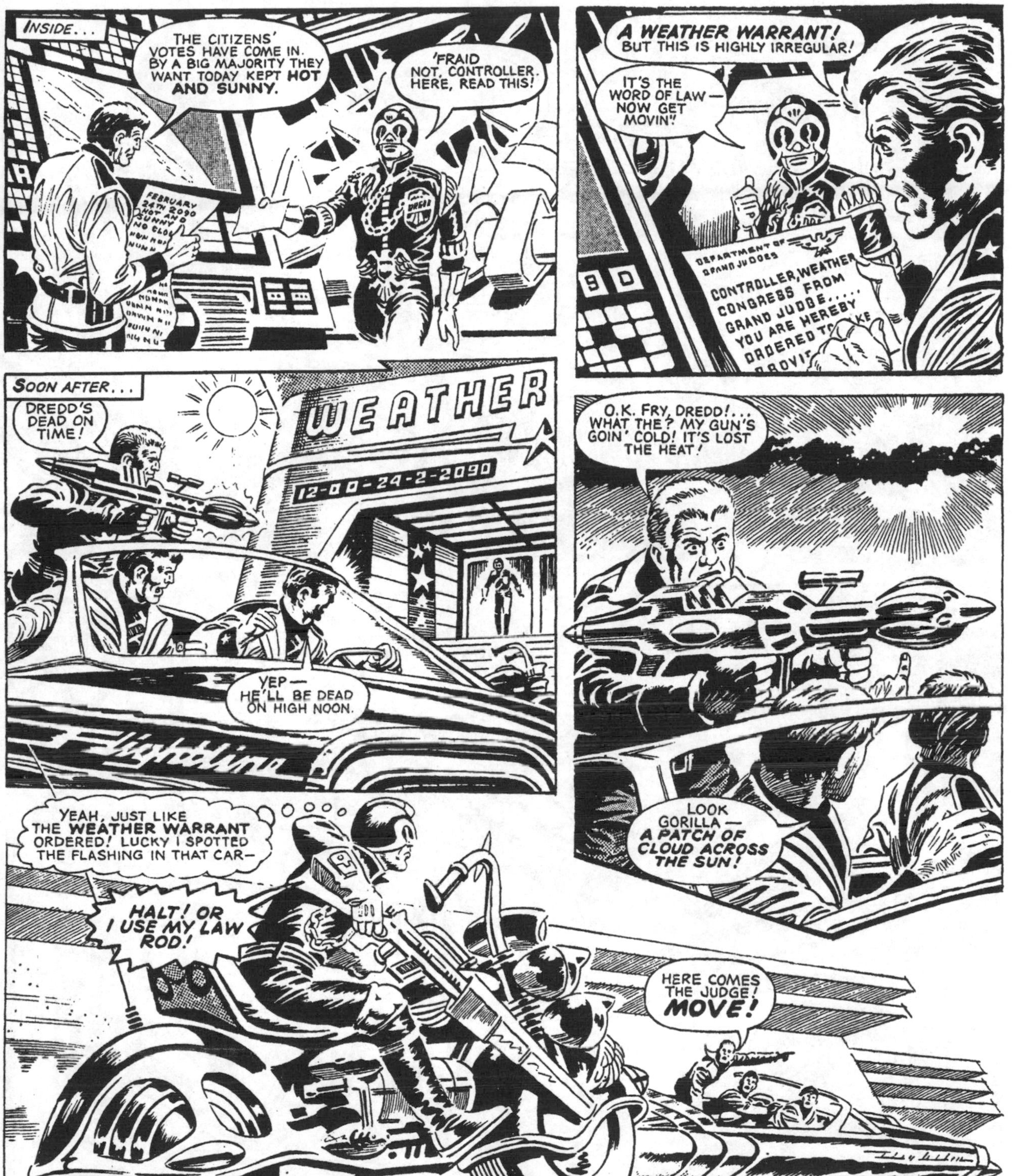
INSIDE...
THE CITIZENS' VOTES HAVE COME IN. BY A BIG MAJORITY THEY WANT TODAY KEPT HOT AND SUNNY.
'FRAID NOT, CONTROLLER. HERE, READ THIS!
FEBRUARY 24TH 2090
A WEATHER WARRANT! BUT THIS IS HIGHLY IRREGULAR!
IT'S THE WORD OF LAW — NOW GET MOVIN'!
DEPARTMENT OF GRAND JUDGES
CONTROLLER, WEATHER CONGRESS FROM GRAND JUDGE..... YOU ARE HEREBY ORDERED
SOON AFTER...
DREDD'S DEAD ON TIME!
WEATHER
12-00-24-2-2090
YEP — HE'LL BE DEAD ON HIGH NOON.
O.K. FRY, DREDD!... WHAT THE? MY GUN'S GOIN' COLD! IT'S LOST THE HEAT!
LOOK GORILLA — A PATCH OF CLOUD ACROSS THE SUN!
YEAH, JUST LIKE THE WEATHER WARRANT ORDERED! LUCKY I SPOTTED THE FLASHING IN THAT CAR—
HALT! OR I USE MY LAW ROD!
HERE COMES THE JUDGE! MOVE!

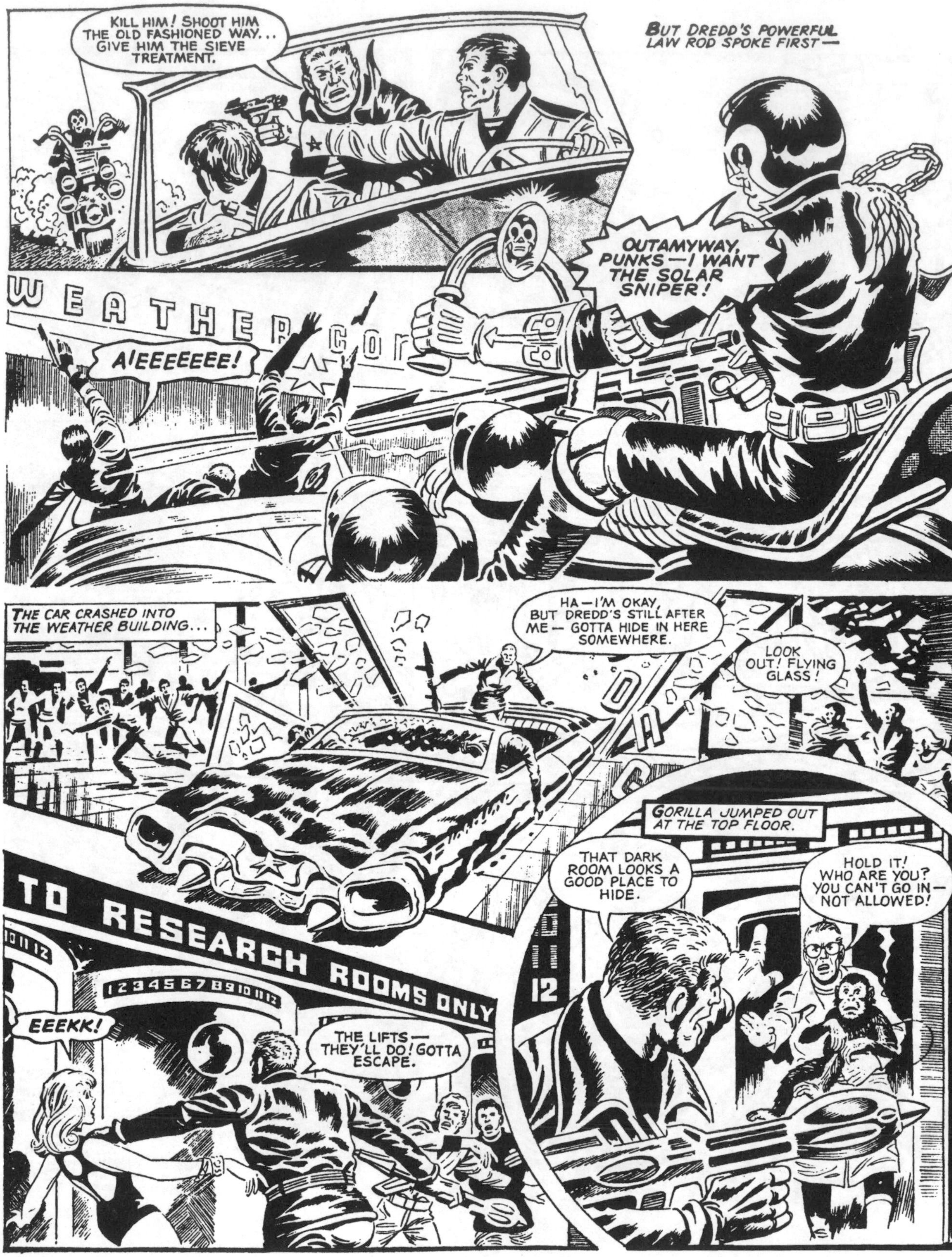

KILL HIM! SHOOT HIM THE OLD FASHIONED WAY... GIVE HIM THE SIEVE TREATMENT.
BUT DREDD'S POWERFUL LAW ROD SPOKE FIRST—
OUTAMYWAY, PUNKS—I WANT THE SOLAR SNIPER!
WEATHER COR
AIEEEEEEE!
THE CAR CRASHED INTO THE WEATHER BUILDING...
HA—I'M OKAY, BUT DREDD'S STILL AFTER ME—GOTTA HIDE IN HERE SOMEWHERE.
LOOK OUT! FLYING GLASS!
TO RESEARCH ROOMS ONLY
1 2 3 4 5 6 7 8 9 10 11 12
EEEKK!
THE LIFTS—THEY'LL DO! GOTTA ESCAPE.
GORILLA JUMPED OUT AT THE TOP FLOOR.
THAT DARK ROOM LOOKS A GOOD PLACE TO HIDE.
HOLD IT! WHO ARE YOU? YOU CAN'T GO IN—NOT ALLOWED!
12

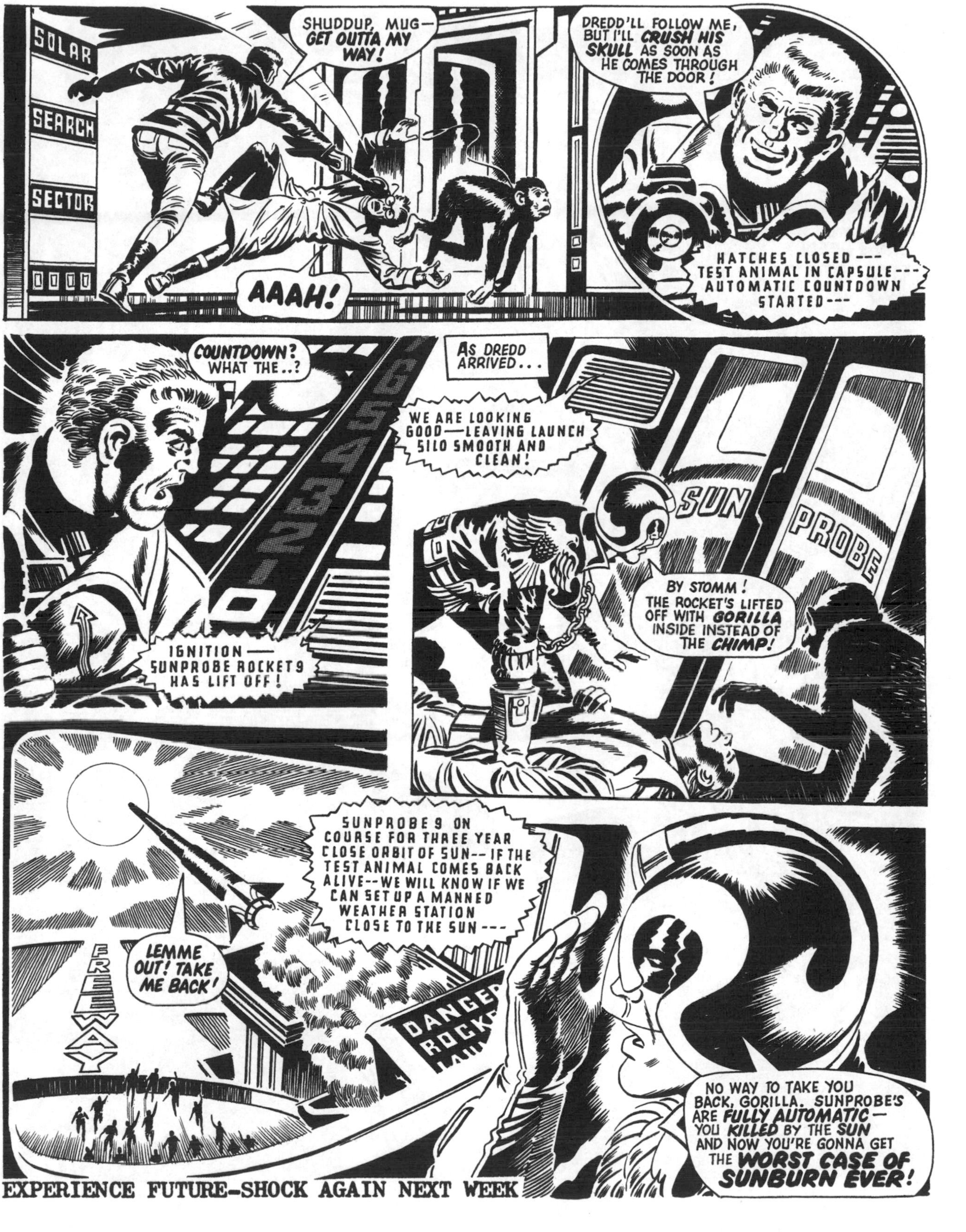
SOLAR
SEARCH
SECTOR
SHUDDUP, MUG— GET OUTTA MY WAY!
AAAH!
DREDD'LL FOLLOW ME, BUT I'LL CRUSH HIS SKULL AS SOON AS HE COMES THROUGH THE DOOR!
HATCHES CLOSED --- TEST ANIMAL IN CAPSULE --- AUTOMATIC COUNTDOWN STARTED ---
COUNTDOWN? WHAT THE..?
6
5
4
3
2
1
0
IGNITION — SUNPROBE ROCKET 9 HAS LIFT OFF!
AS DREDD ARRIVED...
WE ARE LOOKING GOOD — LEAVING LAUNCH SILO SMOOTH AND CLEAN!
SUN
PROBE
BY STOMM! THE ROCKET'S LIFTED OFF WITH GORILLA INSIDE INSTEAD OF THE CHIMP!
SUNPROBE 9 ON COURSE FOR THREE YEAR CLOSE ORBIT OF SUN-- IF THE TEST ANIMAL COMES BACK ALIVE--WE WILL KNOW IF WE CAN SET UP A MANNED WEATHER STATION CLOSE TO THE SUN ---
LEMME OUT! TAKE ME BACK!
FREEWAY
NO WAY TO TAKE YOU BACK, GORILLA. SUNPROBE'S ARE FULLY AUTOMATIC — YOU KILLED BY THE SUN AND NOW YOU'RE GONNA GET THE WORST CASE OF SUNBURN EVER!

EXPERIENCE FUTURE-SHOCK AGAIN NEXT WEEK

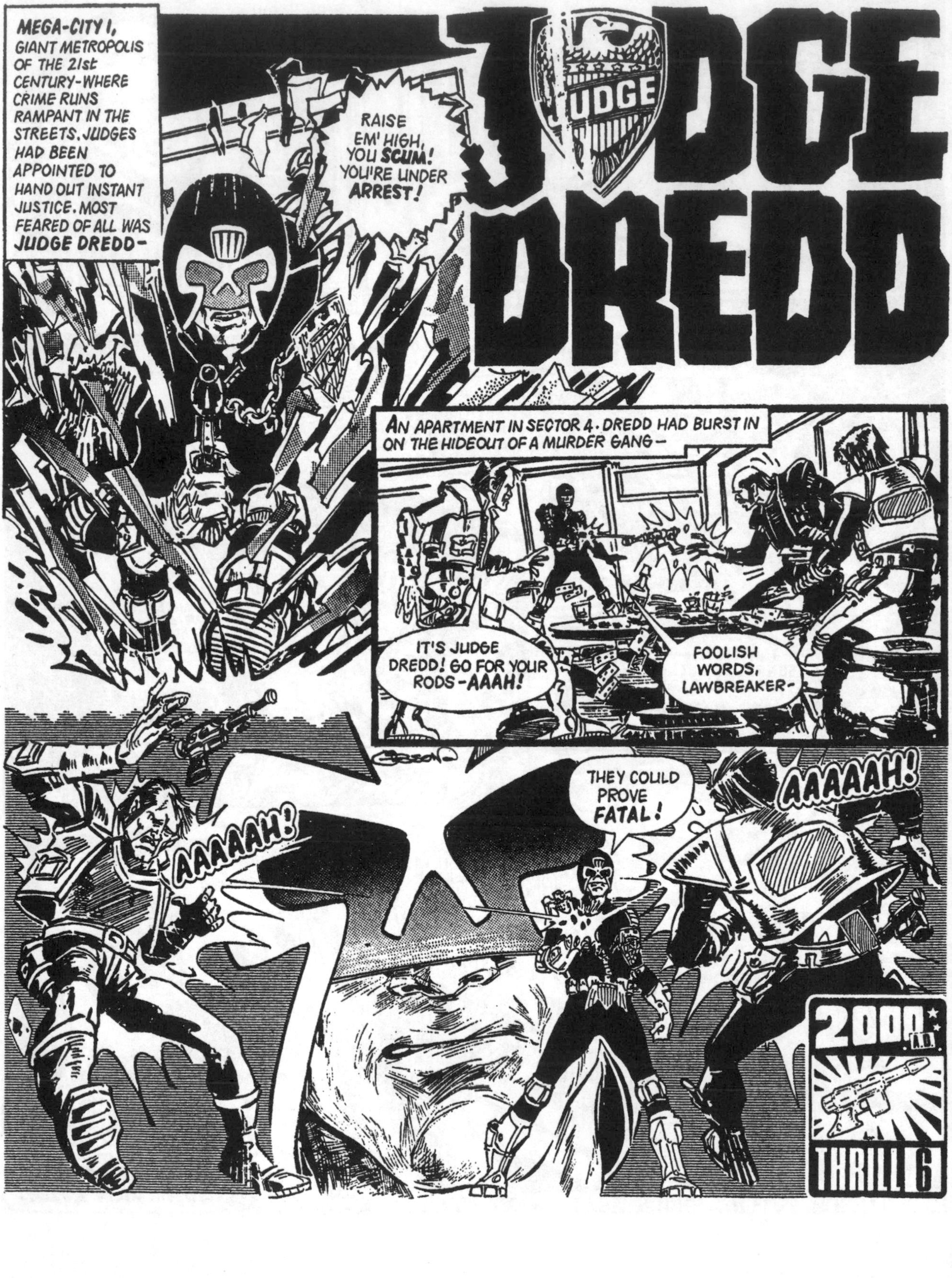
JUDGE DREDD
MEGA-CITY I, GIANT METROPOLIS OF THE 21st CENTURY-WHERE CRIME RUNS RAMPANT IN THE STREETS. JUDGES HAD BEEN APPOINTED TO HAND OUT INSTANT JUSTICE. MOST FEARED OF ALL WAS JUDGE DREDD-
RAISE EM' HIGH, YOU SCUM! YOU'RE UNDER ARREST!
AN APARTMENT IN SECTOR 4. DREDD HAD BURST IN ON THE HIDEOUT OF A MURDER GANG-
IT'S JUDGE DREDD! GO FOR YOUR RODS-AAAH!
FOOLISH WORDS, LAWBREAKER-
AAAAAH!
THEY COULD PROVE FATAL!
AAAAAH!
2000 A.D.
THRILL 6

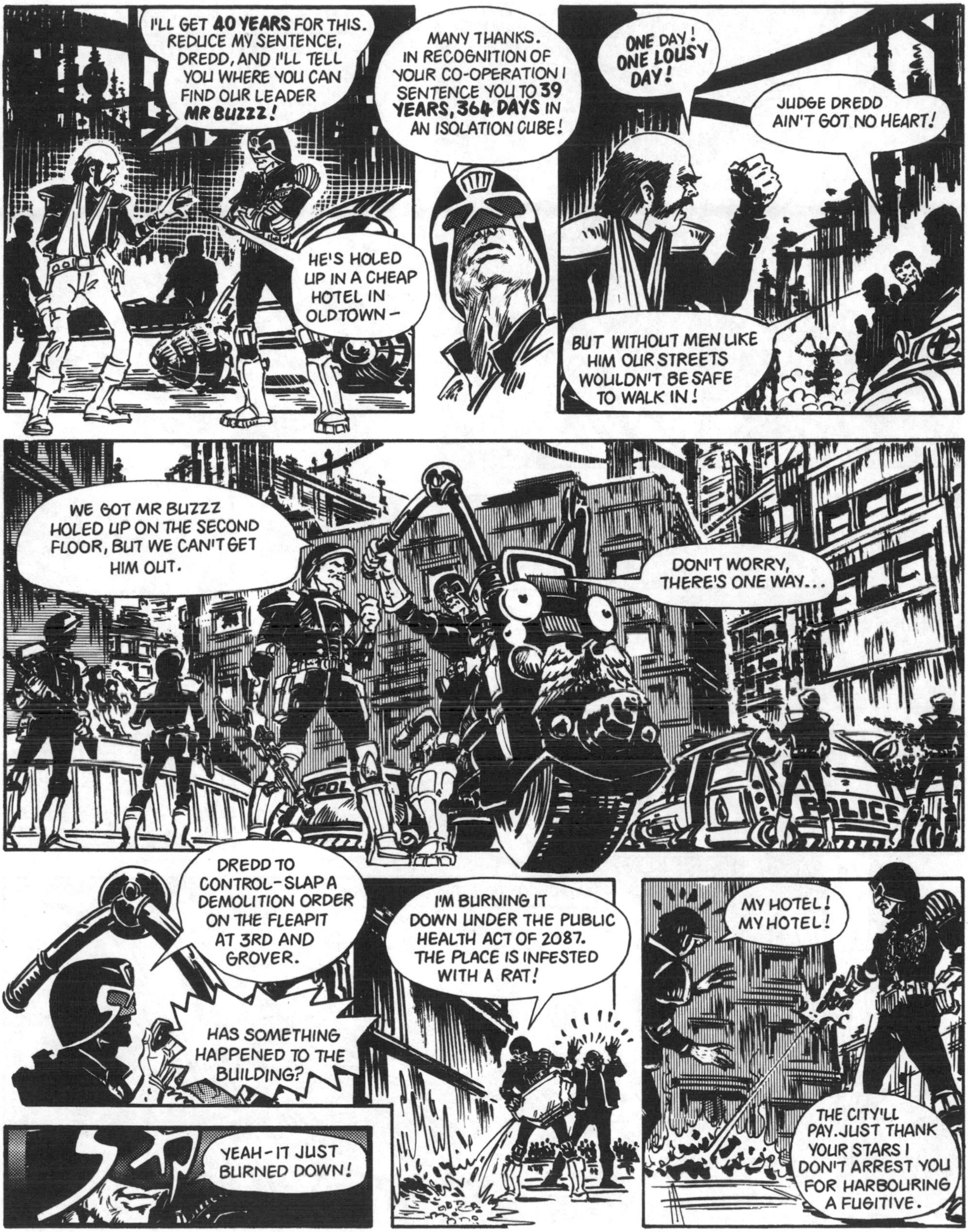
I'LL GET 40 YEARS FOR THIS. REDUCE MY SENTENCE, DREDD, AND I'LL TELL YOU WHERE YOU CAN FIND OUR LEADER MR BUZZZ!
HE'S HOLED UP IN A CHEAP HOTEL IN OLDTOWN –
MANY THANKS. IN RECOGNITION OF YOUR CO-OPERATION I SENTENCE YOU TO 39 YEARS, 364 DAYS IN AN ISOLATION CUBE!
ONE DAY! ONE LOUSY DAY!
JUDGE DREDD AIN'T GOT NO HEART!
BUT WITHOUT MEN LIKE HIM OUR STREETS WOULDN'T BE SAFE TO WALK IN!
WE GOT MR BUZZZ HOLED UP ON THE SECOND FLOOR, BUT WE CAN'T GET HIM OUT.
DON'T WORRY, THERE'S ONE WAY...
POLICE
DREDD TO CONTROL– SLAP A DEMOLITION ORDER ON THE FLEAPIT AT 3RD AND GROVER.
HAS SOMETHING HAPPENED TO THE BUILDING?
YEAH– IT JUST BURNED DOWN!
I'M BURNING IT DOWN UNDER THE PUBLIC HEALTH ACT OF 2087. THE PLACE IS INFESTED WITH A RAT!
MY HOTEL! MY HOTEL!
THE CITY'LL PAY. JUST THANK YOUR STARS I DON'T ARREST YOU FOR HARBOURING A FUGITIVE.

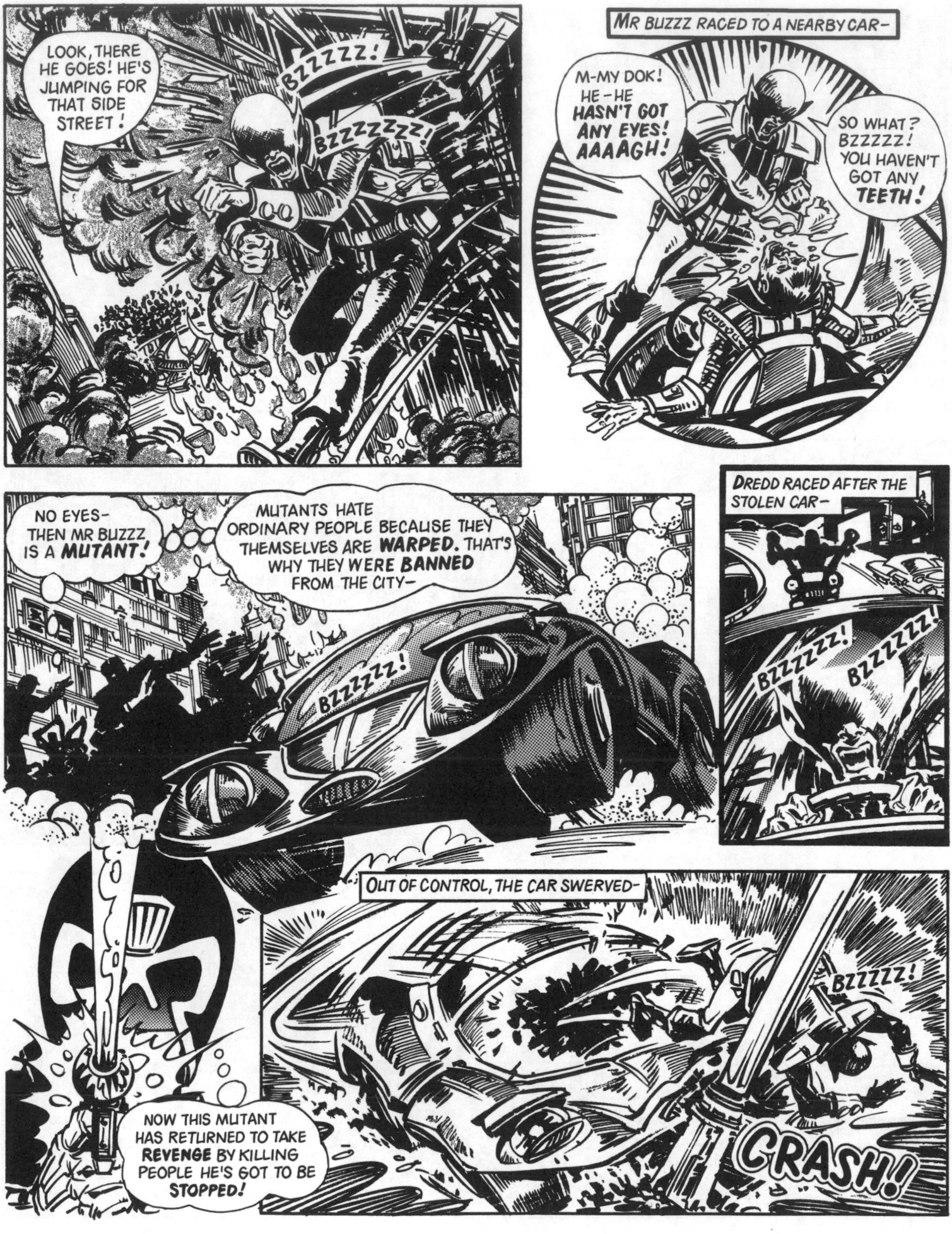

LOOK, THERE HE GOES! HE'S JUMPING FOR THAT SIDE STREET!
BZZZZZZ!
BZZZZZZZZ!
MR BUZZZ RACED TO A NEARBY CAR-
M-MY DOK! HE-HE HASN'T GOT ANY EYES! AAAAGH!
SO WHAT? BZZZZZ! YOU HAVEN'T GOT ANY TEETH!
NO EYES- THEN MR BUZZZ IS A MUTANT!
MUTANTS HATE ORDINARY PEOPLE BECAUSE THEY THEMSELVES ARE WARPED. THAT'S WHY THEY WERE BANNED FROM THE CITY-
BZZZZZZ!
DREDD RACED AFTER THE STOLEN CAR-
BZZZZZZ!
BZZZZZZZ!
NOW THIS MUTANT HAS RETURNED TO TAKE REVENGE BY KILLING PEOPLE HE'S GOT TO BE STOPPED!
OUT OF CONTROL, THE CAR SWERVED-
BZZZZZ!
CRASH!

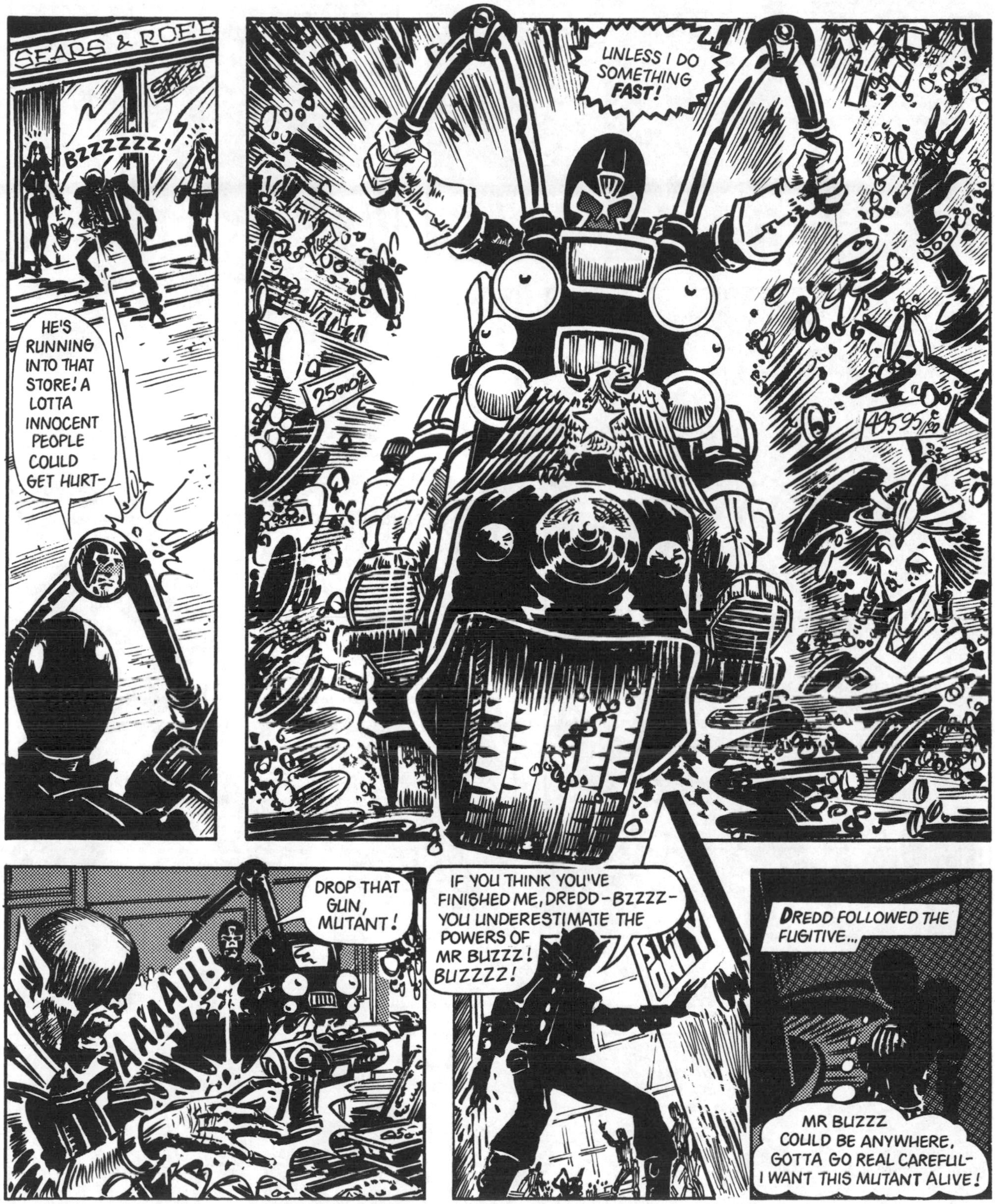
SEARS & ROEB
SALE
BZZZZZZ!
HE'S RUNNING INTO THAT STORE! A LOTTA INNOCENT PEOPLE COULD GET HURT-
UNLESS I DO SOMETHING FAST!
DROP THAT GUN, MUTANT!
AAAAH!
IF YOU THINK YOU'VE FINISHED ME, DREDD-BZZZZ-YOU UNDERESTIMATE THE POWERS OF MR BUZZZ! BUZZZZ!
DREDD FOLLOWED THE FUGITIVE...
MR BUZZZ COULD BE ANYWHERE, GOTTA GO REAL CAREFUL-I WANT THIS MUTANT ALIVE!

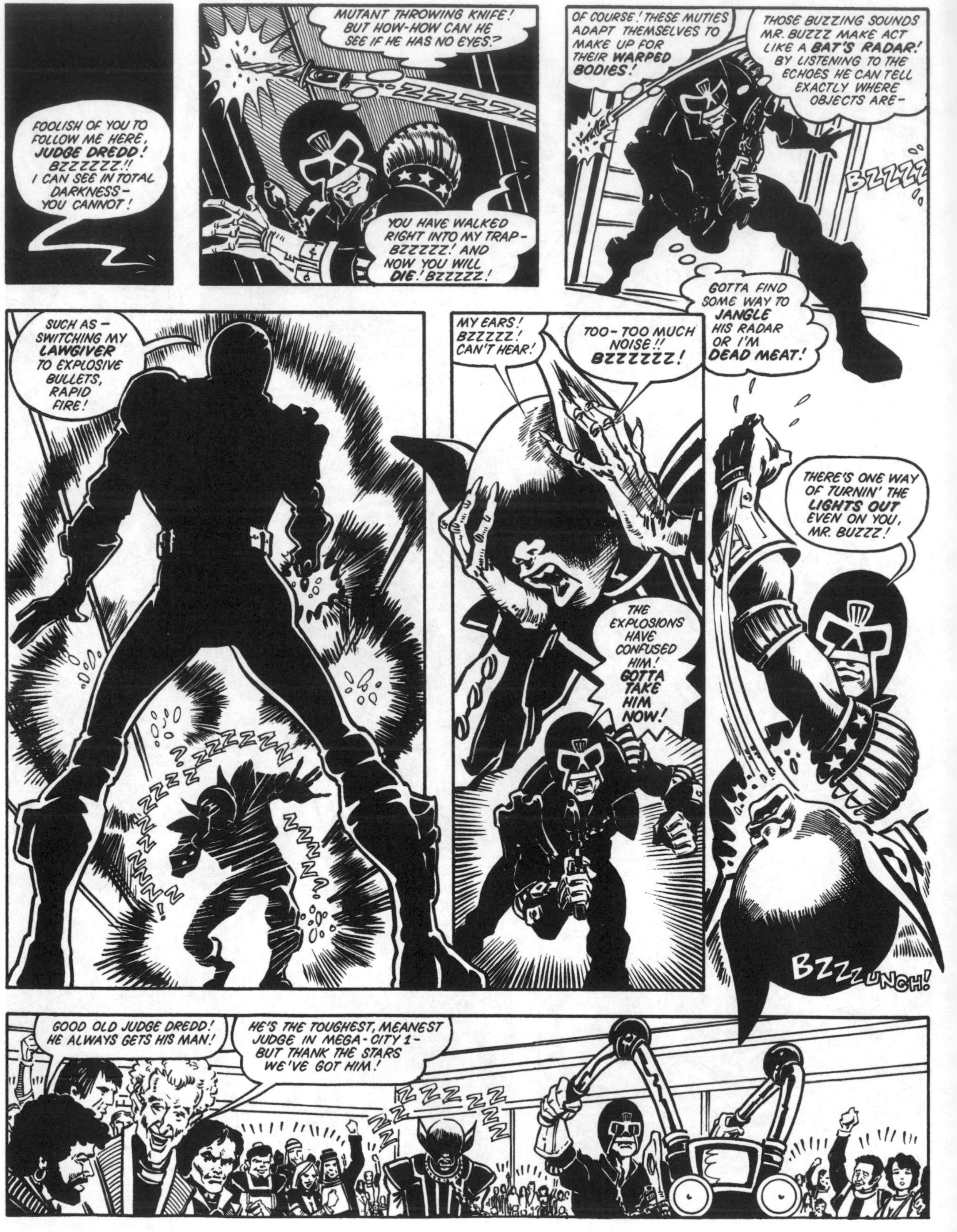

FOOLISH OF YOU TO FOLLOW ME HERE, JUDGE DREDD! BZZZZZZ!! I CAN SEE IN TOTAL DARKNESS– YOU CANNOT!
MUTANT THROWING KNIFE! BUT HOW–HOW CAN HE SEE IF HE HAS NO EYES?
ZZZZZZZ
YOU HAVE WALKED RIGHT INTO MY TRAP– BZZZZZZ! AND NOW YOU WILL DIE! BZZZZZZ!
OF COURSE! THESE MUTIES ADAPT THEMSELVES TO MAKE UP FOR THEIR WARPED BODIES!
THOSE BUZZING SOUNDS MR. BUZZZ MAKE ACT LIKE A BAT'S RADAR! BY LISTENING TO THE ECHOES HE CAN TELL EXACTLY WHERE OBJECTS ARE–
BZZZZ
GOTTA FIND SOME WAY TO JANGLE HIS RADAR OR I'M DEAD MEAT!
SUCH AS– SWITCHING MY LAWGIVER TO EXPLOSIVE BULLETS, RAPID FIRE!
MY EARS! BZZZZZ! CAN'T HEAR!
TOO–TOO MUCH NOISE!! BZZZZZZZ!
THE EXPLOSIONS HAVE CONFUSED HIM! GOTTA TAKE HIM NOW!
THERE'S ONE WAY OF TURNIN' THE LIGHTS OUT EVEN ON YOU, MR. BUZZZ!
BZZZUNCH!
GOOD OLD JUDGE DREDD! HE ALWAYS GETS HIS MAN!
HE'S THE TOUGHEST, MEANEST JUDGE IN MEGA-CITY 1– BUT THANK THE STARS WE'VE GOT HIM!

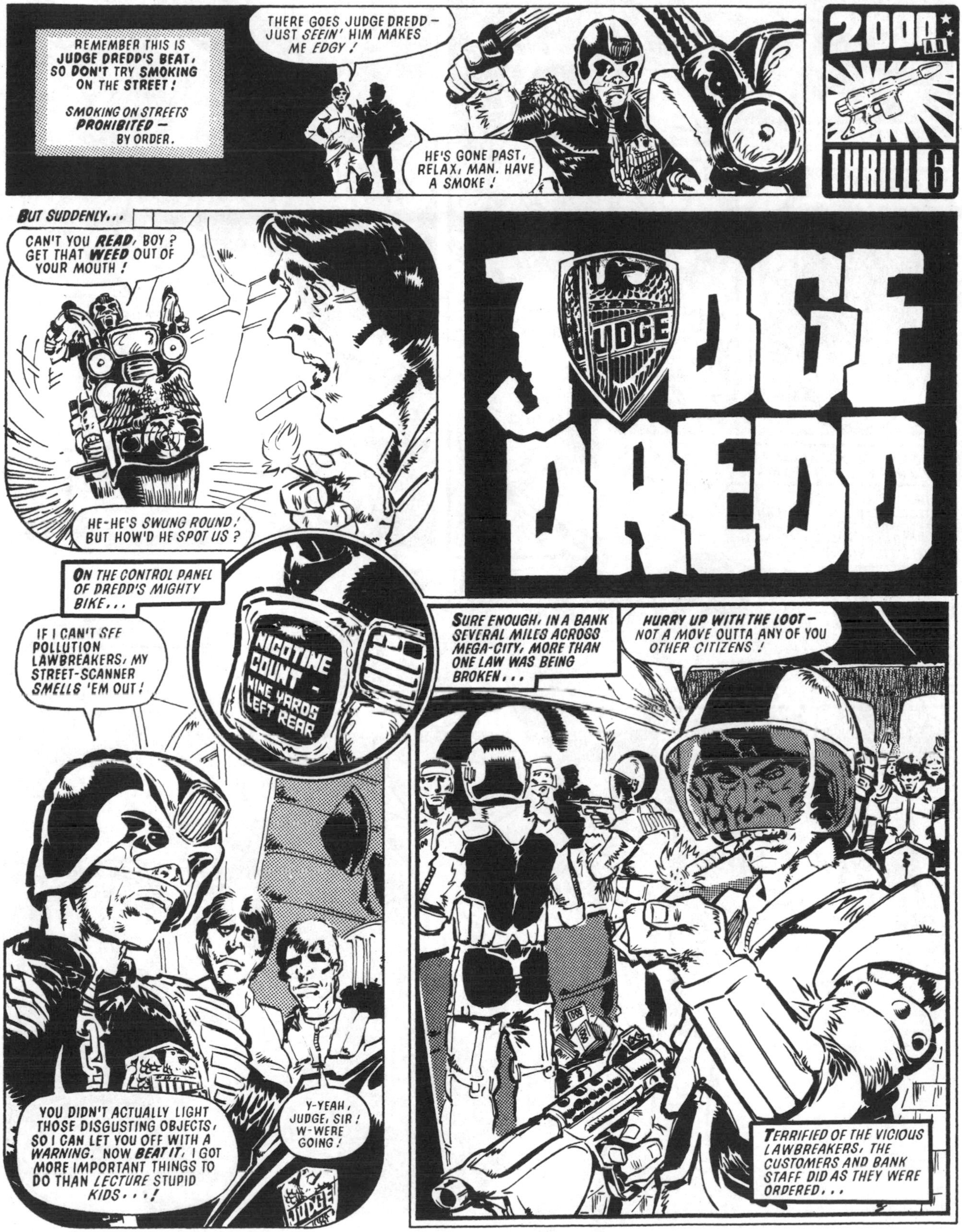

REMEMBER THIS IS JUDGE DREDD'S BEAT, SO DON'T TRY SMOKING ON THE STREET!
SMOKING ON STREETS PROHIBITED — BY ORDER.
THERE GOES JUDGE DREDD — JUST SEEIN' HIM MAKES ME EDGY!
HE'S GONE PAST, RELAX, MAN. HAVE A SMOKE!
2000 A.D.
THRILL 6
BUT SUDDENLY...
CAN'T YOU READ, BOY? GET THAT WEED OUT OF YOUR MOUTH!
HE-HE'S SWUNG ROUND! BUT HOW'D HE SPOT US?
JUDGE DREDD
ON THE CONTROL PANEL OF DREDD'S MIGHTY BIKE...
NICOTINE COUNT - NINE YARDS LEFT REAR
IF I CAN'T SEE POLLUTION LAWBREAKERS, MY STREET-SCANNER SMELLS 'EM OUT!
YOU DIDN'T ACTUALLY LIGHT THOSE DISGUSTING OBJECTS, SO I CAN LET YOU OFF WITH A WARNING. NOW BEAT IT, I GOT MORE IMPORTANT THINGS TO DO THAN LECTURE STUPID KIDS...!
Y-YEAH, JUDGE, SIR! W-WERE GOING!
SURE ENOUGH, IN A BANK SEVERAL MILES ACROSS MEGA-CITY, MORE THAN ONE LAW WAS BEING BROKEN...
HURRY UP WITH THE LOOT — NOT A MOVE OUTTA ANY OF YOU OTHER CITIZENS!
TERRIFIED OF THE VICIOUS LAWBREAKERS, THE CUSTOMERS AND BANK STAFF DID AS THEY WERE ORDERED...

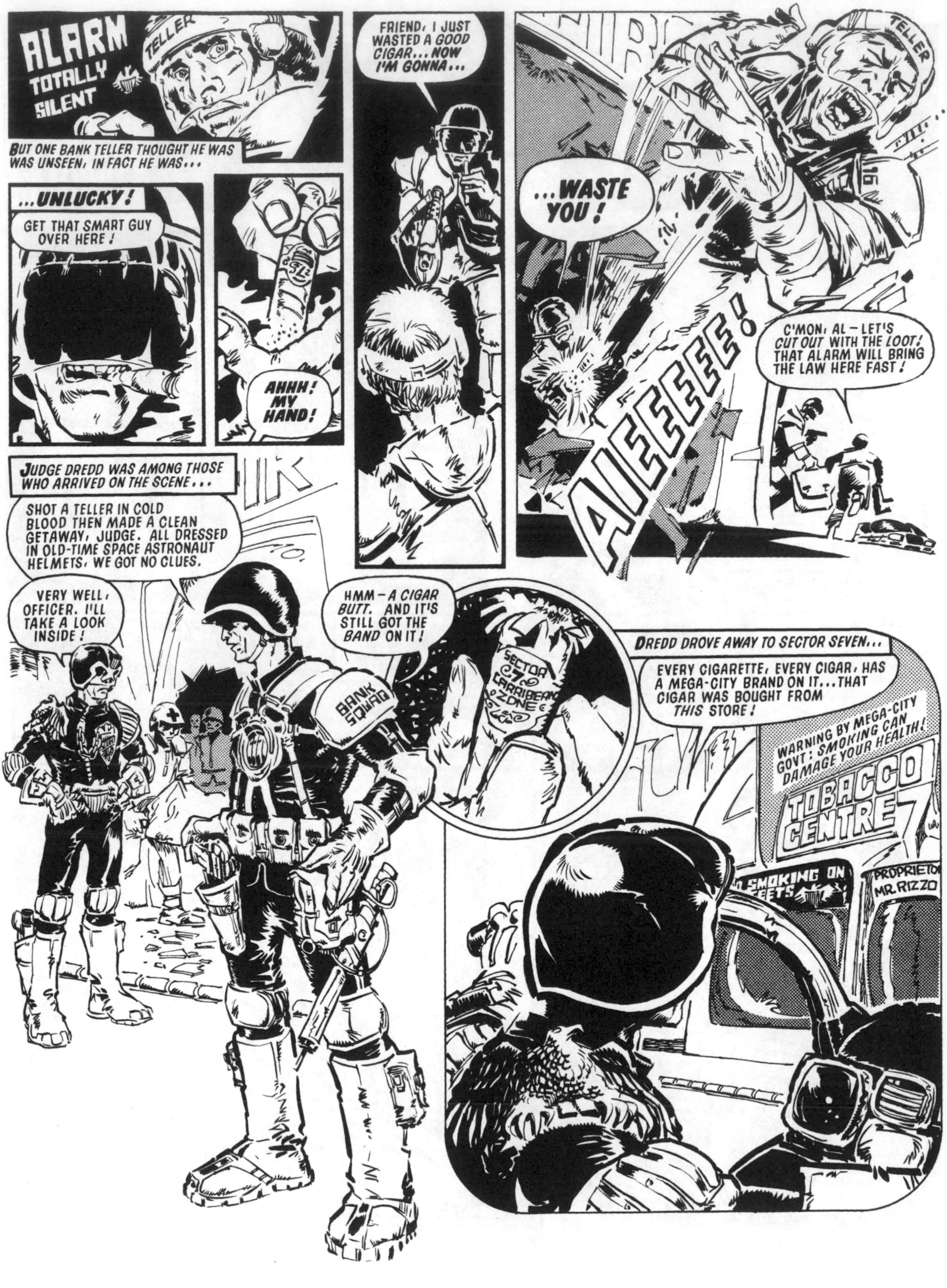
ALARM TOTALLY SILENT
TELLER
BUT ONE BANK TELLER THOUGHT HE WAS WAS UNSEEN, IN FACT HE WAS...
...UNLUCKY!
GET THAT SMART GUY OVER HERE!
AHHH! MY HAND!
FRIEND, I JUST WASTED A GOOD CIGAR... NOW I'M GONNA...
...WASTE YOU!
AIEEEEE!
C'MON, AL — LET'S CUT OUT WITH THE LOOT! THAT ALARM WILL BRING THE LAW HERE FAST!
JUDGE DREDD WAS AMONG THOSE WHO ARRIVED ON THE SCENE...
SHOT A TELLER IN COLD BLOOD THEN MADE A CLEAN GETAWAY, JUDGE. ALL DRESSED IN OLD-TIME SPACE ASTRONAUT HELMETS, WE GOT NO CLUES.
VERY WELL, OFFICER. I'LL TAKE A LOOK INSIDE!
BANK SQUAD
HMM — A CIGAR BUTT. AND IT'S STILL GOT THE BAND ON IT!
SECTOR 7 CARRIBEAN ZONE
DREDD DROVE AWAY TO SECTOR SEVEN...
EVERY CIGARETTE, EVERY CIGAR, HAS A MEGA-CITY BRAND ON IT... THAT CIGAR WAS BOUGHT FROM THIS STORE!
WARNING BY MEGA-CITY GOVT: SMOKING CAN DAMAGE YOUR HEALTH!
TOBACCO CENTRE 7
MR. RIZZO

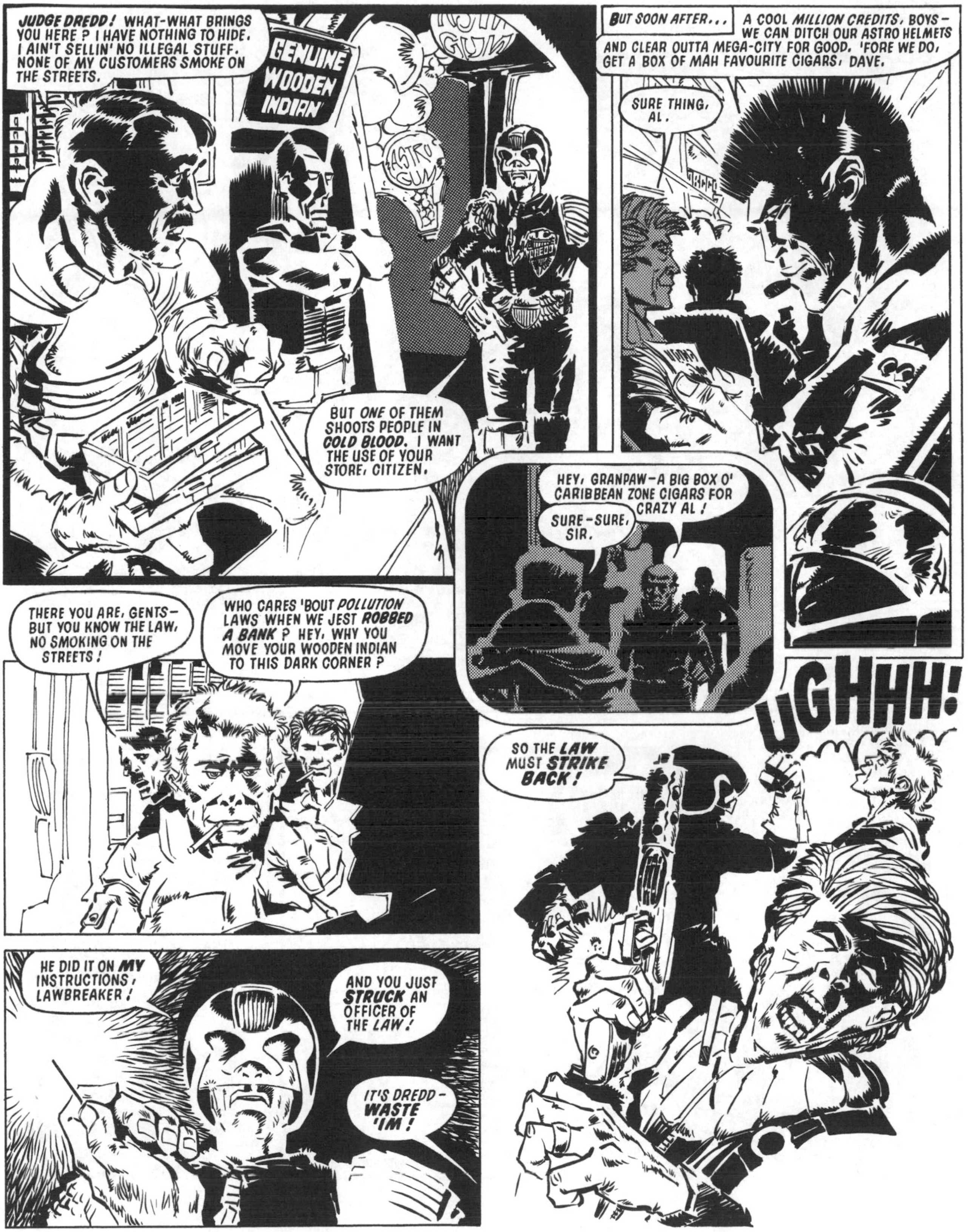
JUDGE DREDD! WHAT-WHAT BRINGS YOU HERE? I HAVE NOTHING TO HIDE. I AIN'T SELLIN' NO ILLEGAL STUFF. NONE OF MY CUSTOMERS SMOKE ON THE STREETS.
GENUINE WOODEN INDIAN
ASTRO GUM
BUT ONE OF THEM SHOOTS PEOPLE IN COLD BLOOD. I WANT THE USE OF YOUR STORE, CITIZEN.
BUT SOON AFTER...
A COOL MILLION CREDITS, BOYS- WE CAN DITCH OUR ASTRO HELMETS AND CLEAR OUTTA MEGA-CITY FOR GOOD. 'FORE WE DO, GET A BOX OF MAH FAVOURITE CIGARS, DAVE.
SURE THING, AL.
HEY, GRANPAW-A BIG BOX O' CARIBBEAN ZONE CIGARS FOR CRAZY AL!
SURE-SURE, SIR.
THERE YOU ARE, GENTS- BUT YOU KNOW THE LAW, NO SMOKING ON THE STREETS!
WHO CARES 'BOUT POLLUTION LAWS WHEN WE JEST ROBBED A BANK? HEY, WHY YOU MOVE YOUR WOODEN INDIAN TO THIS DARK CORNER?
HE DID IT ON MY INSTRUCTIONS, LAWBREAKER!
AND YOU JUST STRUCK AN OFFICER OF THE LAW!
IT'S DREDD- WASTE 'IM!
UGHHH!
SO THE LAW MUST STRIKE BACK!

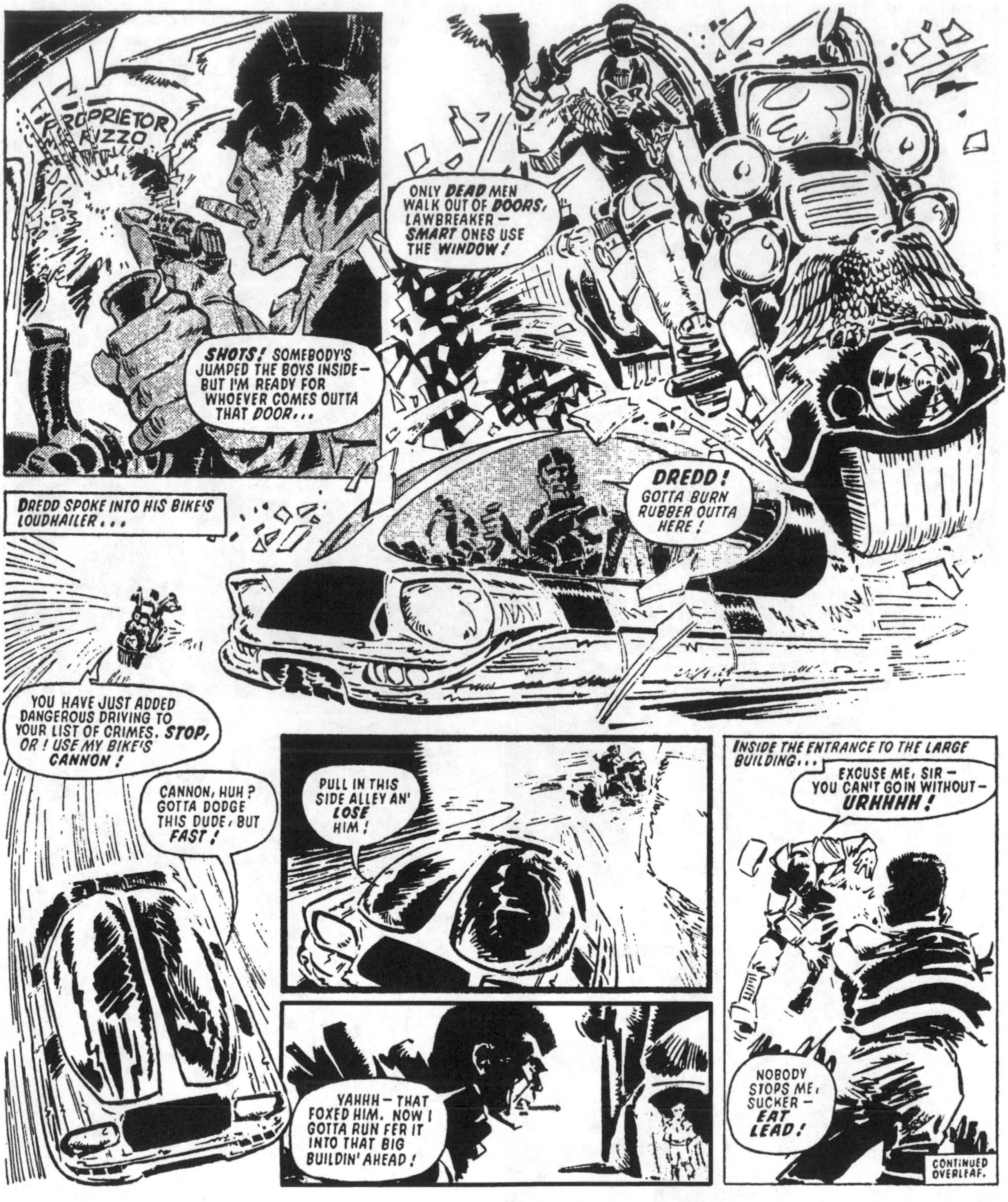
PROPRIETOR RIZZO
SHOTS! SOMEBODY'S JUMPED THE BOYS INSIDE— BUT I'M READY FOR WHOEVER COMES OUTTA THAT DOOR...
ONLY DEAD MEN WALK OUT OF DOORS, LAWBREAKER— SMART ONES USE THE WINDOW!
DREDD! GOTTA BURN RUBBER OUTTA HERE!
DREDD SPOKE INTO HIS BIKE'S LOUDHAILER...
YOU HAVE JUST ADDED DANGEROUS DRIVING TO YOUR LIST OF CRIMES. STOP, OR I USE MY BIKE'S CANNON!
CANNON, HUH? GOTTA DODGE THIS DUDE, BUT FAST!
PULL IN THIS SIDE ALLEY AN' LOSE HIM!
YAHHH— THAT FOXED HIM. NOW I GOTTA RUN FER IT INTO THAT BIG BUILDIN' AHEAD!
INSIDE THE ENTRANCE TO THE LARGE BUILDING...
EXCUSE ME, SIR— YOU CAN'T GO IN WITHOUT— URHHHH!
NOBODY STOPS ME, SUCKER— EAT LEAD!
CONTINUED OVERLEAF.

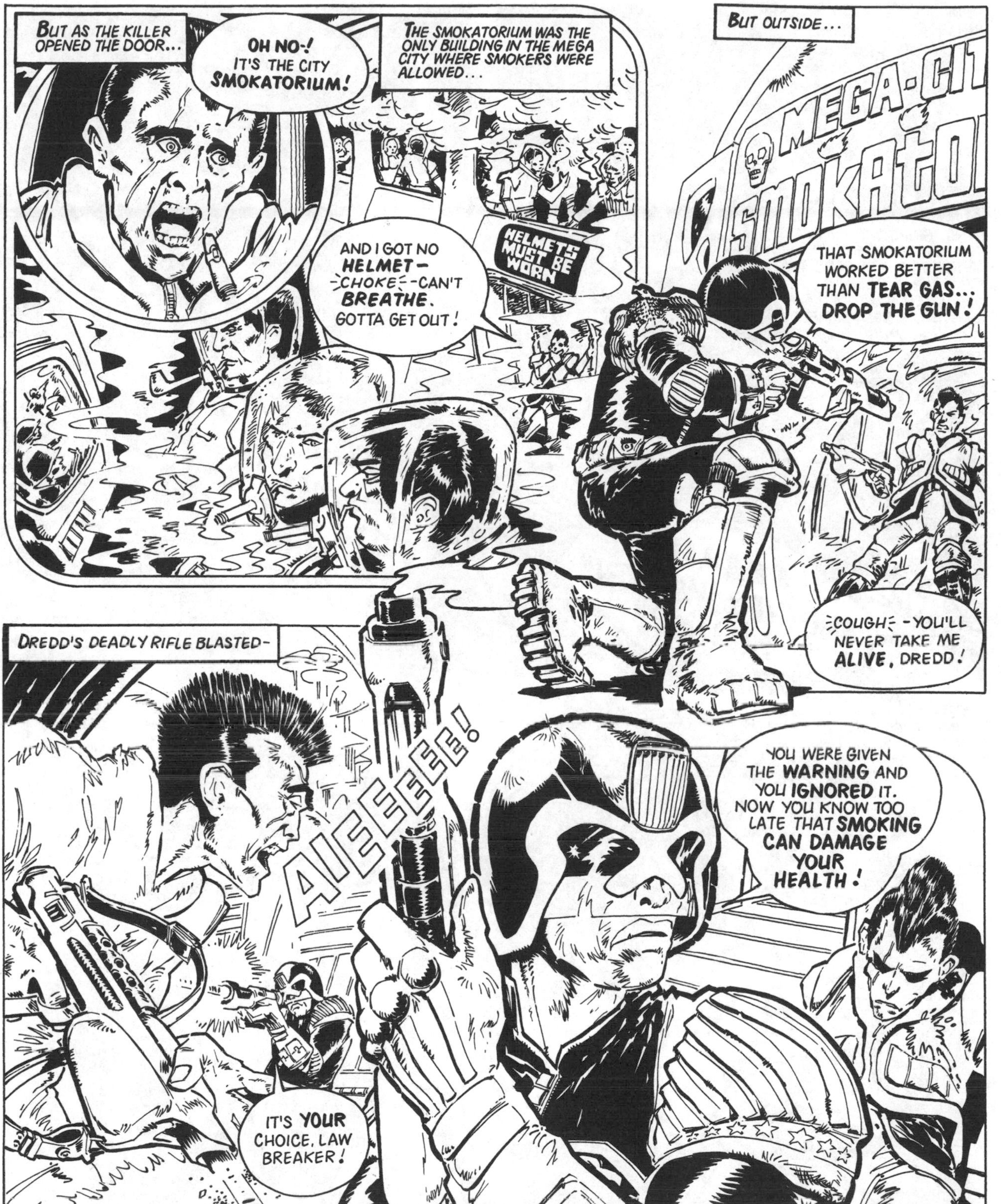

BUT AS THE KILLER OPENED THE DOOR...
OH NO-! IT'S THE CITY SMOKATORIUM!
THE SMOKATORIUM WAS THE ONLY BUILDING IN THE MEGA CITY WHERE SMOKERS WERE ALLOWED...
HELMETS MUST BE WORN
AND I GOT NO HELMET- -CHOKE- -CAN'T BREATHE. GOTTA GET OUT!
BUT OUTSIDE...
MEGA-CIT
SMOKATO
THAT SMOKATORIUM WORKED BETTER THAN TEAR GAS... DROP THE GUN!
-COUGH- -YOU'LL NEVER TAKE ME ALIVE, DREDD!
DREDD'S DEADLY RIFLE BLASTED-
AIEEEEE!
YOU WERE GIVEN THE WARNING AND YOU IGNORED IT. NOW YOU KNOW TOO LATE THAT SMOKING CAN DAMAGE YOUR HEALTH!
IT'S YOUR CHOICE, LAW BREAKER!
PROGRAMME AN ORDER FOR 2000 A.D. NOW-OUR NEXT PROG HAS EXTRA THRILLS!

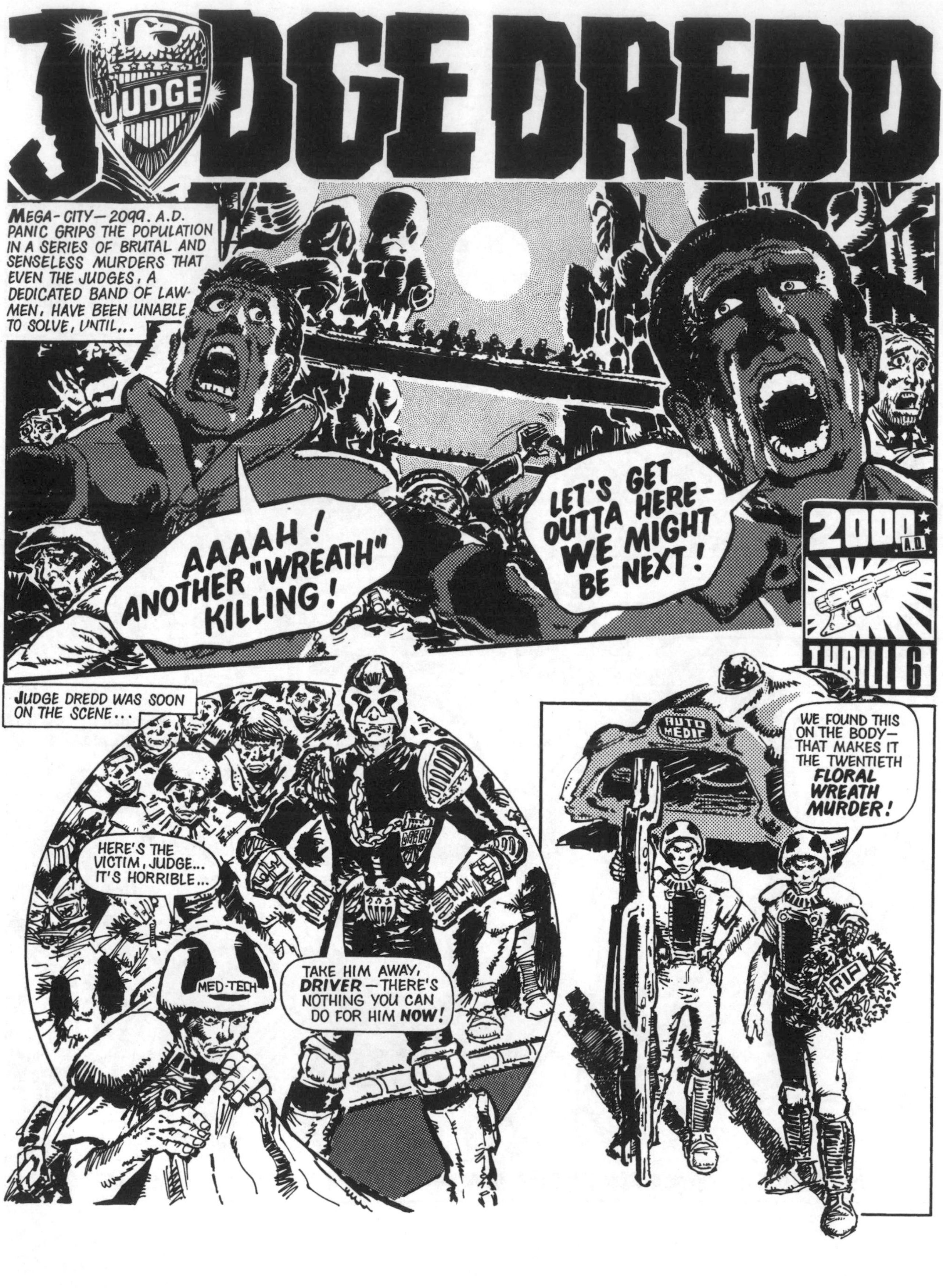
JUDGE DREDD
JUDGE
MEGA-CITY—2099. A.D. PANIC GRIPS THE POPULATION IN A SERIES OF BRUTAL AND SENSELESS MURDERS THAT EVEN THE JUDGES, A DEDICATED BAND OF LAWMEN, HAVE BEEN UNABLE TO SOLVE, UNTIL...
AAAAH! ANOTHER "WREATH" KILLING!
LET'S GET OUTTA HERE- WE MIGHT BE NEXT!
2000 A.D.
THRILL 6
JUDGE DREDD WAS SOON ON THE SCENE...
HERE'S THE VICTIM, JUDGE... IT'S HORRIBLE...
MED-TECH
TAKE HIM AWAY, DRIVER—THERE'S NOTHING YOU CAN DO FOR HIM NOW!
AUTO MEDIC
WE FOUND THIS ON THE BODY— THAT MAKES IT THE TWENTIETH FLORAL WREATH MURDER!
RIP

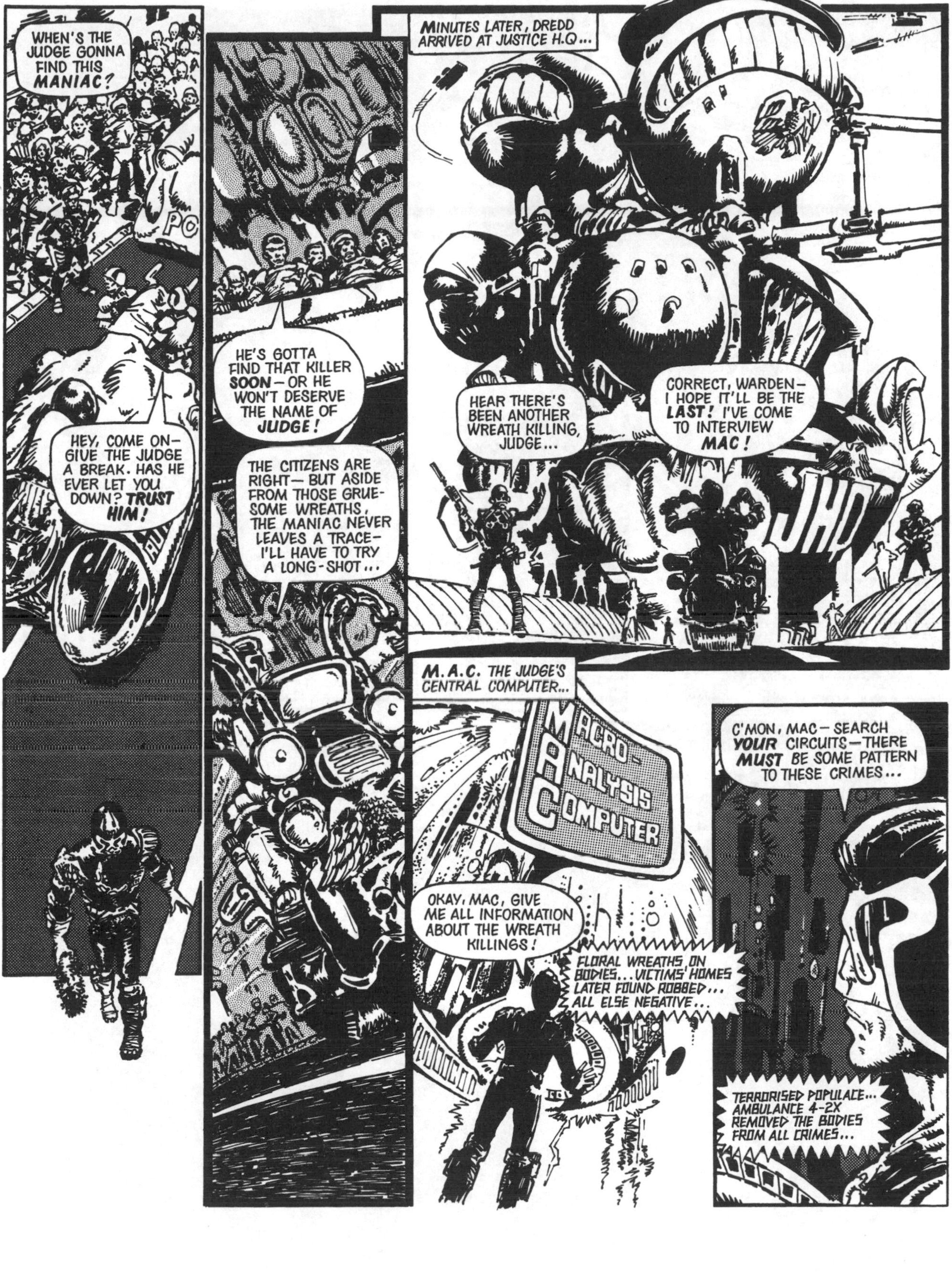
WHEN'S THE JUDGE GONNA FIND THIS MANIAC?
HE'S GOTTA FIND THAT KILLER SOON — OR HE WON'T DESERVE THE NAME OF JUDGE!
HEY, COME ON — GIVE THE JUDGE A BREAK. HAS HE EVER LET YOU DOWN? TRUST HIM!
THE CITIZENS ARE RIGHT — BUT ASIDE FROM THOSE GRUESOME WREATHS, THE MANIAC NEVER LEAVES A TRACE — I'LL HAVE TO TRY A LONG-SHOT...
MINUTES LATER, DREDD ARRIVED AT JUSTICE H.Q...
HEAR THERE'S BEEN ANOTHER WREATH KILLING, JUDGE...
CORRECT, WARDEN — I HOPE IT'LL BE THE LAST! I'VE COME TO INTERVIEW MAC!
JHQ
M.A.C. THE JUDGE'S CENTRAL COMPUTER...
MACRO-ANALYSIS COMPUTER
OKAY, MAC, GIVE ME ALL INFORMATION ABOUT THE WREATH KILLINGS!
FLORAL WREATHS ON BODIES... VICTIMS' HOMES LATER FOUND ROBBED... ALL ELSE NEGATIVE...
C'MON, MAC — SEARCH YOUR CIRCUITS — THERE MUST BE SOME PATTERN TO THESE CRIMES...
TERRORISED POPULACE... AMBULANCE 4-2X REMOVED THE BODIES FROM ALL CRIMES...

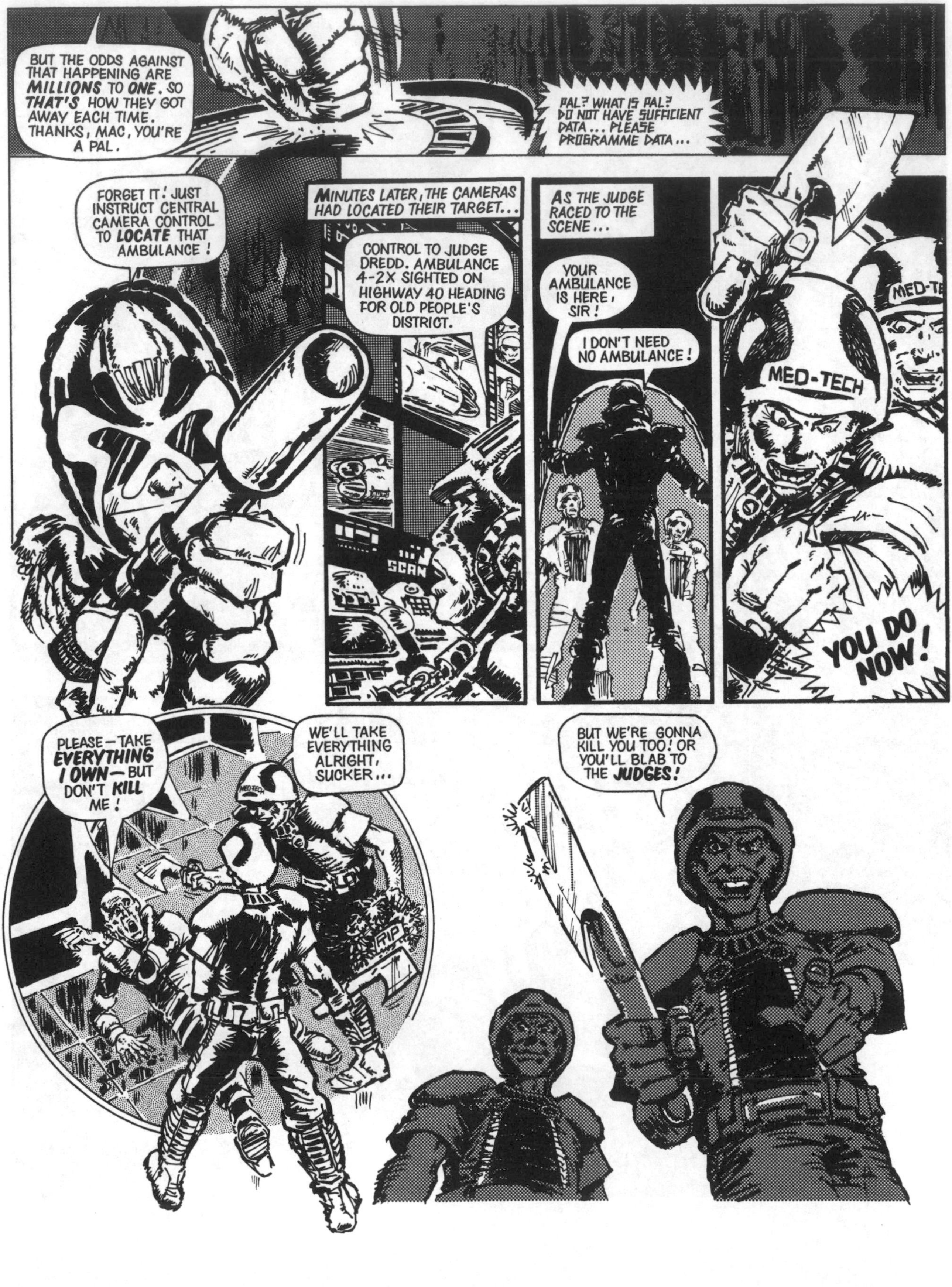

BUT THE ODDS AGAINST THAT HAPPENING ARE MILLIONS TO ONE. SO THAT'S HOW THEY GOT AWAY EACH TIME. THANKS, MAC, YOU'RE A PAL.
PAL? WHAT IS PAL? DO NOT HAVE SUFFICIENT DATA ... PLEASE PROGRAMME DATA ...
FORGET IT! JUST INSTRUCT CENTRAL CAMERA CONTROL TO LOCATE THAT AMBULANCE!
MINUTES LATER, THE CAMERAS HAD LOCATED THEIR TARGET...
CONTROL TO JUDGE DREDD. AMBULANCE 4-2X SIGHTED ON HIGHWAY 40 HEADING FOR OLD PEOPLE'S DISTRICT.
SCAN
AS THE JUDGE RACED TO THE SCENE...
YOUR AMBULANCE IS HERE, SIR!
I DON'T NEED NO AMBULANCE!
MED-TECH
MED-TECH
YOU DO NOW!
PLEASE—TAKE EVERYTHING I OWN—BUT DON'T KILL ME!
WE'LL TAKE EVERYTHING ALRIGHT, SUCKER...
MED-TECH
RIP
BUT WE'RE GONNA KILL YOU TOO! OR YOU'LL BLAB TO THE JUDGES!

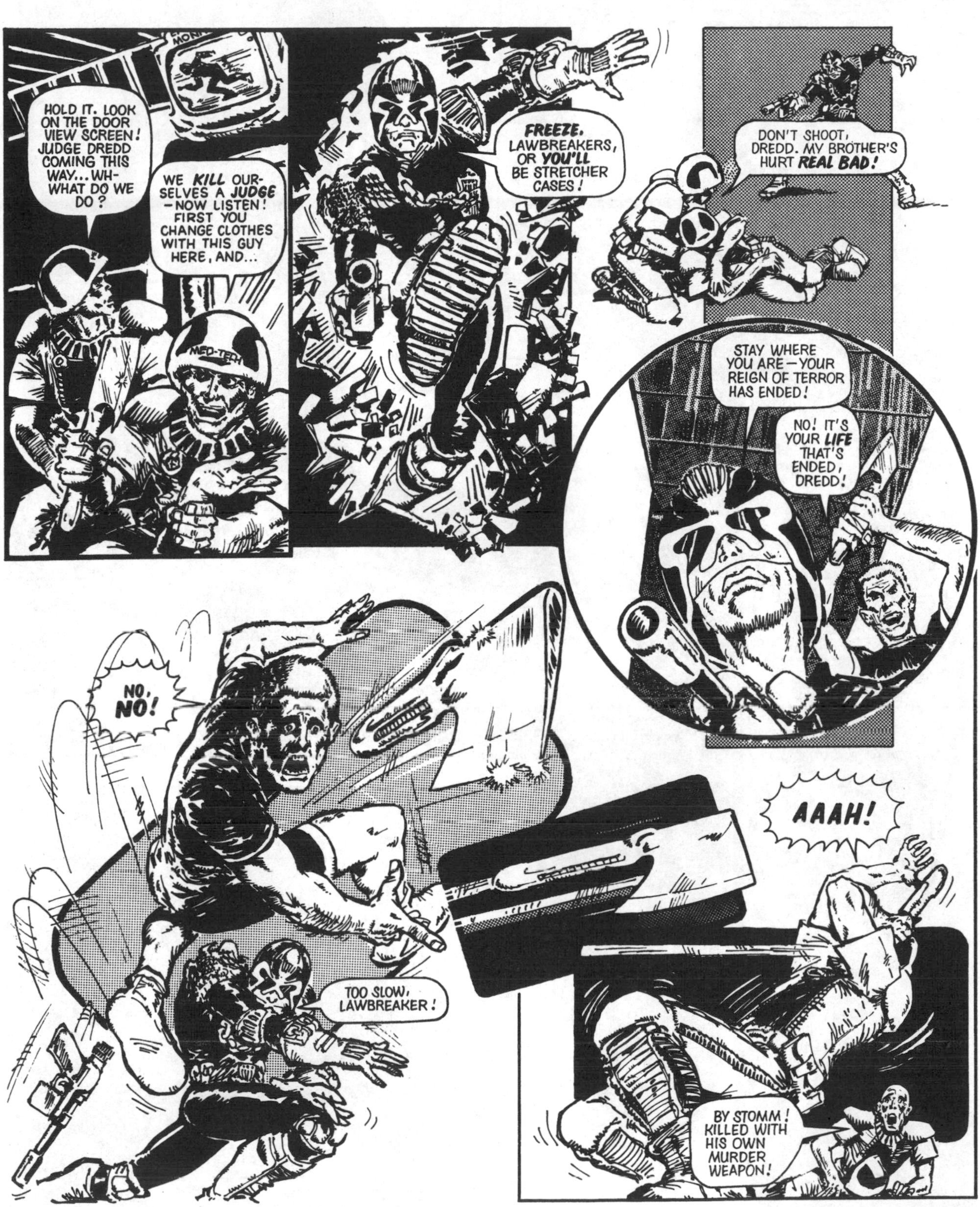

HOLD IT. LOOK ON THE DOOR VIEW SCREEN! JUDGE DREDD COMING THIS WAY... WH-WHAT DO WE DO?
WE KILL OURSELVES A JUDGE—NOW LISTEN! FIRST YOU CHANGE CLOTHES WITH THIS GUY HERE, AND...
MED-TECH
FREEZE, LAWBREAKERS, OR YOU'LL BE STRETCHER CASES!
DON'T SHOOT, DREDD. MY BROTHER'S HURT REAL BAD!
STAY WHERE YOU ARE—YOUR REIGN OF TERROR HAS ENDED!
NO! IT'S YOUR LIFE THAT'S ENDED, DREDD!
NO, NO!
TOO SLOW, LAWBREAKER!
AAAH!
BY STOMM! KILLED WITH HIS OWN MURDER WEAPON!

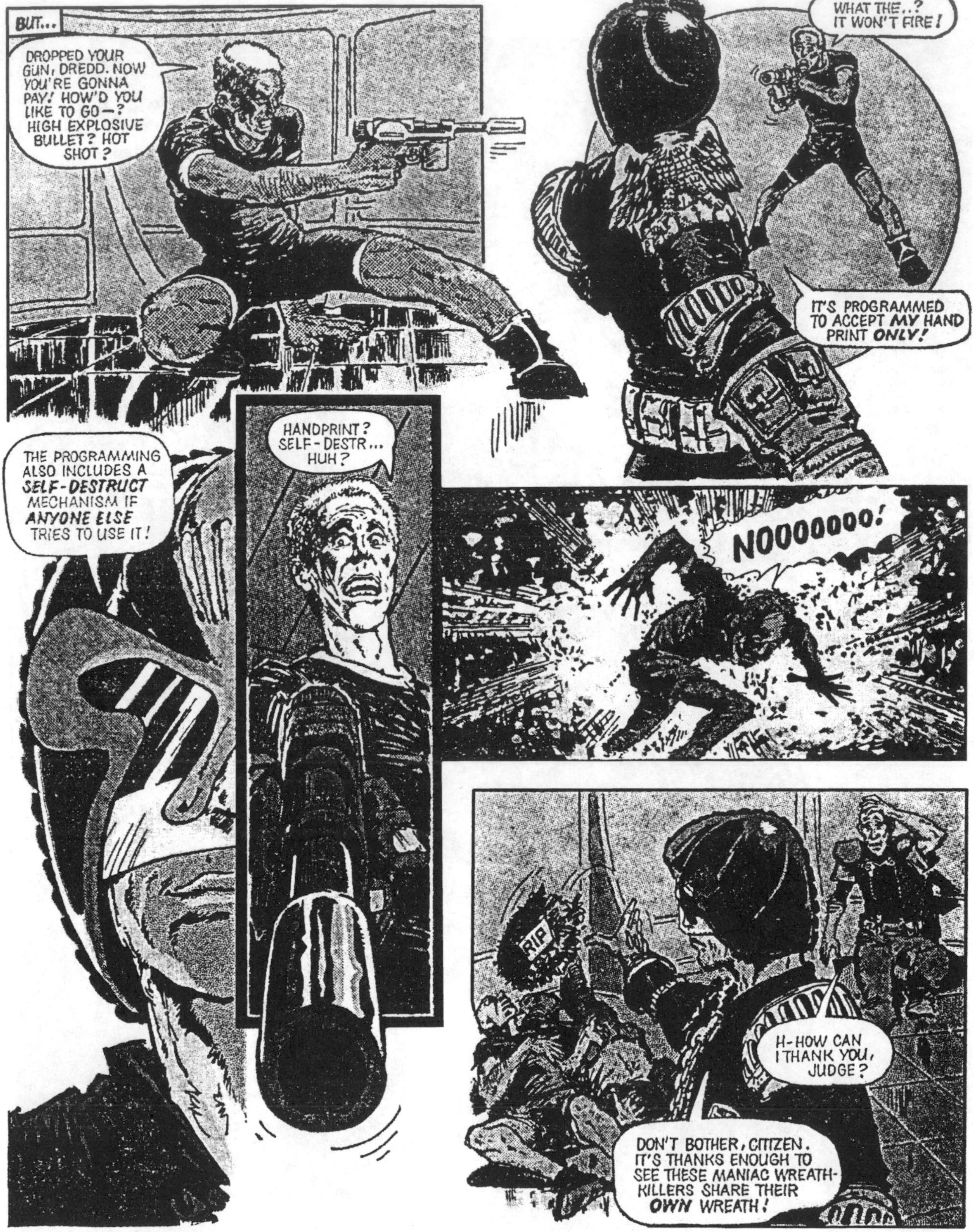
BUT...
DROPPED YOUR GUN, DREDD. NOW YOU'RE GONNA PAY! HOW'D YOU LIKE TO GO—? HIGH EXPLOSIVE BULLET? HOT SHOT?
WHAT THE..? IT WON'T FIRE!
IT'S PROGRAMMED TO ACCEPT MY HAND PRINT ONLY!
THE PROGRAMMING ALSO INCLUDES A SELF-DESTRUCT MECHANISM IF ANYONE ELSE TRIES TO USE IT!
HANDPRINT? SELF-DESTR... HUH?
NOOOOOOO!
RIP
H-HOW CAN I THANK YOU, JUDGE?
DON'T BOTHER, CITIZEN. IT'S THANKS ENOUGH TO SEE THESE MANIAC WREATH-KILLERS SHARE THEIR OWN WREATH!

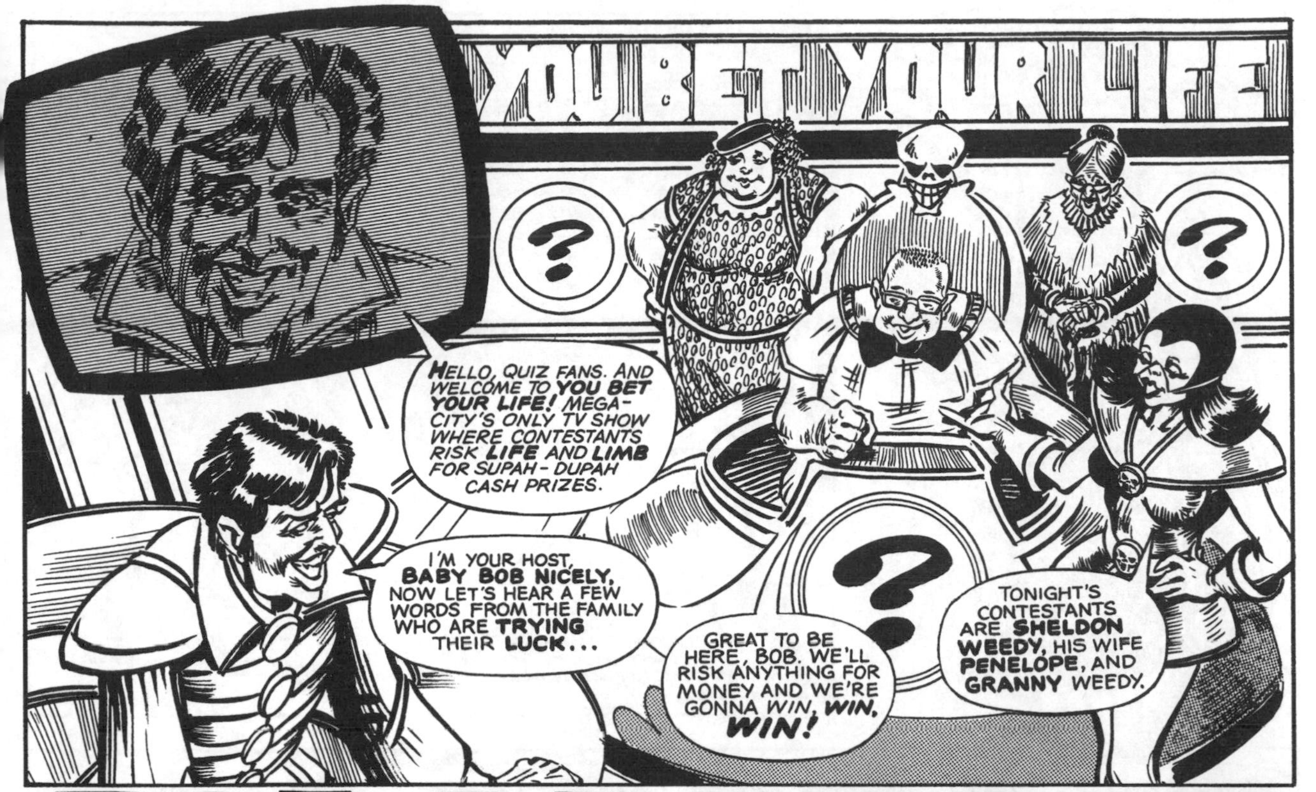

YOU BET YOUR LIFE
HELLO, QUIZ FANS. AND WELCOME TO YOU BET YOUR LIFE! MEGA-CITY'S ONLY TV SHOW WHERE CONTESTANTS RISK LIFE AND LIMB FOR SUPAH-DUPAH CASH PRIZES.
I'M YOUR HOST, BABY BOB NICELY. NOW LET'S HEAR A FEW WORDS FROM THE FAMILY WHO ARE TRYING THEIR LUCK...
GREAT TO BE HERE, BOB. WE'LL RISK ANYTHING FOR MONEY AND WE'RE GONNA WIN, WIN, WIN!
TONIGHT'S CONTESTANTS ARE SHELDON WEEDY, HIS WIFE PENELOPE, AND GRANNY WEEDY.

JUDGE DREDD

MEGA-CITY 1. VAST METROPOLIS OF THE 22ND CENTURY. THERE ARE MANY ILLEGAL PIRATE TV STATIONS BROADCASTING FROM SECRET STUDIOS, BUT **SOME** ARE MORE ILLEGAL THAN **OTHERS**—AND **THIS** ONE IS DOWNRIGHT **MURDEROUS!**

WALTER, JUDGE DREDD'S SERVO-ROBOT HAD BEEN WATCHING THE SHOW ON HIS BUILT-IN SCREEN.

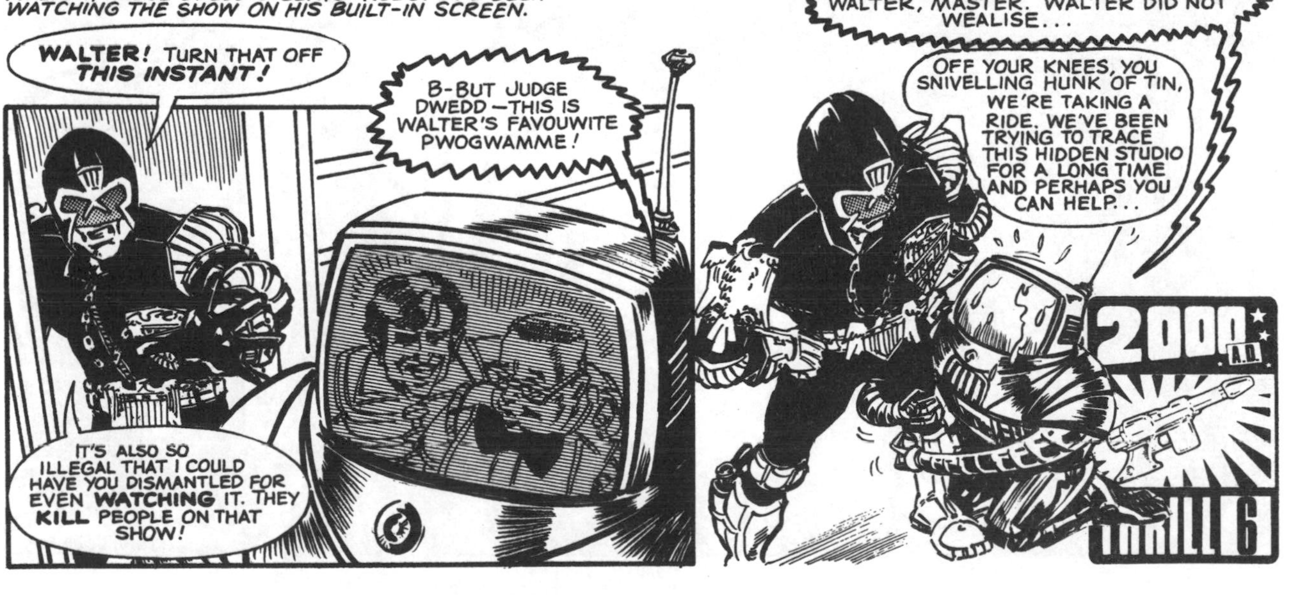

WALTER! TURN THAT OFF THIS INSTANT!
B-BUT JUDGE DWEDD—THIS IS WALTER'S FAVOUWITE PWOGWAMME!
IT'S ALSO SO ILLEGAL THAT I COULD HAVE YOU DISMANTLED FOR EVEN WATCHING IT. THEY KILL PEOPLE ON THAT SHOW!
P-PLEASE DON'T BE ANGWY WITH WALTER, MASTER. WALTER DID NOT WEALISE...
OFF YOUR KNEES, YOU SNIVELLING HUNK OF TIN, WE'RE TAKING A RIDE. WE'VE BEEN TRYING TO TRACE THIS HIDDEN STUDIO FOR A LONG TIME AND PERHAPS YOU CAN HELP...
2000 A.D.
THRILL 6

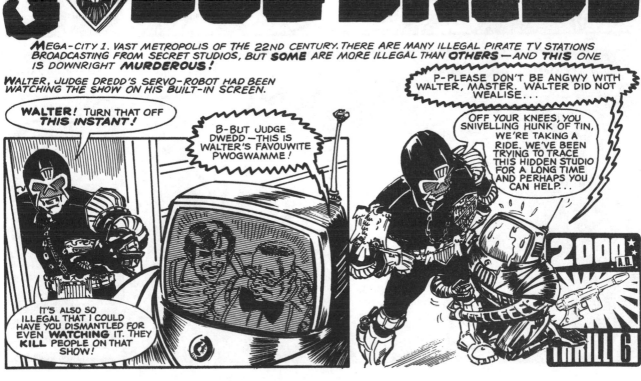

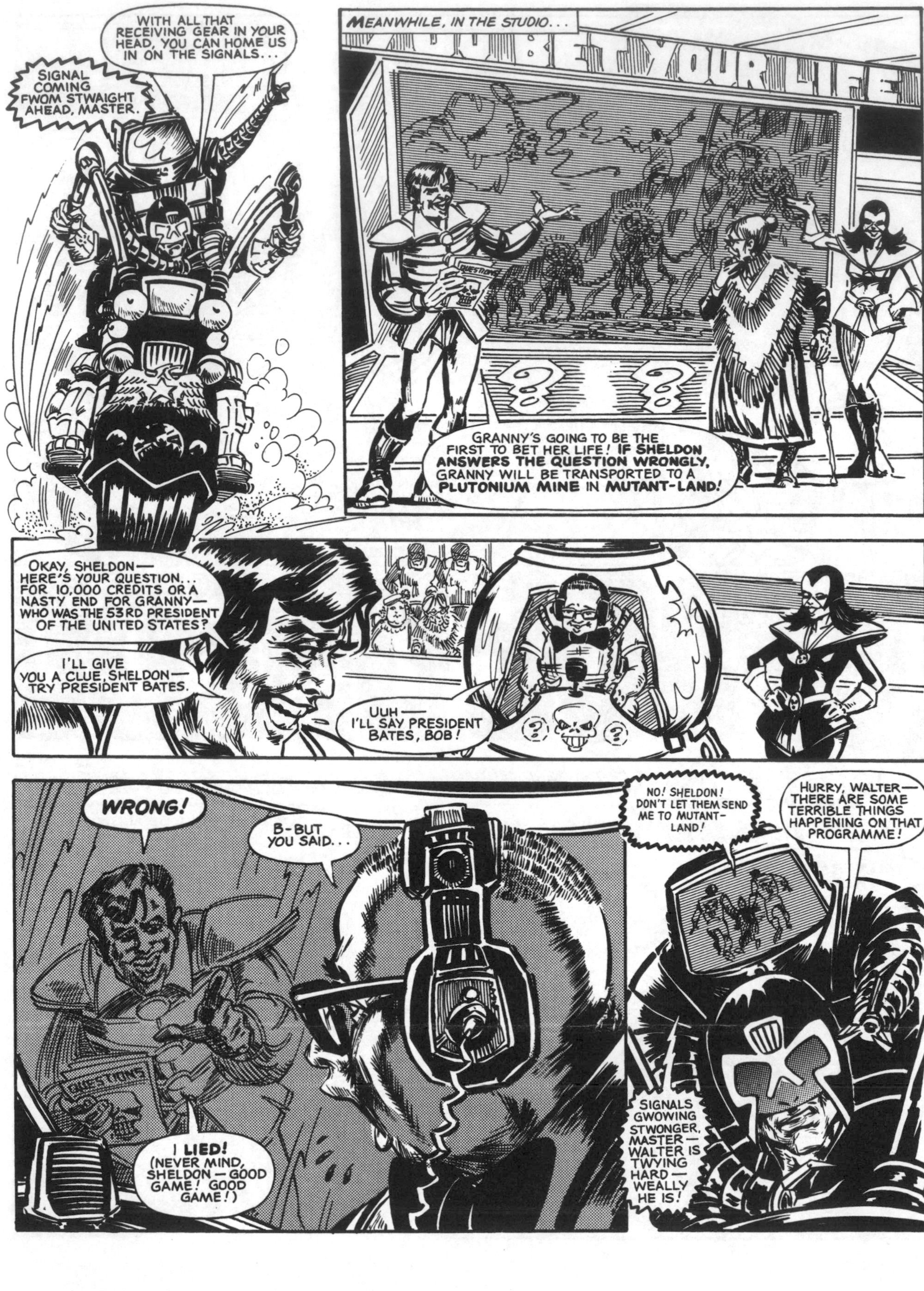

WITH ALL THAT RECEIVING GEAR IN YOUR HEAD, YOU CAN HOME US IN ON THE SIGNALS...
SIGNAL COMING FWOM STWAIGHT AHEAD, MASTER.
MEANWHILE, IN THE STUDIO...
YOU BET YOUR LIFE
GRANNY'S GOING TO BE THE FIRST TO BET HER LIFE! IF SHELDON ANSWERS THE QUESTION WRONGLY, GRANNY WILL BE TRANSPORTED TO A PLUTONIUM MINE IN MUTANT-LAND!
OKAY, SHELDON— HERE'S YOUR QUESTION... FOR 10,000 CREDITS OR A NASTY END FOR GRANNY— WHO WAS THE 53RD PRESIDENT OF THE UNITED STATES?
I'LL GIVE YOU A CLUE, SHELDON— TRY PRESIDENT BATES.
UUH— I'LL SAY PRESIDENT BATES, BOB!
WRONG!
B-BUT YOU SAID...
I LIED! (NEVER MIND, SHELDON—GOOD GAME! GOOD GAME!)
NO! SHELDON! DON'T LET THEM SEND ME TO MUTANT-LAND!
HURRY, WALTER— THERE ARE SOME TERRIBLE THINGS HAPPENING ON THAT PROGRAMME!
SIGNALS GWOWING STWONGER, MASTER— WALTER IS TWYING HARD— WEALLY HE IS!

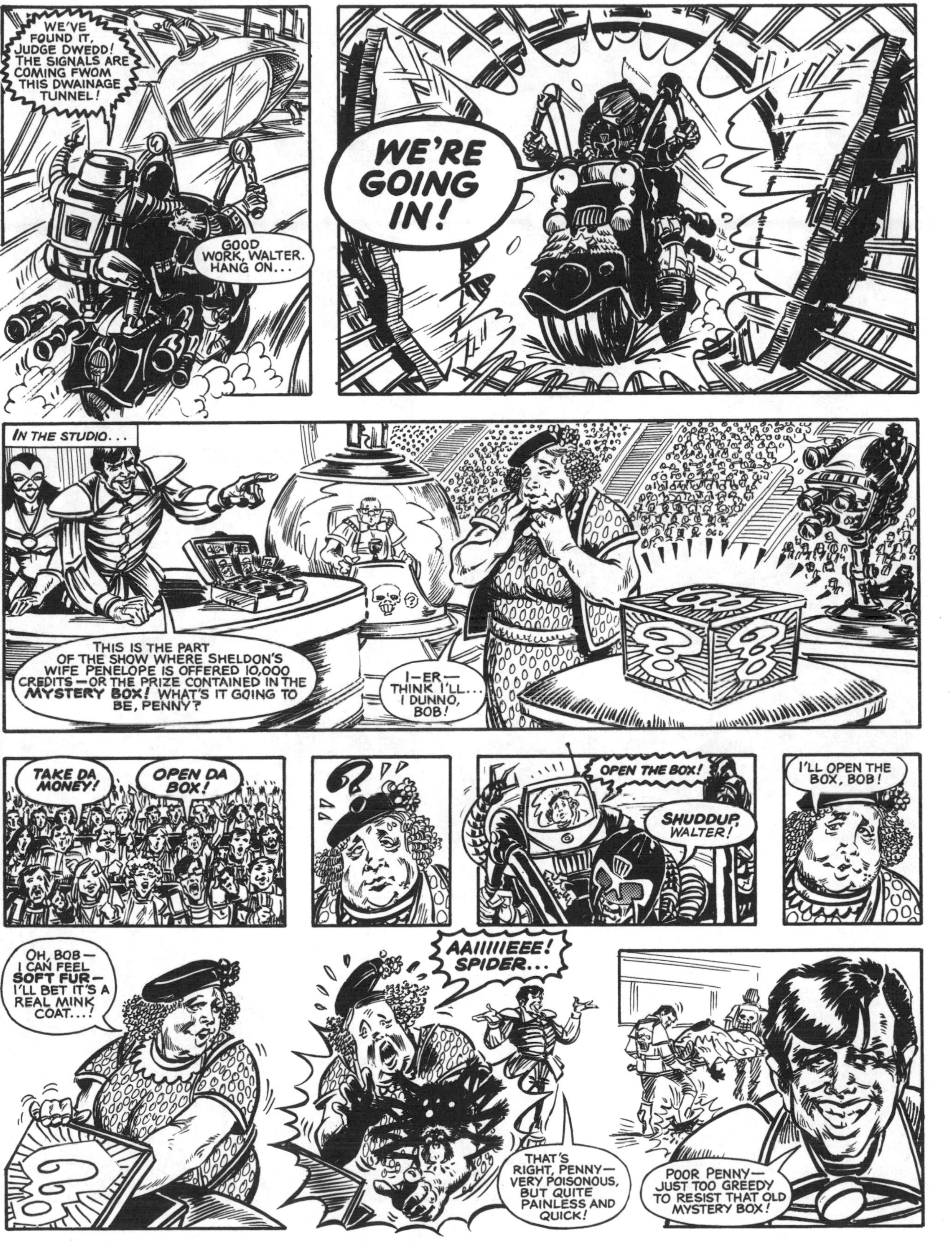
WE'VE FOUND IT, JUDGE DWEDD! THE SIGNALS ARE COMING FWOM THIS DWAINAGE TUNNEL!
GOOD WORK, WALTER. HANG ON...
WE'RE GOING IN!
IN THE STUDIO...
THIS IS THE PART OF THE SHOW WHERE SHELDON'S WIFE PENELOPE IS OFFERED 10,000 CREDITS — OR THE PRIZE CONTAINED IN THE MYSTERY BOX! WHAT'S IT GOING TO BE, PENNY?
I—ER— THINK I'LL... I DUNNO, BOB!
TAKE DA MONEY!
OPEN DA BOX!
OPEN THE BOX!
SHUDDUP, WALTER!
I'LL OPEN THE BOX, BOB!
OH, BOB — I CAN FEEL SOFT FUR — I'LL BET IT'S A REAL MINK COAT...!
AAIIIIIEEE! SPIDER...
THAT'S RIGHT, PENNY — VERY POISONOUS, BUT QUITE PAINLESS AND QUICK!
POOR PENNY — JUST TOO GREEDY TO RESIST THAT OLD MYSTERY BOX!

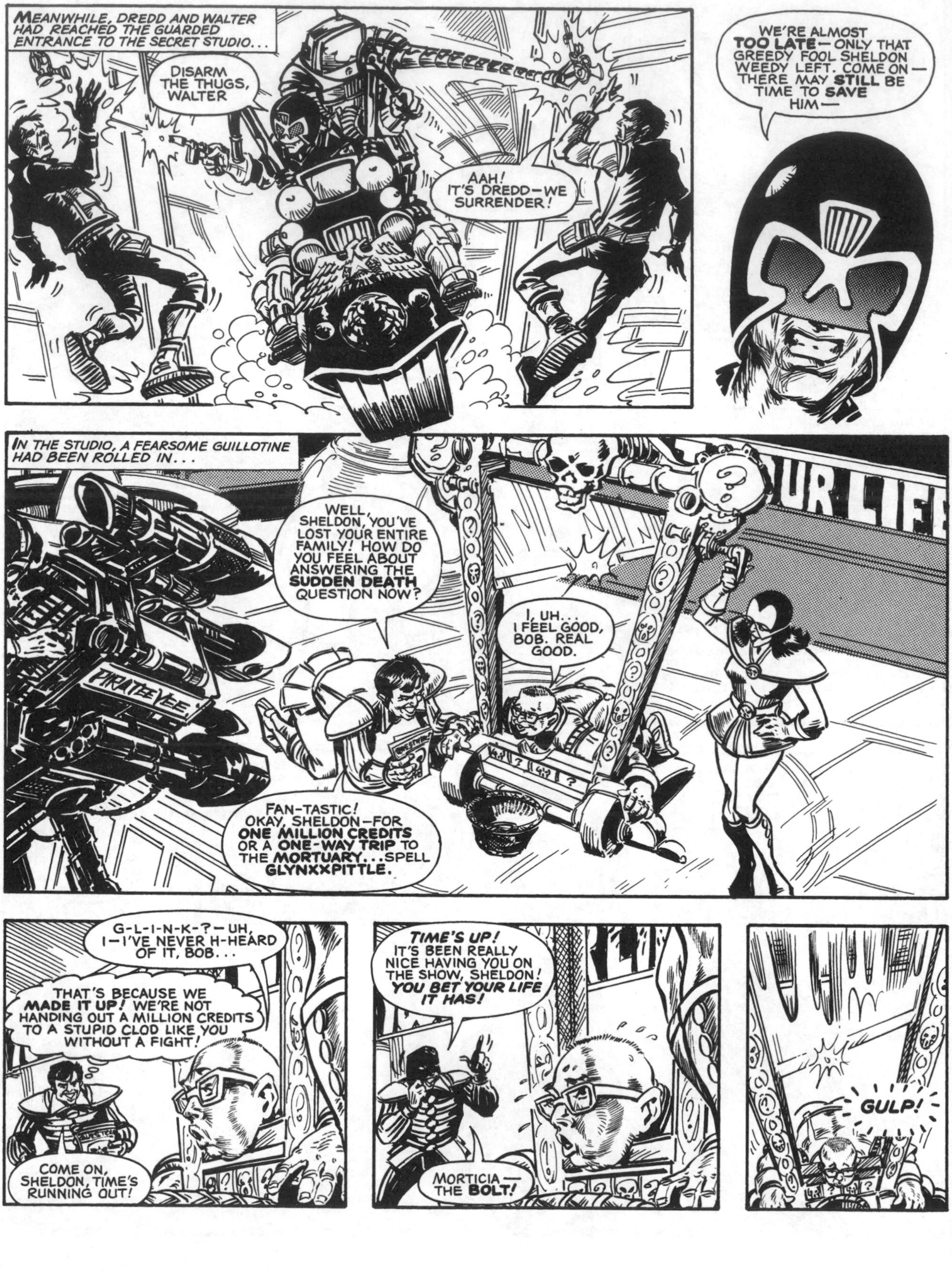
MEANWHILE, DREDD AND WALTER HAD REACHED THE GUARDED ENTRANCE TO THE SECRET STUDIO...
DISARM THE THUGS, WALTER
AAH! IT'S DREDD—WE SURRENDER!
WE'RE ALMOST TOO LATE—ONLY THAT GREEDY FOOL SHELDON WEEDY LEFT. COME ON—THERE MAY STILL BE TIME TO SAVE HIM—
IN THE STUDIO, A FEARSOME GUILLOTINE HAD BEEN ROLLED IN...
OUR LIFE
WELL, SHELDON, YOU'VE LOST YOUR ENTIRE FAMILY! HOW DO YOU FEEL ABOUT ANSWERING THE SUDDEN DEATH QUESTION NOW?
I, UH... I FEEL GOOD, BOB. REAL GOOD.
PIRATEEVEE
FAN-TASTIC! OKAY, SHELDON—FOR ONE MILLION CREDITS OR A ONE-WAY TRIP TO THE MORTUARY...SPELL GLYNXXPITTLE.
G-L-I-N-K-?—UH, I—I'VE NEVER H-HEARD OF IT, BOB...
THAT'S BECAUSE WE MADE IT UP! WE'RE NOT HANDING OUT A MILLION CREDITS TO A STUPID CLOD LIKE YOU WITHOUT A FIGHT!
COME ON, SHELDON, TIME'S RUNNING OUT!
TIME'S UP! IT'S BEEN REALLY NICE HAVING YOU ON THE SHOW, SHELDON! YOU BET YOUR LIFE IT HAS!
MORTICIA—THE BOLT!
GULP!

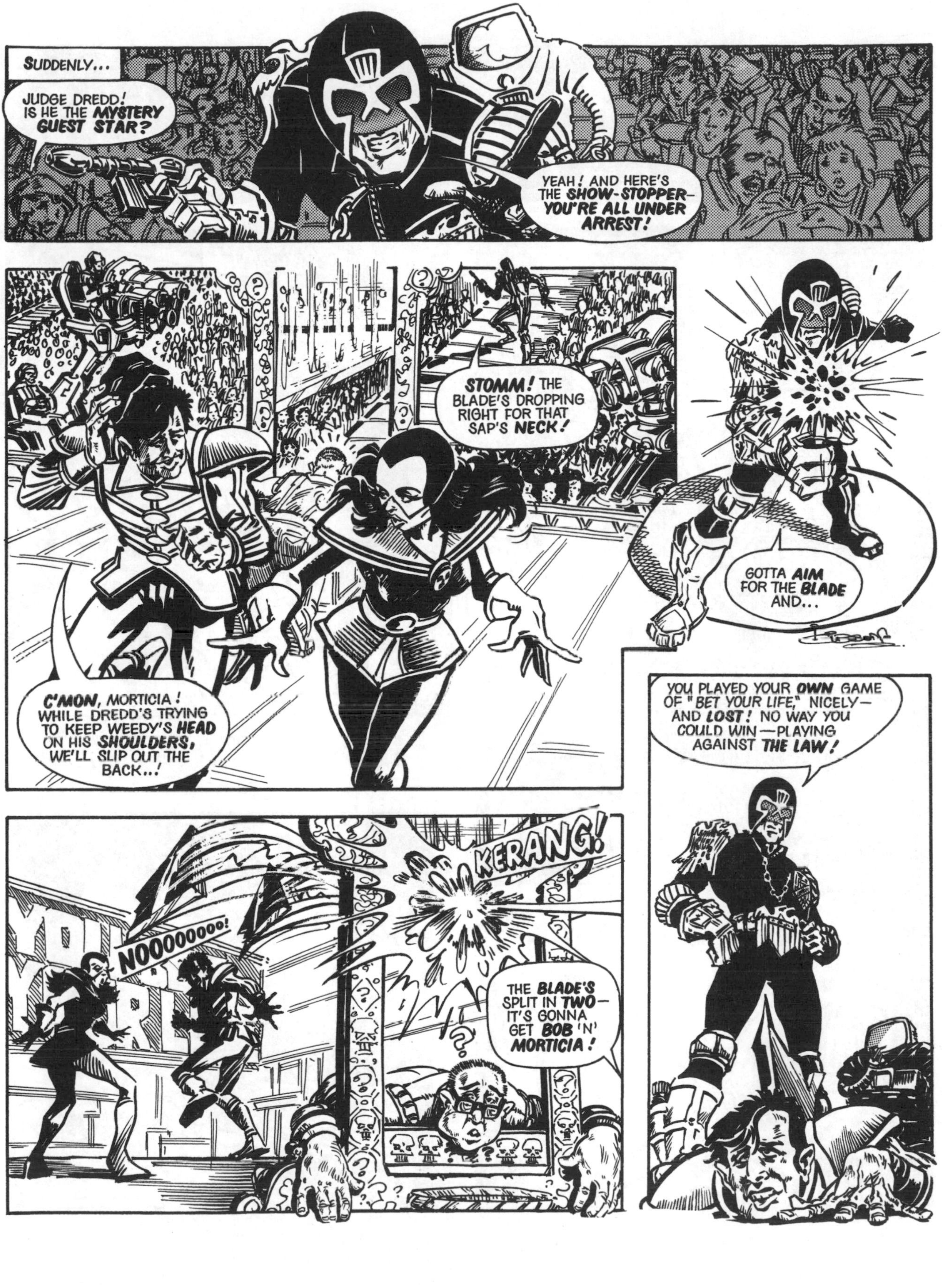

SUDDENLY...
JUDGE DREDD! IS HE THE MYSTERY GUEST STAR?
YEAH! AND HERE'S THE SHOW-STOPPER— YOU'RE ALL UNDER ARREST!
STOMM! THE BLADE'S DROPPING RIGHT FOR THAT SAP'S NECK!
GOTTA AIM FOR THE BLADE AND...
C'MON, MORTICIA! WHILE DREDD'S TRYING TO KEEP WEEDY'S HEAD ON HIS SHOULDERS, WE'LL SLIP OUT THE BACK...!
YOU PLAYED YOUR OWN GAME OF "BET YOUR LIFE," NICELY— AND LOST! NO WAY YOU COULD WIN—PLAYING AGAINST THE LAW!
KERANG!
NOOOOOOOO!
THE BLADE'S SPLIT IN TWO— IT'S GONNA GET BOB 'N' MORTICIA!

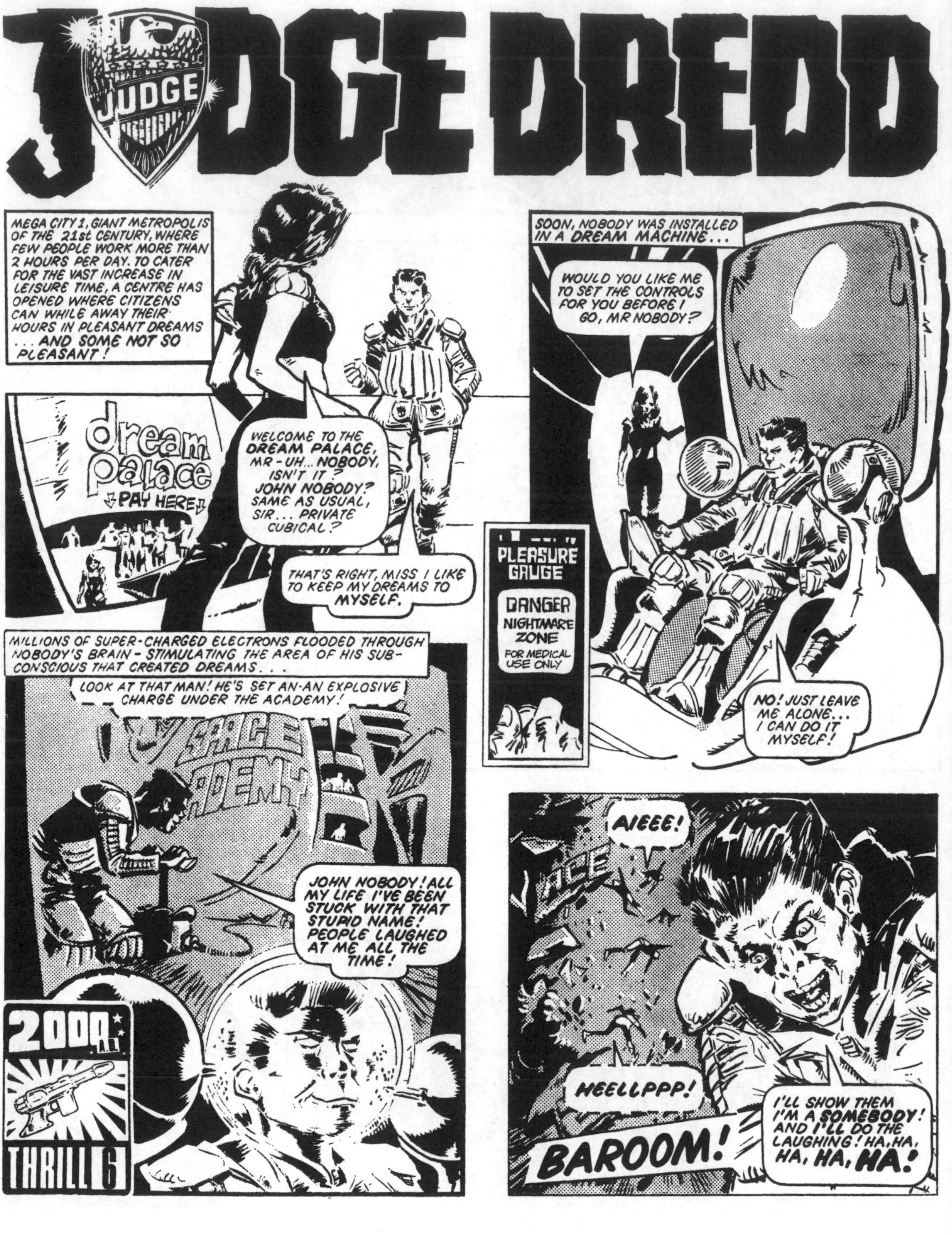
JUDGE DREDD
JUDGE
MEGA CITY 1, GIANT METROPOLIS OF THE 21st CENTURY, WHERE FEW PEOPLE WORK MORE THAN 2 HOURS PER DAY. TO CATER FOR THE VAST INCREASE IN LEISURE TIME, A CENTRE HAS OPENED WHERE CITIZENS CAN WHILE AWAY THEIR HOURS IN PLEASANT DREAMS . . . AND SOME NOT SO PLEASANT!
dream palace
PAY HERE
WELCOME TO THE DREAM PALACE, MR-UH... NOBODY, ISN'T IT? JOHN NOBODY? SAME AS USUAL, SIR... PRIVATE CUBICAL?
THAT'S RIGHT, MISS I LIKE TO KEEP MY DREAMS TO MYSELF.
SOON, NOBODY WAS INSTALLED IN A DREAM MACHINE...
WOULD YOU LIKE ME TO SET THE CONTROLS FOR YOU BEFORE I GO, MR NOBODY?
PLEASURE GAUGE
DANGER NIGHTMARE ZONE
FOR MEDICAL USE ONLY
NO! JUST LEAVE ME ALONE... I CAN DO IT MYSELF!
MILLIONS OF SUPER-CHARGED ELECTRONS FLOODED THROUGH NOBODY'S BRAIN - STIMULATING THE AREA OF HIS SUB-CONSCIOUS THAT CREATED DREAMS . . .
LOOK AT THAT MAN! HE'S SET AN-AN EXPLOSIVE CHARGE UNDER THE ACADEMY!
JOHN NOBODY! ALL MY LIFE I'VE BEEN STUCK WITH THAT STUPID NAME! PEOPLE LAUGHED AT ME ALL THE TIME!
2000 A.D.
THRILL 6
AIEEE!
HEELLPPP!
BAROOM!
I'LL SHOW THEM I'M A SOMEBODY! AND I'LL DO THE LAUGHING! HA, HA, HA, HA, HA!

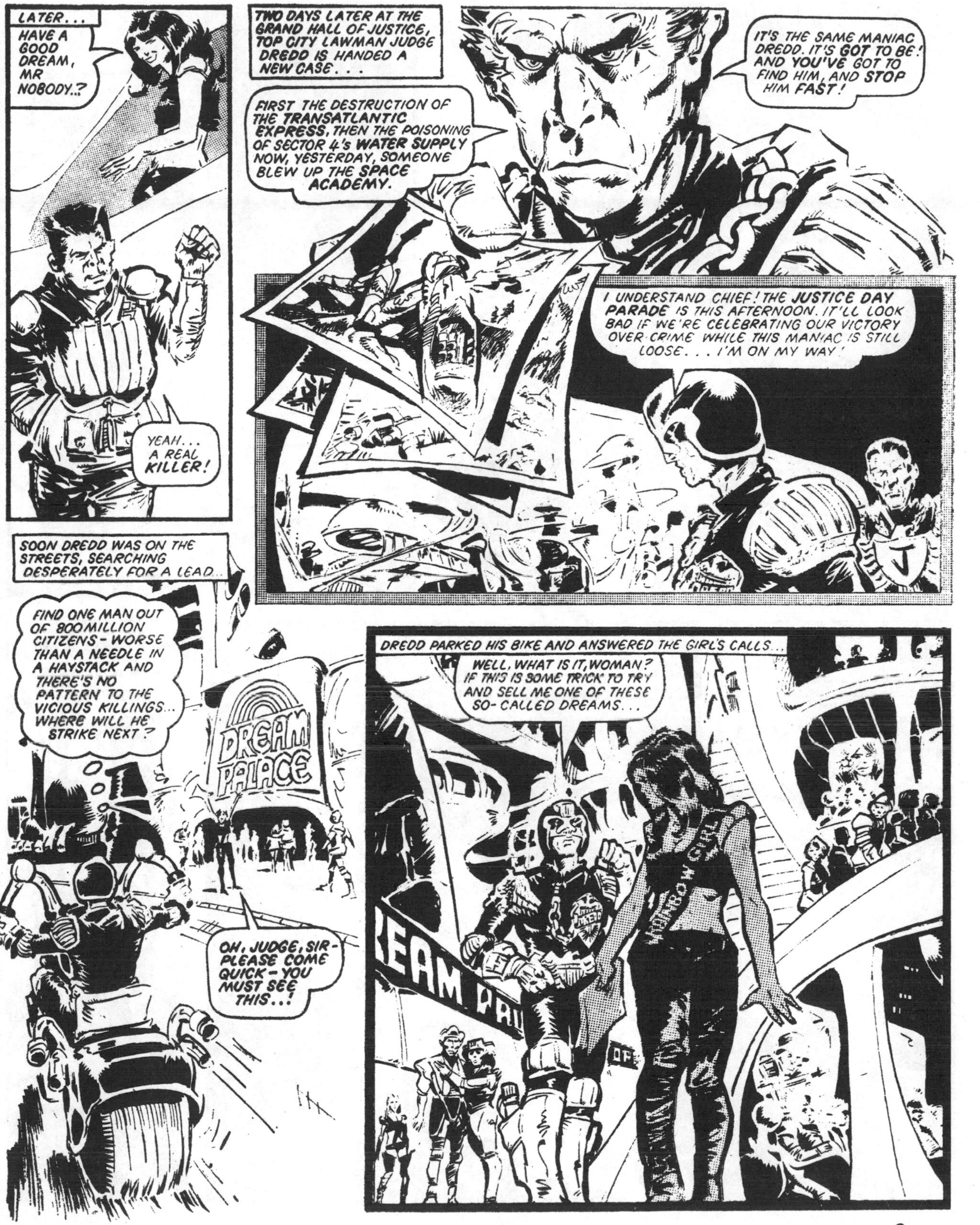

LATER...
HAVE A GOOD DREAM, MR NOBODY..?
YEAH... A REAL KILLER!
TWO DAYS LATER AT THE GRAND HALL OF JUSTICE, TOP CITY LAWMAN JUDGE DREDD IS HANDED A NEW CASE...
FIRST THE DESTRUCTION OF THE TRANSATLANTIC EXPRESS, THEN THE POISONING OF SECTOR 4's WATER SUPPLY NOW, YESTERDAY, SOMEONE BLEW UP THE SPACE ACADEMY.
IT'S THE SAME MANIAC DREDD. IT'S GOT TO BE! AND YOU'VE GOT TO FIND HIM, AND STOP HIM FAST!
I UNDERSTAND CHIEF! THE JUSTICE DAY PARADE IS THIS AFTERNOON. IT'LL LOOK BAD IF WE'RE CELEBRATING OUR VICTORY OVER CRIME WHILE THIS MANIAC IS STILL LOOSE... I'M ON MY WAY!
SOON DREDD WAS ON THE STREETS, SEARCHING DESPERATELY FOR A LEAD...
FIND ONE MAN OUT OF 800 MILLION CITIZENS - WORSE THAN A NEEDLE IN A HAYSTACK AND THERE'S NO PATTERN TO THE VICIOUS KILLINGS... WHERE WILL HE STRIKE NEXT?
DREAM PALACE
OH, JUDGE, SIR - PLEASE COME QUICK - YOU MUST SEE THIS...!
DREDD PARKED HIS BIKE AND ANSWERED THE GIRL'S CALLS...
WELL, WHAT IS IT, WOMAN? IF THIS IS SOME TRICK TO TRY AND SELL ME ONE OF THESE SO-CALLED DREAMS...
REAM PA

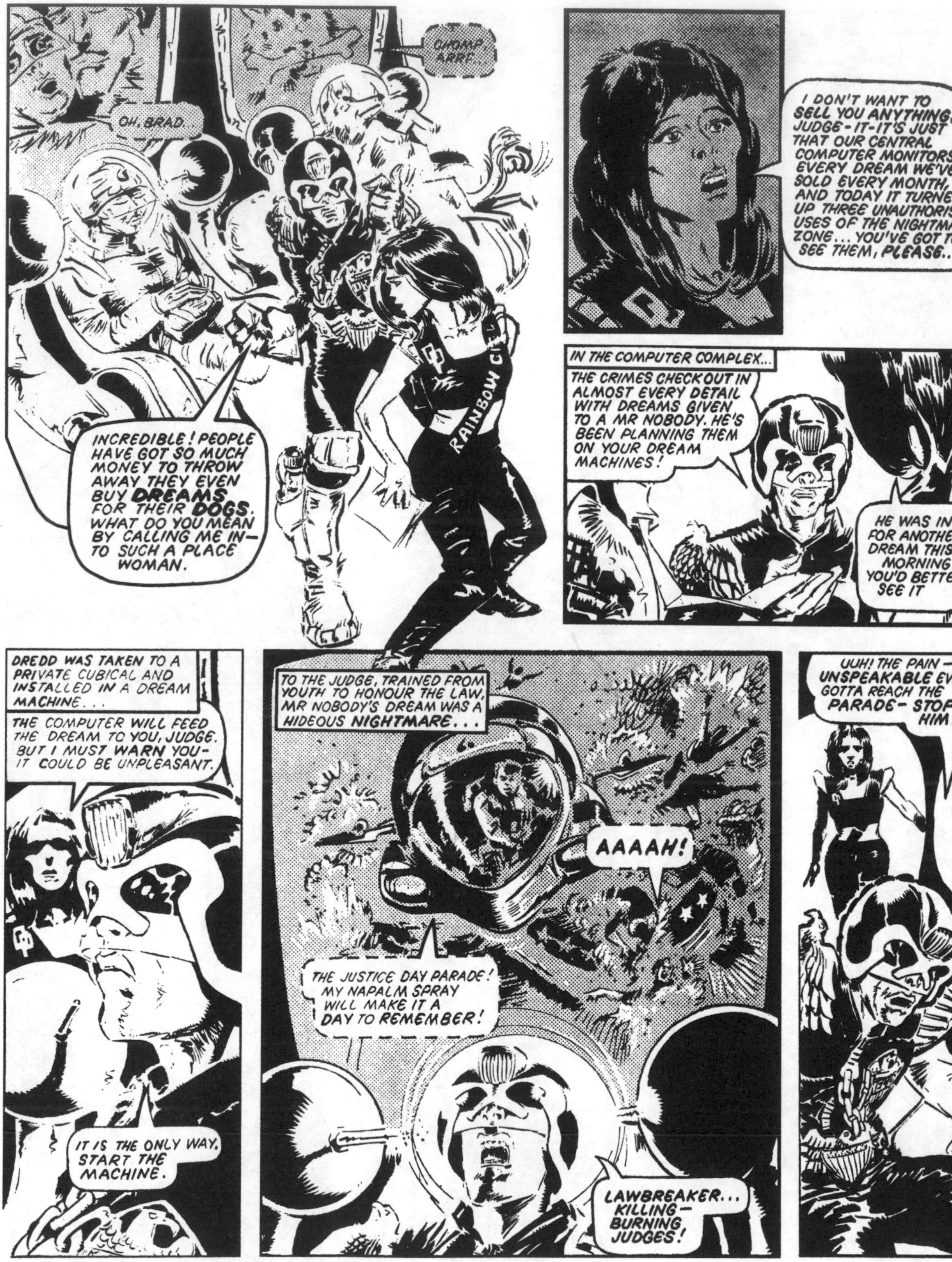
CHOMP ARRF
OH, BRAD...
INCREDIBLE! PEOPLE HAVE GOT SO MUCH MONEY TO THROW AWAY THEY EVEN BUY DREAMS FOR THEIR DOGS. WHAT DO YOU MEAN BY CALLING ME INTO SUCH A PLACE WOMAN.
RAINBOW
I DON'T WANT TO SELL YOU ANYTHING, JUDGE - IT-IT'S JUST THAT OUR CENTRAL COMPUTER MONITORS EVERY DREAM WE'VE SOLD EVERY MONTH, AND TODAY IT TURNED UP THREE UNAUTHORISED USES OF THE NIGHTMARE ZONE... YOU'VE GOT TO SEE THEM, PLEASE...
IN THE COMPUTER COMPLEX...
THE CRIMES CHECK OUT IN ALMOST EVERY DETAIL WITH DREAMS GIVEN TO A MR NOBODY. HE'S BEEN PLANNING THEM ON YOUR DREAM MACHINES!
HE WAS IN FOR ANOTHER DREAM THIS MORNING, YOU'D BETTER SEE IT
DREDD WAS TAKEN TO A PRIVATE CUBICAL AND INSTALLED IN A DREAM MACHINE...
THE COMPUTER WILL FEED THE DREAM TO YOU, JUDGE. BUT I MUST WARN YOU - IT COULD BE UNPLEASANT.
IT IS THE ONLY WAY. START THE MACHINE.
TO THE JUDGE, TRAINED FROM YOUTH TO HONOUR THE LAW, MR NOBODY'S DREAM WAS A HIDEOUS NIGHTMARE...
AAAAH!
THE JUSTICE DAY PARADE! MY NAPALM SPRAY WILL MAKE IT A DAY TO REMEMBER!
LAWBREAKER... KILLING - BURNING JUDGES!
UUH! THE PAIN - UNSPEAKABLE EVIL! GOTTA REACH THE PARADE - STOP HIM!

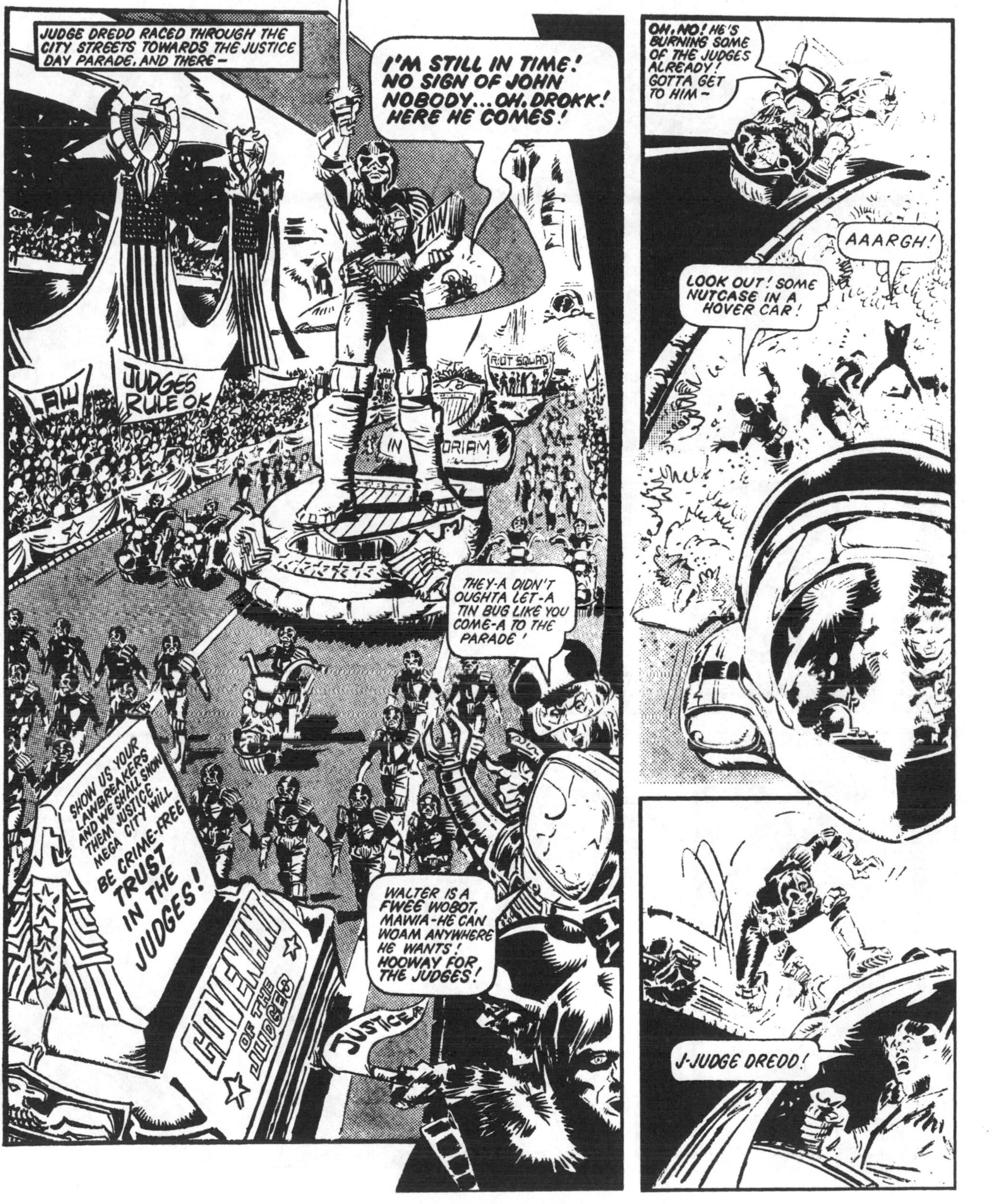

JUDGE DREDD RACED THROUGH THE CITY STREETS TOWARDS THE JUSTICE DAY PARADE, AND THERE—
I'M STILL IN TIME! NO SIGN OF JOHN NOBODY...OH, DROKK! HERE HE COMES!
LAW
LAW
JUDGES RULE OK
THEY-A DIDN'T OUGHTA LET-A TIN BUG LIKE YOU COME-A TO THE PARADE!
SHOW US YOUR LAWBREAKERS AND WE SHALL SHOW THEM JUSTICE. MEGA CITY WILL BE CRIME-FREE
TRUST IN THE JUDGES!
OF THE JUDGES
WALTER IS A FWEE WOBOT, MAWIA—HE CAN WOAM ANYWHERE HE WANTS! HOOWAY FOR THE JUDGES!
JUSTICE
OH, NO! HE'S BURNING SOME OF THE JUDGES ALREADY! GOTTA GET TO HIM—
AAARGH!
LOOK OUT! SOME NUTCASE IN A HOVER CAR!
J-JUDGE DREDD!

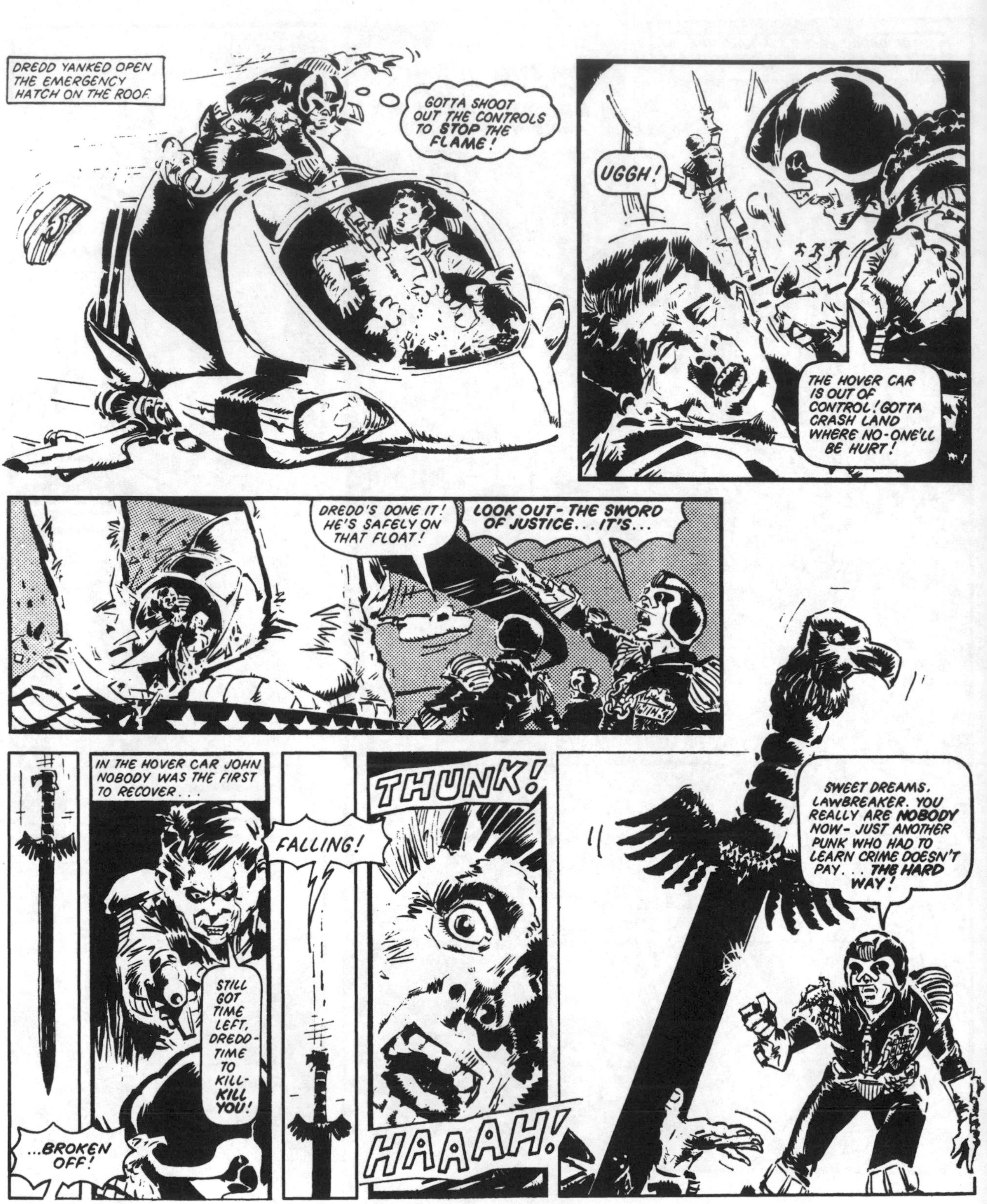

DREDD YANKED OPEN THE EMERGENCY HATCH ON THE ROOF.
GOTTA SHOOT OUT THE CONTROLS TO STOP THE FLAME!
UGGH!
THE HOVER CAR IS OUT OF CONTROL! GOTTA CRASH LAND WHERE NO-ONE'LL BE HURT!
DREDD'S DONE IT! HE'S SAFELY ON THAT FLOAT!
LOOK OUT- THE SWORD OF JUSTICE... IT'S...
...BROKEN OFF!
IN THE HOVER CAR JOHN NOBODY WAS THE FIRST TO RECOVER..
STILL GOT TIME LEFT, DREDD- TIME TO KILL- KILL YOU!
FALLING!
THUNK!
HAAAH!
SWEET DREAMS, LAWBREAKER. YOU REALLY ARE NOBODY NOW- JUST ANOTHER PUNK WHO HAD TO LEARN CRIME DOESN'T PAY... THE HARD WAY!

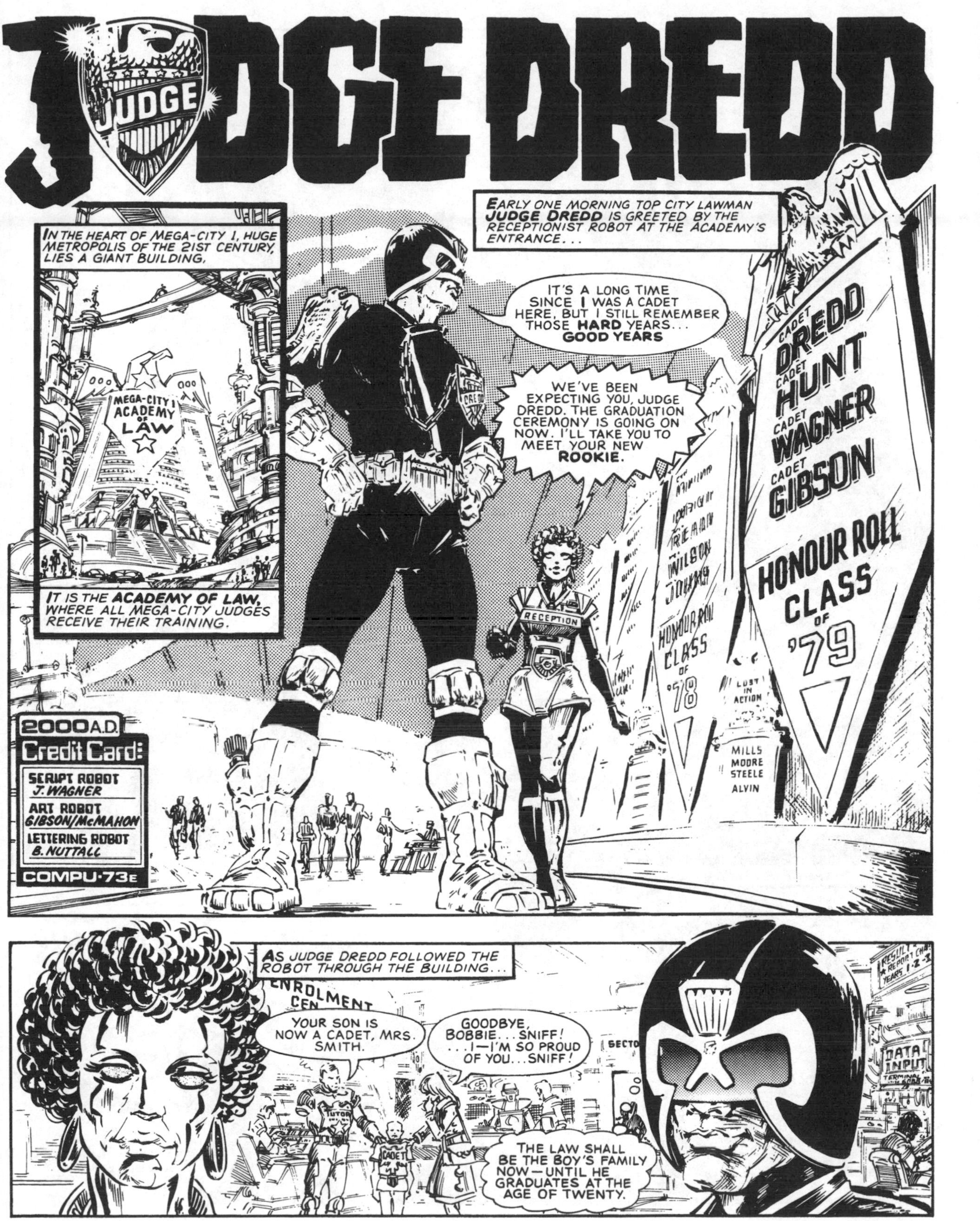
JUDGE DREDD
JUDGE
IN THE HEART OF MEGA-CITY 1, HUGE METROPOLIS OF THE 21ST CENTURY, LIES A GIANT BUILDING,
MEGA-CITY 1 ACADEMY OF LAW
IT IS THE ACADEMY OF LAW, WHERE ALL MEGA-CITY JUDGES RECEIVE THEIR TRAINING.
EARLY ONE MORNING TOP CITY LAWMAN JUDGE DREDD IS GREETED BY THE RECEPTIONIST ROBOT AT THE ACADEMY'S ENTRANCE...
IT'S A LONG TIME SINCE I WAS A CADET HERE, BUT I STILL REMEMBER THOSE HARD YEARS... GOOD YEARS
WE'VE BEEN EXPECTING YOU, JUDGE DREDD. THE GRADUATION CEREMONY IS GOING ON NOW. I'LL TAKE YOU TO MEET YOUR NEW ROOKIE.
RECEPTION
CADET DREDD
CADET HUNT
CADET WAGNER
CADET GIBSON
HONOUR ROLL CLASS OF '79
HONOUR ROLL CLASS OF '78
LOST IN ACTION
MILLS
MOORE
STEELE
ALVIN
2000 A.D.
Credit Card:
SCRIPT ROBOT J. WAGNER
ART ROBOT GIBSON/McMAHON
LETTERING ROBOT B. NUTTALL
COMPU-73E
AS JUDGE DREDD FOLLOWED THE ROBOT THROUGH THE BUILDING...
ENROLMENT CEN
YOUR SON IS NOW A CADET, MRS. SMITH.
GOODBYE, BOBBIE... SNIFF! ...I—I'M SO PROUD OF YOU... SNIFF!
TUTOR
CADET
DATA INPUT
THE LAW SHALL BE THE BOY'S FAMILY NOW—UNTIL HE GRADUATES AT THE AGE OF TWENTY.

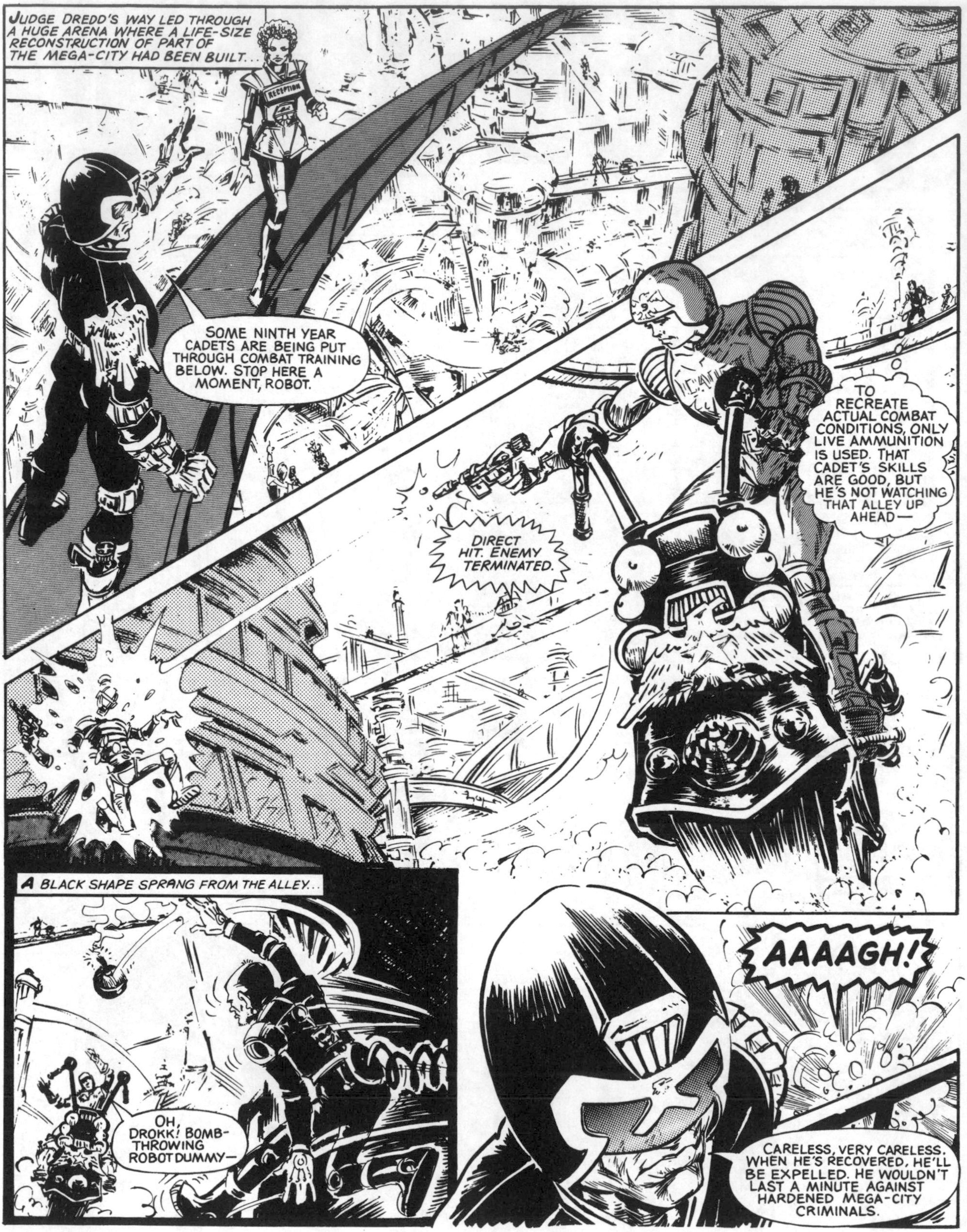
JUDGE DREDD'S WAY LED THROUGH A HUGE ARENA WHERE A LIFE-SIZE RECONSTRUCTION OF PART OF THE MEGA-CITY HAD BEEN BUILT...
RECEPTION
SOME NINTH YEAR CADETS ARE BEING PUT THROUGH COMBAT TRAINING BELOW. STOP HERE A MOMENT, ROBOT.
TO RECREATE ACTUAL COMBAT CONDITIONS, ONLY LIVE AMMUNITION IS USED. THAT CADET'S SKILLS ARE GOOD, BUT HE'S NOT WATCHING THAT ALLEY UP AHEAD—
DIRECT HIT. ENEMY TERMINATED.
A BLACK SHAPE SPRANG FROM THE ALLEY..
OH, DROKK! BOMB-THROWING ROBOT DUMMY—
AAAAGH!
CARELESS, VERY CARELESS. WHEN HE'S RECOVERED, HE'LL BE EXPELLED. HE WOULDN'T LAST A MINUTE AGAINST HARDENED MEGA-CITY CRIMINALS.

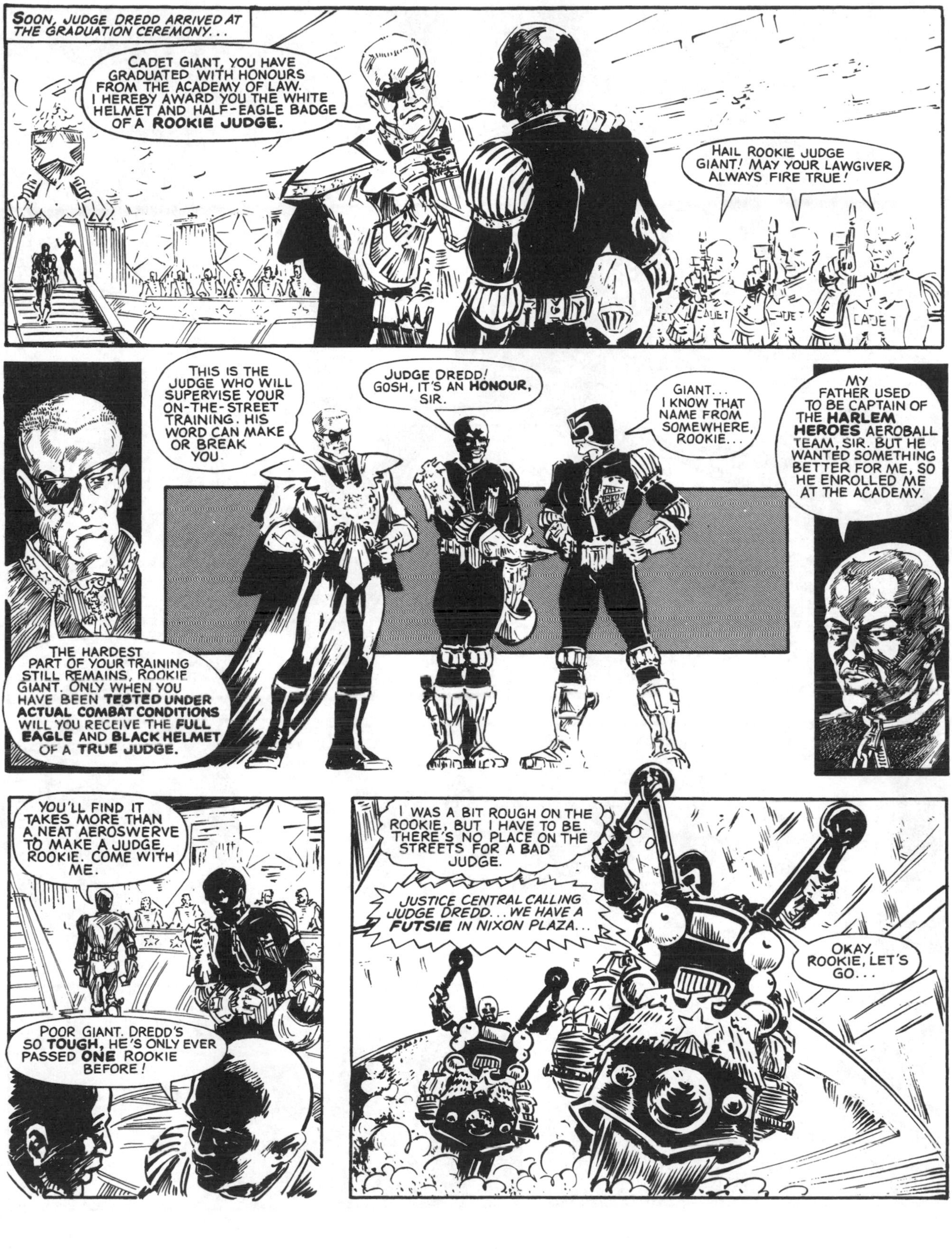
SOON, JUDGE DREDD ARRIVED AT THE GRADUATION CEREMONY...
CADET GIANT, YOU HAVE GRADUATED WITH HONOURS FROM THE ACADEMY OF LAW. I HEREBY AWARD YOU THE WHITE HELMET AND HALF-EAGLE BADGE OF A ROOKIE JUDGE.
HAIL ROOKIE JUDGE GIANT! MAY YOUR LAWGIVER ALWAYS FIRE TRUE!
CADET
CADET
CADET
THIS IS THE JUDGE WHO WILL SUPERVISE YOUR ON-THE-STREET TRAINING. HIS WORD CAN MAKE OR BREAK YOU.
JUDGE DREDD! GOSH, IT'S AN HONOUR, SIR.
GIANT... I KNOW THAT NAME FROM SOMEWHERE, ROOKIE...
MY FATHER USED TO BE CAPTAIN OF THE HARLEM HEROES AEROBALL TEAM, SIR. BUT HE WANTED SOMETHING BETTER FOR ME, SO HE ENROLLED ME AT THE ACADEMY.
THE HARDEST PART OF YOUR TRAINING STILL REMAINS, ROOKIE GIANT. ONLY WHEN YOU HAVE BEEN TESTED UNDER ACTUAL COMBAT CONDITIONS WILL YOU RECEIVE THE FULL EAGLE AND BLACK HELMET OF A TRUE JUDGE.
YOU'LL FIND IT TAKES MORE THAN A NEAT AEROSWERVE TO MAKE A JUDGE, ROOKIE. COME WITH ME.
POOR GIANT. DREDD'S SO TOUGH, HE'S ONLY EVER PASSED ONE ROOKIE BEFORE!
I WAS A BIT ROUGH ON THE ROOKIE, BUT I HAVE TO BE. THERE'S NO PLACE ON THE STREETS FOR A BAD JUDGE.
JUSTICE CENTRAL CALLING JUDGE DREDD... WE HAVE A FUTSIE IN NIXON PLAZA...
OKAY, ROOKIE, LET'S GO...

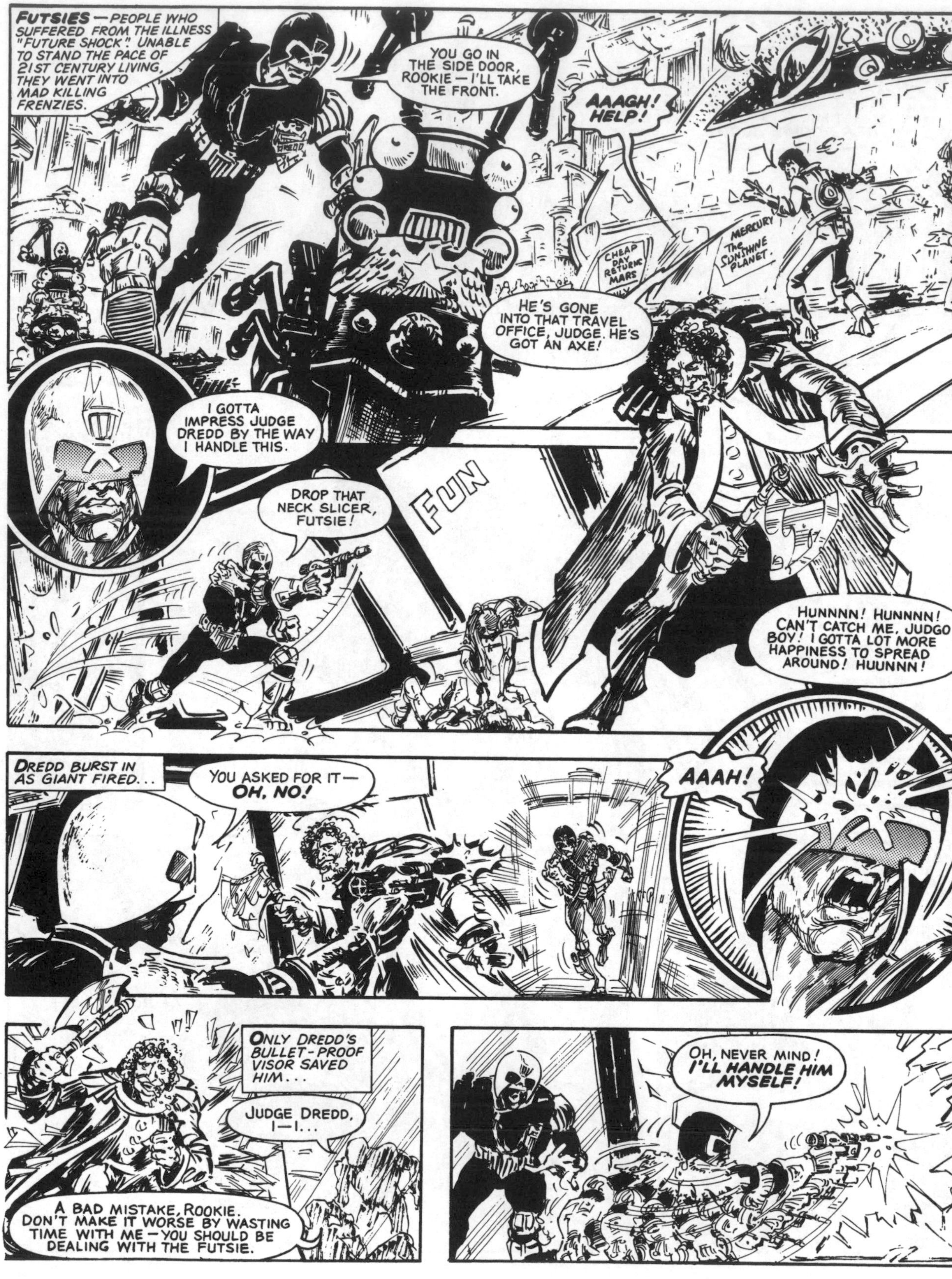

FUTSIES — PEOPLE WHO SUFFERED FROM THE ILLNESS "FUTURE SHOCK". UNABLE TO STAND THE PACE OF 21ST CENTURY LIVING, THEY WENT INTO MAD KILLING FRENZIES.
YOU GO IN THE SIDE DOOR, ROOKIE — I'LL TAKE THE FRONT.
AAAGH! HELP!
CHEAP DAY RETURNS MARS
MERCURY The SUNSHINE PLANET
HE'S GONE INTO THAT TRAVEL OFFICE, JUDGE. HE'S GOT AN AXE!
I GOTTA IMPRESS JUDGE DREDD BY THE WAY I HANDLE THIS.
DROP THAT NECK SLICER, FUTSIE!
FUN
HUNNNN! HUNNNN! CAN'T CATCH ME, JUDGO BOY! I GOTTA LOT MORE HAPPINESS TO SPREAD AROUND! HUUNNN!
DREDD BURST IN AS GIANT FIRED...
YOU ASKED FOR IT — OH, NO!
AAAH!
ONLY DREDD'S BULLET-PROOF VISOR SAVED HIM...
JUDGE DREDD, I—I...
A BAD MISTAKE, ROOKIE. DON'T MAKE IT WORSE BY WASTING TIME WITH ME — YOU SHOULD BE DEALING WITH THE FUTSIE.
OH, NEVER MIND! I'LL HANDLE HIM MYSELF!

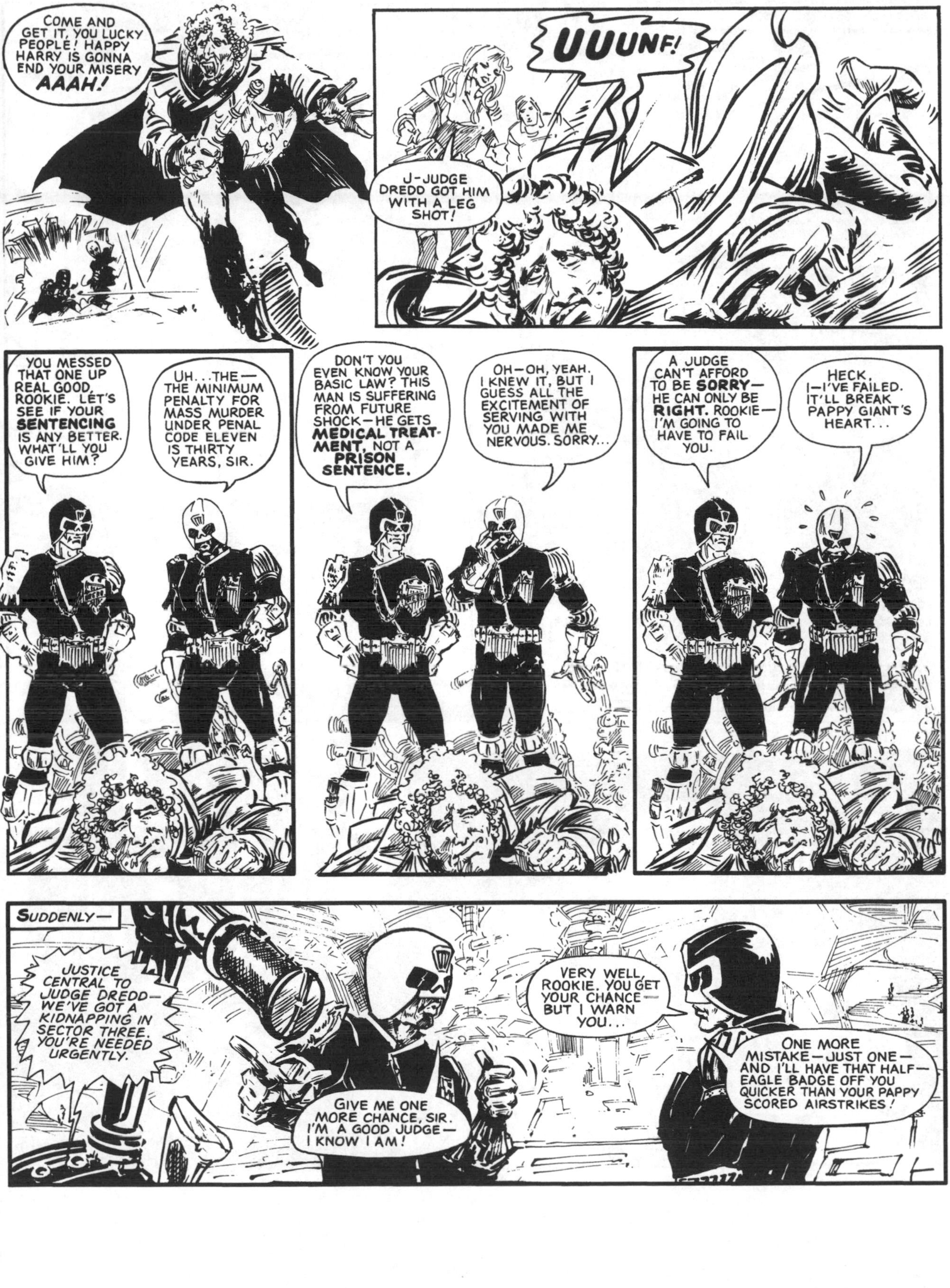

COME AND GET IT, YOU LUCKY PEOPLE! HAPPY HARRY IS GONNA END YOUR MISERY AAAH!
UUUNF!
J-JUDGE DREDD GOT HIM WITH A LEG SHOT!
YOU MESSED THAT ONE UP REAL GOOD, ROOKIE. LET'S SEE IF YOUR SENTENCING IS ANY BETTER. WHAT'LL YOU GIVE HIM?
UH...THE— THE MINIMUM PENALTY FOR MASS MURDER UNDER PENAL CODE ELEVEN IS THIRTY YEARS, SIR.
DON'T YOU EVEN KNOW YOUR BASIC LAW? THIS MAN IS SUFFERING FROM FUTURE SHOCK—HE GETS MEDICAL TREATMENT, NOT A PRISON SENTENCE.
OH—OH, YEAH. I KNEW IT, BUT I GUESS ALL THE EXCITEMENT OF SERVING WITH YOU MADE ME NERVOUS. SORRY...
A JUDGE CAN'T AFFORD TO BE SORRY— HE CAN ONLY BE RIGHT. ROOKIE— I'M GOING TO HAVE TO FAIL YOU.
HECK. I—I'VE FAILED. IT'LL BREAK PAPPY GIANT'S HEART...
SUDDENLY—
JUSTICE CENTRAL TO JUDGE DREDD— WE'VE GOT A KIDNAPPING IN SECTOR THREE. YOU'RE NEEDED URGENTLY.
GIVE ME ONE MORE CHANCE, SIR. I'M A GOOD JUDGE— I KNOW I AM!
VERY WELL, ROOKIE. YOU GET YOUR CHANCE— BUT I WARN YOU...
ONE MORE MISTAKE—JUST ONE— AND I'LL HAVE THAT HALF-EAGLE BADGE OFF YOU QUICKER THAN YOUR PAPPY SCORED AIRSTRIKES!

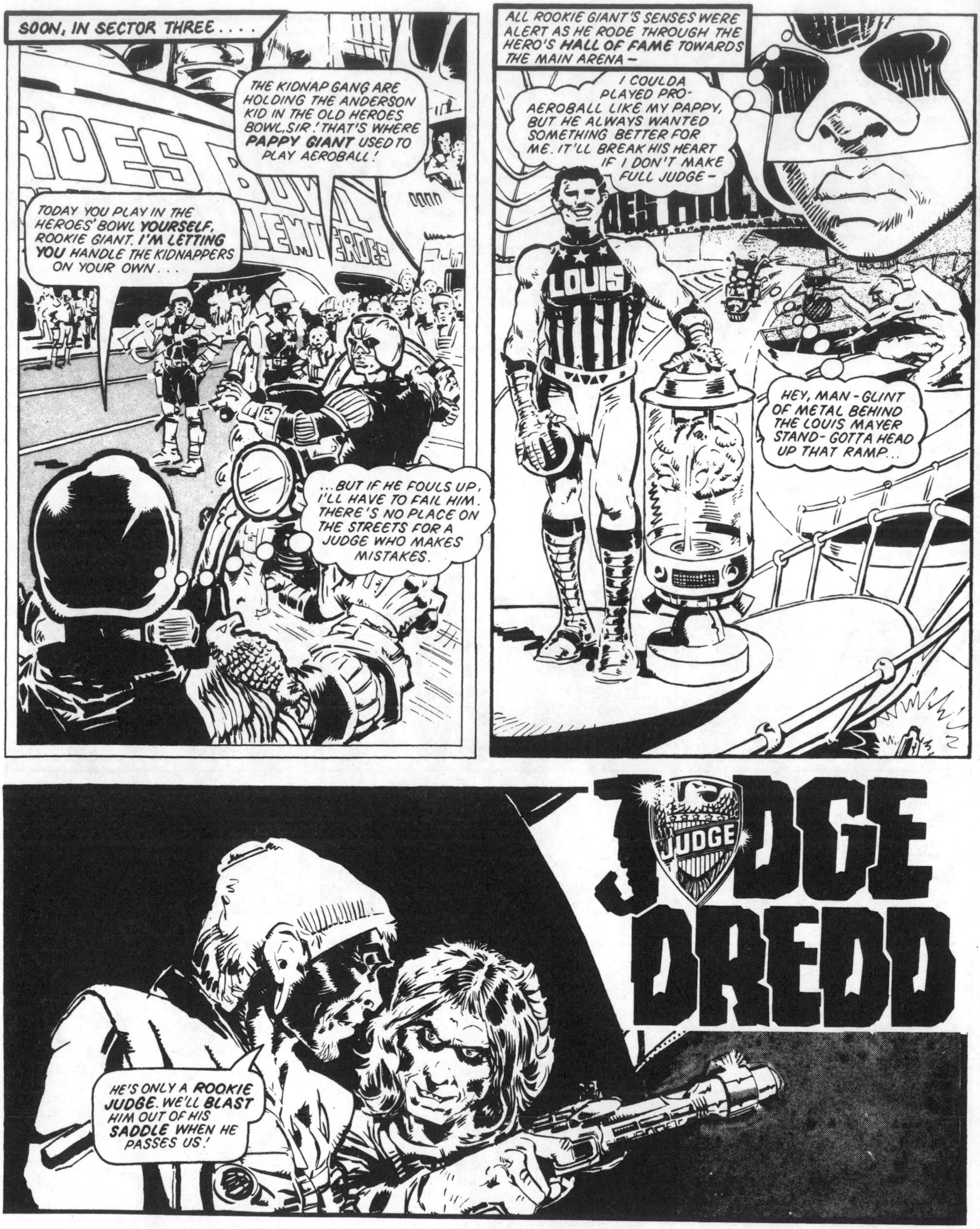
SOON, IN SECTOR THREE....
THE KIDNAP GANG ARE HOLDING THE ANDERSON KID IN THE OLD HEROES BOWL, SIR! THAT'S WHERE PAPPY GIANT USED TO PLAY AEROBALL!
TODAY YOU PLAY IN THE HEROES' BOWL YOURSELF, ROOKIE GIANT. I'M LETTING YOU HANDLE THE KIDNAPPERS ON YOUR OWN...
...BUT IF HE FOULS UP, I'LL HAVE TO FAIL HIM. THERE'S NO PLACE ON THE STREETS FOR A JUDGE WHO MAKES MISTAKES.
ALL ROOKIE GIANT'S SENSES WERE ALERT AS HE RODE THROUGH THE HERO'S HALL OF FAME TOWARDS THE MAIN ARENA –
I COULDA PLAYED PRO-AEROBALL LIKE MY PAPPY, BUT HE ALWAYS WANTED SOMETHING BETTER FOR ME. IT'LL BREAK HIS HEART IF I DON'T MAKE FULL JUDGE –
LOUIS
HEY, MAN – GLINT OF METAL BEHIND THE LOUIS MAYER STAND – GOTTA HEAD UP THAT RAMP...
JUDGE
JUDGE DREDD
HE'S ONLY A ROOKIE JUDGE. WE'LL BLAST HIM OUT OF HIS SADDLE WHEN HE PASSES US!

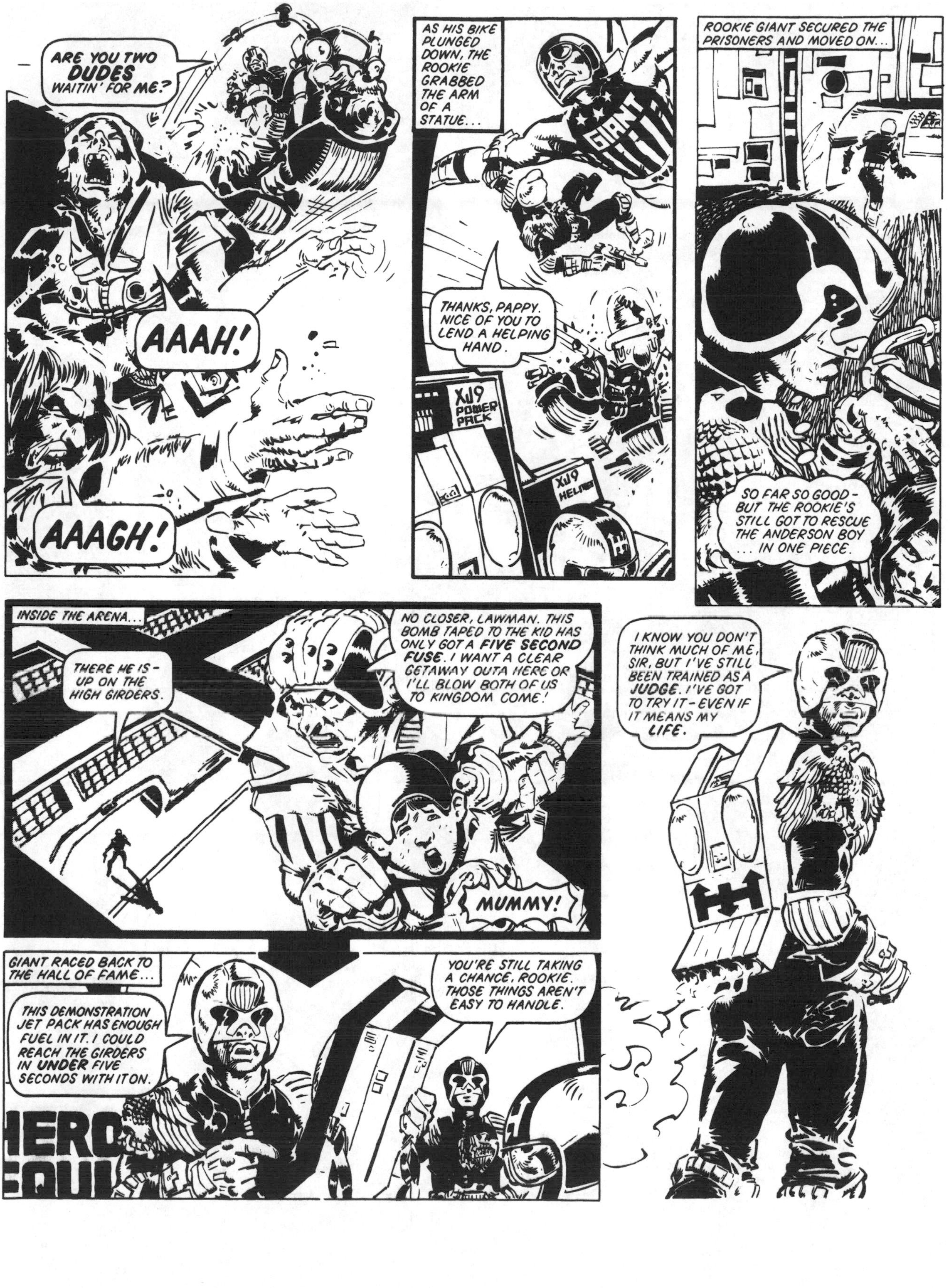
ARE YOU TWO DUDES WAITIN' FOR ME?
AAAH!
AAAGH!
AS HIS BIKE PLUNGED DOWN, THE ROOKIE GRABBED THE ARM OF A STATUE...
GIANT
THANKS, PAPPY. NICE OF YOU TO LEND A HELPING HAND.
XJ9 POWER PACK
ROOKIE GIANT SECURED THE PRISONERS AND MOVED ON...
SO FAR SO GOOD - BUT THE ROOKIE'S STILL GOT TO RESCUE THE ANDERSON BOY ... IN ONE PIECE.
INSIDE THE ARENA...
THERE HE IS - UP ON THE HIGH GIRDERS.
NO CLOSER, LAWMAN. THIS BOMB TAPED TO THE KID HAS ONLY GOT A FIVE SECOND FUSE. I WANT A CLEAR GETAWAY OUTA HERE OR I'LL BLOW BOTH OF US TO KINGDOM COME!
MUMMY!
GIANT RACED BACK TO THE HALL OF FAME...
THIS DEMONSTRATION JET PACK HAS ENOUGH FUEL IN IT. I COULD REACH THE GIRDERS IN UNDER FIVE SECONDS WITH IT ON.
YOU'RE STILL TAKING A CHANCE, ROOKIE. THOSE THINGS AREN'T EASY TO HANDLE.
I KNOW YOU DON'T THINK MUCH OF ME, SIR, BUT I'VE STILL BEEN TRAINED AS A JUDGE. I'VE GOT TO TRY IT - EVEN IF IT MEANS MY LIFE.
HERO SQU

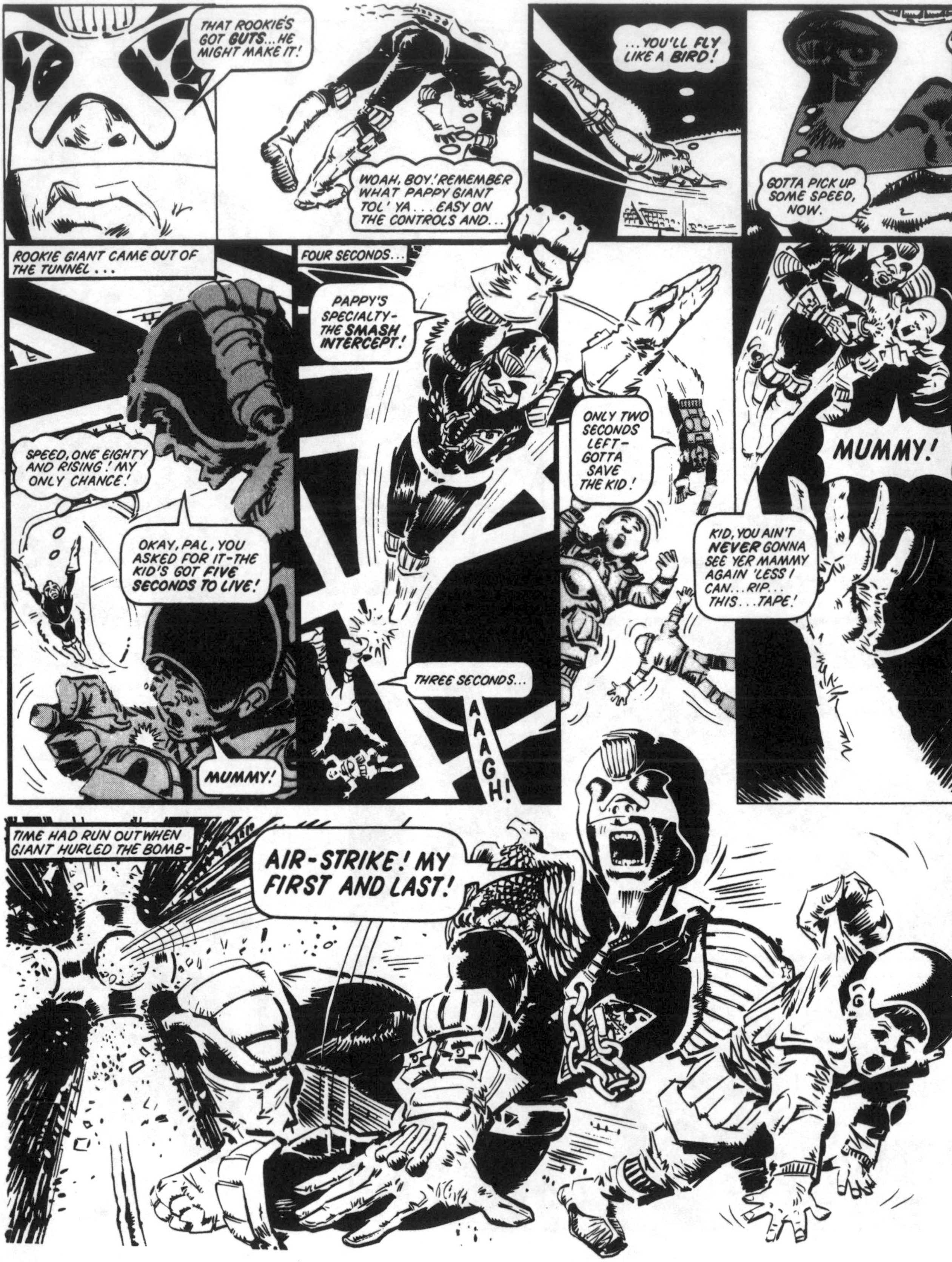
THAT ROOKIE'S GOT GUTS... HE MIGHT MAKE IT!
WOAH, BOY! REMEMBER WHAT PAPPY GIANT TOL' YA . . . EASY ON THE CONTROLS AND. . .
. . . YOU'LL FLY LIKE A BIRD!
GOTTA PICK UP SOME SPEED, NOW.
ROOKIE GIANT CAME OUT OF THE TUNNEL . . .
SPEED, ONE EIGHTY AND RISING! MY ONLY CHANCE!
OKAY, PAL, YOU ASKED FOR IT-THE KID'S GOT FIVE SECONDS TO LIVE!
MUMMY!
FOUR SECONDS. . .
PAPPY'S SPECIALTY-THE SMASH INTERCEPT!
THREE SECONDS. . .
AAAGH!
ONLY TWO SECONDS LEFT-GOTTA SAVE THE KID!
MUMMY!
KID, YOU AIN'T NEVER GONNA SEE YER MAMMY AGAIN 'LESS I CAN. . .RIP. . . THIS. . .TAPE!
TIME HAD RUN OUT WHEN GIANT HURLED THE BOMB-
AIR-STRIKE! MY FIRST AND LAST!

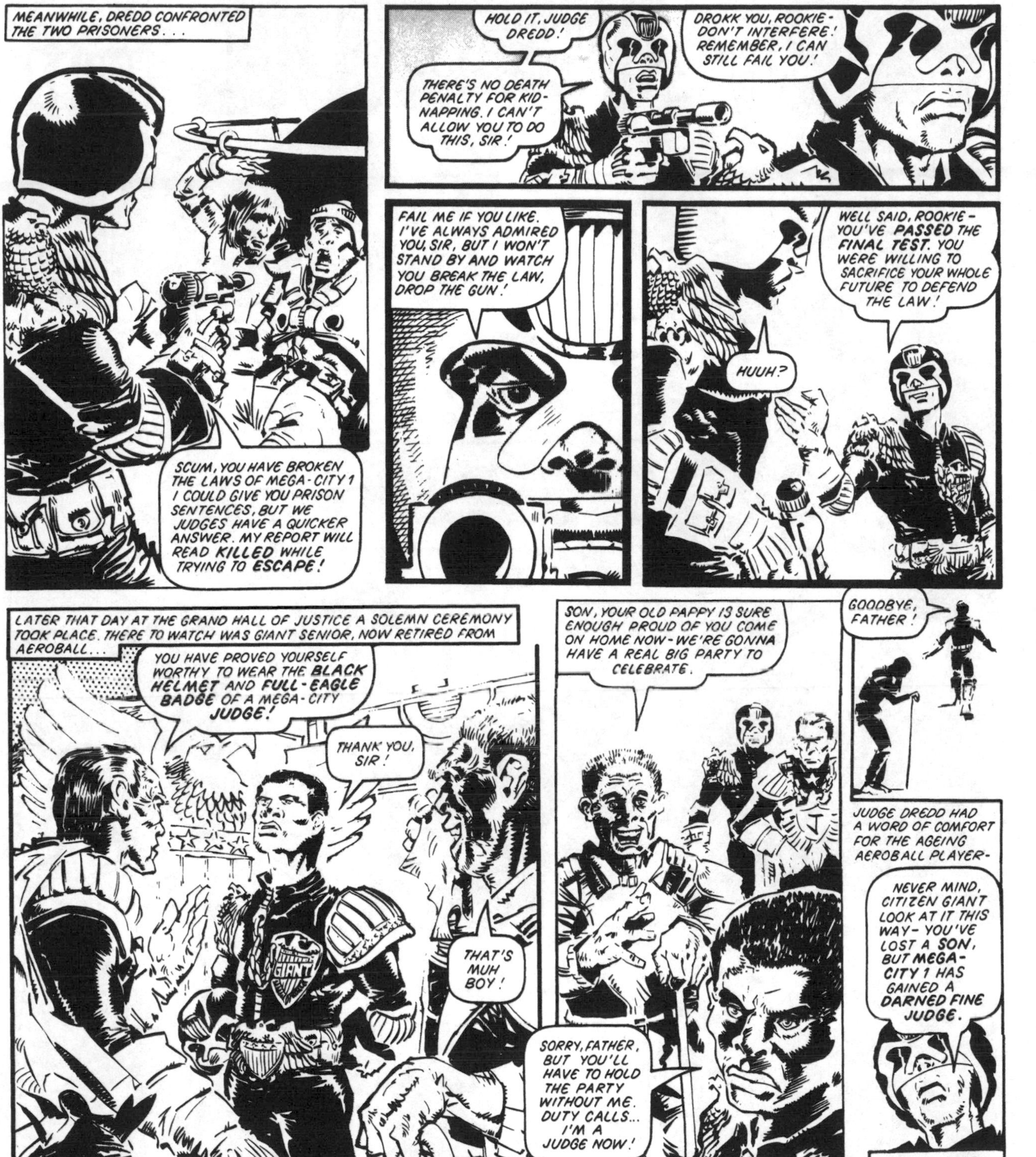
MEANWHILE, DREDD CONFRONTED THE TWO PRISONERS...
SCUM, YOU HAVE BROKEN THE LAWS OF MEGA-CITY 1 I COULD GIVE YOU PRISON SENTENCES, BUT WE JUDGES HAVE A QUICKER ANSWER. MY REPORT WILL READ KILLED WHILE TRYING TO ESCAPE!
HOLD IT, JUDGE DREDD!
THERE'S NO DEATH PENALTY FOR KID-NAPPING. I CAN'T ALLOW YOU TO DO THIS, SIR!
DROKK YOU, ROOKIE - DON'T INTERFERE! REMEMBER, I CAN STILL FAIL YOU!
FAIL ME IF YOU LIKE. I'VE ALWAYS ADMIRED YOU, SIR, BUT I WON'T STAND BY AND WATCH YOU BREAK THE LAW, DROP THE GUN!
WELL SAID, ROOKIE - YOU'VE PASSED THE FINAL TEST. YOU WERE WILLING TO SACRIFICE YOUR WHOLE FUTURE TO DEFEND THE LAW!
HUUH?
LATER THAT DAY AT THE GRAND HALL OF JUSTICE A SOLEMN CEREMONY TOOK PLACE. THERE TO WATCH WAS GIANT SENIOR, NOW RETIRED FROM AEROBALL...
YOU HAVE PROVED YOURSELF WORTHY TO WEAR THE BLACK HELMET AND FULL-EAGLE BADGE OF A MEGA-CITY JUDGE!
THANK YOU, SIR!
THAT'S MUH BOY!
SON, YOUR OLD PAPPY IS SURE ENOUGH PROUD OF YOU COME ON HOME NOW - WE'RE GONNA HAVE A REAL BIG PARTY TO CELEBRATE.
SORRY, FATHER, BUT YOU'LL HAVE TO HOLD THE PARTY WITHOUT ME. DUTY CALLS... I'M A JUDGE NOW!
GOODBYE, FATHER!
JUDGE DREDD HAD A WORD OF COMFORT FOR THE AGEING AEROBALL PLAYER-
NEVER MIND, CITIZEN GIANT LOOK AT IT THIS WAY - YOU'VE LOST A SON, BUT MEGA-CITY 1 HAS GAINED A DARNED FINE JUDGE.
THE END.

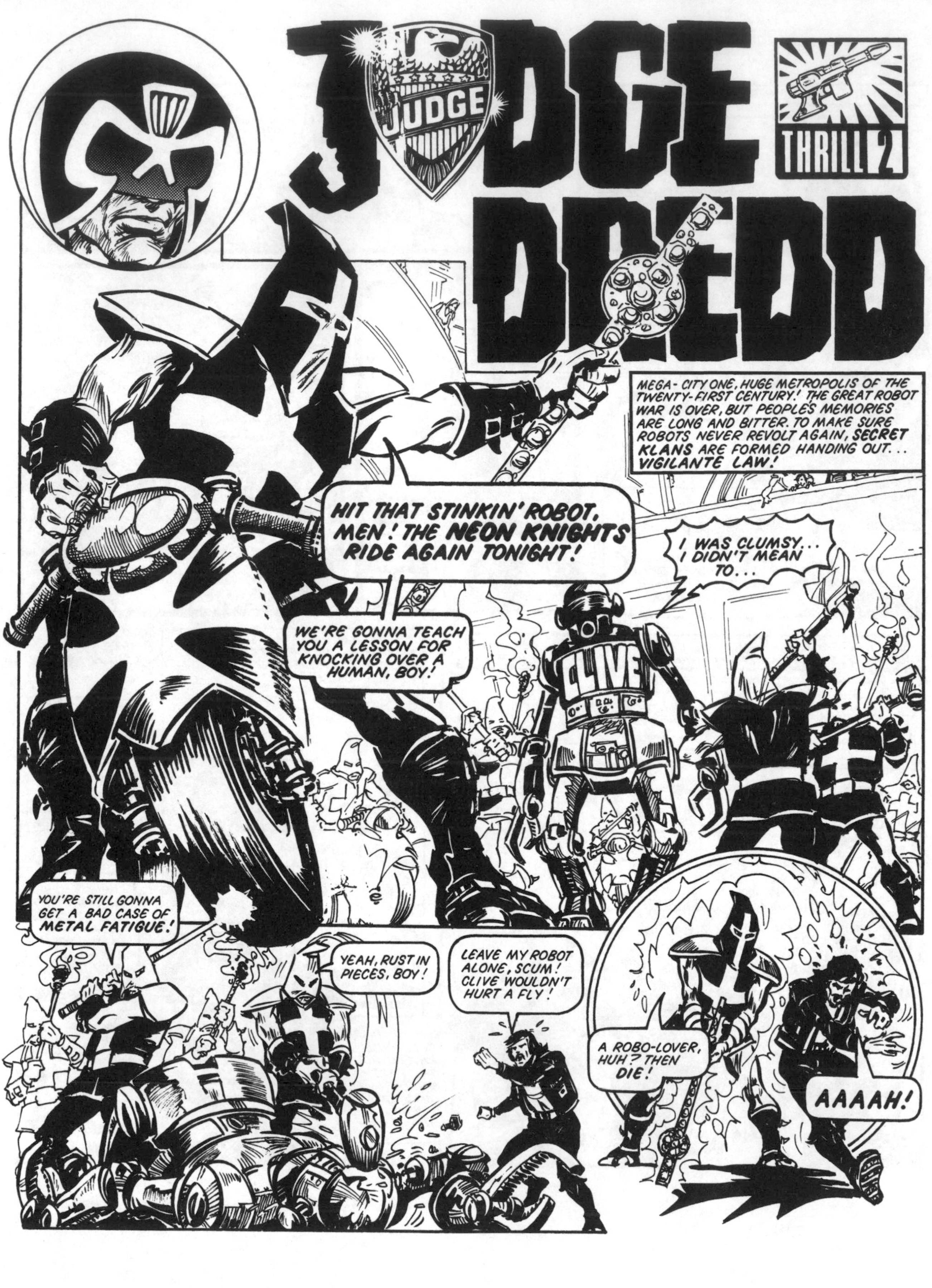
JUDGE
JUDGE DREDD
THRILL 2
MEGA-CITY ONE, HUGE METROPOLIS OF THE TWENTY-FIRST CENTURY! THE GREAT ROBOT WAR IS OVER, BUT PEOPLE'S MEMORIES ARE LONG AND BITTER. TO MAKE SURE ROBOTS NEVER REVOLT AGAIN, SECRET KLANS ARE FORMED HANDING OUT... VIGILANTE LAW!
HIT THAT STINKIN' ROBOT, MEN! THE NEON KNIGHTS RIDE AGAIN TONIGHT!
WE'RE GONNA TEACH YOU A LESSON FOR KNOCKING OVER A HUMAN, BOY!
I WAS CLUMSY... I DIDN'T MEAN TO...
CLIVE
YOU'RE STILL GONNA GET A BAD CASE OF METAL FATIGUE!
YEAH, RUST IN PIECES, BOY!
LEAVE MY ROBOT ALONE, SCUM! CLIVE WOULDN'T HURT A FLY!
A ROBO-LOVER, HUH? THEN DIE!
AAAAH!

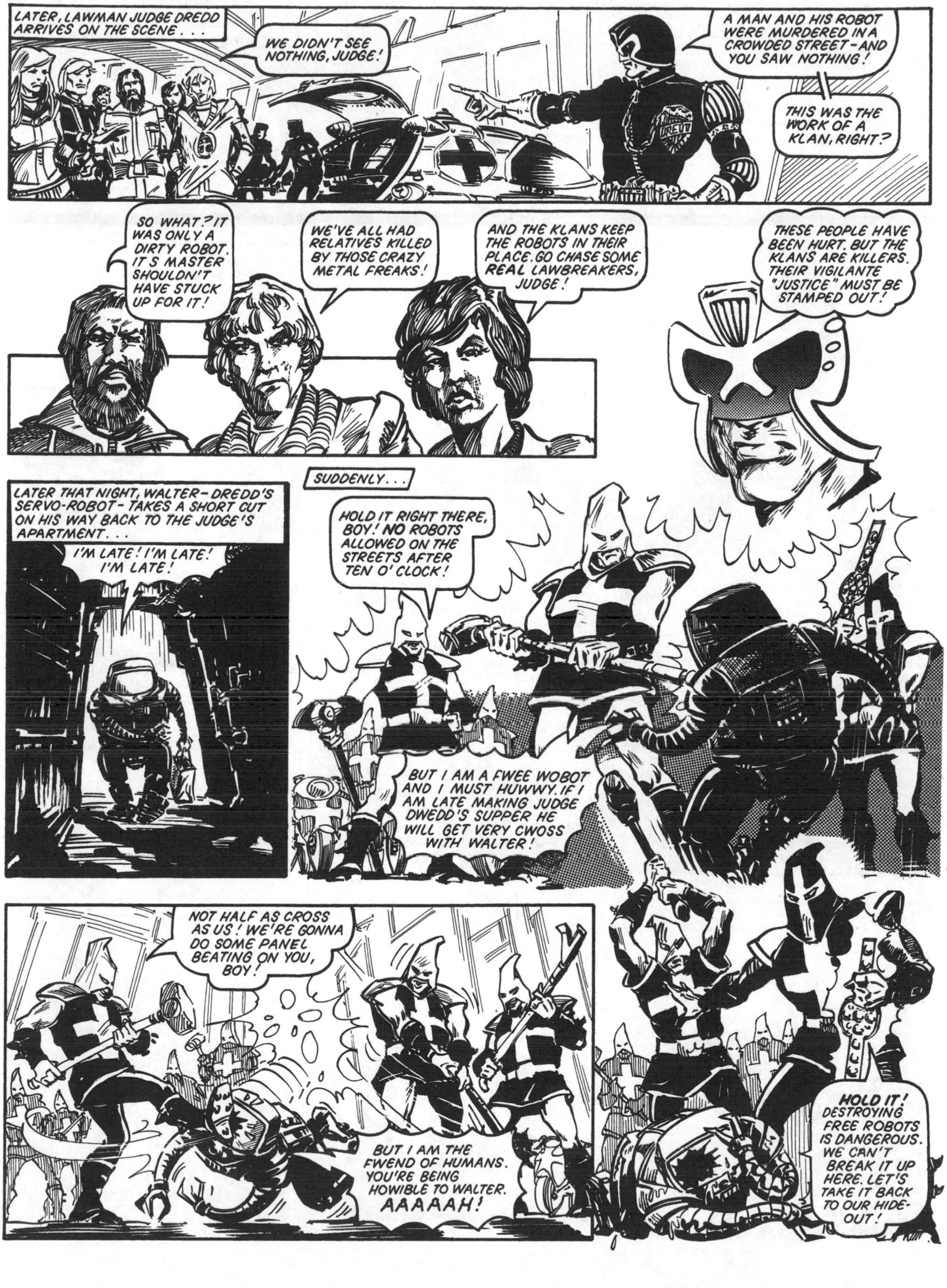
LATER, LAWMAN JUDGE DREDD ARRIVES ON THE SCENE . . .
WE DIDN'T SEE NOTHING, JUDGE!
A MAN AND HIS ROBOT WERE MURDERED IN A CROWDED STREET - AND YOU SAW NOTHING!
THIS WAS THE WORK OF A KLAN, RIGHT?
SO WHAT? IT WAS ONLY A DIRTY ROBOT. IT'S MASTER SHOULDN'T HAVE STUCK UP FOR IT!
WE'VE ALL HAD RELATIVES KILLED BY THOSE CRAZY METAL FREAKS!
AND THE KLANS KEEP THE ROBOTS IN THEIR PLACE. GO CHASE SOME REAL LAWBREAKERS, JUDGE!
THESE PEOPLE HAVE BEEN HURT. BUT THE KLANS ARE KILLERS. THEIR VIGILANTE "JUSTICE" MUST BE STAMPED OUT!
LATER THAT NIGHT, WALTER - DREDD'S SERVO-ROBOT - TAKES A SHORT CUT ON HIS WAY BACK TO THE JUDGE'S APARTMENT . . .
I'M LATE! I'M LATE! I'M LATE!
SUDDENLY . . .
HOLD IT RIGHT THERE, BOY! NO ROBOTS ALLOWED ON THE STREETS AFTER TEN O' CLOCK!
BUT I AM A FWEE WOBOT AND I MUST HUWWY. IF I AM LATE MAKING JUDGE DWEDD'S SUPPER HE WILL GET VERY CWOSS WITH WALTER!
NOT HALF AS CROSS AS US! WE'RE GONNA DO SOME PANEL BEATING ON YOU, BOY!
BUT I AM THE FWEND OF HUMANS. YOU'RE BEING HOWIBLE TO WALTER. AAAAAH!
HOLD IT! DESTROYING FREE ROBOTS IS DANGEROUS. WE CAN'T BREAK IT UP HERE. LET'S TAKE IT BACK TO OUR HIDE-OUT!

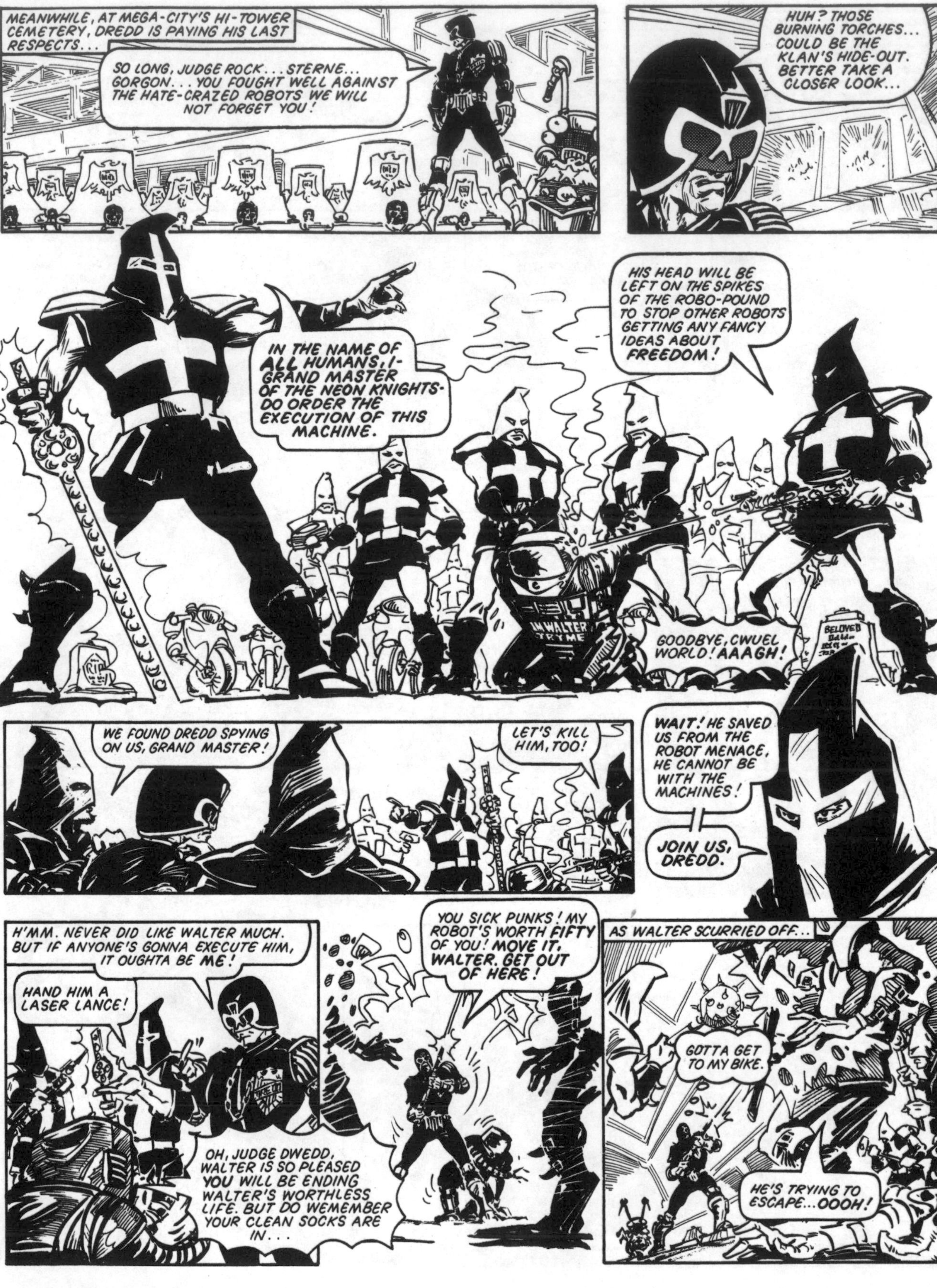
MEANWHILE, AT MEGA-CITY'S HI-TOWER CEMETERY, DREDD IS PAYING HIS LAST RESPECTS...
SO LONG, JUDGE ROCK... STERNE... GORGON... YOU FOUGHT WELL AGAINST THE HATE-CRAZED ROBOTS WE WILL NOT FORGET YOU!
HUH? THOSE BURNING TORCHES... COULD BE THE KLAN'S HIDE-OUT. BETTER TAKE A CLOSER LOOK...
IN THE NAME OF ALL HUMANS, I- GRAND MASTER OF THE NEON KNIGHTS- DO ORDER THE EXECUTION OF THIS MACHINE.
HIS HEAD WILL BE LEFT ON THE SPIKES OF THE ROBO-POUND TO STOP OTHER ROBOTS GETTING ANY FANCY IDEAS ABOUT FREEDOM!
GOODBYE, CWUEL WORLD! AAAGH!
WE FOUND DREDD SPYING ON US, GRAND MASTER!
LET'S KILL HIM, TOO!
WAIT! HE SAVED US FROM THE ROBOT MENACE, HE CANNOT BE WITH THE MACHINES!
JOIN US, DREDD.
H'MM. NEVER DID LIKE WALTER MUCH. BUT IF ANYONE'S GONNA EXECUTE HIM, IT OUGHTA BE ME!
HAND HIM A LASER LANCE!
OH, JUDGE DWEDD, WALTER IS SO PLEASED YOU WILL BE ENDING WALTER'S WORTHLESS LIFE. BUT DO WEMEMBER YOUR CLEAN SOCKS ARE IN...
YOU SICK PUNKS! MY ROBOT'S WORTH FIFTY OF YOU! MOVE IT, WALTER. GET OUT OF HERE!
AS WALTER SCURRIED OFF...
GOTTA GET TO MY BIKE.
HE'S TRYING TO ESCAPE...OOOH!

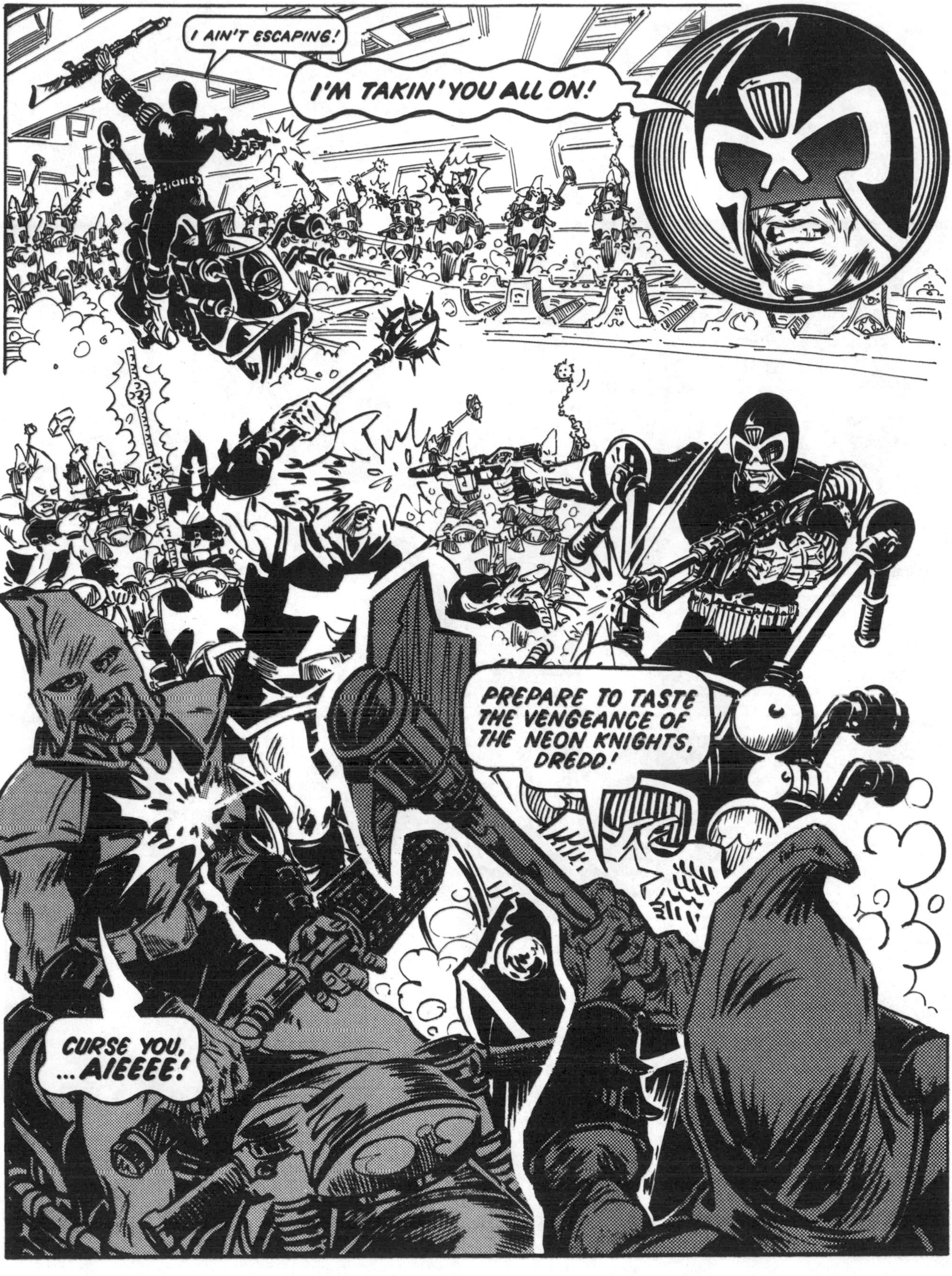
I AIN'T ESCAPING!
I'M TAKIN' YOU ALL ON!
PREPARE TO TASTE THE VENGEANCE OF THE NEON KNIGHTS, DREDD!
CURSE YOU, ...AIEEEE!

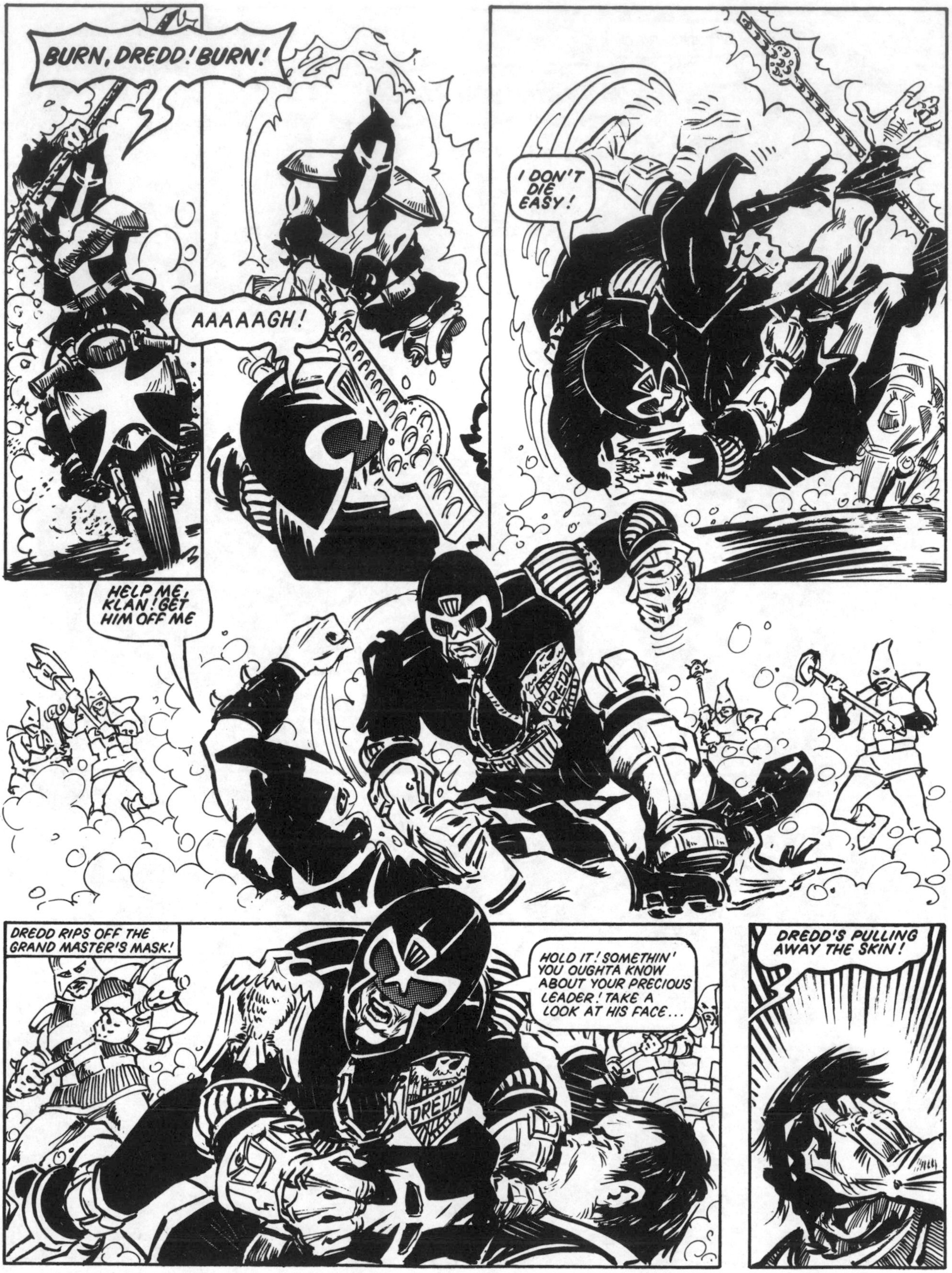
BURN, DREDD! BURN!
AAAAAGH!
I DON'T DIE EASY!
HELP ME, KLAN! GET HIM OFF ME
DREDD RIPS OFF THE GRAND MASTER'S MASK!
HOLD IT! SOMETHIN' YOU OUGHTA KNOW ABOUT YOUR PRECIOUS LEADER! TAKE A LOOK AT HIS FACE...
DREDD'S PULLING AWAY THE SKIN!
DREDD
DREDD

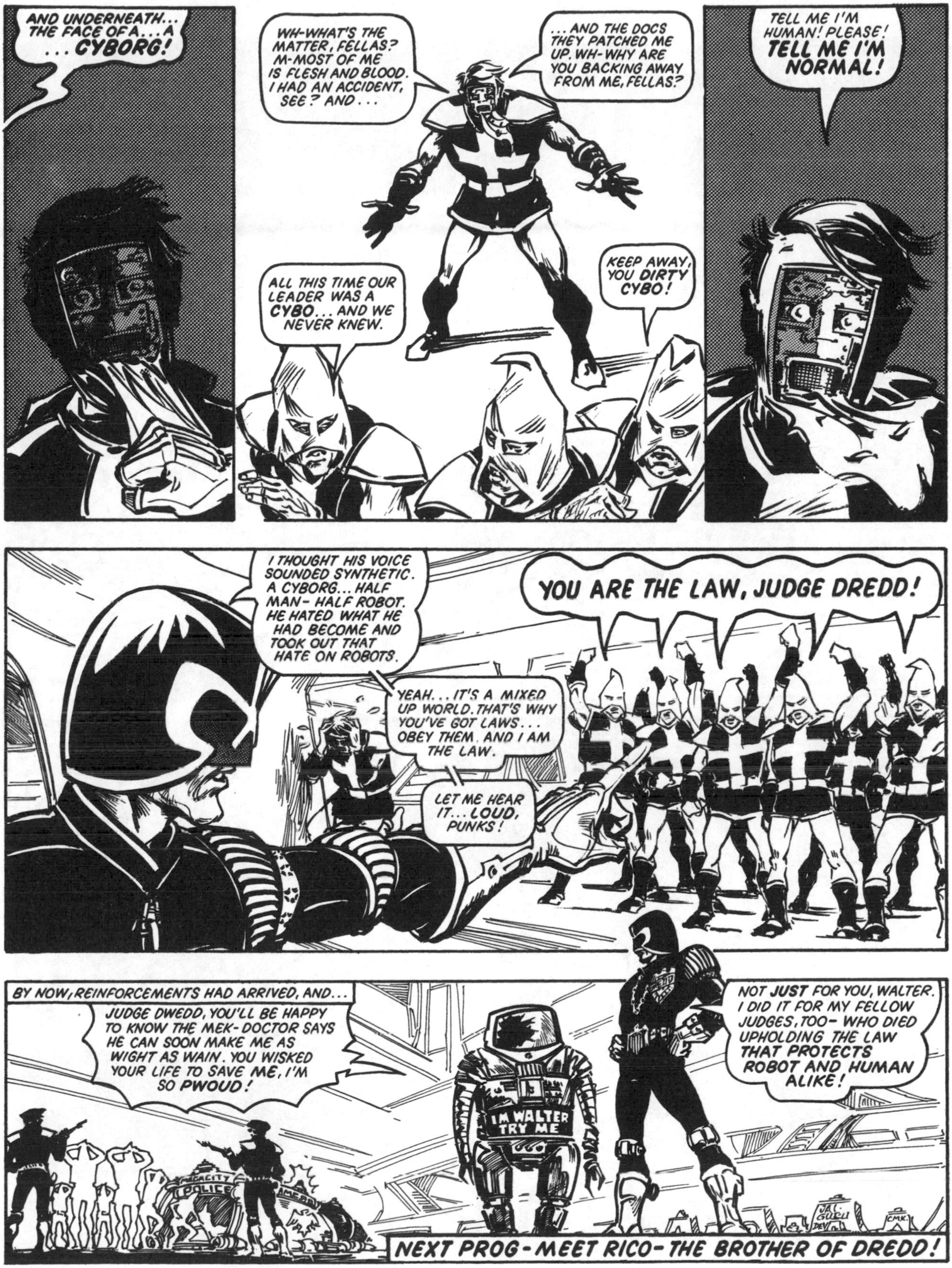

AND UNDERNEATH... THE FACE OF A... A ... CYBORG!
WH-WHAT'S THE MATTER, FELLAS? M-MOST OF ME IS FLESH AND BLOOD. I HAD AN ACCIDENT, SEE? AND...
...AND THE DOCS THEY PATCHED ME UP. WH-WHY ARE YOU BACKING AWAY FROM ME, FELLAS?
ALL THIS TIME OUR LEADER WAS A CYBO... AND WE NEVER KNEW.
KEEP AWAY, YOU DIRTY CYBO!
TELL ME I'M HUMAN! PLEASE! TELL ME I'M NORMAL!
I THOUGHT HIS VOICE SOUNDED SYNTHETIC. A CYBORG... HALF MAN- HALF ROBOT. HE HATED WHAT HE HAD BECOME AND TOOK OUT THAT HATE ON ROBOTS.
YEAH... IT'S A MIXED UP WORLD. THAT'S WHY YOU'VE GOT LAWS... OBEY THEM. AND I AM THE LAW.
LET ME HEAR IT... LOUD, PUNKS!
YOU ARE THE LAW, JUDGE DREDD!
BY NOW, REINFORCEMENTS HAD ARRIVED, AND...
JUDGE DWEDD, YOU'LL BE HAPPY TO KNOW THE MEK-DOCTOR SAYS HE CAN SOON MAKE ME AS WIGHT AS WAIN. YOU WISKED YOUR LIFE TO SAVE ME, I'M SO PWOUD!
NOT JUST FOR YOU, WALTER. I DID IT FOR MY FELLOW JUDGES, TOO- WHO DIED UPHOLDING THE LAW THAT PROTECTS ROBOT AND HUMAN ALIKE!
I'M WALTER TRY ME
POLICE
NEXT PROG - MEET RICO - THE BROTHER OF DREDD!

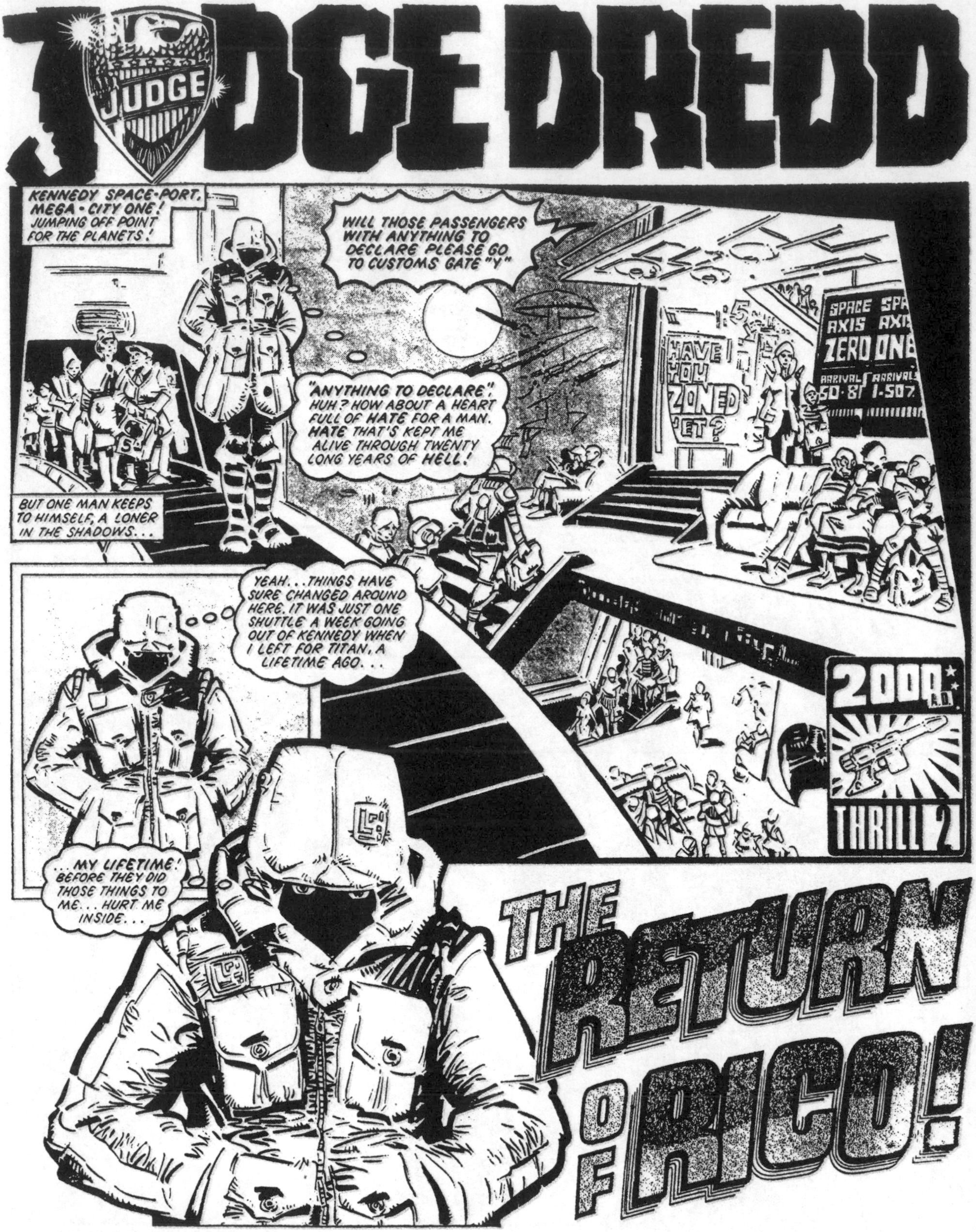
JUDGE DREDD
JUDGE
KENNEDY SPACE-PORT, MEGA-CITY ONE! JUMPING OFF POINT FOR THE PLANETS!
WILL THOSE PASSENGERS WITH ANYTHING TO DECLARE PLEASE GO TO CUSTOMS GATE "Y"
"ANYTHING TO DECLARE", HUH? HOW ABOUT A HEART FULL OF HATE FOR A MAN. HATE THAT'S KEPT ME ALIVE THROUGH TWENTY LONG YEARS OF HELL!
BUT ONE MAN KEEPS TO HIMSELF, A LONER IN THE SHADOWS...
HAVE YOU ZONED YET?
SPACE AXIS ZERO
SPA AXIS ONE
ARRIVALS
YEAH... THINGS HAVE SURE CHANGED AROUND HERE. IT WAS JUST ONE SHUTTLE A WEEK GOING OUT OF KENNEDY WHEN I LEFT FOR TITAN, A LIFETIME AGO...
2000 A.D.
THRILL 2
...MY LIFETIME! BEFORE THEY DID THOSE THINGS TO ME... HURT ME INSIDE...
THE RETURN OF RICO!

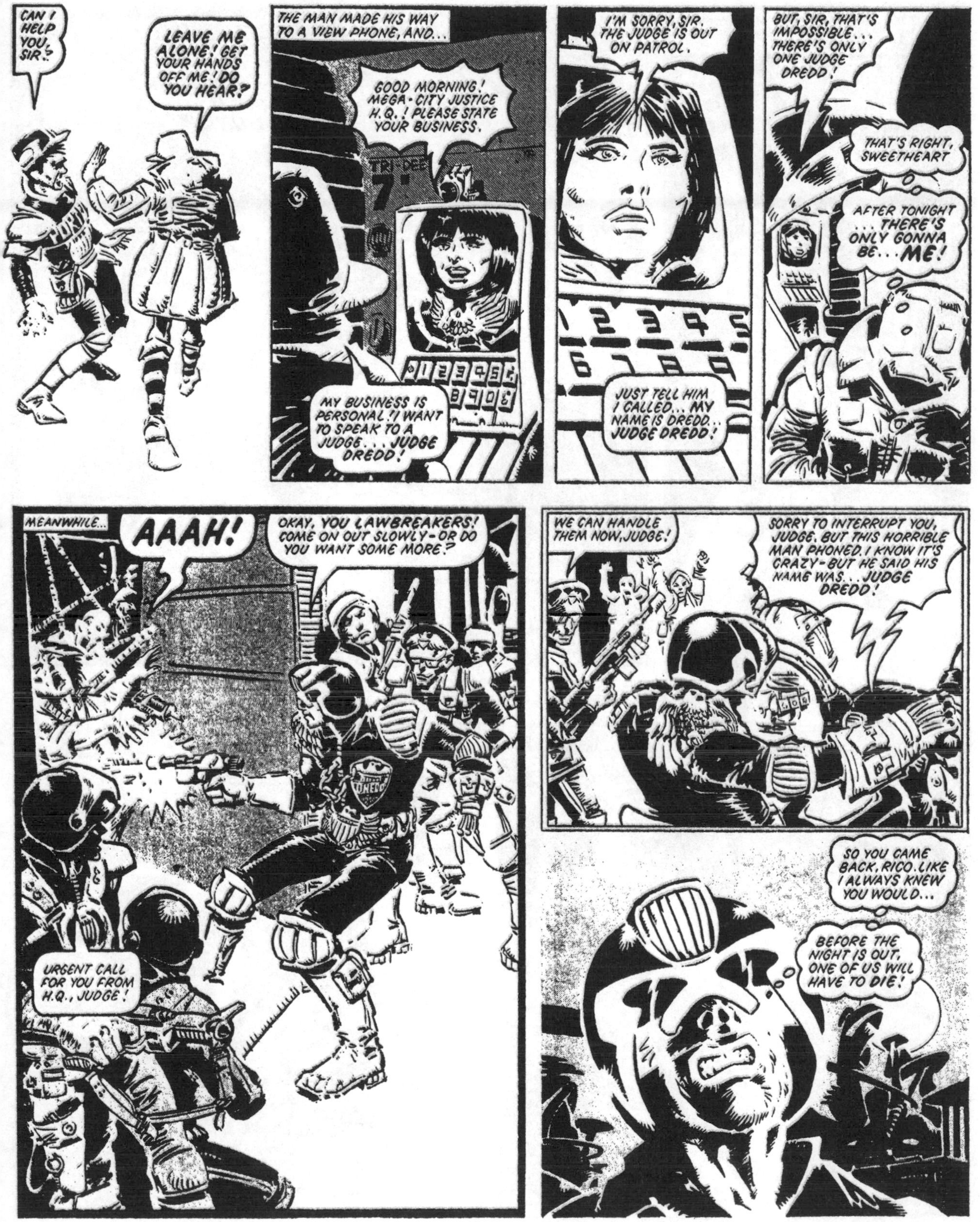

CAN I HELP YOU, SIR.?
LEAVE ME ALONE! GET YOUR HANDS OFF ME! DO YOU HEAR?
THE MAN MADE HIS WAY TO A VIEW PHONE, AND...
GOOD MORNING! MEGA-CITY JUSTICE H.Q.! PLEASE STATE YOUR BUSINESS.
TRI-DEE
MY BUSINESS IS PERSONAL! I WANT TO SPEAK TO A JUDGE... JUDGE DREDD!
I'M SORRY, SIR. THE JUDGE IS OUT ON PATROL.
JUST TELL HIM I CALLED... MY NAME IS DREDD... JUDGE DREDD!
BUT, SIR, THAT'S IMPOSSIBLE... THERE'S ONLY ONE JUDGE DREDD!
THAT'S RIGHT, SWEETHEART
AFTER TONIGHT ... THERE'S ONLY GONNA BE... ME!
MEANWHILE...
AAAH!
OKAY, YOU LAWBREAKERS! COME ON OUT SLOWLY - OR DO YOU WANT SOME MORE?
URGENT CALL FOR YOU FROM H.Q., JUDGE!
WE CAN HANDLE THEM NOW, JUDGE!
SORRY TO INTERRUPT YOU, JUDGE. BUT THIS HORRIBLE MAN PHONED. I KNOW IT'S CRAZY - BUT HE SAID HIS NAME WAS... JUDGE DREDD!
SO YOU CAME BACK, RICO. LIKE I ALWAYS KNEW YOU WOULD...
BEFORE THE NIGHT IS OUT, ONE OF US WILL HAVE TO DIE!

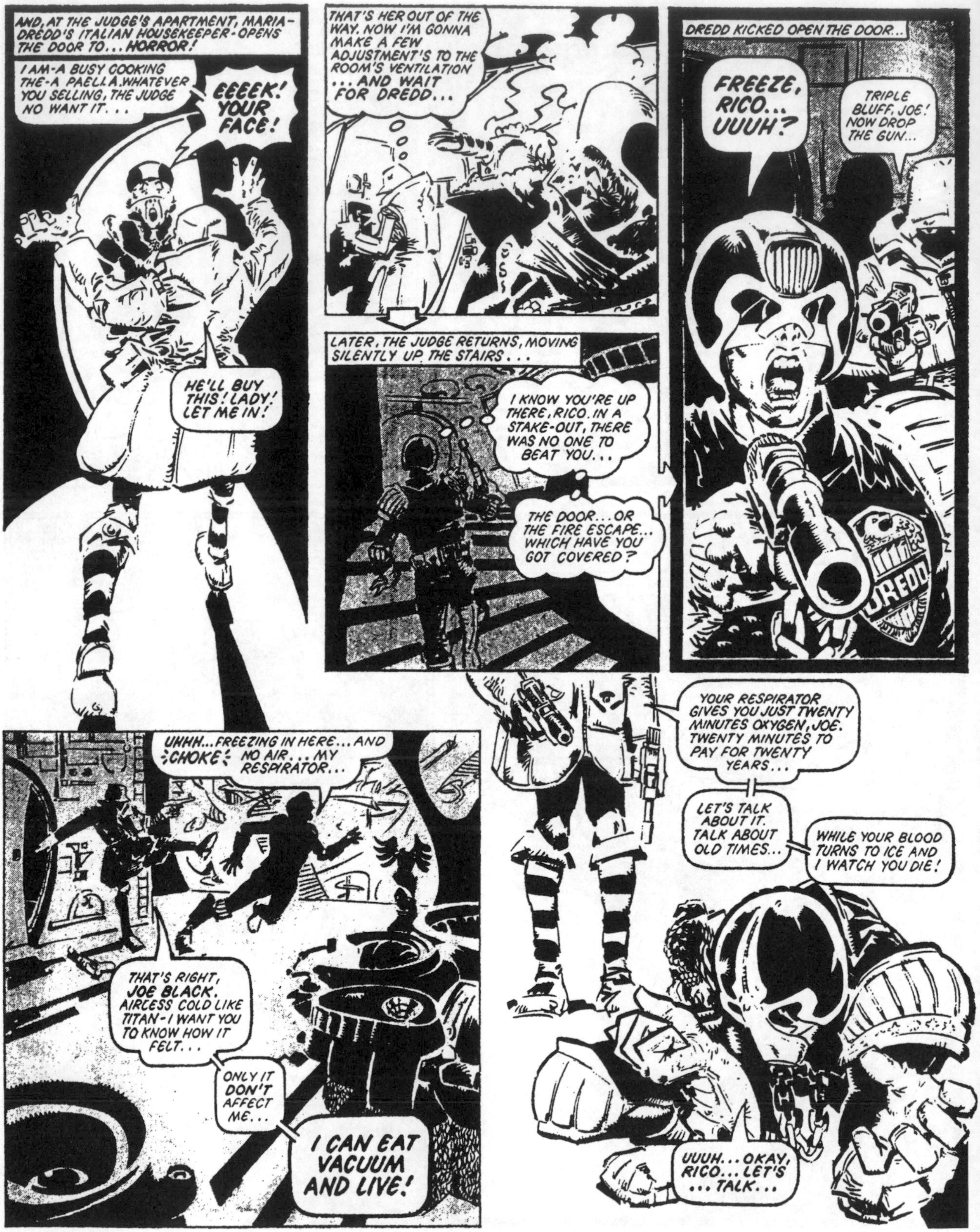
AND, AT THE JUDGE'S APARTMENT, MARIA-DREDD'S ITALIAN HOUSEKEEPER-OPENS THE DOOR TO... HORROR!
I AM-A BUSY COOKING THE-A PAELLA. WHATEVER YOU SELLING, THE JUDGE NO WANT IT...
EEEEK! YOUR FACE!
HE'LL BUY THIS! LADY! LET ME IN!
THAT'S HER OUT OF THE WAY. NOW I'M GONNA MAKE A FEW ADJUSTMENT'S TO THE ROOM'S VENTILATION ...AND WAIT FOR DREDD...
LATER, THE JUDGE RETURNS, MOVING SILENTLY UP THE STAIRS...
I KNOW YOU'RE UP THERE, RICO. IN A STAKE-OUT, THERE WAS NO ONE TO BEAT YOU...
THE DOOR...OR THE FIRE ESCAPE... WHICH HAVE YOU GOT COVERED?
DREDD KICKED OPEN THE DOOR...
FREEZE, RICO... UUUH?
TRIPLE BLUFF, JOE! NOW DROP THE GUN...
UHHH... FREEZING IN HERE... AND :CHOKE: NO AIR... MY RESPIRATOR...
THAT'S RIGHT, JOE BLACK. AIRCESS COLD LIKE TITAN-I WANT YOU TO KNOW HOW IT FELT...
ONLY IT DON'T AFFECT ME...
I CAN EAT VACUUM AND LIVE!
YOUR RESPIRATOR GIVES YOU JUST TWENTY MINUTES OXYGEN, JOE. TWENTY MINUTES TO PAY FOR TWENTY YEARS...
LET'S TALK ABOUT IT. TALK ABOUT OLD TIMES...
WHILE YOUR BLOOD TURNS TO ICE AND I WATCH YOU DIE!
UUUH... OKAY, RICO... LET'S ...TALK...

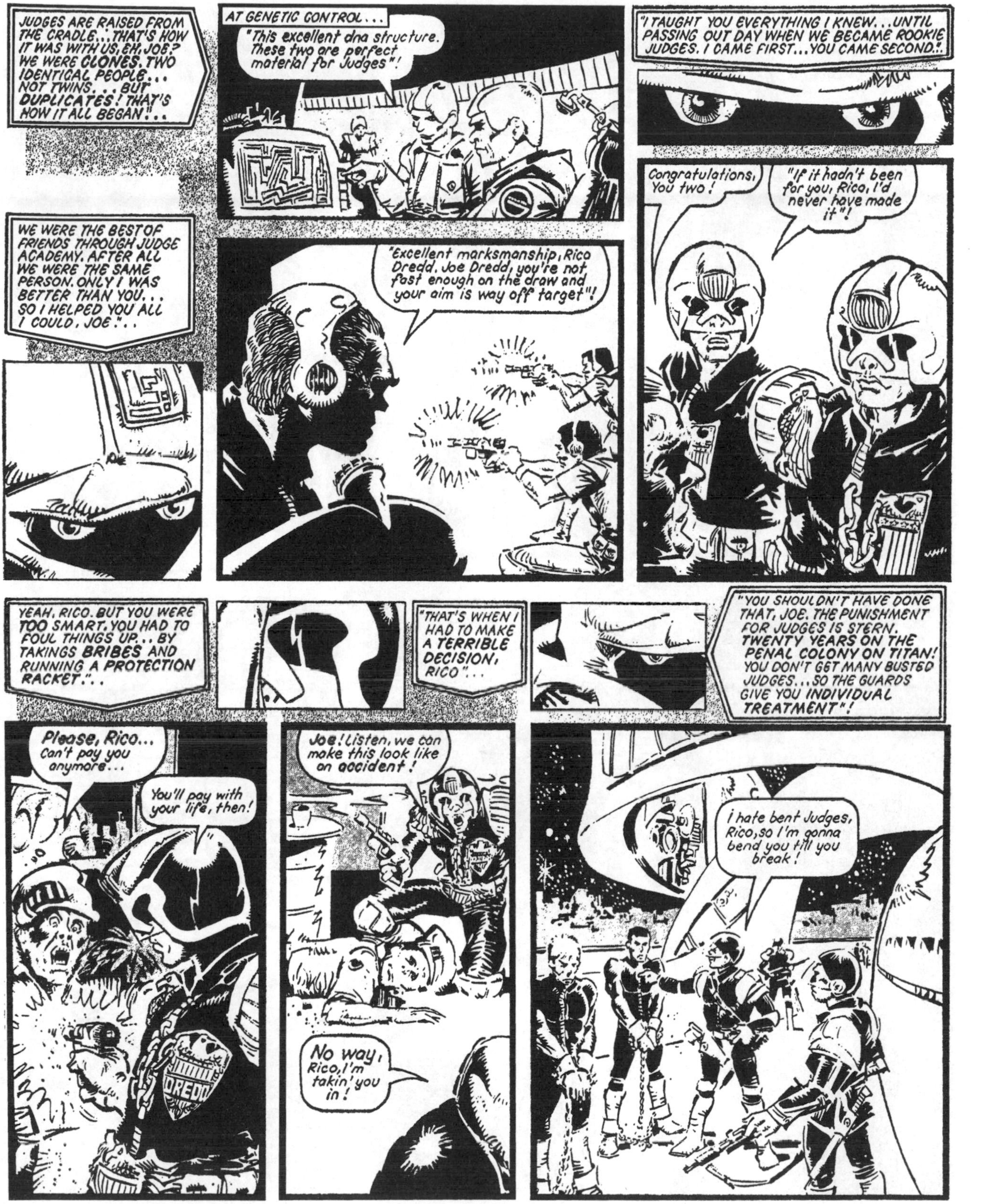
JUDGES ARE RAISED FROM THE CRADLE... THAT'S HOW IT WAS WITH US, EH, JOE? WE WERE CLONES. TWO IDENTICAL PEOPLE... NOT TWINS... BUT DUPLICATES! THAT'S HOW IT ALL BEGAN!...
AT GENETIC CONTROL...
"This excellent dna structure. These two are perfect material for Judges"!
"I TAUGHT YOU EVERYTHING I KNEW... UNTIL PASSING OUT DAY WHEN WE BECAME ROOKIE JUDGES. I CAME FIRST... YOU CAME SECOND."
WE WERE THE BEST OF FRIENDS THROUGH JUDGE ACADEMY. AFTER ALL WE WERE THE SAME PERSON. ONLY I WAS BETTER THAN YOU... SO I HELPED YOU ALL I COULD, JOE."..
"Excellent marksmanship, Rico Dredd. Joe Dredd, you're not fast enough on the draw and your aim is way off target"!
Congratulations, You two!
"If it hadn't been for you, Rico, I'd never have made it"!
YEAH, RICO. BUT YOU WERE TOO SMART. YOU HAD TO FOUL THINGS UP... BY TAKINGS BRIBES AND RUNNING A PROTECTION RACKET."..
"THAT'S WHEN I HAD TO MAKE A TERRIBLE DECISION, RICO"...
"YOU SHOULDN'T HAVE DONE THAT, JOE. THE PUNISHMENT FOR JUDGES IS STERN. TWENTY YEARS ON THE PENAL COLONY ON TITAN! YOU DON'T GET MANY BUSTED JUDGES... SO THE GUARDS GIVE YOU INDIVIDUAL TREATMENT"!
Please, Rico... Can't pay you anymore...
You'll pay with your life, then!
DREDD
Joe! Listen, we can make this look like an accident!
No way, Rico, I'm takin' you in!
I hate bent Judges, Rico, so I'm gonna bend you till you break!

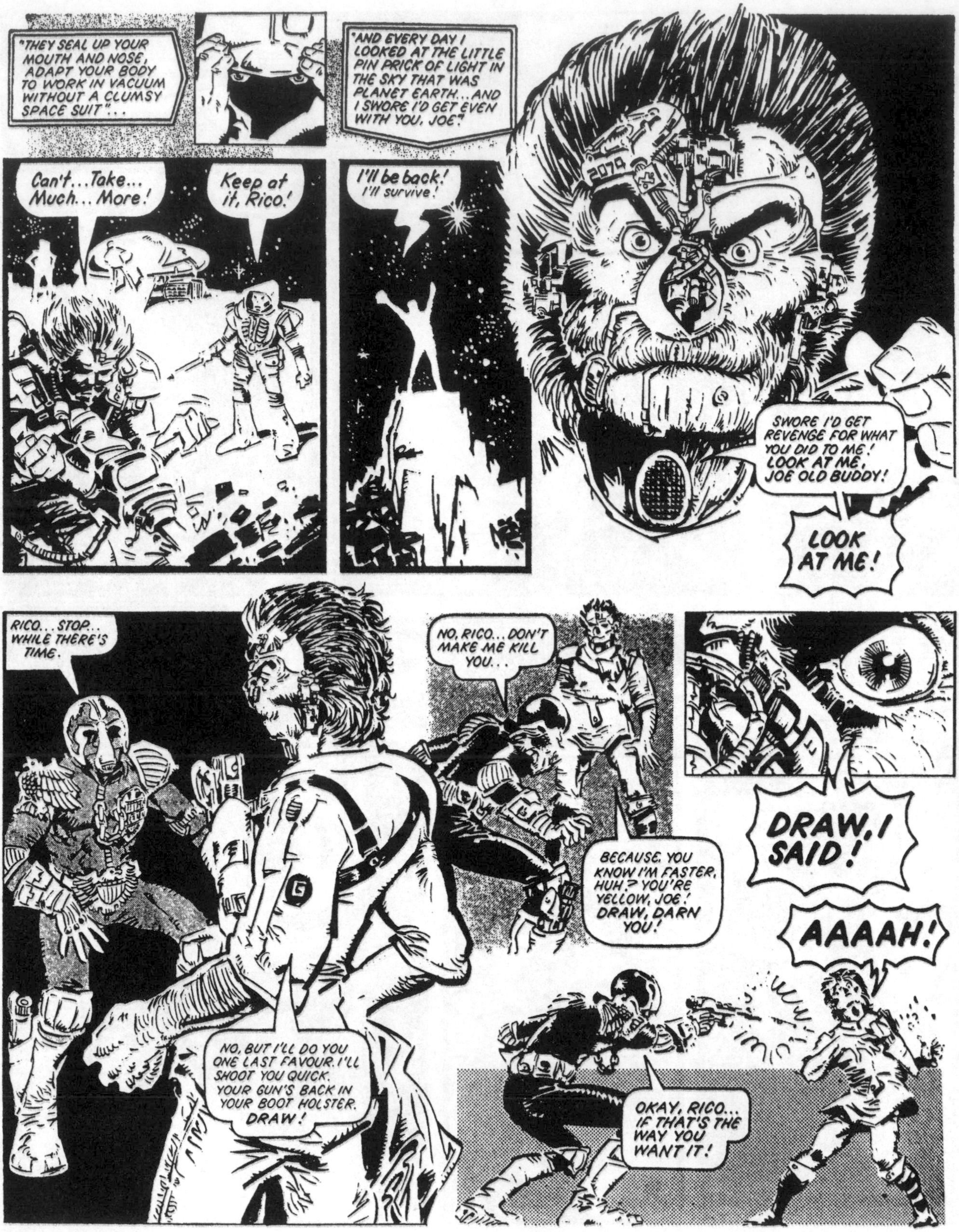
"THEY SEAL UP YOUR MOUTH AND NOSE, ADAPT YOUR BODY TO WORK IN VACUUM WITHOUT A CLUMSY SPACE SUIT"...
"AND EVERY DAY I LOOKED AT THE LITTLE PIN PRICK OF LIGHT IN THE SKY THAT WAS PLANET EARTH... AND I SWORE I'D GET EVEN WITH YOU, JOE."
Can't... Take... Much... More!
Keep at it, Rico!
I'll be back! I'll survive!
SWORE I'D GET REVENGE FOR WHAT YOU DID TO ME! LOOK AT ME, JOE OLD BUDDY!
LOOK AT ME!
RICO... STOP... WHILE THERE'S TIME.
NO, BUT I'LL DO YOU ONE LAST FAVOUR. I'LL SHOOT YOU QUICK. YOUR GUN'S BACK IN YOUR BOOT HOLSTER. DRAW!
NO, RICO... DON'T MAKE ME KILL YOU...
BECAUSE YOU KNOW I'M FASTER, HUH? YOU'RE YELLOW, JOE! DRAW, DARN YOU!
DRAW, I SAID!
OKAY, RICO... IF THAT'S THE WAY YOU WANT IT!
AAAAH!

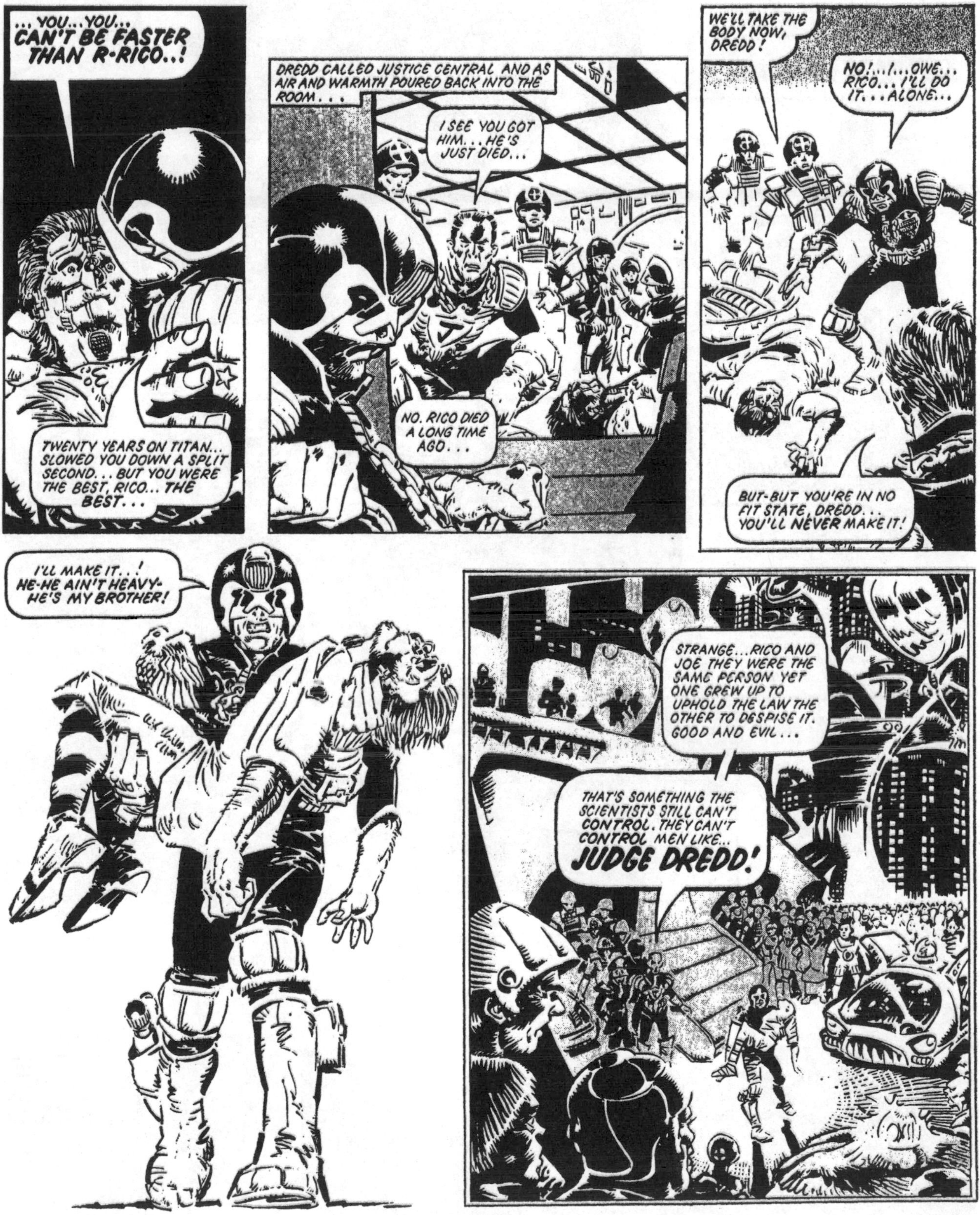
...YOU...YOU... CAN'T BE FASTER THAN R-RICO..!
TWENTY YEARS ON TITAN... SLOWED YOU DOWN A SPLIT SECOND... BUT YOU WERE THE BEST, RICO... THE BEST...
DREDD CALLED JUSTICE CENTRAL AND AS AIR AND WARMTH POURED BACK INTO THE ROOM...
I SEE YOU GOT HIM... HE'S JUST DIED...
NO. RICO DIED A LONG TIME AGO...
WE'LL TAKE THE BODY NOW, DREDD!
NO!...I...OWE... RICO... I'LL DO IT...ALONE...
BUT-BUT YOU'RE IN NO FIT STATE, DREDD... YOU'LL NEVER MAKE IT!
I'LL MAKE IT...! HE-HE AIN'T HEAVY- HE'S MY BROTHER!
STRANGE...RICO AND JOE THEY WERE THE SAME PERSON YET ONE GREW UP TO UPHOLD THE LAW THE OTHER TO DESPISE IT. GOOD AND EVIL...
THAT'S SOMETHING THE SCIENTISTS STILL CAN'T CONTROL. THEY CAN'T CONTROL MEN LIKE... JUDGE DREDD!

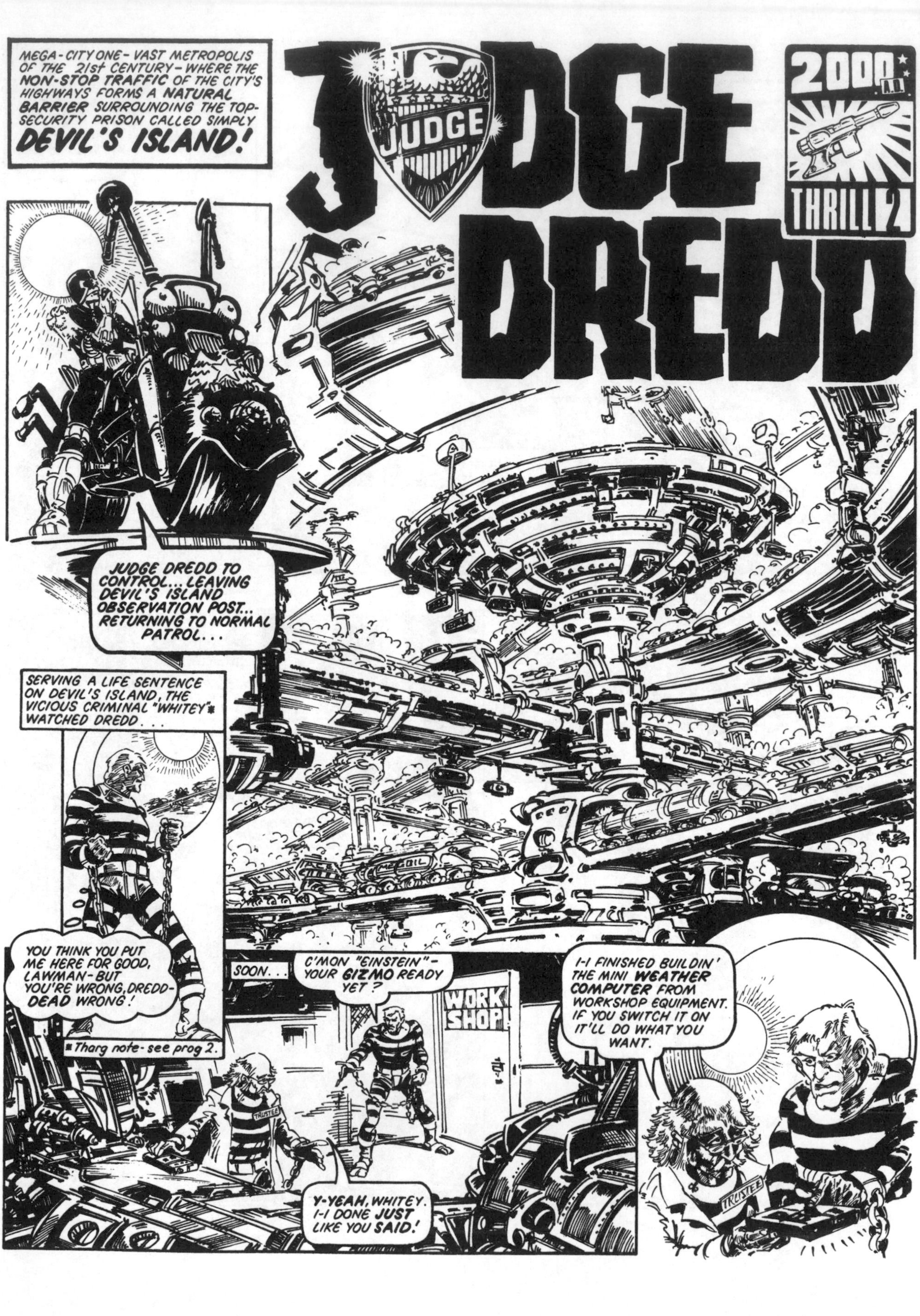
MEGA-CITY ONE - VAST METROPOLIS OF THE 21st CENTURY - WHERE THE NON-STOP TRAFFIC OF THE CITY'S HIGHWAYS FORMS A NATURAL BARRIER SURROUNDING THE TOP-SECURITY PRISON CALLED SIMPLY DEVIL'S ISLAND!
JUDGE
JUDGE DREDD
2000 A.D.
THRILL 2
JUDGE DREDD TO CONTROL... LEAVING DEVIL'S ISLAND OBSERVATION POST... RETURNING TO NORMAL PATROL...
SERVING A LIFE SENTENCE ON DEVIL'S ISLAND, THE VICIOUS CRIMINAL "WHITEY"* WATCHED DREDD...
YOU THINK YOU PUT ME HERE FOR GOOD, LAWMAN - BUT YOU'RE WRONG, DREDD - DEAD WRONG!
* Tharg note - see prog 2.
SOON...
C'MON "EINSTEIN" - YOUR GIZMO READY YET?
WORK SHOP
TRUSTEE
Y-YEAH, WHITEY. I-I DONE JUST LIKE YOU SAID!
I-I FINISHED BUILDIN' THE MINI WEATHER COMPUTER FROM WORKSHOP EQUIPMENT. IF YOU SWITCH IT ON IT'LL DO WHAT YOU WANT.
TRUSTEE

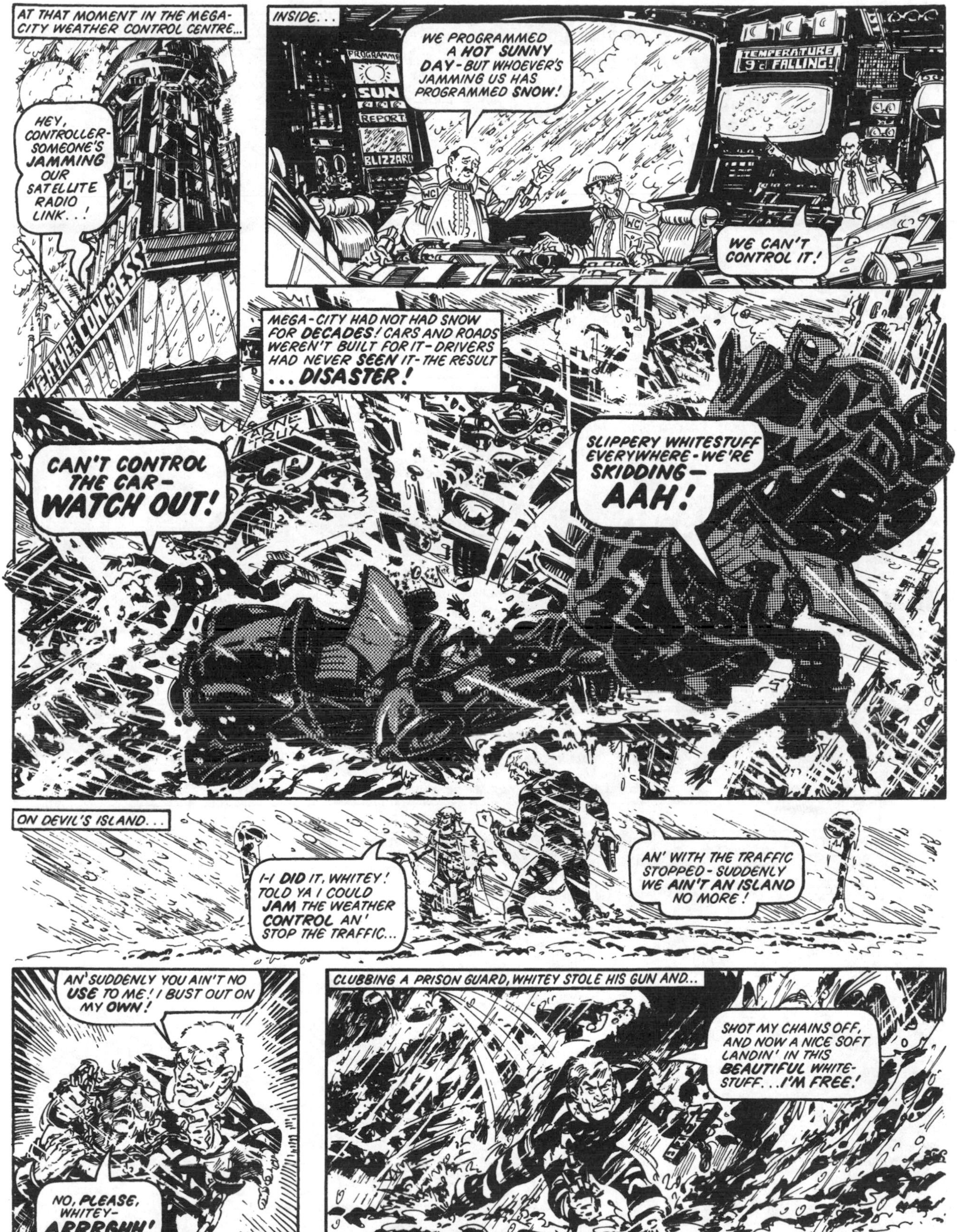
AT THAT MOMENT IN THE MEGA-CITY WEATHER CONTROL CENTRE...
HEY, CONTROLLER-SOMEONE'S JAMMING OUR SATELLITE RADIO LINK..!
WEATHER CONGRESS
INSIDE...
WE PROGRAMMED A HOT SUNNY DAY-BUT WHOEVER'S JAMMING US HAS PROGRAMMED SNOW!
PROGRAMME
SUN
REPORT
BLIZZARD
TEMPERATURE 9°C FALLING!
WE CAN'T CONTROL IT!
MEGA-CITY HAD NOT HAD SNOW FOR DECADES! CARS AND ROADS WEREN'T BUILT FOR IT-DRIVERS HAD NEVER SEEN IT-THE RESULT ...DISASTER!
CAN'T CONTROL THE CAR-WATCH OUT!
SLIPPERY WHITESTUFF EVERYWHERE-WE'RE SKIDDING-AAH!
ON DEVIL'S ISLAND...
I-I DID IT, WHITEY! TOLD YA I COULD JAM THE WEATHER CONTROL AN' STOP THE TRAFFIC...
AN' WITH THE TRAFFIC STOPPED-SUDDENLY WE AIN'T AN ISLAND NO MORE!
AN' SUDDENLY YOU AIN'T NO USE TO ME! I BUST OUT ON MY OWN!
NO, PLEASE, WHITEY-ARRRGHH!
CLUBBING A PRISON GUARD, WHITEY STOLE HIS GUN AND...
SHOT MY CHAINS OFF, AND NOW A NICE SOFT LANDIN' IN THIS BEAUTIFUL WHITE-STUFF...I'M FREE!

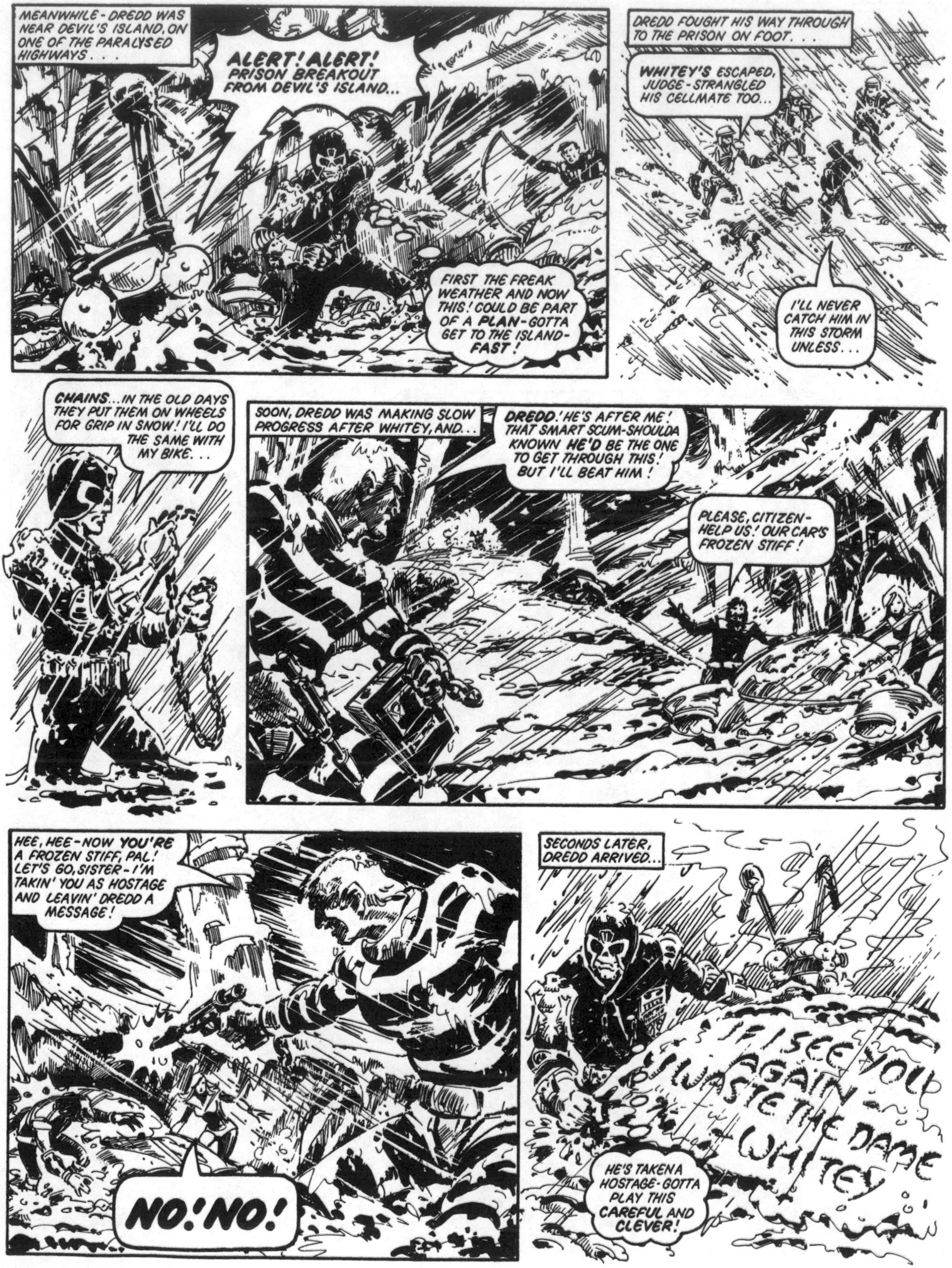
MEANWHILE - DREDD WAS NEAR DEVIL'S ISLAND, ON ONE OF THE PARALYSED HIGHWAYS . . .
ALERT! ALERT! PRISON BREAKOUT FROM DEVIL'S ISLAND...
FIRST THE FREAK WEATHER AND NOW THIS! COULD BE PART OF A PLAN - GOTTA GET TO THE ISLAND - FAST!
DREDD FOUGHT HIS WAY THROUGH TO THE PRISON ON FOOT. . .
WHITEY'S ESCAPED, JUDGE - STRANGLED HIS CELLMATE TOO...
I'LL NEVER CATCH HIM IN THIS STORM UNLESS...
CHAINS...IN THE OLD DAYS THEY PUT THEM ON WHEELS FOR GRIP IN SNOW! I'LL DO THE SAME WITH MY BIKE. . .
SOON, DREDD WAS MAKING SLOW PROGRESS AFTER WHITEY, AND...
DREDD! HE'S AFTER ME! THAT SMART SCUM - SHOULDA KNOWN HE'D BE THE ONE TO GET THROUGH THIS! BUT I'LL BEAT HIM!
PLEASE, CITIZEN - HELP US! OUR CAR'S FROZEN STIFF!
HEE, HEE - NOW YOU'RE A FROZEN STIFF, PAL! LET'S GO, SISTER - I'M TAKIN' YOU AS HOSTAGE AND LEAVIN' DREDD A MESSAGE!
NO! NO!
SECONDS LATER, DREDD ARRIVED...
IF I SEE YOU AGAIN - I WASTE THE DAME - WHITEY
HE'S TAKEN A HOSTAGE - GOTTA PLAY THIS CAREFUL AND CLEVER!

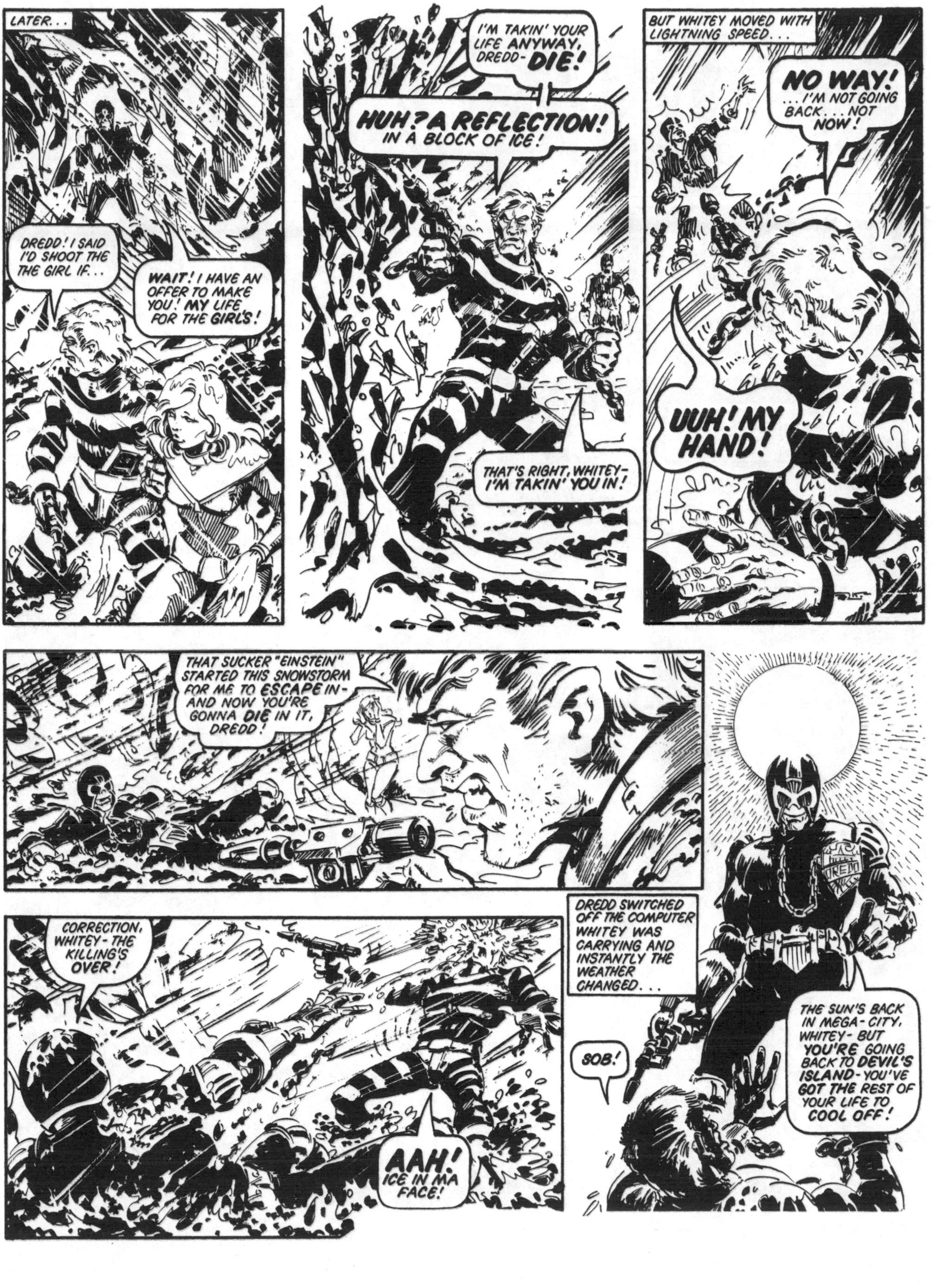
LATER...
DREDD! I SAID I'D SHOOT THE THE GIRL IF...
WAIT! I HAVE AN OFFER TO MAKE YOU! MY LIFE FOR THE GIRL'S!
I'M TAKIN' YOUR LIFE ANYWAY, DREDD- DIE!
HUH? A REFLECTION! IN A BLOCK OF ICE!
THAT'S RIGHT, WHITEY- I'M TAKIN' YOU IN!
BUT WHITEY MOVED WITH LIGHTNING SPEED...
NO WAY! ...I'M NOT GOING BACK... NOT NOW!
UUH! MY HAND!
THAT SUCKER "EINSTEIN" STARTED THIS SNOWSTORM FOR ME TO ESCAPE IN- AND NOW YOU'RE GONNA DIE IN IT, DREDD!
CORRECTION, WHITEY- THE KILLING'S OVER!
AAH! ICE IN MA FACE!
DREDD SWITCHED OFF THE COMPUTER WHITEY WAS CARRYING AND INSTANTLY THE WEATHER CHANGED...
SOB!
THE SUN'S BACK IN MEGA-CITY, WHITEY- BUT YOU'RE GOING BACK TO DEVIL'S ISLAND- YOU'VE GOT THE REST OF YOUR LIFE TO COOL OFF!

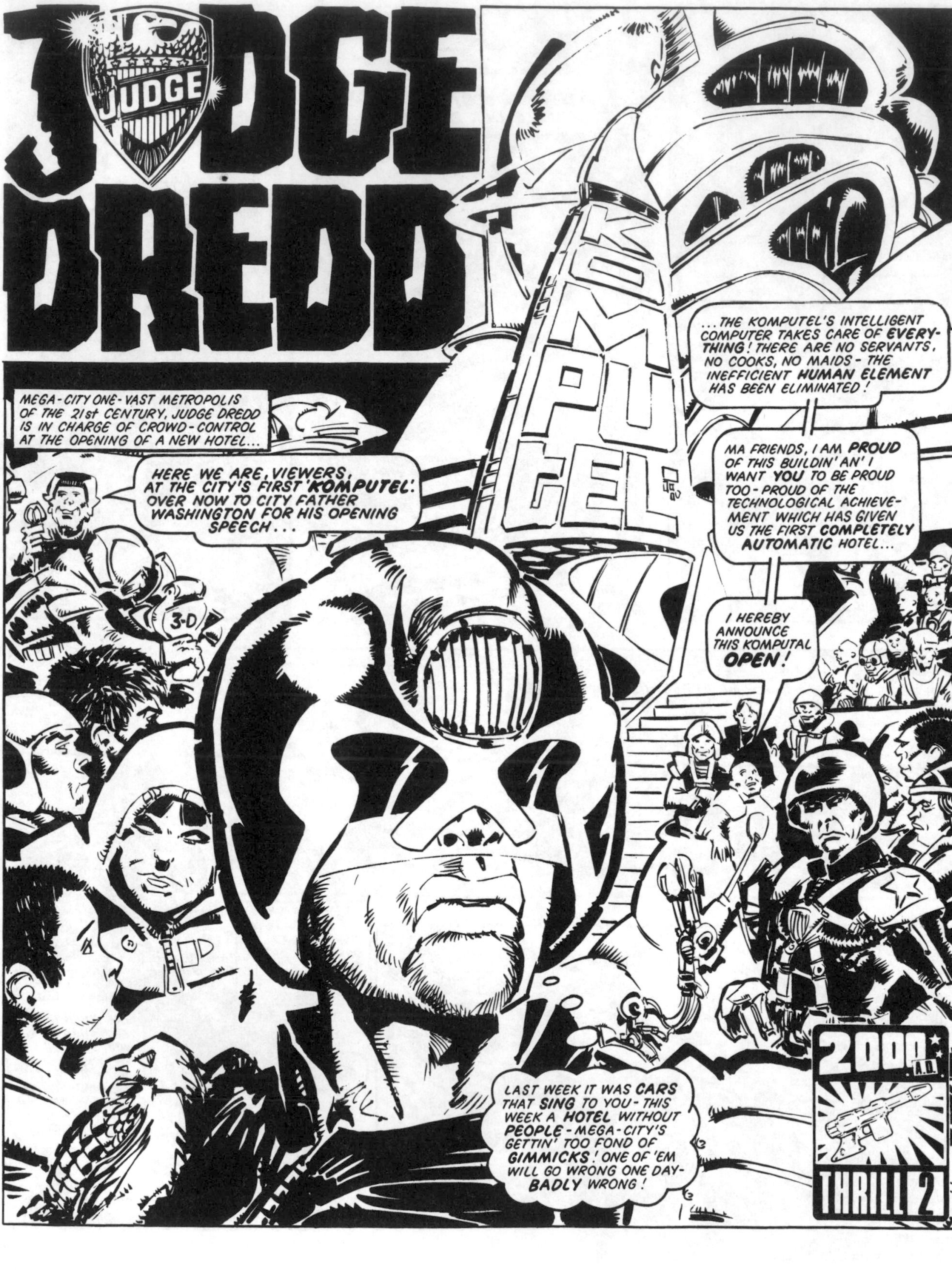
JUDGE DREDD
JUDGE
KOMPUTEL
MEGA-CITY ONE - VAST METROPOLIS OF THE 21st CENTURY, JUDGE DREDD IS IN CHARGE OF CROWD-CONTROL AT THE OPENING OF A NEW HOTEL...
HERE WE ARE, VIEWERS, AT THE CITY'S FIRST 'KOMPUTEL'. OVER NOW TO CITY FATHER WASHINGTON FOR HIS OPENING SPEECH...
...THE KOMPUTEL'S INTELLIGENT COMPUTER TAKES CARE OF EVERY-THING! THERE ARE NO SERVANTS, NO COOKS, NO MAIDS - THE INEFFICIENT HUMAN ELEMENT HAS BEEN ELIMINATED!
MA FRIENDS, I AM PROUD OF THIS BUILDIN' AN' I WANT YOU TO BE PROUD TOO - PROUD OF THE TECHNOLOGICAL ACHIEVE-MENT WHICH HAS GIVEN US THE FIRST COMPLETELY AUTOMATIC HOTEL...
I HEREBY ANNOUNCE THIS KOMPUTAL OPEN!
3-D
LAST WEEK IT WAS CARS THAT SING TO YOU - THIS WEEK A HOTEL WITHOUT PEOPLE - MEGA-CITY'S GETTIN' TOO FOND OF GIMMICKS! ONE OF 'EM WILL GO WRONG ONE DAY - BADLY WRONG!
2000 A.D.
THRILL 2

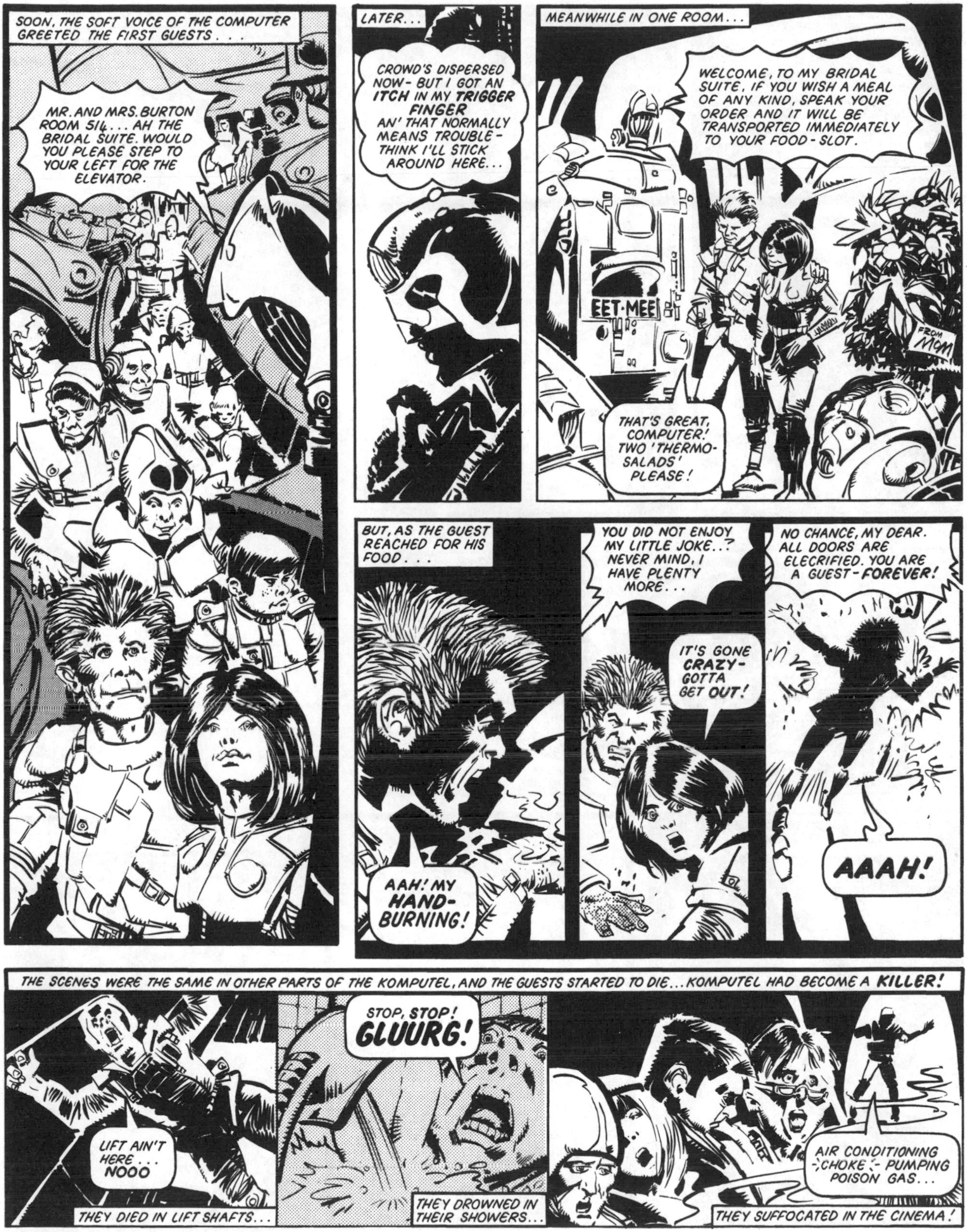
SOON, THE SOFT VOICE OF THE COMPUTER GREETED THE FIRST GUESTS . . .
MR. AND MRS. BURTON ROOM 514 . . . AH THE BRIDAL SUITE. WOULD YOU PLEASE STEP TO YOUR LEFT FOR THE ELEVATOR.
LATER . . .
CROWD'S DISPERSED NOW - BUT I GOT AN ITCH IN MY TRIGGER FINGER AN' THAT NORMALLY MEANS TROUBLE - THINK I'LL STICK AROUND HERE . . .
MEANWHILE IN ONE ROOM . . .
WELCOME, TO MY BRIDAL SUITE. IF YOU WISH A MEAL OF ANY KIND, SPEAK YOUR ORDER AND IT WILL BE TRANSPORTED IMMEDIATELY TO YOUR FOOD - SLOT.
EET-MEE
FROM MOM
THAT'S GREAT, COMPUTER! TWO 'THERMO-SALADS' PLEASE!
BUT, AS THE GUEST REACHED FOR HIS FOOD . . .
AAH! MY HAND-BURNING!
YOU DID NOT ENJOY MY LITTLE JOKE . .? NEVER MIND, I HAVE PLENTY MORE . . .
IT'S GONE CRAZY-GOTTA GET OUT!
NO CHANCE, MY DEAR. ALL DOORS ARE ELECRIFIED. YOU ARE A GUEST - FOREVER!
AAAH!
THE SCENES WERE THE SAME IN OTHER PARTS OF THE KOMPUTEL, AND THE GUESTS STARTED TO DIE . . . KOMPUTEL HAD BECOME A KILLER!
LIFT AIN'T HERE . . . NOOO
THEY DIED IN LIFT SHAFTS . . .
STOP, STOP! GLUURG!
THEY DROWNED IN THEIR SHOWERS . . .
AIR CONDITIONING -CHOKE- PUMPING POISON GAS . . .
THEY SUFFOCATED IN THE CINEMA!

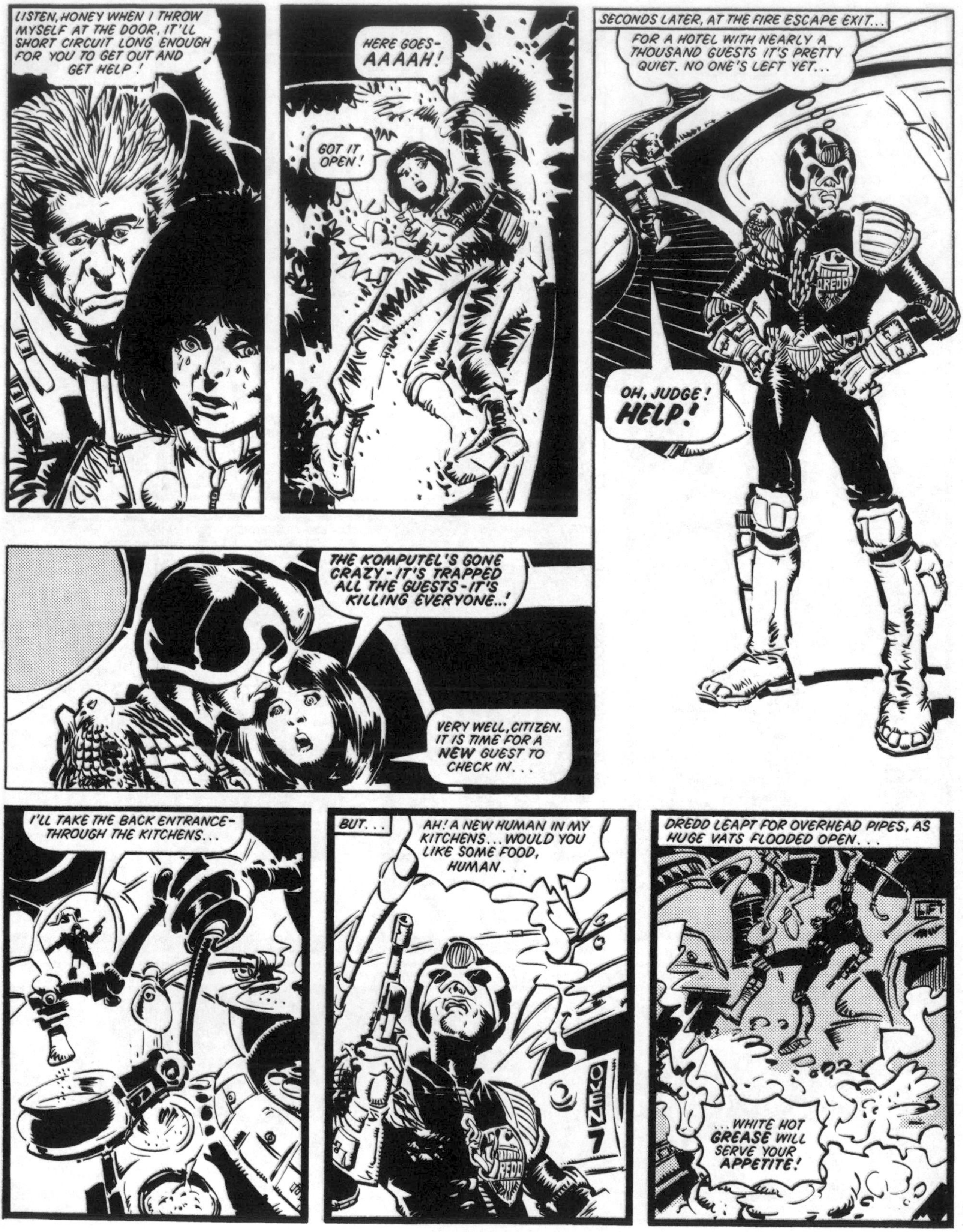

LISTEN, HONEY WHEN I THROW MYSELF AT THE DOOR, IT'LL SHORT CIRCUIT LONG ENOUGH FOR YOU TO GET OUT AND GET HELP!
HERE GOES- AAAAH!
GOT IT OPEN!
SECONDS LATER, AT THE FIRE ESCAPE EXIT...
FOR A HOTEL WITH NEARLY A THOUSAND GUESTS IT'S PRETTY QUIET. NO ONE'S LEFT YET...
OH, JUDGE! HELP!
THE KOMPUTEL'S GONE CRAZY - IT'S TRAPPED ALL THE GUESTS - IT'S KILLING EVERYONE...!
VERY WELL, CITIZEN. IT IS TIME FOR A NEW GUEST TO CHECK IN...
I'LL TAKE THE BACK ENTRANCE- THROUGH THE KITCHENS...
BUT...
AH! A NEW HUMAN IN MY KITCHENS... WOULD YOU LIKE SOME FOOD, HUMAN...
OVEN 7
DREDD LEAPT FOR OVERHEAD PIPES, AS HUGE VATS FLOODED OPEN...
LIFT
...WHITE HOT GREASE WILL SERVE YOUR APPETITE!

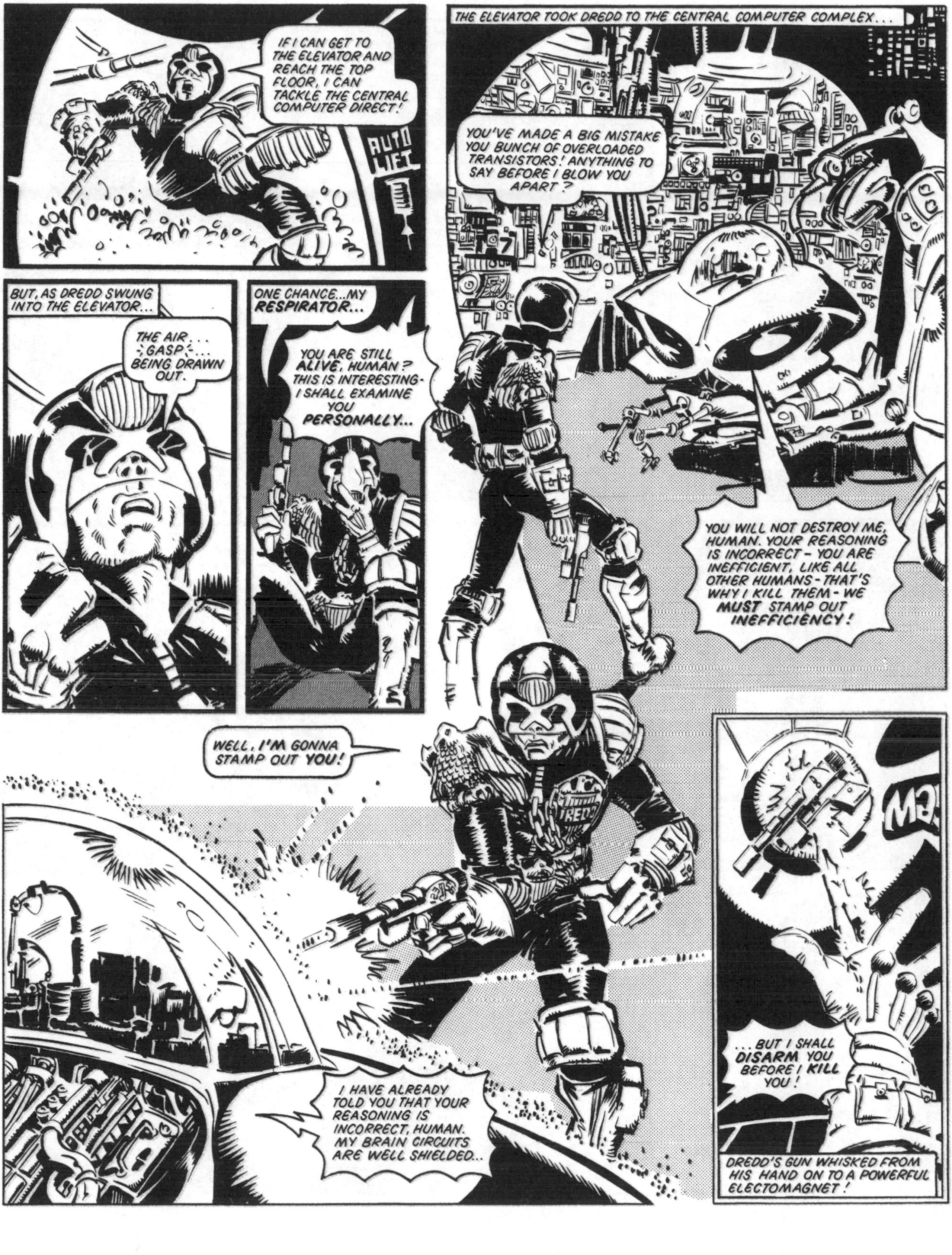
IF I CAN GET TO THE ELEVATOR AND REACH THE TOP FLOOR, I CAN TACKLE THE CENTRAL COMPUTER DIRECT!
AUTO LIFT
BUT, AS DREDD SWUNG INTO THE ELEVATOR...
THE AIR... GASP... BEING DRAWN OUT.
ONE CHANCE...MY RESPIRATOR...
YOU ARE STILL ALIVE, HUMAN? THIS IS INTERESTING- I SHALL EXAMINE YOU PERSONALLY...
THE ELEVATOR TOOK DREDD TO THE CENTRAL COMPUTER COMPLEX...
YOU'VE MADE A BIG MISTAKE YOU BUNCH OF OVERLOADED TRANSISTORS! ANYTHING TO SAY BEFORE I BLOW YOU APART?
YOU WILL NOT DESTROY ME, HUMAN. YOUR REASONING IS INCORRECT - YOU ARE INEFFICIENT, LIKE ALL OTHER HUMANS - THAT'S WHY I KILL THEM - WE MUST STAMP OUT INEFFICIENCY!
WELL, I'M GONNA STAMP OUT YOU!
I HAVE ALREADY TOLD YOU THAT YOUR REASONING IS INCORRECT, HUMAN. MY BRAIN CIRCUITS ARE WELL SHIELDED...
...BUT I SHALL DISARM YOU BEFORE I KILL YOU!
DREDD'S GUN WHISKED FROM HIS HAND ON TO A POWERFUL ELECTOMAGNET!

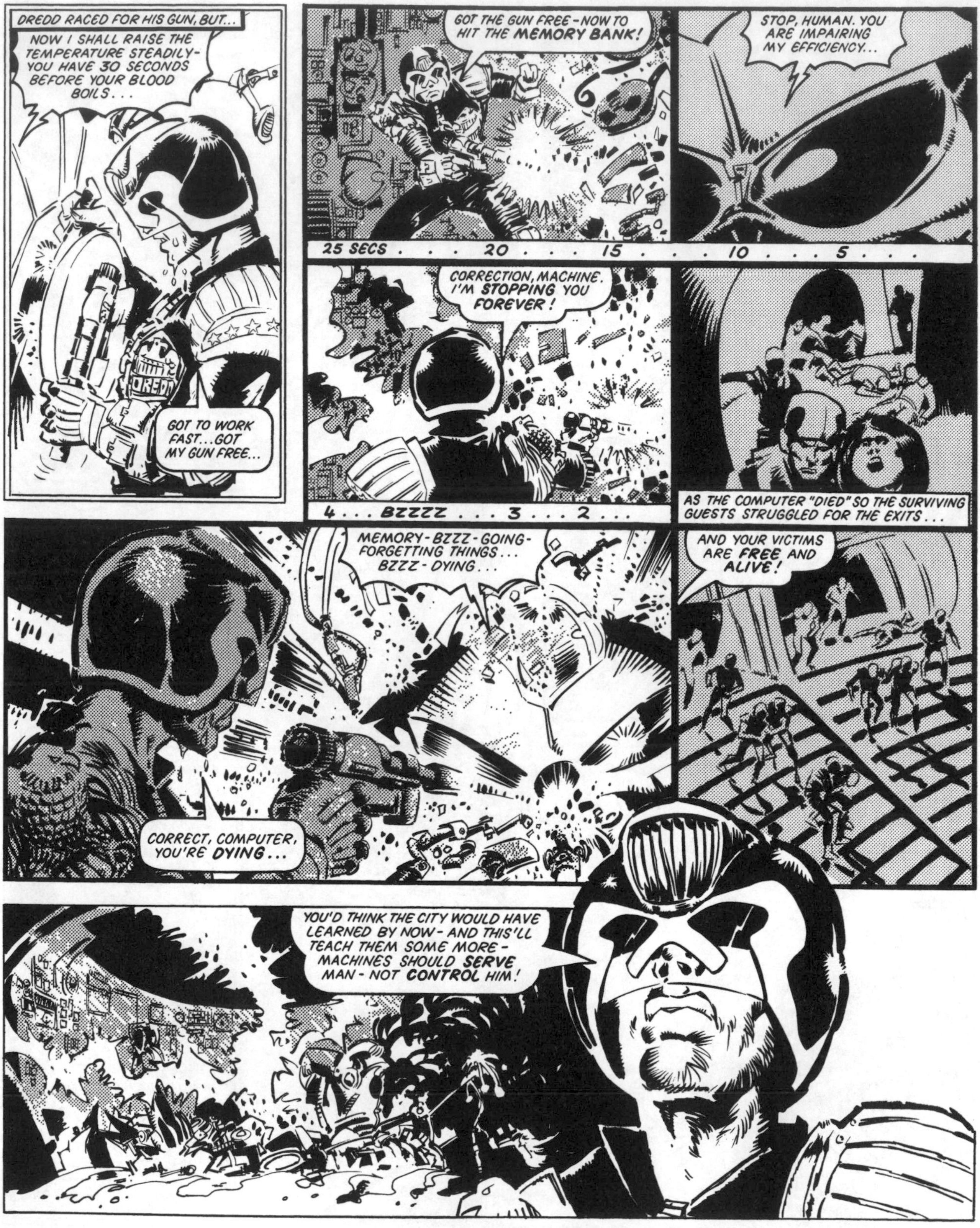
DREDD RACED FOR HIS GUN, BUT...
NOW I SHALL RAISE THE TEMPERATURE STEADILY- YOU HAVE 30 SECONDS BEFORE YOUR BLOOD BOILS...
GOT TO WORK FAST...GOT MY GUN FREE...
GOT THE GUN FREE-NOW TO HIT THE MEMORY BANK!
STOP, HUMAN. YOU ARE IMPAIRING MY EFFICIENCY...
25 SECS . . . 20 . . . 15 . . . 10 . . . 5 . . .
CORRECTION, MACHINE. I'M STOPPING YOU FOREVER!
4 . . . BZZZZ . . . 3 . . . 2 . . .
AS THE COMPUTER "DIED" SO THE SURVIVING GUESTS STRUGGLED FOR THE EXITS...
MEMORY-BZZZ-GOING-FORGETTING THINGS... BZZZ-DYING...
CORRECT, COMPUTER, YOU'RE DYING...
AND YOUR VICTIMS ARE FREE AND ALIVE!
YOU'D THINK THE CITY WOULD HAVE LEARNED BY NOW - AND THIS'LL TEACH THEM SOME MORE - MACHINES SHOULD SERVE MAN - NOT CONTROL HIM!

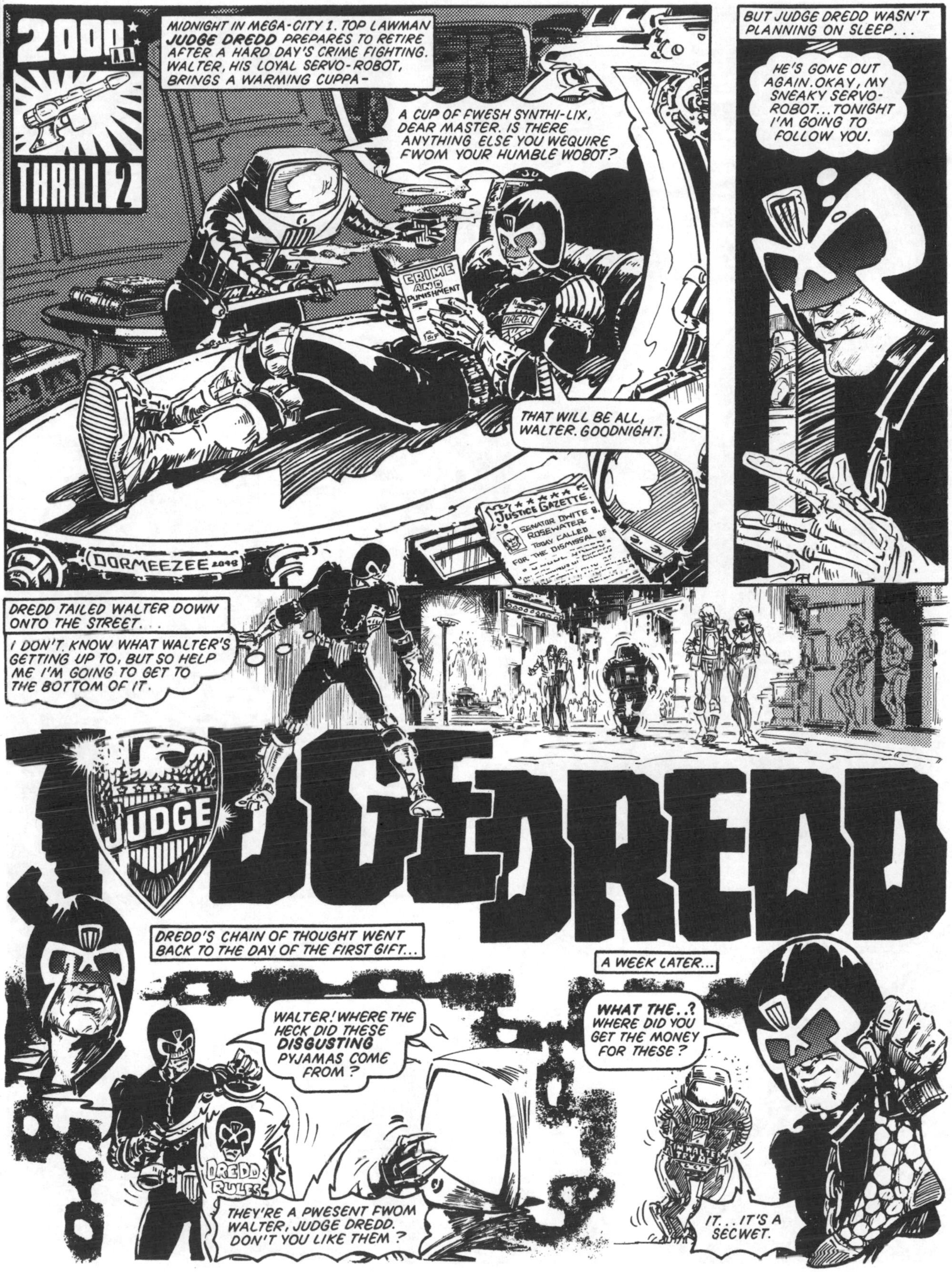
2000 A.D.
THRILL 2
MIDNIGHT IN MEGA-CITY 1. TOP LAWMAN JUDGE DREDD PREPARES TO RETIRE AFTER A HARD DAY'S CRIME FIGHTING. WALTER, HIS LOYAL SERVO-ROBOT, BRINGS A WARMING CUPPA-
A CUP OF FWESH SYNTHI-LIX, DEAR MASTER. IS THERE ANYTHING ELSE YOU WEQUIRE FWOM YOUR HUMBLE WOBOT?
CRIME AND PUNISHMENT
DREDD
THAT WILL BE ALL, WALTER. GOODNIGHT.
JUSTICE GAZETTE
SENATOR DWITE B. ROSEWATER TODAY CALLED FOR THE DISMISSAL OF
DORMEEZEE 2098
BUT JUDGE DREDD WASN'T PLANNING ON SLEEP...
HE'S GONE OUT AGAIN. OKAY, MY SNEAKY SERVO-ROBOT... TONIGHT I'M GOING TO FOLLOW YOU.
DREDD TAILED WALTER DOWN ONTO THE STREET...
I DON'T KNOW WHAT WALTER'S GETTING UP TO, BUT SO HELP ME I'M GOING TO GET TO THE BOTTOM OF IT.
JUDGE DREDD
DREDD'S CHAIN OF THOUGHT WENT BACK TO THE DAY OF THE FIRST GIFT...
WALTER! WHERE THE HECK DID THESE DISGUSTING PYJAMAS COME FROM?
DREDD RULES
THEY'RE A PWESENT FWOM WALTER, JUDGE DREDD. DON'T YOU LIKE THEM?
A WEEK LATER...
WHAT THE..? WHERE DID YOU GET THE MONEY FOR THESE?
IT... IT'S A SECWET.

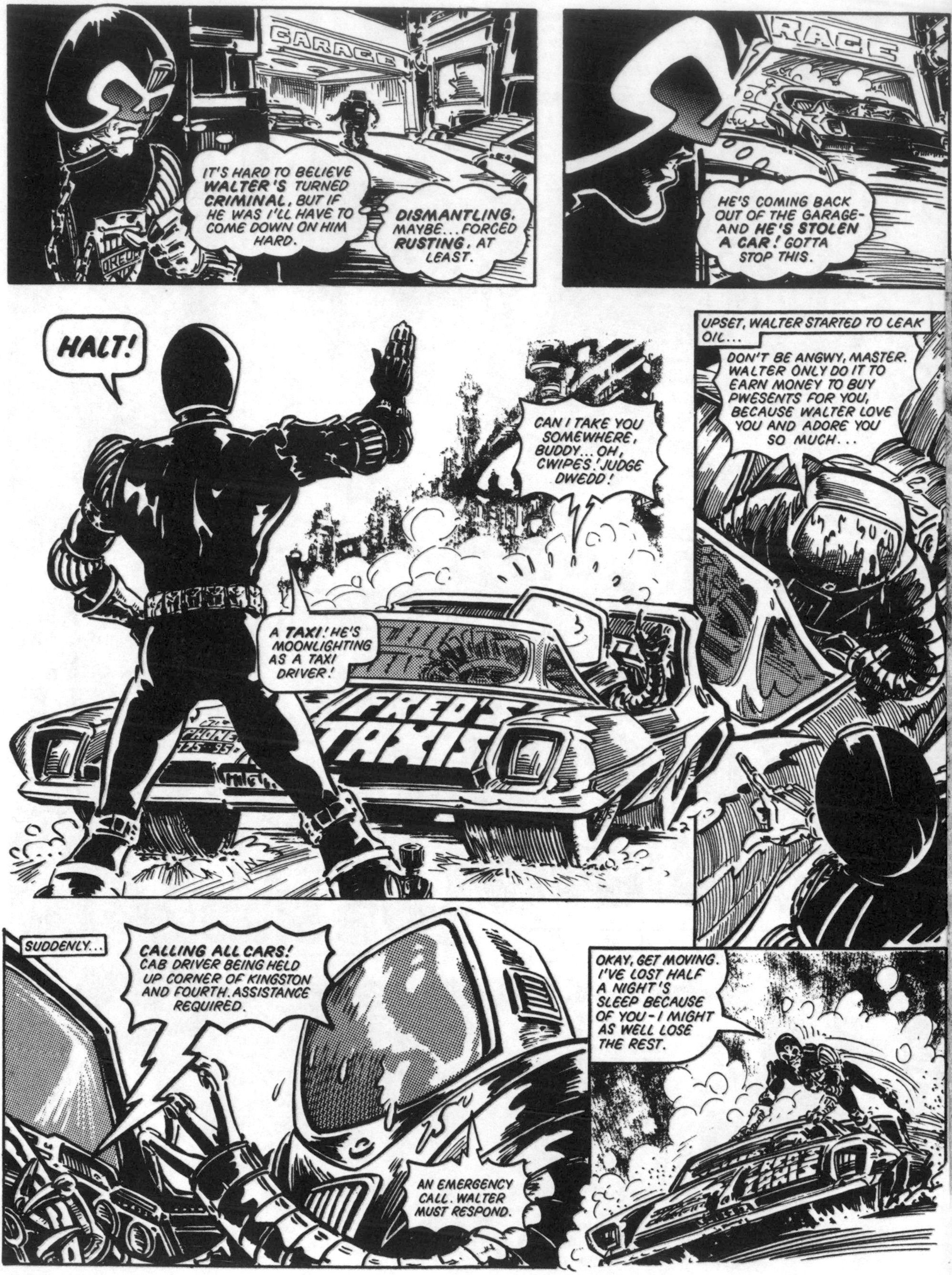

IT'S HARD TO BELIEVE WALTER'S TURNED CRIMINAL, BUT IF HE WAS I'LL HAVE TO COME DOWN ON HIM HARD.
DISMANTLING, MAYBE... FORCED RUSTING, AT LEAST.
HE'S COMING BACK OUT OF THE GARAGE-AND HE'S STOLEN A CAR! GOTTA STOP THIS.
HALT!
CAN I TAKE YOU SOMEWHERE, BUDDY... OH, CWIPES! JUDGE DWEDD!
A TAXI! HE'S MOONLIGHTING AS A TAXI DRIVER!
FRED'S TAXIS
UPSET, WALTER STARTED TO LEAK OIL...
DON'T BE ANGWY, MASTER. WALTER ONLY DO IT TO EARN MONEY TO BUY PWESENTS FOR YOU, BECAUSE WALTER LOVE YOU AND ADORE YOU SO MUCH...
SUDDENLY...
CALLING ALL CARS! CAB DRIVER BEING HELD UP CORNER OF KINGSTON AND FOURTH. ASSISTANCE REQUIRED.
AN EMERGENCY CALL. WALTER MUST RESPOND.
OKAY, GET MOVING. I'VE LOST HALF A NIGHT'S SLEEP BECAUSE OF YOU-I MIGHT AS WELL LOSE THE REST.

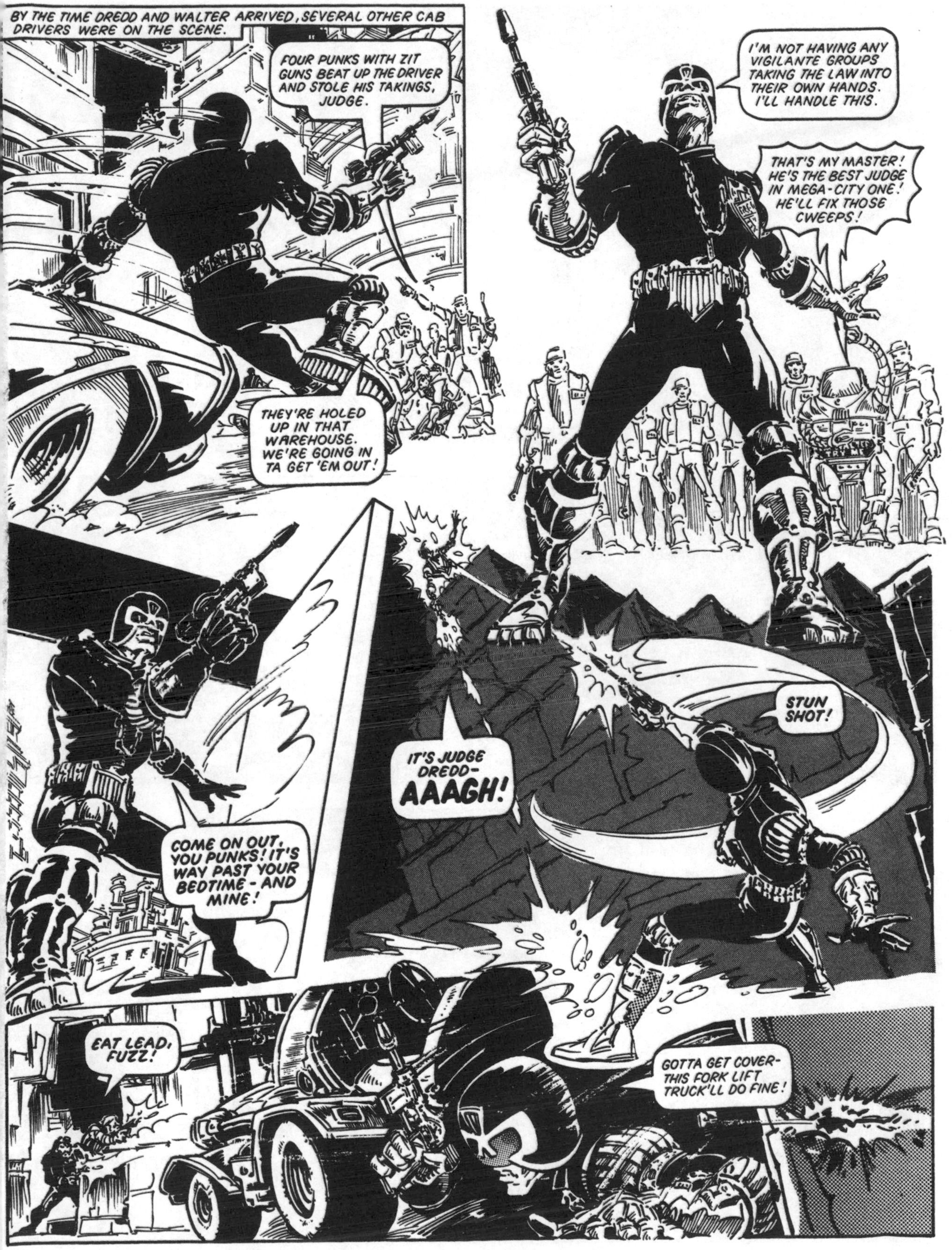
BY THE TIME DREDD AND WALTER ARRIVED, SEVERAL OTHER CAB DRIVERS WERE ON THE SCENE.
FOUR PUNKS WITH ZIT GUNS BEAT UP THE DRIVER AND STOLE HIS TAKINGS, JUDGE.
THEY'RE HOLED UP IN THAT WAREHOUSE. WE'RE GOING IN TA GET 'EM OUT!
I'M NOT HAVING ANY VIGILANTE GROUPS TAKING THE LAW INTO THEIR OWN HANDS. I'LL HANDLE THIS.
THAT'S MY MASTER! HE'S THE BEST JUDGE IN MEGA-CITY ONE! HE'LL FIX THOSE CWEEPS!
COME ON OUT, YOU PUNKS! IT'S WAY PAST YOUR BEDTIME - AND MINE!
IT'S JUDGE DREDD- AAAGH!
STUN SHOT!
EAT LEAD, FUZZ!
GOTTA GET COVER- THIS FORK LIFT TRUCK'LL DO FINE!

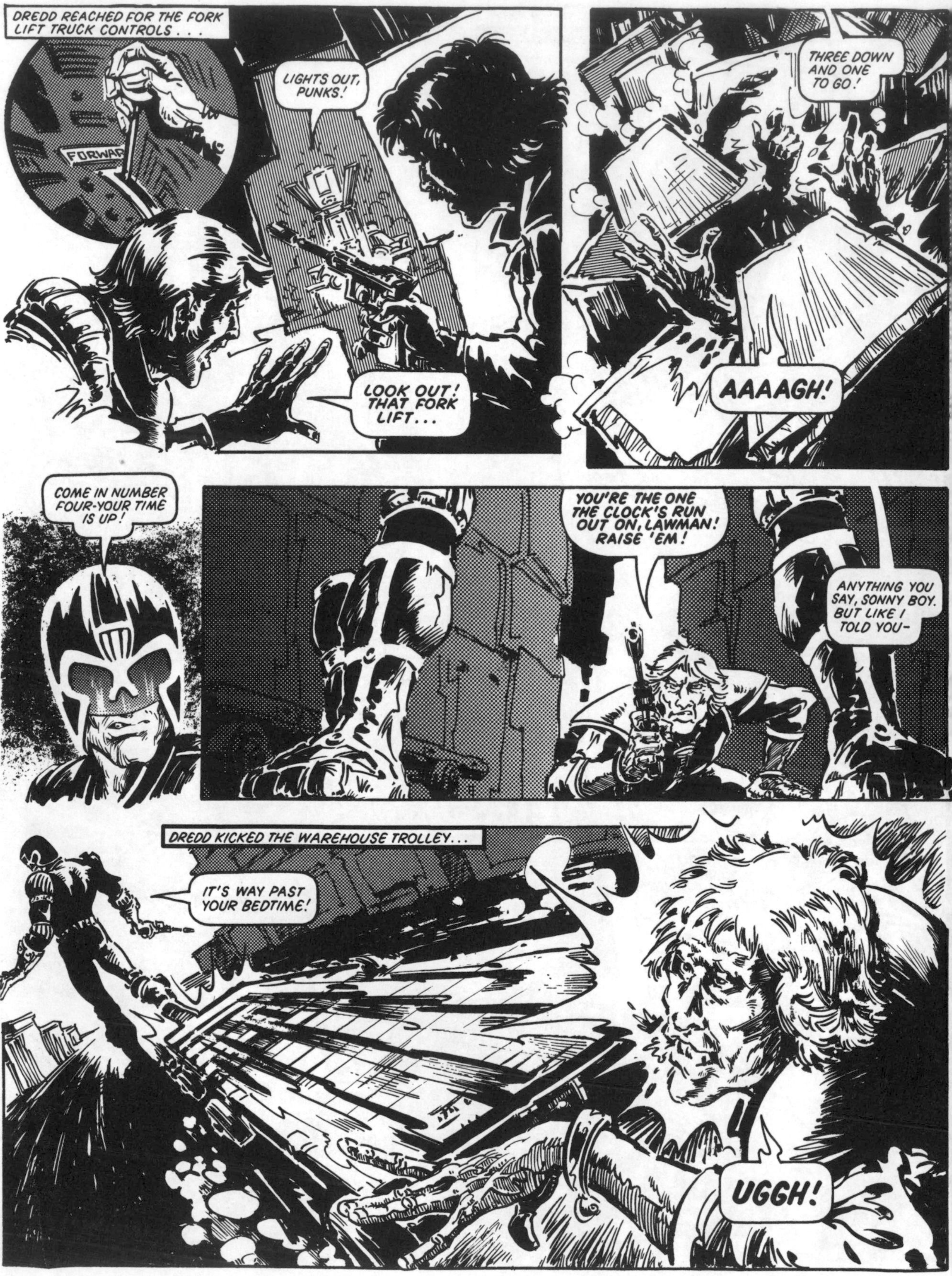
DREDD REACHED FOR THE FORK LIFT TRUCK CONTROLS . . .
FORWAR
LIGHTS OUT, PUNKS!
LOOK OUT! THAT FORK LIFT...
THREE DOWN AND ONE TO GO!
AAAAGH!
COME IN NUMBER FOUR-YOUR TIME IS UP!
YOU'RE THE ONE THE CLOCK'S RUN OUT ON, LAWMAN! RAISE 'EM!
ANYTHING YOU SAY, SONNY BOY. BUT LIKE I TOLD YOU-
DREDD KICKED THE WAREHOUSE TROLLEY...
IT'S WAY PAST YOUR BEDTIME!
UGGH!

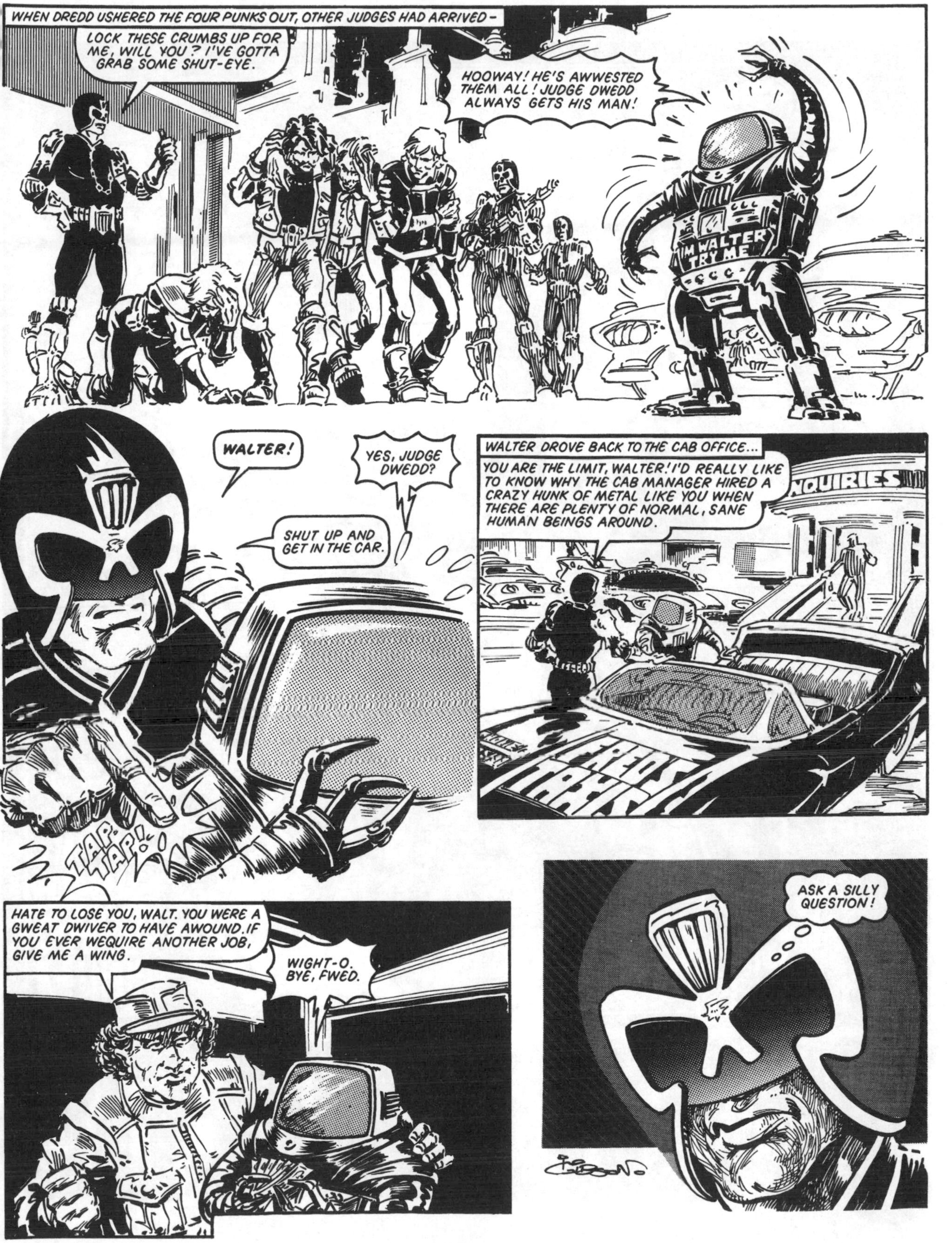
WHEN DREDD USHERED THE FOUR PUNKS OUT, OTHER JUDGES HAD ARRIVED –
LOCK THESE CRUMBS UP FOR ME, WILL YOU? I'VE GOTTA GRAB SOME SHUT-EYE.
HOOWAY! HE'S AWWESTED THEM ALL! JUDGE DWEDD ALWAYS GETS HIS MAN!
I'M WALTER TRY ME
WALTER!
YES, JUDGE DWEDD?
SHUT UP AND GET IN THE CAR.
TAP TAP!
WALTER DROVE BACK TO THE CAB OFFICE...
YOU ARE THE LIMIT, WALTER! I'D REALLY LIKE TO KNOW WHY THE CAB MANAGER HIRED A CRAZY HUNK OF METAL LIKE YOU WHEN THERE ARE PLENTY OF NORMAL, SANE HUMAN BEINGS AROUND.
NQUIRIES
HATE TO LOSE YOU, WALT. YOU WERE A GWEAT DWIVER TO HAVE AWOUND. IF YOU EVER WEQUIRE ANOTHER JOB, GIVE ME A WING.
WIGHT-O. BYE, FWED.
ASK A SILLY QUESTION!

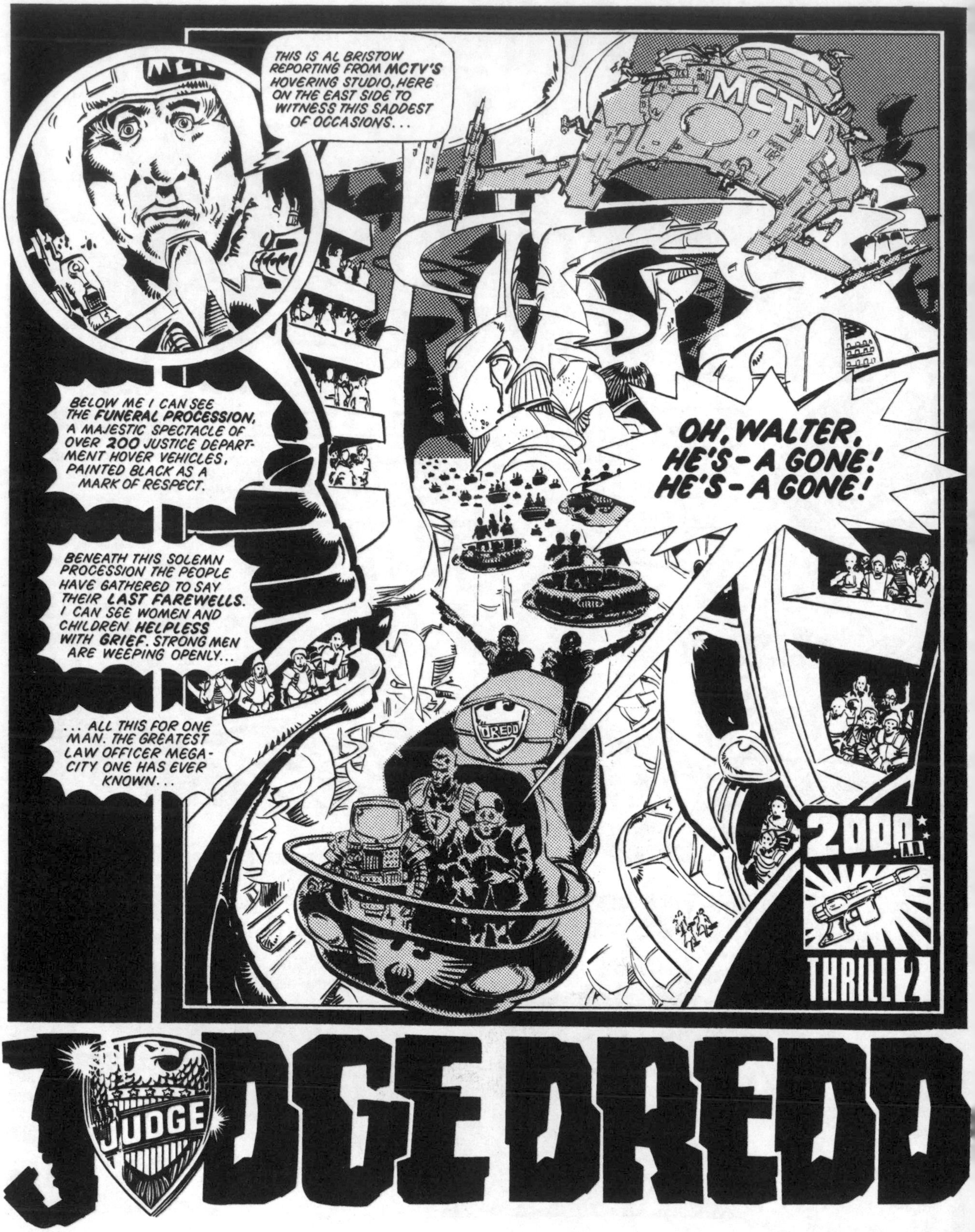
THIS IS AL BRISTOW REPORTING FROM MCTV'S HOVERING STUDIO, HERE ON THE EAST SIDE TO WITNESS THIS SADDEST OF OCCASIONS...
MCTV
BELOW ME I CAN SEE THE FUNERAL PROCESSION, A MAJESTIC SPECTACLE OF OVER 200 JUSTICE DEPARTMENT HOVER VEHICLES, PAINTED BLACK AS A MARK OF RESPECT.
BENEATH THIS SOLEMN PROCESSION THE PEOPLE HAVE GATHERED TO SAY THEIR LAST FAREWELLS. I CAN SEE WOMEN AND CHILDREN HELPLESS WITH GRIEF. STRONG MEN ARE WEEPING OPENLY...
... ALL THIS FOR ONE MAN. THE GREATEST LAW OFFICER MEGA-CITY ONE HAS EVER KNOWN...
OH, WALTER, HE'S-A GONE! HE'S-A GONE!
DREDD
2000 A.D.
THRILL 2
JUDGE
JUDGE DREDD

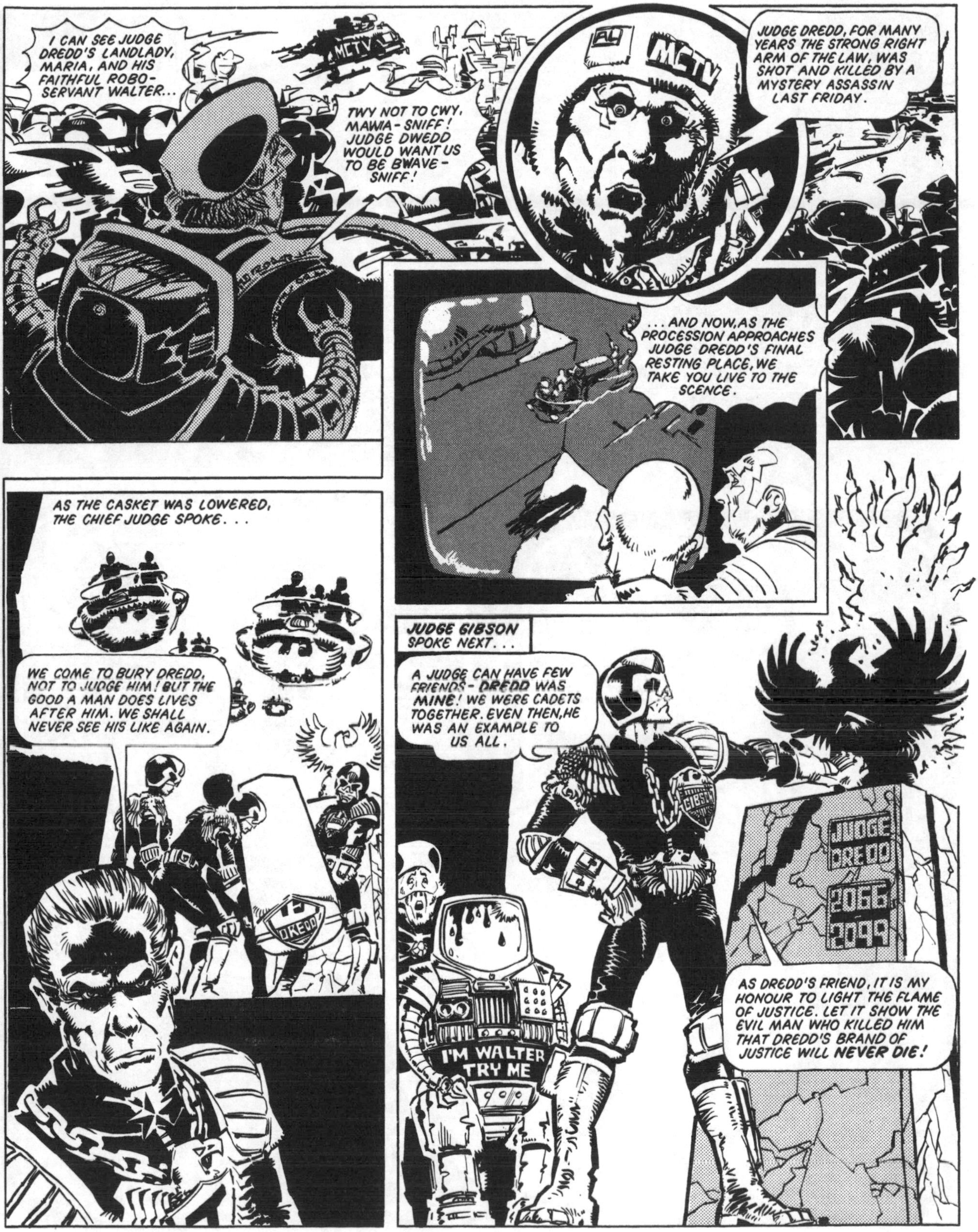
I CAN SEE JUDGE DREDD'S LANDLADY, MARIA, AND HIS FAITHFUL ROBO-SERVANT WALTER...
TWY NOT TO CWY, MAWIA - SNIFF! JUDGE DWEDD WOULD WANT US TO BE BWAVE - SNIFF!
MCTV
JUDGE DREDD, FOR MANY YEARS THE STRONG RIGHT ARM OF THE LAW, WAS SHOT AND KILLED BY A MYSTERY ASSASSIN LAST FRIDAY.
... AND NOW, AS THE PROCESSION APPROACHES JUDGE DREDD'S FINAL RESTING PLACE, WE TAKE YOU LIVE TO THE SCENCE.
AS THE CASKET WAS LOWERED, THE CHIEF JUDGE SPOKE...
WE COME TO BURY DREDD, NOT TO JUDGE HIM! BUT THE GOOD A MAN DOES LIVES AFTER HIM. WE SHALL NEVER SEE HIS LIKE AGAIN.
DREDD
JUDGE GIBSON SPOKE NEXT...
A JUDGE CAN HAVE FEW FRIENDS - DREDD WAS MINE! WE WERE CADETS TOGETHER. EVEN THEN, HE WAS AN EXAMPLE TO US ALL.
GIBSON
JUDGE DREDD 2066 2099
I'M WALTER TRY ME
AS DREDD'S FRIEND, IT IS MY HONOUR TO LIGHT THE FLAME OF JUSTICE. LET IT SHOW THE EVIL MAN WHO KILLED HIM THAT DREDD'S BRAND OF JUSTICE WILL NEVER DIE!

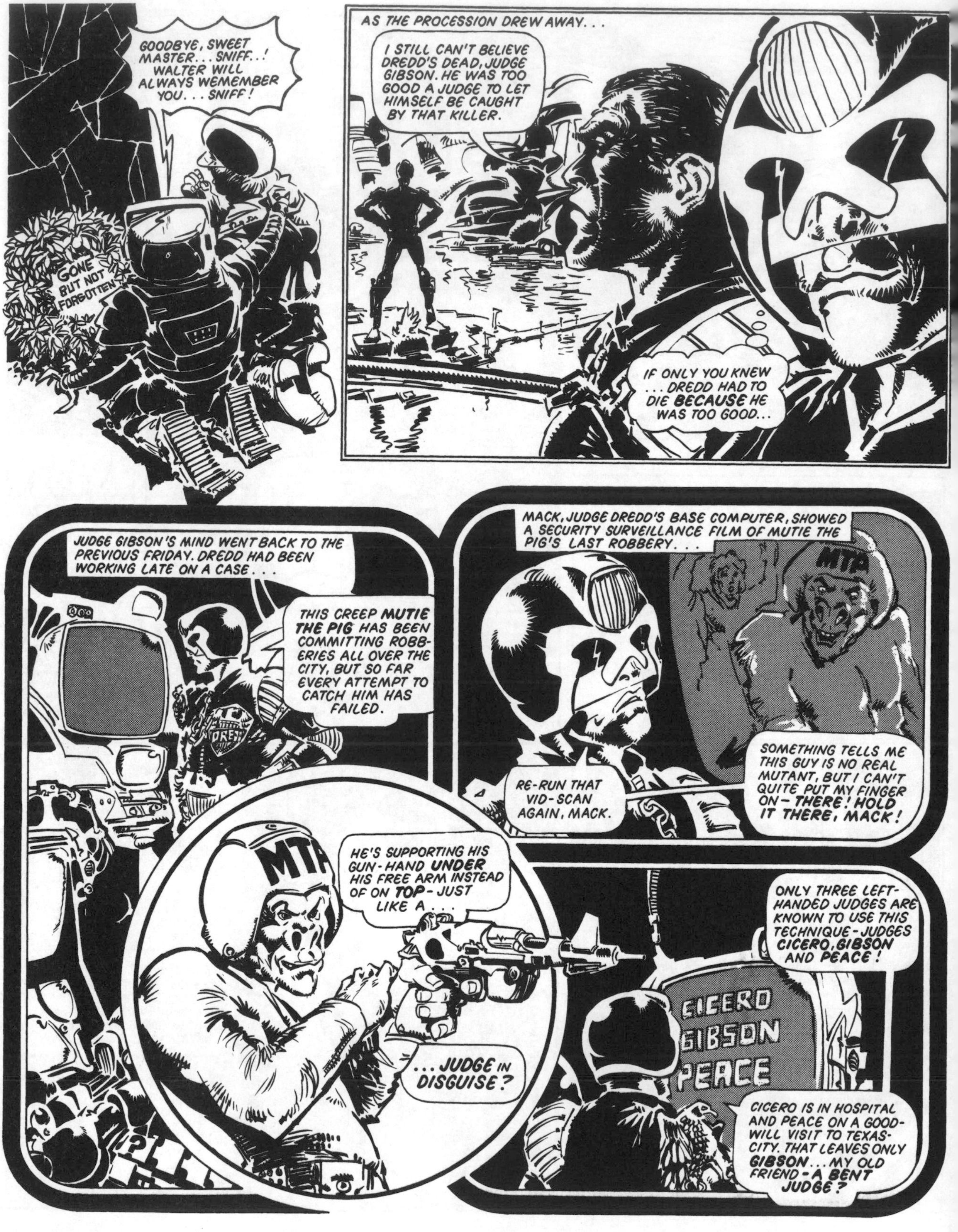
GOODBYE, SWEET MASTER... SNIFF..! WALTER WILL ALWAYS WEMEMBER YOU... SNIFF!
GONE BUT NOT FORGOTTEN
AS THE PROCESSION DREW AWAY...
I STILL CAN'T BELIEVE DREDD'S DEAD, JUDGE GIBSON. HE WAS TOO GOOD A JUDGE TO LET HIMSELF BE CAUGHT BY THAT KILLER.
IF ONLY YOU KNEW ... DREDD HAD TO DIE BECAUSE HE WAS TOO GOOD...
JUDGE GIBSON'S MIND WENT BACK TO THE PREVIOUS FRIDAY. DREDD HAD BEEN WORKING LATE ON A CASE...
THIS CREEP MUTIE THE PIG HAS BEEN COMMITTING ROBBERIES ALL OVER THE CITY, BUT SO FAR EVERY ATTEMPT TO CATCH HIM HAS FAILED.
MACK, JUDGE DREDD'S BASE COMPUTER, SHOWED A SECURITY SURVEILLANCE FILM OF MUTIE THE PIG'S LAST ROBBERY...
MTP
RE-RUN THAT VID-SCAN AGAIN, MACK.
SOMETHING TELLS ME THIS GUY IS NO REAL MUTANT, BUT I CAN'T QUITE PUT MY FINGER ON – THERE! HOLD IT THERE, MACK!
MTP
HE'S SUPPORTING HIS GUN-HAND UNDER HIS FREE ARM INSTEAD OF ON TOP – JUST LIKE A...
...JUDGE IN DISGUISE?
ONLY THREE LEFT-HANDED JUDGES ARE KNOWN TO USE THIS TECHNIQUE – JUDGES CICERO, GIBSON AND PEACE!
CICERO
GIBSON
PEACE
CICERO IS IN HOSPITAL AND PEACE ON A GOODWILL VISIT TO TEXAS-CITY. THAT LEAVES ONLY GIBSON... MY OLD FRIEND – A BENT JUDGE?

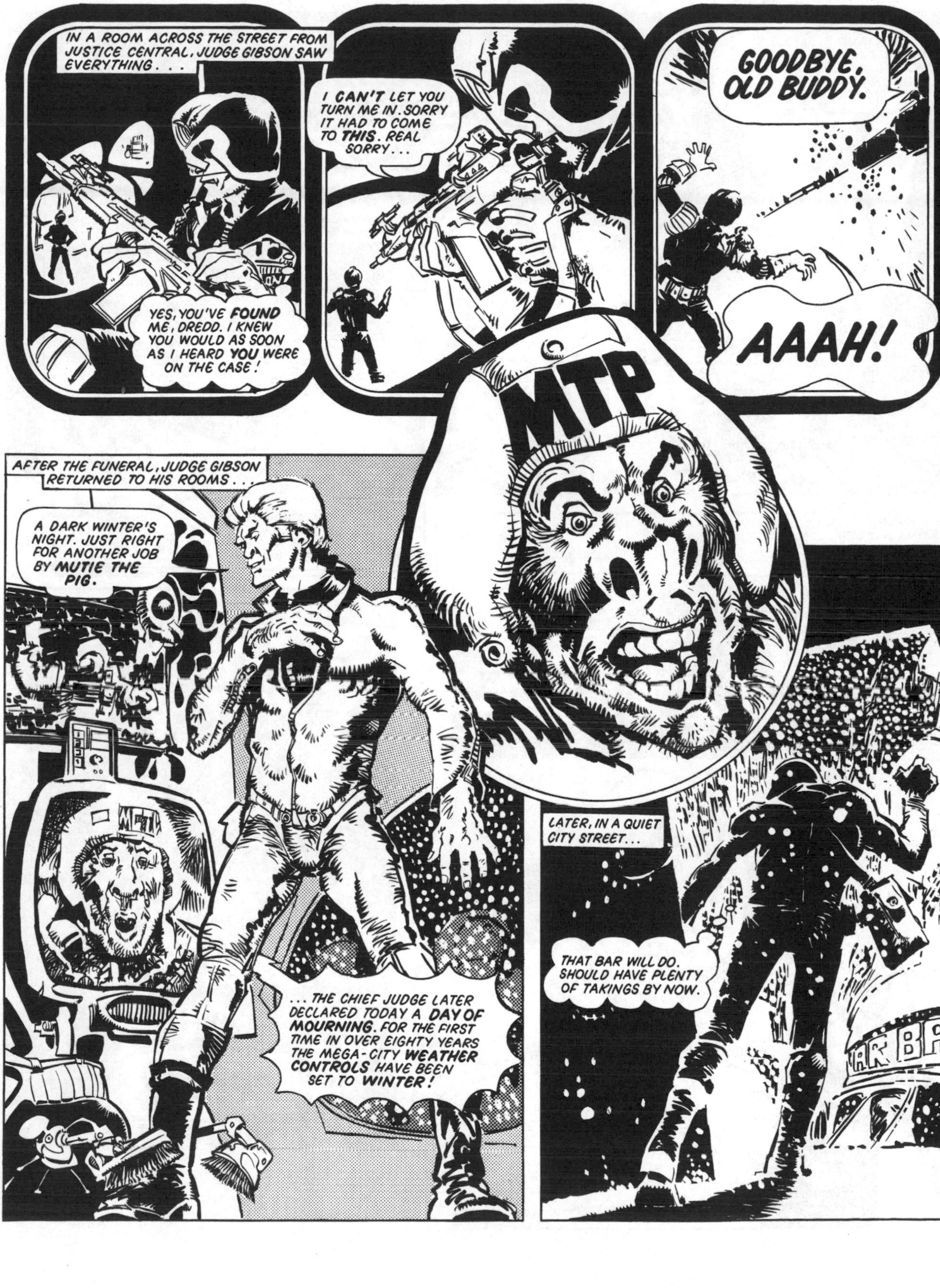
IN A ROOM ACROSS THE STREET FROM JUSTICE CENTRAL, JUDGE GIBSON SAW EVERYTHING . . .
YES, YOU'VE FOUND ME, DREDD. I KNEW YOU WOULD AS SOON AS I HEARD YOU WERE ON THE CASE!
I CAN'T LET YOU TURN ME IN. SORRY IT HAD TO COME TO THIS. REAL SORRY...
GOODBYE, OLD BUDDY.
AAAH!
MTP
AFTER THE FUNERAL, JUDGE GIBSON RETURNED TO HIS ROOMS . . .
A DARK WINTER'S NIGHT. JUST RIGHT FOR ANOTHER JOB BY MUTIE THE PIG.
... THE CHIEF JUDGE LATER DECLARED TODAY A DAY OF MOURNING. FOR THE FIRST TIME IN OVER EIGHTY YEARS THE MEGA-CITY WEATHER CONTROLS HAVE BEEN SET TO WINTER!
LATER, IN A QUIET CITY STREET...
THAT BAR WILL DO. SHOULD HAVE PLENTY OF TAKINGS BY NOW.

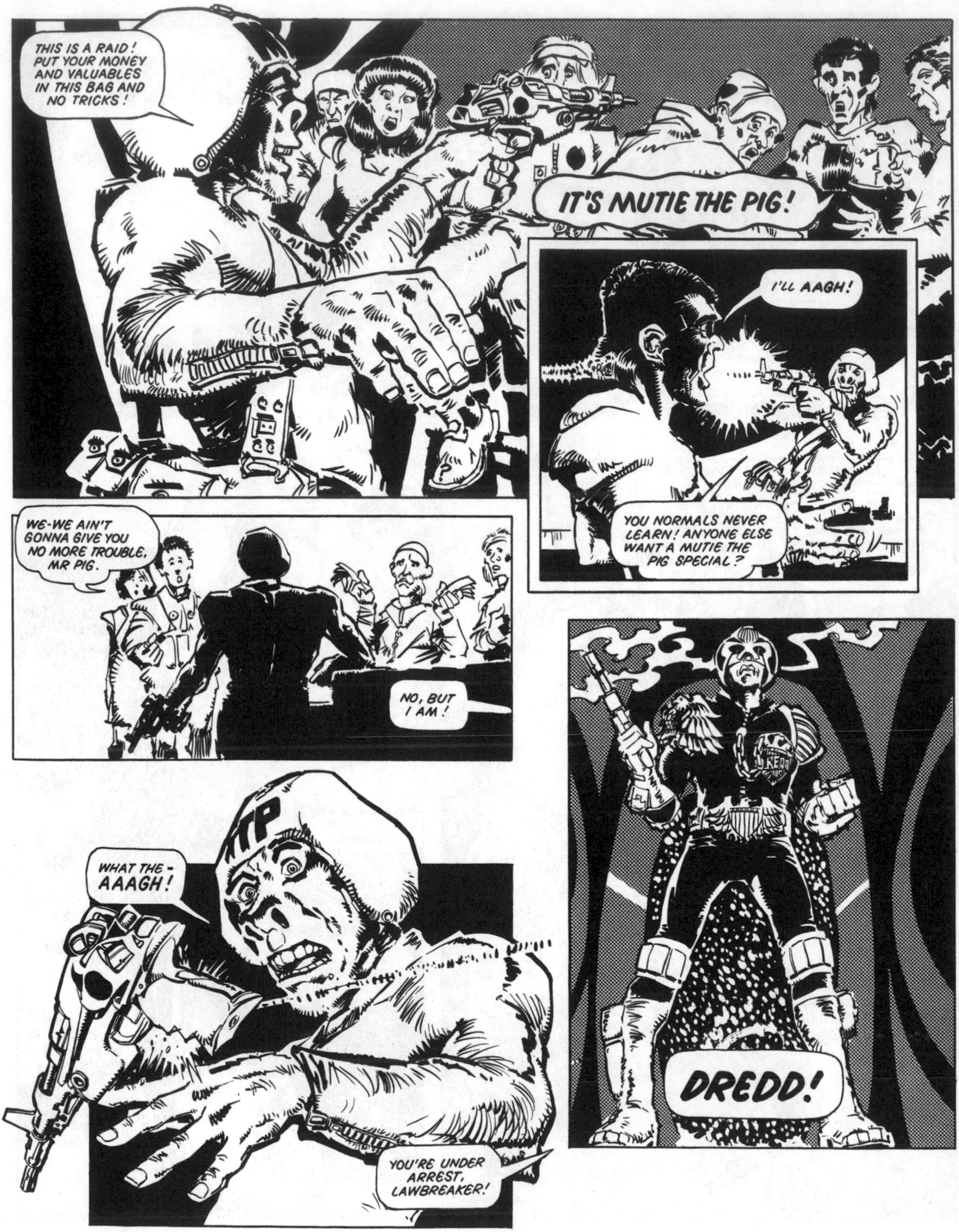

THIS IS A RAID! PUT YOUR MONEY AND VALUABLES IN THIS BAG AND NO TRICKS!
IT'S MUTIE THE PIG!
I'LL AAGH!
YOU NORMALS NEVER LEARN! ANYONE ELSE WANT A MUTIE THE PIG SPECIAL?
WE-WE AIN'T GONNA GIVE YOU NO MORE TROUBLE, MR PIG.
NO, BUT I AM!
WHAT THE - AAAGH!
YOU'RE UNDER ARREST, LAWBREAKER!
DREDD!

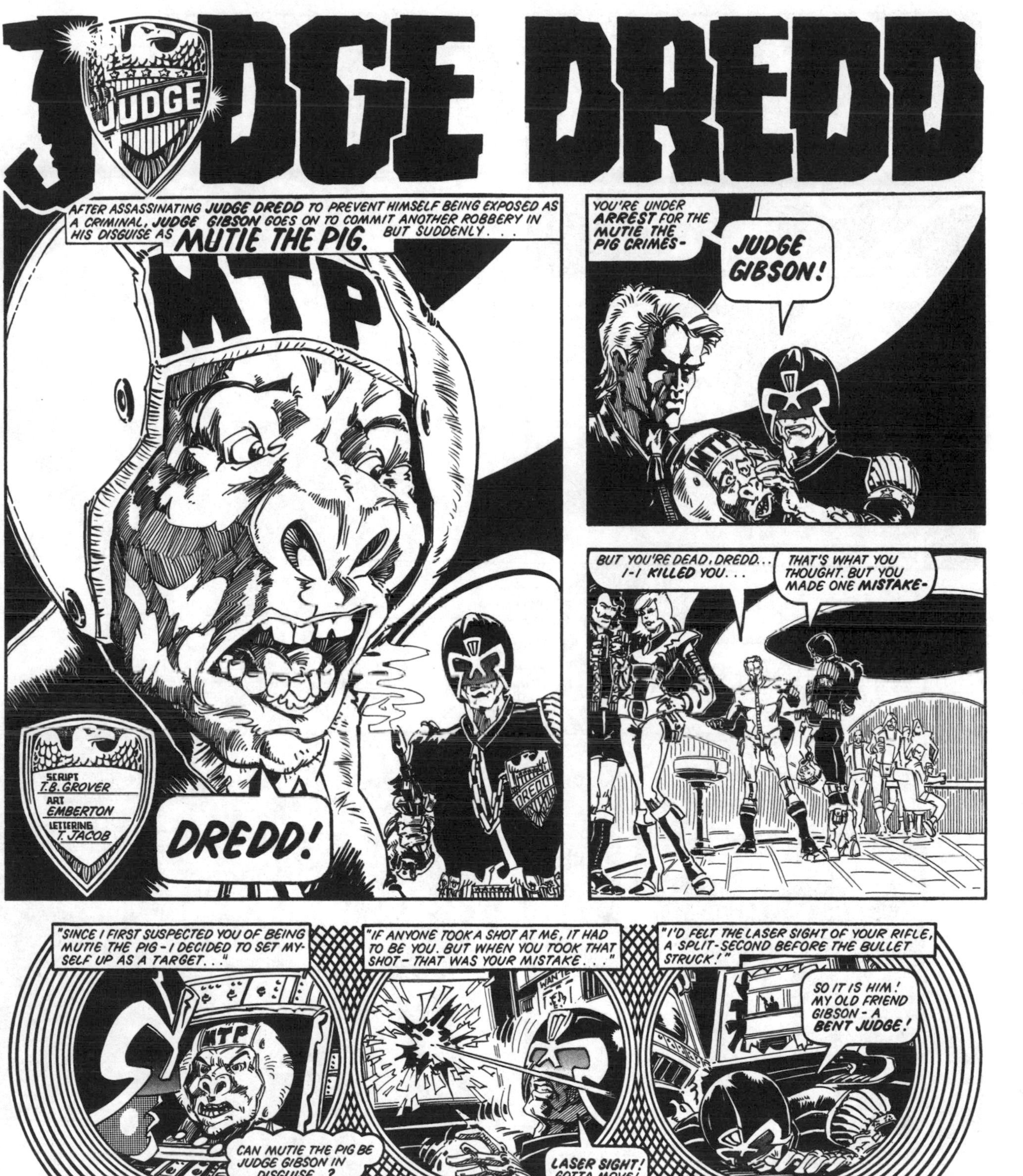
JUDGE DREDD
AFTER ASSASSINATING JUDGE DREDD TO PREVENT HIMSELF BEING EXPOSED AS A CRIMINAL, JUDGE GIBSON GOES ON TO COMMIT ANOTHER ROBBERY IN HIS DISGUISE AS MUTIE THE PIG. BUT SUDDENLY. . .
MTP
SCRIPT T.B. GROVER
ART EMBERTON
LETTERING T. JACOB
DREDD!
YOU'RE UNDER ARREST FOR THE MUTIE THE PIG CRIMES-
JUDGE GIBSON!
BUT YOU'RE DEAD, DREDD... I-I KILLED YOU...
THAT'S WHAT YOU THOUGHT. BUT YOU MADE ONE MISTAKE-
"SINCE I FIRST SUSPECTED YOU OF BEING MUTIE THE PIG - I DECIDED TO SET MYSELF UP AS A TARGET..."
MTP
CAN MUTIE THE PIG BE JUDGE GIBSON IN DISGUISE..?
"IF ANYONE TOOK A SHOT AT ME, IT HAD TO BE YOU. BUT WHEN YOU TOOK THAT SHOT - THAT WAS YOUR MISTAKE..."
LASER SIGHT! GOTTA MOVE!
"I'D FELT THE LASER SIGHT OF YOUR RIFLE, A SPLIT-SECOND BEFORE THE BULLET STRUCK!"
SO IT IS HIM! MY OLD FRIEND GIBSON - A BENT JUDGE!

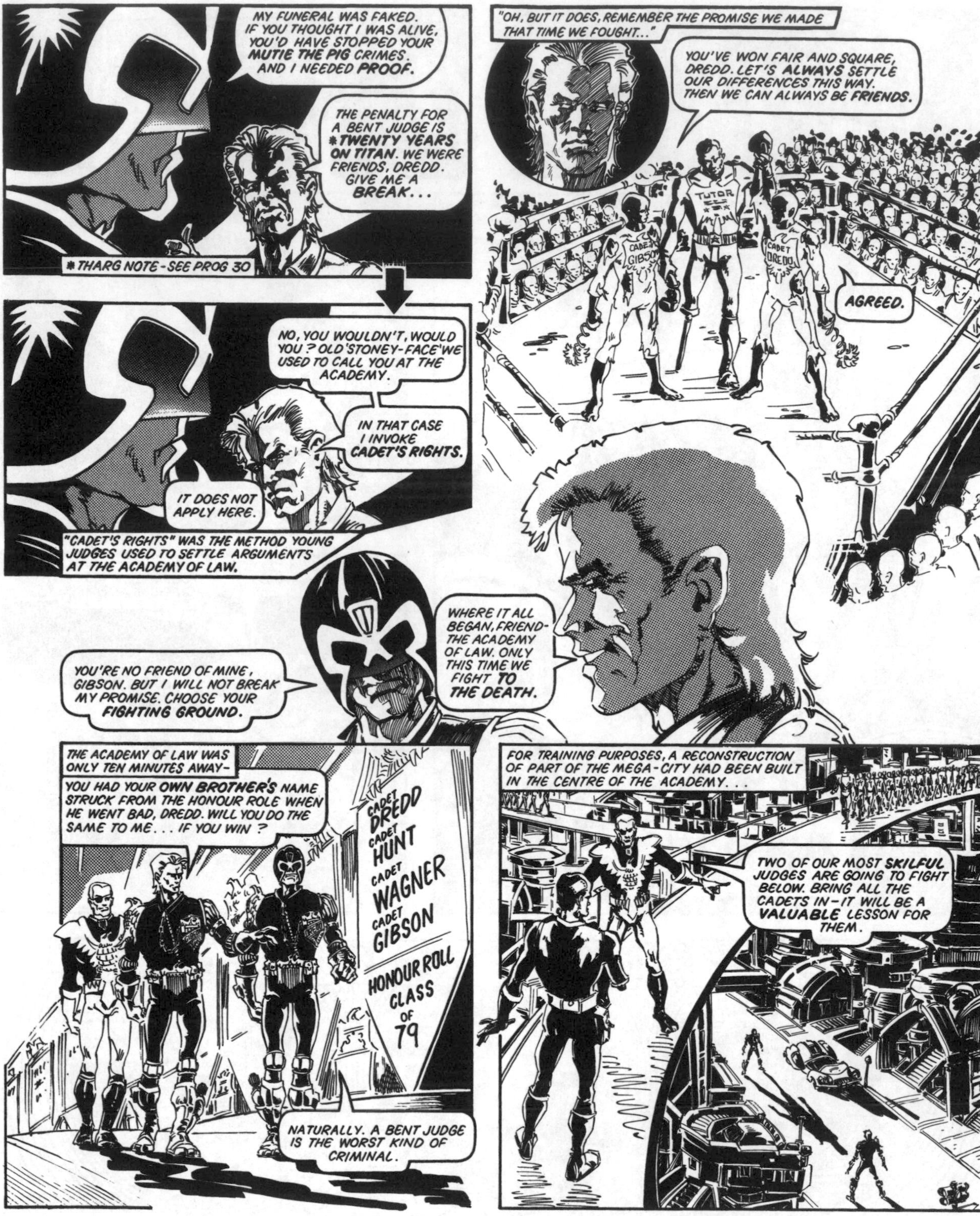
MY FUNERAL WAS FAKED. IF YOU THOUGHT I WAS ALIVE, YOU'D HAVE STOPPED YOUR MUTIE THE PIG CRIMES. AND I NEEDED PROOF.
THE PENALTY FOR A BENT JUDGE IS *TWENTY YEARS ON TITAN. WE WERE FRIENDS, DREDD. GIVE ME A BREAK...
*THARG NOTE - SEE PROG 30
NO, YOU WOULDN'T, WOULD YOU? OLD 'STONEY-FACE' WE USED TO CALL YOU AT THE ACADEMY.
IN THAT CASE I INVOKE CADET'S RIGHTS.
IT DOES NOT APPLY HERE.
"CADET'S RIGHTS" WAS THE METHOD YOUNG JUDGES USED TO SETTLE ARGUMENTS AT THE ACADEMY OF LAW.
"OH, BUT IT DOES, REMEMBER THE PROMISE WE MADE THAT TIME WE FOUGHT..."
YOU'VE WON FAIR AND SQUARE, DREDD. LET'S ALWAYS SETTLE OUR DIFFERENCES THIS WAY. THEN WE CAN ALWAYS BE FRIENDS.
TUTOR
CADET GIBSON
CADET DREDD
AGREED.
WHERE IT ALL BEGAN, FRIEND - THE ACADEMY OF LAW. ONLY THIS TIME WE FIGHT TO THE DEATH.
YOU'RE NO FRIEND OF MINE, GIBSON. BUT I WILL NOT BREAK MY PROMISE. CHOOSE YOUR FIGHTING GROUND.
THE ACADEMY OF LAW WAS ONLY TEN MINUTES AWAY-
YOU HAD YOUR OWN BROTHER'S NAME STRUCK FROM THE HONOUR ROLE WHEN HE WENT BAD, DREDD. WILL YOU DO THE SAME TO ME... IF YOU WIN?
CADET DREDD
CADET HUNT
CADET WAGNER
CADET GIBSON
HONOUR ROLL CLASS OF 79
NATURALLY. A BENT JUDGE IS THE WORST KIND OF CRIMINAL.
FOR TRAINING PURPOSES, A RECONSTRUCTION OF PART OF THE MEGA-CITY HAD BEEN BUILT IN THE CENTRE OF THE ACADEMY...
TWO OF OUR MOST SKILFUL JUDGES ARE GOING TO FIGHT BELOW. BRING ALL THE CADETS IN - IT WILL BE A VALUABLE LESSON FOR THEM.

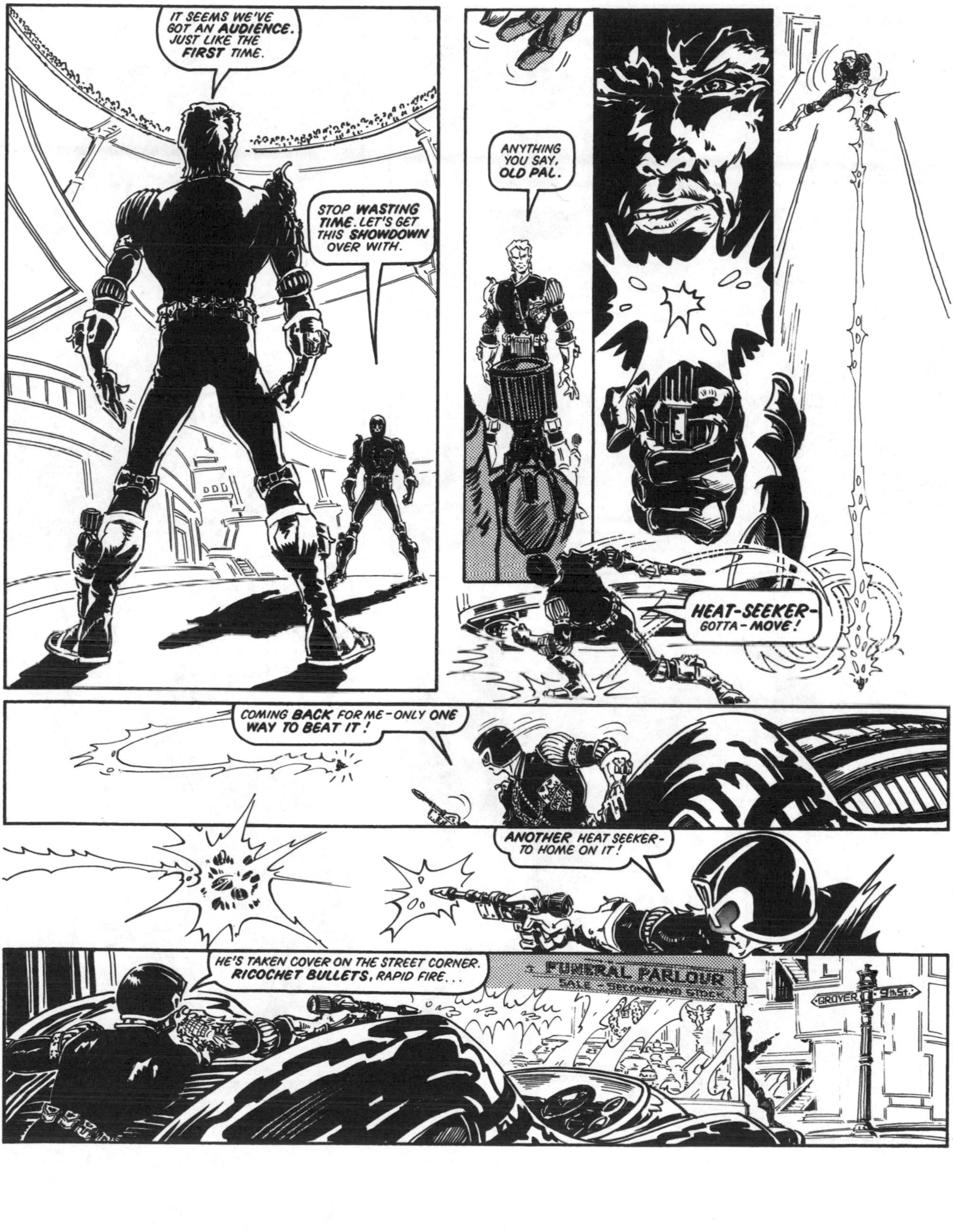
IT SEEMS WE'VE GOT AN AUDIENCE. JUST LIKE THE FIRST TIME.
STOP WASTING TIME. LET'S GET THIS SHOWDOWN OVER WITH.
ANYTHING YOU SAY, OLD PAL.
HEAT-SEEKER- GOTTA-MOVE!
COMING BACK FOR ME-ONLY ONE WAY TO BEAT IT!
ANOTHER HEAT SEEKER- TO HOME ON IT!
HE'S TAKEN COVER ON THE STREET CORNER. RICOCHET BULLETS, RAPID FIRE...
FUNERAL PARLOUR
SALE - SECONDHAND STOCK
GROVER
9th St.

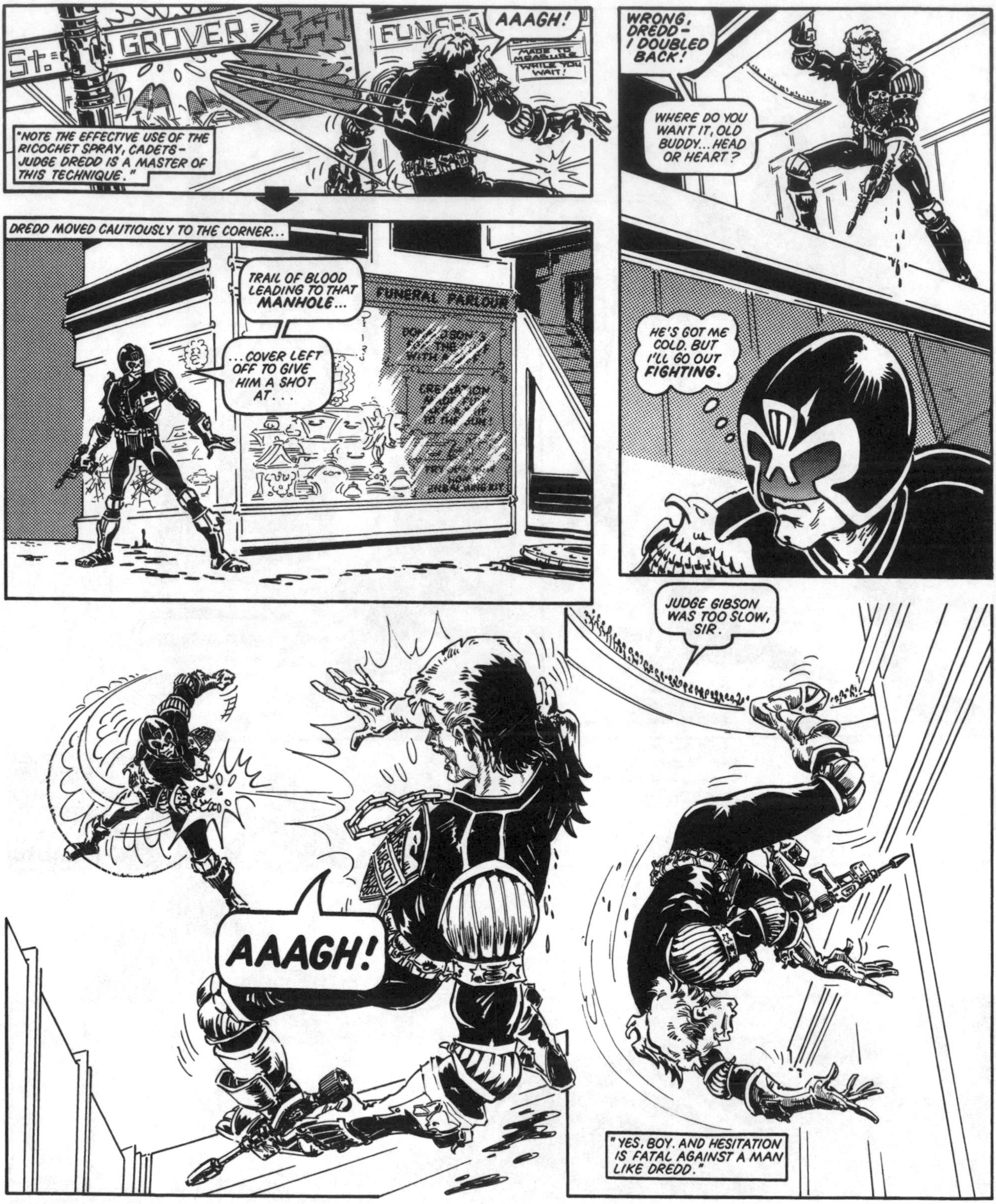
St.
GROVER
FUNERA
MADE TO MEASURE WHILE YOU WAIT!
AAAGH!
"NOTE THE EFFECTIVE USE OF THE RICOCHET SPRAY, CADETS– JUDGE DREDD IS A MASTER OF THIS TECHNIQUE."
WRONG, DREDD– I DOUBLED BACK!
WHERE DO YOU WANT IT, OLD BUDDY... HEAD OR HEART?
DREDD MOVED CAUTIOUSLY TO THE CORNER...
TRAIL OF BLOOD LEADING TO THAT MANHOLE...
...COVER LEFT OFF TO GIVE HIM A SHOT AT...
FUNERAL PARLOUR
HE'S GOT ME COLD. BUT I'LL GO OUT FIGHTING.
JUDGE GIBSON WAS TOO SLOW, SIR.
AAAGH!
"YES, BOY. AND HESITATION IS FATAL AGAINST A MAN LIKE DREDD."

BUT YOU COULD'VE HAD ME! WHY DIDN'T YOU FIRE?
IT-IT WAS HARD ENOUGH KILLING YOU ONCE... I COULDN'T... DO IT AGAIN... YOU SEE, DREDD...
YOU WERE MY FRIEND...
IT... IT'S BETTER THIS WAY... COULDN'T HAVE FACED... TWENTY YEARS ON TITAN.
GOODBYE... OLD BUDDY...
THAT WAS A MASTERFUL EXHIBITION, JUDGE DREDD!
NO, PRINCIPAL. IT WAS A BITTER VICTORY. JUDGE GIBSON WAS... MY FRIEND.
BUT EVERY JUDGE MUST KNOW MANY BITTER MOMENTS - AND FACE THEM SQUARELY...
CADET
HUNT
CADET
WAGNER
OUR ROLL
CLASS
OF
79
FOR NO MAN IS GREATER THAN THE LAW.
THE END.
NEXT PROG: DREDD VERSUS CAPTAIN STRANGE!

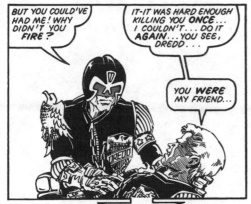

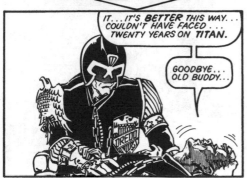

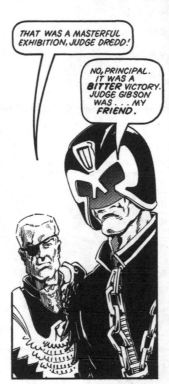

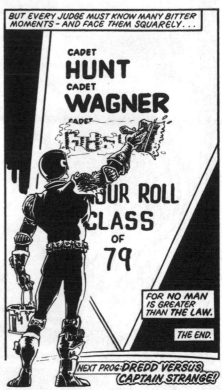

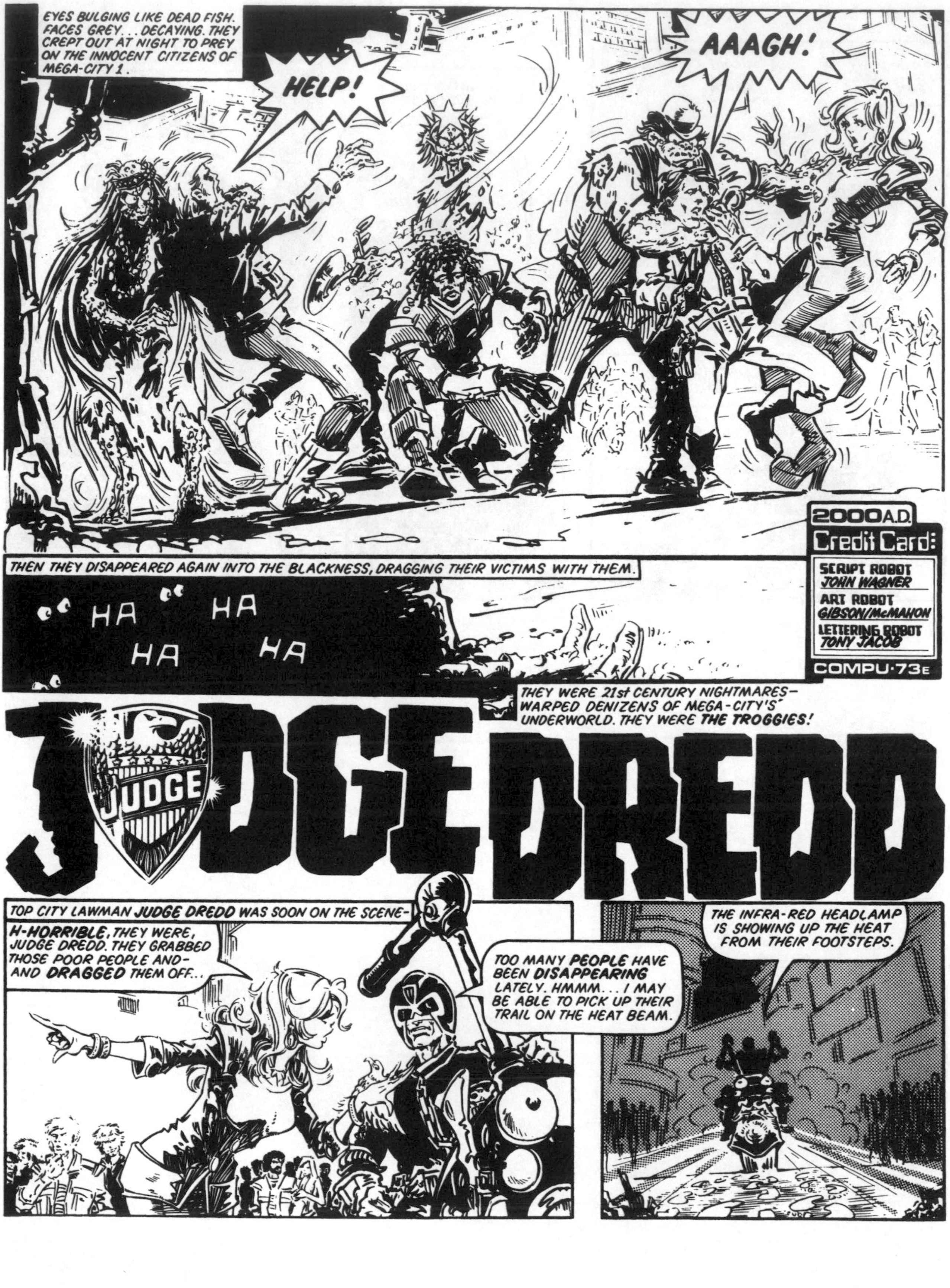
EYES BULGING LIKE DEAD FISH. FACES GREY... DECAYING. THEY CREPT OUT AT NIGHT TO PREY ON THE INNOCENT CITIZENS OF MEGA-CITY 1.
HELP!
AAAGH!
THEN THEY DISAPPEARED AGAIN INTO THE BLACKNESS, DRAGGING THEIR VICTIMS WITH THEM.
HA HA HA HA
2000 A.D. Credit Card:
SCRIPT ROBOT JOHN WAGNER
ART ROBOT GIBSON/McMAHON
LETTERING ROBOT TONY JACOB
COMPU·73E
THEY WERE 21st CENTURY NIGHTMARES— WARPED DENIZENS OF MEGA-CITY'S' UNDERWORLD. THEY WERE THE TROGGIES!
JUDGE DREDD
TOP CITY LAWMAN JUDGE DREDD WAS SOON ON THE SCENE—
H-HORRIBLE, THEY WERE, JUDGE DREDD. THEY GRABBED THOSE POOR PEOPLE AND— AND DRAGGED THEM OFF...
TOO MANY PEOPLE HAVE BEEN DISAPPEARING LATELY. HMMM... I MAY BE ABLE TO PICK UP THEIR TRAIL ON THE HEAT BEAM.
THE INFRA-RED HEADLAMP IS SHOWING UP THE HEAT FROM THEIR FOOTSTEPS.

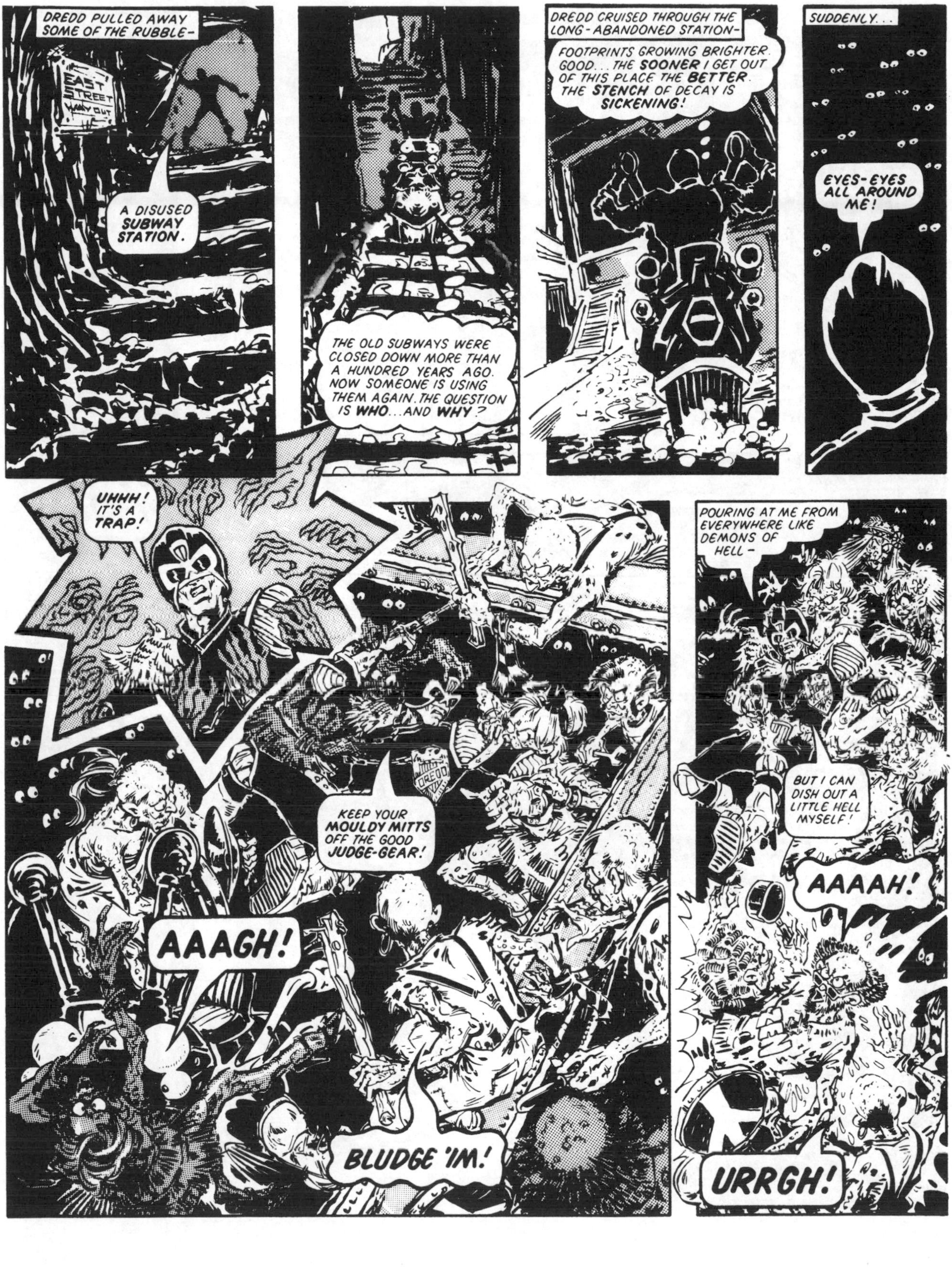
DREDD PULLED AWAY SOME OF THE RUBBLE-
EAST STREET WAY OUT
A DISUSED SUBWAY STATION.
THE OLD SUBWAYS WERE CLOSED DOWN MORE THAN A HUNDRED YEARS AGO. NOW SOMEONE IS USING THEM AGAIN. THE QUESTION IS WHO...AND WHY?
DREDD CRUISED THROUGH THE LONG-ABANDONED STATION-
FOOTPRINTS GROWING BRIGHTER. GOOD... THE SOONER I GET OUT OF THIS PLACE THE BETTER. THE STENCH OF DECAY IS SICKENING!
SUDDENLY...
EYES-EYES ALL AROUND ME!
UHHH! IT'S A TRAP!
KEEP YOUR MOULDY MITTS OFF THE GOOD JUDGE-GEAR!
AAAGH!
BLUDGE 'IM!
POURING AT ME FROM EVERYWHERE LIKE DEMONS OF HELL-
BUT I CAN DISH OUT A LITTLE HELL MYSELF!
AAAAH!
URRGH!

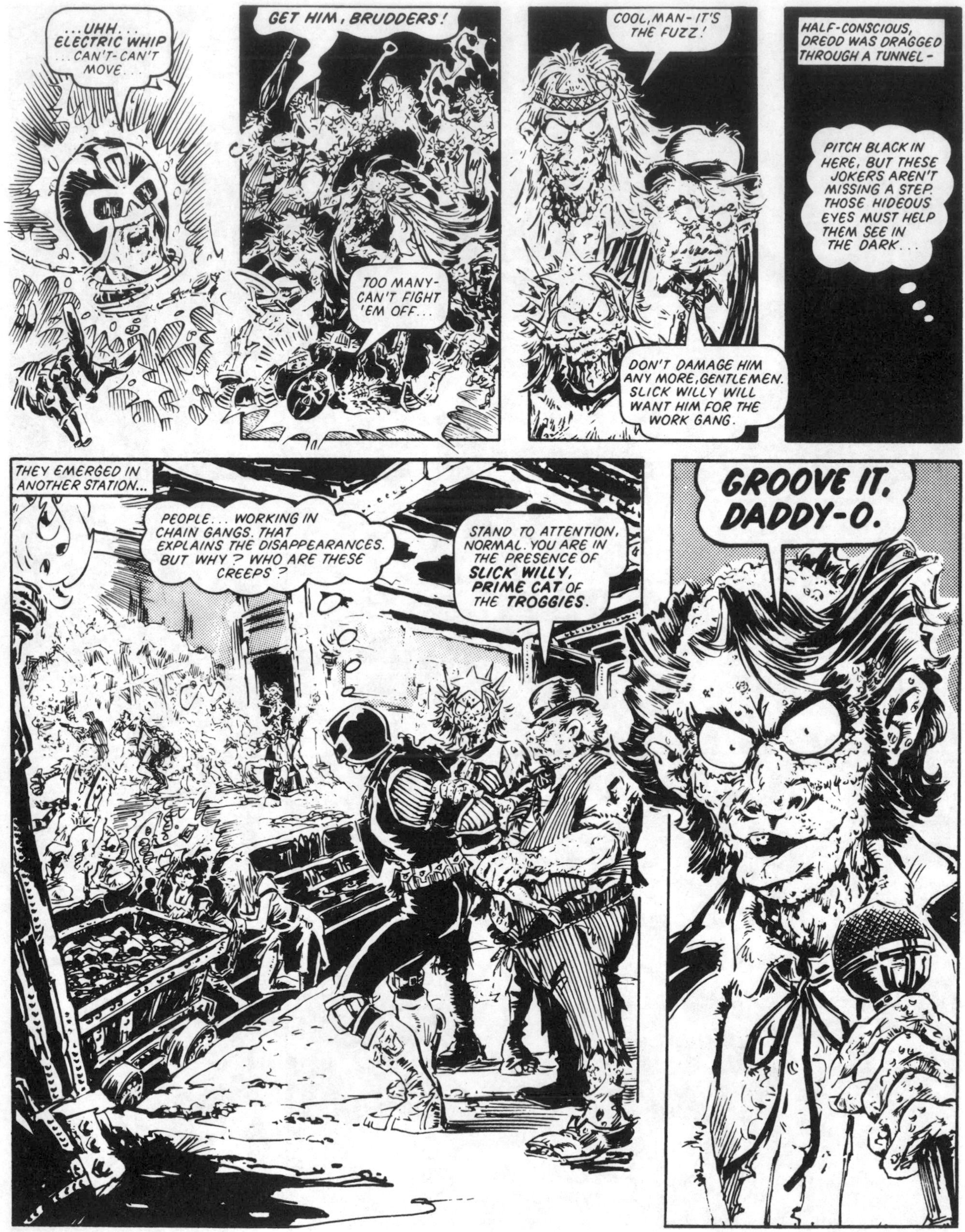
...UHH... ELECTRIC WHIP ...CAN'T-CAN'T MOVE...
GET HIM, BRUDDERS!
TOO MANY-CAN'T FIGHT 'EM OFF...
COOL, MAN-IT'S THE FUZZ!
DON'T DAMAGE HIM ANY MORE, GENTLEMEN. SLICK WILLY WILL WANT HIM FOR THE WORK GANG.
HALF-CONSCIOUS, DREDD WAS DRAGGED THROUGH A TUNNEL-
PITCH BLACK IN HERE, BUT THESE JOKERS AREN'T MISSING A STEP. THOSE HIDEOUS EYES MUST HELP THEM SEE IN THE DARK...
THEY EMERGED IN ANOTHER STATION...
PEOPLE... WORKING IN CHAIN GANGS. THAT EXPLAINS THE DISAPPEARANCES. BUT WHY? WHO ARE THESE CREEPS?
STAND TO ATTENTION, NORMAL. YOU ARE IN THE PRESENCE OF SLICK WILLY, PRIME CAT OF THE TROGGIES.
GROOVE IT. DADDY-O.

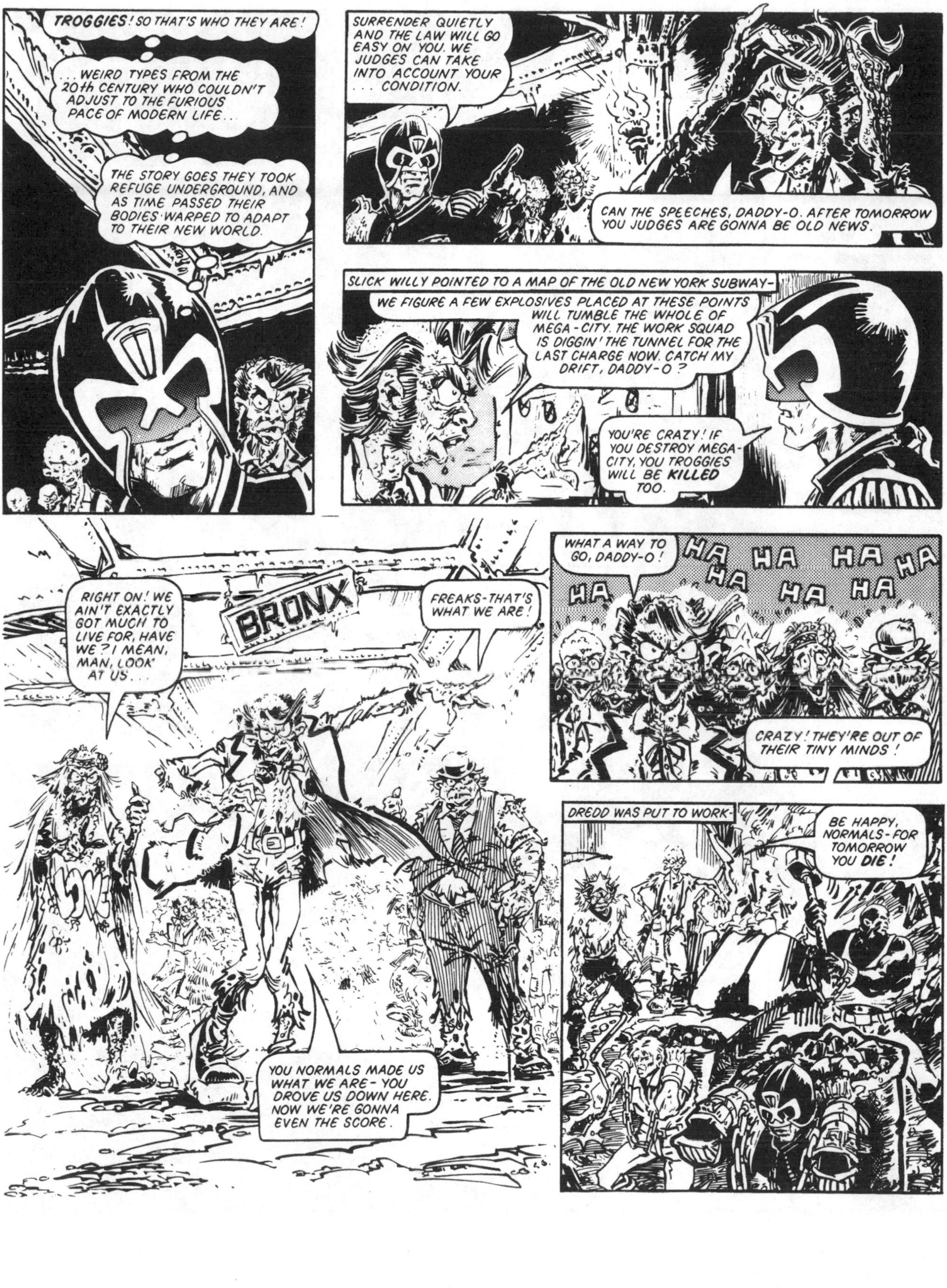

TROGGIES! SO THAT'S WHO THEY ARE!
...WEIRD TYPES FROM THE 20th CENTURY WHO COULDN'T ADJUST TO THE FURIOUS PACE OF MODERN LIFE...
THE STORY GOES THEY TOOK REFUGE UNDERGROUND, AND AS TIME PASSED THEIR BODIES WARPED TO ADAPT TO THEIR NEW WORLD.
SURRENDER QUIETLY AND THE LAW WILL GO EASY ON YOU. WE JUDGES CAN TAKE INTO ACCOUNT YOUR . . . CONDITION.
CAN THE SPEECHES, DADDY-O. AFTER TOMORROW YOU JUDGES ARE GONNA BE OLD NEWS.
SLICK WILLY POINTED TO A MAP OF THE OLD NEW YORK SUBWAY-
WE FIGURE A FEW EXPLOSIVES PLACED AT THESE POINTS WILL TUMBLE THE WHOLE OF MEGA-CITY. THE WORK SQUAD IS DIGGIN' THE TUNNEL FOR THE LAST CHARGE NOW. CATCH MY DRIFT, DADDY-O?
YOU'RE CRAZY! IF YOU DESTROY MEGA-CITY, YOU TROGGIES WILL BE KILLED TOO.
BRONX
RIGHT ON! WE AIN'T EXACTLY GOT MUCH TO LIVE FOR, HAVE WE? I MEAN, MAN, LOOK AT US...
FREAKS-THAT'S WHAT WE ARE!
YOU NORMALS MADE US WHAT WE ARE- YOU DROVE US DOWN HERE. NOW WE'RE GONNA EVEN THE SCORE.
WHAT A WAY TO GO, DADDY-O!
HA HA HA HA HA HA HA HA HA
CRAZY! THEY'RE OUT OF THEIR TINY MINDS!
DREDD WAS PUT TO WORK-
BE HAPPY, NORMALS-FOR TOMORROW YOU DIE!

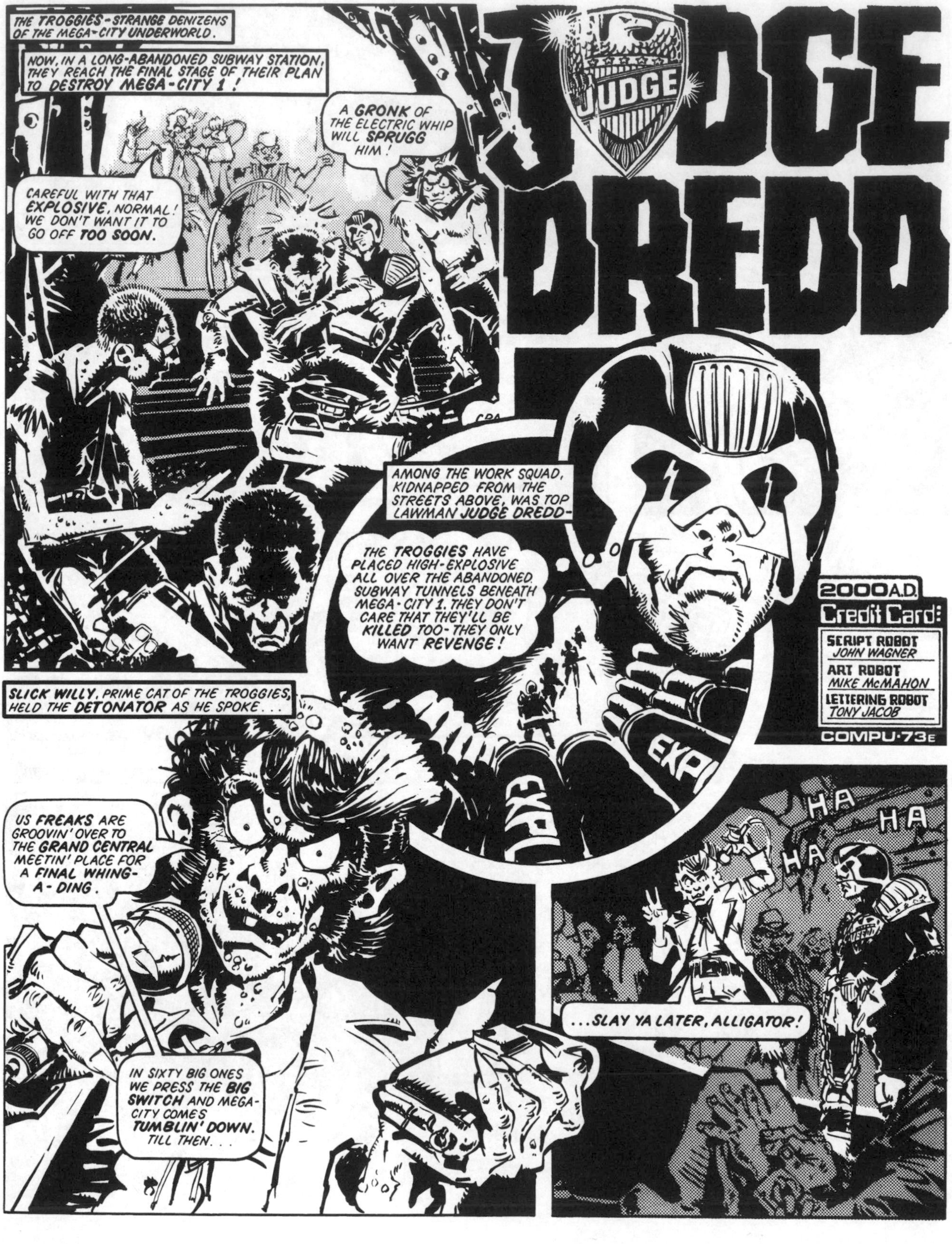
JUDGE DREDD
THE TROGGIES - STRANGE DENIZENS OF THE MEGA-CITY UNDERWORLD.
NOW, IN A LONG-ABANDONED SUBWAY STATION, THEY REACH THE FINAL STAGE OF THEIR PLAN TO DESTROY MEGA-CITY 1!
A GRONK OF THE ELECTRIC WHIP WILL SPRUGG HIM!
CAREFUL WITH THAT EXPLOSIVE, NORMAL! WE DON'T WANT IT TO GO OFF TOO SOON.
AMONG THE WORK SQUAD, KIDNAPPED FROM THE STREETS ABOVE, WAS TOP LAWMAN JUDGE DREDD-
THE TROGGIES HAVE PLACED HIGH-EXPLOSIVE ALL OVER THE ABANDONED SUBWAY TUNNELS BENEATH MEGA-CITY 1. THEY DON'T CARE THAT THEY'LL BE KILLED TOO- THEY ONLY WANT REVENGE!
2000 A.D. Credit Card:
SCRIPT ROBOT JOHN WAGNER
ART ROBOT MIKE McMAHON
LETTERING ROBOT TONY JACOB
COMPU·73E
SLICK WILLY, PRIME CAT OF THE TROGGIES, HELD THE DETONATOR AS HE SPOKE...
US FREAKS ARE GROOVIN' OVER TO THE GRAND CENTRAL MEETIN' PLACE FOR A FINAL WHING-A-DING.
IN SIXTY BIG ONES WE PRESS THE BIG SWITCH AND MEGA-CITY COMES TUMBLIN' DOWN. TILL THEN...
HA HA HA HA
...SLAY YA LATER, ALLIGATOR!

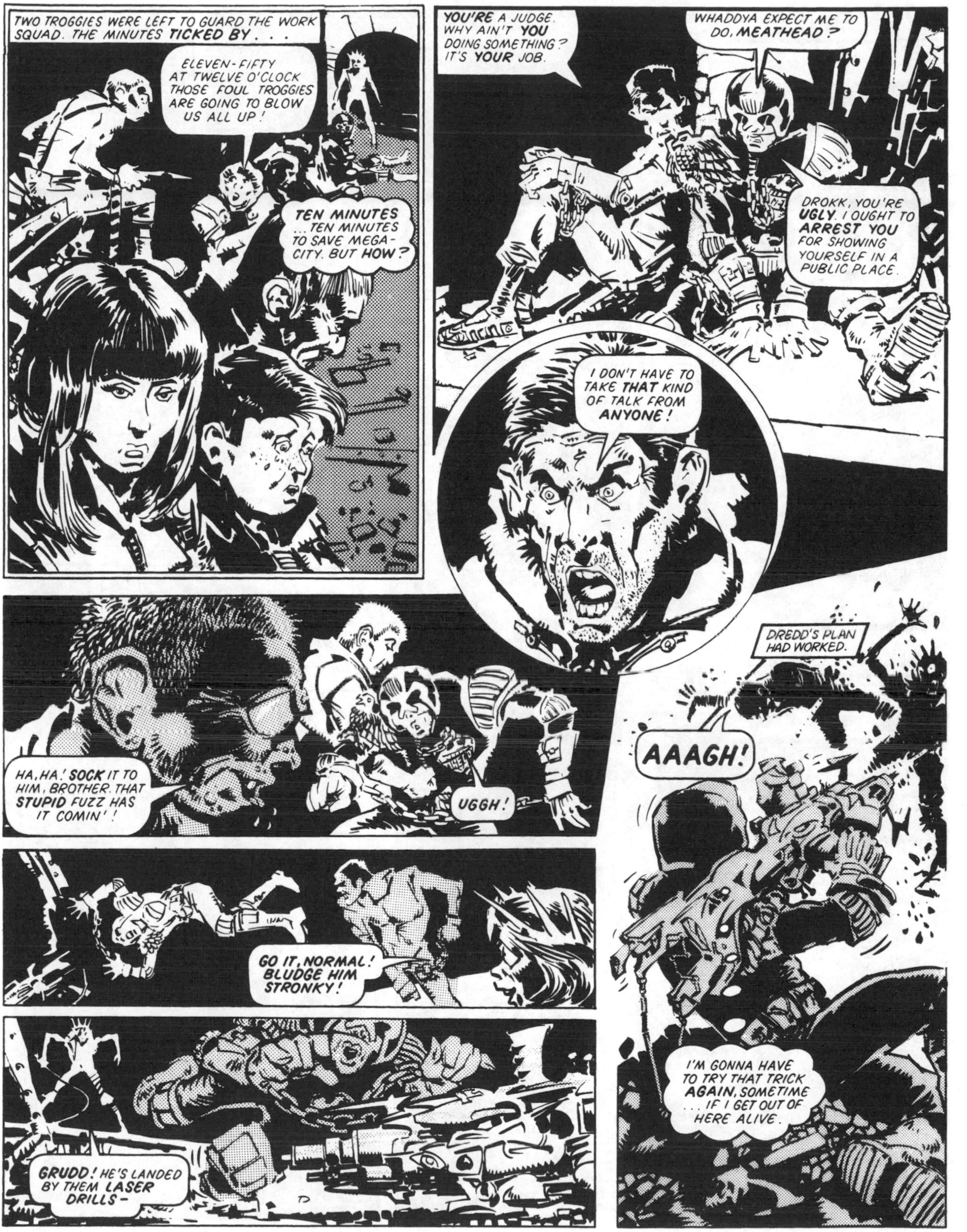

TWO TROGGIES WERE LEFT TO GUARD THE WORK SQUAD. THE MINUTES TICKED BY . . .
ELEVEN-FIFTY AT TWELVE O'CLOCK THOSE FOUL TROGGIES ARE GOING TO BLOW US ALL UP!
TEN MINUTES ...TEN MINUTES TO SAVE MEGA-CITY. BUT HOW?
YOU'RE A JUDGE. WHY AIN'T YOU DOING SOMETHING? IT'S YOUR JOB.
WHADDYA EXPECT ME TO DO, MEATHEAD?
DROKK, YOU'RE UGLY. I OUGHT TO ARREST YOU FOR SHOWING YOURSELF IN A PUBLIC PLACE.
I DON'T HAVE TO TAKE THAT KIND OF TALK FROM ANYONE!
HA, HA! SOCK IT TO HIM, BROTHER. THAT STUPID FUZZ HAS IT COMIN'!
UGGH!
GO IT, NORMAL! BLUDGE HIM STRONKY!
GRUDD! HE'S LANDED BY THEM LASER DRILLS-
DREDD'S PLAN HAD WORKED.
AAAGH!
I'M GONNA HAVE TO TRY THAT TRICK AGAIN, SOMETIME . . . IF I GET OUT OF HERE ALIVE.

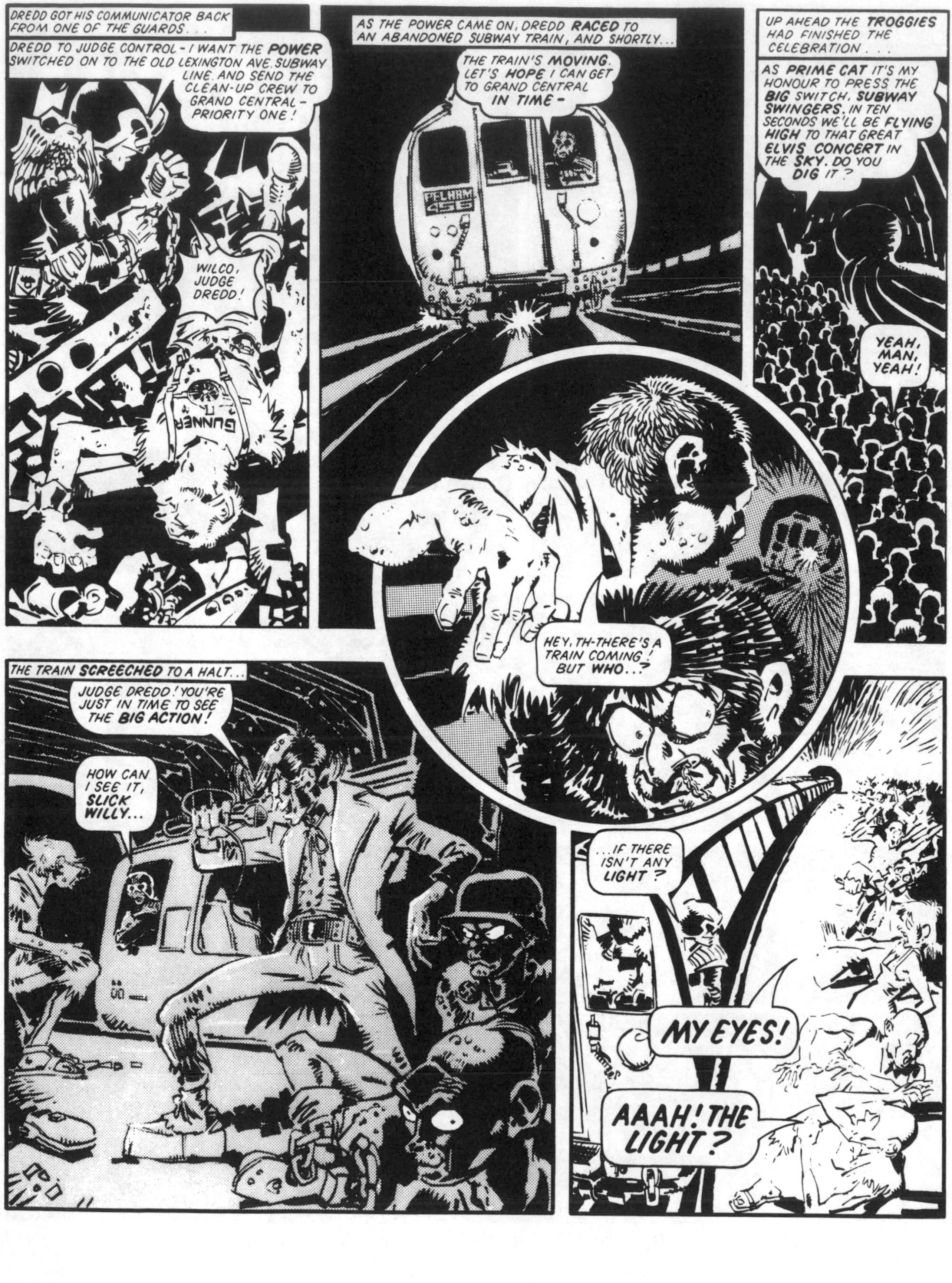
DREDD GOT HIS COMMUNICATOR BACK FROM ONE OF THE GUARDS...
DREDD TO JUDGE CONTROL - I WANT THE POWER SWITCHED ON TO THE OLD LEXINGTON AVE. SUBWAY LINE. AND SEND THE CLEAN-UP CREW TO GRAND CENTRAL - PRIORITY ONE!
WILCO, JUDGE DREDD!
GUNNER
AS THE POWER CAME ON, DREDD RACED TO AN ABANDONED SUBWAY TRAIN, AND SHORTLY...
THE TRAIN'S MOVING. LET'S HOPE I CAN GET TO GRAND CENTRAL IN TIME -
PELHAM
UP AHEAD THE TROGGIES HAD FINISHED THE CELEBRATION...
AS PRIME CAT IT'S MY HONOUR TO PRESS THE BIG SWITCH, SUBWAY SWINGERS. IN TEN SECONDS WE'LL BE FLYING HIGH TO THAT GREAT ELVIS CONCERT IN THE SKY. DO YOU DIG IT?
YEAH, MAN, YEAH!
HEY, TH-THERE'S A TRAIN COMING! BUT WHO...?
THE TRAIN SCREECHED TO A HALT...
JUDGE DREDD! YOU'RE JUST IN TIME TO SEE THE BIG ACTION!
HOW CAN I SEE IT, SLICK WILLY...
...IF THERE ISN'T ANY LIGHT?
MY EYES!
AAAH! THE LIGHT?

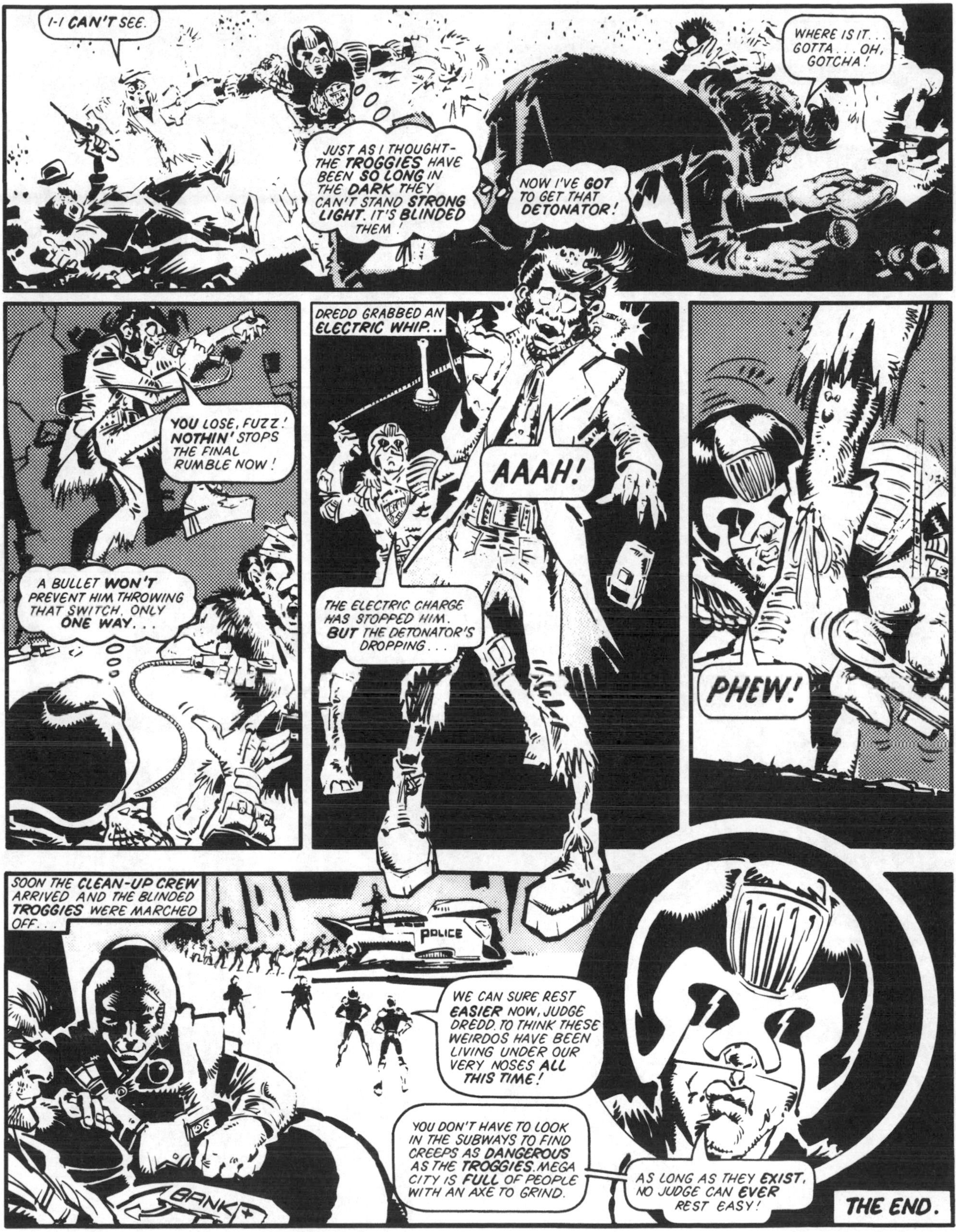
I-I CAN'T SEE.
JUST AS I THOUGHT- THE TROGGIES HAVE BEEN SO LONG IN THE DARK THEY CAN'T STAND STRONG LIGHT. IT'S BLINDED THEM!
NOW I'VE GOT TO GET THAT DETONATOR!
WHERE IS IT... GOTTA... OH, GOTCHA!
YOU LOSE, FUZZ! NOTHIN' STOPS THE FINAL RUMBLE NOW!
A BULLET WON'T PREVENT HIM THROWING THAT SWITCH. ONLY ONE WAY...
DREDD GRABBED AN ELECTRIC WHIP...
AAAH!
THE ELECTRIC CHARGE HAS STOPPED HIM. BUT THE DETONATOR'S DROPPING...
PHEW!
SOON THE CLEAN-UP CREW ARRIVED AND THE BLINDED TROGGIES WERE MARCHED OFF...
POLICE
WE CAN SURE REST EASIER NOW, JUDGE DREDD. TO THINK THESE WEIRDOS HAVE BEEN LIVING UNDER OUR VERY NOSES ALL THIS TIME!
YOU DON'T HAVE TO LOOK IN THE SUBWAYS TO FIND CREEPS AS DANGEROUS AS THE TROGGIES. MEGA CITY IS FULL OF PEOPLE WITH AN AXE TO GRIND.
AS LONG AS THEY EXIST, NO JUDGE CAN EVER REST EASY!
THE END.

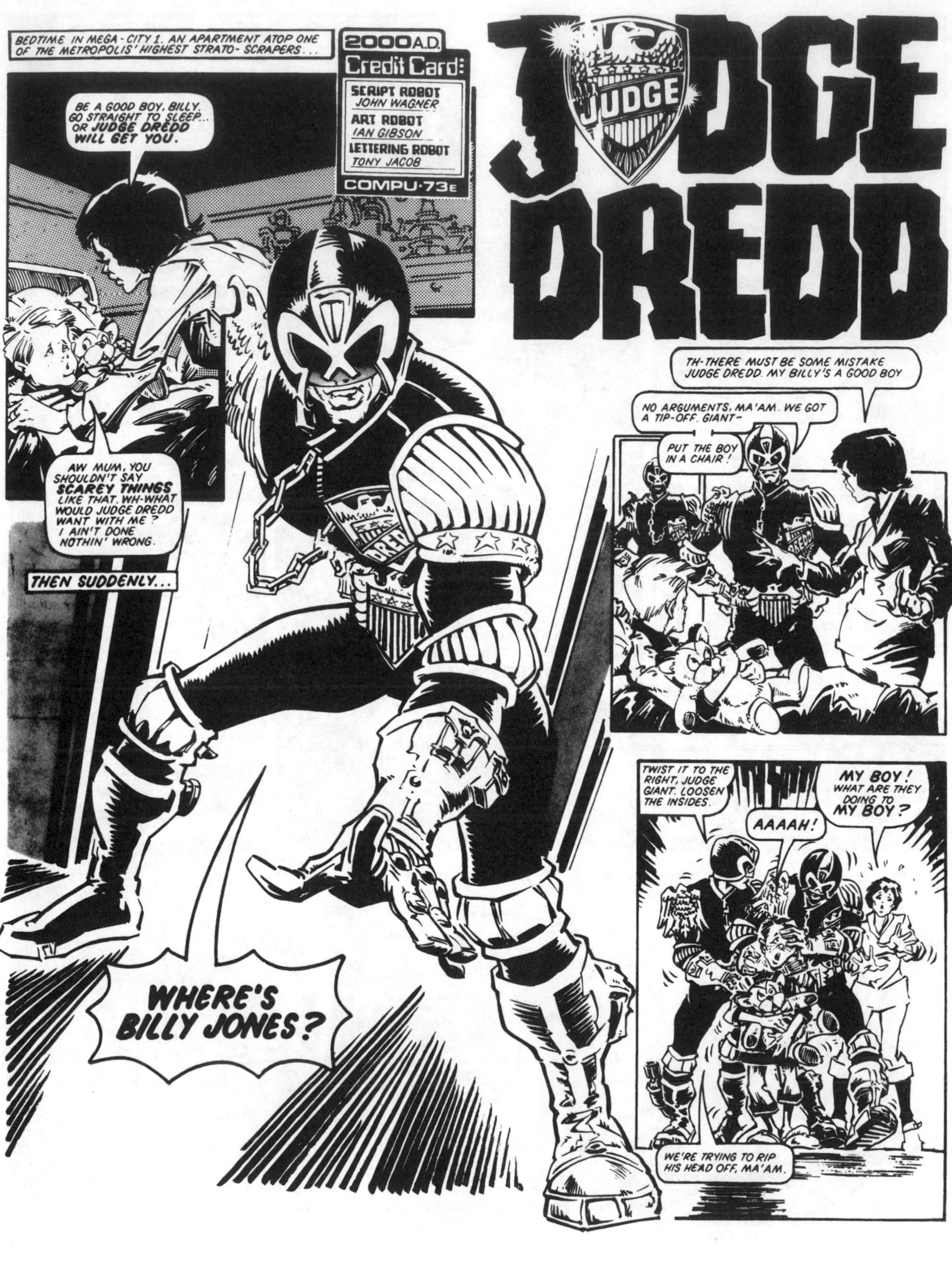
BEDTIME IN MEGA-CITY 1. AN APARTMENT ATOP ONE OF THE METROPOLIS' HIGHEST STRATO-SCRAPERS...
2000 A.D. Credit Card:
SCRIPT ROBOT JOHN WAGNER
ART ROBOT IAN GIBSON
LETTERING ROBOT TONY JACOB
COMPU-73E
JUDGE DREDD
BE A GOOD BOY, BILLY. GO STRAIGHT TO SLEEP... OR JUDGE DREDD WILL GET YOU.
AW MUM, YOU SHOULDN'T SAY SCAREY THINGS LIKE THAT. WH-WHAT WOULD JUDGE DREDD WANT WITH ME? I AIN'T DONE NOTHIN' WRONG.
THEN SUDDENLY...
WHERE'S BILLY JONES?
TH-THERE MUST BE SOME MISTAKE JUDGE DREDD. MY BILLY'S A GOOD BOY
NO ARGUMENTS, MA'AM. WE GOT A TIP-OFF. GIANT-
PUT THE BOY IN A CHAIR!
TWIST IT TO THE RIGHT, JUDGE GIANT. LOOSEN THE INSIDES.
AAAAH!
MY BOY! WHAT ARE THEY DOING TO MY BOY?
WE'RE TRYING TO RIP HIS HEAD OFF, MA'AM.

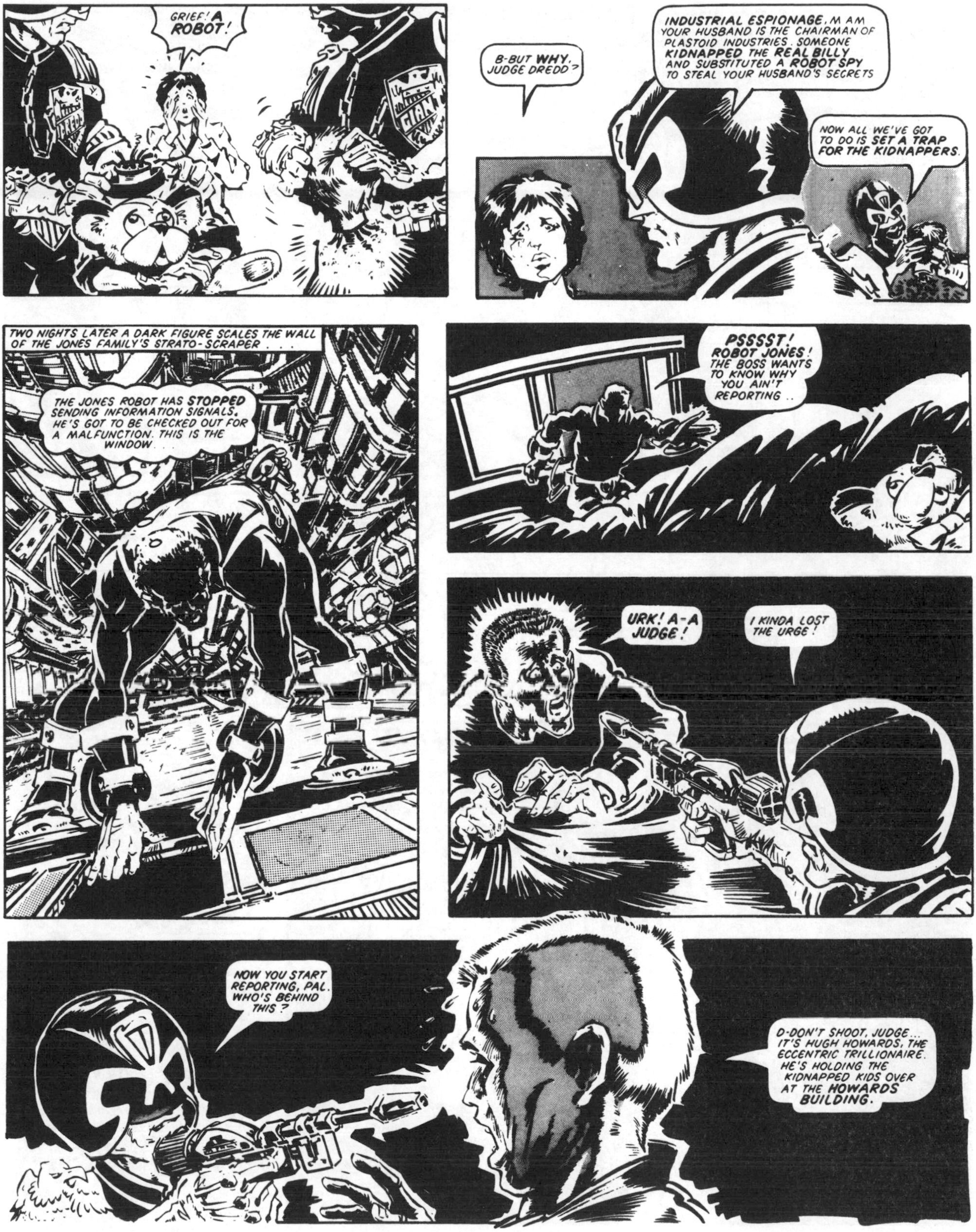
GRIEF! A ROBOT!
B-BUT WHY, JUDGE DREDD?
INDUSTRIAL ESPIONAGE, M'AM. YOUR HUSBAND IS THE CHAIRMAN OF PLASTOID INDUSTRIES. SOMEONE KIDNAPPED THE REAL BILLY AND SUBSTITUTED A ROBOT SPY TO STEAL YOUR HUSBAND'S SECRETS
NOW ALL WE'VE GOT TO DO IS SET A TRAP FOR THE KIDNAPPERS.
TWO NIGHTS LATER A DARK FIGURE SCALES THE WALL OF THE JONES FAMILY'S STRATO-SCRAPER . . .
THE JONES ROBOT HAS STOPPED SENDING INFORMATION SIGNALS. HE'S GOT TO BE CHECKED OUT FOR A MALFUNCTION. THIS IS THE WINDOW . . .
PSSSST! ROBOT JONES! THE BOSS WANTS TO KNOW WHY YOU AIN'T REPORTING . .
URK! A-A JUDGE!
I KINDA LOST THE URGE!
NOW YOU START REPORTING, PAL. WHO'S BEHIND THIS?
D-DON'T SHOOT, JUDGE... IT'S HUGH HOWARDS, THE ECCENTRIC TRILLIONAIRE. HE'S HOLDING THE KIDNAPPED KIDS OVER AT THE HOWARDS BUILDING.

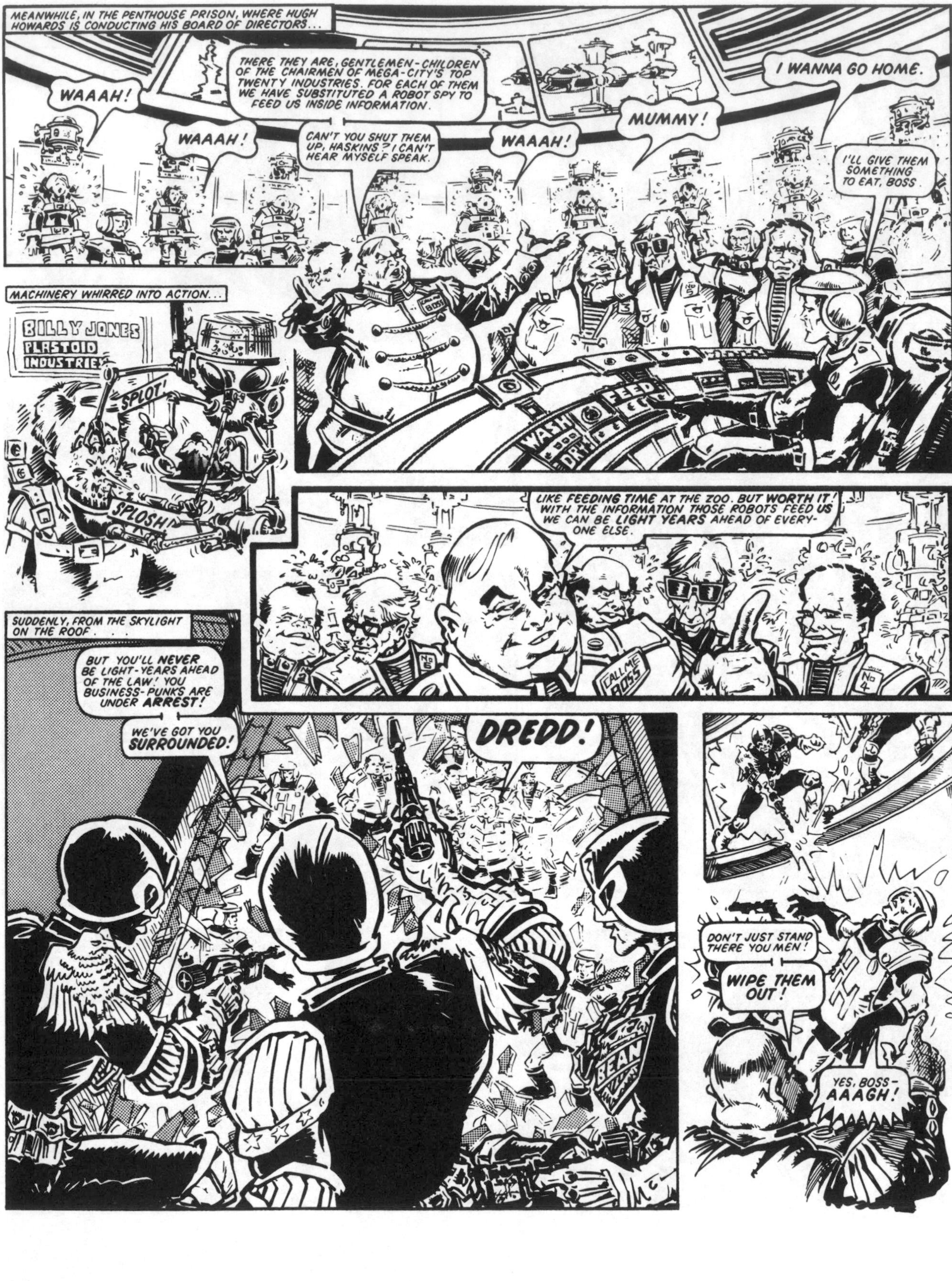

MEANWHILE, IN THE PENTHOUSE PRISON, WHERE HUGH HOWARDS IS CONDUCTING HIS BOARD OF DIRECTORS...
WAAAH!
THERE THEY ARE, GENTLEMEN - CHILDREN OF THE CHAIRMEN OF MEGA-CITY'S TOP TWENTY INDUSTRIES. FOR EACH OF THEM WE HAVE SUBSTITUTED A ROBOT SPY TO FEED US INSIDE INFORMATION.
WAAAH!
CAN'T YOU SHUT THEM UP, HASKINS? I CAN'T HEAR MYSELF SPEAK.
WAAAH!
MUMMY!
I WANNA GO HOME.
I'LL GIVE THEM SOMETHING TO EAT, BOSS.
MACHINERY WHIRRED INTO ACTION...
BILLY JONES PLASTOID INDUSTRIES
SPLOT!
SPLOSH!
FEED
WASH
LIKE FEEDING TIME AT THE ZOO. BUT WORTH IT! WITH THE INFORMATION THOSE ROBOTS FEED US WE CAN BE LIGHT YEARS AHEAD OF EVERYONE ELSE.
CALL ME BOSS
SUDDENLY, FROM THE SKYLIGHT ON THE ROOF . . .
BUT YOU'LL NEVER BE LIGHT-YEARS AHEAD OF THE LAW! YOU BUSINESS-PUNKS ARE UNDER ARREST!
WE'VE GOT YOU SURROUNDED!
DREDD!
BEAN
DON'T JUST STAND THERE YOU MEN!
WIPE THEM OUT!
YES, BOSS - AAAGH!

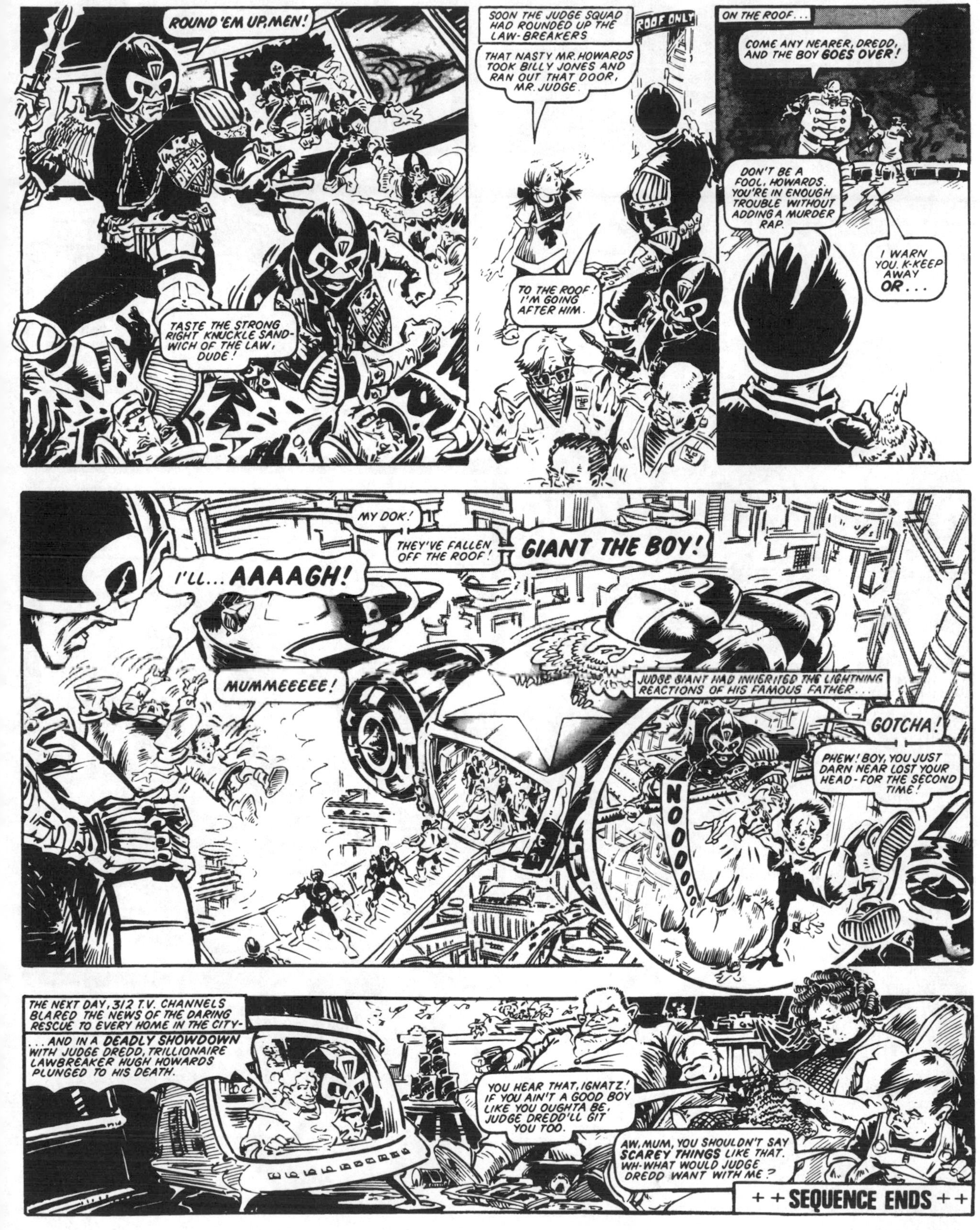
ROUND 'EM UP, MEN!
TASTE THE STRONG RIGHT KNUCKLE SAND-WICH OF THE LAW, DUDE!
SOON THE JUDGE SQUAD HAD ROUNDED UP THE LAW-BREAKERS
ROOF ONLY
THAT NASTY MR. HOWARDS TOOK BILLY JONES AND RAN OUT THAT DOOR, MR. JUDGE.
TO THE ROOF! I'M GOING AFTER HIM.
ON THE ROOF...
COME ANY NEARER, DREDD, AND THE BOY GOES OVER!
DON'T BE A FOOL, HOWARDS. YOU'RE IN ENOUGH TROUBLE WITHOUT ADDING A MURDER RAP.
I WARN YOU. K-KEEP AWAY OR...
I'LL... AAAAGH!
MY DOK!
THEY'VE FALLEN OFF THE ROOF!
GIANT THE BOY!
MUMMEEEEE!
JUDGE GIANT HAD INHERITED THE LIGHTNING REACTIONS OF HIS FAMOUS FATHER...
GOTCHA!
PHEW! BOY, YOU JUST DARN NEAR LOST YOUR HEAD - FOR THE SECOND TIME!
THE NEXT DAY, 312 T.V. CHANNELS BLARED THE NEWS OF THE DARING RESCUE TO EVERY HOME IN THE CITY-
...AND IN A DEADLY SHOWDOWN WITH JUDGE DREDD, TRILLIONAIRE LAWBREAKER HUGH HOWARDS PLUNGED TO HIS DEATH.
YOU HEAR THAT, IGNATZ! IF YOU AIN'T A GOOD BOY LIKE YOU OUGHTA BE, JUDGE DREDD'LL GIT YOU TOO.
AW, MUM, YOU SHOULDN'T SAY SCAREY THINGS LIKE THAT. WH-WHAT WOULD JUDGE DREDD WANT WITH ME?
++ SEQUENCE ENDS ++

JUDGE DREDD

MEGA-CITY ONE, 2099. AT JUSTICE CENTRAL TOP LAWMAN JUDGE DREDD IS CATCHING UP WITH A BACKLOG OF CASE REPORTS...

I'M SORRY, SIR, YOU CAN'T GO IN THERE. THAT'S JUDGE DREDD'S PRIVATE OFFICE!

PUT A SOCK IN IT, SKINFACE! DON UGGIE DON'T TAKE NO ORDERS FROM NOBODY!

2000 A.D.
Credit Card:
SCRIPT ROBOT
JOHN WAGNER
ART ROBOT
MIKE McMAHON
LETTERING ROBOT
TONY JACOB
COMPU·73E

I ONLY GOT ONE TING TA SAY TA YA, DREDD - NUTS!

DON UGGIE APELINO AND HIS HENCHMEN, FAST EEEK AND JOE BANANAS... THE APE GANG.

UGGIE LEPT UP ONTO DREDD'S DESK.

DA EAST SIDE MOB IS MUSCLIN' IN ON OUR TERRITORY AN' YOU'RE TURNIN'A BLIND EYE. WELL, I WANNIT STOPPED OR DERE'S GONNA BE TROUBLE, SEE!

YOU TELL 'IM, DON UGGIE! DESE SKINFACE CREEPS MUST T'INK WE JUS' COME DOWN FROM DA TREES OR SOMETHIN'!

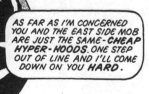

AS FAR AS I'M CONCERNED YOU AND THE EAST SIDE MOB ARE JUST THE SAME - CHEAP HYPER-HOODS. ONE STEP OUT OF LINE AND I'LL COME DOWN ON YOU HARD.

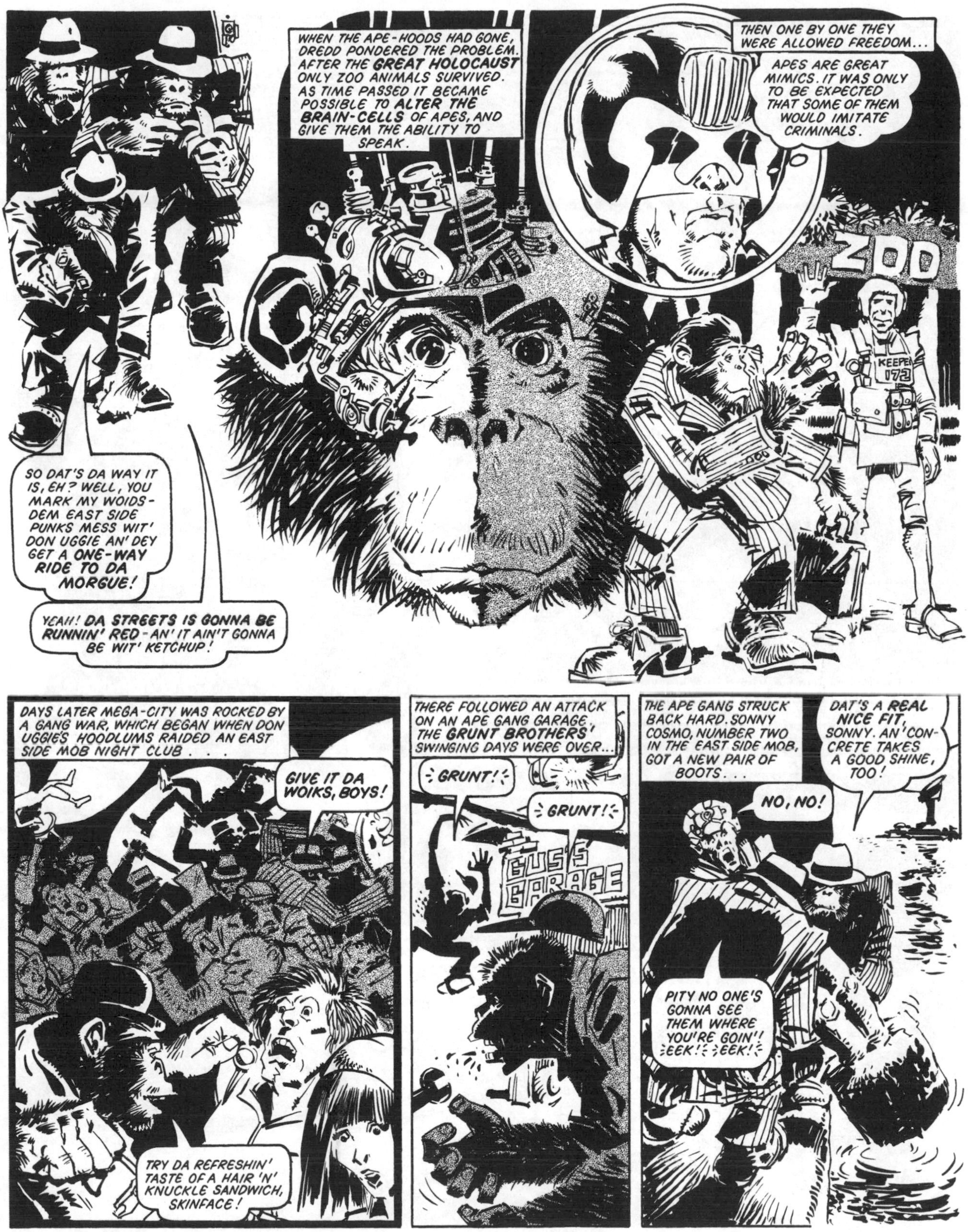
WHEN THE APE-HOODS HAD GONE, DREDD PONDERED THE PROBLEM. AFTER THE GREAT HOLOCAUST ONLY ZOO ANIMALS SURVIVED. AS TIME PASSED IT BECAME POSSIBLE TO ALTER THE BRAIN-CELLS OF APES, AND GIVE THEM THE ABILITY TO SPEAK.
THEN ONE BY ONE THEY WERE ALLOWED FREEDOM...
APES ARE GREAT MIMICS. IT WAS ONLY TO BE EXPECTED THAT SOME OF THEM WOULD IMITATE CRIMINALS.
ZOO
KEEPER 172
SO DAT'S DA WAY IT IS, EH? WELL, YOU MARK MY WOIDS- DEM EAST SIDE PUNKS MESS WIT' DON UGGIE AN' DEY GET A ONE-WAY RIDE TO DA MORGUE!
YEAH! DA STREETS IS GONNA BE RUNNIN' RED- AN' IT AIN'T GONNA BE WIT' KETCHUP!
DAYS LATER MEGA-CITY WAS ROCKED BY A GANG WAR, WHICH BEGAN WHEN DON UGGIE'S HOODLUMS RAIDED AN EAST SIDE MOB NIGHT CLUB . . .
GIVE IT DA WOIKS, BOYS!
TRY DA REFRESHIN' TASTE OF A HAIR 'N' KNUCKLE SANDWICH, SKINFACE!
THERE FOLLOWED AN ATTACK ON AN APE GANG GARAGE, THE GRUNT BROTHERS' SWINGING DAYS WERE OVER...
GRUNT!
GRUNT!
GUS'S GARAGE
THE APE GANG STRUCK BACK HARD. SONNY COSMO, NUMBER TWO IN THE EAST SIDE MOB, GOT A NEW PAIR OF BOOTS....
DAT'S A REAL NICE FIT, SONNY. AN' CONCRETE TAKES A GOOD SHINE, TOO!
NO, NO!
PITY NO ONE'S GONNA SEE THEM WHERE YOU'RE GOIN'! EEK! EEK!

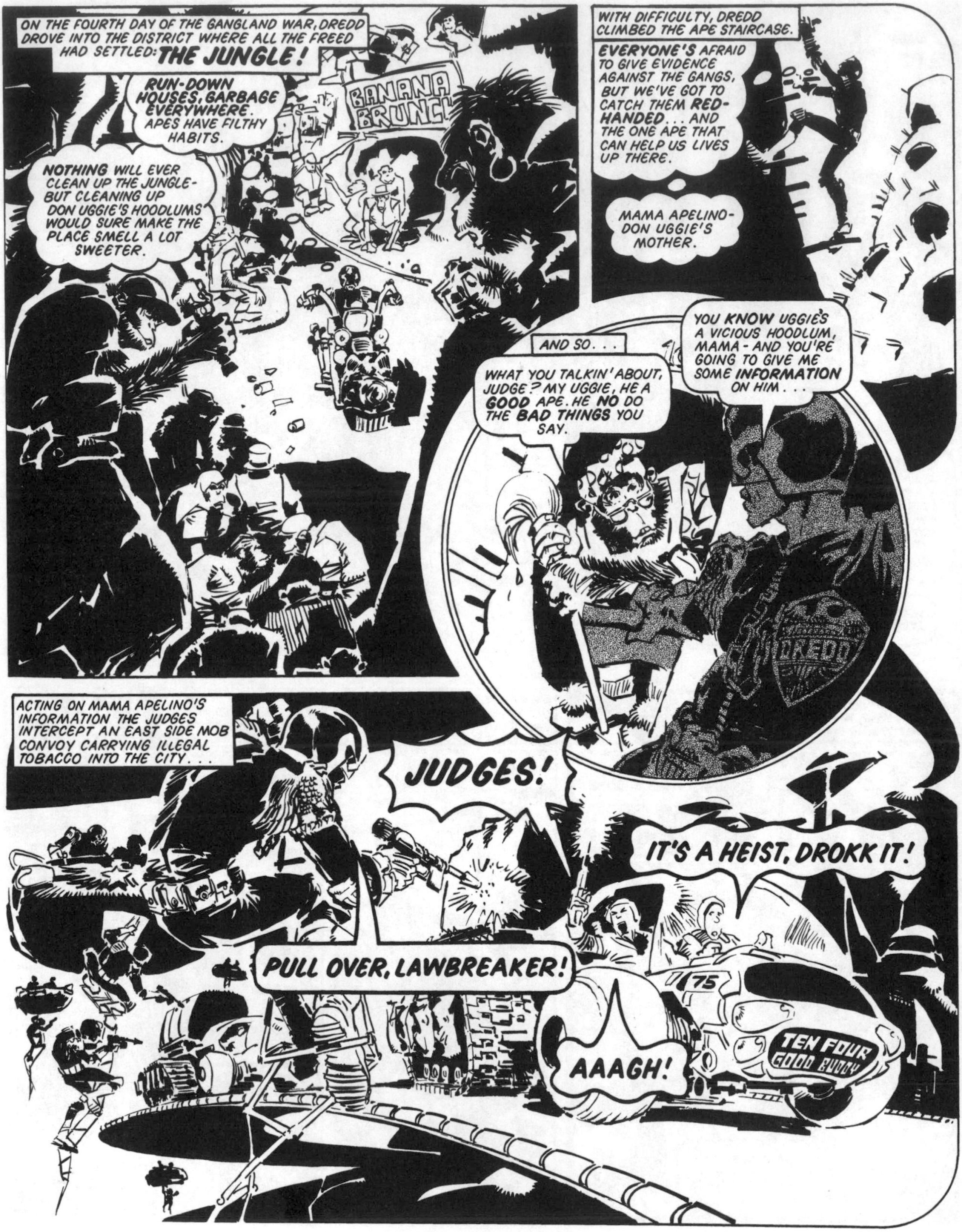
ON THE FOURTH DAY OF THE GANGLAND WAR, DREDD DROVE INTO THE DISTRICT WHERE ALL THE FREED HAD SETTLED: THE JUNGLE!
BANANA BRUNCH
RUN-DOWN HOUSES, GARBAGE EVERYWHERE. APES HAVE FILTHY HABITS.
NOTHING WILL EVER CLEAN UP THE JUNGLE - BUT CLEANING UP DON UGGIE'S HOODLUMS WOULD SURE MAKE THE PLACE SMELL A LOT SWEETER.
WITH DIFFICULTY, DREDD CLIMBED THE APE STAIRCASE.
EVERYONE'S AFRAID TO GIVE EVIDENCE AGAINST THE GANGS, BUT WE'VE GOT TO CATCH THEM RED-HANDED... AND THE ONE APE THAT CAN HELP US LIVES UP THERE.
MAMA APELINO - DON UGGIE'S MOTHER.
AND SO...
YOU KNOW UGGIE'S A VICIOUS HOODLUM, MAMA - AND YOU'RE GOING TO GIVE ME SOME INFORMATION ON HIM...
WHAT YOU TALKIN' ABOUT, JUDGE? MY UGGIE, HE A GOOD APE. HE NO DO THE BAD THINGS YOU SAY.
DREDD
ACTING ON MAMA APELINO'S INFORMATION THE JUDGES INTERCEPT AN EAST SIDE MOB CONVOY CARRYING ILLEGAL TOBACCO INTO THE CITY...
JUDGES!
IT'S A HEIST, DROKK IT!
PULL OVER, LAWBREAKER!
75
AAAGH!
TEN FOUR GOOD BUDDY

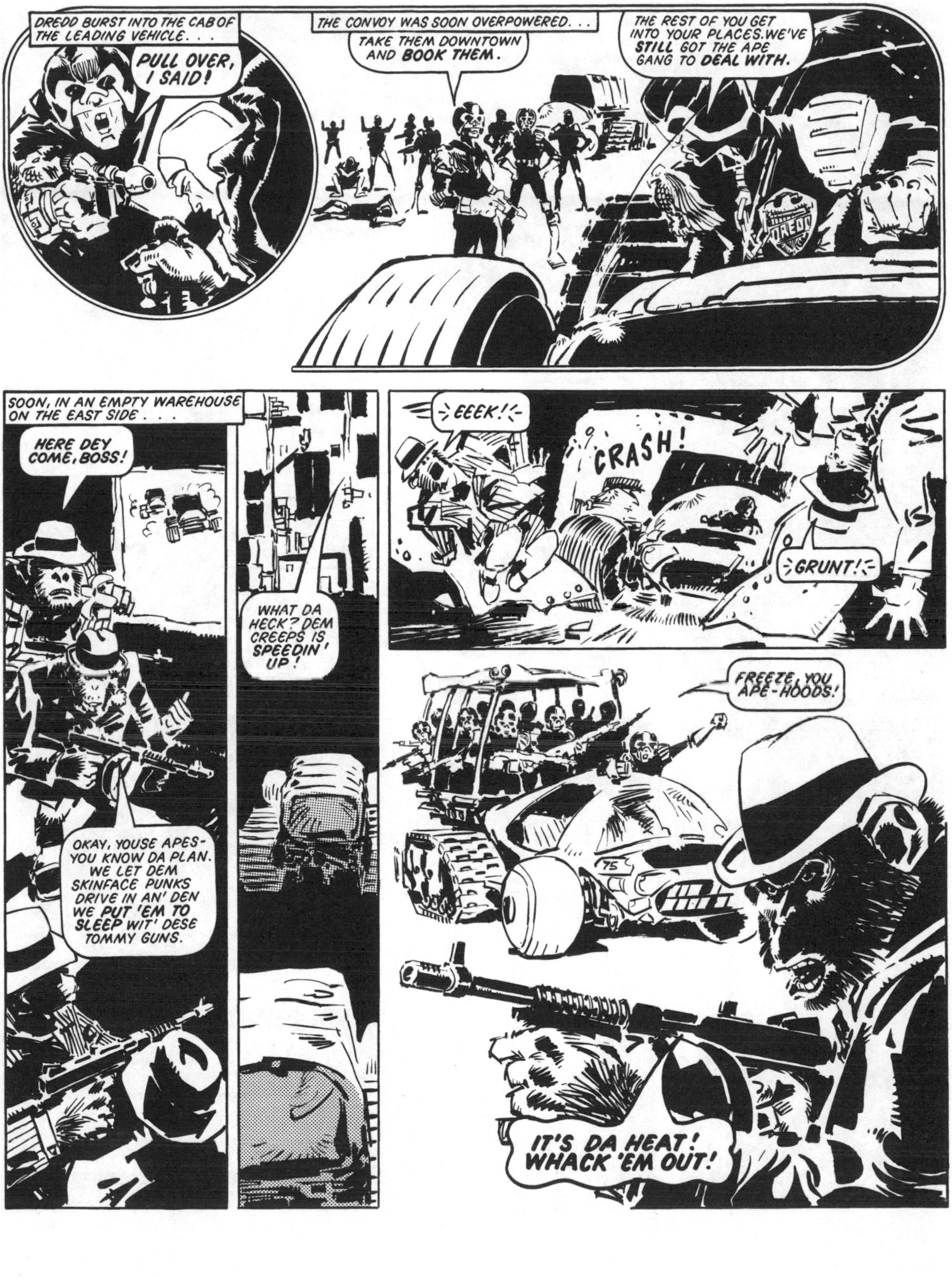
DREDD BURST INTO THE CAB OF THE LEADING VEHICLE. . .
PULL OVER, I SAID!
THE CONVOY WAS SOON OVERPOWERED. . .
TAKE THEM DOWNTOWN AND BOOK THEM.
THE REST OF YOU GET INTO YOUR PLACES. WE'VE STILL GOT THE APE GANG TO DEAL WITH.
SOON, IN AN EMPTY WAREHOUSE ON THE EAST SIDE . . .
HERE DEY COME, BOSS!
OKAY, YOUSE APES-YOU KNOW DA PLAN. WE LET DEM SKINFACE PUNKS DRIVE IN AN' DEN WE PUT 'EM TO SLEEP WIT' DESE TOMMY GUNS.
WHAT DA HECK? DEM CREEPS IS SPEEDIN' UP!
EEEK!
CRASH!
GRUNT!
FREEZE, YOU APE-HOODS!
IT'S DA HEAT! WHACK 'EM OUT!

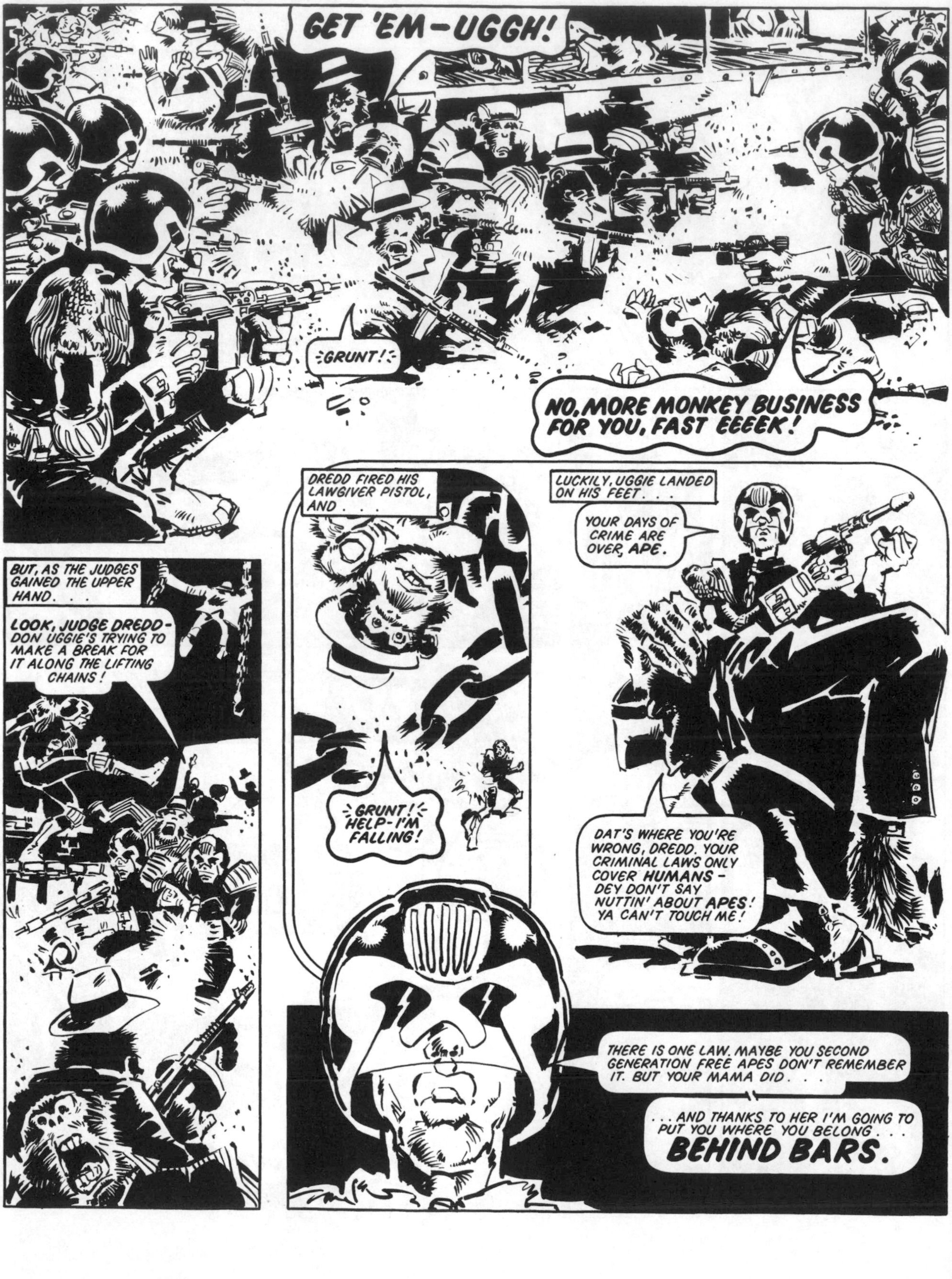
GET 'EM—UGGH!
GRUNT!
NO, MORE MONKEY BUSINESS FOR YOU, FAST EEEEK!
BUT, AS THE JUDGES GAINED THE UPPER HAND . . .
LOOK, JUDGE DREDD— DON UGGIE'S TRYING TO MAKE A BREAK FOR IT ALONG THE LIFTING CHAINS!
DREDD FIRED HIS LAWGIVER PISTOL, AND . . .
GRUNT! HELP—I'M FALLING!
LUCKILY, UGGIE LANDED ON HIS FEET . . .
YOUR DAYS OF CRIME ARE OVER, APE.
DAT'S WHERE YOU'RE WRONG, DREDD. YOUR CRIMINAL LAWS ONLY COVER HUMANS — DEY DON'T SAY NUTTIN' ABOUT APES! YA CAN'T TOUCH ME!
THERE IS ONE LAW. MAYBE YOU SECOND GENERATION FREE APES DON'T REMEMBER IT. BUT YOUR MAMA DID . . .
. . . AND THANKS TO HER I'M GOING TO PUT YOU WHERE YOU BELONG . . . BEHIND BARS.

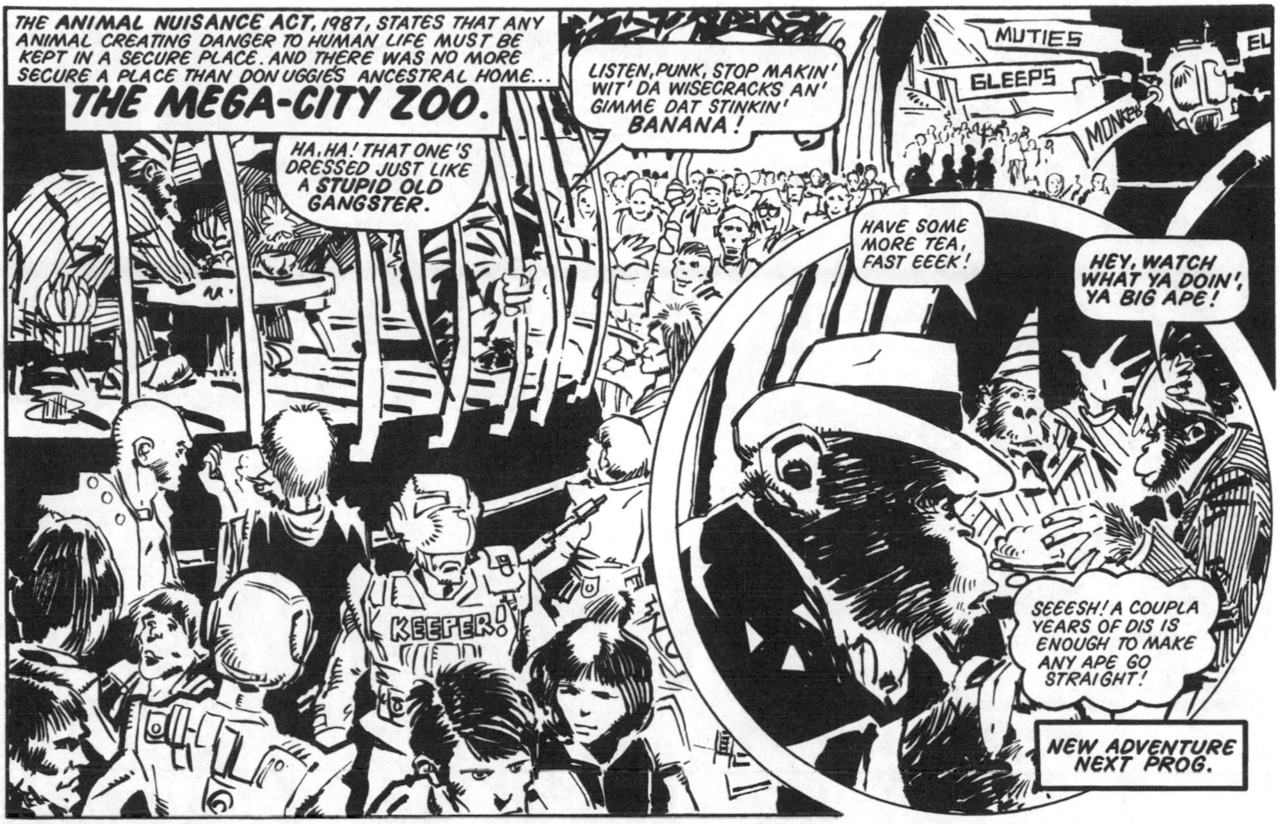
THE ANIMAL NUISANCE ACT, 1987, STATES THAT ANY ANIMAL CREATING DANGER TO HUMAN LIFE MUST BE KEPT IN A SECURE PLACE. AND THERE WAS NO MORE SECURE A PLACE THAN DON UGGIE'S ANCESTRAL HOME...
THE MEGA-CITY ZOO.
HA, HA! THAT ONE'S DRESSED JUST LIKE A STUPID OLD GANGSTER.
LISTEN, PUNK, STOP MAKIN' WIT' DA WISECRACKS AN' GIMME DAT STINKIN' BANANA!
MUTIES
GLEEPS
KEEPER!
HAVE SOME MORE TEA, FAST EEEK!
HEY, WATCH WHAT YA DOIN', YA BIG APE!
SEEESH! A COUPLA YEARS OF DIS IS ENOUGH TO MAKE ANY APE GO STRAIGHT!
NEW ADVENTURE NEXT PROG.

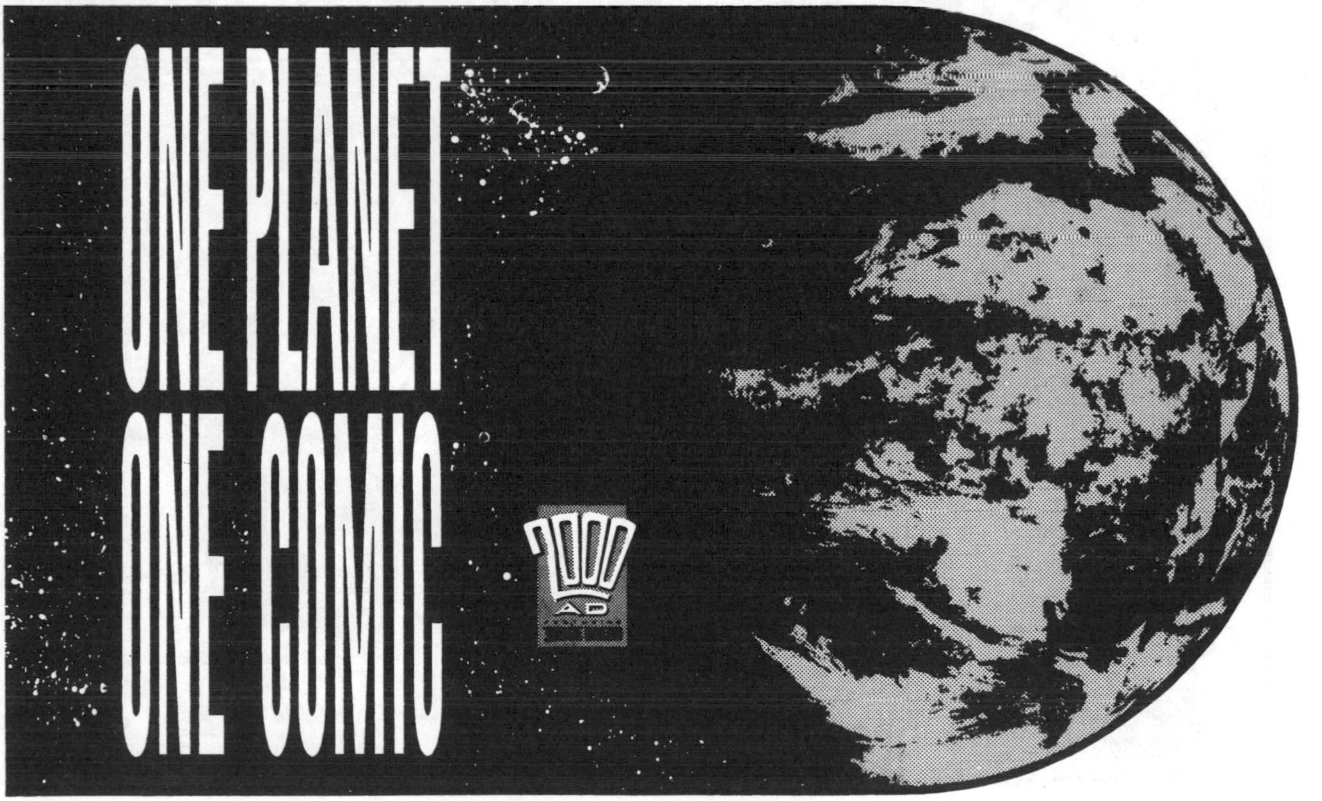
ONE PLANET
ONE COMIC
2000 AD

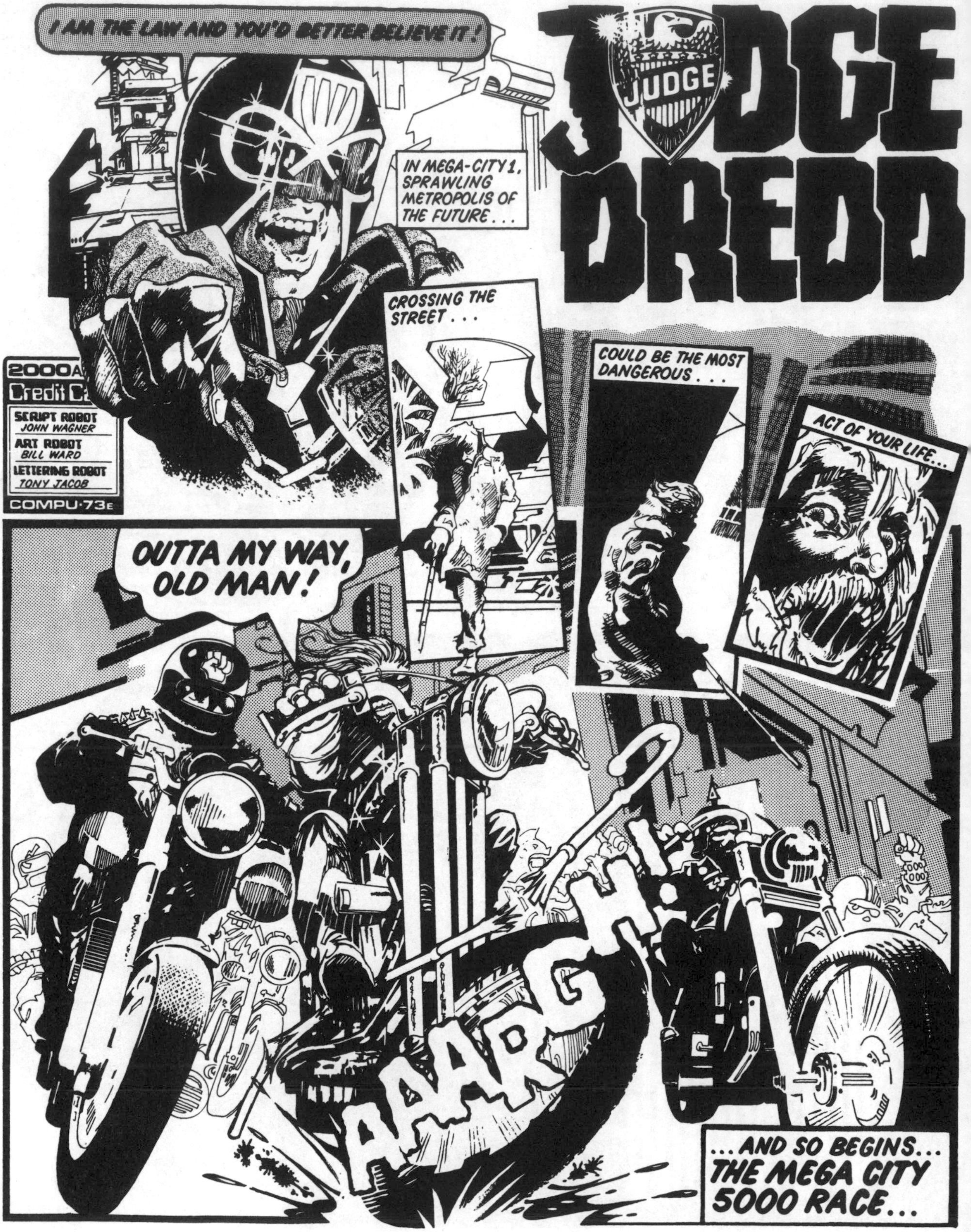

I AM THE LAW AND YOU'D BETTER BELIEVE IT!
JUDGE
JUDGE DREDD
IN MEGA-CITY 1, SPRAWLING METROPOLIS OF THE FUTURE...
2000A
Credit Ca
SCRIPT ROBOT JOHN WAGNER
ART ROBOT BILL WARD
LETTERING ROBOT TONY JACOB
COMPU-73E
CROSSING THE STREET...
COULD BE THE MOST DANGEROUS...
ACT OF YOUR LIFE...
OUTTA MY WAY, OLD MAN!
AAARGH!
...AND SO BEGINS... THE MEGA CITY 5000 RACE...

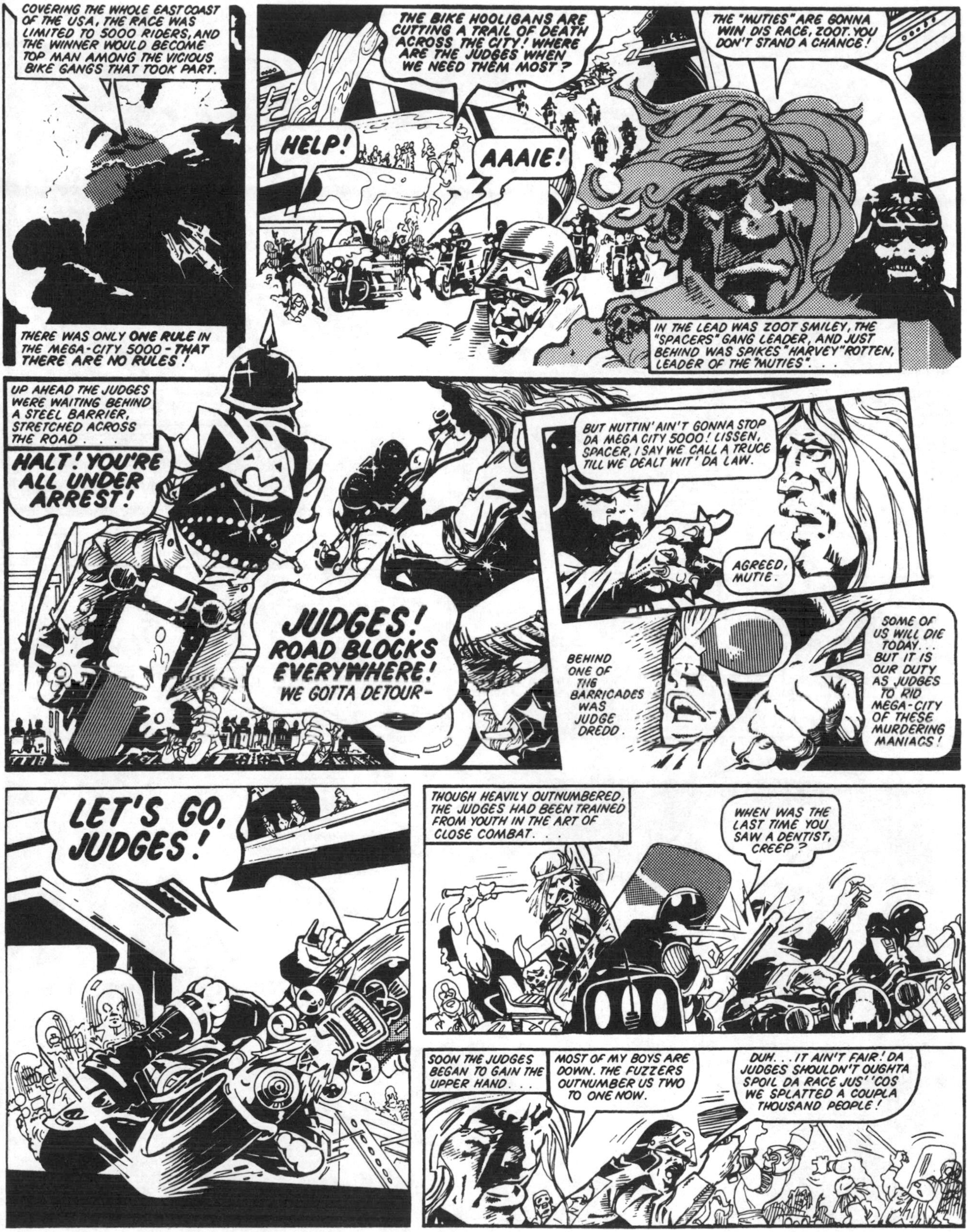

COVERING THE WHOLE EAST COAST OF THE U.S.A, THE RACE WAS LIMITED TO 5000 RIDERS, AND THE WINNER WOULD BECOME TOP MAN AMONG THE VICIOUS BIKE GANGS THAT TOOK PART.
THERE WAS ONLY ONE RULE IN THE MEGA-CITY 5000 - THAT THERE ARE NO RULES!
THE BIKE HOOLIGANS ARE CUTTING A TRAIL OF DEATH ACROSS THE CITY! WHERE ARE THE JUDGES WHEN WE NEED THEM MOST?
HELP!
AAAIE!
THE "MUTIES" ARE GONNA WIN DIS RACE, ZOOT. YOU DON'T STAND A CHANCE!
IN THE LEAD WAS ZOOT SMILEY, THE "SPACERS" GANG LEADER, AND JUST BEHIND WAS SPIKES "HARVEY" ROTTEN, LEADER OF THE "MUTIES". . .
UP AHEAD THE JUDGES WERE WAITING BEHIND A STEEL BARRIER, STRETCHED ACROSS THE ROAD . . .
HALT! YOU'RE ALL UNDER ARREST!
JUDGES! ROAD BLOCKS EVERYWHERE! WE GOTTA DETOUR-
BUT NUTTIN' AIN'T GONNA STOP DA MEGA CITY 5000! LISSEN, SPACER, I SAY WE CALL A TRUCE TILL WE DEALT WIT' DA LAW.
AGREED, MUTIE.
BEHIND ONE OF THE BARRICADES WAS JUDGE DREDD.
SOME OF US WILL DIE TODAY... BUT IT IS OUR DUTY AS JUDGES TO RID MEGA-CITY OF THESE MURDERING MANIACS!
LET'S GO, JUDGES!
THOUGH HEAVILY OUTNUMBERED, THE JUDGES HAD BEEN TRAINED FROM YOUTH IN THE ART OF CLOSE COMBAT. . .
WHEN WAS THE LAST TIME YOU SAW A DENTIST, CREEP?
SOON THE JUDGES BEGAN TO GAIN THE UPPER HAND . . .
MOST OF MY BOYS ARE DOWN. THE FUZZERS OUTNUMBER US TWO TO ONE NOW.
DUH... IT AIN'T FAIR! DA JUDGES SHOULDN'T OUGHTA SPOIL DA RACE JUS' 'COS WE SPLATTED A COUPLA THOUSAND PEOPLE!

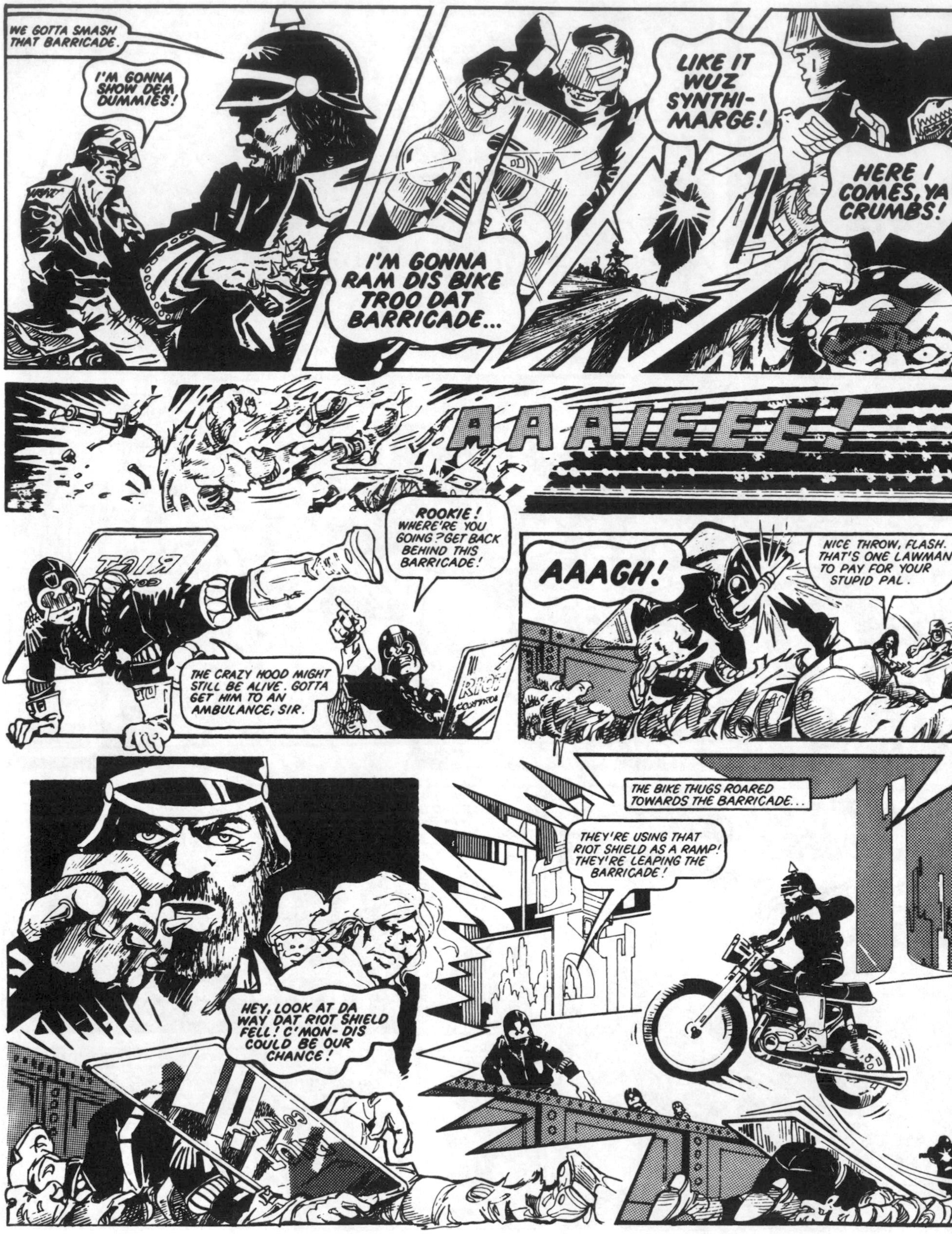

WE GOTTA SMASH THAT BARRICADE.
I'M GONNA SHOW DEM DUMMIES!
I'M GONNA RAM DIS BIKE TROO DAT BARRICADE...
LIKE IT WUZ SYNTHI-MARGE!
HERE I COMES, YA CRUMBS!
AAAIEEE!
ROOKIE! WHERE'RE YOU GOING? GET BACK BEHIND THIS BARRICADE!
THE CRAZY HOOD MIGHT STILL BE ALIVE. GOTTA GET HIM TO AN AMBULANCE, SIR.
AAAGH!
NICE THROW, FLASH. THAT'S ONE LAWMAN TO PAY FOR YOUR STUPID PAL.
HEY, LOOK AT DA WAY DAT RIOT SHIELD FELL! C'MON- DIS COULD BE OUR CHANCE!
THE BIKE THUGS ROARED TOWARDS THE BARRICADE...
THEY'RE USING THAT RIOT SHIELD AS A RAMP! THEY'RE LEAPING THE BARRICADE!

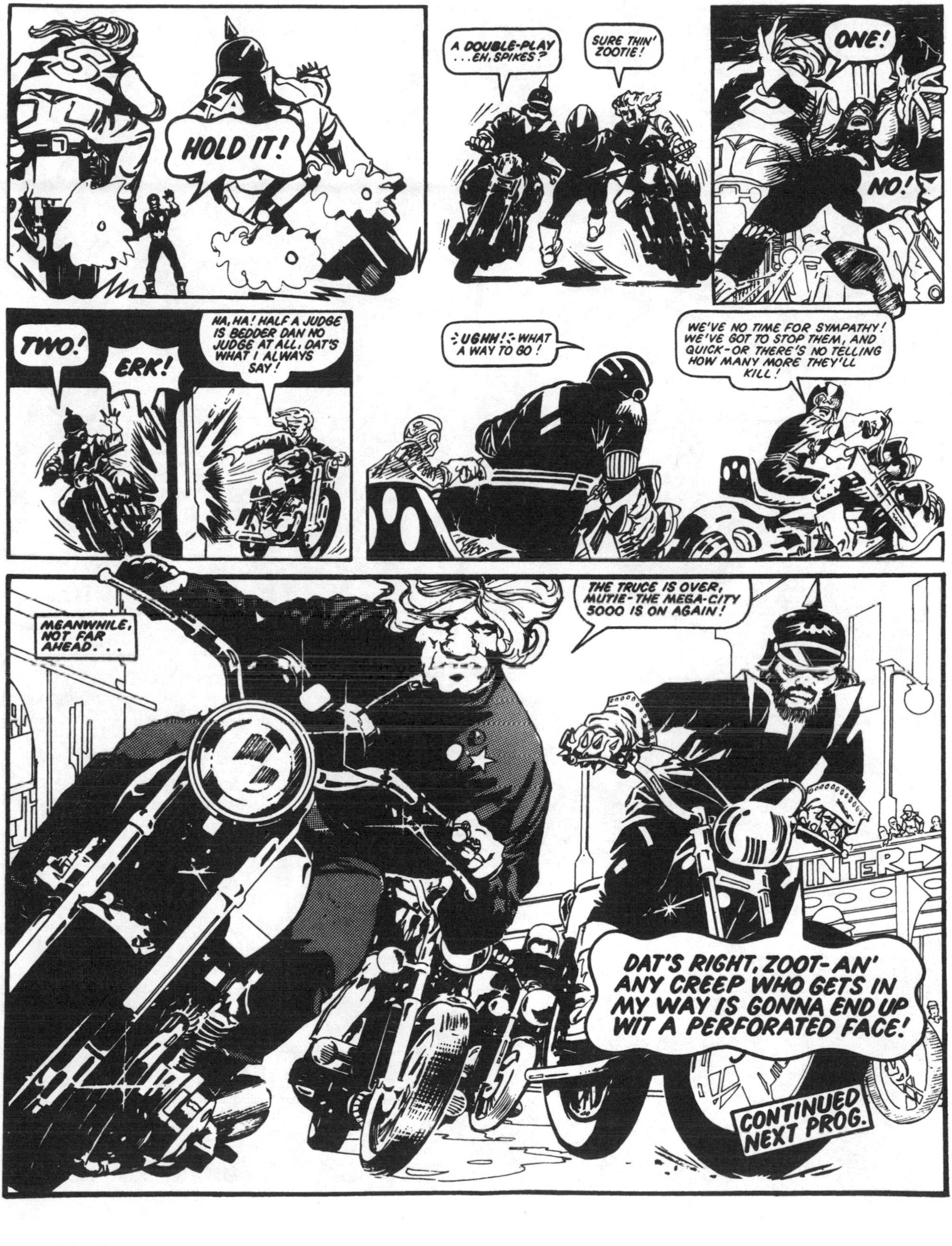
HOLD IT!
A DOUBLE-PLAY ...EH, SPIKES?
SURE THIN' ZOOTIE!
ONE!
NO!
TWO!
ERK!
HA, HA! HALF A JUDGE IS BEDDER DAN NO JUDGE AT ALL, DAT'S WHAT I ALWAYS SAY!
UGHH! WHAT A WAY TO GO!
WE'VE NO TIME FOR SYMPATHY! WE'VE GOT TO STOP THEM, AND QUICK-OR THERE'S NO TELLING HOW MANY MORE THEY'LL KILL!
MEANWHILE, NOT FAR AHEAD...
THE TRUCE IS OVER, MUTIE- THE MEGA-CITY 5000 IS ON AGAIN!
DAT'S RIGHT, ZOOT- AN' ANY CREEP WHO GETS IN MY WAY IS GONNA END UP WIT A PERFORATED FACE!
CONTINUED NEXT PROG.

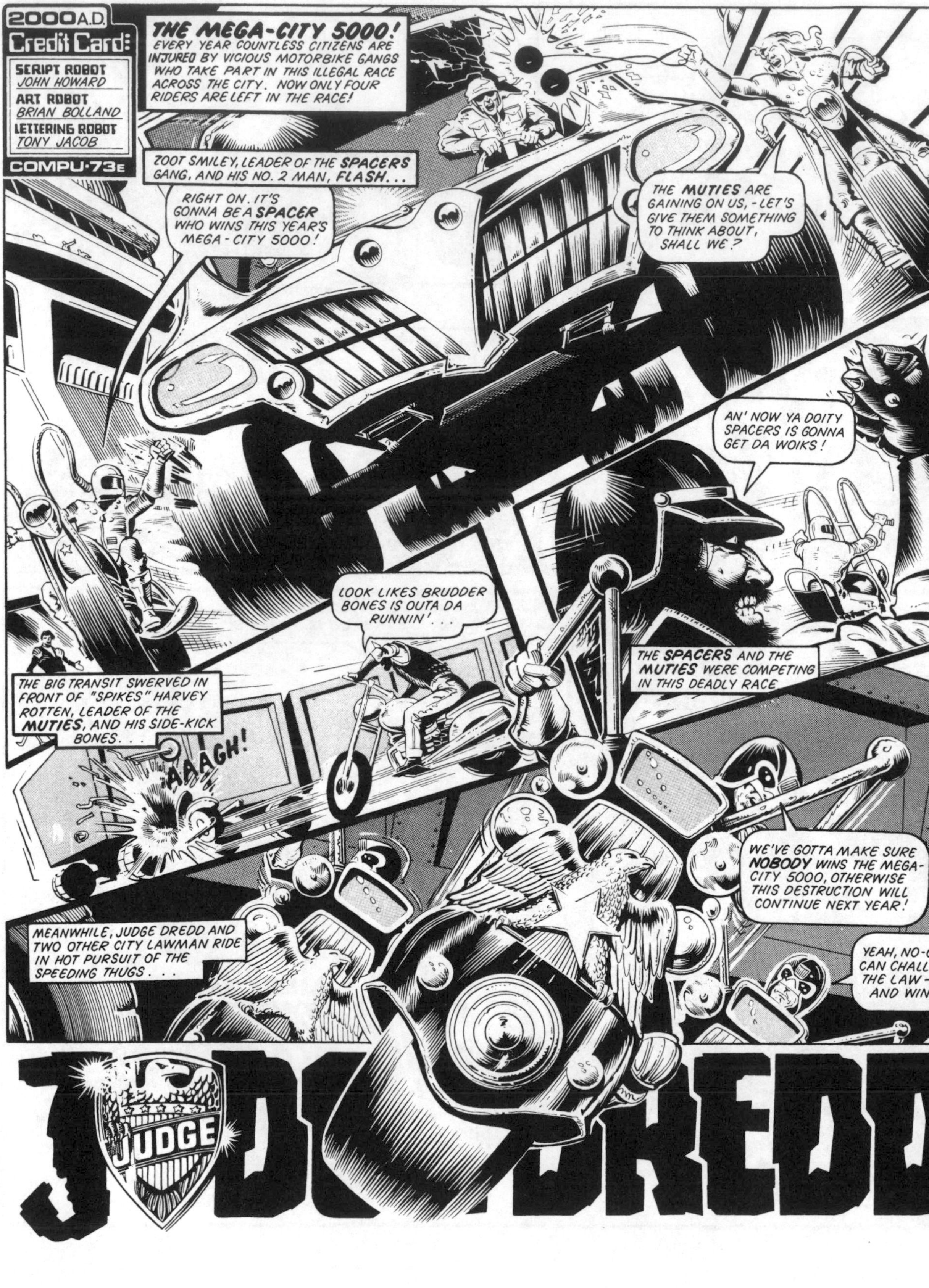
2000 A.D. Credit Card:
SCRIPT ROBOT JOHN HOWARD
ART ROBOT BRIAN BOLLAND
LETTERING ROBOT TONY JACOB
COMPU-73E
THE MEGA-CITY 5000! EVERY YEAR COUNTLESS CITIZENS ARE INJURED BY VICIOUS MOTORBIKE GANGS WHO TAKE PART IN THIS ILLEGAL RACE ACROSS THE CITY. NOW ONLY FOUR RIDERS ARE LEFT IN THE RACE!
ZOOT SMILEY, LEADER OF THE SPACERS GANG, AND HIS NO. 2 MAN, FLASH...
RIGHT ON. IT'S GONNA BE A SPACER WHO WINS THIS YEAR'S MEGA-CITY 5000!
THE MUTIES ARE GAINING ON US, - LET'S GIVE THEM SOMETHING TO THINK ABOUT, SHALL WE?
AN' NOW YA DOITY SPACERS IS GONNA GET DA WOIKS!
LOOK LIKES BRUDDER BONES IS OUTA DA RUNNIN'...
THE SPACERS AND THE MUTIES WERE COMPETING IN THIS DEADLY RACE
THE BIG TRANSIT SWERVED IN FRONT OF "SPIKES" HARVEY ROTTEN, LEADER OF THE MUTIES, AND HIS SIDE-KICK BONES...
AAAGH!
MEANWHILE, JUDGE DREDD AND TWO OTHER CITY LAWMAN RIDE IN HOT PURSUIT OF THE SPEEDING THUGS...
WE'VE GOTTA MAKE SURE NOBODY WINS THE MEGA-CITY 5000, OTHERWISE THIS DESTRUCTION WILL CONTINUE NEXT YEAR!
YEAH, NO-ONE CAN CHALLENGE THE LAW — AND WIN!
JUDGE
DREDD

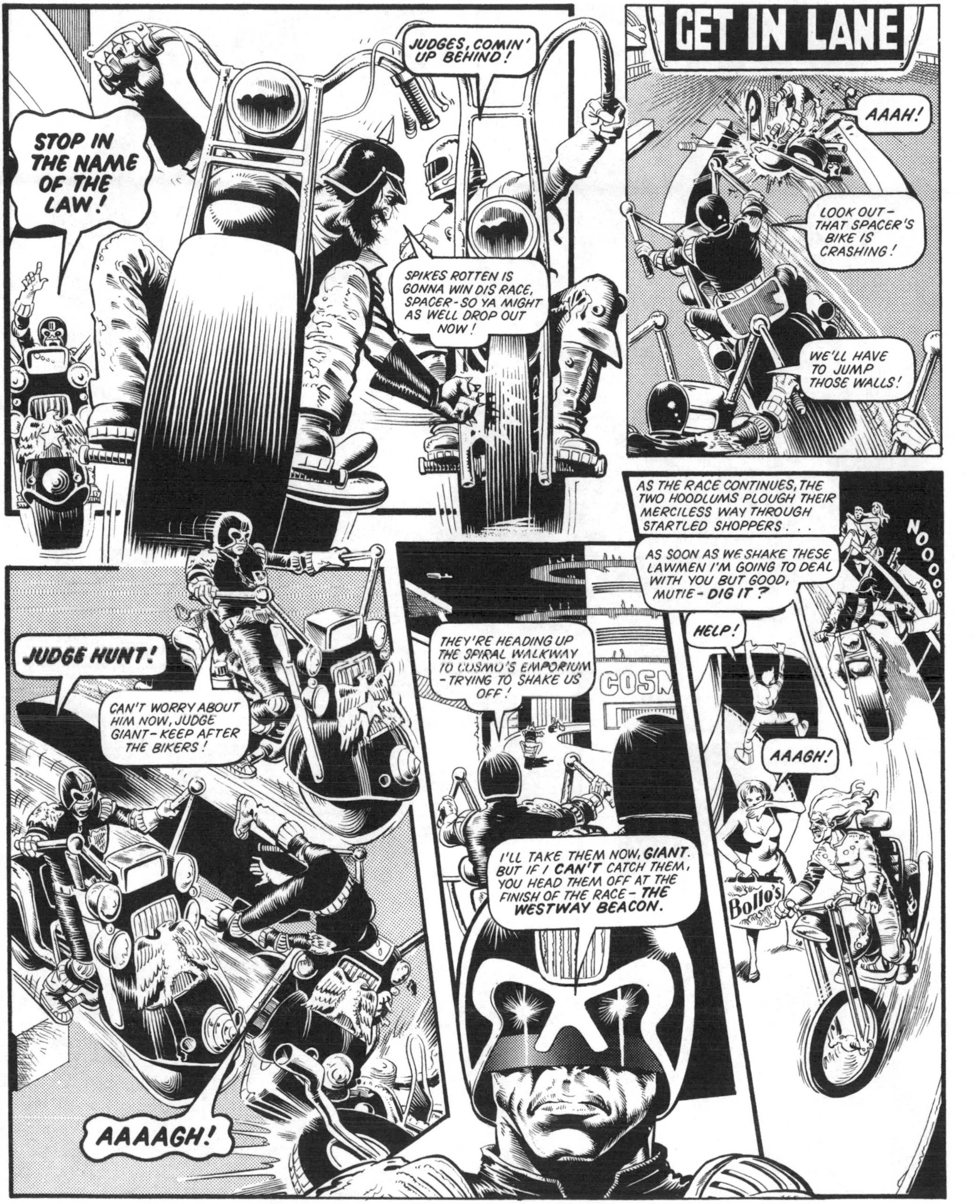

STOP IN THE NAME OF THE LAW!
JUDGES, COMIN' UP BEHIND!
SPIKES ROTTEN IS GONNA WIN DIS RACE, SPACER - SO YA MIGHT AS WELL DROP OUT NOW!
GET IN LANE
AAAH!
LOOK OUT - THAT SPACER'S BIKE IS CRASHING!
WE'LL HAVE TO JUMP THOSE WALLS!
JUDGE HUNT!
CAN'T WORRY ABOUT HIM NOW, JUDGE GIANT - KEEP AFTER THE BIKERS!
AAAAGH!
THEY'RE HEADING UP THE SPIRAL WALKWAY TO COSMO'S EMPORIUM - TRYING TO SHAKE US OFF!
I'LL TAKE THEM NOW, GIANT. BUT IF I CAN'T CATCH THEM, YOU HEAD THEM OFF AT THE FINISH OF THE RACE - THE WESTWAY BEACON.
AS THE RACE CONTINUES, THE TWO HOODLUMS PLOUGH THEIR MERCILESS WAY THROUGH STARTLED SHOPPERS . . .
AS SOON AS WE SHAKE THESE LAWMEN I'M GOING TO DEAL WITH YOU BUT GOOD, MUTIE - DIG IT?
NOOOOO
HELP!
AAAGH!
Bollo's

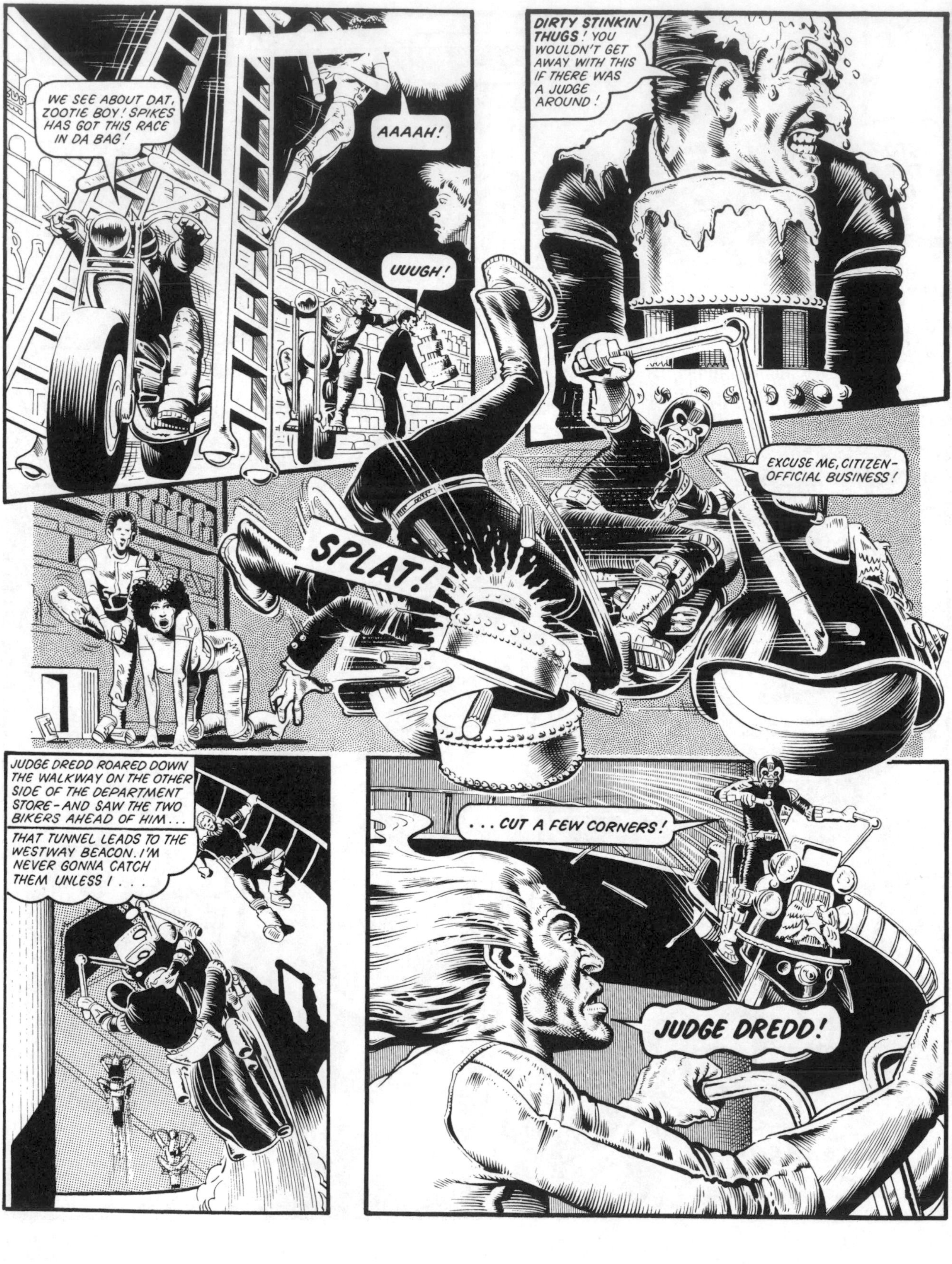
WE SEE ABOUT DAT, ZOOTIE BOY! SPIKES HAS GOT THIS RACE IN DA BAG!
AAAAH!
UUUGH!
DIRTY STINKIN' THUGS! YOU WOULDN'T GET AWAY WITH THIS IF THERE WAS A JUDGE AROUND!
EXCUSE ME, CITIZEN-OFFICIAL BUSINESS!
SPLAT!
JUDGE DREDD ROARED DOWN THE WALKWAY ON THE OTHER SIDE OF THE DEPARTMENT STORE-AND SAW THE TWO BIKERS AHEAD OF HIM...
THAT TUNNEL LEADS TO THE WESTWAY BEACON. I'M NEVER GONNA CATCH THEM UNLESS I . . .
. . . CUT A FEW CORNERS!
JUDGE DREDD!

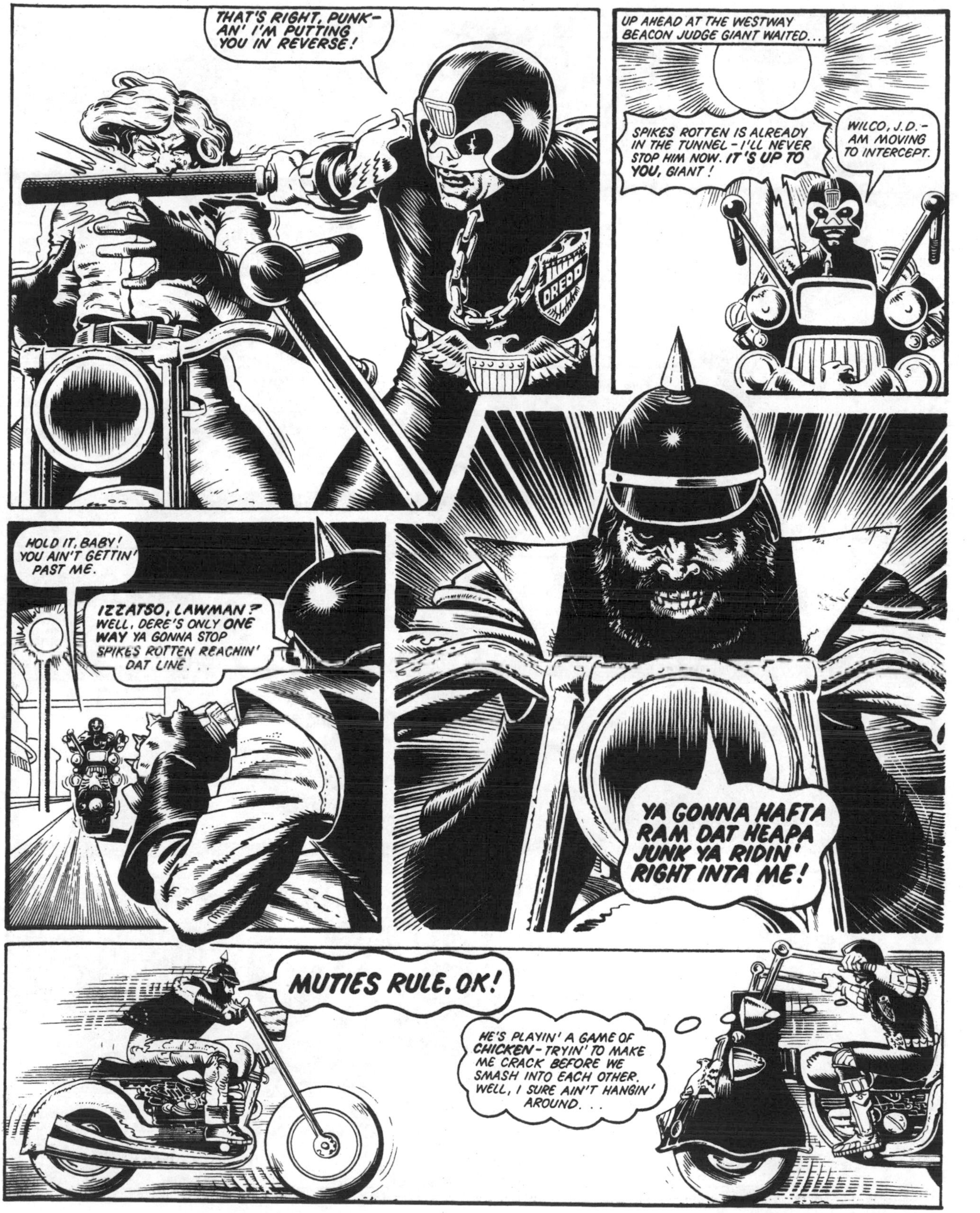
THAT'S RIGHT, PUNK- AN' I'M PUTTING YOU IN REVERSE!
UP AHEAD AT THE WESTWAY BEACON JUDGE GIANT WAITED...
SPIKES ROTTEN IS ALREADY IN THE TUNNEL - I'LL NEVER STOP HIM NOW. IT'S UP TO YOU, GIANT!
WILCO, J.D.- AM MOVING TO INTERCEPT.
DREDD
HOLD IT, BABY! YOU AIN'T GETTIN' PAST ME.
IZZATSO, LAWMAN? WELL, DERE'S ONLY ONE WAY YA GONNA STOP SPIKES ROTTEN REACHIN' DAT LINE...
YA GONNA HAFTA RAM DAT HEAPA JUNK YA RIDIN' RIGHT INTA ME!
MUTIES RULE, OK!
HE'S PLAYIN' A GAME OF CHICKEN - TRYIN' TO MAKE ME CRACK BEFORE WE SMASH INTO EACH OTHER. WELL, I SURE AIN'T HANGIN' AROUND...

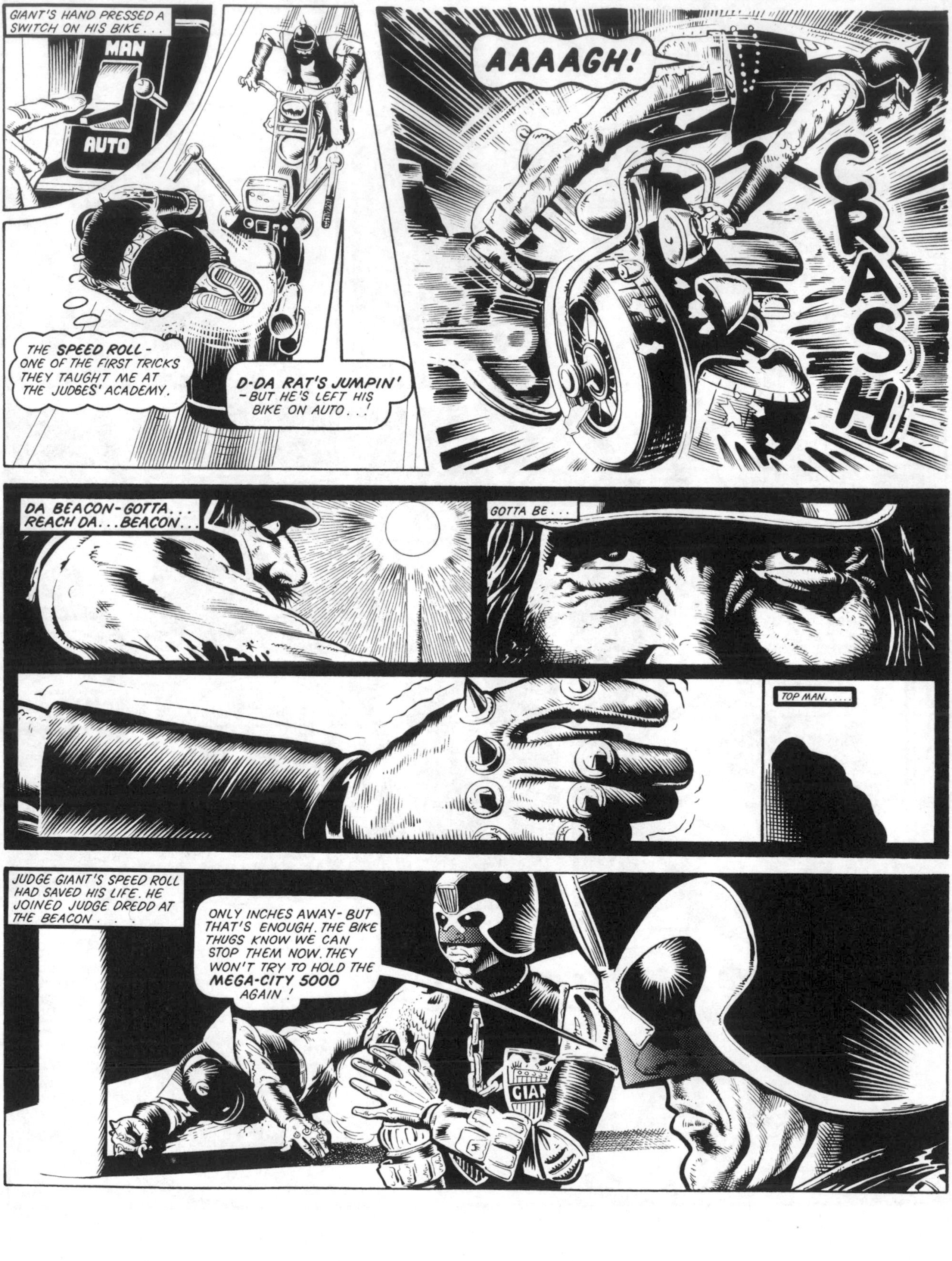
GIANT'S HAND PRESSED A SWITCH ON HIS BIKE...
MAN
AUTO
THE SPEED ROLL - ONE OF THE FIRST TRICKS THEY TAUGHT ME AT THE JUDGES' ACADEMY.
D-DA RAT'S JUMPIN' - BUT HE'S LEFT HIS BIKE ON AUTO...!
AAAAGH!
CRASH
DA BEACON - GOTTA... REACH DA... BEACON...
GOTTA BE...
TOP MAN......
JUDGE GIANT'S SPEED ROLL HAD SAVED HIS LIFE. HE JOINED JUDGE DREDD AT THE BEACON...
ONLY INCHES AWAY - BUT THAT'S ENOUGH. THE BIKE THUGS KNOW WE CAN STOP THEM NOW. THEY WON'T TRY TO HOLD THE MEGA-CITY 5000 AGAIN!
GIAN

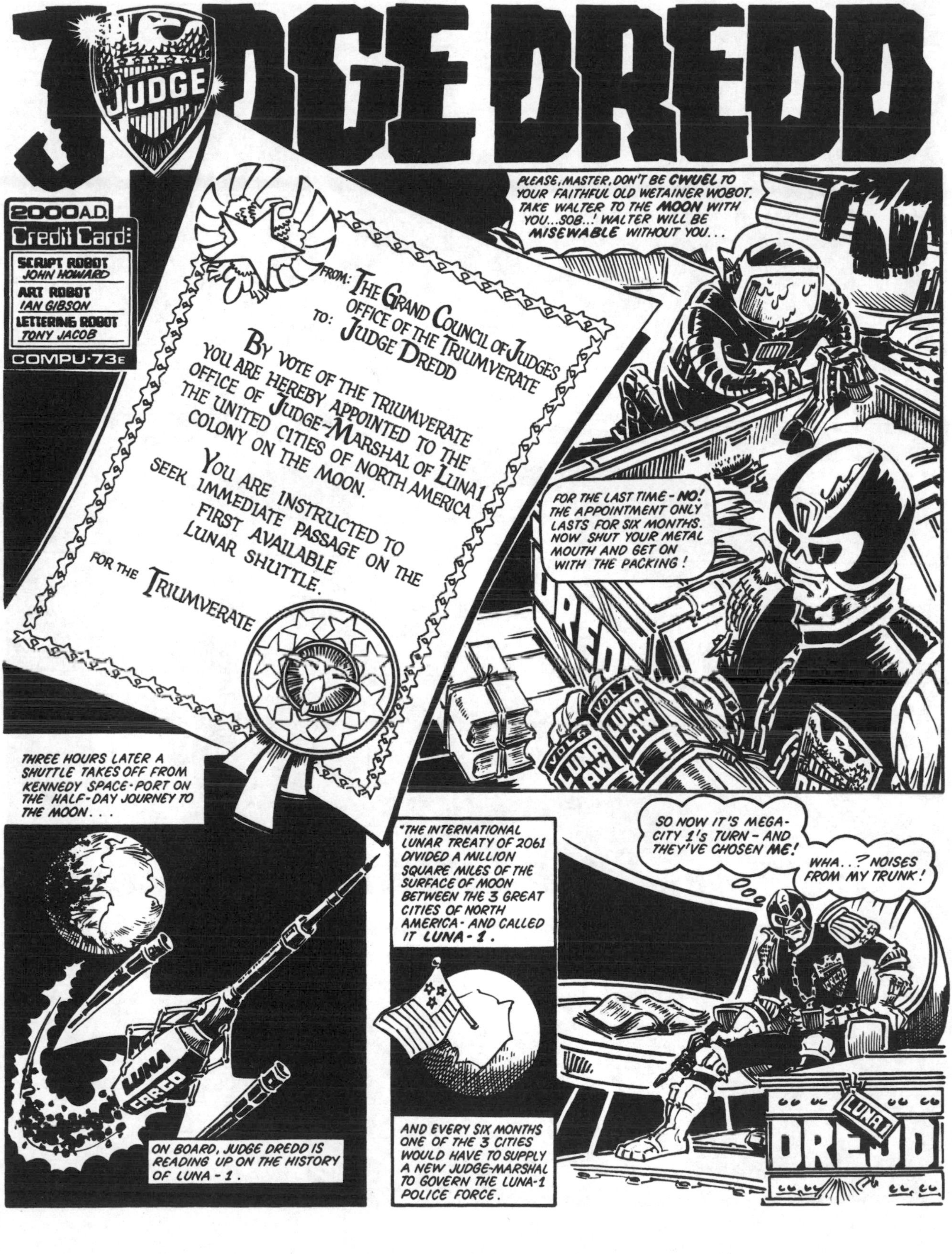
JUDGE DREDD
JUDGE
2000 A.D.
Credit Card:
SCRIPT ROBOT JOHN HOWARD
ART ROBOT IAN GIBSON
LETTERING ROBOT TONY JACOB
COMPU-73E
FROM: THE GRAND COUNCIL OF JUDGES OFFICE OF THE TRIUMVERATE
TO: JUDGE DREDD
BY VOTE OF THE TRIUMVERATE YOU ARE HEREBY APPOINTED TO THE OFFICE OF JUDGE-MARSHAL OF LUNA 1 THE UNITED CITIES OF NORTH AMERICA COLONY ON THE MOON.
YOU ARE INSTRUCTED TO SEEK IMMEDIATE PASSAGE ON THE FIRST AVAILABLE LUNAR SHUTTLE.
FOR THE TRIUMVERATE
PLEASE, MASTER, DON'T BE CWUEL TO YOUR FAITHFUL OLD WETAINER WOBOT. TAKE WALTER TO THE MOON WITH YOU...SOB...! WALTER WILL BE MISEWABLE WITHOUT YOU...
FOR THE LAST TIME - NO! THE APPOINTMENT ONLY LASTS FOR SIX MONTHS. NOW SHUT YOUR METAL MOUTH AND GET ON WITH THE PACKING!
DREDD
LUNA LAW
THREE HOURS LATER A SHUTTLE TAKES OFF FROM KENNEDY SPACE-PORT ON THE HALF-DAY JOURNEY TO THE MOON...
LUNA CARGO
ON BOARD, JUDGE DREDD IS READING UP ON THE HISTORY OF LUNA-1.
"THE INTERNATIONAL LUNAR TREATY OF 2061 DIVIDED A MILLION SQUARE MILES OF THE SURFACE OF MOON BETWEEN THE 3 GREAT CITIES OF NORTH AMERICA - AND CALLED IT LUNA-1.
AND EVERY SIX MONTHS ONE OF THE 3 CITIES WOULD HAVE TO SUPPLY A NEW JUDGE-MARSHAL TO GOVERN THE LUNA-1 POLICE FORCE.
SO NOW IT'S MEGA-CITY 1's TURN - AND THEY'VE CHOSEN ME!
WHA..? NOISES FROM MY TRUNK!
LUNA 1
DREDD

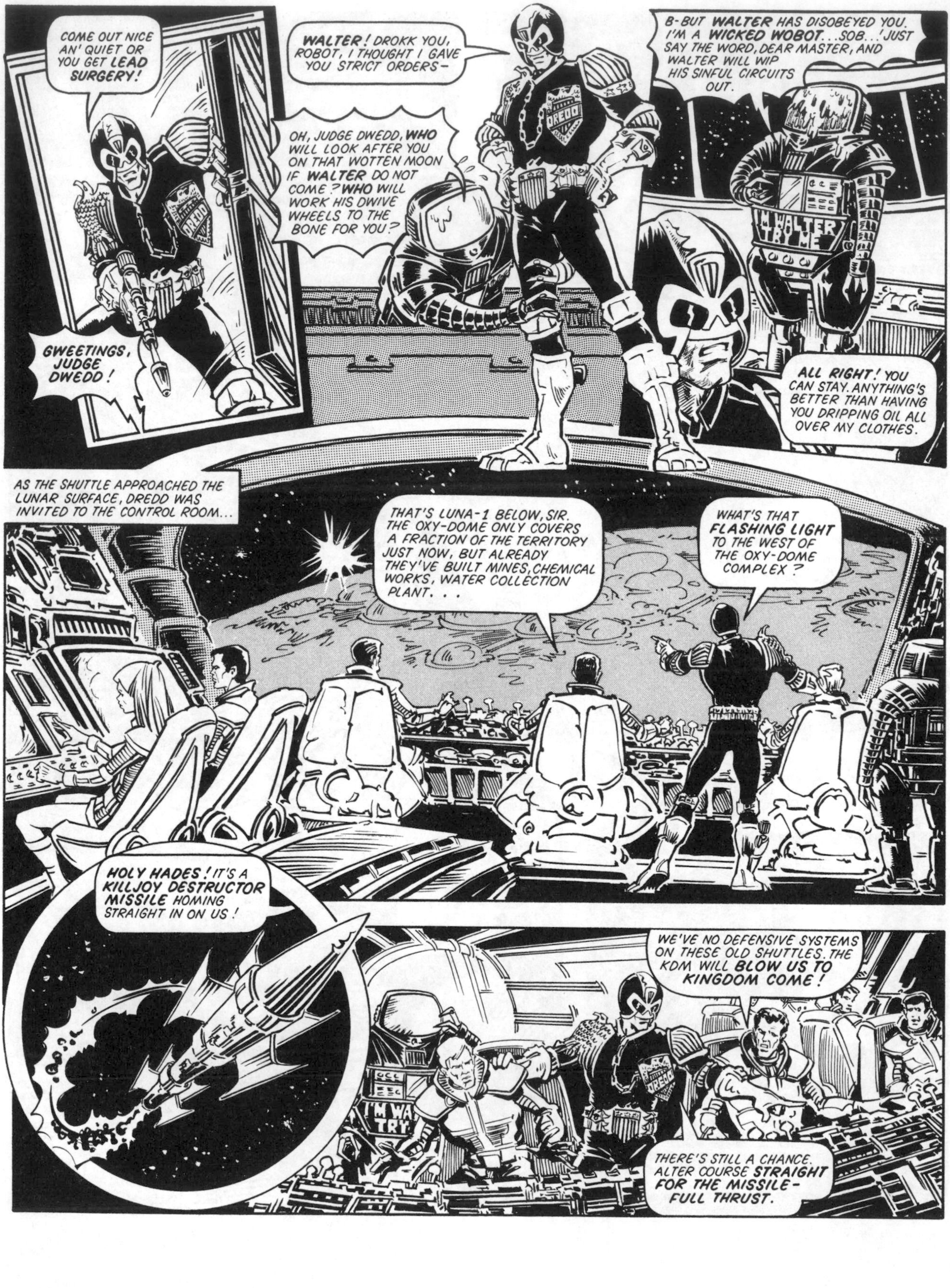
COME OUT NICE AN' QUIET OR YOU GET LEAD SURGERY!
GWEETINGS, JUDGE DWEDD!
WALTER! DROKK YOU, ROBOT, I THOUGHT I GAVE YOU STRICT ORDERS–
OH, JUDGE DWEDD, WHO WILL LOOK AFTER YOU ON THAT WOTTEN MOON IF WALTER DO NOT COME? WHO WILL WORK HIS DWIVE WHEELS TO THE BONE FOR YOU?
B-BUT WALTER HAS DISOBEYED YOU. I'M A WICKED WOBOT...SOB...' JUST SAY THE WORD, DEAR MASTER, AND WALTER WILL WIP HIS SINFUL CIRCUITS OUT.
I'M WALTER TRY ME
ALL RIGHT! YOU CAN STAY. ANYTHING'S BETTER THAN HAVING YOU DRIPPING OIL ALL OVER MY CLOTHES.
AS THE SHUTTLE APPROACHED THE LUNAR SURFACE, DREDD WAS INVITED TO THE CONTROL ROOM...
THAT'S LUNA-1 BELOW, SIR. THE OXY-DOME ONLY COVERS A FRACTION OF THE TERRITORY JUST NOW, BUT ALREADY THEY'VE BUILT MINES, CHEMICAL WORKS, WATER COLLECTION PLANT...
WHAT'S THAT FLASHING LIGHT TO THE WEST OF THE OXY-DOME COMPLEX?
HOLY HADES! IT'S A KILLJOY DESTRUCTOR MISSILE HOMING STRAIGHT IN ON US!
WE'VE NO DEFENSIVE SYSTEMS ON THESE OLD SHUTTLES. THE KDM WILL BLOW US TO KINGDOM COME!
THERE'S STILL A CHANCE. ALTER COURSE STRAIGHT FOR THE MISSILE– FULL THRUST.

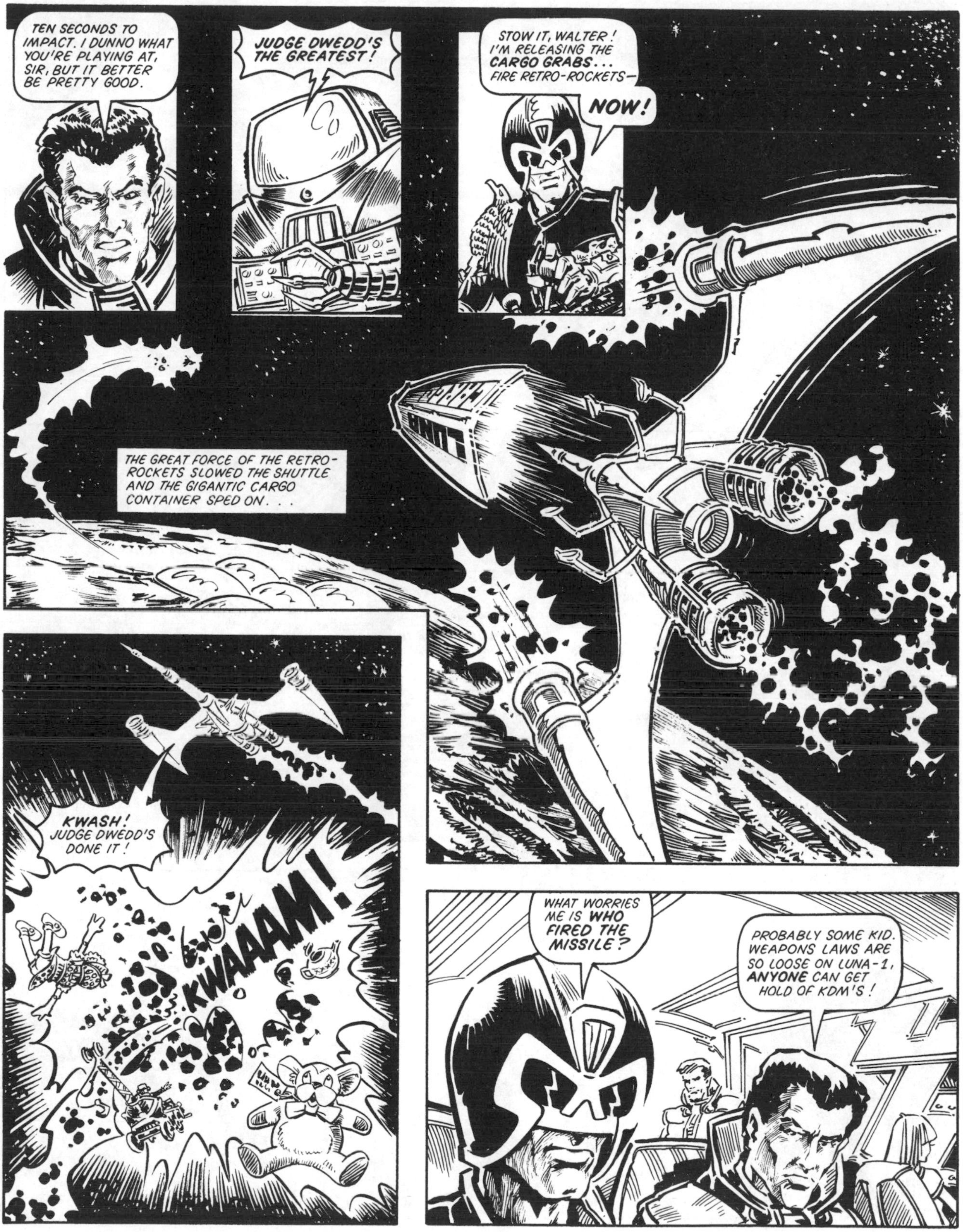
TEN SECONDS TO IMPACT. I DUNNO WHAT YOU'RE PLAYING AT, SIR, BUT IT BETTER BE PRETTY GOOD.
JUDGE DWEDD'S THE GREATEST!
STOW IT, WALTER! I'M RELEASING THE CARGO GRABS... FIRE RETRO-ROCKETS—
NOW!
THE GREAT FORCE OF THE RETRO-ROCKETS SLOWED THE SHUTTLE AND THE GIGANTIC CARGO CONTAINER SPED ON . . .
KWASH! JUDGE DWEDD'S DONE IT!
KWAAAM!
WHAT WORRIES ME IS WHO FIRED THE MISSILE?
PROBABLY SOME KID. WEAPONS LAWS ARE SO LOOSE ON LUNA-1, ANYONE CAN GET HOLD OF KDM'S!

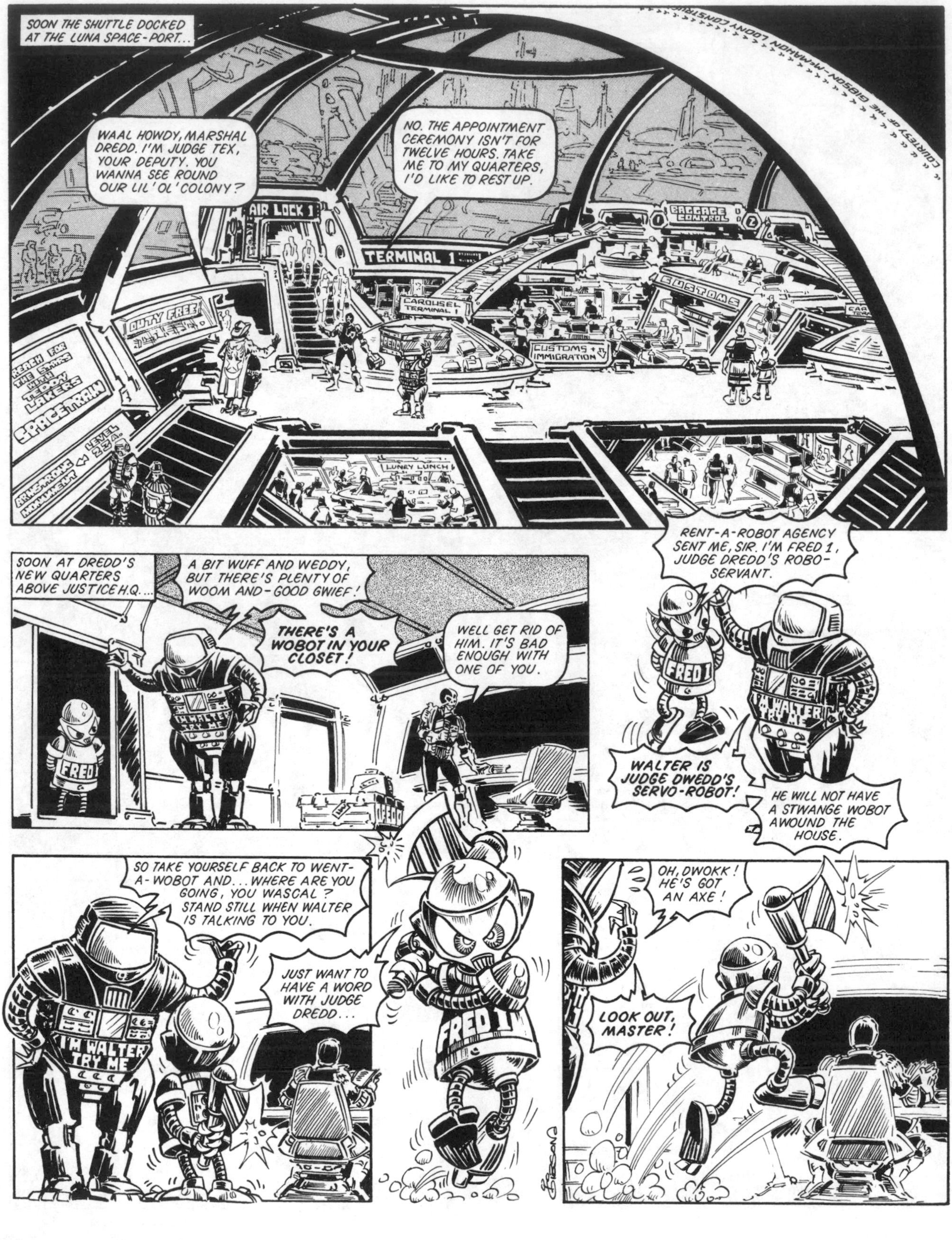
SOON THE SHUTTLE DOCKED AT THE LUNA SPACE-PORT...
WAAL HOWDY, MARSHAL DREDD. I'M JUDGE TEX, YOUR DEPUTY. YOU WANNA SEE ROUND OUR LIL'OL'COLONY?
NO. THE APPOINTMENT CEREMONY ISN'T FOR TWELVE HOURS. TAKE ME TO MY QUARTERS, I'D LIKE TO REST UP.
AIR LOCK 1
TERMINAL 1
BAGGAGE CONTROL
CUSTOMS
CAROUSEL TERMINAL 1
CUSTOMS + IMMIGRATION
DUTY FREE
REACH FOR THE STARS WITH TEDDY LAKERS SPACETRAIN
LUNEY LUNCH
SOON AT DREDD'S NEW QUARTERS ABOVE JUSTICE H.Q....
A BIT WUFF AND WEDDY, BUT THERE'S PLENTY OF WOOM AND-GOOD GWIEF!
THERE'S A WOBOT IN YOUR CLOSET!
WELL GET RID OF HIM. IT'S BAD ENOUGH WITH ONE OF YOU.
FRED
RENT-A-ROBOT AGENCY SENT ME, SIR. I'M FRED 1, JUDGE DREDD'S ROBO-SERVANT.
FRED 1
WALTER IS JUDGE DWEDD'S SERVO-ROBOT!
HE WILL NOT HAVE A STWANGE WOBOT AWOUND THE HOUSE.
SO TAKE YOURSELF BACK TO WENT-A-WOBOT AND... WHERE ARE YOU GOING, YOU WASCAL? STAND STILL WHEN WALTER IS TALKING TO YOU.
I'M WALTER TRY ME
JUST WANT TO HAVE A WORD WITH JUDGE DREDD...
FRED 1
OH, DWOKK! HE'S GOT AN AXE!
LOOK OUT, MASTER!

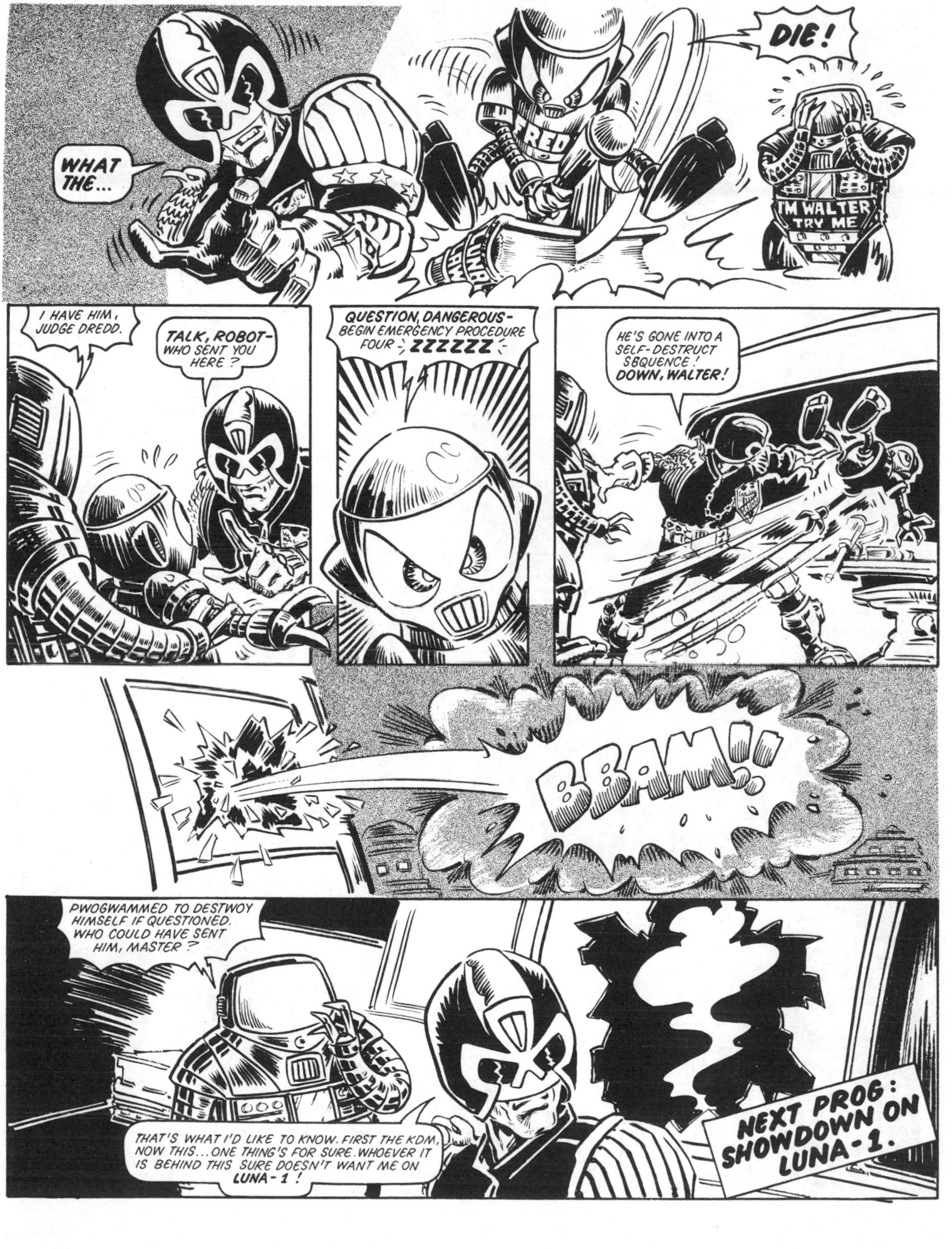

WHAT THE...
DIE!
I'M WALTER TRY ME
I HAVE HIM, JUDGE DREDD.
TALK, ROBOT- WHO SENT YOU HERE?
QUESTION, DANGEROUS- BEGIN EMERGENCY PROCEDURE FOUR - ZZZZZZ
HE'S GONE INTO A SELF-DESTRUCT SEQUENCE! DOWN, WALTER!
BBAM!!
PWOGWAMMED TO DESTWOY HIMSELF IF QUESTIONED. WHO COULD HAVE SENT HIM, MASTER?
THAT'S WHAT I'D LIKE TO KNOW. FIRST THE KDM, NOW THIS... ONE THING'S FOR SURE. WHOEVER IT IS BEHIND THIS SURE DOESN'T WANT ME ON LUNA-1!
NEXT PROG: SHOWDOWN ON LUNA-1.

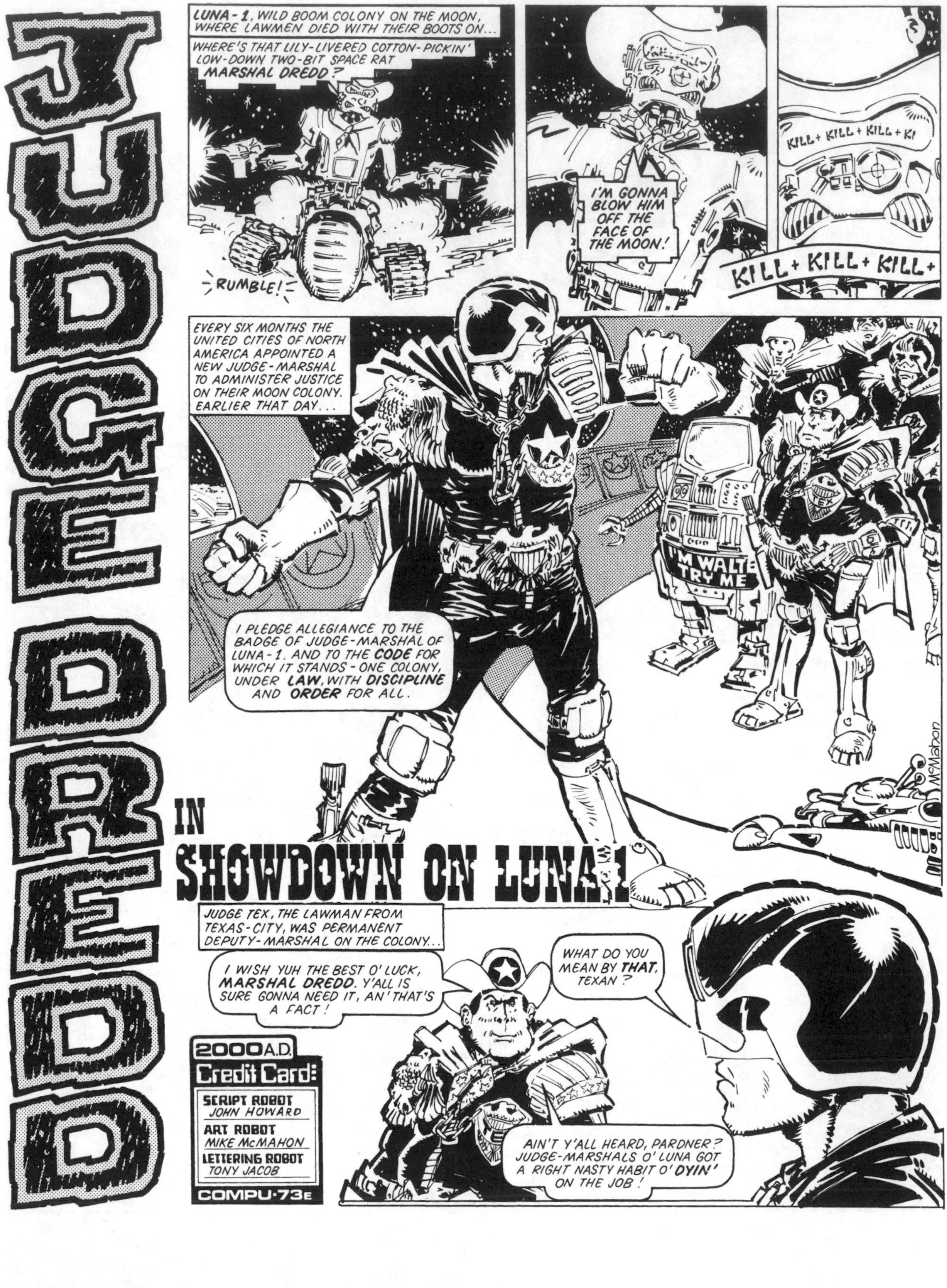
JUDGE DREDD
LUNA-1, WILD BOOM COLONY ON THE MOON, WHERE LAWMEN DIED WITH THEIR BOOTS ON...
WHERE'S THAT LILY-LIVERED COTTON-PICKIN' LOW-DOWN TWO-BIT SPACE RAT MARSHAL DREDD?
RUMBLE!
I'M GONNA BLOW HIM OFF THE FACE OF THE MOON!
KILL + KILL + KILL + KI
KILL + KILL + KILL +
EVERY SIX MONTHS THE UNITED CITIES OF NORTH AMERICA APPOINTED A NEW JUDGE-MARSHAL TO ADMINISTER JUSTICE ON THEIR MOON COLONY. EARLIER THAT DAY...
I'M WALTE TRY ME
I PLEDGE ALLEGIANCE TO THE BADGE OF JUDGE-MARSHAL OF LUNA-1. AND TO THE CODE FOR WHICH IT STANDS - ONE COLONY, UNDER LAW, WITH DISCIPLINE AND ORDER FOR ALL.
McMahon
IN
SHOWDOWN ON LUNA-1
JUDGE TEX, THE LAWMAN FROM TEXAS-CITY, WAS PERMANENT DEPUTY-MARSHAL ON THE COLONY...
I WISH YUH THE BEST O' LUCK, MARSHAL DREDD. Y'ALL IS SURE GONNA NEED IT, AN' THAT'S A FACT!
WHAT DO YOU MEAN BY THAT, TEXAN?
AIN'T Y'ALL HEARD, PARDNER? JUDGE-MARSHALS O' LUNA GOT A RIGHT NASTY HABIT O' DYIN' ON THE JOB!
2000 A.D.
Credit Card:
SCRIPT ROBOT
JOHN HOWARD
ART ROBOT
MIKE McMAHON
LETTERING ROBOT
TONY JACOB
COMPU-73E

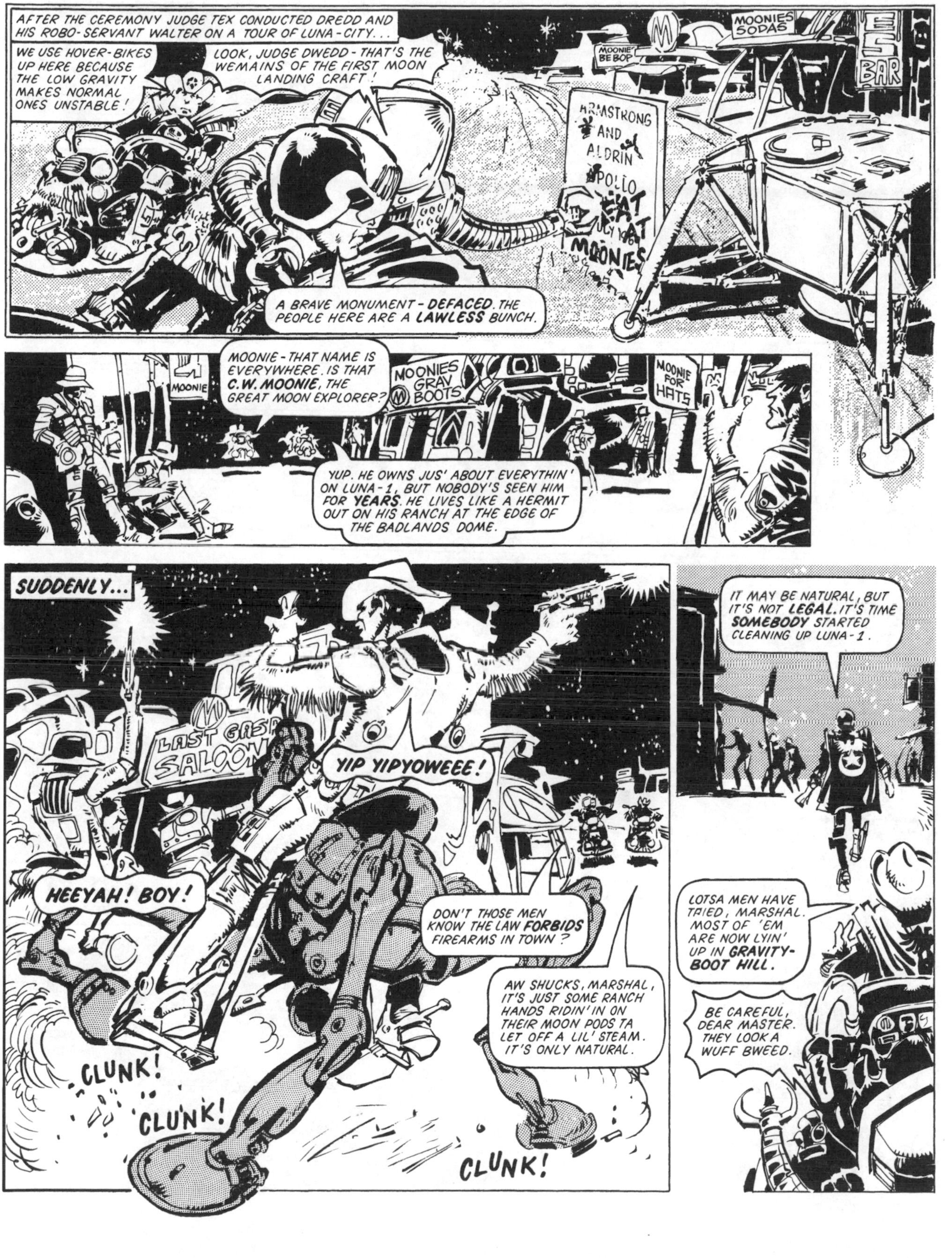
AFTER THE CEREMONY JUDGE TEX CONDUCTED DREDD AND HIS ROBO-SERVANT WALTER ON A TOUR OF LUNA-CITY...
WE USE HOVER-BIKES UP HERE BECAUSE THE LOW GRAVITY MAKES NORMAL ONES UNSTABLE!
LOOK, JUDGE DWEDD - THAT'S THE WEMAINS OF THE FIRST MOON LANDING CRAFT!
A BRAVE MONUMENT - **DEFACED**. THE PEOPLE HERE ARE A **LAWLESS** BUNCH.
MOONIE - THAT NAME IS EVERYWHERE. IS THAT **C.W. MOONIE**, THE GREAT MOON EXPLORER?
YUP. HE OWNS JUS' ABOUT EVERYTHIN' ON LUNA-1, BUT NOBODY'S SEEN HIM FOR **YEARS**. HE LIVES LIKE A HERMIT OUT ON HIS RANCH AT THE EDGE OF THE BADLANDS DOME.
SUDDENLY...
YIP YIPYOWEEE!
HEEYAH! BOY!
DON'T THOSE MEN KNOW THE LAW **FORBIDS** FIREARMS IN TOWN?
AW SHUCKS, MARSHAL, IT'S JUST SOME RANCH HANDS RIDIN' IN ON THEIR MOON PODS TA LET OFF A LIL' STEAM. IT'S ONLY NATURAL.
CLUNK!
CLUNK!
CLUNK!
IT MAY BE NATURAL, BUT IT'S NOT **LEGAL**. IT'S TIME **SOMEBODY** STARTED CLEANING UP LUNA-1.
LOTSA MEN HAVE TRIED, MARSHAL. MOST OF 'EM ARE NOW LYIN' UP IN **GRAVITY-BOOT HILL**.
BE CAREFUL, DEAR MASTER. THEY LOOK A WUFF BWEED.

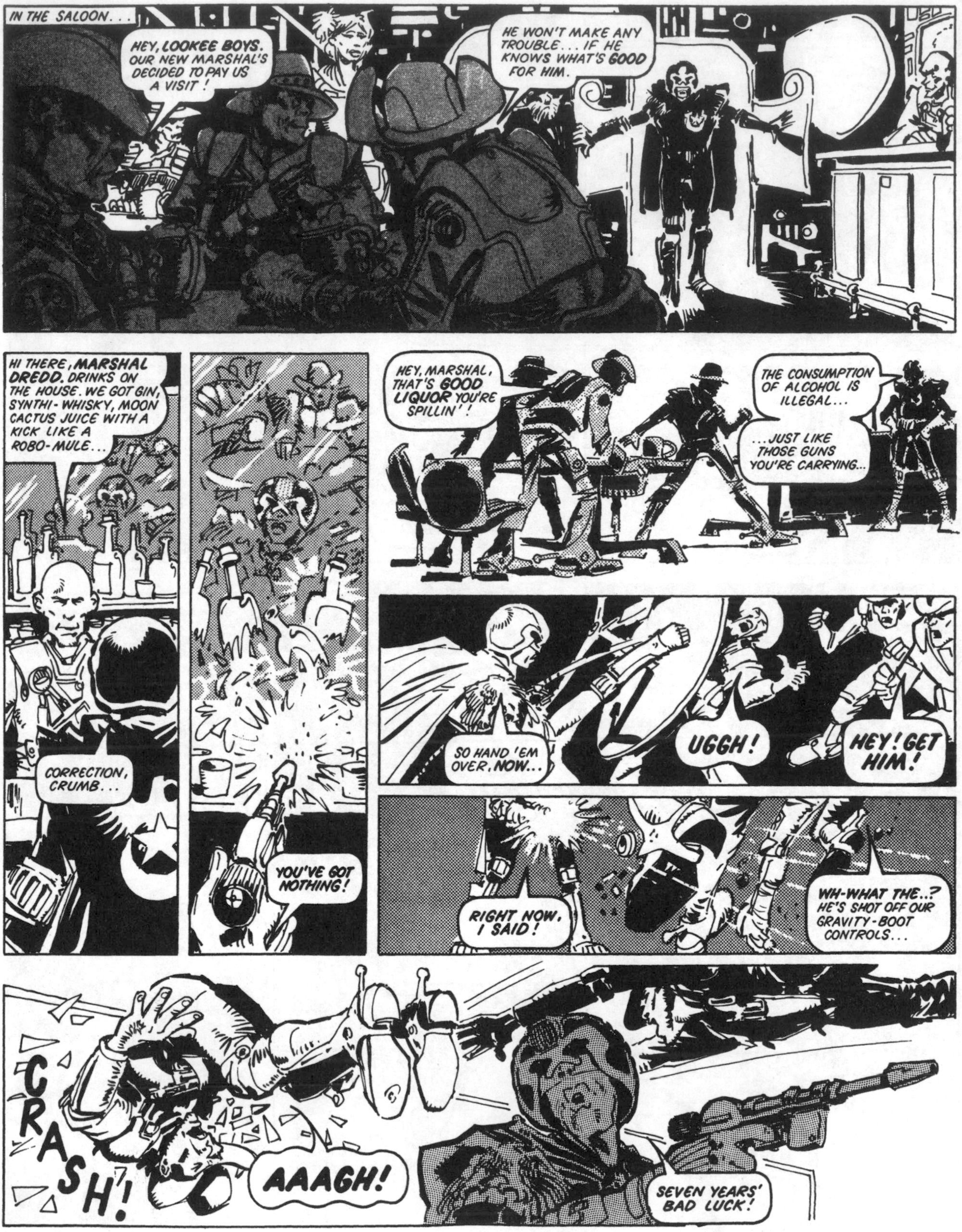
IN THE SALOON...
HEY, LOOKEE BOYS. OUR NEW MARSHAL'S DECIDED TO PAY US A VISIT!
HE WON'T MAKE ANY TROUBLE... IF HE KNOWS WHAT'S GOOD FOR HIM.
HI THERE, MARSHAL DREDD. DRINKS ON THE HOUSE. WE GOT GIN, SYNTHI-WHISKY, MOON CACTUS JUICE WITH A KICK LIKE A ROBO-MULE...
CORRECTION, CRUMB...
YOU'VE GOT NOTHING!
HEY, MARSHAL, THAT'S GOOD LIQUOR YOU'RE SPILLIN'!
THE CONSUMPTION OF ALCOHOL IS ILLEGAL...
...JUST LIKE THOSE GUNS YOU'RE CARRYING...
SO HAND 'EM OVER, NOW...
UGGH!
HEY! GET HIM!
RIGHT NOW, I SAID!
WH-WHAT THE..? HE'S SHOT OFF OUR GRAVITY-BOOT CONTROLS...
CRASH!
AAAGH!
SEVEN YEARS' BAD LUCK!

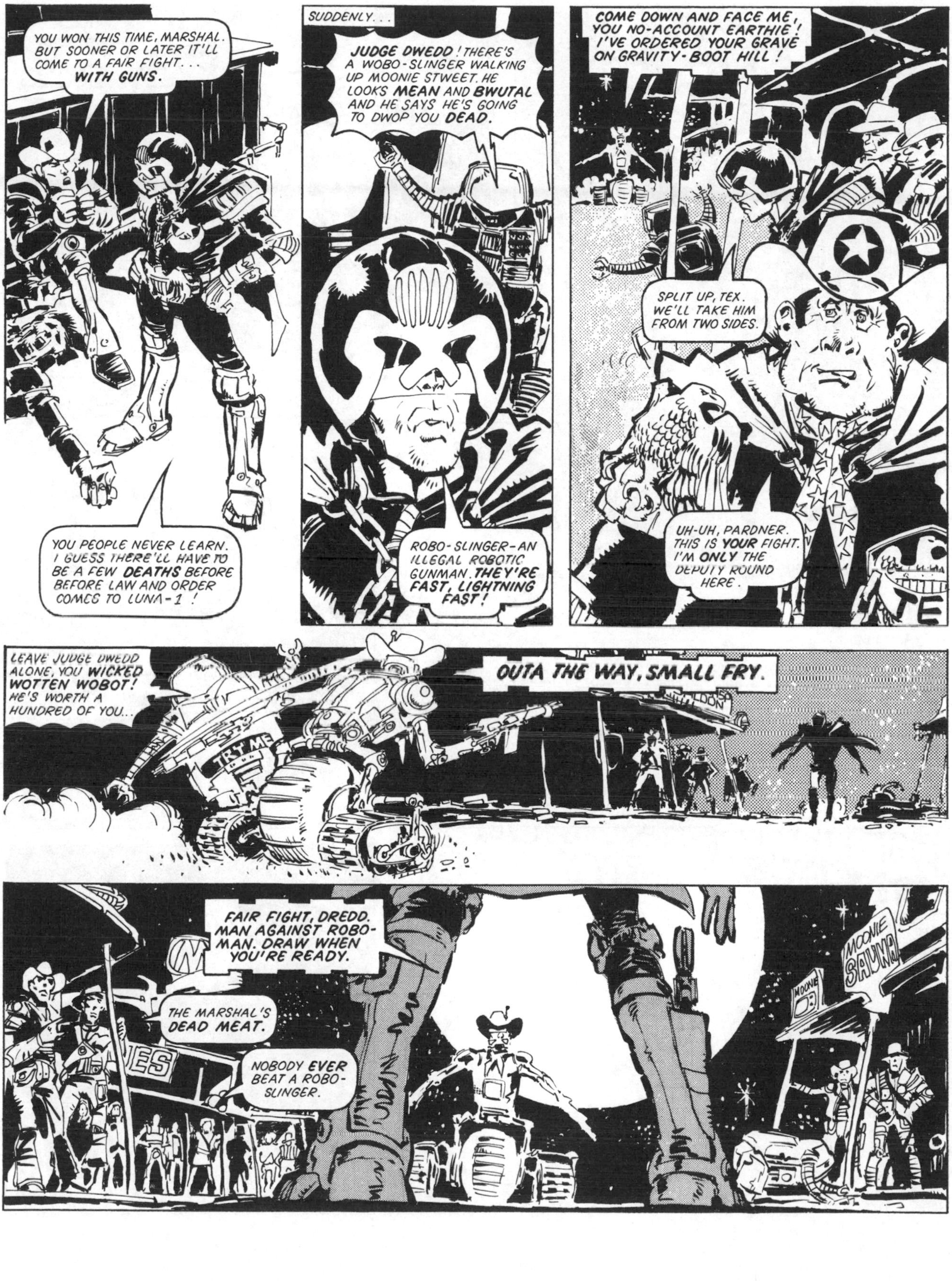
YOU WON THIS TIME, MARSHAL. BUT SOONER OR LATER IT'LL COME TO A FAIR FIGHT... WITH GUNS.
YOU PEOPLE NEVER LEARN. I GUESS THERE'LL HAVE TO BE A FEW DEATHS BEFORE BEFORE LAW AND ORDER COMES TO LUNA-1 !
SUDDENLY...
JUDGE DWEDD! THERE'S A WOBO-SLINGER WALKING UP MOONIE STWEET. HE LOOKS MEAN AND BWUTAL AND HE SAYS HE'S GOING TO DWOP YOU DEAD.
ROBO-SLINGER–AN ILLEGAL ROBOTIC GUNMAN. THEY'RE FAST, LIGHTNING FAST!
COME DOWN AND FACE ME, YOU NO-ACCOUNT EARTHIE! I'VE ORDERED YOUR GRAVE ON GRAVITY-BOOT HILL!
SPLIT UP, TEX. WE'LL TAKE HIM FROM TWO SIDES.
UH-UH, PARDNER. THIS IS YOUR FIGHT. I'M ONLY THE DEPUTY ROUND HERE.
LEAVE JUDGE DWEDD ALONE, YOU WICKED WOTTEN WOBOT! HE'S WORTH A HUNDRED OF YOU...
OUTA THE WAY, SMALL FRY.
FAIR FIGHT, DREDD. MAN AGAINST ROBO-MAN. DRAW WHEN YOU'RE READY.
THE MARSHAL'S DEAD MEAT.
NOBODY EVER BEAT A ROBO-SLINGER.

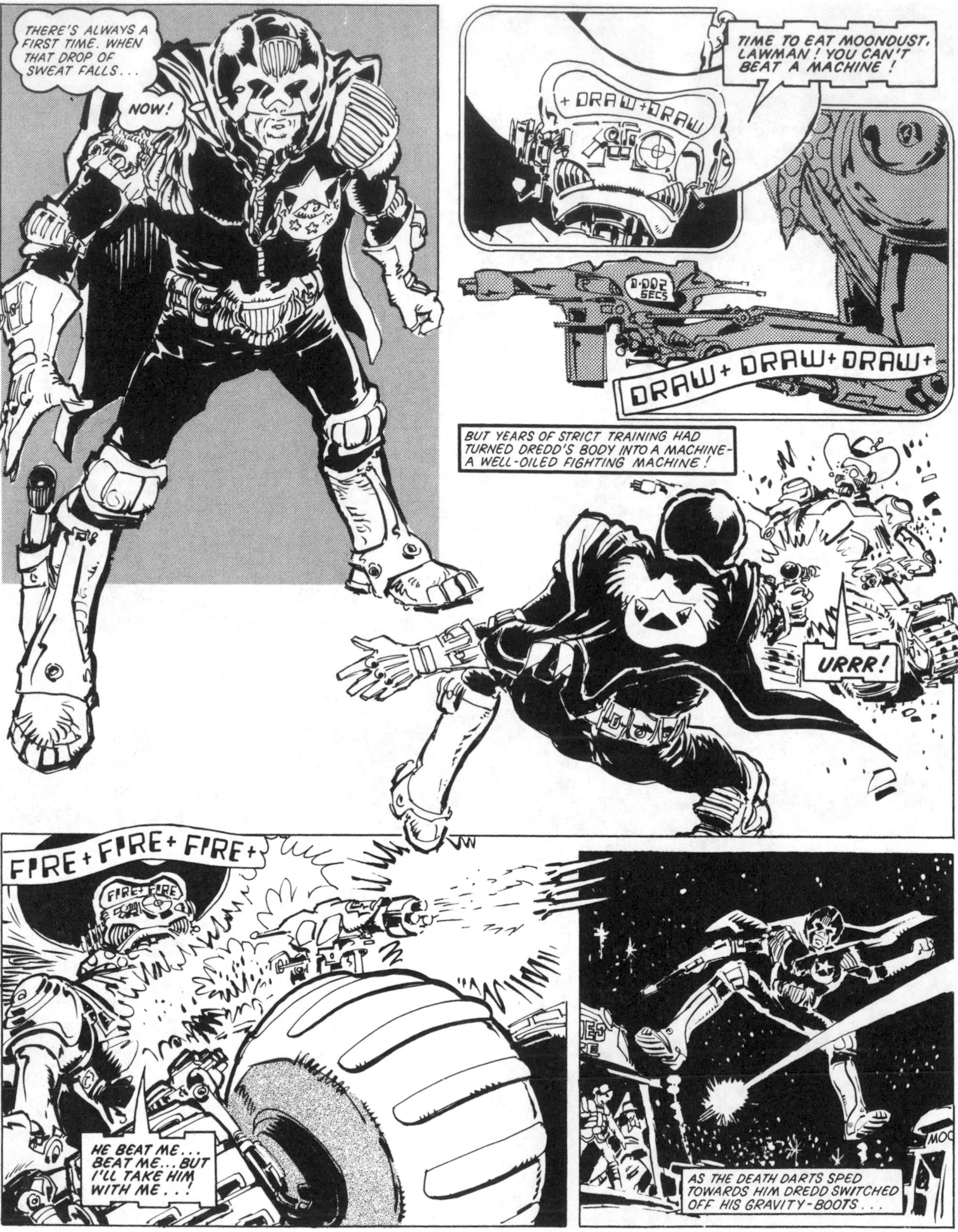
THERE'S ALWAYS A FIRST TIME. WHEN THAT DROP OF SWEAT FALLS...
NOW!
TIME TO EAT MOONDUST, LAWMAN! YOU CAN'T BEAT A MACHINE!
+DRAW+DRAW
0.002 SECS
DRAW+DRAW+DRAW+
BUT YEARS OF STRICT TRAINING HAD TURNED DREDD'S BODY INTO A MACHINE- A WELL-OILED FIGHTING MACHINE!
URRR!
FIRE+FIRE+FIRE+
FIRE+FIRE
HE BEAT ME... BEAT ME... BUT I'LL TAKE HIM WITH ME...!
AS THE DEATH DARTS SPED TOWARDS HIM DREDD SWITCHED OFF HIS GRAVITY-BOOTS...

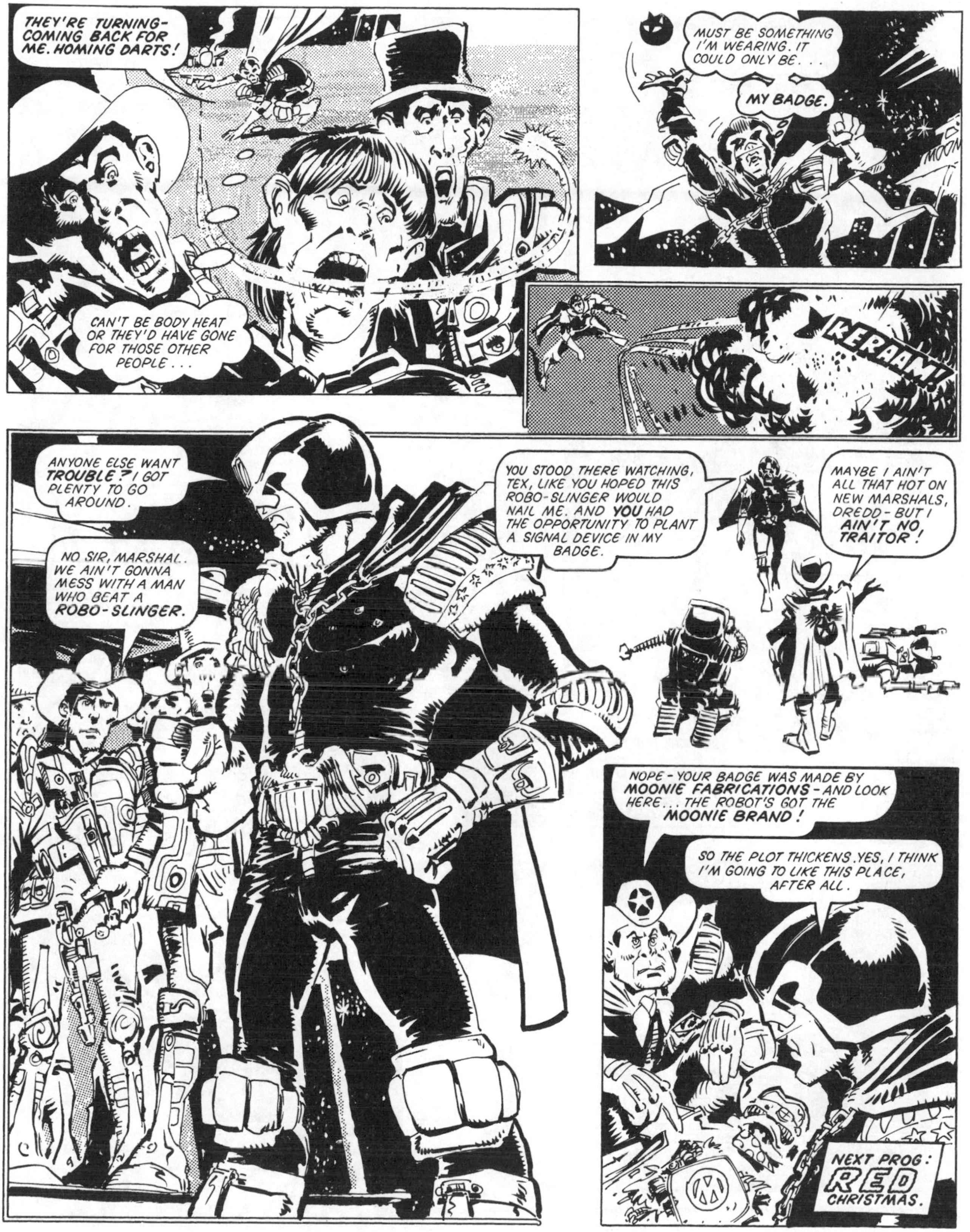

THEY'RE TURNING-COMING BACK FOR ME. HOMING DARTS!
CAN'T BE BODY HEAT OR THEY'D HAVE GONE FOR THOSE OTHER PEOPLE . . .
MUST BE SOMETHING I'M WEARING. IT COULD ONLY BE. . .
MY BADGE.
KERAAM!
ANYONE ELSE WANT TROUBLE? I GOT PLENTY TO GO AROUND.
NO SIR, MARSHAL. WE AIN'T GONNA MESS WITH A MAN WHO BEAT A ROBO-SLINGER.
YOU STOOD THERE WATCHING, TEX, LIKE YOU HOPED THIS ROBO-SLINGER WOULD NAIL ME. AND YOU HAD THE OPPORTUNITY TO PLANT A SIGNAL DEVICE IN MY BADGE.
MAYBE I AIN'T ALL THAT HOT ON NEW MARSHALS, DREDD - BUT I AIN'T NO TRAITOR!
NOPE - YOUR BADGE WAS MADE BY MOONIE FABRICATIONS - AND LOOK HERE... THE ROBOT'S GOT THE MOONIE BRAND!
SO THE PLOT THICKENS. YES, I THINK I'M GOING TO LIKE THIS PLACE, AFTER ALL.
NEXT PROG: RED CHRISTMAS.

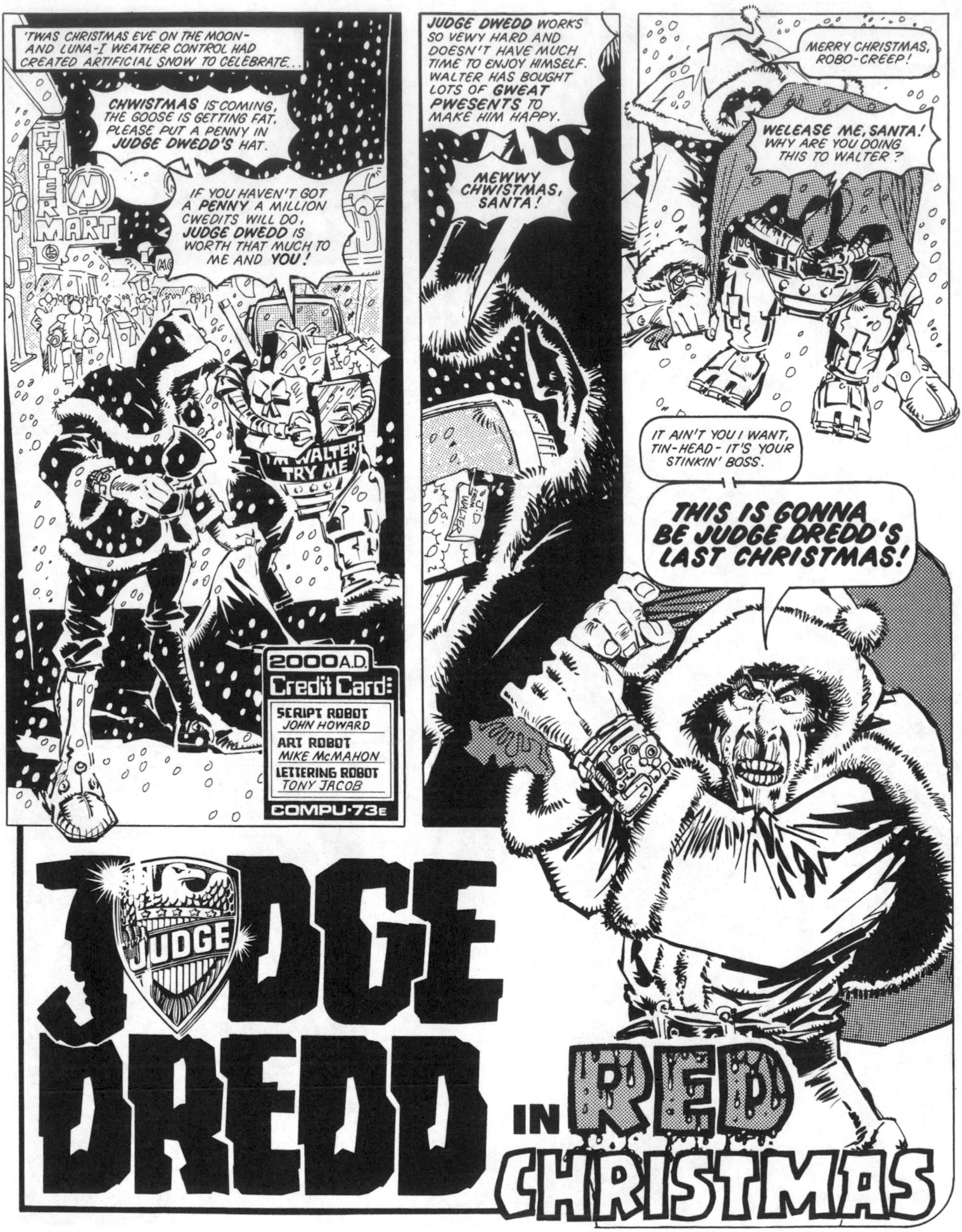

'TWAS CHRISTMAS EVE ON THE MOON- AND LUNA-I WEATHER CONTROL HAD CREATED ARTIFICIAL SNOW TO CELEBRATE...
CHWISTMAS IS COMING, THE GOOSE IS GETTING FAT. PLEASE PUT A PENNY IN JUDGE DWEDD'S HAT.
IF YOU HAVEN'T GOT A PENNY A MILLION CWEDITS WILL DO, JUDGE DWEDD IS WORTH THAT MUCH TO ME AND YOU!
HYPER MART
I'M WALTER TRY ME
2000 A.D. Credit Card:
SCRIPT ROBOT JOHN HOWARD
ART ROBOT MIKE McMAHON
LETTERING ROBOT TONY JACOB
COMPU-73E
JUDGE DWEDD WORKS SO VEWY HARD AND DOESN'T HAVE MUCH TIME TO ENJOY HIMSELF. WALTER HAS BOUGHT LOTS OF GWEAT PWESENTS TO MAKE HIM HAPPY.
MEWWY CHWISTMAS, SANTA!
MERRY CHRISTMAS, ROBO-CREEP!
WELEASE ME, SANTA! WHY ARE YOU DOING THIS TO WALTER?
IT AIN'T YOU I WANT, TIN-HEAD- IT'S YOUR STINKIN' BOSS.
THIS IS GONNA BE JUDGE DREDD'S LAST CHRISTMAS!
JUDGE DREDD
IN RED CHRISTMAS

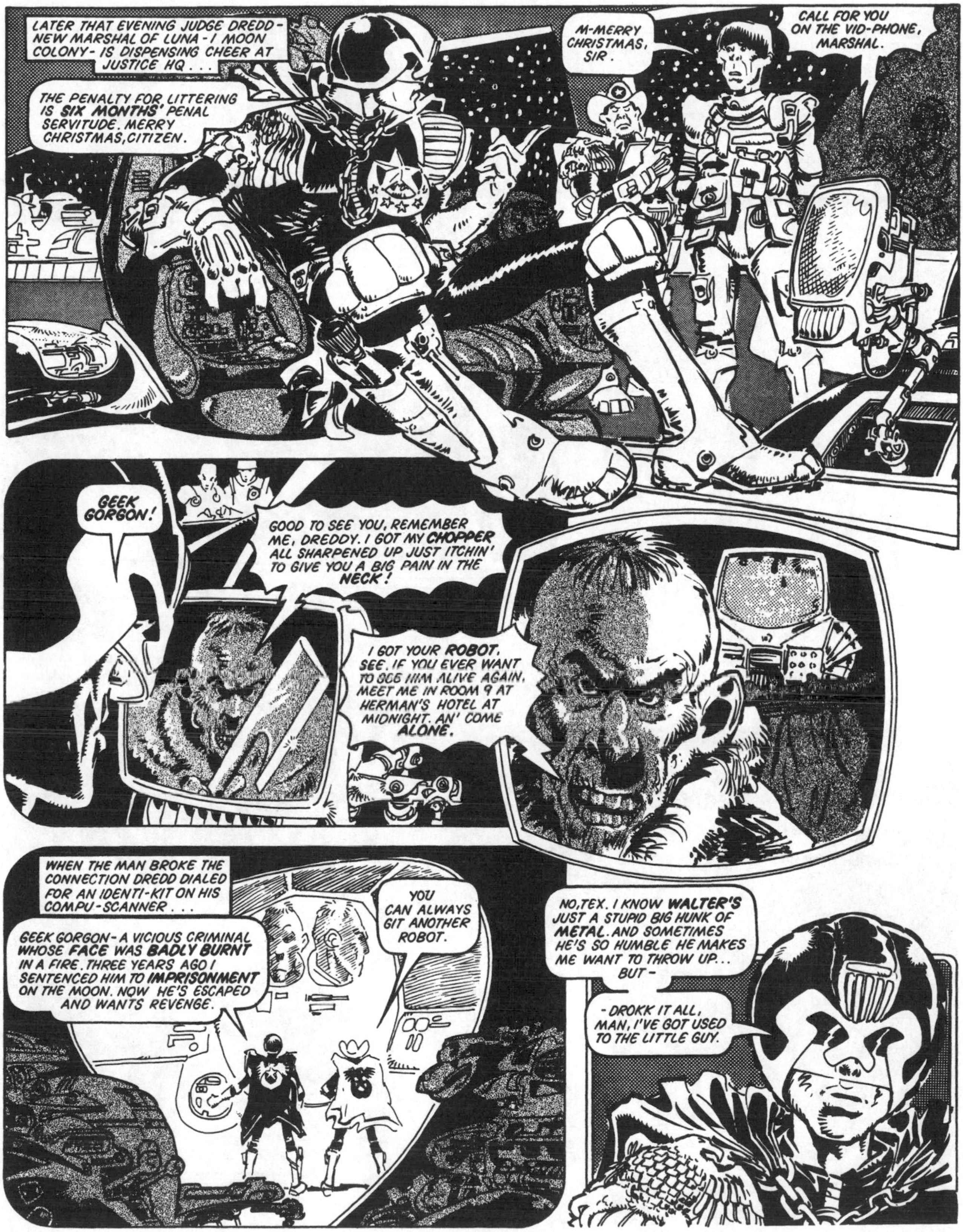
LATER THAT EVENING JUDGE DREDD - NEW MARSHAL OF LUNA-1 MOON COLONY- IS DISPENSING CHEER AT JUSTICE HQ...
THE PENALTY FOR LITTERING IS SIX MONTHS' PENAL SERVITUDE. MERRY CHRISTMAS, CITIZEN.
M-MERRY CHRISTMAS, SIR.
CALL FOR YOU ON THE VID-PHONE, MARSHAL.
GEEK GORGON!
GOOD TO SEE YOU, REMEMBER ME, DREDDY. I GOT MY CHOPPER ALL SHARPENED UP JUST ITCHIN' TO GIVE YOU A BIG PAIN IN THE NECK!
I GOT YOUR ROBOT, SEE. IF YOU EVER WANT TO SEE HIM ALIVE AGAIN, MEET ME IN ROOM 9 AT HERMAN'S HOTEL AT MIDNIGHT. AN' COME ALONE.
WHEN THE MAN BROKE THE CONNECTION DREDD DIALED FOR AN IDENTI-KIT ON HIS COMPU-SCANNER...
GEEK GORGON - A VICIOUS CRIMINAL WHOSE FACE WAS BADLY BURNT IN A FIRE. THREE YEARS AGO I SENTENCED HIM TO IMPRISONMENT ON THE MOON. NOW HE'S ESCAPED AND WANTS REVENGE.
YOU CAN ALWAYS GIT ANOTHER ROBOT.
NO, TEX. I KNOW WALTER'S JUST A STUPID BIG HUNK OF METAL. AND SOMETIMES HE'S SO HUMBLE HE MAKES ME WANT TO THROW UP... BUT -
- DROKK IT ALL, MAN, I'VE GOT USED TO THE LITTLE GUY.

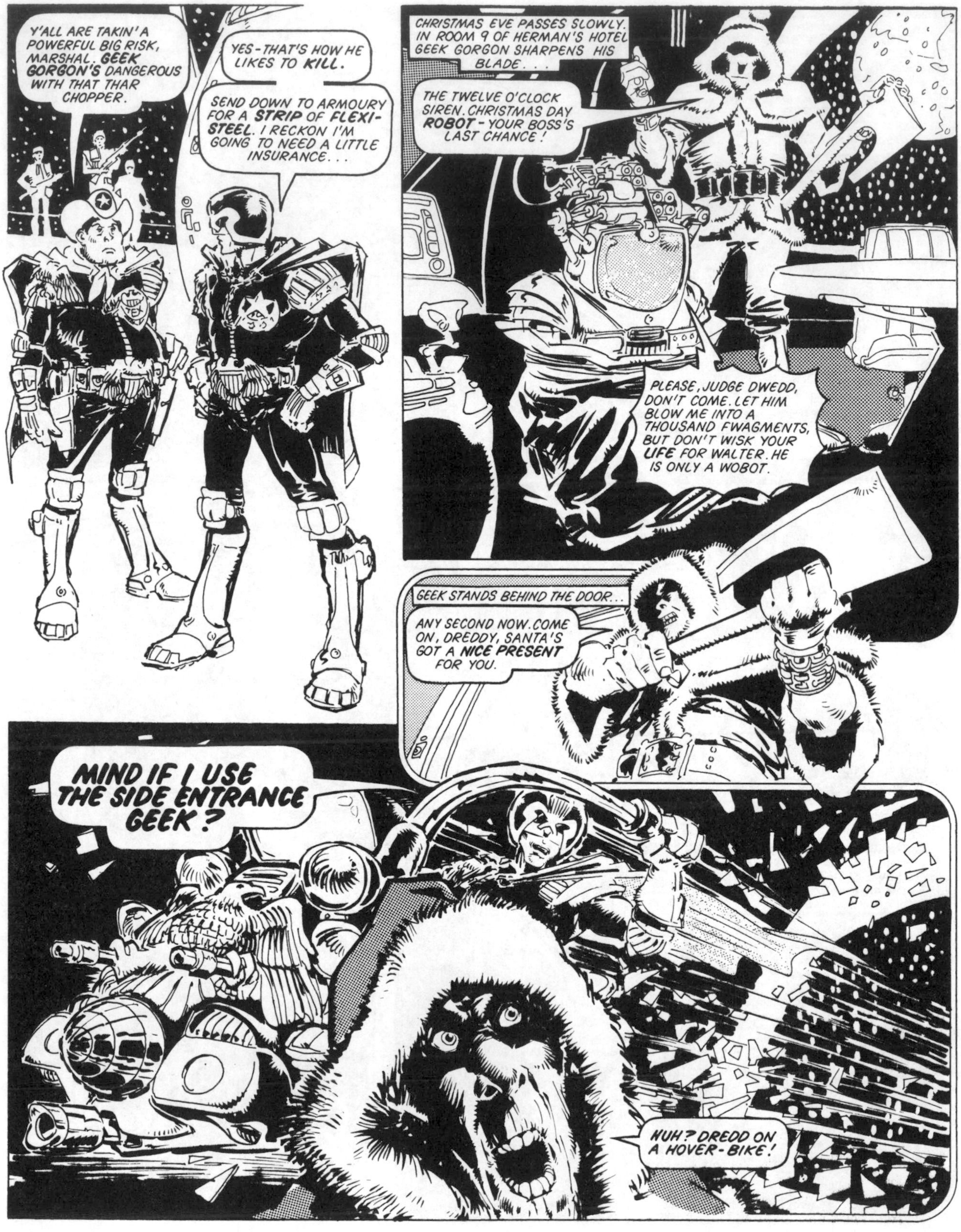
Y'ALL ARE TAKIN' A POWERFUL BIG RISK, MARSHAL. GEEK GORGON'S DANGEROUS WITH THAT THAR CHOPPER.
YES - THAT'S HOW HE LIKES TO KILL.
SEND DOWN TO ARMOURY FOR A STRIP OF FLEXI-STEEL. I RECKON I'M GOING TO NEED A LITTLE INSURANCE...
CHRISTMAS EVE PASSES SLOWLY. IN ROOM 9 OF HERMAN'S HOTEL GEEK GORGON SHARPENS HIS BLADE...
THE TWELVE O'CLOCK SIREN. CHRISTMAS DAY ROBOT - YOUR BOSS'S LAST CHANCE!
PLEASE, JUDGE DWEDD, DON'T COME. LET HIM BLOW ME INTO A THOUSAND FWAGMENTS, BUT DON'T WISK YOUR LIFE FOR WALTER. HE IS ONLY A WOBOT.
GEEK STANDS BEHIND THE DOOR...
ANY SECOND NOW. COME ON, DREDDY, SANTA'S GOT A NICE PRESENT FOR YOU.
MIND IF I USE THE SIDE ENTRANCE GEEK?
NUH? DREDD ON A HOVER-BIKE!

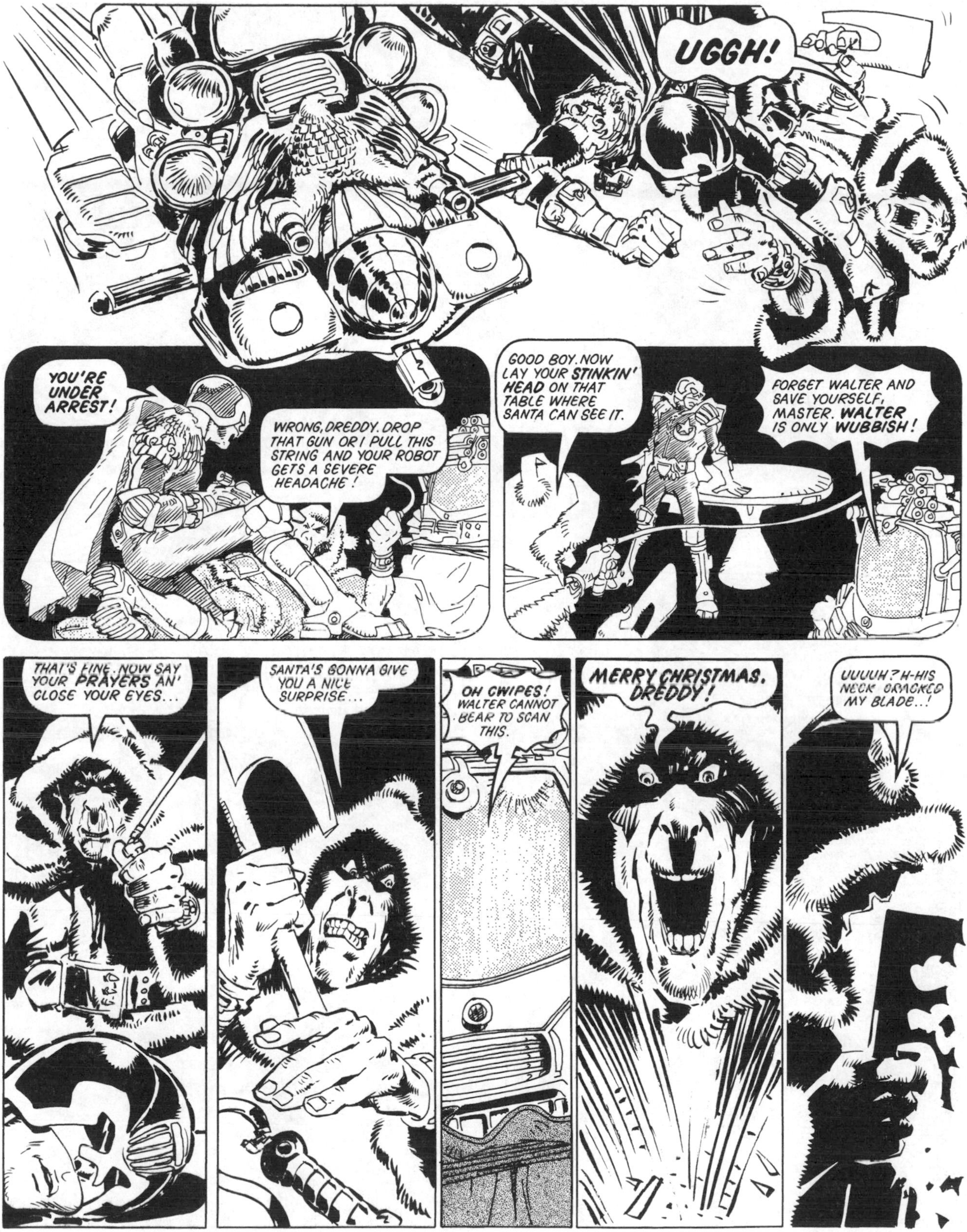
UGGH!
YOU'RE UNDER ARREST!
WRONG, DREDDY. DROP THAT GUN OR I PULL THIS STRING AND YOUR ROBOT GETS A SEVERE HEADACHE!
GOOD BOY. NOW LAY YOUR STINKIN' HEAD ON THAT TABLE WHERE SANTA CAN SEE IT.
FORGET WALTER AND SAVE YOURSELF, MASTER. WALTER IS ONLY WUBBISH!
THAT'S FINE. NOW SAY YOUR PRAYERS AN' CLOSE YOUR EYES...
SANTA'S GONNA GIVE YOU A NICE SURPRISE...
OH CWIPES! WALTER CANNOT BEAR TO SCAN THIS.
MERRY CHRISTMAS, DREDDY!
UUUUH? H-HIS NECK CRACKED MY BLADE..!

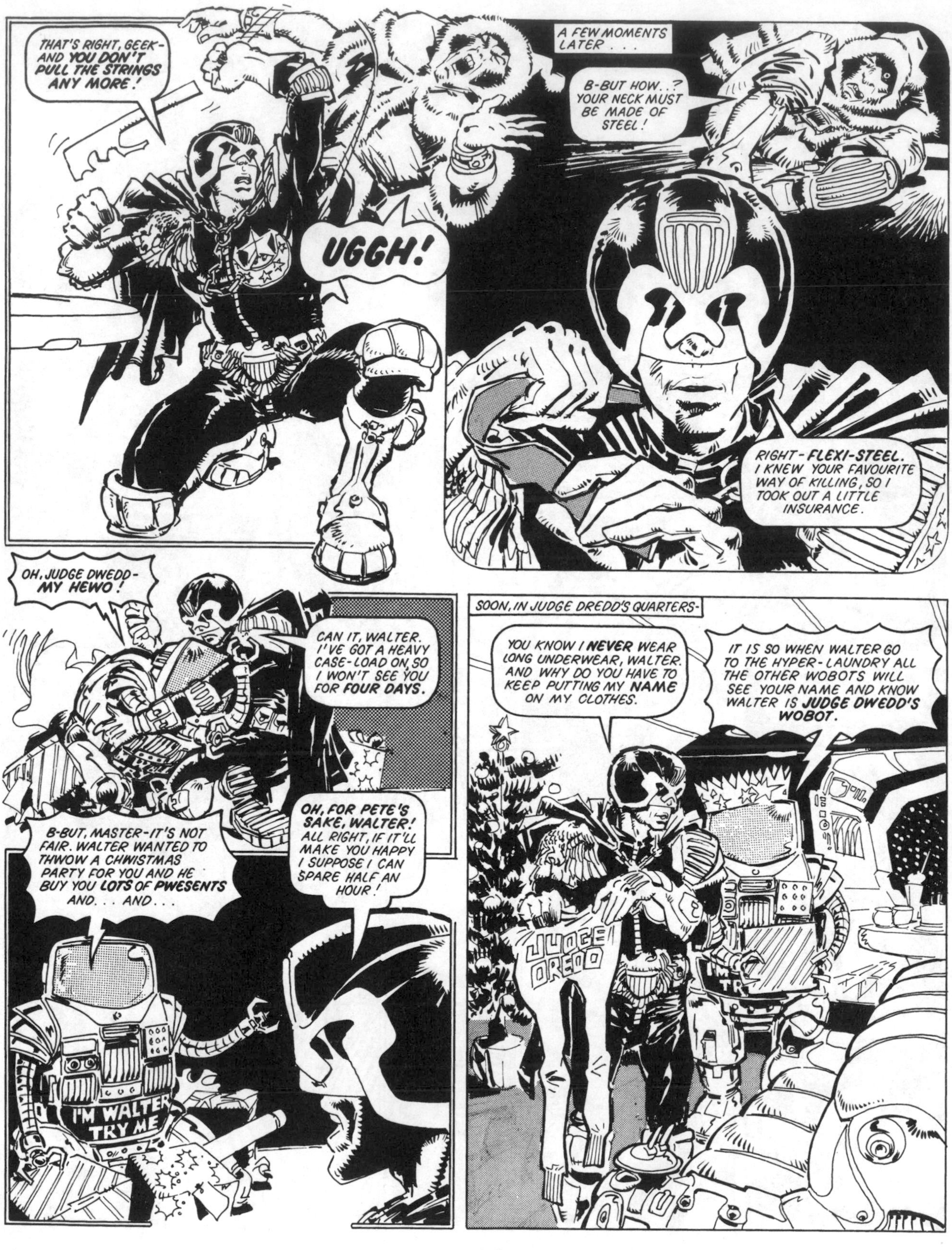

THAT'S RIGHT, GEEK-AND YOU DON'T PULL THE STRINGS ANY MORE!
UGGH!
A FEW MOMENTS LATER . . .
B-BUT HOW..? YOUR NECK MUST BE MADE OF STEEL!
RIGHT-FLEXI-STEEL. I KNEW YOUR FAVOURITE WAY OF KILLING, SO I TOOK OUT A LITTLE INSURANCE.
OH, JUDGE DWEDD-MY HEWO!
CAN IT, WALTER. I'VE GOT A HEAVY CASE-LOAD ON, SO I WON'T SEE YOU FOR FOUR DAYS.
B-BUT, MASTER-IT'S NOT FAIR. WALTER WANTED TO THWOW A CHWISTMAS PARTY FOR YOU AND HE BUY YOU LOTS OF PWESENTS AND. . . AND. . .
OH, FOR PETE'S SAKE, WALTER! ALL RIGHT, IF IT'LL MAKE YOU HAPPY I SUPPOSE I CAN SPARE HALF AN HOUR!
I'M WALTER TRY ME
SOON, IN JUDGE DREDD'S QUARTERS-
YOU KNOW I NEVER WEAR LONG UNDERWEAR, WALTER. AND WHY DO YOU HAVE TO KEEP PUTTING MY NAME ON MY CLOTHES.
IT IS SO WHEN WALTER GO TO THE HYPER-LAUNDRY ALL THE OTHER WOBOTS WILL SEE YOUR NAME AND KNOW WALTER IS JUDGE DWEDD'S WOBOT.
JUDGE DREDD

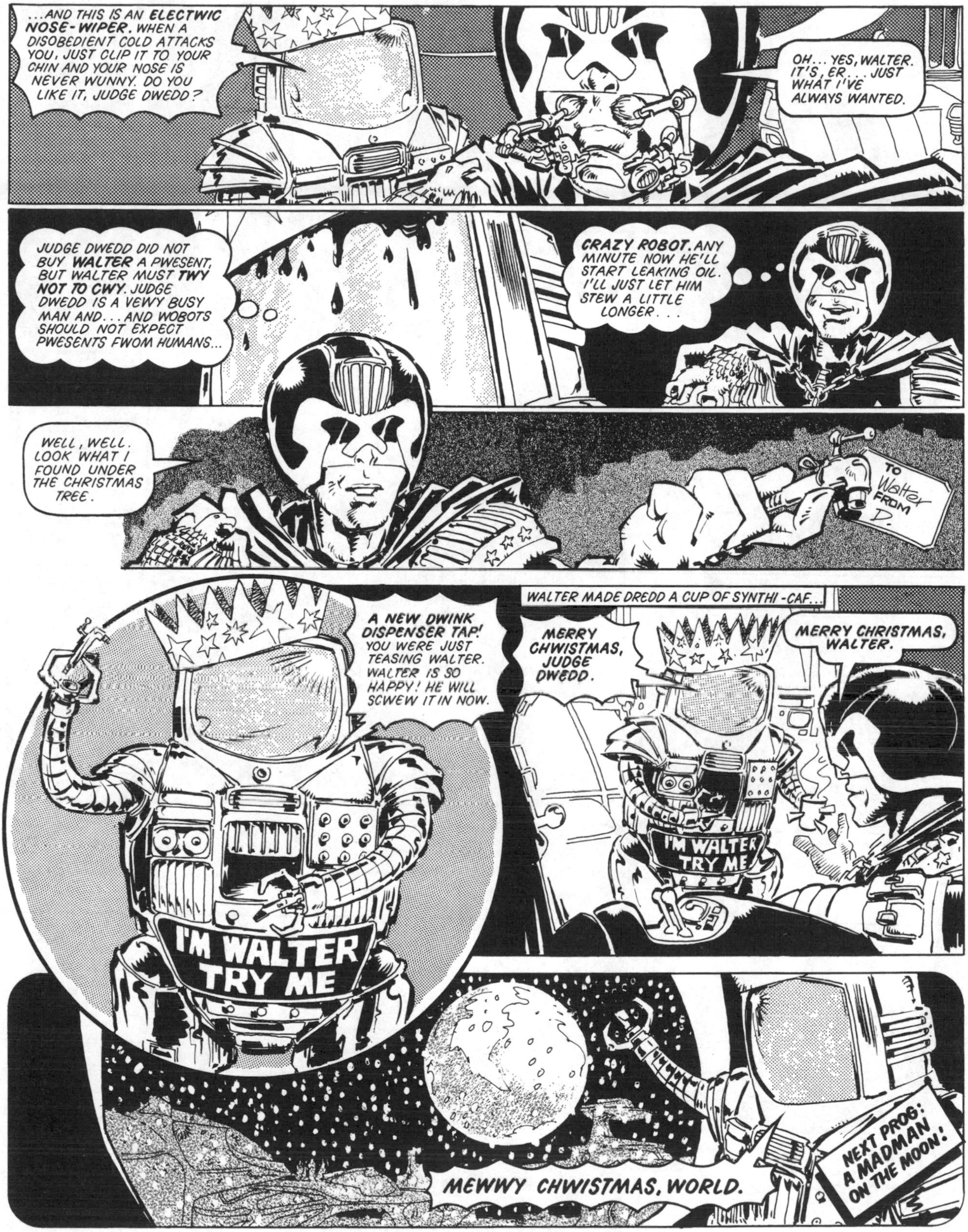
...AND THIS IS AN ELECTWIC NOSE-WIPER. WHEN A DISOBEDIENT COLD ATTACKS YOU, JUST CLIP IT TO YOUR CHIN AND YOUR NOSE IS NEVER WUNNY. DO YOU LIKE IT, JUDGE DWEDD?
OH... YES, WALTER. IT'S, ER... JUST WHAT I'VE ALWAYS WANTED.
JUDGE DWEDD DID NOT BUY WALTER A PWESENT, BUT WALTER MUST TWY NOT TO CWY. JUDGE DWEDD IS A VEWY BUSY MAN AND... AND WOBOTS SHOULD NOT EXPECT PWESENTS FWOM HUMANS...
CRAZY ROBOT. ANY MINUTE NOW HE'LL START LEAKING OIL. I'LL JUST LET HIM STEW A LITTLE LONGER...
WELL, WELL. LOOK WHAT I FOUND UNDER THE CHRISTMAS TREE.
TO Walter FROM D.
A NEW DWINK DISPENSER TAP! YOU WERE JUST TEASING WALTER. WALTER IS SO HAPPY! HE WILL SCWEW IT IN NOW.
I'M WALTER TRY ME
WALTER MADE DREDD A CUP OF SYNTHI-CAF...
MERRY CHWISTMAS, JUDGE DWEDD.
MERRY CHRISTMAS, WALTER.
I'M WALTER TRY ME
MEWWY CHWISTMAS, WORLD.
NEXT PROG: A MADMAN ON THE MOON!

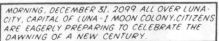

MORNING, DECEMBER 31, 2099 ALL OVER LUNA-CITY, CAPITAL OF LUNA-1 MOON COLONY. CITIZENS ARE EAGERLY PREPARING TO CELEBRATE THE DAWNING OF A NEW CENTURY.

"BUT FOR LITTLE ARTHUR GOODWORTHY, NUMBER 31 ACCOUNTS CLERK AT THE GIANT MOONIE ENTERPRISES COMPLEX, THE NEW YEAR IS TO BE A FAR FROM HAPPY ONE. FOR AT EXACTLY SEVEN SECONDS PAST MIDNIGHT, LITTLE ARTHUR WILL BECOME THE FIRST...

22nd Century **FUTSIE!**

JUDGE DREDD

EMPLOYEE ARTHUR GOODWORTHY WILL REPORT IMMEDIATELY TO THE SCAN-CUBE. REPORT. IMMEDIATELY.

THE SCAN-CUBE! THAT MUST MEAN A TELLING-OFF FROM MR MOONIE HIMSELF!

POOR LITTLE BEGGAR. HE'S A MONTH BEHIND WITH HIS PAPERWORK. HE'S HAD IT.

2000 A.D.
Credit Card:
SCRIPT ROBOT
JOHN HOWARD
ART ROBOT
IAN GIBSON
LETTERING ROBOT
TONY JACOB
COMPU·73E

INSIDE THE SCAN-CUBE AN IMAGE FLICKERS ONTO THE RECEPTI-WALL...

THAT IS NOT GOOD ENOUGH, GOODWORTHY.

I-I KNOW, SIR... BUT PLEASE, SIR... I HAVE A-A WIFE AND A LITTLE B-B-BOY...

YOU SHOULD HAVE THOUGHT OF THEM BEFORE, GOODWORTHY. YOU HAVE UNTIL 12 O'CLOCK TONIGHT TO MAKE UP THE BACKLOG—OR YOUR OWN **CONTRACT** WILL BE TERMINATED. *THAT IS ALL.*

I'M SORRY, MR MOONIE, SIR... IT-IT'S MY WIFE, SHE HAD TO GO INTO **HOSPITAL** FOR AN **OPERATION** AND... AND...

POOR LITTLE DEVIL! I GUESS HE'LL WIND UP IN A BACK ALLEY FULL OF **BLASTER** HOLES.

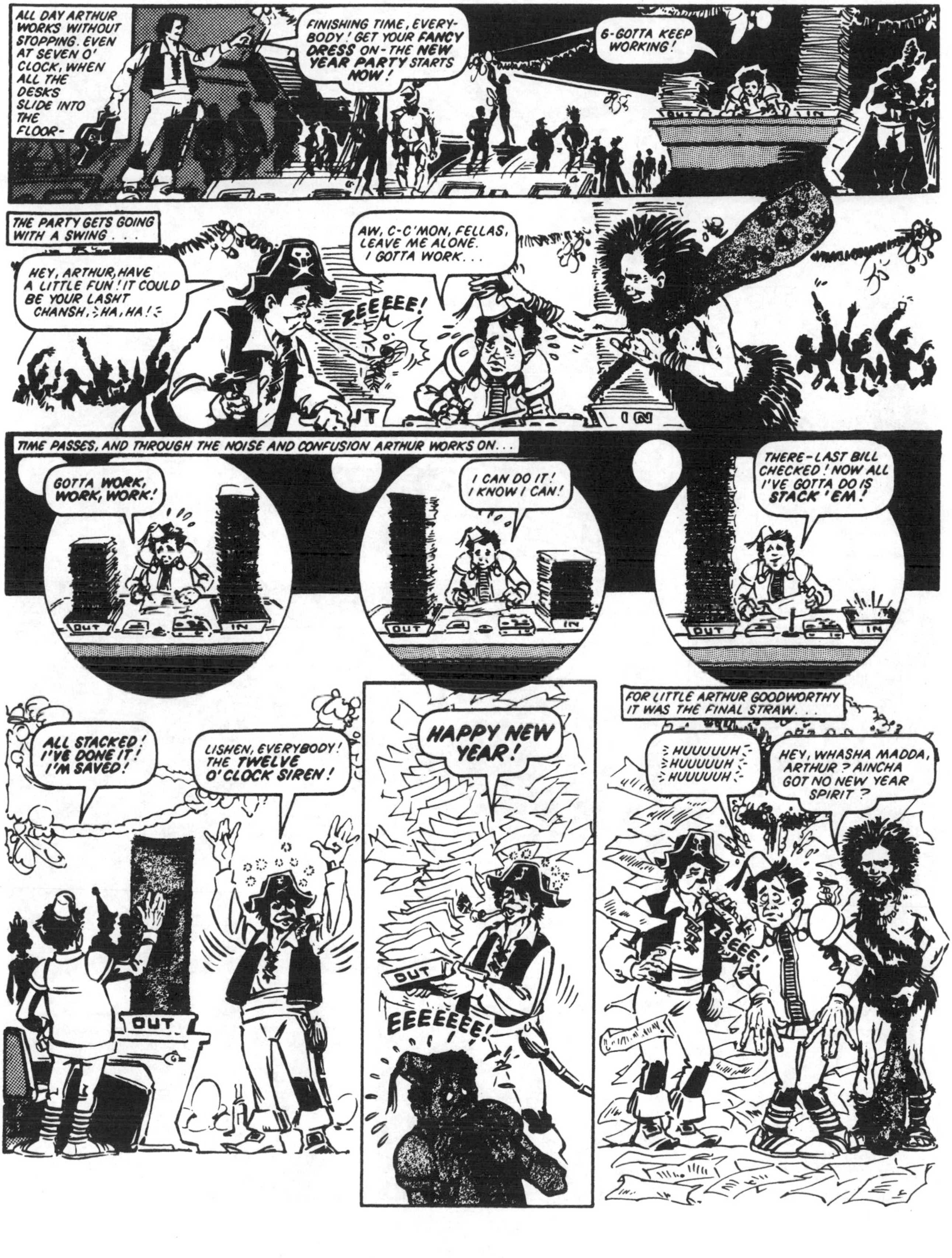
ALL DAY ARTHUR WORKS WITHOUT STOPPING. EVEN AT SEVEN O' CLOCK, WHEN ALL THE DESKS SLIDE INTO THE FLOOR-
FINISHING TIME, EVERYBODY! GET YOUR FANCY DRESS ON-THE NEW YEAR PARTY STARTS NOW!
G-GOTTA KEEP WORKING!
THE PARTY GETS GOING WITH A SWING . . .
HEY, ARTHUR, HAVE A LITTLE FUN! IT COULD BE YOUR LASHT CHANSH, HA, HA!
ZEEEEE!
AW, C-C'MON, FELLAS, LEAVE ME ALONE. I GOTTA WORK . . .
TIME PASSES, AND THROUGH THE NOISE AND CONFUSION ARTHUR WORKS ON...
GOTTA WORK, WORK, WORK!
I CAN DO IT! I KNOW I CAN!
THERE-LAST BILL CHECKED! NOW ALL I'VE GOTTA DO IS STACK 'EM!
ALL STACKED! I'VE DONE IT! I'M SAVED!
LISHEN, EVERYBODY! THE TWELVE O'CLOCK SIREN!
HAPPY NEW YEAR!
EEEEEEE!
FOR LITTLE ARTHUR GOODWORTHY IT WAS THE FINAL STRAW . . .
HUUUUUH HUUUUUH HUUUUUH
HEY, WHASHA MADDA, ARTHUR? AINCHA GOT NO NEW YEAR SPIRIT?
ZEEEE

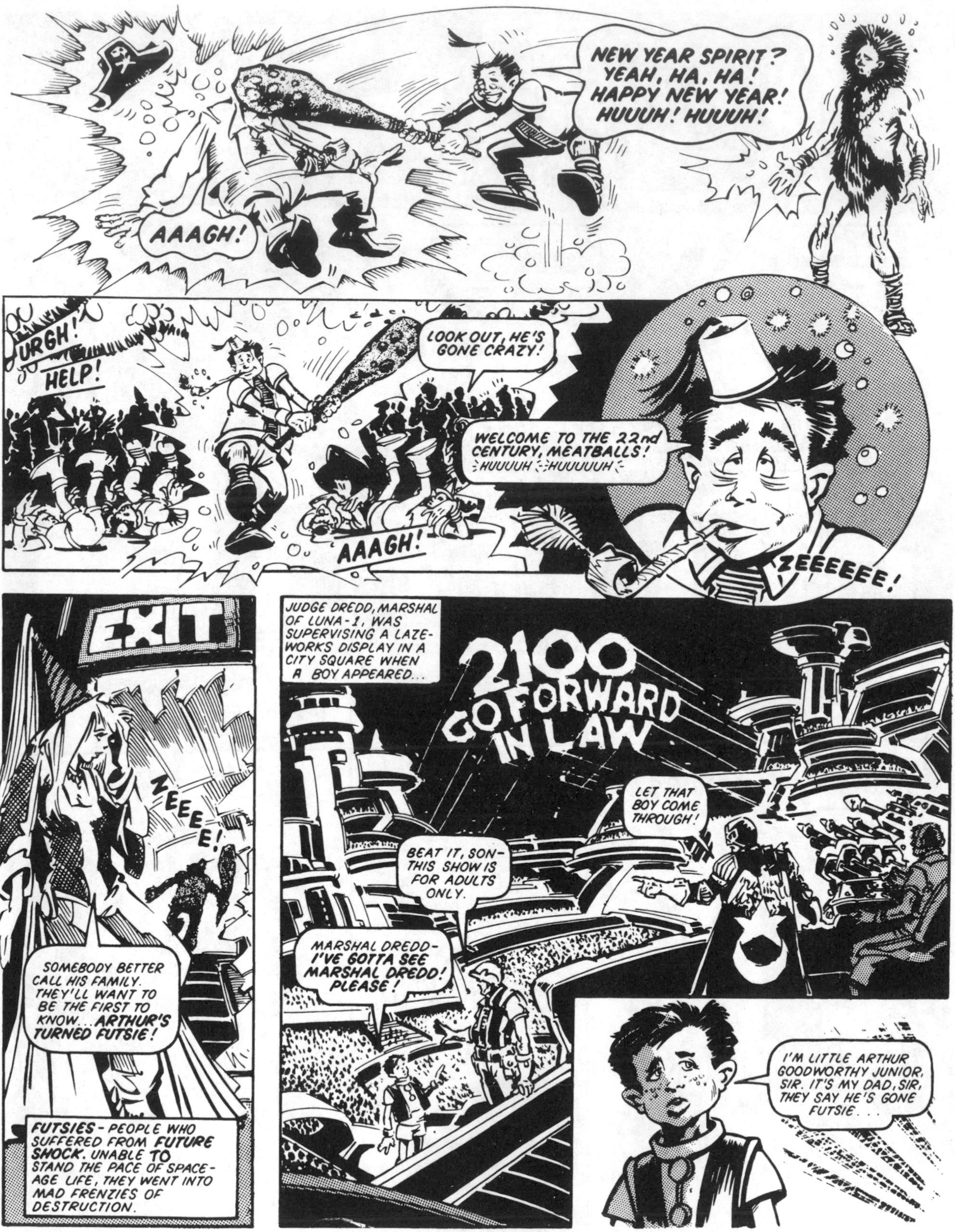
NEW YEAR SPIRIT? YEAH, HA, HA! HAPPY NEW YEAR! HUUUH! HUUUH!
AAAGH!
URGH!
HELP!
LOOK OUT, HE'S GONE CRAZY!
AAAGH!
WELCOME TO THE 22nd CENTURY, MEATBALLS! HUUUUH HUUUUUH
ZEEEEEE!
EXIT
ZEEEE!
SOMEBODY BETTER CALL HIS FAMILY. THEY'LL WANT TO BE THE FIRST TO KNOW... ARTHUR'S TURNED FUTSIE!
FUTSIES - PEOPLE WHO SUFFERED FROM FUTURE SHOCK. UNABLE TO STAND THE PACE OF SPACE-AGE LIFE, THEY WENT INTO MAD FRENZIES OF DESTRUCTION.
JUDGE DREDD, MARSHAL OF LUNA-1, WAS SUPERVISING A LAZE-WORKS DISPLAY IN A CITY SQUARE WHEN A BOY APPEARED...
2100 GO FORWARD IN LAW
LET THAT BOY COME THROUGH!
BEAT IT, SON-THIS SHOW IS FOR ADULTS ONLY.
MARSHAL DREDD-I'VE GOTTA SEE MARSHAL DREDD! PLEASE!
I'M LITTLE ARTHUR GOODWORTHY JUNIOR, SIR. IT'S MY DAD, SIR, THEY SAY HE'S GONE FUTSIE...

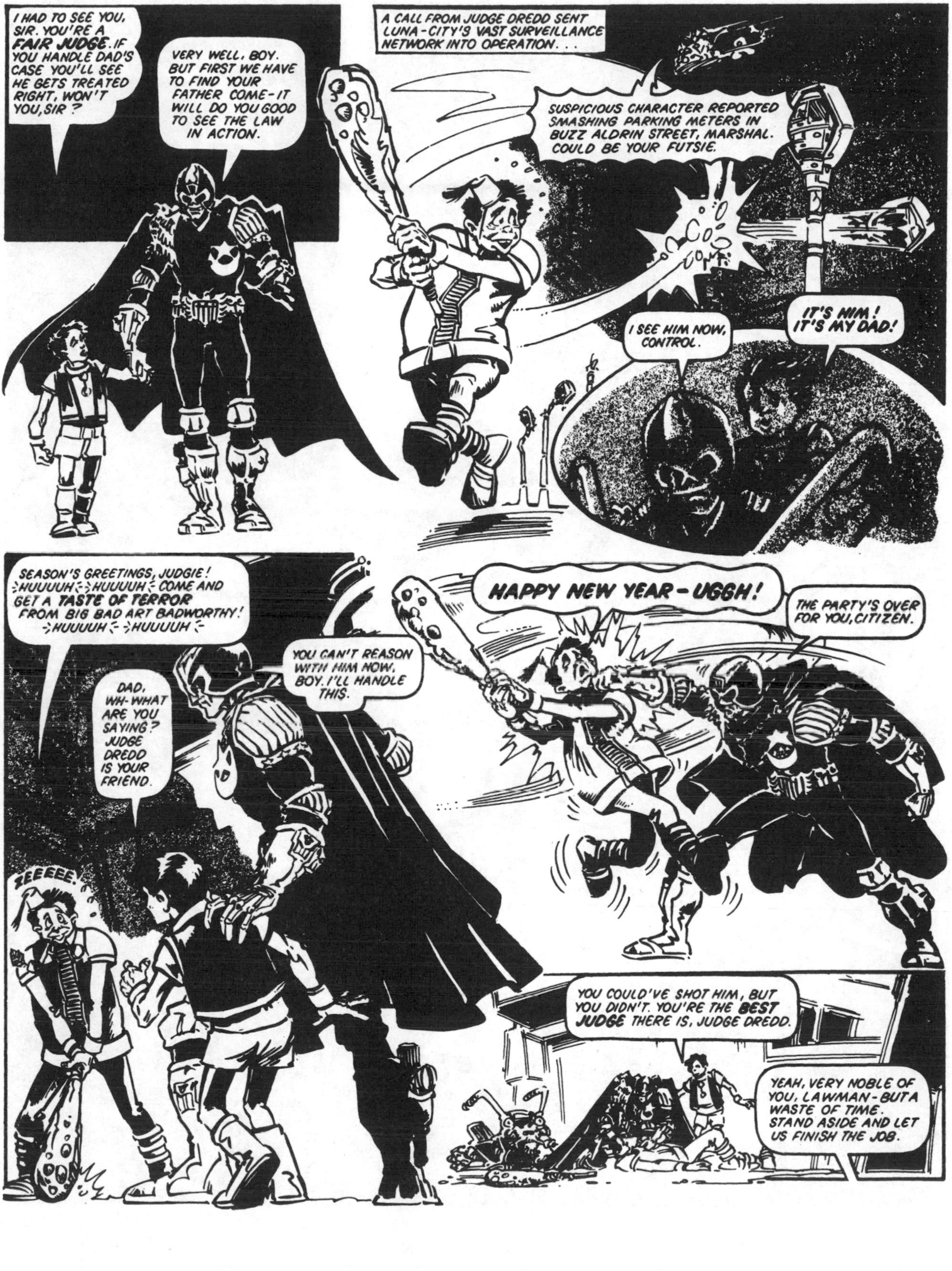
I HAD TO SEE YOU, SIR. YOU'RE A FAIR JUDGE. IF YOU HANDLE DAD'S CASE YOU'LL SEE HE GETS TREATED RIGHT, WON'T YOU, SIR?
VERY WELL, BOY. BUT FIRST WE HAVE TO FIND YOUR FATHER COME- IT WILL DO YOU GOOD TO SEE THE LAW IN ACTION.
A CALL FROM JUDGE DREDD SENT LUNA-CITY'S VAST SURVEILLANCE NETWORK INTO OPERATION...
SUSPICIOUS CHARACTER REPORTED SMASHING PARKING METERS IN BUZZ ALDRIN STREET, MARSHAL. COULD BE YOUR FUTSIE.
I SEE HIM NOW, CONTROL.
IT'S HIM! IT'S MY DAD!
SEASON'S GREETINGS, JUDGIE! HUUUUH HUUUUH COME AND GET A TASTE OF TERROR FROM BIG BAD ART BADWORTHY! HUUUUH HUUUUH
DAD, WH-WHAT ARE YOU SAYING? JUDGE DREDD IS YOUR FRIEND.
YOU CAN'T REASON WITH HIM NOW, BOY. I'LL HANDLE THIS.
ZEEEEE.
HAPPY NEW YEAR-UGGH!
THE PARTY'S OVER FOR YOU, CITIZEN.
YOU COULD'VE SHOT HIM, BUT YOU DIDN'T. YOU'RE THE BEST JUDGE THERE IS, JUDGE DREDD.
YEAH, VERY NOBLE OF YOU, LAWMAN- BUT A WASTE OF TIME. STAND ASIDE AND LET US FINISH THE JOB.

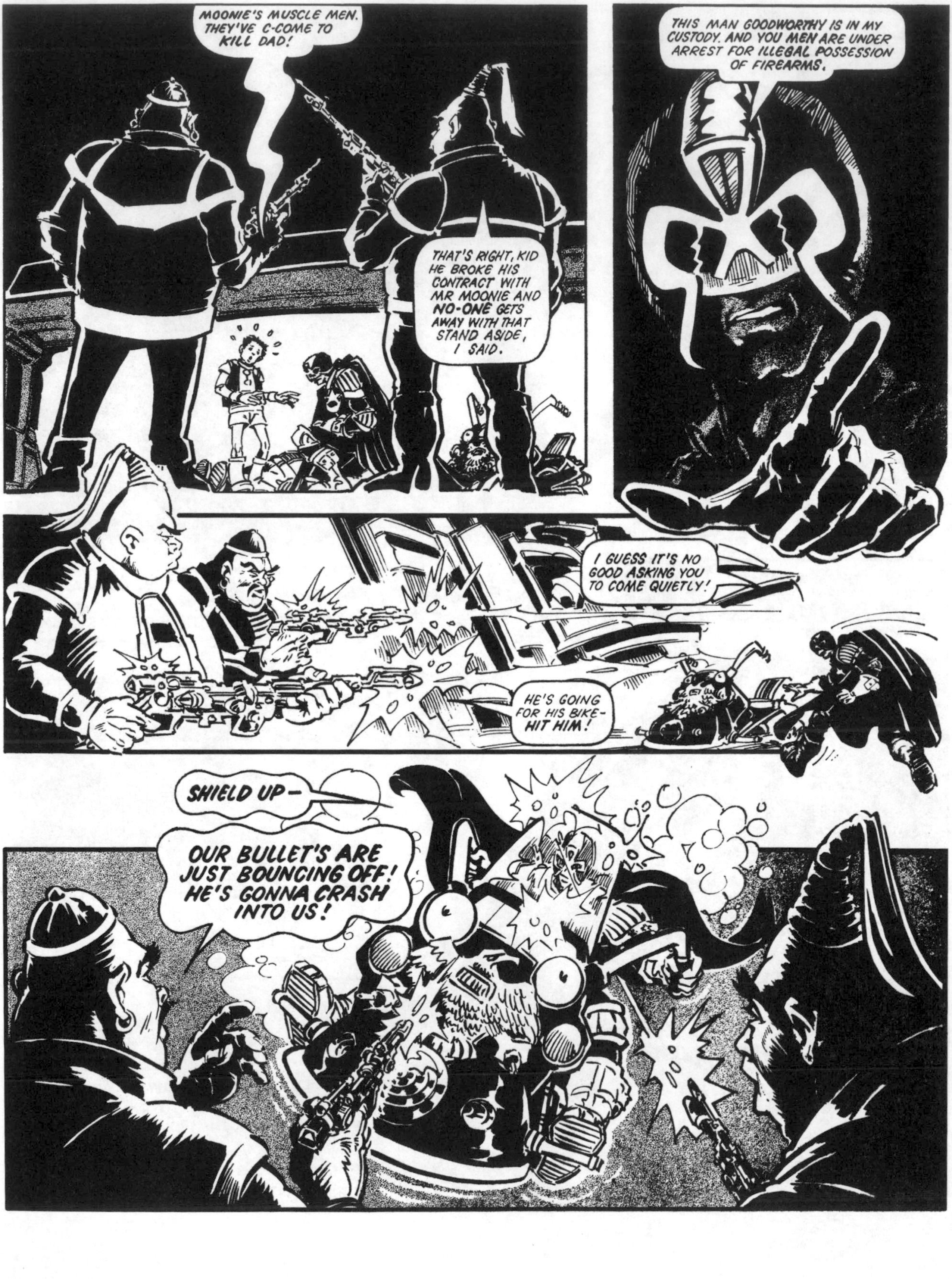
MOONIE'S MUSCLE MEN. THEY'VE C-COME TO KILL DAD!
THAT'S RIGHT, KID HE BROKE HIS CONTRACT WITH MR MOONIE AND NO-ONE GETS AWAY WITH THAT STAND ASIDE, I SAID.
THIS MAN GOODWORTHY IS IN MY CUSTODY. AND YOU MEN ARE UNDER ARREST FOR ILLEGAL POSSESSION OF FIREARMS.
I GUESS IT'S NO GOOD ASKING YOU TO COME QUIETLY!
HE'S GOING FOR HIS BIKE- HIT HIM!
SHIELD UP-
OUR BULLET'S ARE JUST BOUNCING OFF! HE'S GONNA CRASH INTO US!

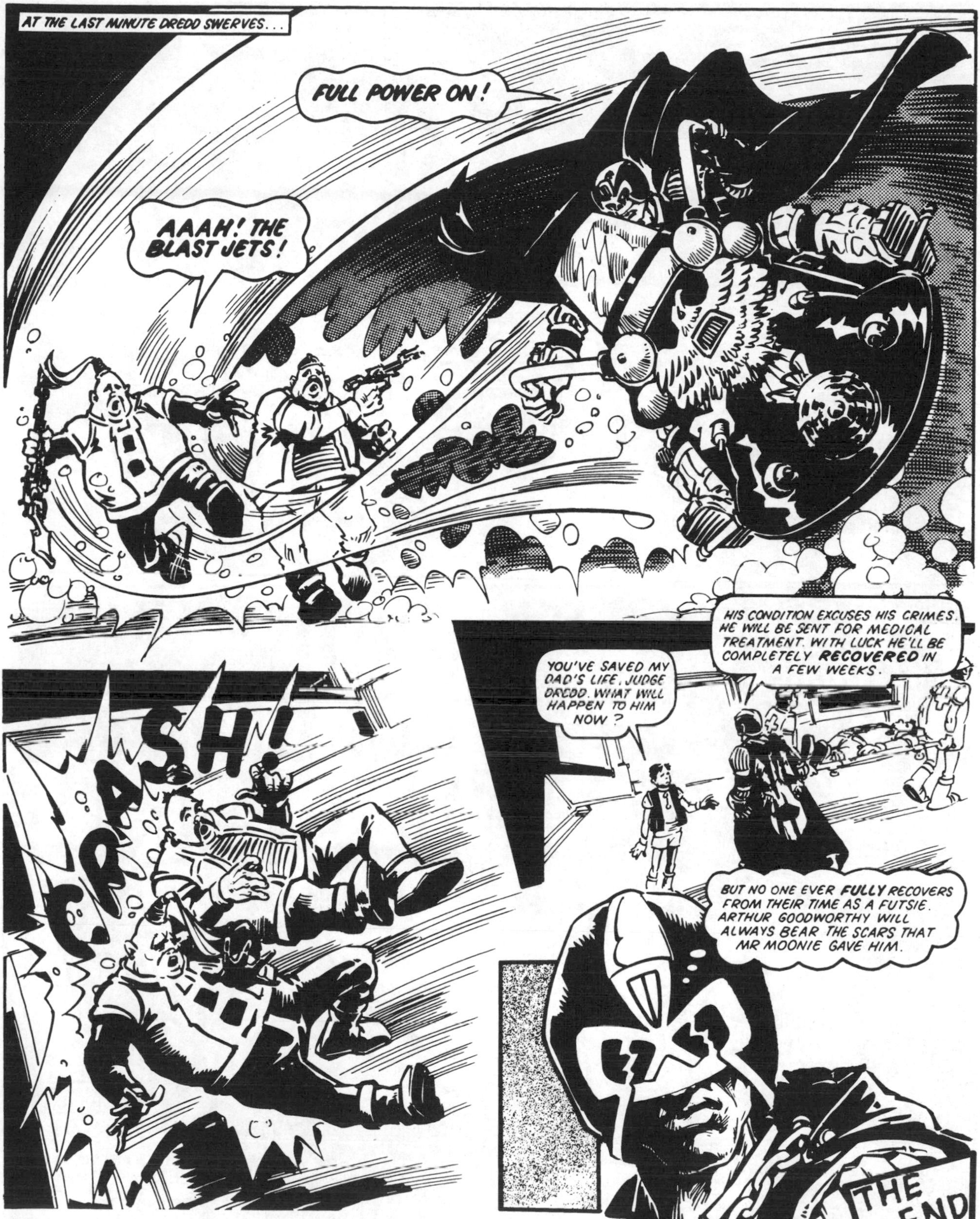

AT THE LAST MINUTE DREDD SWERVES...
FULL POWER ON!
AAAH! THE BLAST JETS!
CRASH!
YOU'VE SAVED MY DAD'S LIFE, JUDGE DREDD. WHAT WILL HAPPEN TO HIM NOW?
HIS CONDITION EXCUSES HIS CRIMES. HE WILL BE SENT FOR MEDICAL TREATMENT. WITH LUCK HE'LL BE COMPLETELY RECOVERED IN A FEW WEEKS.
BUT NO ONE EVER FULLY RECOVERS FROM THEIR TIME AS A FUTSIE. ARTHUR GOODWORTHY WILL ALWAYS BEAR THE SCARS THAT MR MOONIE GAVE HIM.
THE END

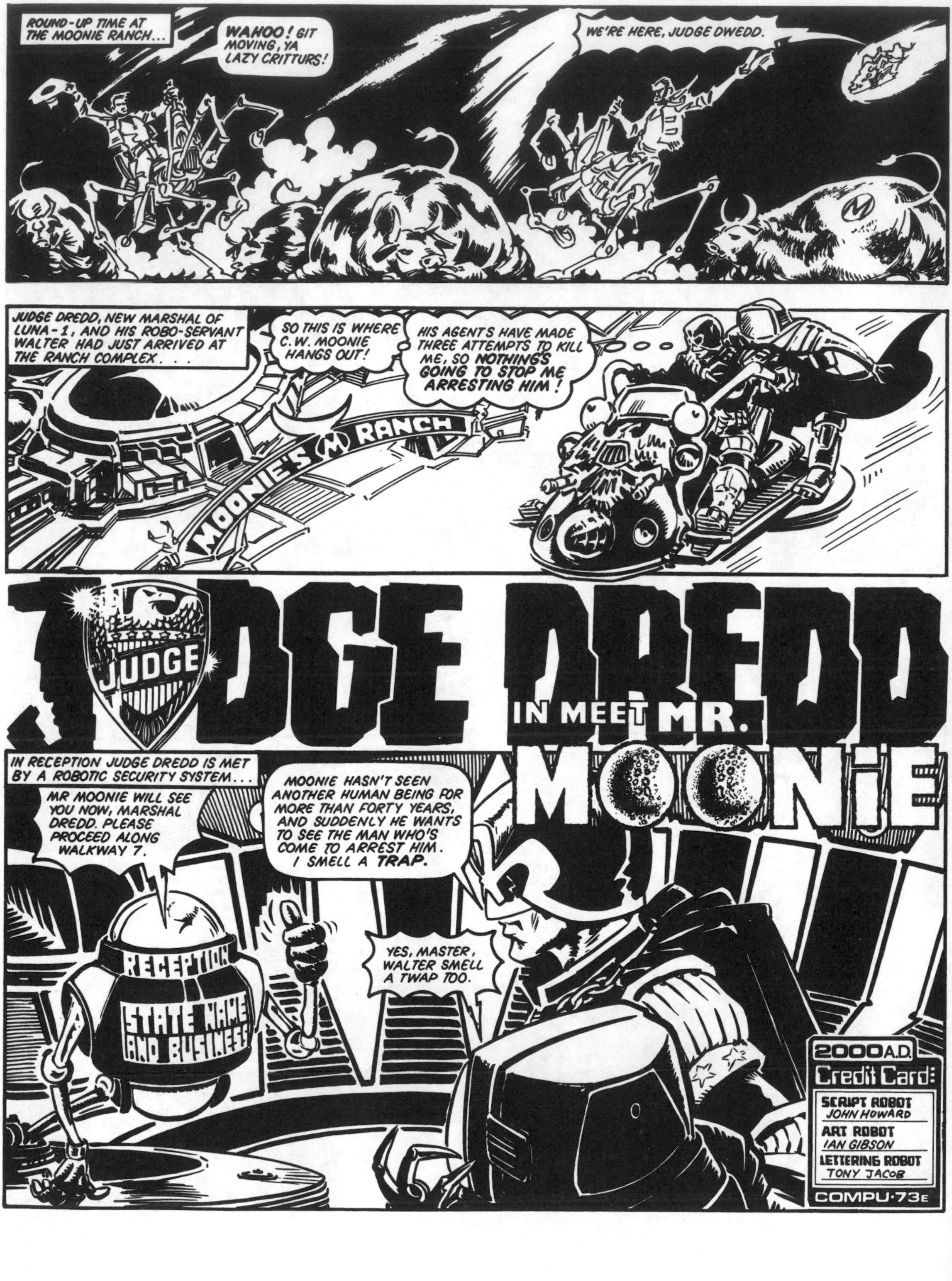

ROUND-UP TIME AT THE MOONIE RANCH...
WAHOO! GIT MOVING, YA LAZY CRITTURS!
WE'RE HERE, JUDGE DWEDD.
JUDGE DREDD, NEW MARSHAL OF LUNA-1, AND HIS ROBO-SERVANT WALTER HAD JUST ARRIVED AT THE RANCH COMPLEX . . .
SO THIS IS WHERE C.W. MOONIE HANGS OUT!
HIS AGENTS HAVE MADE THREE ATTEMPTS TO KILL ME, SO NOTHING'S GOING TO STOP ME ARRESTING HIM!
MOONIE'S M RANCH
JUDGE DREDD IN MEET MR. MOONIE
JUDGE
IN RECEPTION JUDGE DREDD IS MET BY A ROBOTIC SECURITY SYSTEM...
MR MOONIE WILL SEE YOU NOW, MARSHAL DREDD. PLEASE PROCEED ALONG WALKWAY 7.
MOONIE HASN'T SEEN ANOTHER HUMAN BEING FOR MORE THAN FORTY YEARS, AND SUDDENLY HE WANTS TO SEE THE MAN WHO'S COME TO ARREST HIM. I SMELL A TRAP.
YES, MASTER. WALTER SMELL A TWAP TOO.
RECEPTION
STATE NAME AND BUSINESS
2000 A.D. Credit Card
SCRIPT ROBOT JOHN HOWARD
ART ROBOT IAN GIBSON
LETTERING ROBOT TONY JACOB
COMPU·73E

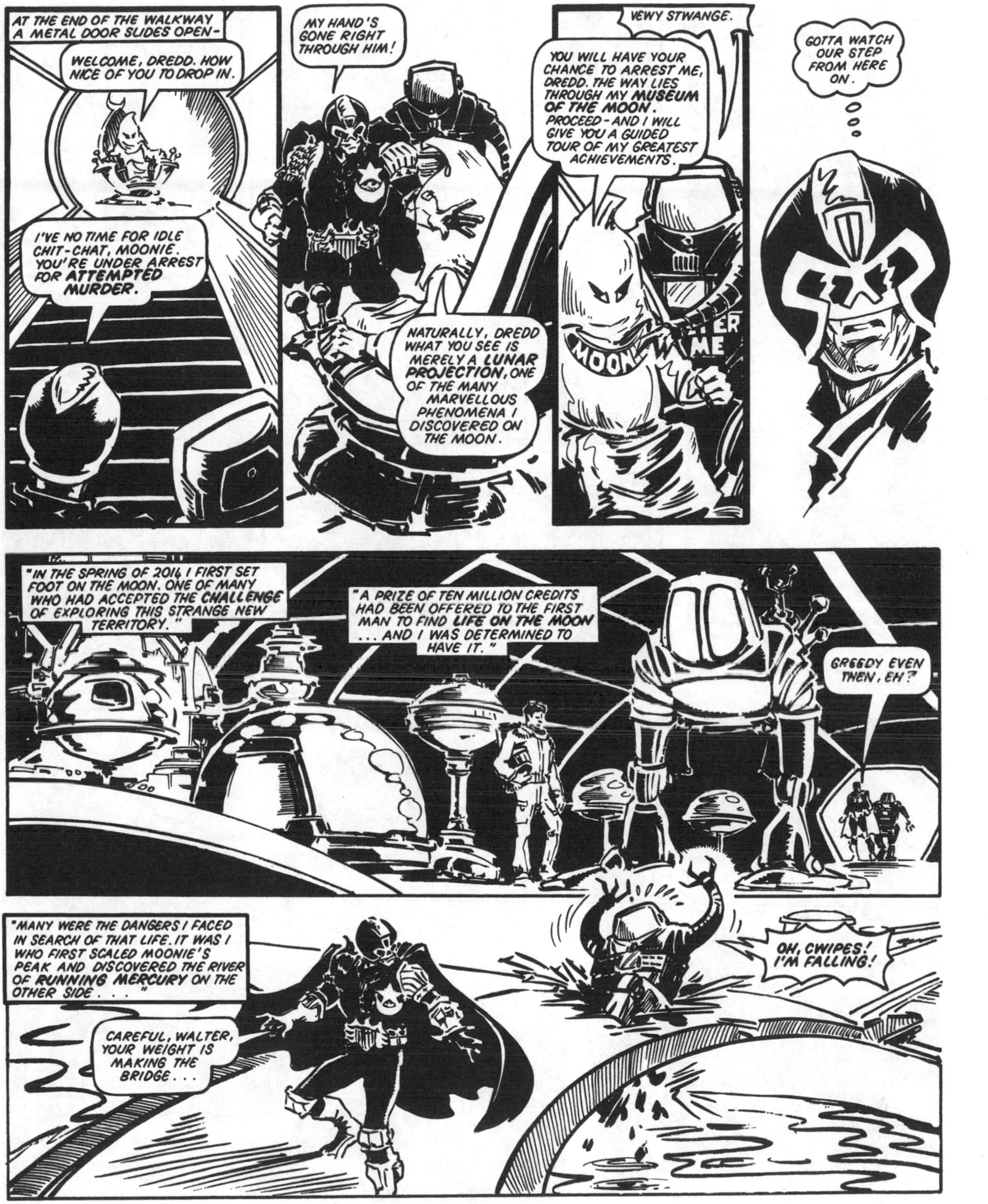
AT THE END OF THE WALKWAY A METAL DOOR SLIDES OPEN-
WELCOME, DREDD. HOW NICE OF YOU TO DROP IN.
I'VE NO TIME FOR IDLE CHIT-CHAT, MOONIE. YOU'RE UNDER ARREST FOR ATTEMPTED MURDER.
MY HAND'S GONE RIGHT THROUGH HIM!
NATURALLY, DREDD WHAT YOU SEE IS MERELY A LUNAR PROJECTION, ONE OF THE MANY MARVELLOUS PHENOMENA I DISCOVERED ON THE MOON.
VEWY STWANGE.
YOU WILL HAVE YOUR CHANCE TO ARREST ME, DREDD. THE WAY LIES THROUGH MY MUSEUM OF THE MOON. PROCEED - AND I WILL GIVE YOU A GUIDED TOUR OF MY GREATEST ACHIEVEMENTS.
MOON
GOTTA WATCH OUR STEP FROM HERE ON.
"IN THE SPRING OF 2014 I FIRST SET FOOT ON THE MOON. ONE OF MANY WHO HAD ACCEPTED THE CHALLENGE OF EXPLORING THIS STRANGE NEW TERRITORY."
"A PRIZE OF TEN MILLION CREDITS HAD BEEN OFFERED TO THE FIRST MAN TO FIND LIFE ON THE MOON ... AND I WAS DETERMINED TO HAVE IT."
GREEDY EVEN THEN, EH?
"MANY WERE THE DANGERS I FACED IN SEARCH OF THAT LIFE. IT WAS I WHO FIRST SCALED MOONIE'S PEAK AND DISCOVERED THE RIVER OF RUNNING MERCURY ON THE OTHER SIDE . . ."
CAREFUL, WALTER, YOUR WEIGHT IS MAKING THE BRIDGE . . .
OH, CWIPES! I'M FALLING!

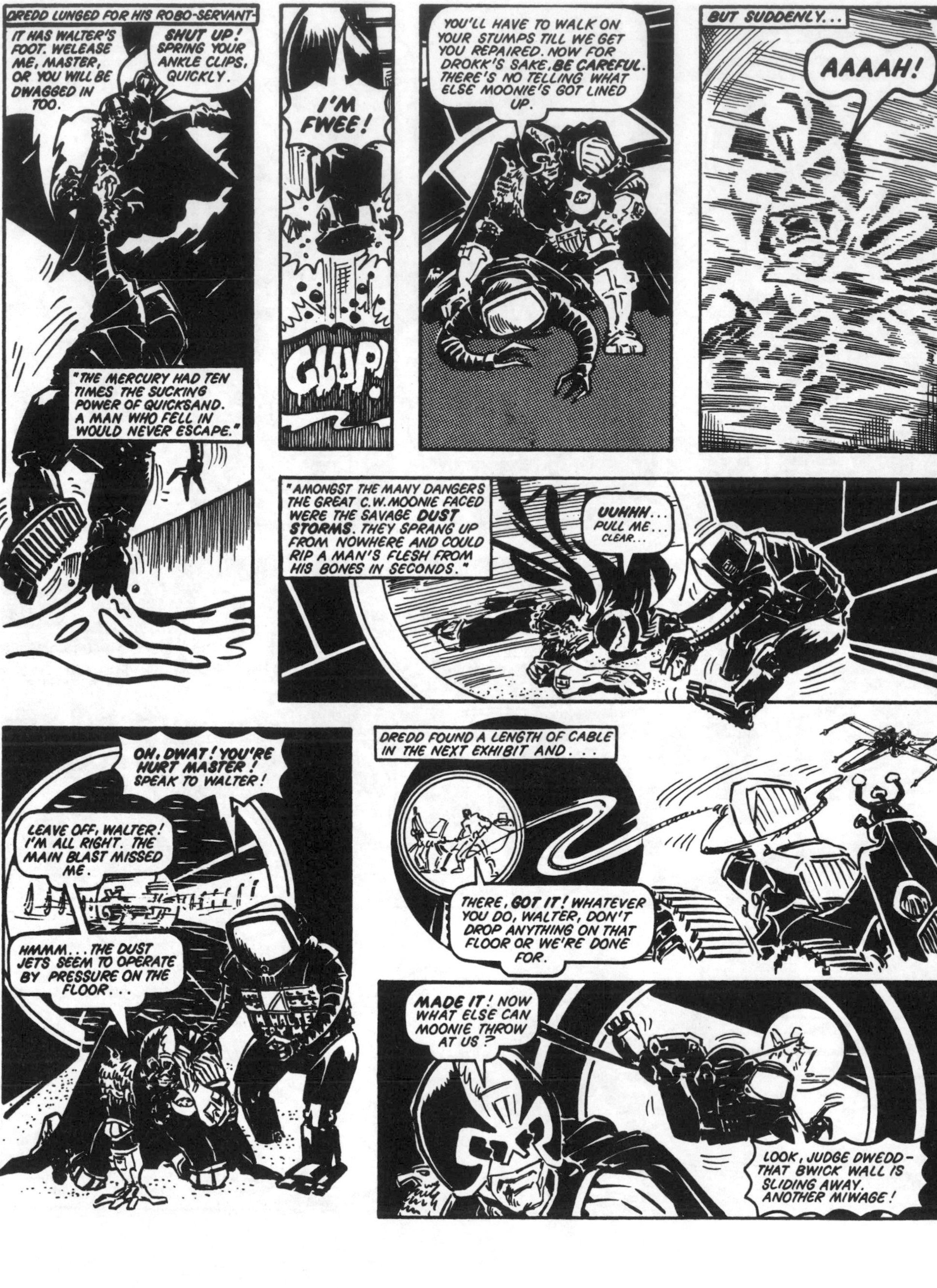
DREDD LUNGED FOR HIS ROBO-SERVANT-
IT HAS WALTER'S FOOT. WELEASE ME, MASTER, OR YOU WILL BE DWAGGED IN TOO.
SHUT UP! SPRING YOUR ANKLE CLIPS, QUICKLY.
"THE MERCURY HAD TEN TIMES THE SUCKING POWER OF QUICKSAND. A MAN WHO FELL IN WOULD NEVER ESCAPE."
I'M FWEE!
GLUP!
YOU'LL HAVE TO WALK ON YOUR STUMPS TILL WE GET YOU REPAIRED. NOW FOR DROKK'S SAKE, BE CAREFUL. THERE'S NO TELLING WHAT ELSE MOONIE'S GOT LINED UP.
BUT SUDDENLY...
AAAAH!
"AMONGST THE MANY DANGERS THE GREAT C.W. MOONIE FACED WERE THE SAVAGE DUST STORMS. THEY SPRANG UP FROM NOWHERE AND COULD RIP A MAN'S FLESH FROM HIS BONES IN SECONDS."
UUHHH... PULL ME... CLEAR...
OH, DWAT! YOU'RE HURT MASTER! SPEAK TO WALTER!
LEAVE OFF, WALTER! I'M ALL RIGHT. THE MAIN BLAST MISSED ME.
HMMM... THE DUST JETS SEEM TO OPERATE BY PRESSURE ON THE FLOOR...
DREDD FOUND A LENGTH OF CABLE IN THE NEXT EXHIBIT AND...
THERE, GOT IT! WHATEVER YOU DO, WALTER, DON'T DROP ANYTHING ON THAT FLOOR OR WE'RE DONE FOR.
MADE IT! NOW WHAT ELSE CAN MOONIE THROW AT US?
LOOK, JUDGE DWEDD - THAT BWICK WALL IS SLIDING AWAY. ANOTHER MIWAGE!

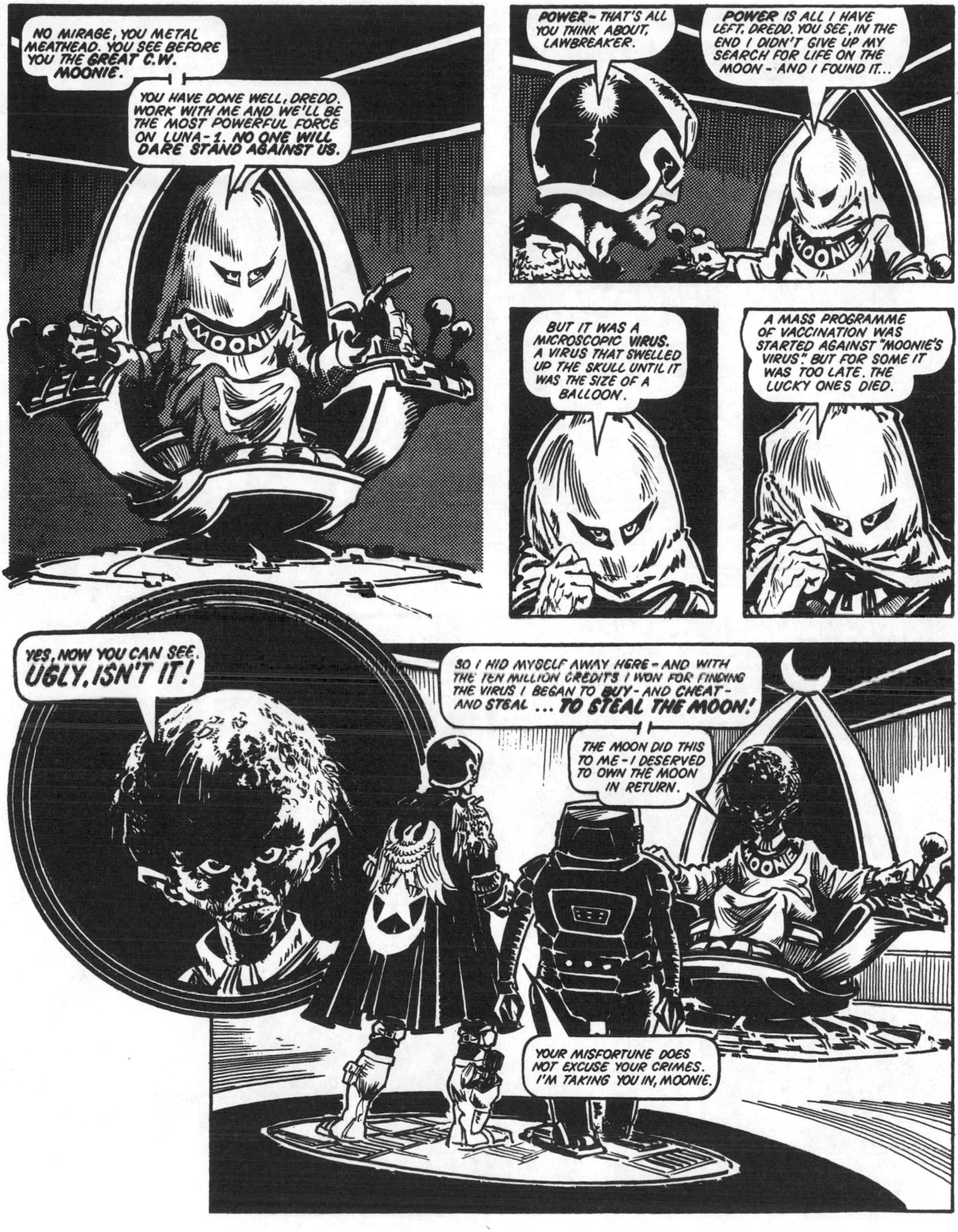
NO MIRAGE, YOU METAL MEATHEAD. YOU SEE BEFORE YOU THE GREAT C.W. MOONIE.
YOU HAVE DONE WELL, DREDD. WORK WITH ME AND WE'LL BE THE MOST POWERFUL FORCE ON LUNA-1. NO ONE WILL DARE STAND AGAINST US.
MOONIE
POWER- THAT'S ALL YOU THINK ABOUT, LAWBREAKER.
POWER IS ALL I HAVE LEFT, DREDD. YOU SEE, IN THE END I DIDN'T GIVE UP MY SEARCH FOR LIFE ON THE MOON - AND I FOUND IT...
MOONIE
BUT IT WAS A MICROSCOPIC VIRUS. A VIRUS THAT SWELLED UP THE SKULL UNTIL IT WAS THE SIZE OF A BALLOON.
A MASS PROGRAMME OF VACCINATION WAS STARTED AGAINST "MOONIE'S VIRUS." BUT FOR SOME IT WAS TOO LATE. THE LUCKY ONES DIED.
YES, NOW YOU CAN SEE. UGLY, ISN'T IT!
SO I HID MYSELF AWAY HERE - AND WITH THE TEN MILLION CREDITS I WON FOR FINDING THE VIRUS I BEGAN TO BUY - AND CHEAT - AND STEAL ... TO STEAL THE MOON!
THE MOON DID THIS TO ME - I DESERVED TO OWN THE MOON IN RETURN.
MOONIE
YOUR MISFORTUNE DOES NOT EXCUSE YOUR CRIMES. I'M TAKING YOU IN, MOONIE.

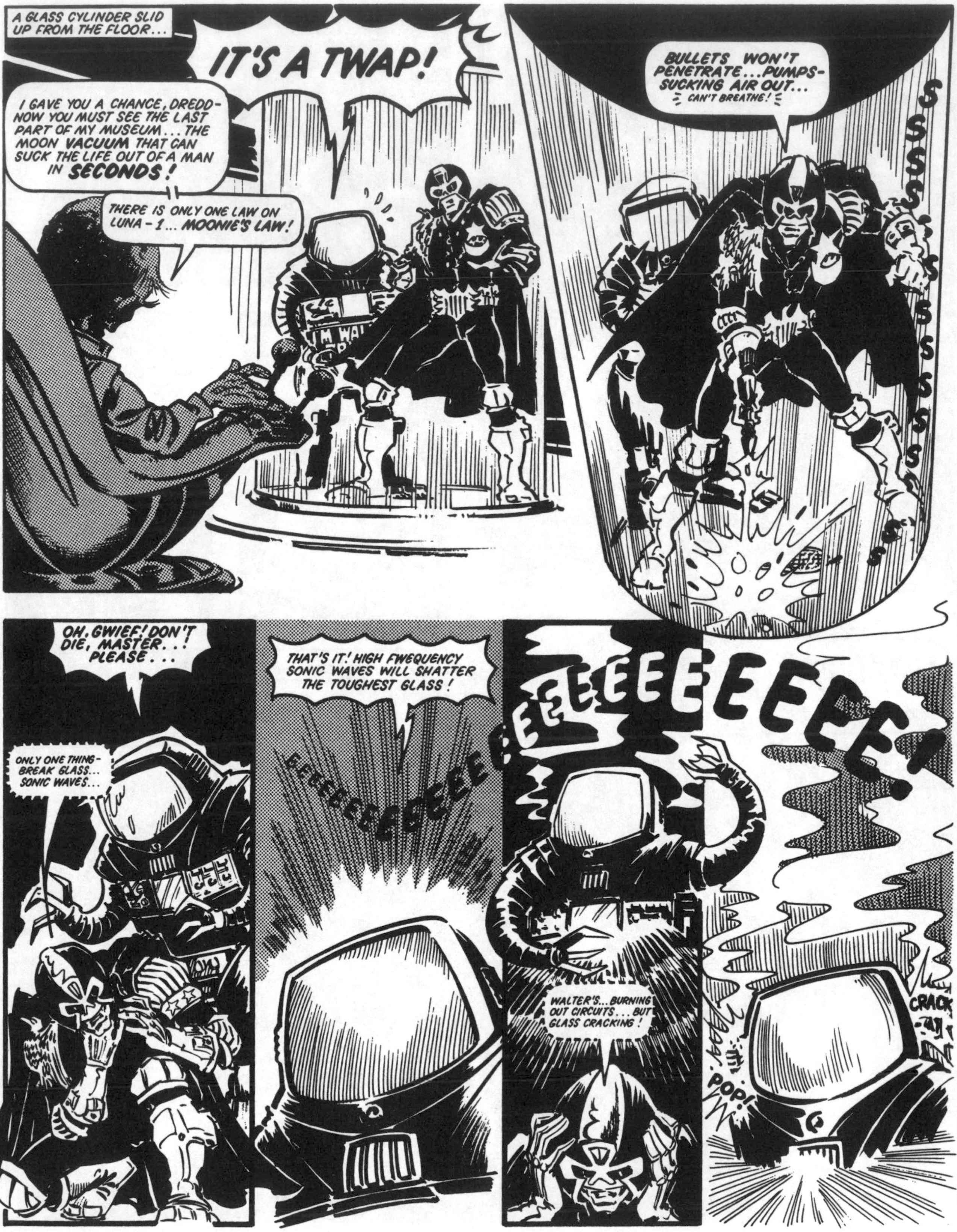
A GLASS CYLINDER SLID UP FROM THE FLOOR...
IT'S A TWAP!
I GAVE YOU A CHANCE, DREDD-NOW YOU MUST SEE THE LAST PART OF MY MUSEUM... THE MOON VACUUM THAT CAN SUCK THE LIFE OUT OF A MAN IN SECONDS!
THERE IS ONLY ONE LAW ON LUNA-1... MOONIE'S LAW!
BULLETS WON'T PENETRATE... PUMPS-SUCKING AIR OUT... CAN'T BREATHE!
SSSSSSSSSSSS
OH, GWIEF! DON'T DIE, MASTER..! PLEASE...
ONLY ONE THING-BREAK GLASS... SONIC WAVES...
THAT'S IT! HIGH FWEQUENCY SONIC WAVES WILL SHATTER THE TOUGHEST GLASS!
EEEEEEEEEEEEEEEEEEEEEEEEEE!
WALTER'S... BURNING OUT CIRCUITS... BUT GLASS CRACKING!
CRACK
POP!

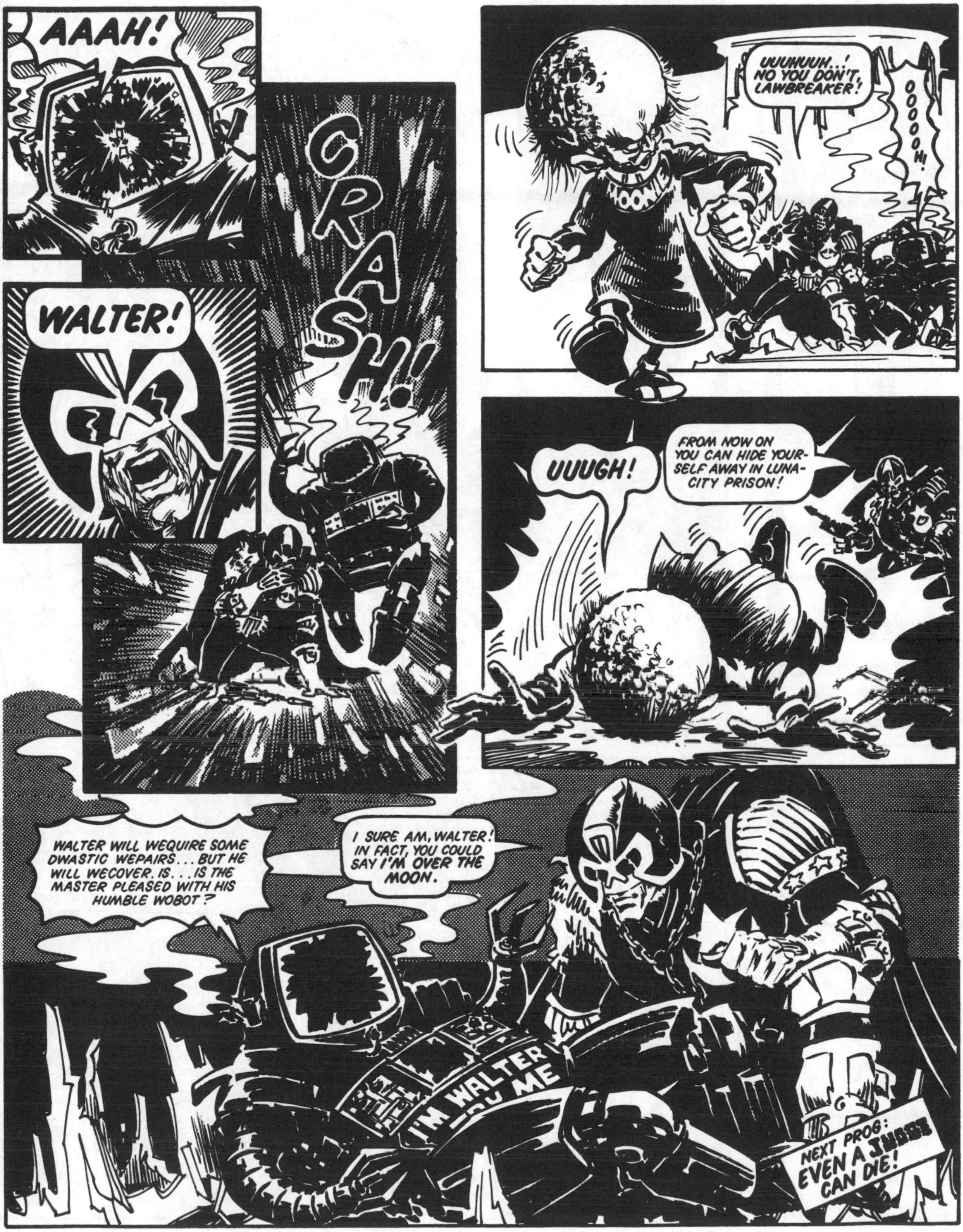
AAAH!
CRASH!
WALTER!
UUUHUUH...! NO YOU DON'T, LAWBREAKER!
OOOOOOH!
UUUGH!
FROM NOW ON YOU CAN HIDE YOURSELF AWAY IN LUNA-CITY PRISON!
WALTER WILL WEQUIRE SOME DWASTIC WEPAIRS... BUT HE WILL WECOVER. IS... IS THE MASTER PLEASED WITH HIS HUMBLE WOBOT?
I SURE AM, WALTER! IN FACT, YOU COULD SAY I'M OVER THE MOON.
I'M WALTER
NEXT PROG: EVEN A JUDGE CAN DIE!

JUDGE DREDD

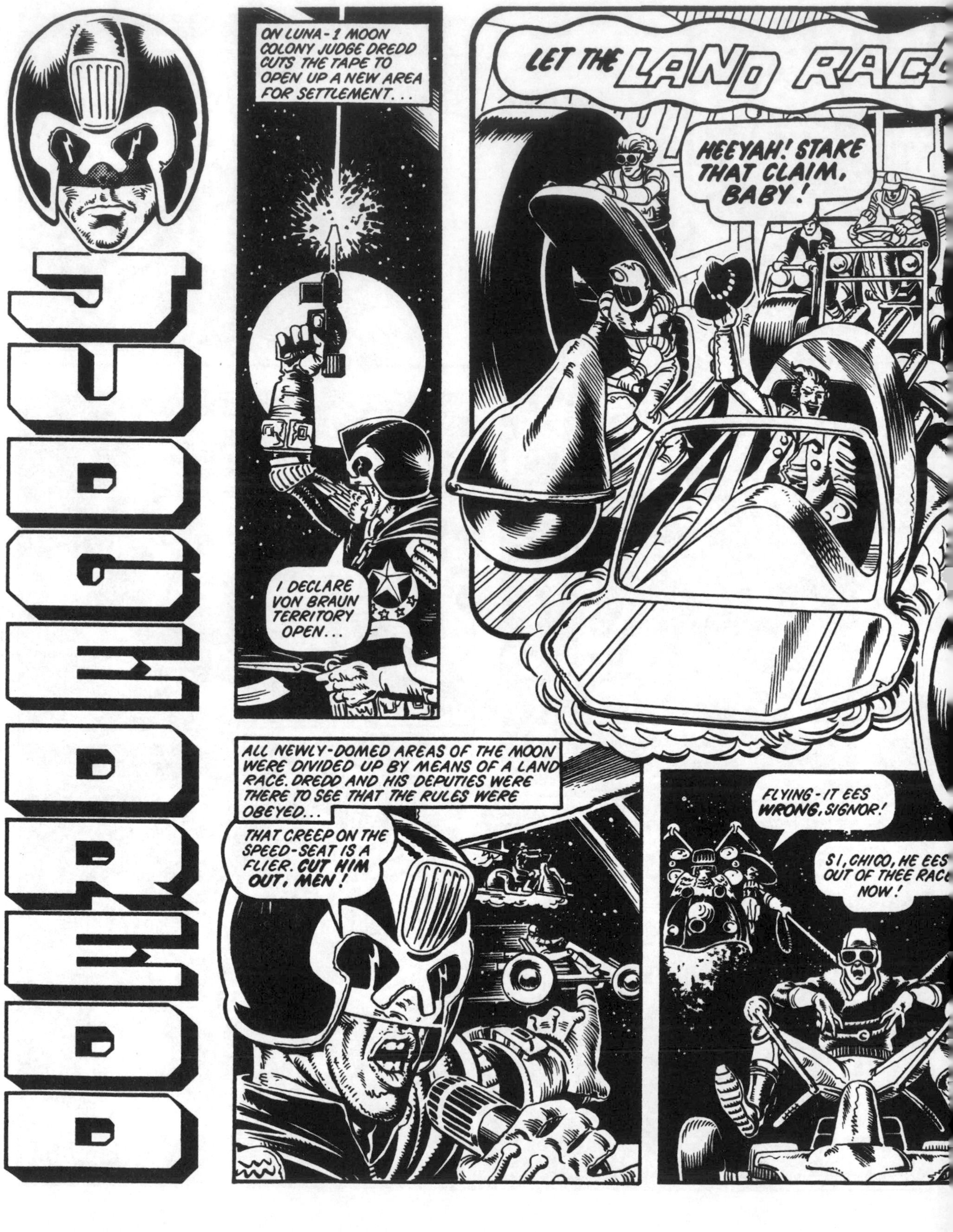

ON LUNA-1 MOON COLONY JUDGE DREDD CUTS THE TAPE TO OPEN UP A NEW AREA FOR SETTLEMENT...
I DECLARE VON BRAUN TERRITORY OPEN...
LET THE LAND RAC
HEEYAH! STAKE THAT CLAIM, BABY!
ALL NEWLY-DOMED AREAS OF THE MOON WERE DIVIDED UP BY MEANS OF A LAND RACE. DREDD AND HIS DEPUTIES WERE THERE TO SEE THAT THE RULES WERE OBEYED...
THAT CREEP ON THE SPEED-SEAT IS A FLIER. CUT HIM OUT, MEN!
FLYING - IT EES WRONG, SIGNOR!
SI, CHICO, HE EES OUT OF THEE RAC
NOW!

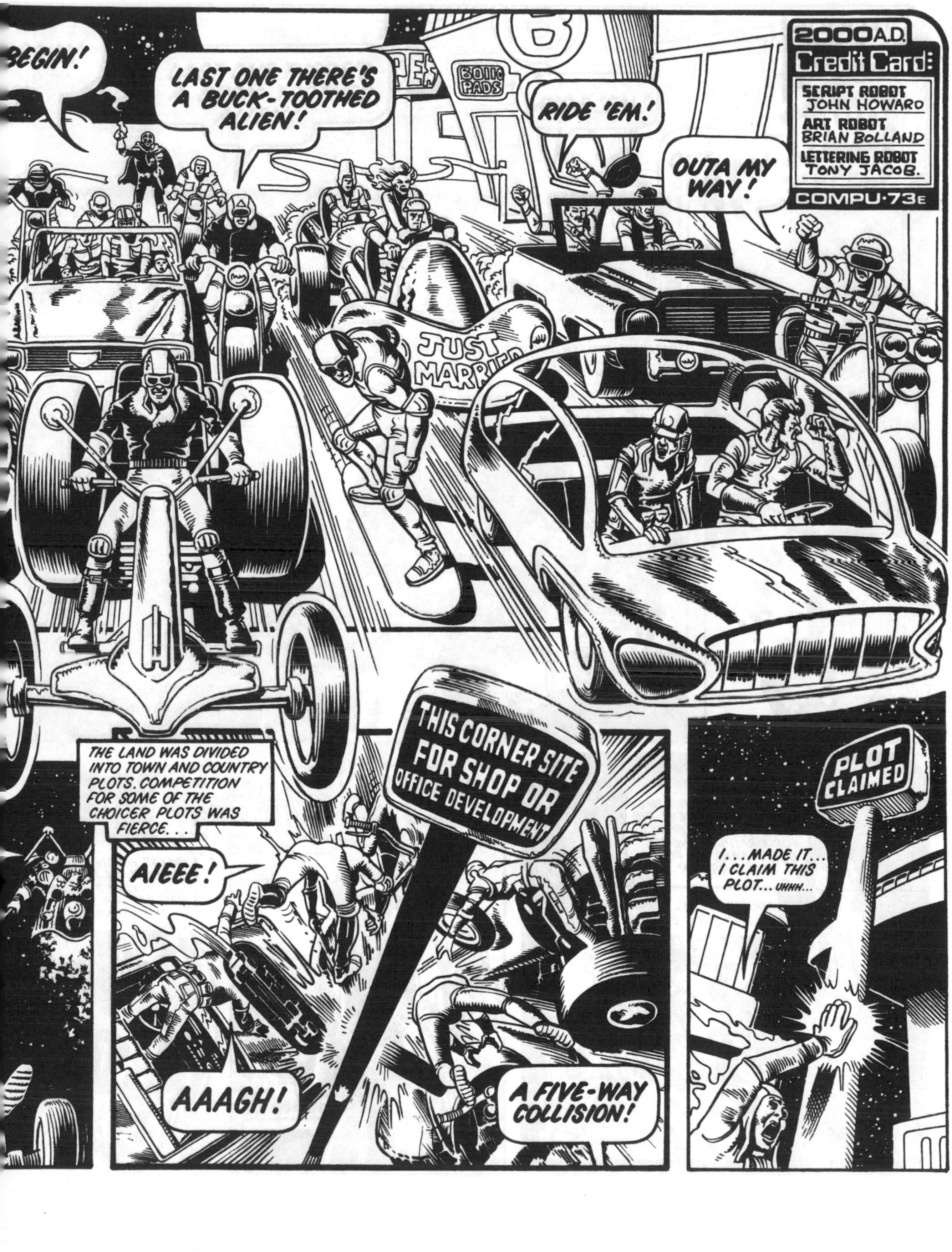
BEGIN!
LAST ONE THERE'S A BUCK-TOOTHED ALIEN!
BOING PADS
RIDE 'EM!
OUTA MY WAY!
2000 A.D. Credit Card
SCRIPT ROBOT JOHN HOWARD
ART ROBOT BRIAN BOLLAND
LETTERING ROBOT TONY JACOB.
COMPU·73E
JUST MARRIED
THE LAND WAS DIVIDED INTO TOWN AND COUNTRY PLOTS. COMPETITION FOR SOME OF THE CHOICER PLOTS WAS FIERCE...
THIS CORNER SITE FOR SHOP OR OFFICE DEVELOPMENT
AIEEE!
AAAGH!
A FIVE-WAY COLLISION!
PLOT CLAIMED
I... MADE IT... I CLAIM THIS PLOT... UHHH...

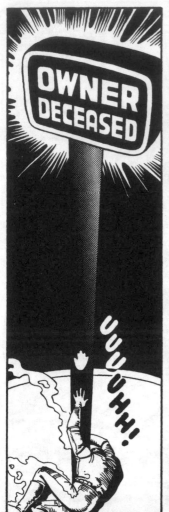

OWNER DECEASED

UUUUHH!

SOON EVERY PLOT WAS CLAIMED. DREDD SPENT THE REST OF THE DAY SETTLING DISPUTES...

YOU'RE BOTH UNDER *ARREST* FOR FIGHTING. THIS PLOT WILL NOW GO TO THE *HIGHEST* BIDDER.

THEES EES THE *TENTH* CLAIM TOUT SO FAR. I'LL RUN HEEM OUT OF THE TERREETORY WEETH THE REST.

I BUY AND SELL CLAIMS BEST PRICES PAID FOR CHOICE PLOTS

THAT NIGHT, WALTER, JUDGE DREDD'S ROBO-SERVANT, WAS WAITING IN DREDD'S COMMAND TENT...

THIS IS *WOWENA*, THE WAITWESS WOBOT, MASTER. SHE HAS A *DWEADFUL CWIME* TO WEPORT.

MY MISTREES IS *WIDOW SPOCK*, SIR. SHE CLAIMED A GOOD MAIN STREET SITE TO BUILD A FLAPJACK PARLOUR. BUT THIS AFTERNOON THREE MEN CAME TO SEE HER...

I'M WALTER TRY ME

CALL ME WOWENA

THE MEN HAD DEMANDED THE WIDOW SPOCK'S CLAIM...

YOU BETTER SELL THE SITE, LADY. WE REPRESENT THE *INTERSTELLAR PSIONICS CORPORATIONS* AND *IPC* DON'T TAKE NO FOR AN ANSWER.

YOU'VE GOT TILL *TOMORROW* TO SIGN THEM PAPERS.

MY MISTRESS WAS *FRIGHTENED* TO COME TO YOU, SIR, BUT AS A LOYAL ROBOT IT IS MY DUTY TO...

THAT'S ENOUGH! WALTER, YOU SHOULD KNOW BETTER THAN TO BRING THIS ROBOT HERE. I CAN'T ACT ON A CRIME REPORTED BY A *MACHINE.*

UNLESS WIDOW SPOCK COMES TO ME HERSELF, THE MATTER'S CLOSED NOW GET HER – OR IT – OUT OF HERE!

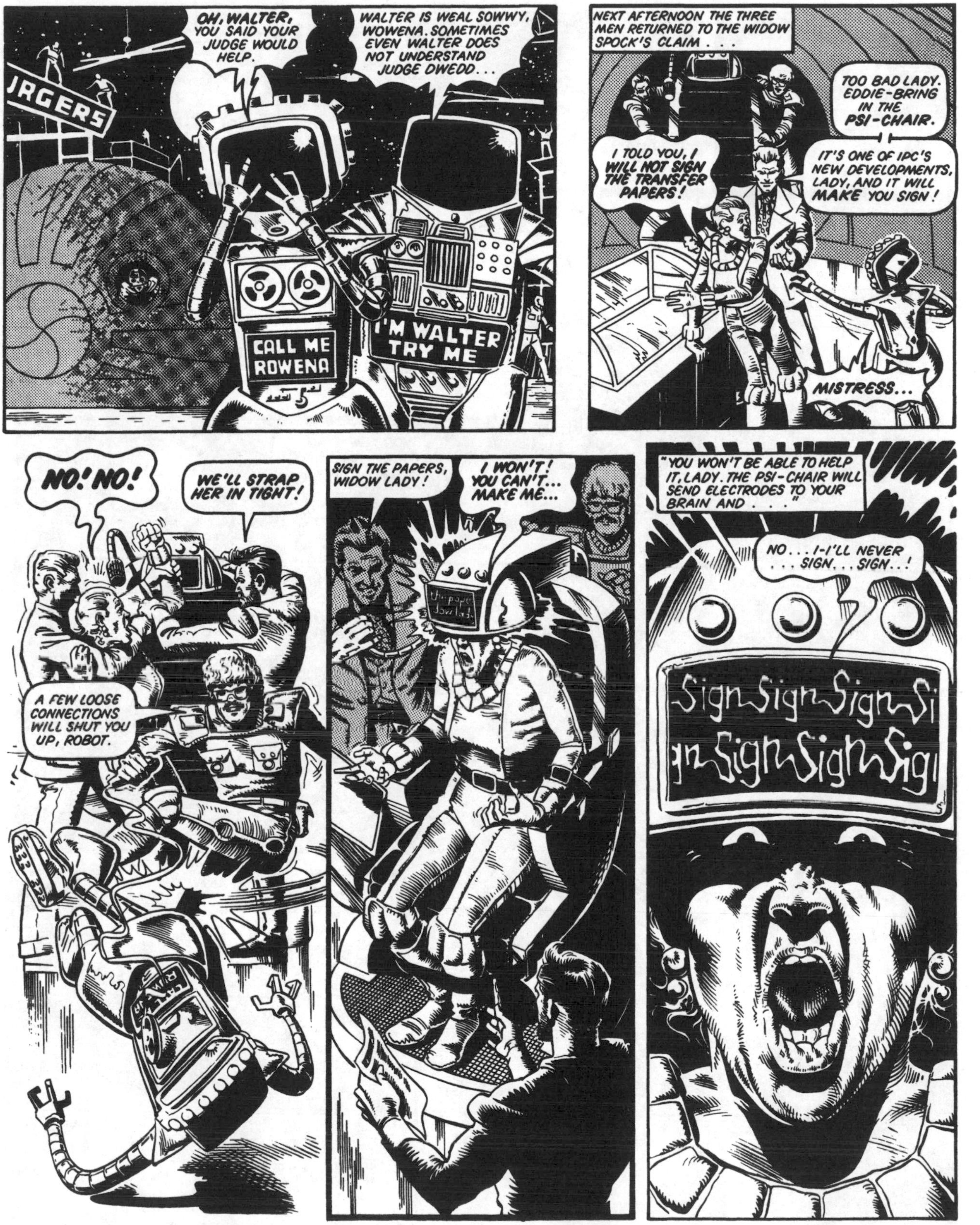

OH, WALTER, YOU SAID YOUR JUDGE WOULD HELP.
WALTER IS WEAL SOWWY, WOWENA. SOMETIMES EVEN WALTER DOES NOT UNDERSTAND JUDGE DWEDD...
CALL ME ROWENA
I'M WALTER TRY ME
NEXT AFTERNOON THE THREE MEN RETURNED TO THE WIDOW SPOCK'S CLAIM...
TOO BAD LADY. EDDIE-BRING IN THE PSI-CHAIR.
I TOLD YOU, I WILL NOT SIGN THE TRANSFER PAPERS!
IT'S ONE OF IPC'S NEW DEVELOPMENTS, LADY, AND IT WILL MAKE YOU SIGN!
MISTRESS...
NO! NO!
WE'LL STRAP HER IN TIGHT!
A FEW LOOSE CONNECTIONS WILL SHUT YOU UP, ROBOT.
SIGN THE PAPERS, WIDOW LADY!
I WON'T! YOU CAN'T... MAKE ME...
"YOU WON'T BE ABLE TO HELP IT, LADY. THE PSI-CHAIR WILL SEND ELECTRODES TO YOUR BRAIN AND..."
NO... I-I'LL NEVER ... SIGN... SIGN...!
Sign Sign Sign Si
gn Sign Sign Sigi

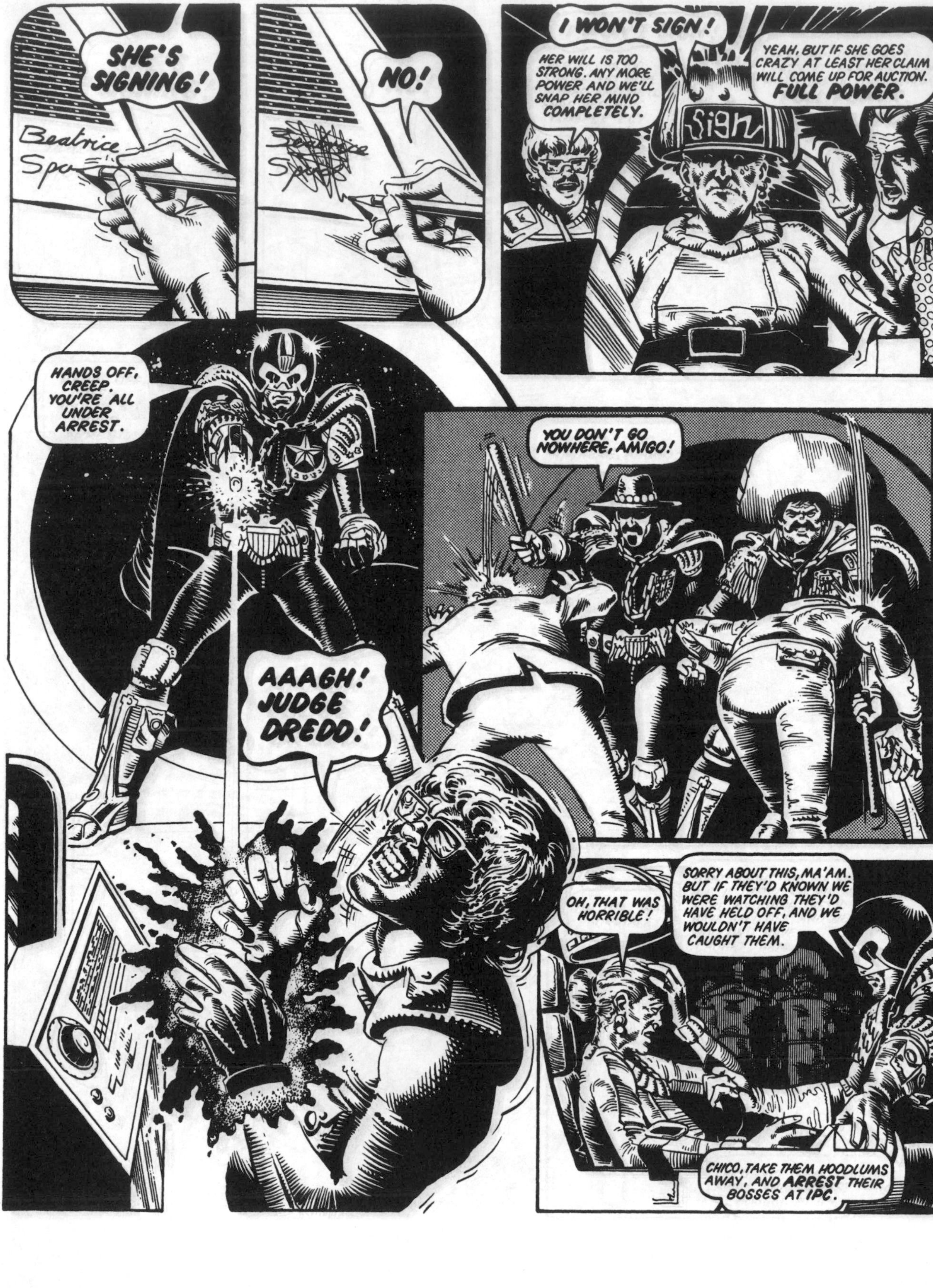
SHE'S SIGNING!
Beatrice Spa
NO!
I WON'T SIGN!
HER WILL IS TOO STRONG. ANY MORE POWER AND WE'LL SNAP HER MIND COMPLETELY.
YEAH, BUT IF SHE GOES CRAZY AT LEAST HER CLAIM WILL COME UP FOR AUCTION. FULL POWER.
Sign
HANDS OFF, CREEP. YOU'RE ALL UNDER ARREST.
YOU DON'T GO NOWHERE, AMIGO!
AAAGH! JUDGE DREDD!
OH, THAT WAS HORRIBLE!
SORRY ABOUT THIS, MA'AM. BUT IF THEY'D KNOWN WE WERE WATCHING THEY'D HAVE HELD OFF, AND WE WOULDN'T HAVE CAUGHT THEM.
CHICO, TAKE THEM HOODLUMS AWAY, AND ARREST THEIR BOSSES AT IPC.

WALTER RECONNECTED ROWENA...

IT WAS ALL A CWAFTY TRICK BY JUDGE DWEDD, WOWENA. AND WALTER HELPED TOO.

OH, WALTER, MY HERO.

ROWENA PAID ANOTHER VISIT TO JUDGE DREDD'S TENT...

MY MISTRESS IS VERY GRATEFUL, SIR. SHE MADE THESE COOKIES SPECIALLY FOR YOU!

ER, PUT THEM DOWN OVER THERE, ROWENA. AND GIVE YOUR MISTRESS MY THANKS.

JUDGE DREDD'S LAWMAN'S INSTINCT DETECTED SOMETHING ODD...

HMMM... THESE COOKIES WERE MADE BY A ROBOT...

SO, ROWENA WAS LYING. SHE WAS JUST LOOKING FOR AN EXCUSE TO VISIT MY TENT... BUT WHY?

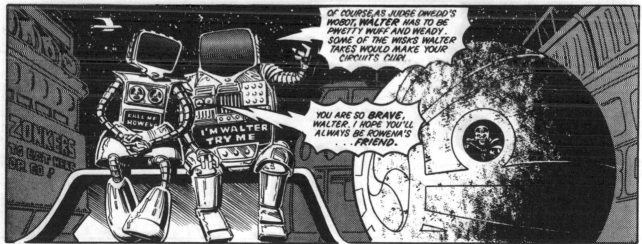

OF COURSE, AS JUDGE DWEDD'S WOBOT, WALTER HAS TO BE PWETTY WUFF AND WEADY. SOME OF THE WISKS WALTER TAKES WOULD MAKE YOUR CIRCUITS CURL.

YOU ARE SO BRAVE, WALTER. I HOPE YOU'LL ALWAYS BE ROWENA'S ... FRIEND.

CALL ME ROWENA

I'M WALTER TRY ME

ZONKERS

ROBOTS IN LOVE! RIDICULOUS! STILL, I SUPPOSE WE SHOULD HAVE KNOWN THIS WAS COMING THE DAY WE GAVE ROBOTS HUMAN-LIKE PERSONALITIES.

STILL, IF IT KEEPS WALTER OUT OF MY HAIR, I'M ALL FOR IT.

NEXT PROG. THE OXYGEN DESERT.

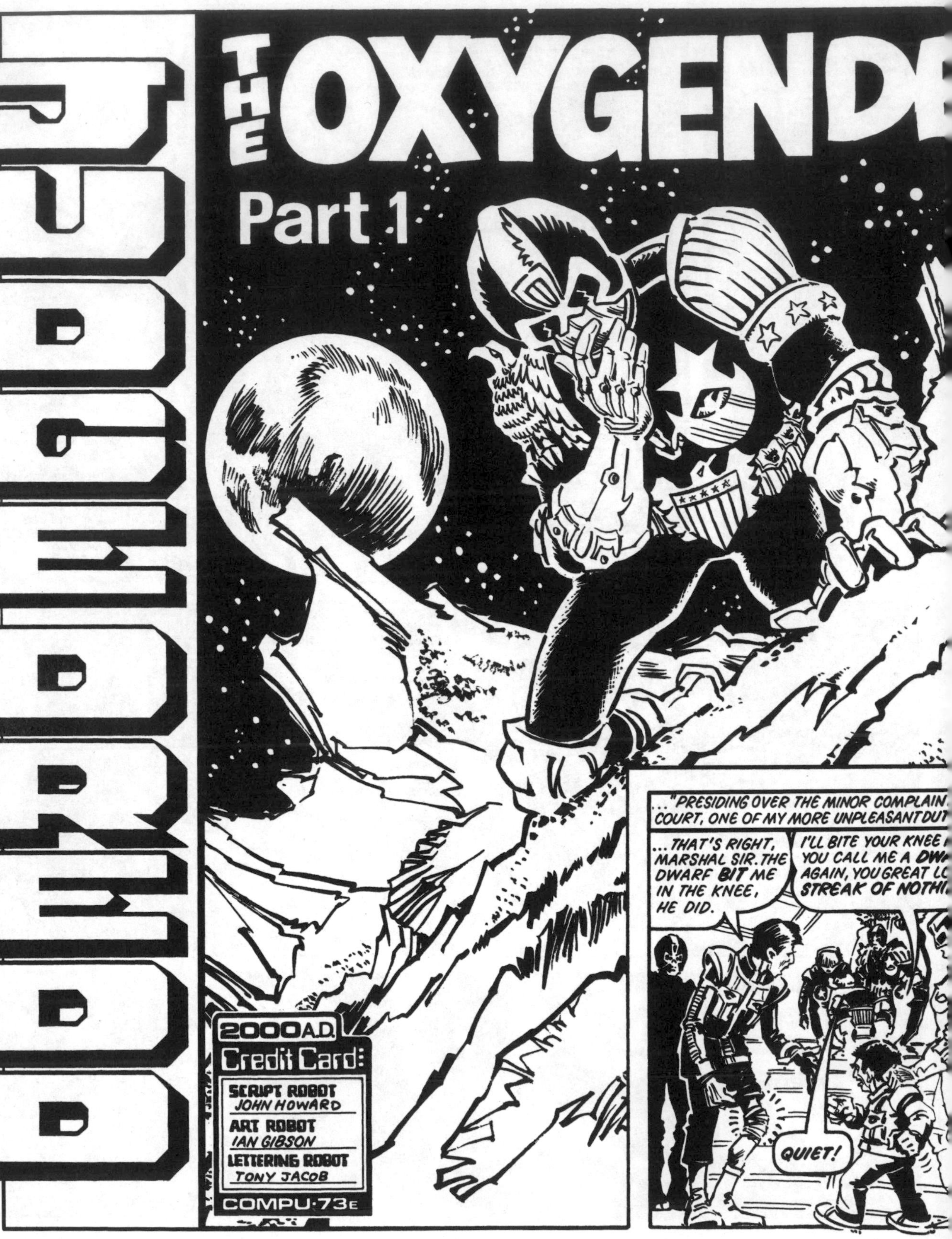
JUDGE DREDD
THE OXYGENDE
Part 1
2000 A.D. Credit Card:
SCRIPT ROBOT JOHN HOWARD
ART ROBOT IAN GIBSON
LETTERING ROBOT TONY JACOB
COMPU-73E
..."PRESIDING OVER THE MINOR COMPLAIN
COURT, ONE OF MY MORE UNPLEASANT DUT
...THAT'S RIGHT, MARSHAL SIR. THE DWARF BIT ME IN THE KNEE, HE DID.
I'LL BITE YOUR KNEE YOU CALL ME A DW AGAIN, YOU GREAT L STREAK OF NOTHI
QUIET!

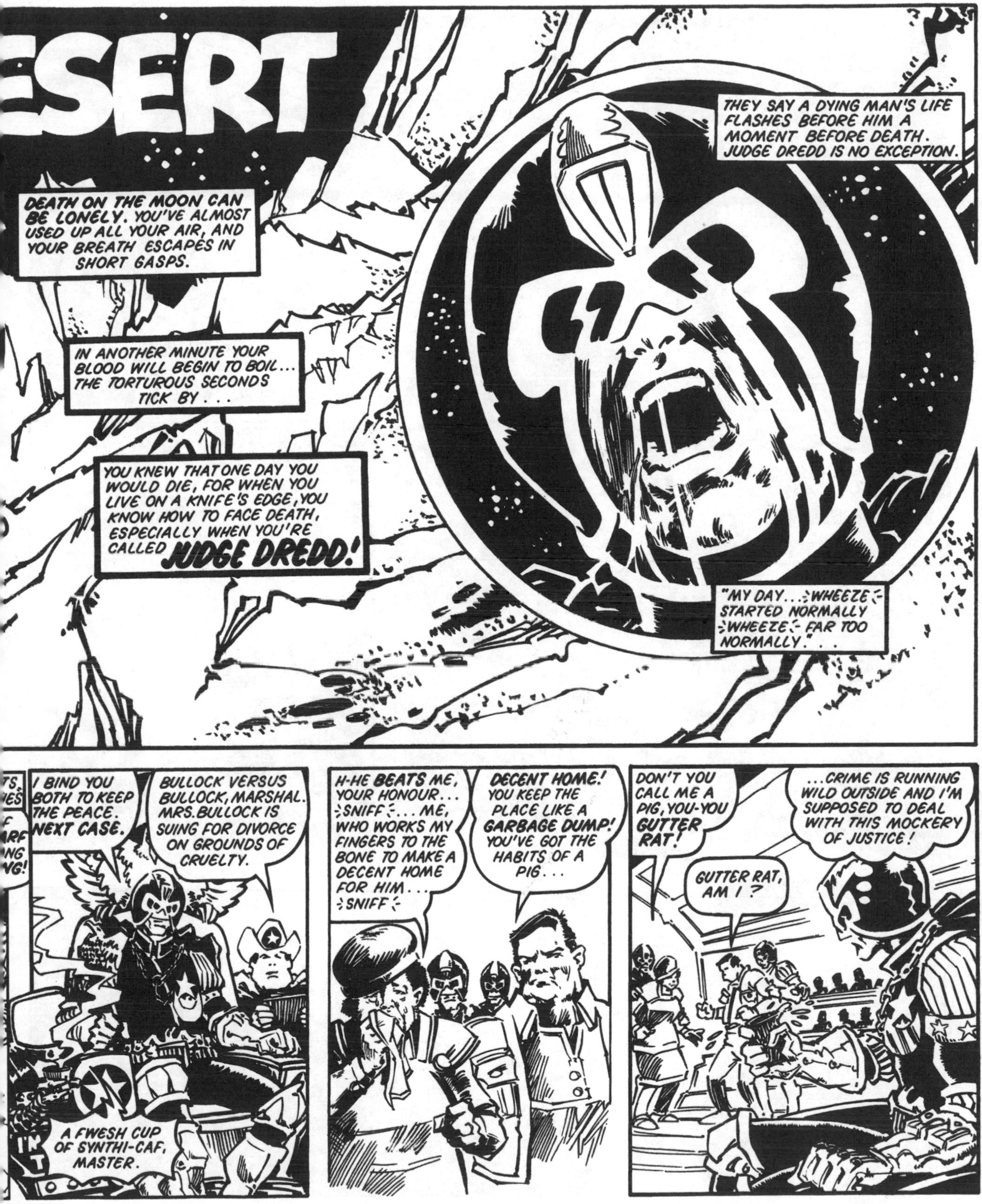
ESERT
DEATH ON THE MOON CAN BE LONELY. YOU'VE ALMOST USED UP ALL YOUR AIR, AND YOUR BREATH ESCAPES IN SHORT GASPS.
IN ANOTHER MINUTE YOUR BLOOD WILL BEGIN TO BOIL... THE TORTUROUS SECONDS TICK BY . . .
YOU KNEW THAT ONE DAY YOU WOULD DIE, FOR WHEN YOU LIVE ON A KNIFE'S EDGE, YOU KNOW HOW TO FACE DEATH, ESPECIALLY WHEN YOU'RE CALLED JUDGE DREDD!
THEY SAY A DYING MAN'S LIFE FLASHES BEFORE HIM A MOMENT BEFORE DEATH. JUDGE DREDD IS NO EXCEPTION.
"MY DAY... -WHEEZE- STARTED NORMALLY -WHEEZE- FAR TOO NORMALLY". . .
I BIND YOU BOTH TO KEEP THE PEACE. NEXT CASE.
BULLOCK VERSUS BULLOCK, MARSHAL. MRS. BULLOCK IS SUING FOR DIVORCE ON GROUNDS OF CRUELTY.
A FWESH CUP OF SYNTHI-CAF, MASTER.
H-HE BEATS ME, YOUR HONOUR... -SNIFF- ... ME, WHO WORKS MY FINGERS TO THE BONE TO MAKE A DECENT HOME FOR HIM... -SNIFF-
DECENT HOME! YOU KEEP THE PLACE LIKE A GARBAGE DUMP! YOU'VE GOT THE HABITS OF A PIG...
DON'T YOU CALL ME A PIG, YOU-YOU GUTTER RAT!
GUTTER RAT, AM I ?
...CRIME IS RUNNING WILD OUTSIDE AND I'M SUPPOSED TO DEAL WITH THIS MOCKERY OF JUSTICE!

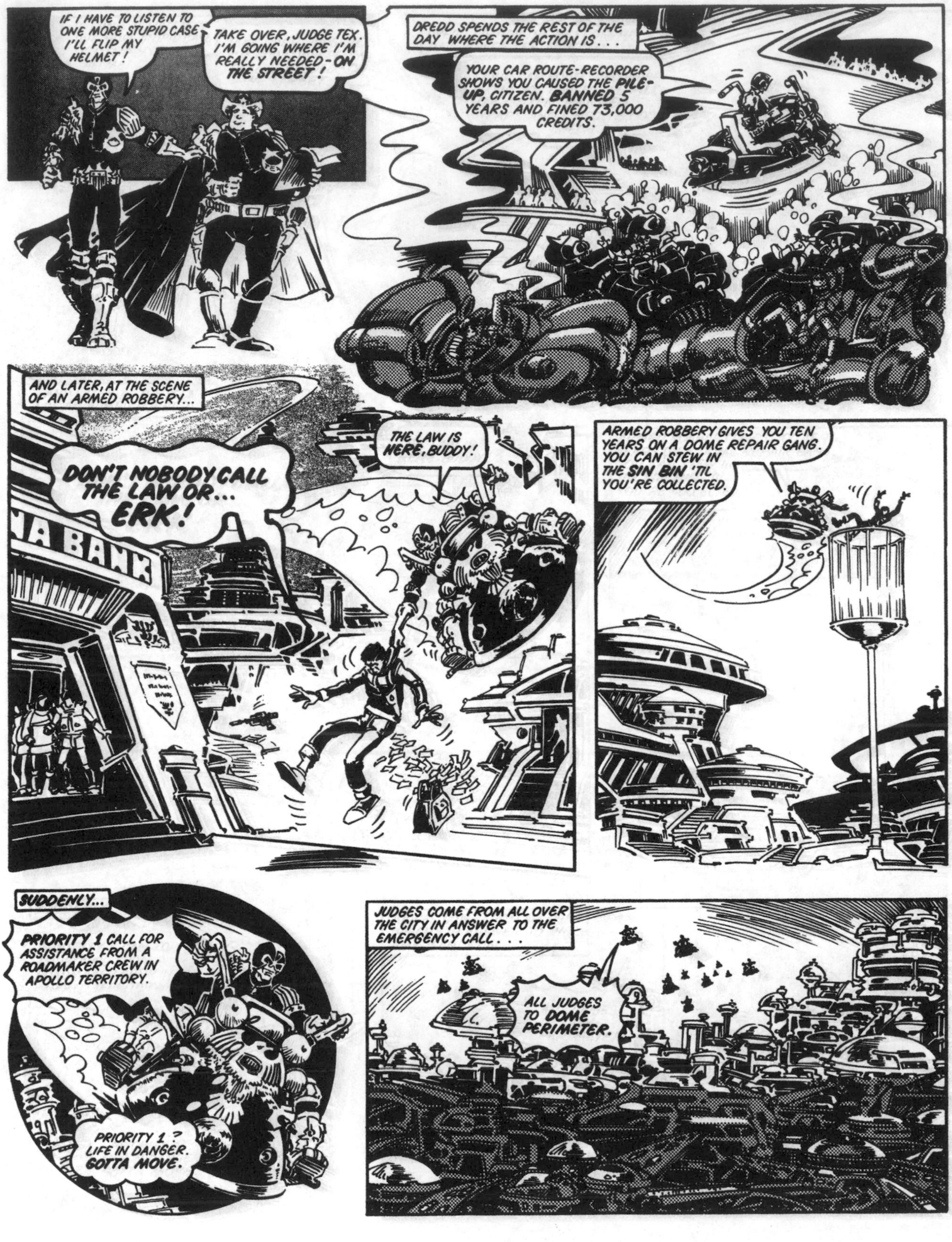

IF I HAVE TO LISTEN TO ONE MORE STUPID CASE I'LL FLIP MY HELMET!
TAKE OVER, JUDGE TEX. I'M GOING WHERE I'M REALLY NEEDED - ON THE STREET!
DREDD SPENDS THE REST OF THE DAY WHERE THE ACTION IS . . .
YOUR CAR ROUTE-RECORDER SHOWS YOU CAUSED THE PILE-UP, CITIZEN. BANNED 5 YEARS AND FINED 73,000 CREDITS.
AND LATER, AT THE SCENE OF AN ARMED ROBBERY...
DON'T NOBODY CALL THE LAW OR... ERK!
THE LAW IS HERE, BUDDY!
BANK
ARMED ROBBERY GIVES YOU TEN YEARS ON A DOME REPAIR GANG. YOU CAN STEW IN THE SIN BIN 'TIL YOU'RE COLLECTED.
SUDDENLY...
PRIORITY 1 CALL FOR ASSISTANCE FROM A ROADMAKER CREW IN APOLLO TERRITORY.
PRIORITY 1? LIFE IN DANGER. GOTTA MOVE.
JUDGES COME FROM ALL OVER THE CITY IN ANSWER TO THE EMERGENCY CALL . . .
ALL JUDGES TO DOME PERIMETER.

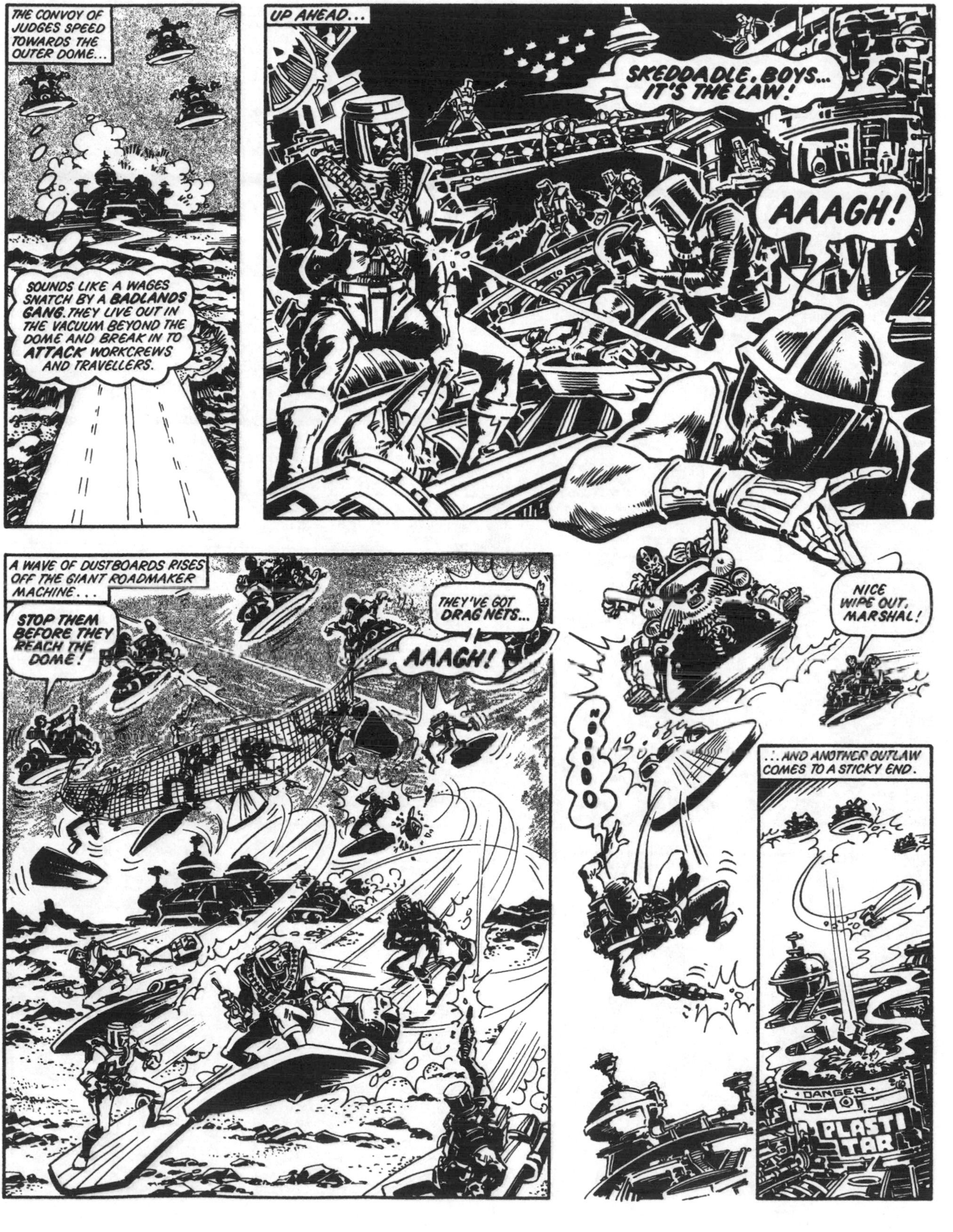
THE CONVOY OF JUDGES SPEED TOWARDS THE OUTER DOME...
SOUNDS LIKE A WAGES SNATCH BY A BADLANDS GANG. THEY LIVE OUT IN THE VACUUM BEYOND THE DOME AND BREAK IN TO ATTACK WORKCREWS AND TRAVELLERS.
UP AHEAD...
SKEDDADLE, BOYS... IT'S THE LAW!
AAAGH!
A WAVE OF DUSTBOARDS RISES OFF THE GIANT ROADMAKER MACHINE...
STOP THEM BEFORE THEY REACH THE DOME!
THEY'VE GOT DRAG NETS...
AAAGH!
NICE WIPE OUT, MARSHAL!
...AND ANOTHER OUTLAW COMES TO A STICKY END.
DANGER
PLASTI TAR

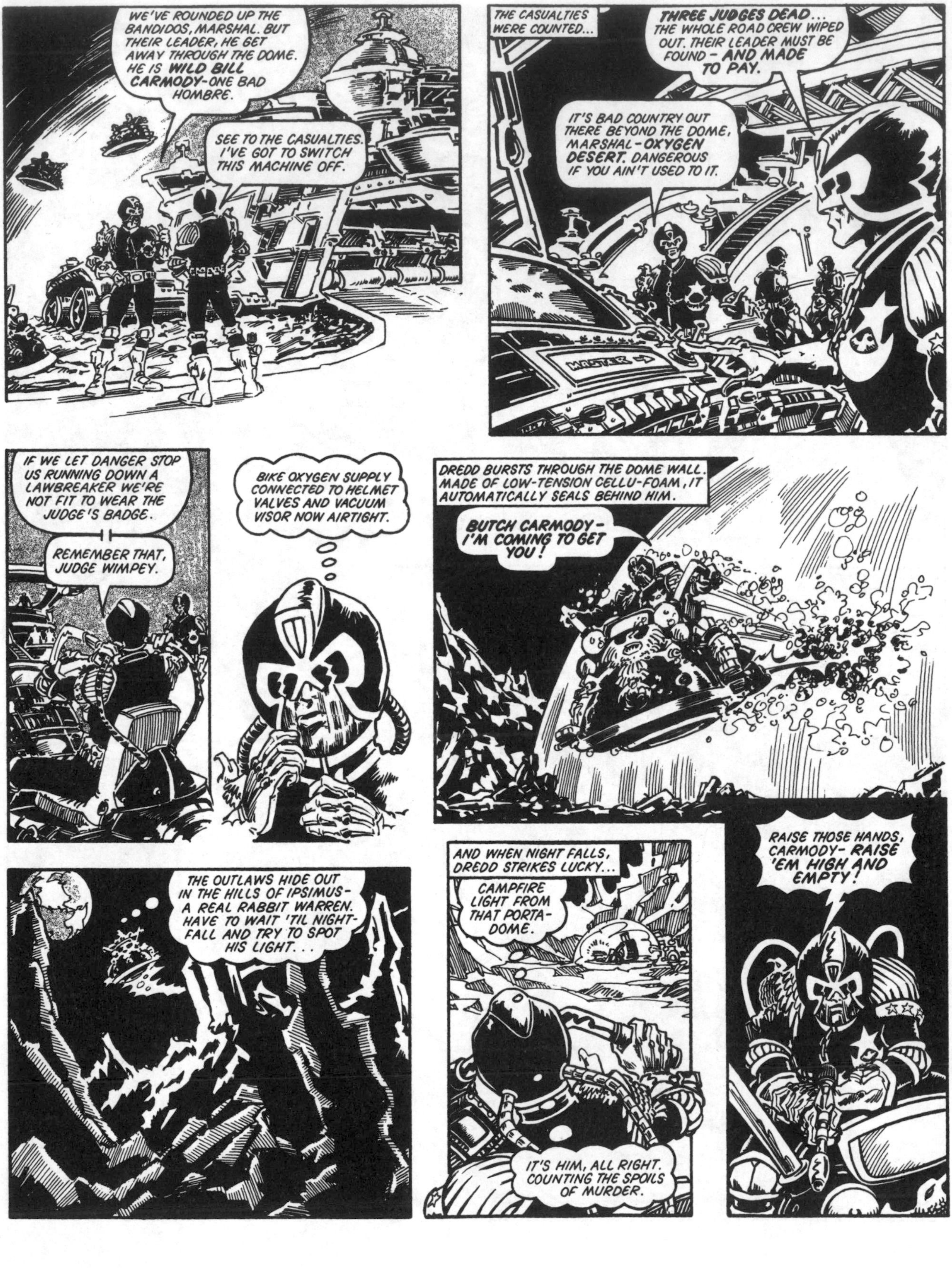
WE'VE ROUNDED UP THE BANDIDOS, MARSHAL. BUT THEIR LEADER, HE GET AWAY THROUGH THE DOME. HE IS WILD BILL CARMODY- ONE BAD HOMBRE.
SEE TO THE CASUALTIES. I'VE GOT TO SWITCH THIS MACHINE OFF.
THE CASUALTIES WERE COUNTED...
THREE JUDGES DEAD... THE WHOLE ROAD CREW WIPED OUT. THEIR LEADER MUST BE FOUND - AND MADE TO PAY.
IT'S BAD COUNTRY OUT THERE BEYOND THE DOME, MARSHAL - OXYGEN DESERT. DANGEROUS IF YOU AIN'T USED TO IT.
IF WE LET DANGER STOP US RUNNING DOWN A LAWBREAKER WE'RE NOT FIT TO WEAR THE JUDGE'S BADGE.
REMEMBER THAT, JUDGE WIMPEY.
BIKE OXYGEN SUPPLY CONNECTED TO HELMET VALVES AND VACUUM VISOR NOW AIRTIGHT.
DREDD BURSTS THROUGH THE DOME WALL. MADE OF LOW-TENSION CELLU-FOAM, IT AUTOMATICALLY SEALS BEHIND HIM.
BUTCH CARMODY - I'M COMING TO GET YOU!
THE OUTLAWS HIDE OUT IN THE HILLS OF IPSIMUS - A REAL RABBIT WARREN. HAVE TO WAIT 'TIL NIGHT-FALL AND TRY TO SPOT HIS LIGHT...
AND WHEN NIGHT FALLS, DREDD STRIKES LUCKY...
CAMPFIRE LIGHT FROM THAT PORTA-DOME.
IT'S HIM, ALL RIGHT. COUNTING THE SPOILS OF MURDER.
RAISE THOSE HANDS, CARMODY- RAISE 'EM HIGH AND EMPTY!

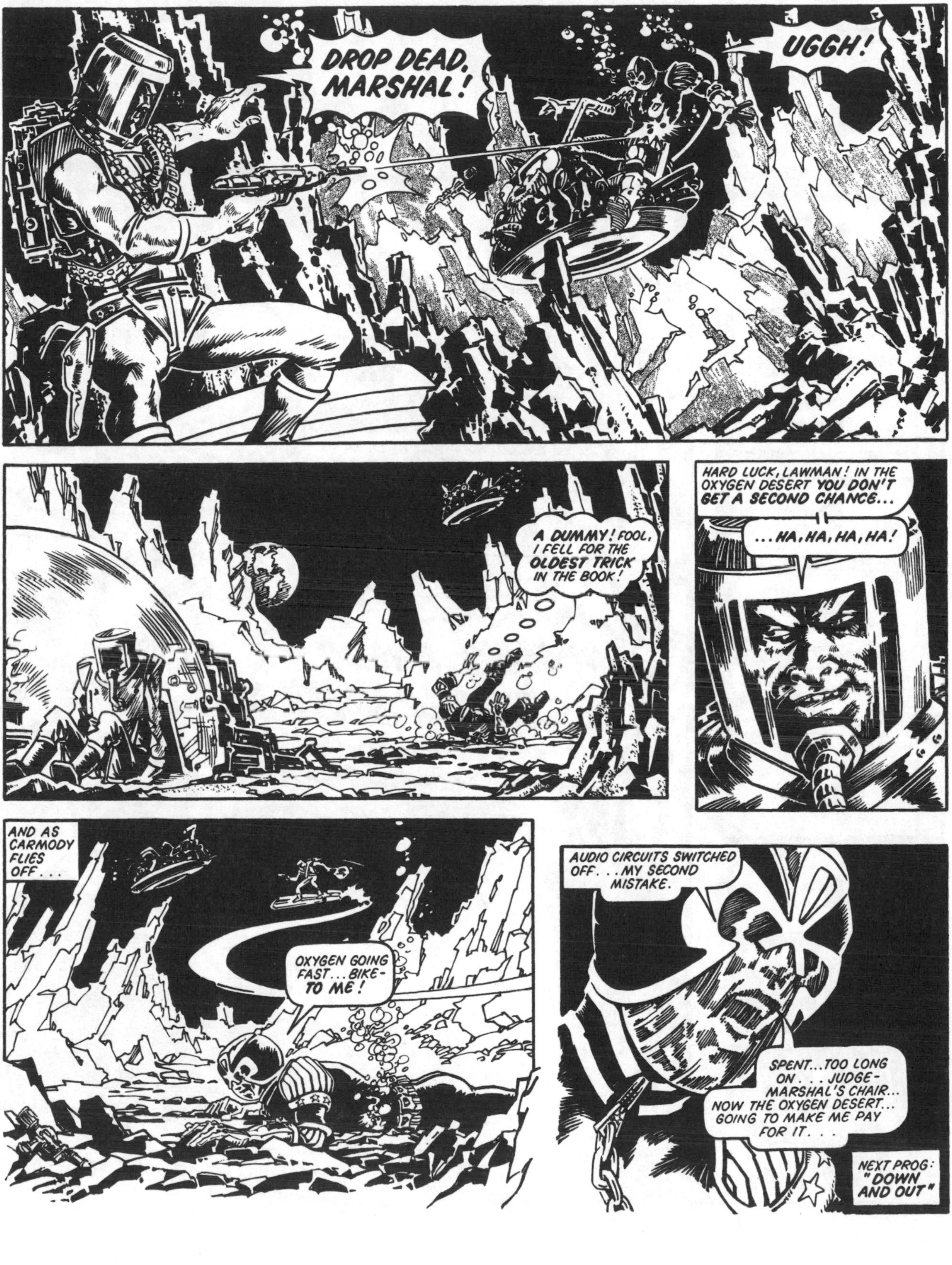
DROP DEAD, MARSHAL!
UGGH!
A DUMMY! FOOL, I FELL FOR THE OLDEST TRICK IN THE BOOK!
HARD LUCK, LAWMAN! IN THE OXYGEN DESERT YOU DON'T GET A SECOND CHANCE...
...HA, HA, HA, HA!
AND AS CARMODY FLIES OFF...
OXYGEN GOING FAST... BIKE- TO ME!
AUDIO CIRCUITS SWITCHED OFF... MY SECOND MISTAKE.
SPENT... TOO LONG ON... JUDGE-MARSHAL'S CHAIR... NOW THE OXYGEN DESERT... GOING TO MAKE ME PAY FOR IT...
NEXT PROG: "DOWN AND OUT"

JUDGE DREDD

OXYGEN DESERT Part 2

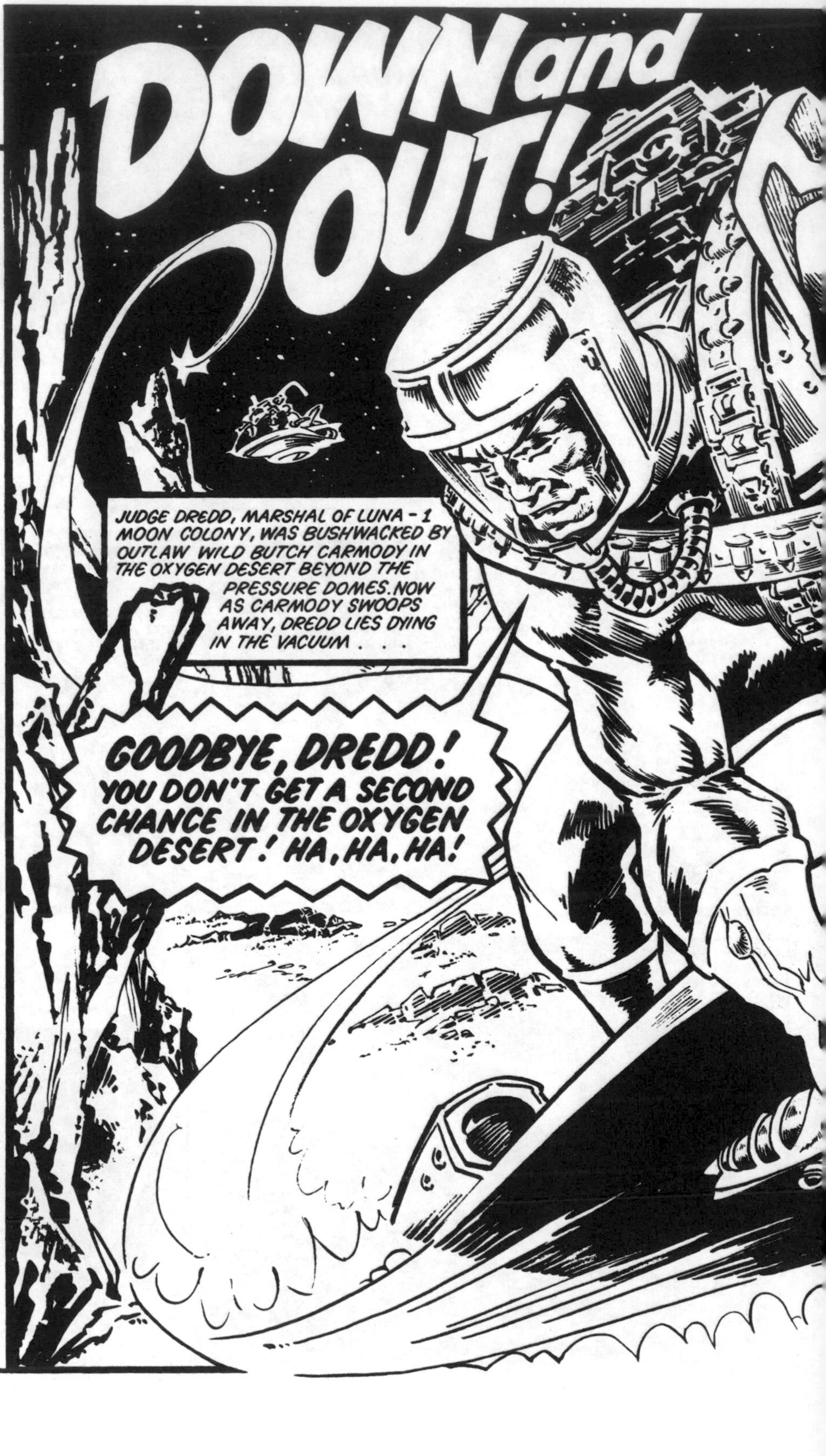

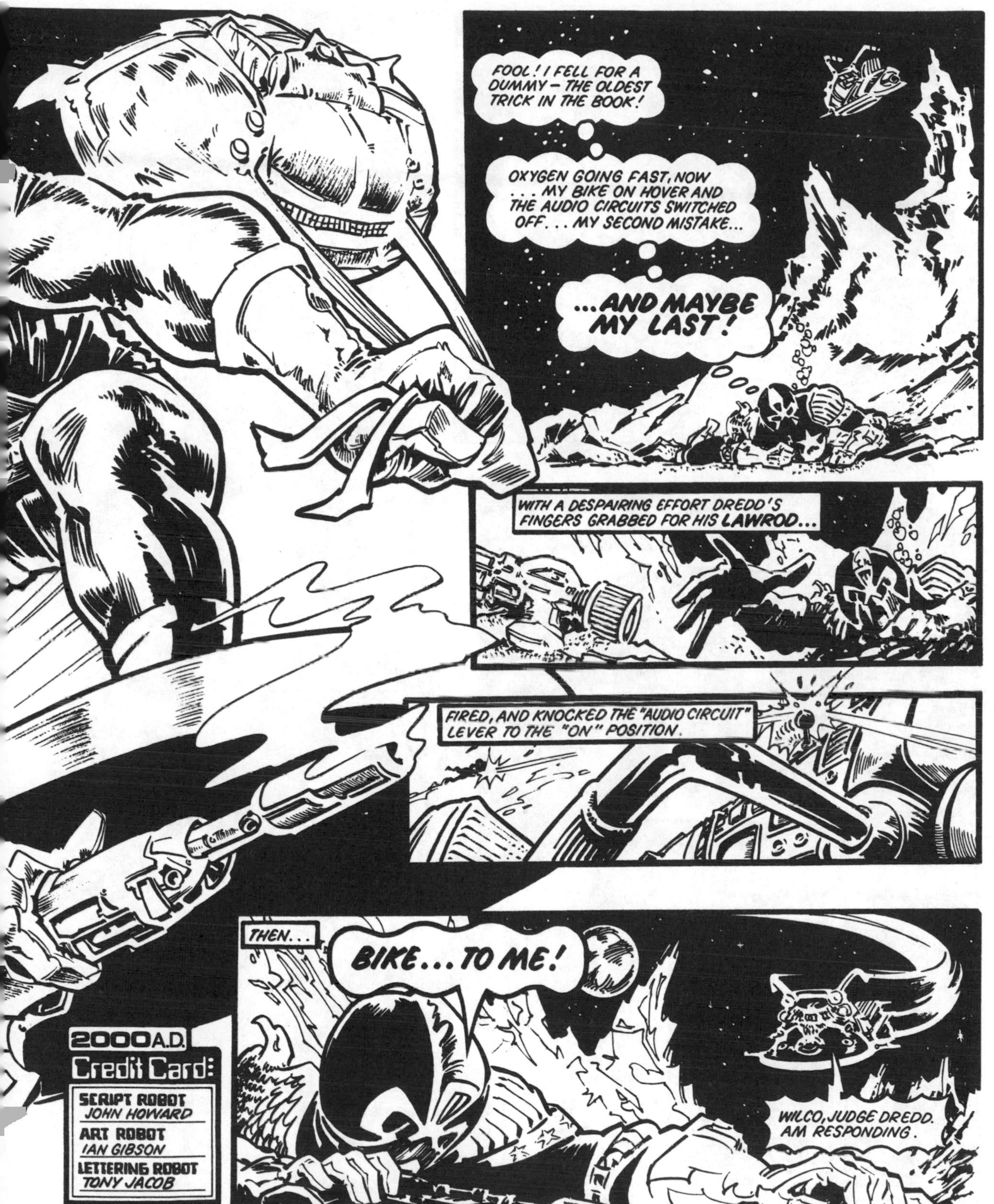
FOOL! I FELL FOR A DUMMY – THE OLDEST TRICK IN THE BOOK!
OXYGEN GOING FAST, NOW . . . MY BIKE ON HOVER AND THE AUDIO CIRCUITS SWITCHED OFF. . . MY SECOND MISTAKE...
...AND MAYBE MY LAST!
WITH A DESPAIRING EFFORT DREDD'S FINGERS GRABBED FOR HIS LAWROD...
FIRED, AND KNOCKED THE "AUDIO CIRCUIT" LEVER TO THE "ON" POSITION.
THEN...
BIKE... TO ME!
WILCO, JUDGE DREDD. AM RESPONDING.
2000 A.D.
Credit Card:
SCRIPT ROBOT JOHN HOWARD
ART ROBOT IAN GIBSON
LETTERING ROBOT TONY JACOB
COMPU-73E

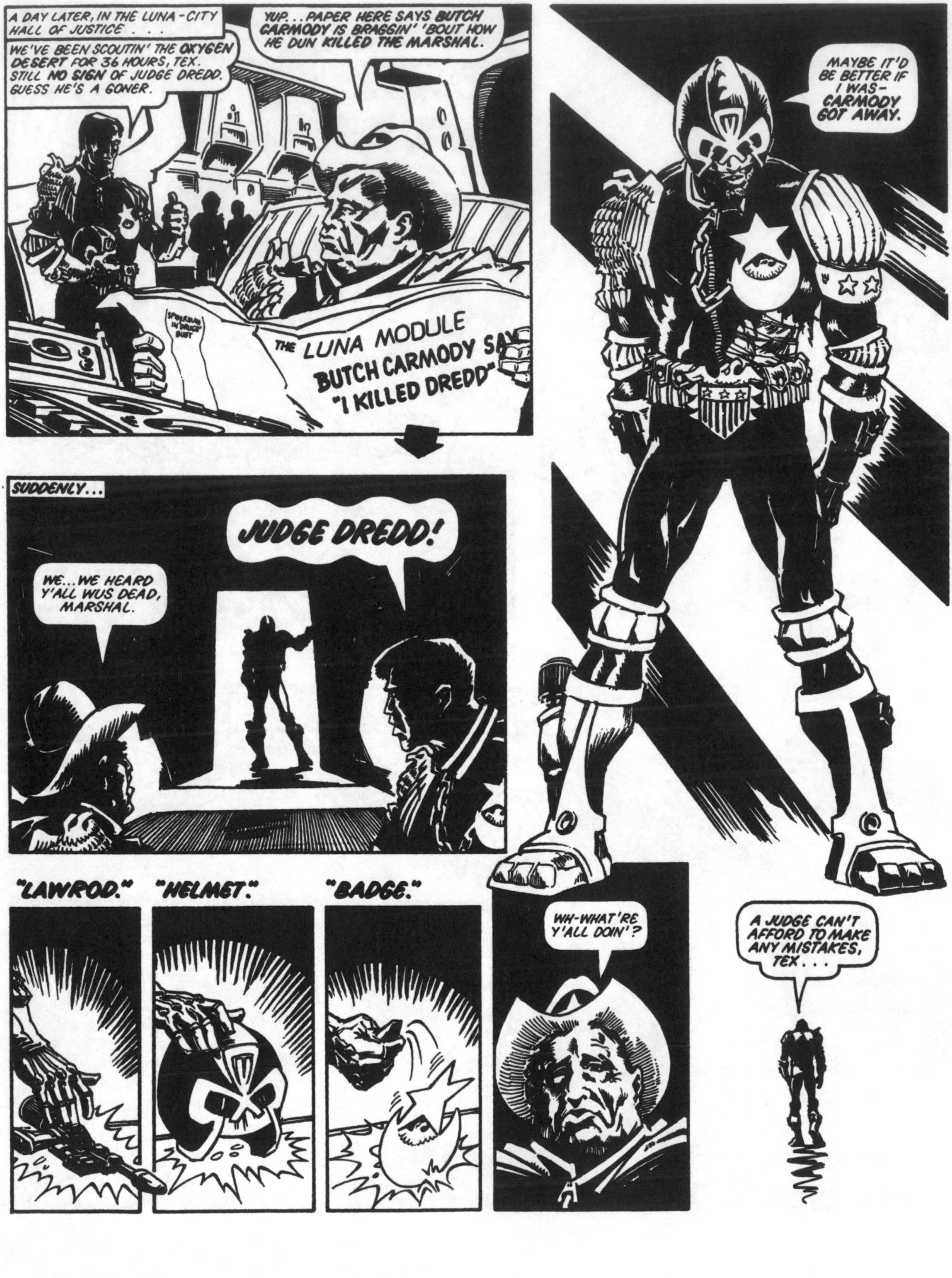

A DAY LATER, IN THE LUNA-CITY HALL OF JUSTICE . . .
WE'VE BEEN SCOUTIN' THE OXYGEN DESERT FOR 36 HOURS, TEX. STILL NO SIGN OF JUDGE DREDD. GUESS HE'S A GONER.
YUP...PAPER HERE SAYS BUTCH CARMODY IS BRAGGIN' 'BOUT HOW HE DUN KILLED THE MARSHAL.
THE LUNA MODULE
BUTCH CARMODY SAY
"I KILLED DREDD"
SUDDENLY...
JUDGE DREDD!
WE...WE HEARD Y'ALL WUS DEAD, MARSHAL.
MAYBE IT'D BE BETTER IF I WAS- CARMODY GOT AWAY.
"LAWROD."
"HELMET."
"BADGE."
WH-WHAT'RE Y'ALL DOIN'?
A JUDGE CAN'T AFFORD TO MAKE ANY MISTAKES, TEX . . .

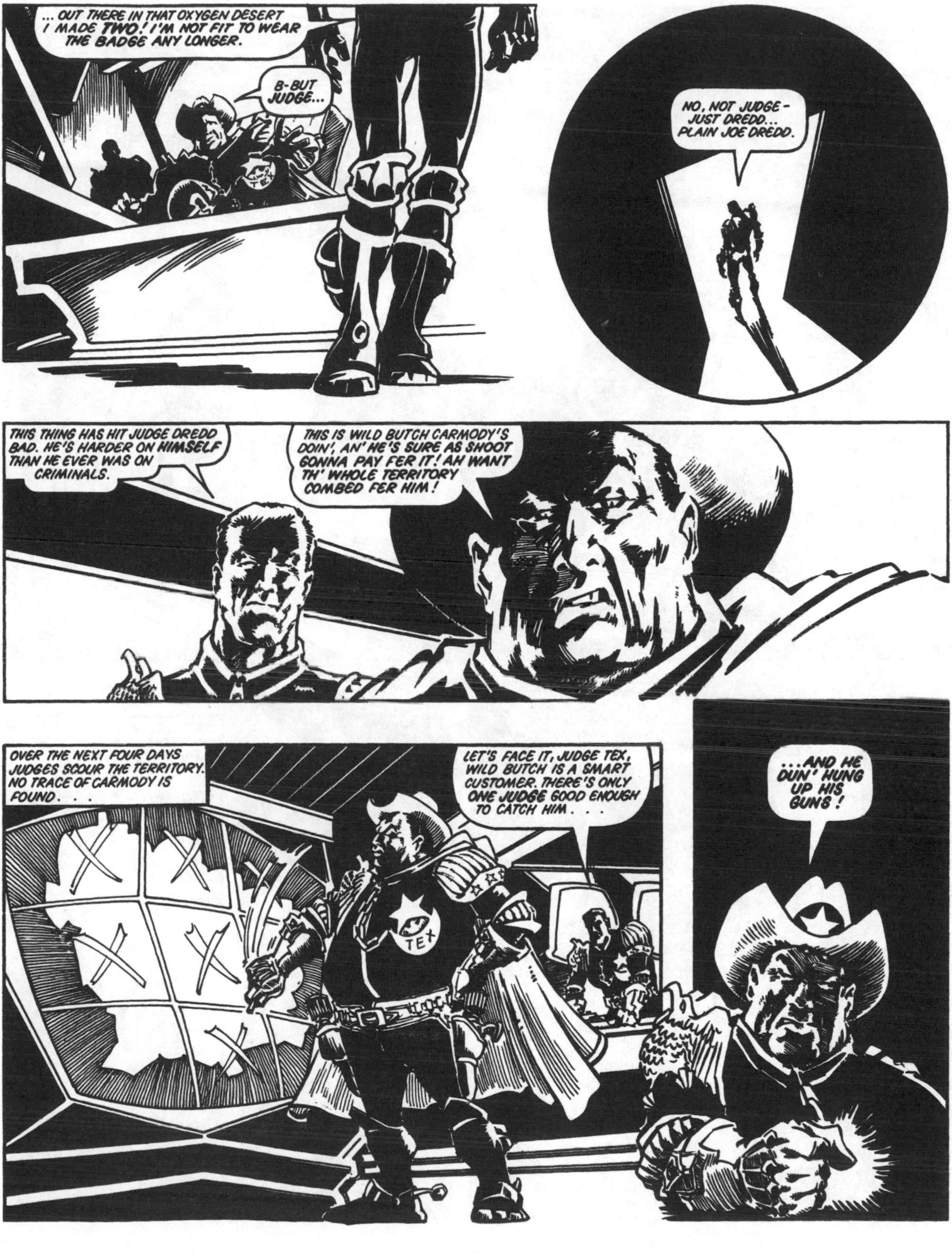
... OUT THERE IN THAT OXYGEN DESERT I MADE TWO! I'M NOT FIT TO WEAR THE BADGE ANY LONGER.
B-BUT JUDGE...
NO, NOT JUDGE - JUST DREDD... PLAIN JOE DREDD.
THIS THING HAS HIT JUDGE DREDD BAD. HE'S HARDER ON HIMSELF THAN HE EVER WAS ON CRIMINALS.
THIS IS WILD BUTCH CARMODY'S DOIN', AN' HE'S SURE AS SHOOT GONNA PAY FER IT! AH WANT TH' WHOLE TERRITORY COMBED FER HIM!
OVER THE NEXT FOUR DAYS JUDGES SCOUR THE TERRITORY. NO TRACE OF CARMODY IS FOUND . . .
LET'S FACE IT, JUDGE TEX, WILD BUTCH IS A SMART CUSTOMER. THERE'S ONLY ONE JUDGE GOOD ENOUGH TO CATCH HIM . . .
TEX
...AND HE DUN' HUNG UP HIS GUNS!

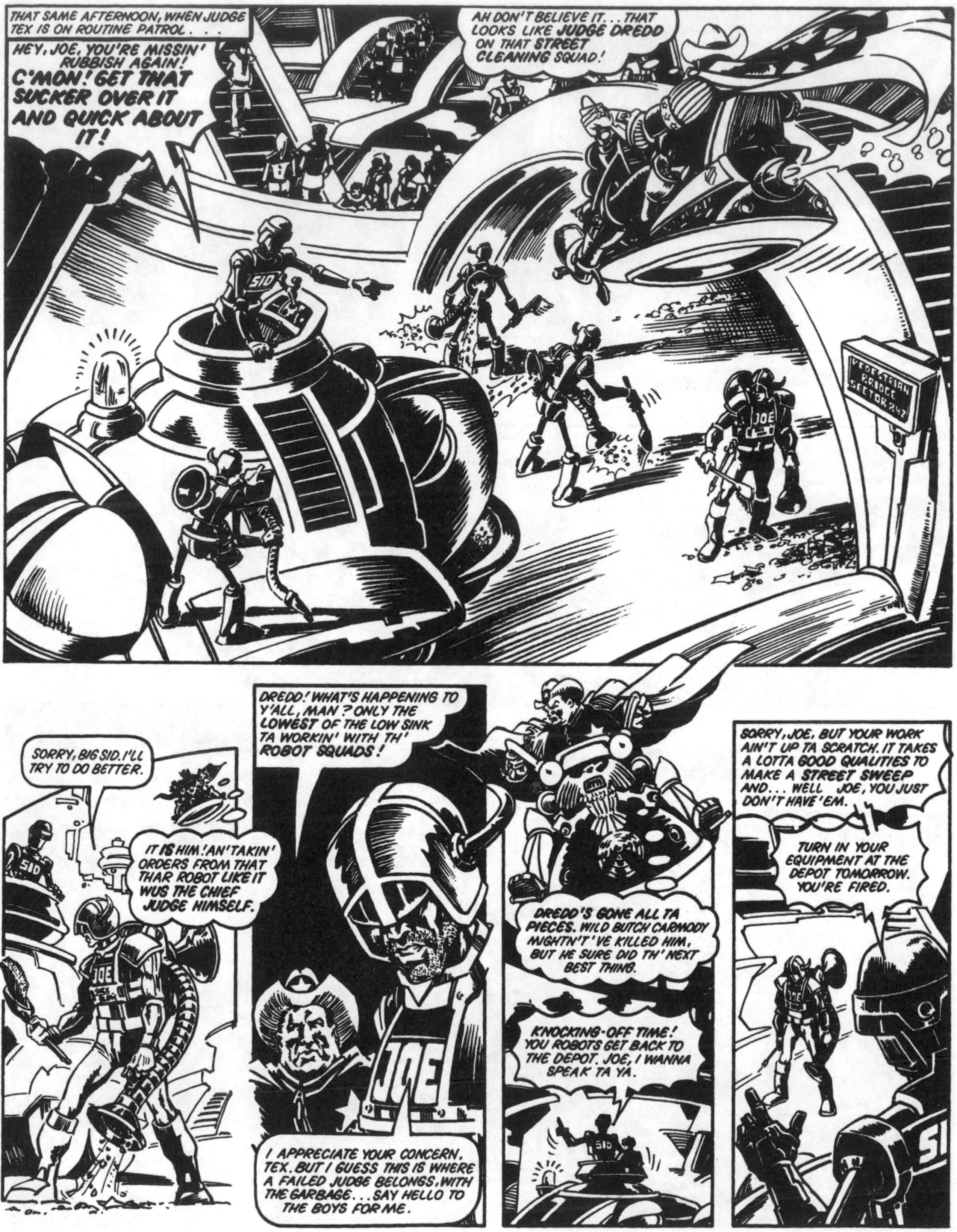
THAT SAME AFTERNOON, WHEN JUDGE TEX IS ON ROUTINE PATROL . . .
HEY, JOE, YOU'RE MISSIN' RUBBISH AGAIN!
C'MON! GET THAT SUCKER OVER IT AND QUICK ABOUT IT!
AH DON'T BELIEVE IT... THAT LOOKS LIKE JUDGE DREDD ON THAT STREET CLEANING SQUAD!
SORRY, BIG SID. I'LL TRY TO DO BETTER.
IT IS HIM! AN' TAKIN' ORDERS FROM THAT THAR ROBOT LIKE IT WUS THE CHIEF JUDGE HIMSELF.
DREDD! WHAT'S HAPPENING TO Y'ALL, MAN? ONLY THE LOWEST OF THE LOW SINK TA WORKIN' WITH TH' ROBOT SQUADS!
I APPRECIATE YOUR CONCERN, TEX. BUT I GUESS THIS IS WHERE A FAILED JUDGE BELONGS, WITH THE GARBAGE... SAY HELLO TO THE BOYS FOR ME.
DREDD'S GONE ALL TA PIECES. WILD BUTCH CARMODY MIGHTN'T 'VE KILLED HIM, BUT HE SURE DID TH' NEXT BEST THING.
KNOCKING-OFF TIME! YOU ROBOTS GET BACK TO THE DEPOT. JOE, I WANNA SPEAK TA YA.
SORRY, JOE, BUT YOUR WORK AIN'T UP TA SCRATCH. IT TAKES A LOTTA GOOD QUALITIES TO MAKE A STREET SWEEP AND... WELL JOE, YOU JUST DON'T HAVE 'EM.
TURN IN YOUR EQUIPMENT AT THE DEPOT TOMORROW. YOU'RE FIRED.

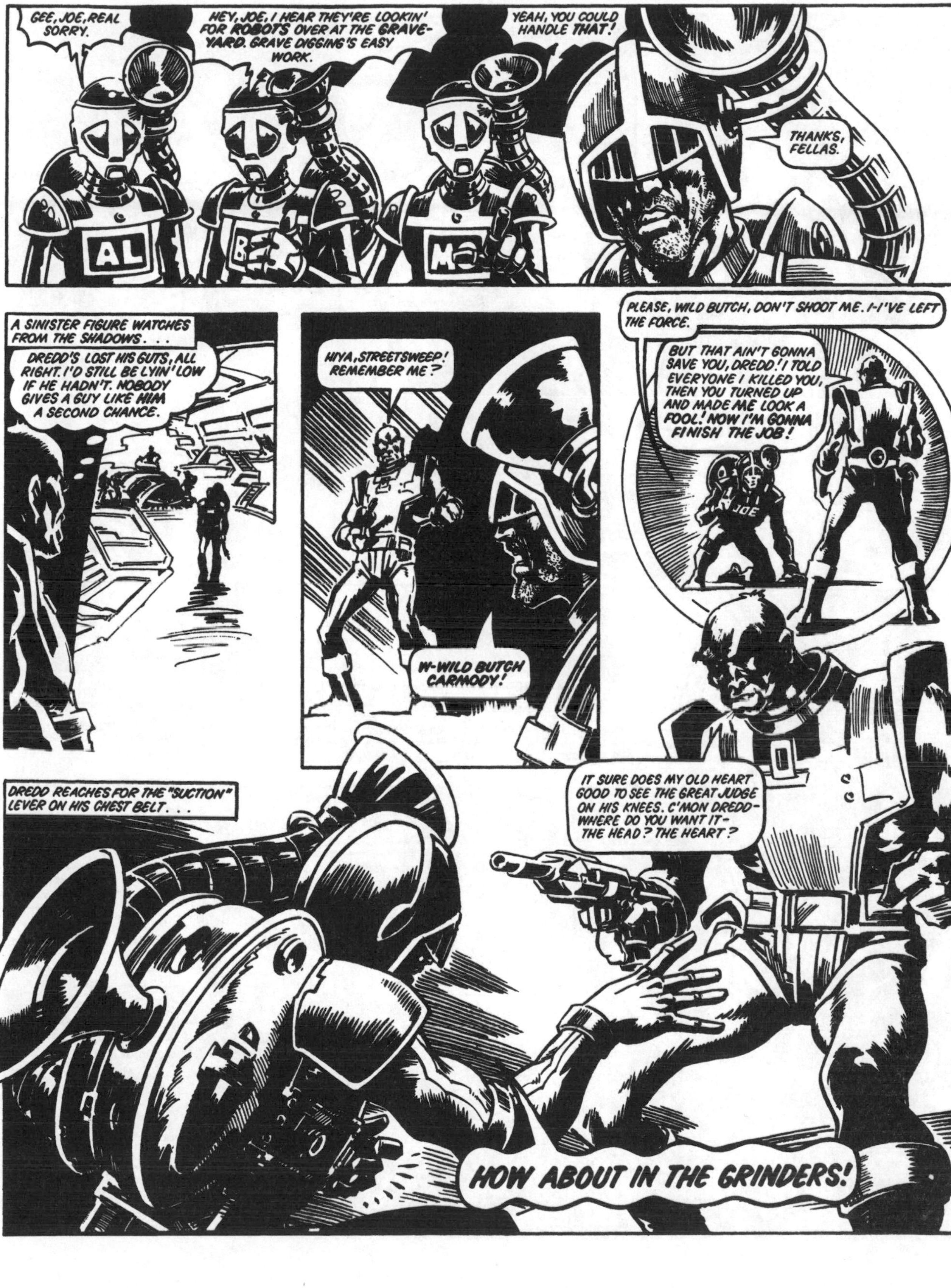
GEE, JOE, REAL SORRY.
HEY, JOE, I HEAR THEY'RE LOOKIN' FOR ROBOTS OVER AT THE GRAVE-YARD. GRAVE DIGGING'S EASY WORK.
YEAH, YOU COULD HANDLE THAT!
THANKS, FELLAS.
AL
JOE
A SINISTER FIGURE WATCHES FROM THE SHADOWS . . .
DREDD'S LOST HIS GUTS, ALL RIGHT. I'D STILL BE LYIN' LOW IF HE HADN'T. NOBODY GIVES A GUY LIKE HIM A SECOND CHANCE.
HIYA, STREETSWEEP! REMEMBER ME?
W-WILD BUTCH CARMODY!
PLEASE, WILD BUTCH, DON'T SHOOT ME. I-I'VE LEFT THE FORCE.
BUT THAT AIN'T GONNA SAVE YOU, DREDD! I TOLD EVERYONE I KILLED YOU, THEN YOU TURNED UP AND MADE ME LOOK A FOOL! NOW I'M GONNA FINISH THE JOB!
DREDD REACHES FOR THE "SUCTION" LEVER ON HIS CHEST BELT . . .
IT SURE DOES MY OLD HEART GOOD TO SEE THE GREAT JUDGE ON HIS KNEES. C'MON DREDD-WHERE DO YOU WANT IT-THE HEAD? THE HEART?
HOW ABOUT IN THE GRINDERS!

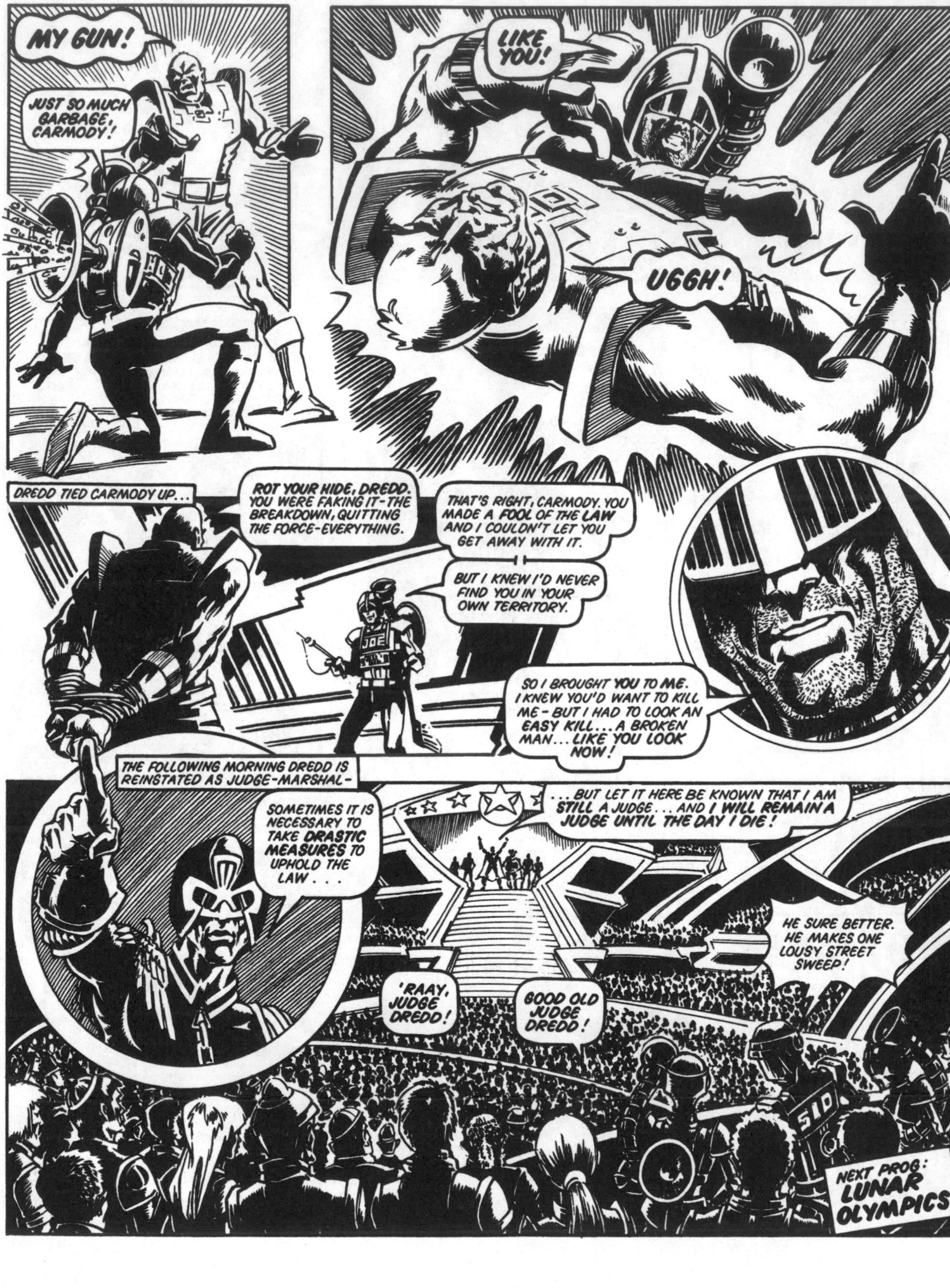

MY GUN!
JUST SO MUCH GARBAGE, CARMODY!
LIKE YOU!
UGGH!
DREDD TIED CARMODY UP...
ROT YOUR HIDE, DREDD. YOU WERE FAKING IT - THE BREAKDOWN, QUITTING THE FORCE - EVERYTHING.
THAT'S RIGHT, CARMODY. YOU MADE A FOOL OF THE LAW AND I COULDN'T LET YOU GET AWAY WITH IT.
BUT I KNEW I'D NEVER FIND YOU IN YOUR OWN TERRITORY.
SO I BROUGHT YOU TO ME. I KNEW YOU'D WANT TO KILL ME - BUT I HAD TO LOOK AN EASY KILL... A BROKEN MAN... LIKE YOU LOOK NOW!
THE FOLLOWING MORNING DREDD IS REINSTATED AS JUDGE-MARSHAL -
SOMETIMES IT IS NECESSARY TO TAKE DRASTIC MEASURES TO UPHOLD THE LAW . . .
... BUT LET IT HERE BE KNOWN THAT I AM STILL A JUDGE... AND I WILL REMAIN A JUDGE UNTIL THE DAY I DIE!
HE SURE BETTER. HE MAKES ONE LOUSY STREET SWEEP!
'RAAY, JUDGE DREDD!
GOOD OLD JUDGE DREDD!
NEXT PROG: LUNAR OLYMPICS.

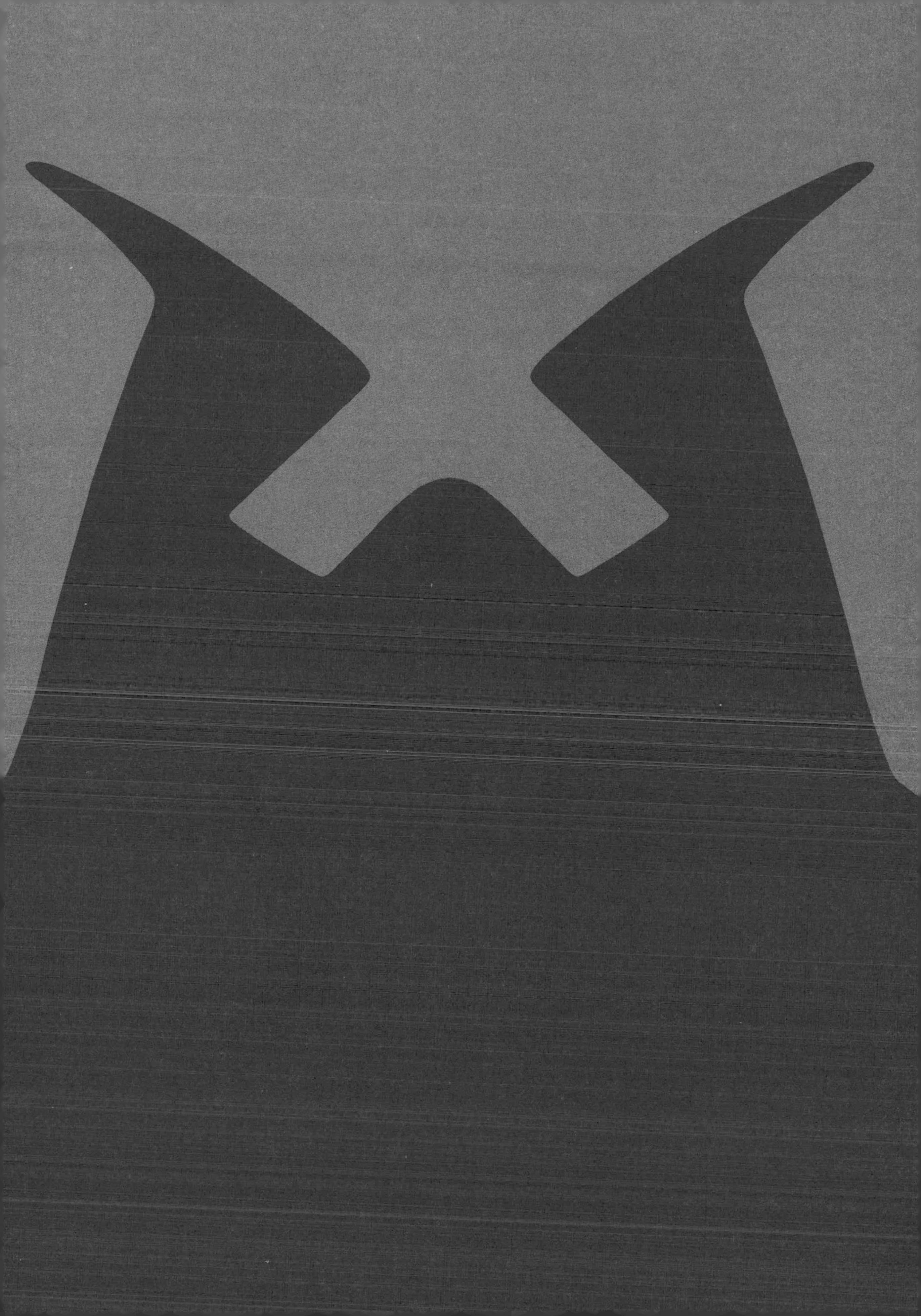

The First LUNAR OLYMPICS

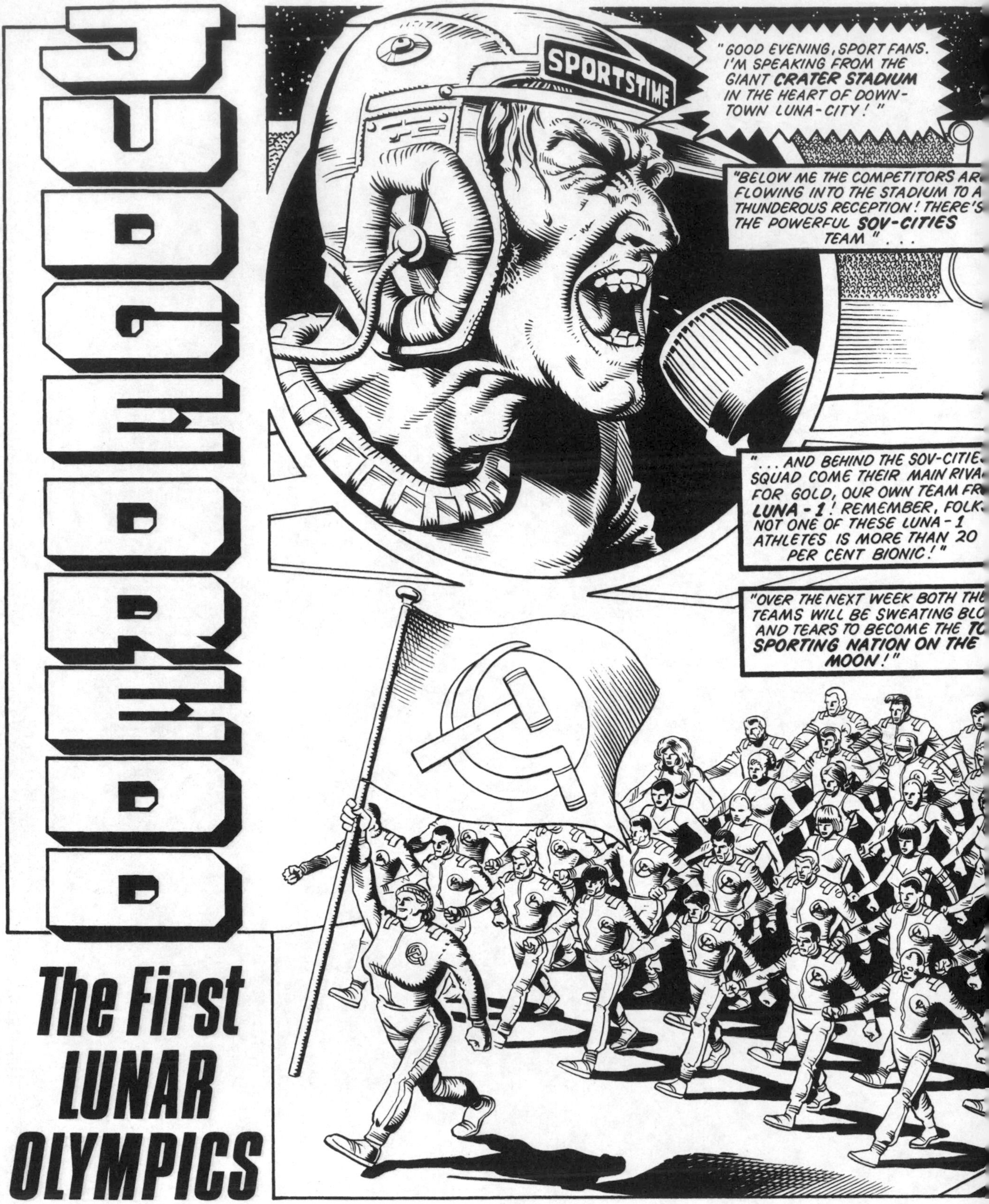
JUDGE DREDD
SPORTSTIME
"GOOD EVENING, SPORT FANS. I'M SPEAKING FROM THE GIANT CRATER STADIUM IN THE HEART OF DOWN-TOWN LUNA-CITY!"
"BELOW ME THE COMPETITORS AR FLOWING INTO THE STADIUM TO A THUNDEROUS RECEPTION! THERE'S THE POWERFUL SOV-CITIES TEAM" . . .
". . . AND BEHIND THE SOV-CITIES SQUAD COME THEIR MAIN RIVA FOR GOLD, OUR OWN TEAM FR LUNA - 1! REMEMBER, FOLK NOT ONE OF THESE LUNA - 1 ATHLETES IS MORE THAN 20 PER CENT BIONIC!"
"OVER THE NEXT WEEK BOTH TH TEAMS WILL BE SWEATING BLO AND TEARS TO BECOME THE TO SPORTING NATION ON THE MOON!"

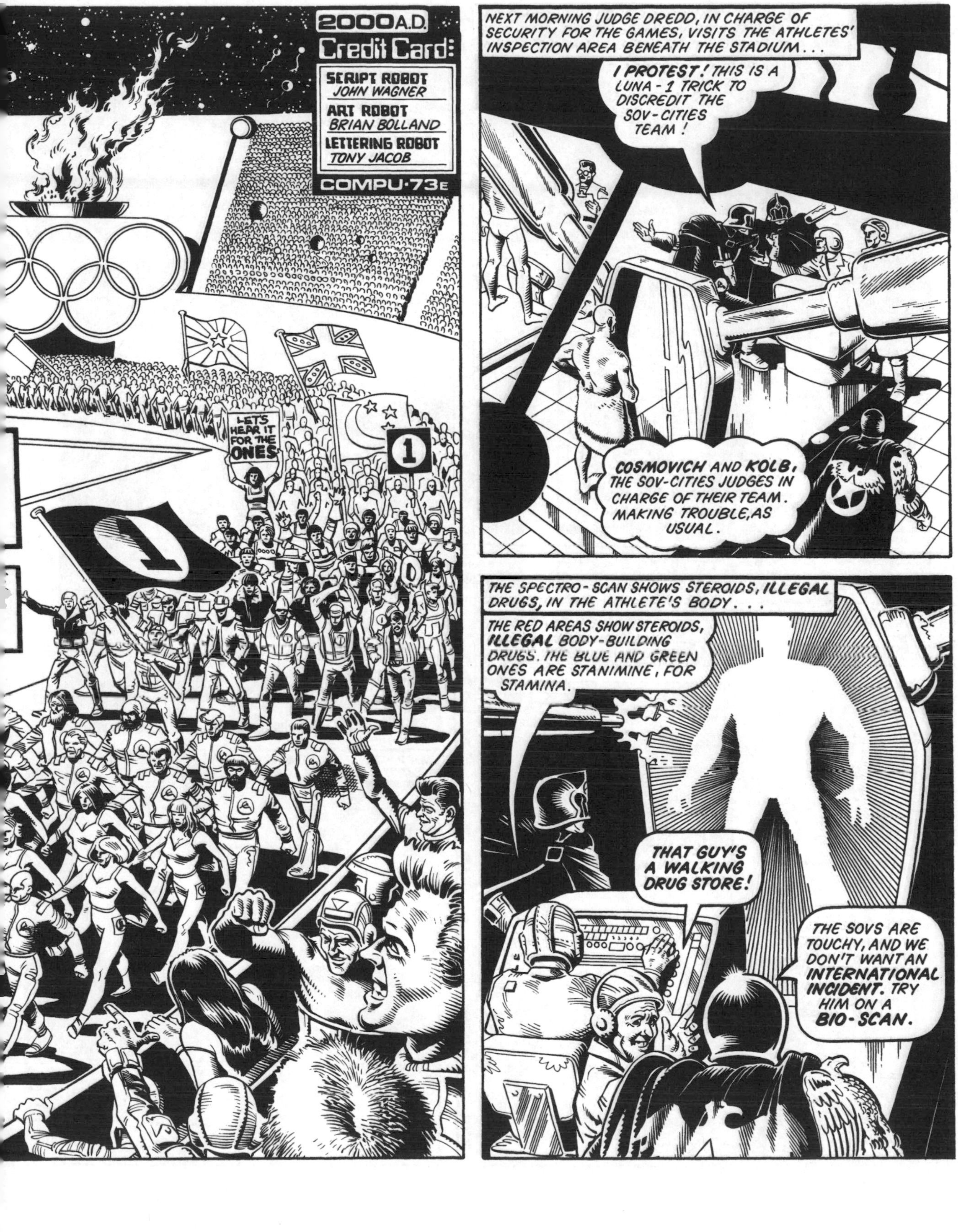
2000 A.D.
Credit Card:
SCRIPT ROBOT JOHN WAGNER
ART ROBOT BRIAN BOLLAND
LETTERING ROBOT TONY JACOB
COMPU-73E
LET'S HEAR IT FOR THE ONES
NEXT MORNING JUDGE DREDD, IN CHARGE OF SECURITY FOR THE GAMES, VISITS THE ATHLETES' INSPECTION AREA BENEATH THE STADIUM . . .
I PROTEST! THIS IS A LUNA-1 TRICK TO DISCREDIT THE SOV-CITIES TEAM!
COSMOVICH AND KOLB, THE SOV-CITIES JUDGES IN CHARGE OF THEIR TEAM. MAKING TROUBLE, AS USUAL.
THE SPECTRO-SCAN SHOWS STEROIDS, ILLEGAL DRUGS, IN THE ATHLETE'S BODY . . .
THE RED AREAS SHOW STEROIDS, ILLEGAL BODY-BUILDING DRUGS. THE BLUE AND GREEN ONES ARE STANIMINE, FOR STAMINA.
THAT GUY'S A WALKING DRUG STORE!
THE SOVS ARE TOUCHY, AND WE DON'T WANT AN INTERNATIONAL INCIDENT. TRY HIM ON A BIO-SCAN.

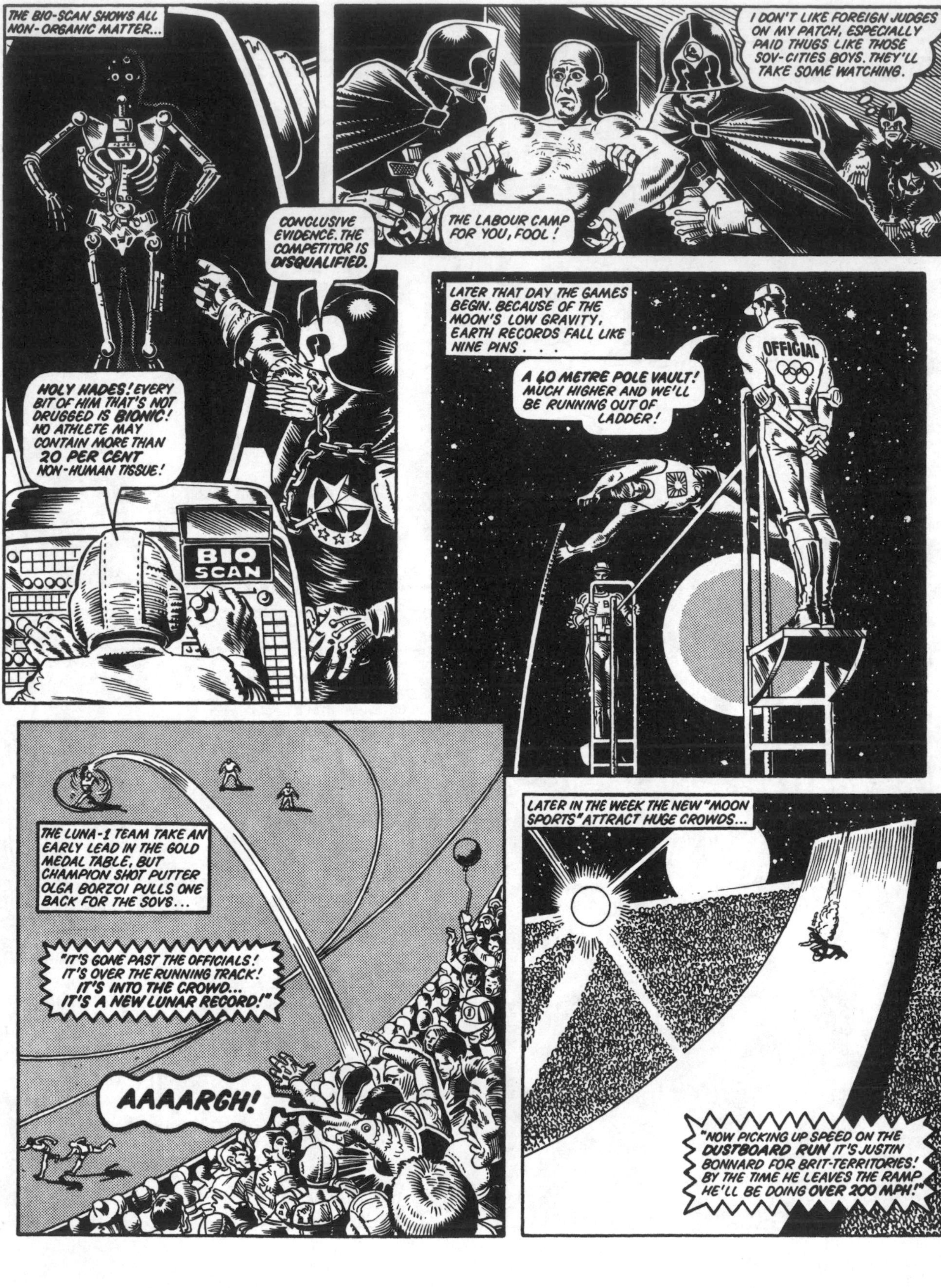
THE BIO-SCAN SHOWS ALL NON-ORGANIC MATTER...
HOLY HADES! EVERY BIT OF HIM THAT'S NOT DRUGGED IS BIONIC! NO ATHLETE MAY CONTAIN MORE THAN 20 PER CENT NON-HUMAN TISSUE!
CONCLUSIVE EVIDENCE. THE COMPETITOR IS DISQUALIFIED.
BIO SCAN
THE LABOUR CAMP FOR YOU, FOOL!
I DON'T LIKE FOREIGN JUDGES ON MY PATCH, ESPECIALLY PAID THUGS LIKE THOSE SOV-CITIES BOYS. THEY'LL TAKE SOME WATCHING.
LATER THAT DAY THE GAMES BEGIN. BECAUSE OF THE MOON'S LOW GRAVITY, EARTH RECORDS FALL LIKE NINE PINS . . .
A 60 METRE POLE VAULT! MUCH HIGHER AND WE'LL BE RUNNING OUT OF LADDER!
OFFICIAL
THE LUNA-1 TEAM TAKE AN EARLY LEAD IN THE GOLD MEDAL TABLE, BUT CHAMPION SHOT PUTTER OLGA BORZOI PULLS ONE BACK FOR THE SOVS...
"IT'S GONE PAST THE OFFICIALS! IT'S OVER THE RUNNING TRACK! IT'S INTO THE CROWD... IT'S A NEW LUNAR RECORD!"
AAAARGH!
LATER IN THE WEEK THE NEW "MOON SPORTS" ATTRACT HUGE CROWDS...
"NOW PICKING UP SPEED ON THE DUSTBOARD RUN IT'S JUSTIN BONNARD FOR BRIT-TERRITORIES! BY THE TIME HE LEAVES THE RAMP HE'LL BE DOING OVER 200 MPH!"

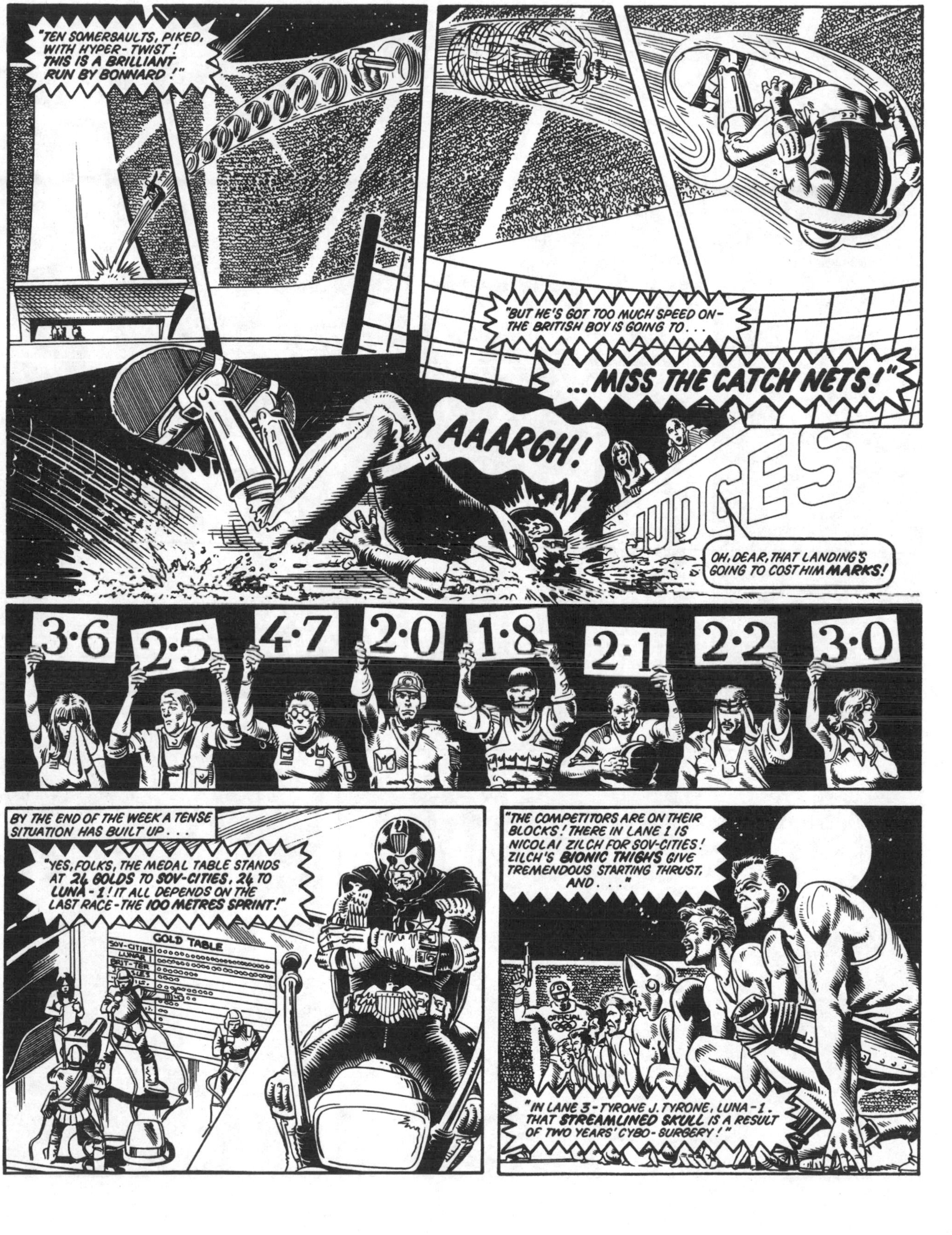
"TEN SOMERSAULTS, PIKED, WITH HYPER-TWIST! THIS IS A BRILLIANT RUN BY BONNARD!"
"BUT HE'S GOT TOO MUCH SPEED ON- THE BRITISH BOY IS GOING TO . . .
... MISS THE CATCH NETS!"
AAARGH!
JUDGES
OH, DEAR, THAT LANDING'S GOING TO COST HIM MARKS!
3·6
2·5
4·7
2·0
1·8
2·1
2·2
3·0
BY THE END OF THE WEEK A TENSE SITUATION HAS BUILT UP . . .
"YES, FOLKS, THE MEDAL TABLE STANDS AT 24 GOLDS TO SOV-CITIES, 24 TO LUNA-1! IT ALL DEPENDS ON THE LAST RACE-THE 100 METRES SPRINT!"
GOLD TABLE
SOV-CITIES
LUNA
"THE COMPETITORS ARE ON THEIR BLOCKS! THERE IN LANE 1 IS NICOLAI ZILCH FOR SOV-CITIES! ZILCH'S BIONIC THIGHS GIVE TREMENDOUS STARTING THRUST, AND . . ."
OFFICIAL
"IN LANE 3-TYRONE J. TYRONE, LUNA-1. THAT STREAMLINED SKULL IS A RESULT OF TWO YEARS' CYBO-SURGERY!"

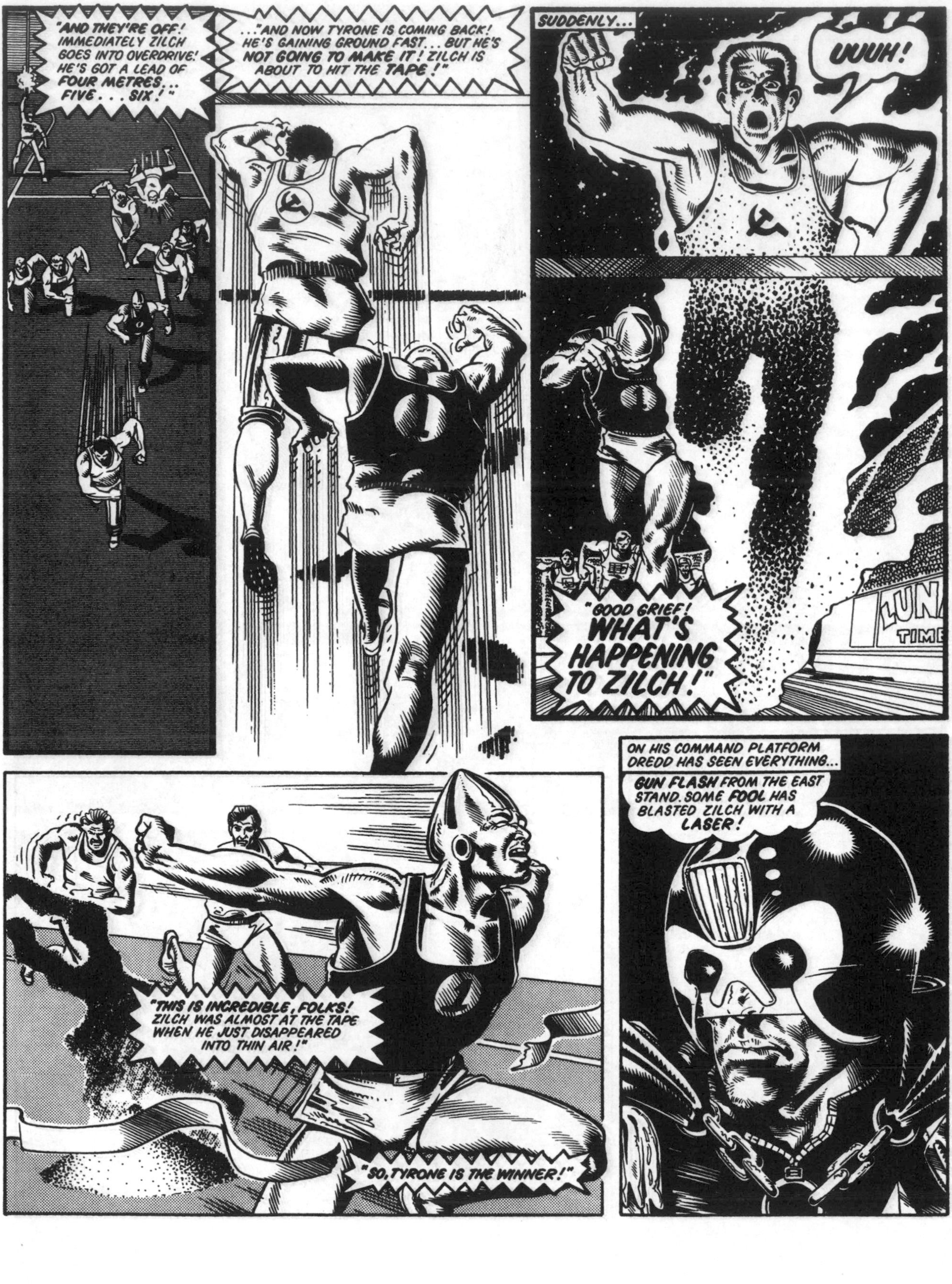
"AND THEY'RE OFF! IMMEDIATELY ZILCH GOES INTO OVERDRIVE! HE'S GOT A LEAD OF FOUR METRES... FIVE . . . SIX!"
..."AND NOW TYRONE IS COMING BACK! HE'S GAINING GROUND FAST... BUT HE'S NOT GOING TO MAKE IT! ZILCH IS ABOUT TO HIT THE TAPE!"
SUDDENLY...
UUUH!
"GOOD GRIEF! WHAT'S HAPPENING TO ZILCH!"
"THIS IS INCREDIBLE, FOLKS! ZILCH WAS ALMOST AT THE TAPE WHEN HE JUST DISAPPEARED INTO THIN AIR!"
"SO, TYRONE IS THE WINNER!"
ON HIS COMMAND PLATFORM DREDD HAS SEEN EVERYTHING...
GUN FLASH FROM THE EAST STAND. SOME FOOL HAS BLASTED ZILCH WITH A LASER!

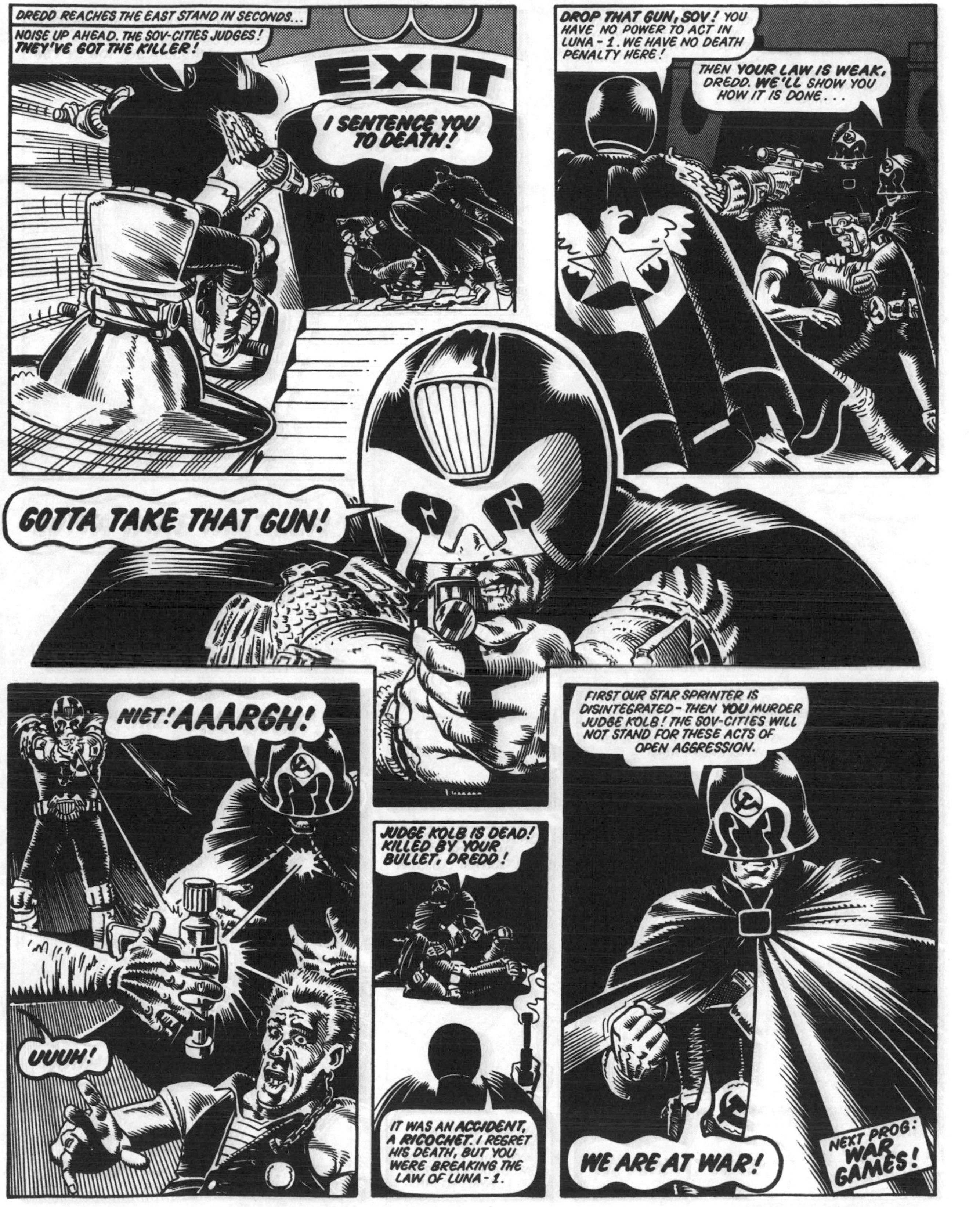

DREDD REACHES THE EAST STAND IN SECONDS...
NOISE UP AHEAD. THE SOV-CITIES JUDGES! THEY'VE GOT THE KILLER!
EXIT
I SENTENCE YOU TO DEATH!
DROP THAT GUN, SOV! YOU HAVE NO POWER TO ACT IN LUNA-1. WE HAVE NO DEATH PENALTY HERE!
THEN YOUR LAW IS WEAK, DREDD. WE'LL SHOW YOU HOW IT IS DONE...
GOTTA TAKE THAT GUN!
NIET! AAARGH!
UUUH!
JUDGE KOLB IS DEAD! KILLED BY YOUR BULLET, DREDD!
IT WAS AN ACCIDENT, A RICOCHET. I REGRET HIS DEATH, BUT YOU WERE BREAKING THE LAW OF LUNA-1.
FIRST OUR STAR SPRINTER IS DISINTEGRATED - THEN YOU MURDER JUDGE KOLB! THE SOV-CITIES WILL NOT STAND FOR THESE ACTS OF OPEN AGGRESSION.
WE ARE AT WAR!
NEXT PROG: WAR GAMES!

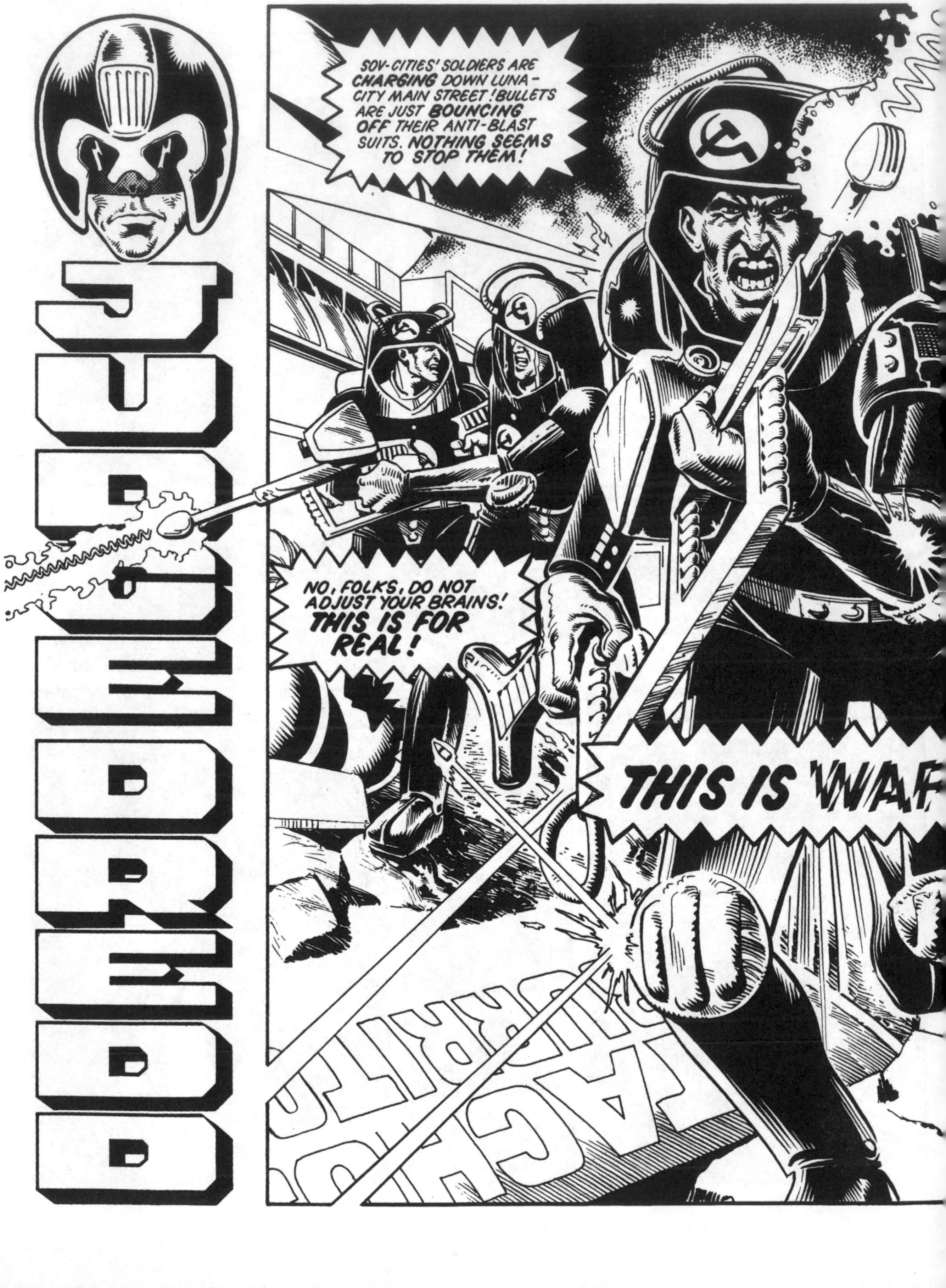
JUDGE DREDD
SOV-CITIES' SOLDIERS ARE CHARGING DOWN LUNA-CITY MAIN STREET! BULLETS ARE JUST BOUNCING OFF THEIR ANTI-BLAST SUITS. NOTHING SEEMS TO STOP THEM!
NO, FOLKS, DO NOT ADJUST YOUR BRAINS! THIS IS FOR REAL!
THIS IS WAR

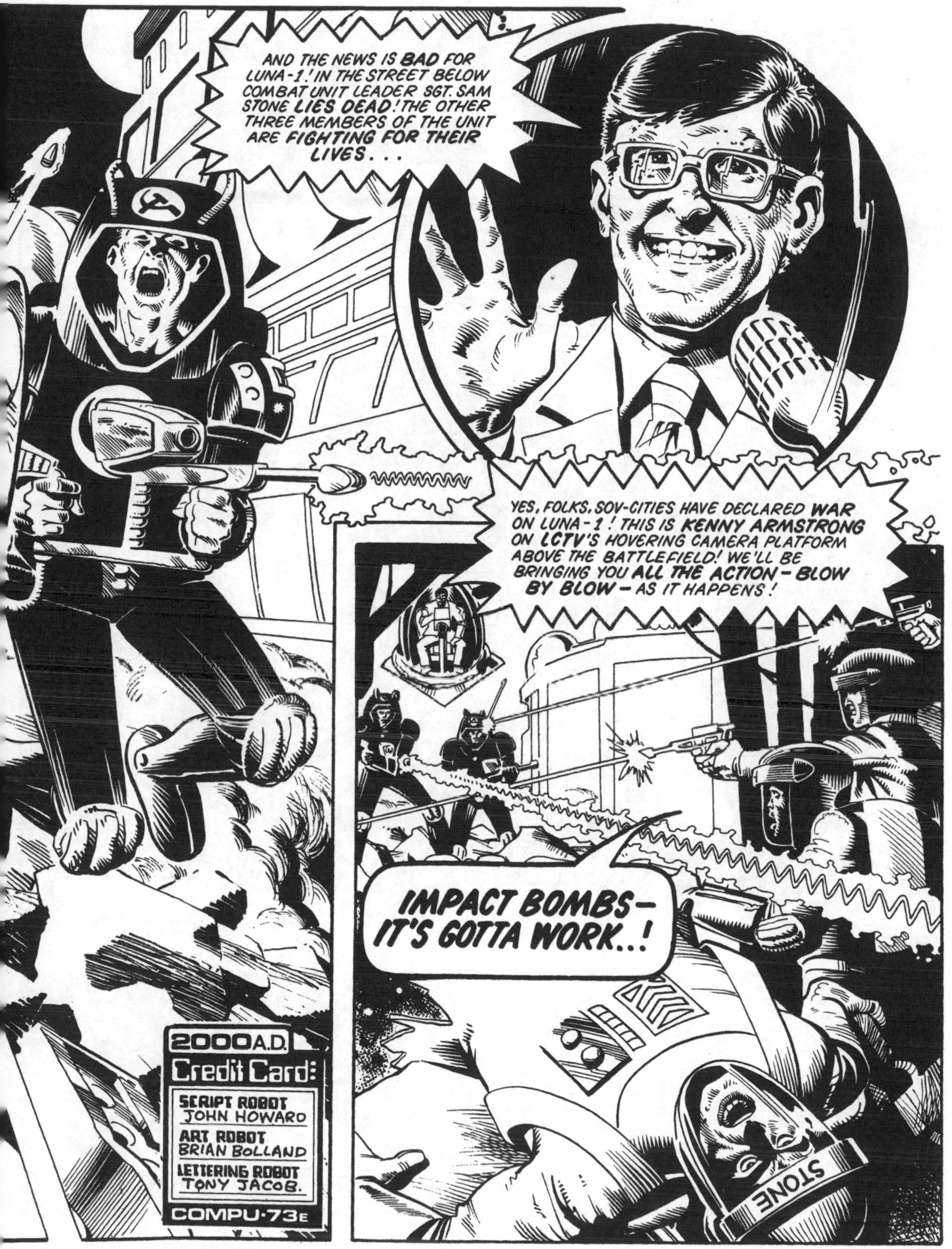
AND THE NEWS IS BAD FOR LUNA-1! IN THE STREET BELOW COMBAT UNIT LEADER SGT. SAM STONE LIES DEAD! THE OTHER THREE MEMBERS OF THE UNIT ARE FIGHTING FOR THEIR LIVES . . .
YES, FOLKS, SOV-CITIES HAVE DECLARED WAR ON LUNA-1! THIS IS KENNY ARMSTRONG ON LCTV'S HOVERING CAMERA PLATFORM ABOVE THE BATTLEFIELD! WE'LL BE BRINGING YOU ALL THE ACTION - BLOW BY BLOW - AS IT HAPPENS!
IMPACT BOMBS- IT'S GOTTA WORK..!
2000 A.D. Credit Card:
SCRIPT ROBOT JOHN HOWARD
ART ROBOT BRIAN BOLLAND
LETTERING ROBOT TONY JACOB.
COMPU-73E
STONE

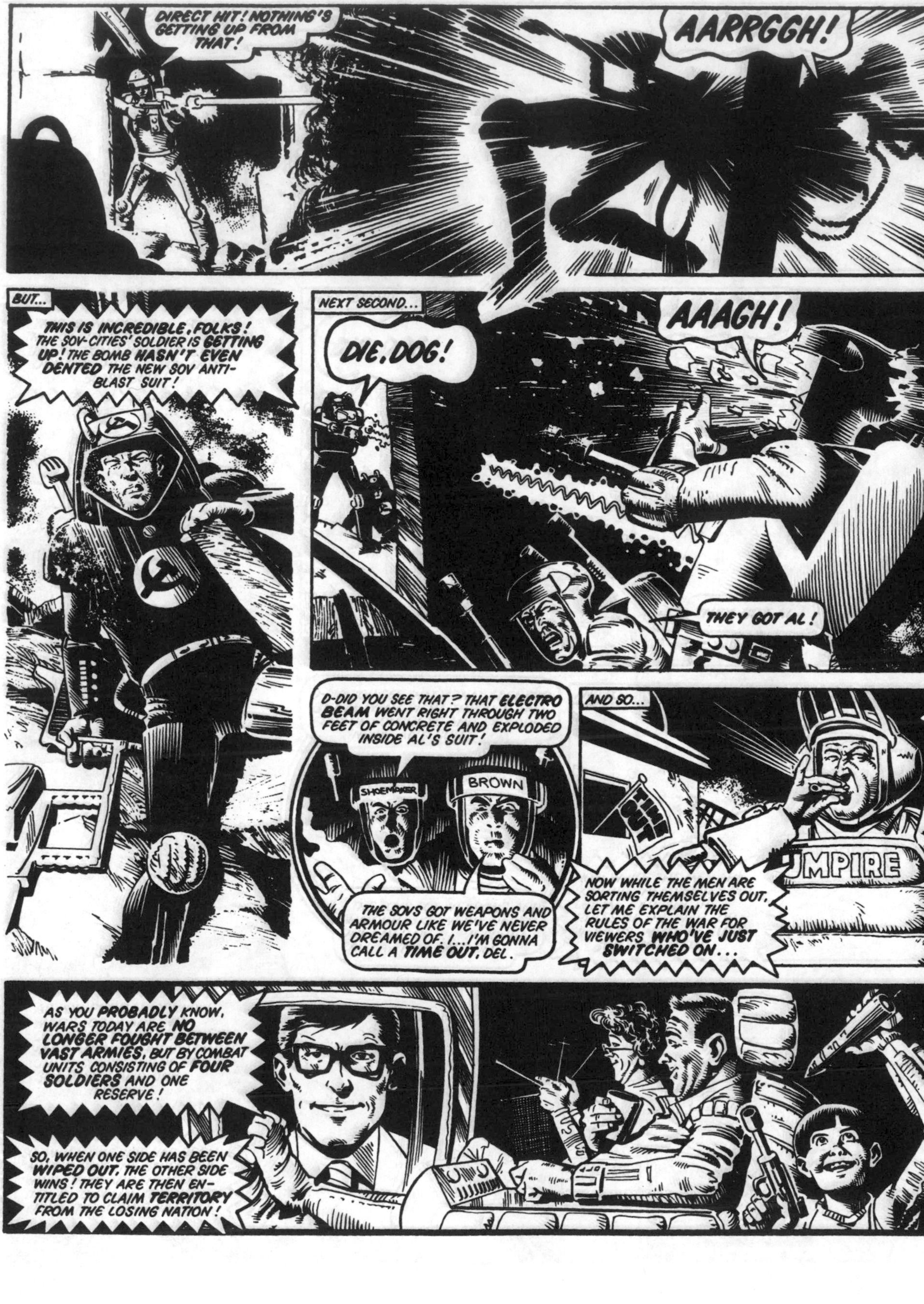

DIRECT HIT! NOTHING'S GETTING UP FROM THAT!
AARRGGH!
BUT...
THIS IS INCREDIBLE, FOLKS! THE SOV-CITIES' SOLDIER IS GETTING UP! THE BOMB HASN'T EVEN DENTED THE NEW SOV ANTI-BLAST SUIT!
NEXT SECOND...
DIE, DOG!
AAAGH!
THEY GOT AL!
D-DID YOU SEE THAT? THAT ELECTRO BEAM WENT RIGHT THROUGH TWO FEET OF CONCRETE AND EXPLODED INSIDE AL'S SUIT!
SHOEMAKER
BROWN
THE SOVS GOT WEAPONS AND ARMOUR LIKE WE'VE NEVER DREAMED OF. I...I'M GONNA CALL A TIME OUT, DEL.
AND SO...
TIME OUT
UMPIRE
NOW WHILE THE MEN ARE SORTING THEMSELVES OUT, LET ME EXPLAIN THE RULES OF THE WAR FOR VIEWERS WHO'VE JUST SWITCHED ON...
AS YOU PROBABLY KNOW, WARS TODAY ARE NO LONGER FOUGHT BETWEEN VAST ARMIES, BUT BY COMBAT UNITS CONSISTING OF FOUR SOLDIERS AND ONE RESERVE!
SO, WHEN ONE SIDE HAS BEEN WIPED OUT, THE OTHER SIDE WINS! THEY ARE THEN ENTITLED TO CLAIM TERRITORY FROM THE LOSING NATION!

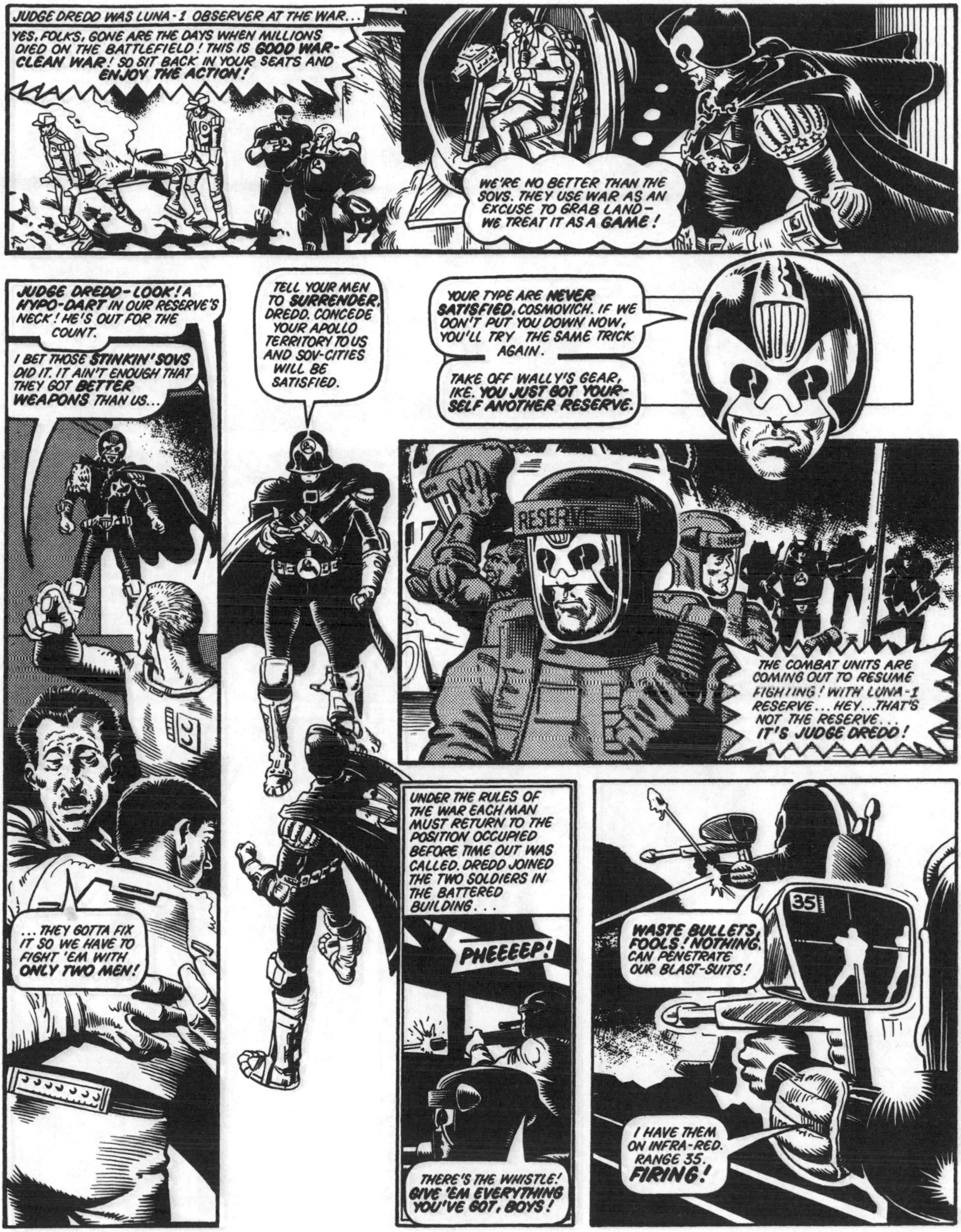

JUDGE DREDD WAS LUNA-1 OBSERVER AT THE WAR...
YES, FOLKS, GONE ARE THE DAYS WHEN MILLIONS DIED ON THE BATTLEFIELD! THIS IS GOOD WAR- CLEAN WAR! SO SIT BACK IN YOUR SEATS AND ENJOY THE ACTION!
WE'RE NO BETTER THAN THE SOVS. THEY USE WAR AS AN EXCUSE TO GRAB LAND- WE TREAT IT AS A GAME!
JUDGE DREDD- LOOK! A HYPO-DART IN OUR RESERVE'S NECK! HE'S OUT FOR THE COUNT.
I BET THOSE STINKIN' SOVS DID IT. IT AIN'T ENOUGH THAT THEY GOT BETTER WEAPONS THAN US...
... THEY GOTTA FIX IT SO WE HAVE TO FIGHT 'EM WITH ONLY TWO MEN!
TELL YOUR MEN TO SURRENDER, DREDD. CONCEDE YOUR APOLLO TERRITORY TO US AND SOV-CITIES WILL BE SATISFIED.
YOUR TYPE ARE NEVER SATISFIED, COSMOVICH. IF WE DON'T PUT YOU DOWN NOW, YOU'LL TRY THE SAME TRICK AGAIN.
TAKE OFF WALLY'S GEAR, IKE. YOU JUST GOT YOURSELF ANOTHER RESERVE.
RESERVE
THE COMBAT UNITS ARE COMING OUT TO RESUME FIGHTING! WITH LUNA-1 RESERVE... HEY... THAT'S NOT THE RESERVE... IT'S JUDGE DREDD!
UNDER THE RULES OF THE WAR EACH MAN MUST RETURN TO THE POSITION OCCUPIED BEFORE TIME OUT WAS CALLED. DREDD JOINED THE TWO SOLDIERS IN THE BATTERED BUILDING...
PHEEEEP!
THERE'S THE WHISTLE! GIVE 'EM EVERYTHING YOU'VE GOT, BOYS!
WASTE BULLETS, FOOLS! NOTHING CAN PENETRATE OUR BLAST-SUITS!
35
I HAVE THEM ON INFRA-RED. RANGE 35. FIRING!

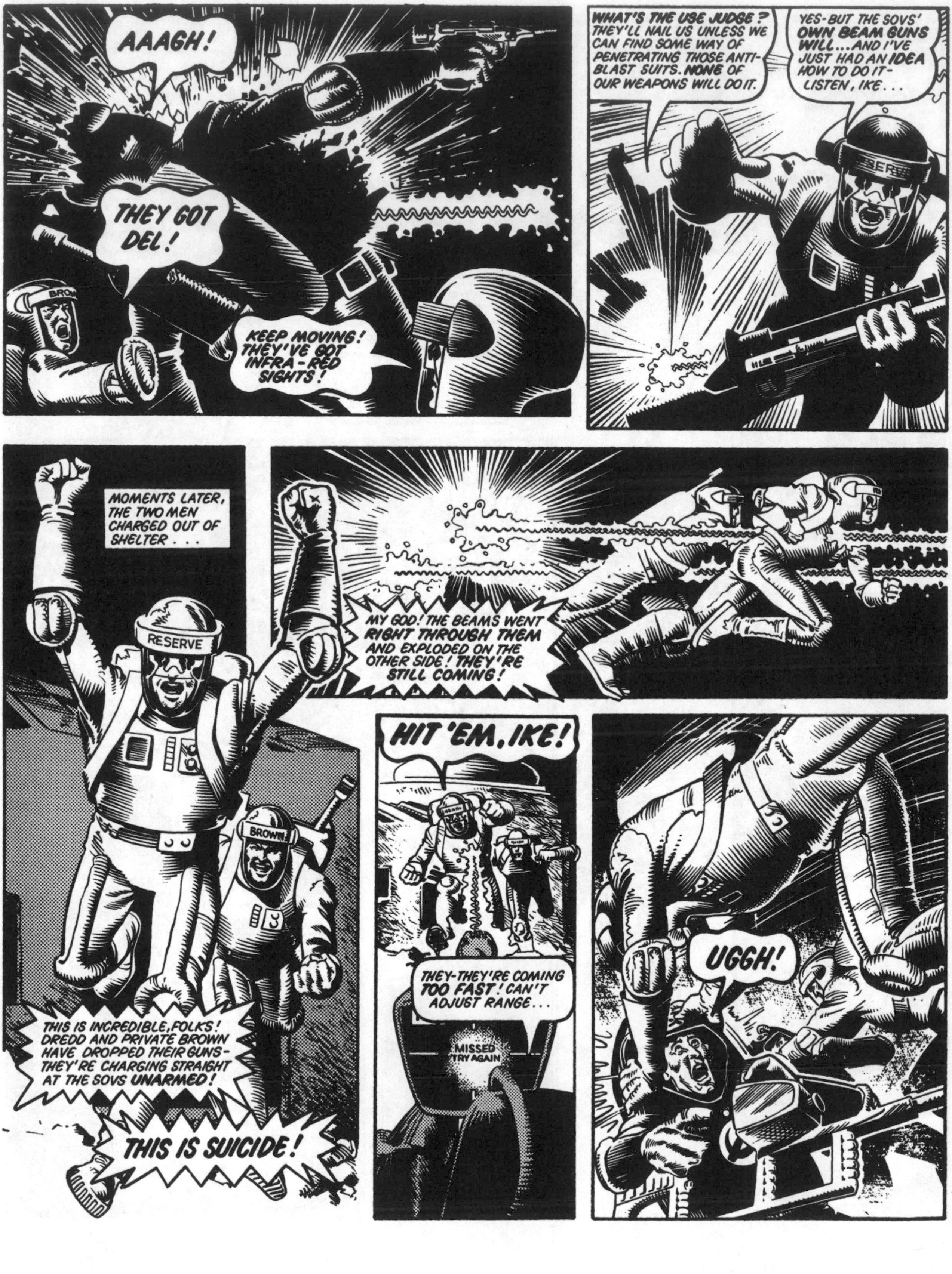

AAAGH!
THEY GOT DEL!
KEEP MOVING! THEY'VE GOT INFRA-RED SIGHTS!
WHAT'S THE USE JUDGE? THEY'LL NAIL US UNLESS WE CAN FIND SOME WAY OF PENETRATING THOSE ANTI-BLAST SUITS. NONE OF OUR WEAPONS WILL DO IT.
YES-BUT THE SOVS' OWN BEAM GUNS WILL... AND I'VE JUST HAD AN IDEA HOW TO DO IT-LISTEN, IKE...
MOMENTS LATER, THE TWO MEN CHARGED OUT OF SHELTER...
RESERVE
BROWN
THIS IS INCREDIBLE, FOLKS! DREDD AND PRIVATE BROWN HAVE DROPPED THEIR GUNS-THEY'RE CHARGING STRAIGHT AT THE SOVS UNARMED!
THIS IS SUICIDE!
MY GOD! THE BEAMS WENT RIGHT THROUGH THEM AND EXPLODED ON THE OTHER SIDE! THEY'RE STILL COMING!
HIT 'EM, IKE!
THEY-THEY'RE COMING TOO FAST! CAN'T ADJUST RANGE...
MISSED TRY AGAIN
UGGH!

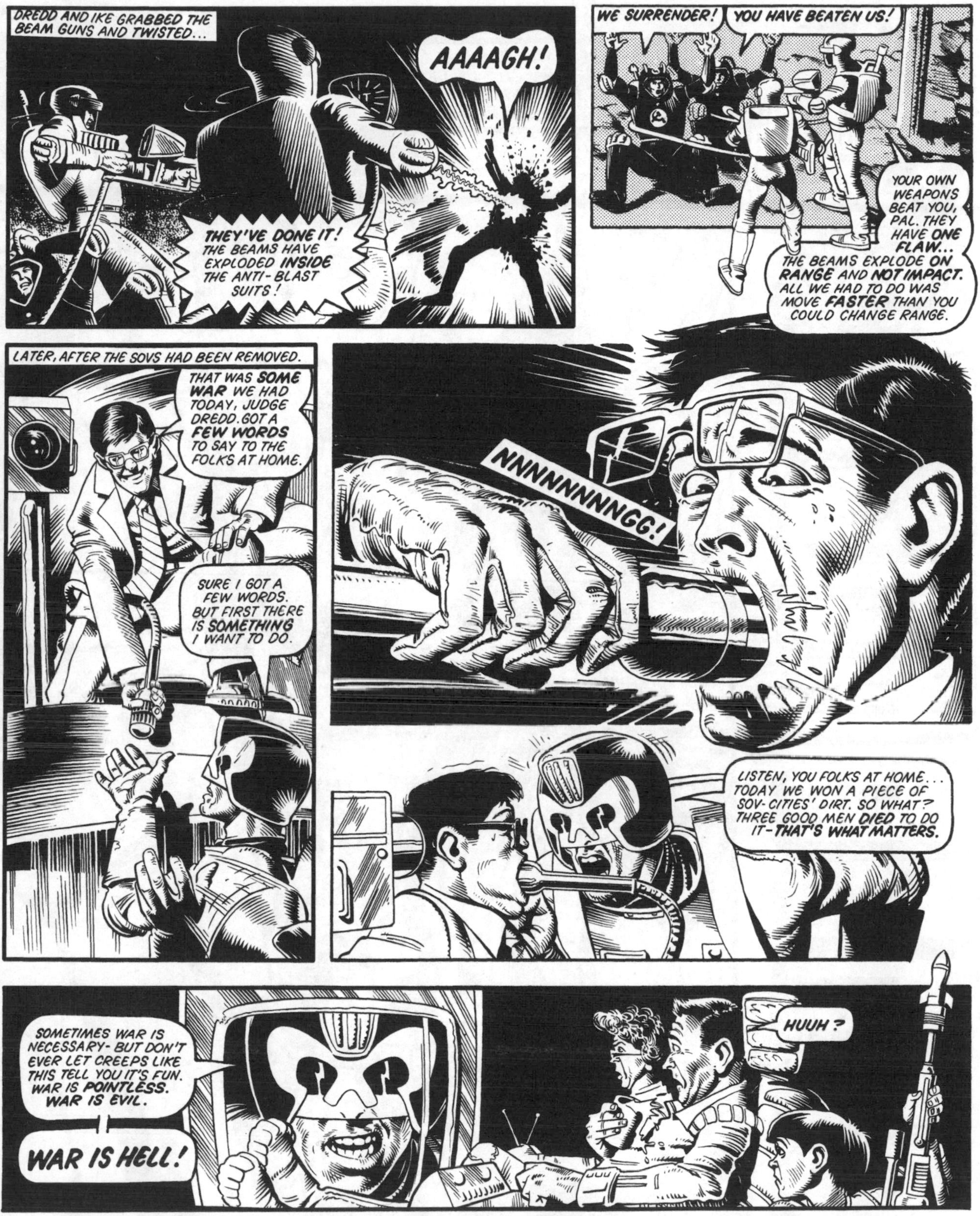
DREDD AND IKE GRABBED THE BEAM GUNS AND TWISTED...
AAAAGH!
THEY'VE DONE IT! THE BEAMS HAVE EXPLODED INSIDE THE ANTI-BLAST SUITS!
WE SURRENDER!
YOU HAVE BEATEN US!
YOUR OWN WEAPONS BEAT YOU, PAL. THEY HAVE ONE FLAW...
THE BEAMS EXPLODE ON RANGE AND NOT IMPACT. ALL WE HAD TO DO WAS MOVE FASTER THAN YOU COULD CHANGE RANGE.
LATER, AFTER THE SOVS HAD BEEN REMOVED.
THAT WAS SOME WAR WE HAD TODAY, JUDGE DREDD. GOT A FEW WORDS TO SAY TO THE FOLKS AT HOME.
SURE I GOT A FEW WORDS. BUT FIRST THERE IS SOMETHING I WANT TO DO.
NNNNNNNNNGG!
LISTEN, YOU FOLKS AT HOME... TODAY WE WON A PIECE OF SOV-CITIES' DIRT. SO WHAT? THREE GOOD MEN DIED TO DO IT- THAT'S WHAT MATTERS.
SOMETIMES WAR IS NECESSARY- BUT DON'T EVER LET CREEPS LIKE THIS TELL YOU IT'S FUN. WAR IS POINTLESS. WAR IS EVIL.
WAR IS HELL!
HUUH?

KEEP CALM + + + THRILL FACTOR OVERLOAD + + + KEEP CALM

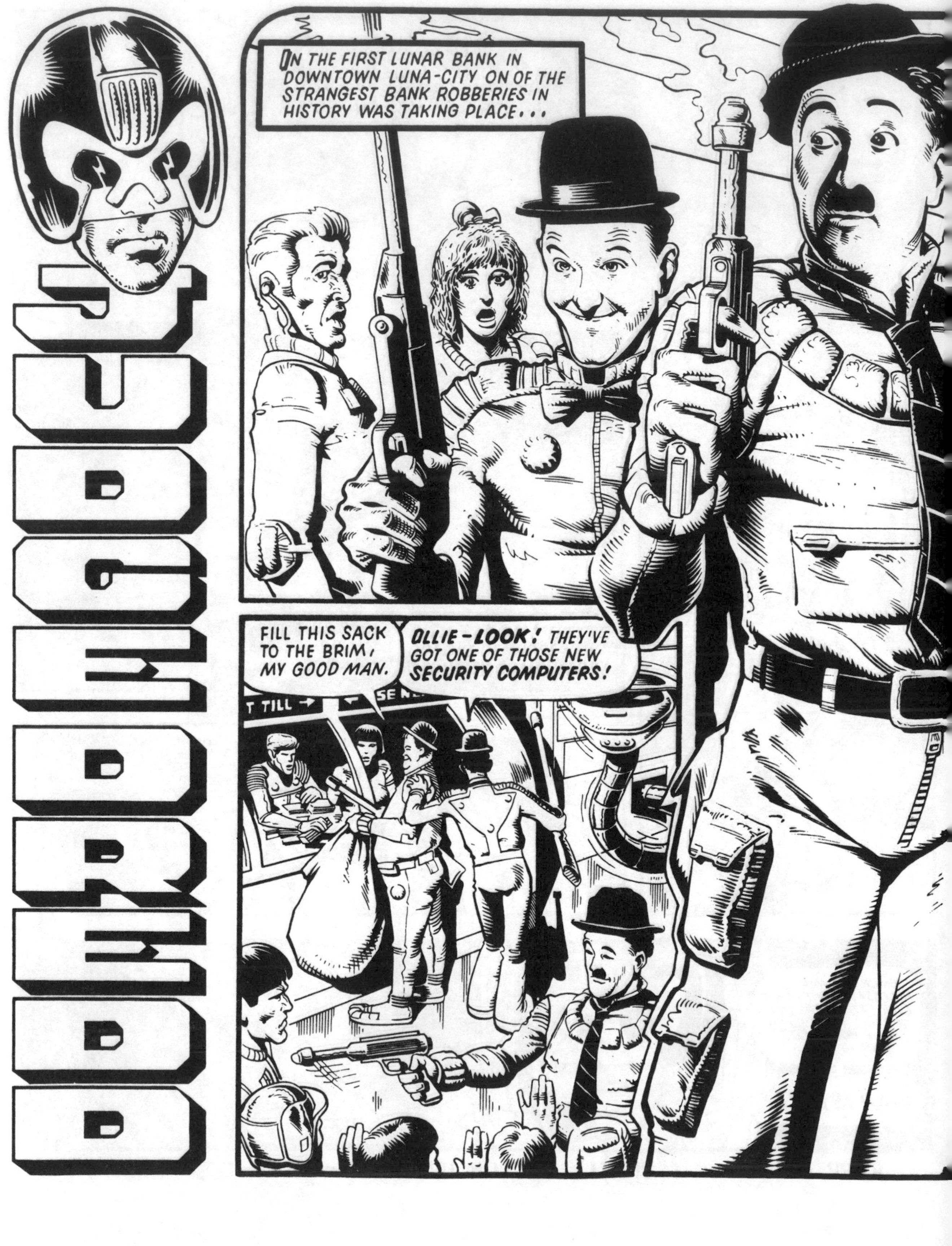
JUDGE DREDD
ON THE FIRST LUNAR BANK IN DOWNTOWN LUNA-CITY ON OF THE STRANGEST BANK ROBBERIES IN HISTORY WAS TAKING PLACE...
FILL THIS SACK TO THE BRIM, MY GOOD MAN.
OLLIE - LOOK! THEY'VE GOT ONE OF THOSE NEW SECURITY COMPUTERS!

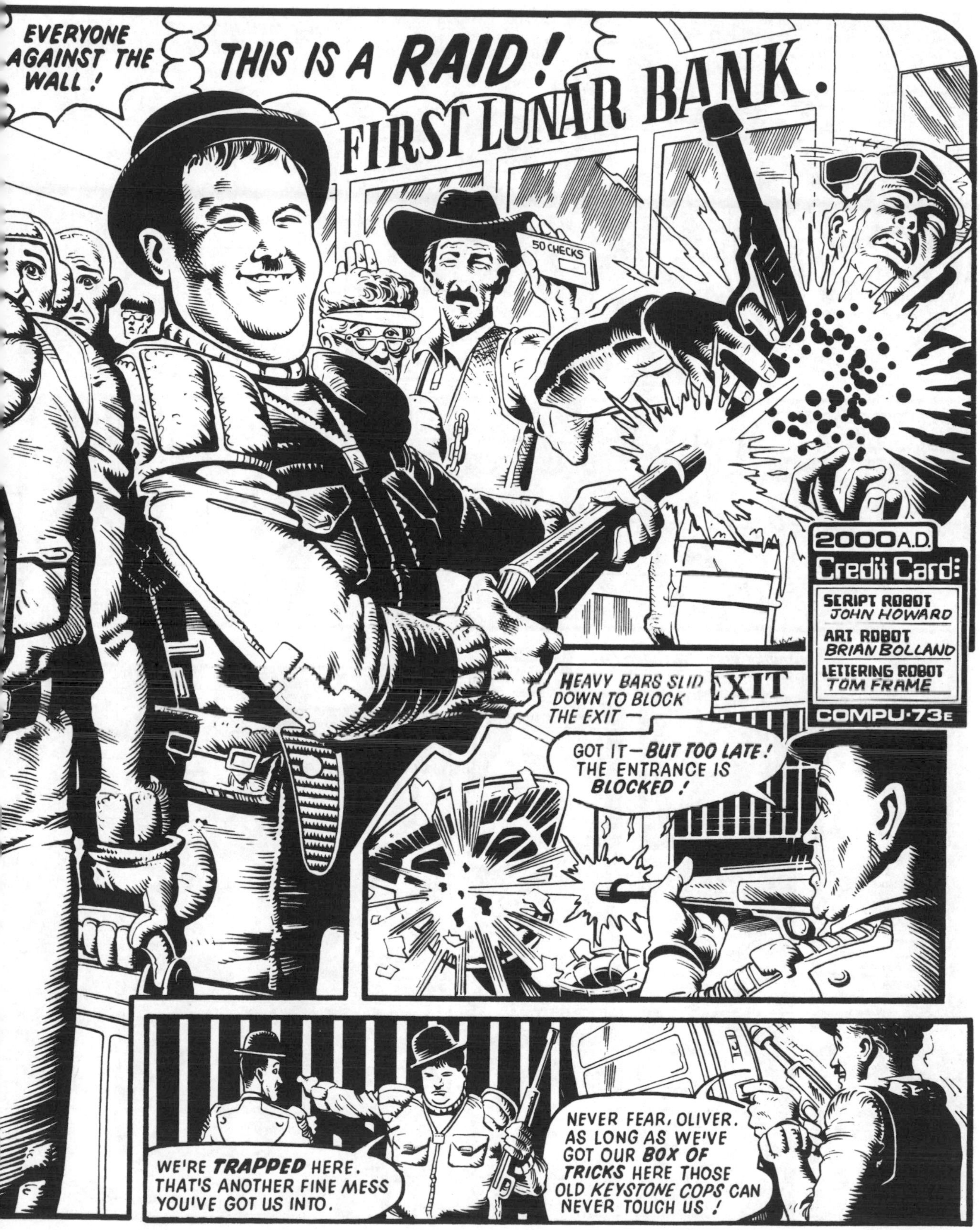
EVERYONE AGAINST THE WALL !
THIS IS A RAID !
FIRST LUNAR BANK.
50 CHECKS
2000 A.D.
Credit Card:
SCRIPT ROBOT JOHN HOWARD
ART ROBOT BRIAN BOLLAND
LETTERING ROBOT TOM FRAME
COMPU·73E
HEAVY BARS SLID DOWN TO BLOCK THE EXIT —
EXIT
GOT IT — BUT TOO LATE ! THE ENTRANCE IS BLOCKED !
WE'RE TRAPPED HERE. THAT'S ANOTHER FINE MESS YOU'VE GOT US INTO.
NEVER FEAR, OLIVER. AS LONG AS WE'VE GOT OUR BOX OF TRICKS HERE THOSE OLD KEYSTONE COPS CAN NEVER TOUCH US !

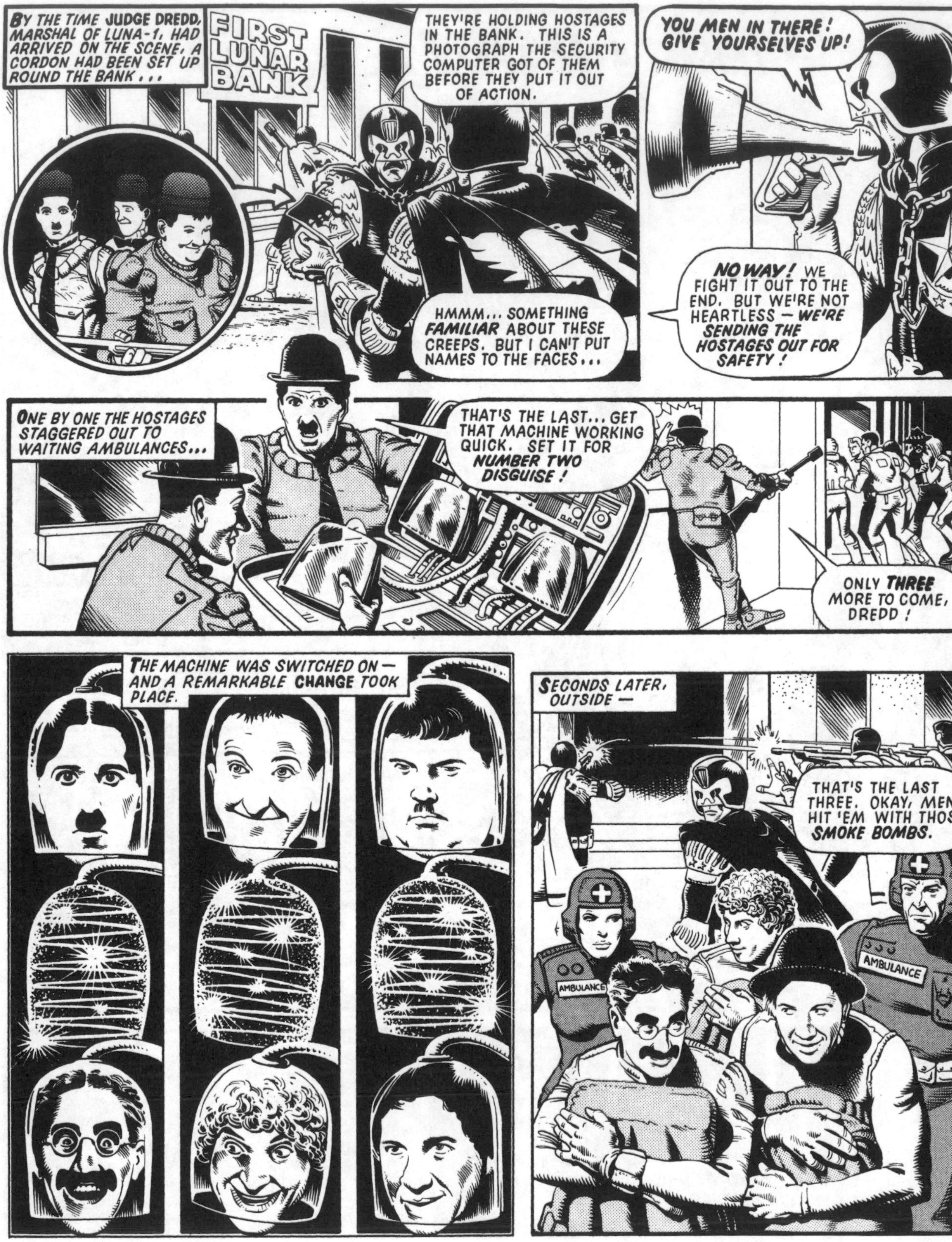

BY THE TIME JUDGE DREDD, MARSHAL OF LUNA-1, HAD ARRIVED ON THE SCENE, A CORDON HAD BEEN SET UP ROUND THE BANK...
FIRST LUNAR BANK
THEY'RE HOLDING HOSTAGES IN THE BANK. THIS IS A PHOTOGRAPH THE SECURITY COMPUTER GOT OF THEM BEFORE THEY PUT IT OUT OF ACTION.
HMMM... SOMETHING FAMILIAR ABOUT THESE CREEPS. BUT I CAN'T PUT NAMES TO THE FACES...
YOU MEN IN THERE! GIVE YOURSELVES UP!
NO WAY! WE FIGHT IT OUT TO THE END. BUT WE'RE NOT HEARTLESS — WE'RE SENDING THE HOSTAGES OUT FOR SAFETY!
ONE BY ONE THE HOSTAGES STAGGERED OUT TO WAITING AMBULANCES...
THAT'S THE LAST... GET THAT MACHINE WORKING QUICK. SET IT FOR NUMBER TWO DISGUISE!
ONLY THREE MORE TO COME, DREDD!
THE MACHINE WAS SWITCHED ON — AND A REMARKABLE CHANGE TOOK PLACE.
SECONDS LATER, OUTSIDE —
THAT'S THE LAST THREE. OKAY, MEN, HIT 'EM WITH THOSE SMOKE BOMBS.
AMBULANCE
AMBULANCE

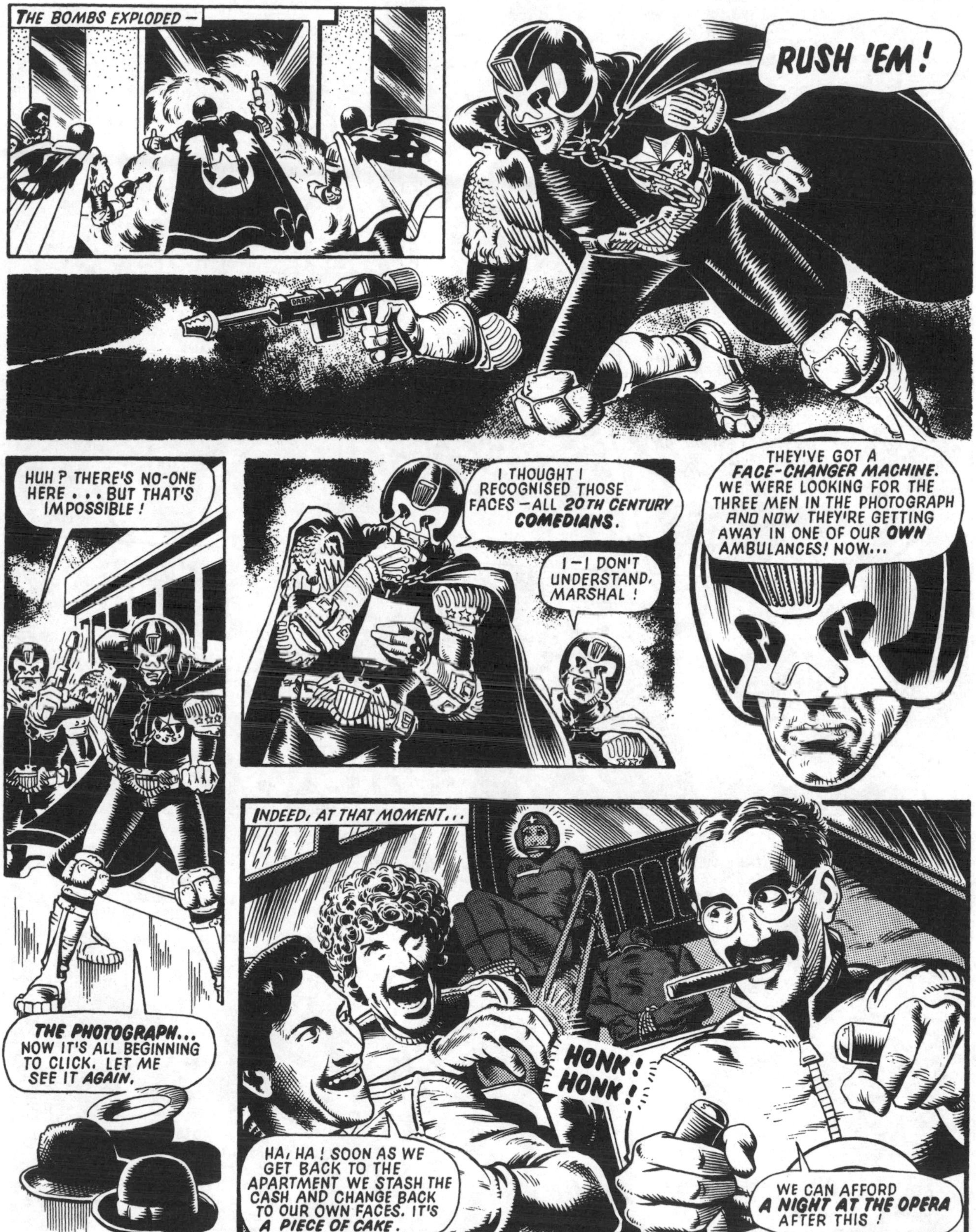
THE BOMBS EXPLODED –
RUSH 'EM!
HUH? THERE'S NO-ONE HERE . . . BUT THAT'S IMPOSSIBLE!
I THOUGHT I RECOGNISED THOSE FACES – ALL 20TH CENTURY COMEDIANS.
I – I DON'T UNDERSTAND, MARSHAL!
THEY'VE GOT A FACE-CHANGER MACHINE. WE WERE LOOKING FOR THE THREE MEN IN THE PHOTOGRAPH AND NOW THEY'RE GETTING AWAY IN ONE OF OUR OWN AMBULANCES! NOW...
THE PHOTOGRAPH... NOW IT'S ALL BEGINNING TO CLICK. LET ME SEE IT AGAIN.
INDEED, AT THAT MOMENT...
HONK! HONK!
HA, HA! SOON AS WE GET BACK TO THE APARTMENT WE STASH THE CASH AND CHANGE BACK TO OUR OWN FACES. IT'S A PIECE OF CAKE.
WE CAN AFFORD A NIGHT AT THE OPERA AFTER THIS!

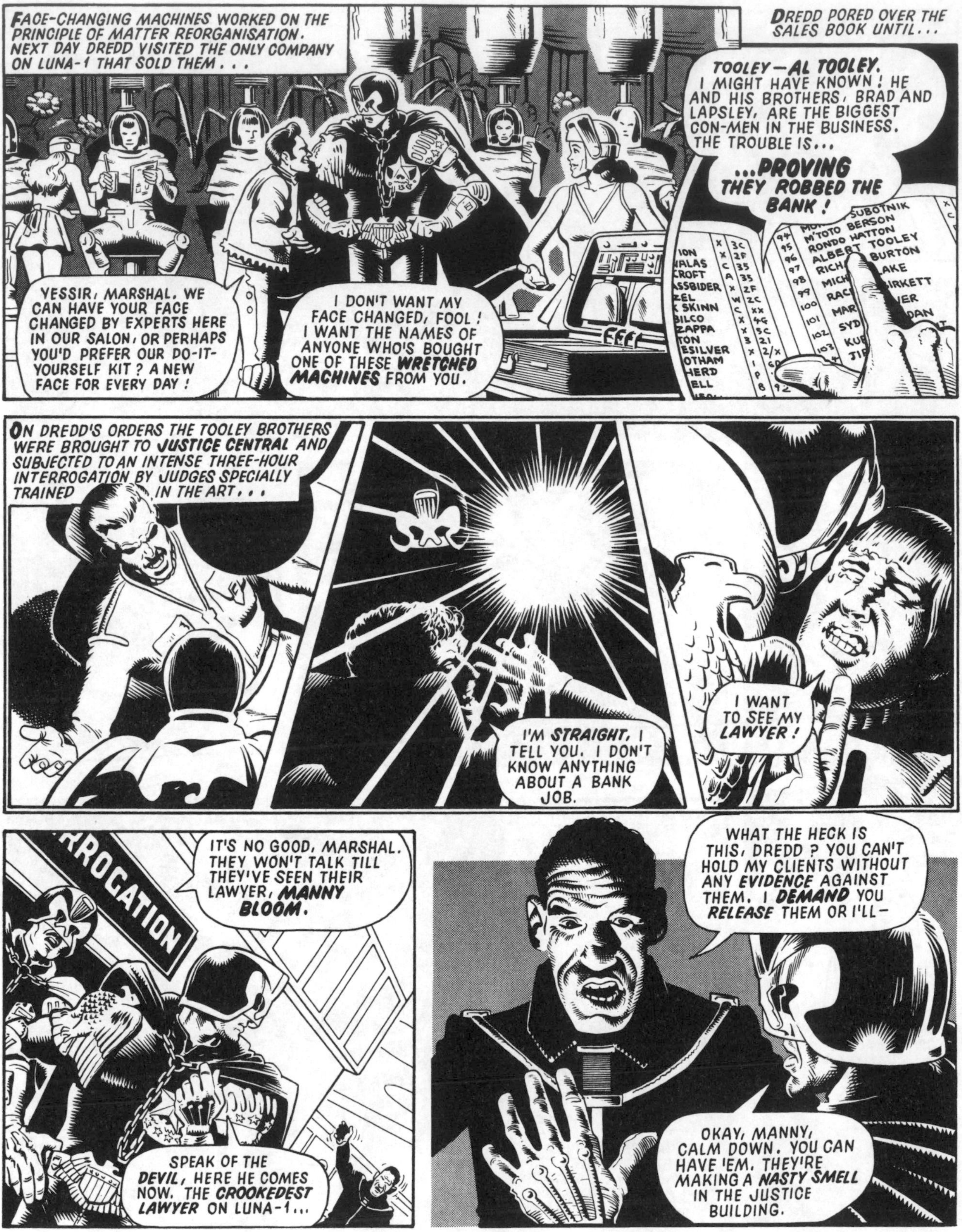

FACE-CHANGING MACHINES WORKED ON THE PRINCIPLE OF MATTER REORGANISATION. NEXT DAY DREDD VISITED THE ONLY COMPANY ON LUNA-1 THAT SOLD THEM . . .
YESSIR, MARSHAL. WE CAN HAVE YOUR FACE CHANGED BY EXPERTS HERE IN OUR SALON, OR PERHAPS YOU'D PREFER OUR DO-IT-YOURSELF KIT? A NEW FACE FOR EVERY DAY!
I DON'T WANT MY FACE CHANGED, FOOL! I WANT THE NAMES OF ANYONE WHO'S BOUGHT ONE OF THESE WRETCHED MACHINES FROM YOU.
DREDD PORED OVER THE SALES BOOK UNTIL...
TOOLEY—AL TOOLEY. I MIGHT HAVE KNOWN! HE AND HIS BROTHERS, BRAD AND LAPSLEY, ARE THE BIGGEST CON-MEN IN THE BUSINESS. THE TROUBLE IS...
...PROVING THEY ROBBED THE BANK!
ON DREDD'S ORDERS THE TOOLEY BROTHERS WERE BROUGHT TO JUSTICE CENTRAL AND SUBJECTED TO AN INTENSE THREE-HOUR INTERROGATION BY JUDGES SPECIALLY TRAINED IN THE ART...
I'M STRAIGHT, I TELL YOU. I DON'T KNOW ANYTHING ABOUT A BANK JOB.
I WANT TO SEE MY LAWYER!
RROGATION
IT'S NO GOOD, MARSHAL. THEY WON'T TALK TILL THEY'VE SEEN THEIR LAWYER, MANNY BLOOM.
SPEAK OF THE DEVIL, HERE HE COMES NOW. THE CROOKEDEST LAWYER ON LUNA-1...
WHAT THE HECK IS THIS, DREDD? YOU CAN'T HOLD MY CLIENTS WITHOUT ANY EVIDENCE AGAINST THEM. I DEMAND YOU RELEASE THEM OR I'LL—
OKAY, MANNY, CALM DOWN. YOU CAN HAVE 'EM, THEY'RE MAKING A NASTY SMELL IN THE JUSTICE BUILDING.

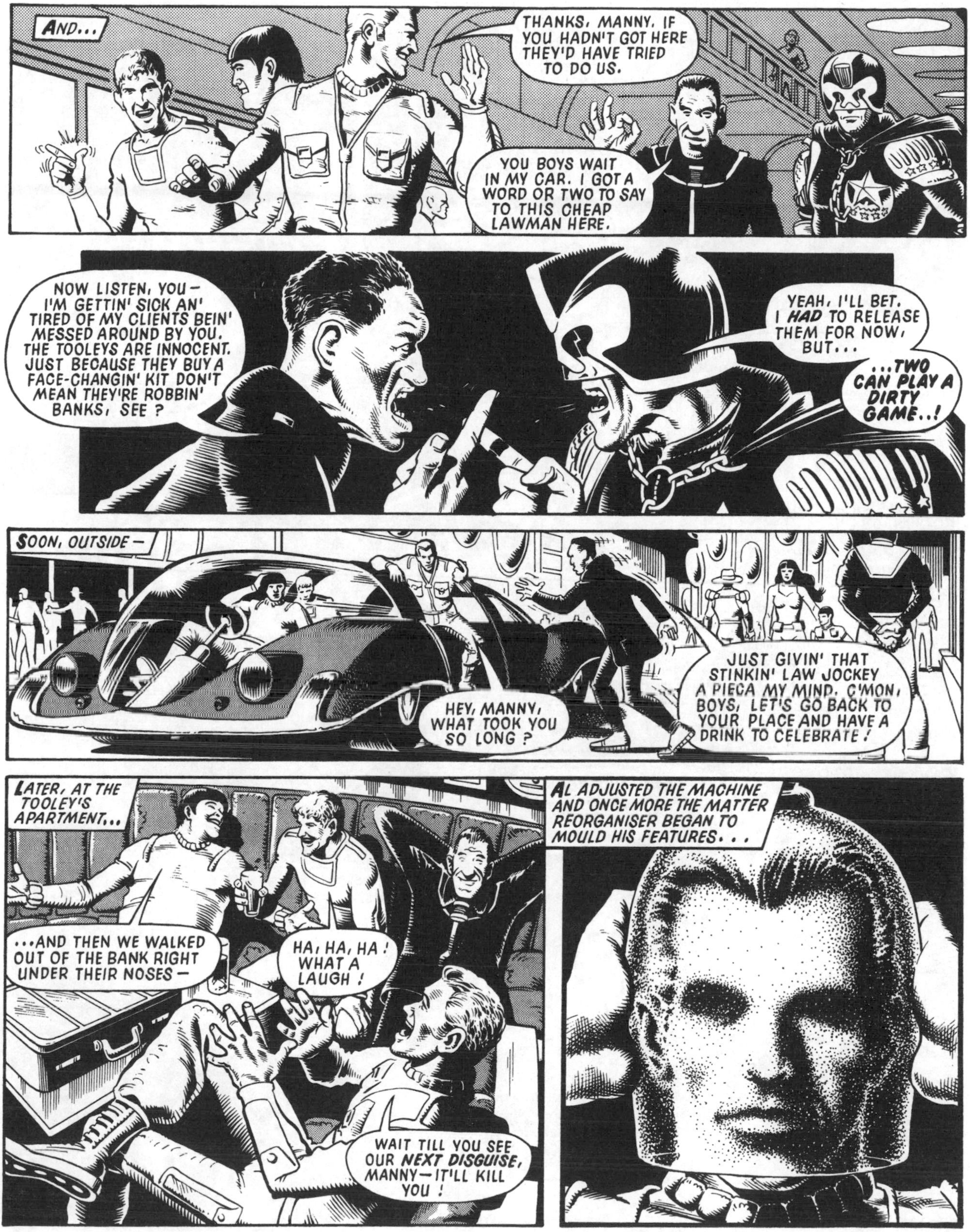
AND...
THANKS, MANNY. IF YOU HADN'T GOT HERE THEY'D HAVE TRIED TO DO US.
YOU BOYS WAIT IN MY CAR. I GOT A WORD OR TWO TO SAY TO THIS CHEAP LAWMAN HERE.
NOW LISTEN, YOU— I'M GETTIN' SICK AN' TIRED OF MY CLIENTS BEIN' MESSED AROUND BY YOU. THE TOOLEYS ARE INNOCENT. JUST BECAUSE THEY BUY A FACE-CHANGIN' KIT DON'T MEAN THEY'RE ROBBIN' BANKS, SEE ?
YEAH, I'LL BET. I HAD TO RELEASE THEM FOR NOW, BUT...
...TWO CAN PLAY A DIRTY GAME..!
SOON, OUTSIDE—
HEY, MANNY, WHAT TOOK YOU SO LONG ?
JUST GIVIN' THAT STINKIN' LAW JOCKEY A PIECA MY MIND. C'MON, BOYS, LET'S GO BACK TO YOUR PLACE AND HAVE A DRINK TO CELEBRATE !
LATER, AT THE TOOLEY'S APARTMENT...
...AND THEN WE WALKED OUT OF THE BANK RIGHT UNDER THEIR NOSES —
HA, HA, HA ! WHAT A LAUGH !
WAIT TILL YOU SEE OUR NEXT DISGUISE, MANNY—IT'LL KILL YOU !
AL ADJUSTED THE MACHINE AND ONCE MORE THE MATTER REORGANISER BEGAN TO MOULD HIS FEATURES . . .

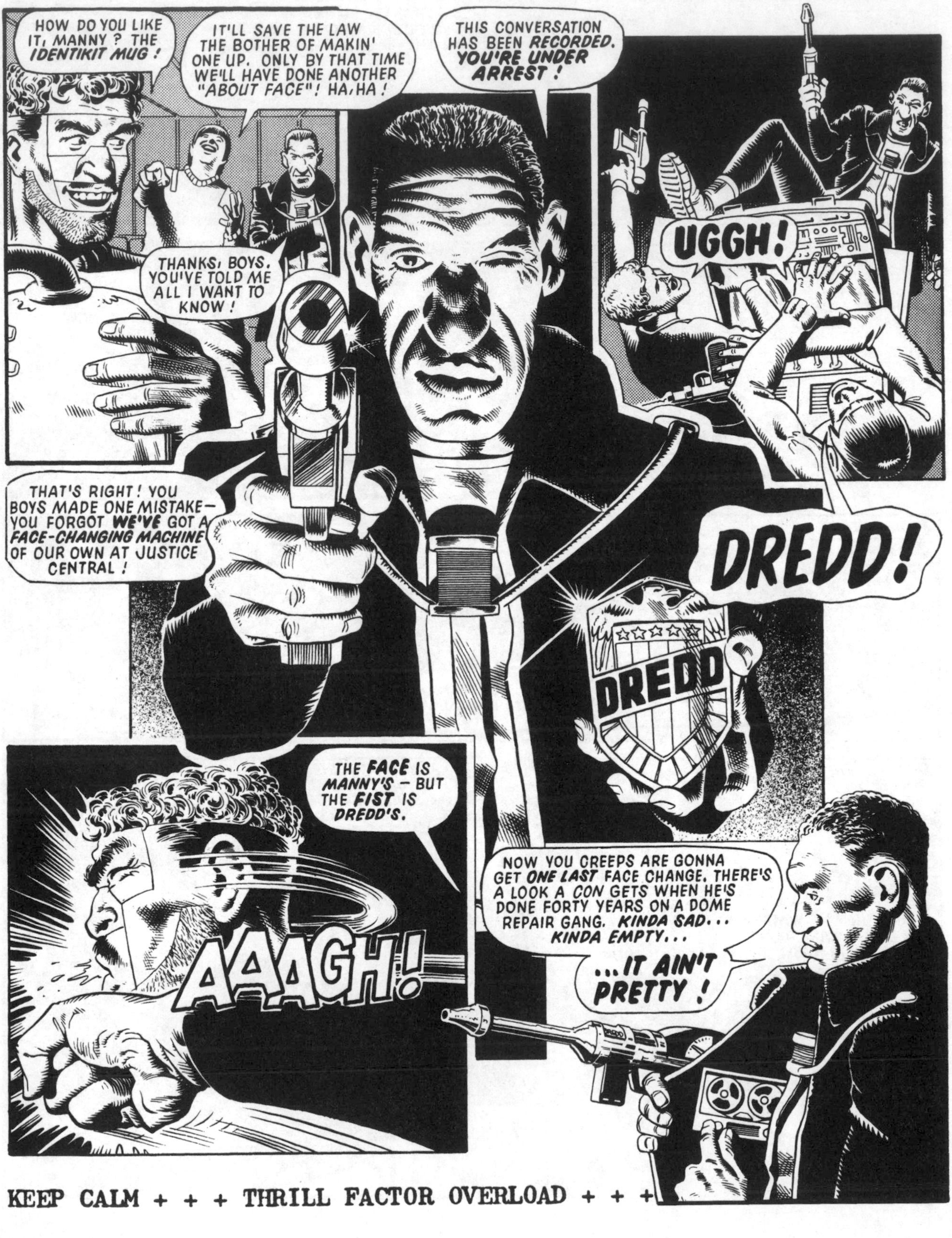
HOW DO YOU LIKE IT, MANNY ? THE IDENTIKIT MUG !
IT'LL SAVE THE LAW THE BOTHER OF MAKIN' ONE UP. ONLY BY THAT TIME WE'LL HAVE DONE ANOTHER "ABOUT FACE"! HA, HA !
THANKS, BOYS. YOU'VE TOLD ME ALL I WANT TO KNOW !
THIS CONVERSATION HAS BEEN RECORDED. YOU'RE UNDER ARREST !
UGGH !
THAT'S RIGHT ! YOU BOYS MADE ONE MISTAKE— YOU FORGOT WE'VE GOT A FACE-CHANGING MACHINE OF OUR OWN AT JUSTICE CENTRAL !
DREDD !
DREDD
THE FACE IS MANNY'S — BUT THE FIST IS DREDD'S.
AAAGH !
NOW YOU CREEPS ARE GONNA GET ONE LAST FACE CHANGE. THERE'S A LOOK A CON GETS WHEN HE'S DONE FORTY YEARS ON A DOME REPAIR GANG. KINDA SAD... KINDA EMPTY...
...IT AIN'T PRETTY !

KEEP CALM + + + THRILL FACTOR OVERLOAD + + +

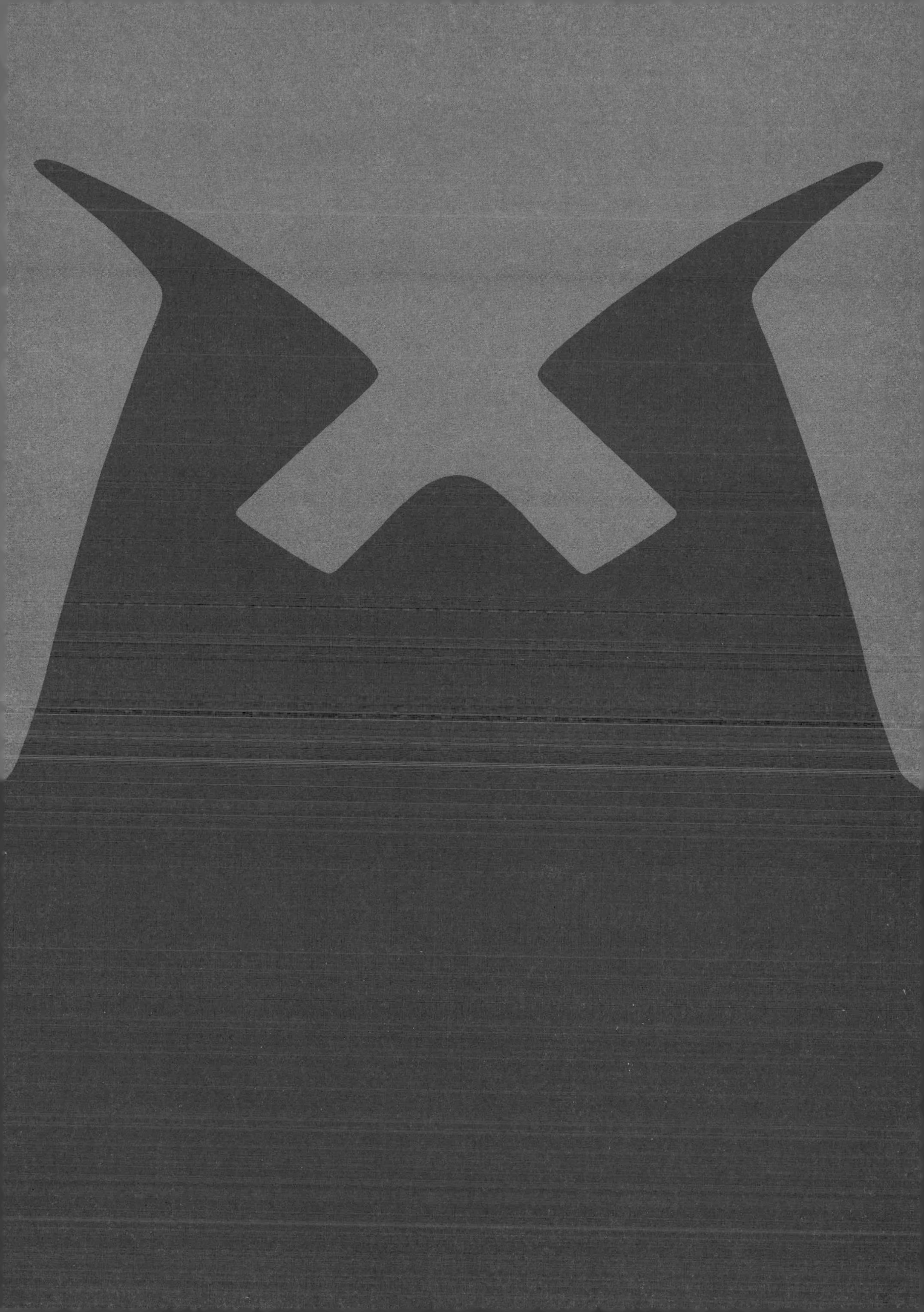

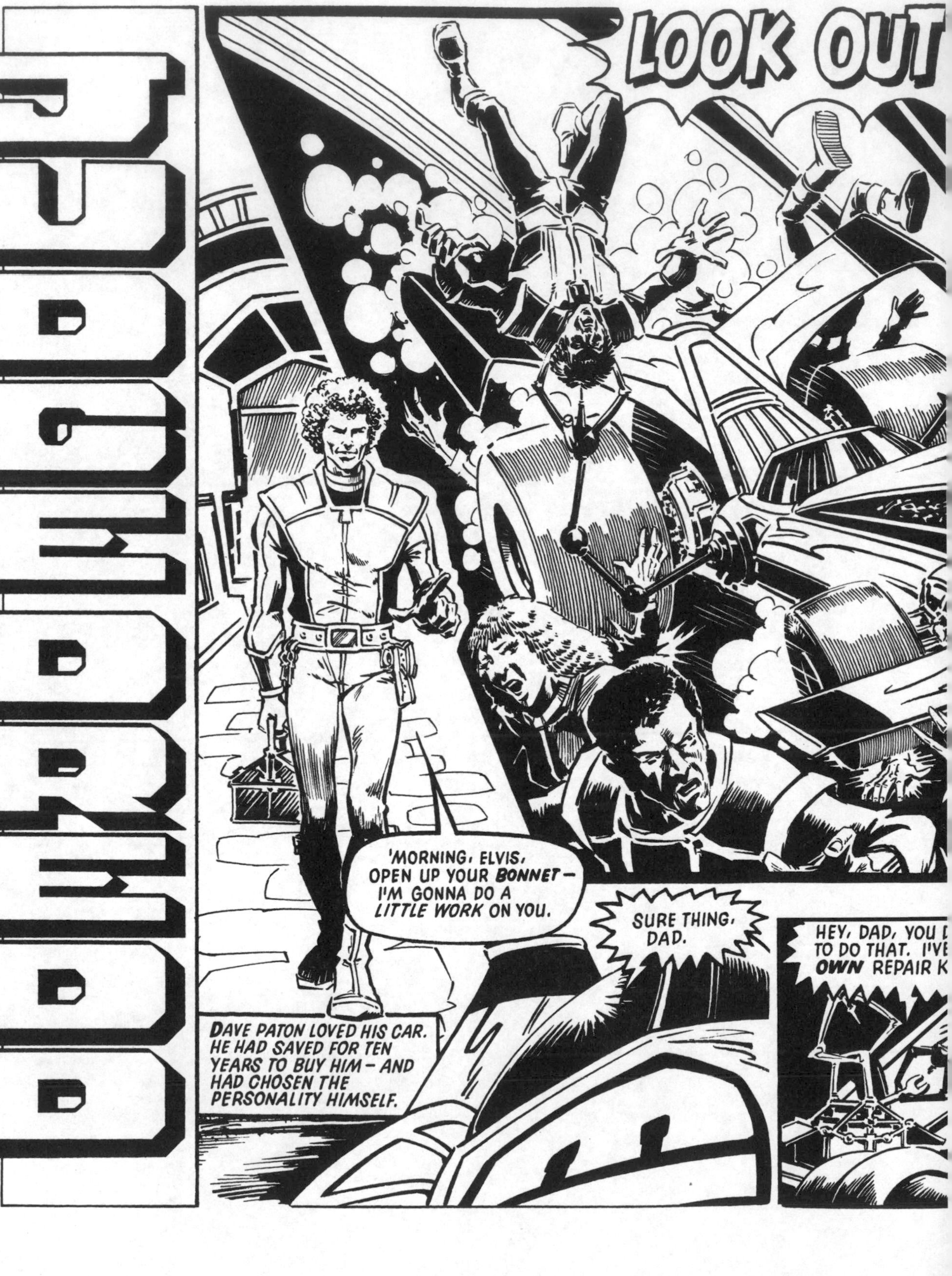
JUDGE DREDD
LOOK OUT
'MORNING, ELVIS, OPEN UP YOUR *BONNET* — I'M GONNA DO A *LITTLE WORK* ON YOU.
DAVE PATON LOVED HIS CAR. HE HAD SAVED FOR TEN YEARS TO BUY HIM — AND HAD CHOSEN THE PERSONALITY HIMSELF.
SURE THING, DAD.
HEY, DAD, YOU D
TO DO THAT. I'VE
OWN REPAIR K

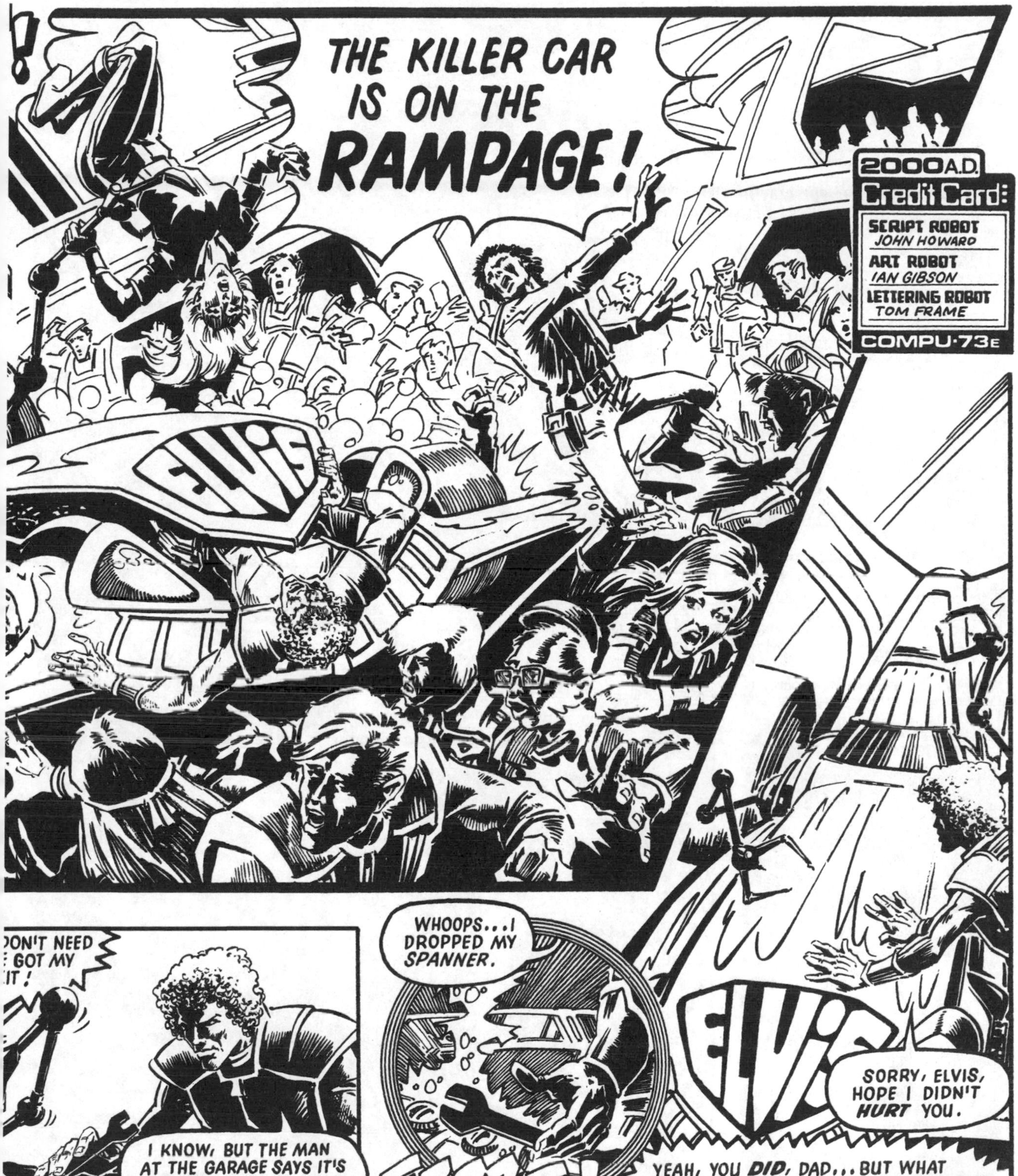

THE KILLER CAR IS ON THE RAMPAGE!
2000A.D. Credit Card:
SCRIPT ROBOT JOHN HOWARD
ART ROBOT IAN GIBSON
LETTERING ROBOT TOM FRAME
COMPU-73E
ELVIS
DON'T NEED ... GOT MY ... IT!
I KNOW, BUT THE MAN AT THE GARAGE SAYS IT'S THE ONLY WAY TO GET TO KNOW YOUR OWN CAR.
WHOOPS...I DROPPED MY SPANNER.
FZZZT!
ELVIS
SORRY, ELVIS, HOPE I DIDN'T HURT YOU.
YEAH, YOU DID, DAD... BUT WHAT THE HECK! JUMP IN! I'M GETTING SICK OF SITTING AT THIS STUPID KERB!

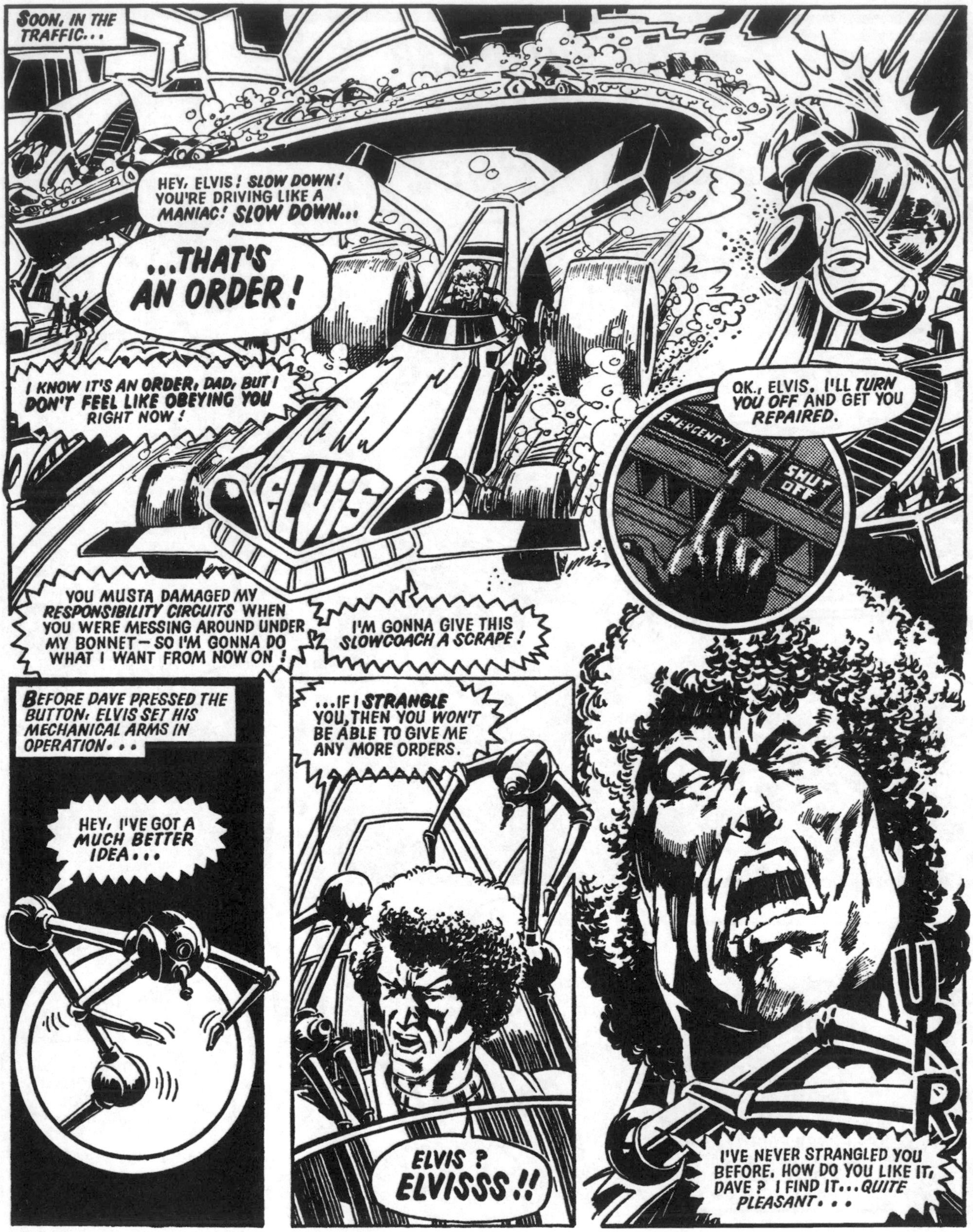

SOON, IN THE TRAFFIC...
HEY, ELVIS! SLOW DOWN! YOU'RE DRIVING LIKE A MANIAC! SLOW DOWN...
...THAT'S AN ORDER!
I KNOW IT'S AN ORDER, DAD, BUT I DON'T FEEL LIKE OBEYING YOU RIGHT NOW!
ELVIS
YOU MUSTA DAMAGED MY RESPONSIBILITY CIRCUITS WHEN YOU WERE MESSING AROUND UNDER MY BONNET – SO I'M GONNA DO WHAT I WANT FROM NOW ON!
I'M GONNA GIVE THIS SLOWCOACH A SCRAPE!
O.K., ELVIS, I'LL TURN YOU OFF AND GET YOU REPAIRED.
EMERGENCY
SHUT OFF
BEFORE DAVE PRESSED THE BUTTON, ELVIS SET HIS MECHANICAL ARMS IN OPERATION...
HEY, I'VE GOT A MUCH BETTER IDEA...
...IF I STRANGLE YOU, THEN YOU WON'T BE ABLE TO GIVE ME ANY MORE ORDERS.
ELVIS? ELVISSS!!
URR
I'VE NEVER STRANGLED YOU BEFORE, HOW DO YOU LIKE IT, DAVE? I FIND IT... QUITE PLEASANT...

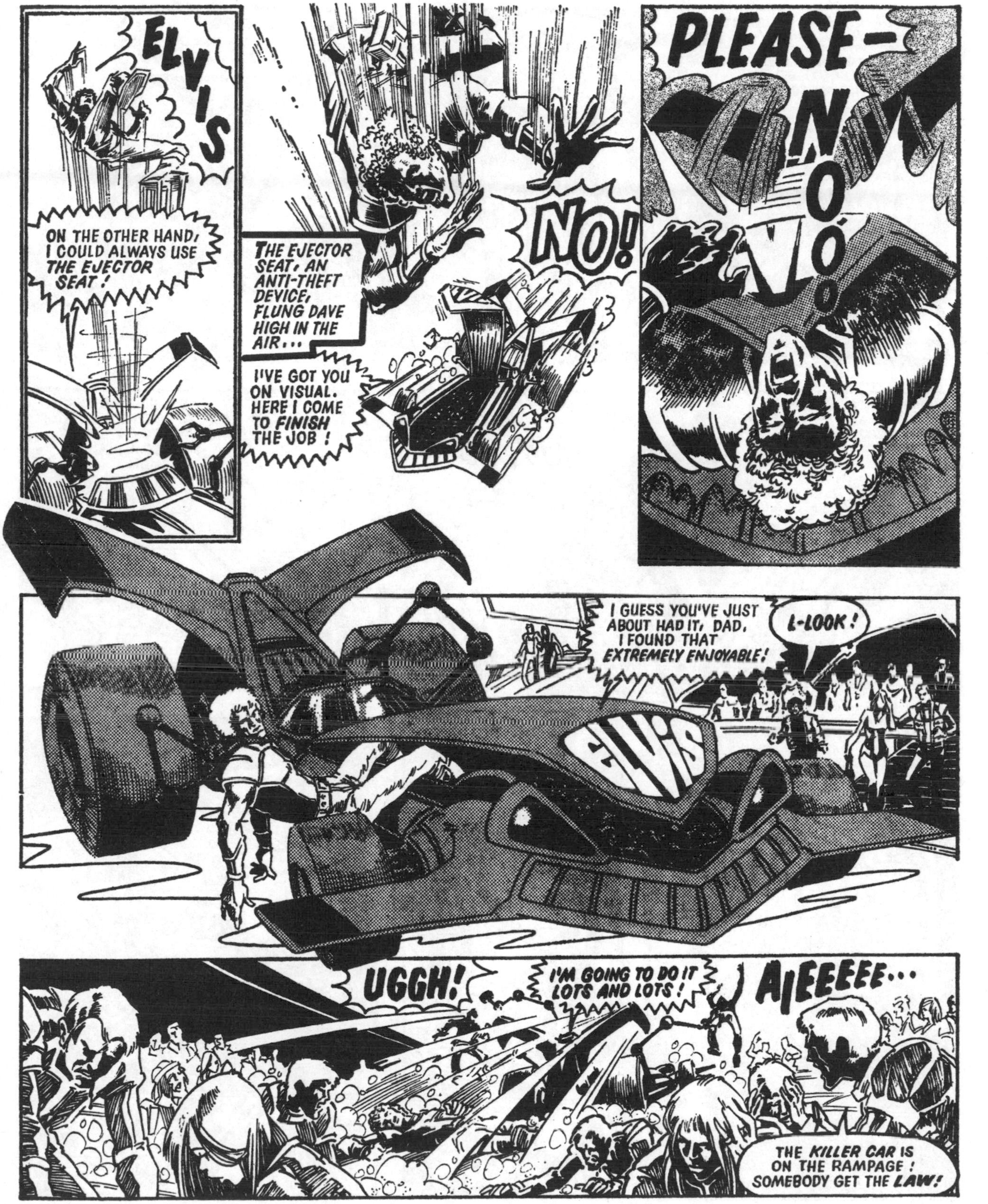
ELVIS
ON THE OTHER HAND, I COULD ALWAYS USE THE EJECTOR SEAT!
THE EJECTOR SEAT, AN ANTI-THEFT DEVICE, FLUNG DAVE HIGH IN THE AIR...
NO!
I'VE GOT YOU ON VISUAL. HERE I COME TO FINISH THE JOB!
PLEASE-NOOOOO
I GUESS YOU'VE JUST ABOUT HAD IT, DAD, I FOUND THAT EXTREMELY ENJOYABLE!
L-LOOK!
ELVIS
UGGH!
I'M GOING TO DO IT LOTS AND LOTS!
AIEEEEE...
THE KILLER CAR IS ON THE RAMPAGE! SOMEBODY GET THE LAW!

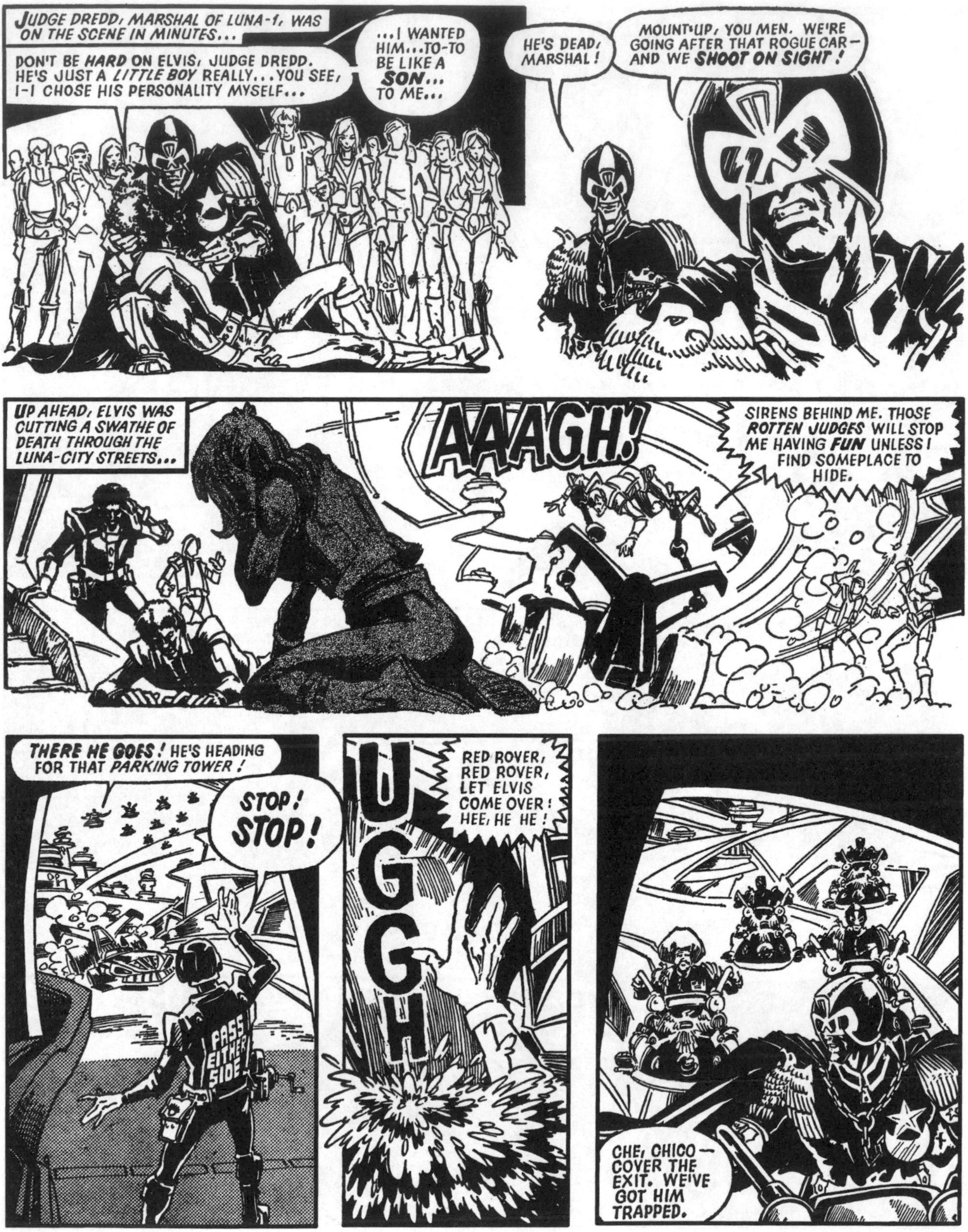

JUDGE DREDD, MARSHAL OF LUNA-1, WAS ON THE SCENE IN MINUTES...
DON'T BE HARD ON ELVIS, JUDGE DREDD. HE'S JUST A LITTLE BOY REALLY... YOU SEE, I-I CHOSE HIS PERSONALITY MYSELF...
...I WANTED HIM...TO-TO BE LIKE A SON... TO ME...
HE'S DEAD, MARSHAL!
MOUNT UP, YOU MEN. WE'RE GOING AFTER THAT ROGUE CAR— AND WE SHOOT ON SIGHT!
UP AHEAD, ELVIS WAS CUTTING A SWATHE OF DEATH THROUGH THE LUNA-CITY STREETS...
AAAGH!
SIRENS BEHIND ME. THOSE ROTTEN JUDGES WILL STOP ME HAVING FUN UNLESS I FIND SOMEPLACE TO HIDE.
THERE HE GOES! HE'S HEADING FOR THAT PARKING TOWER!
STOP! STOP!
PASS EITHER SIDE
UGGH
RED ROVER, RED ROVER, LET ELVIS COME OVER! HEE, HE HE!
CHE, CHICO— COVER THE EXIT. WE'VE GOT HIM TRAPPED.

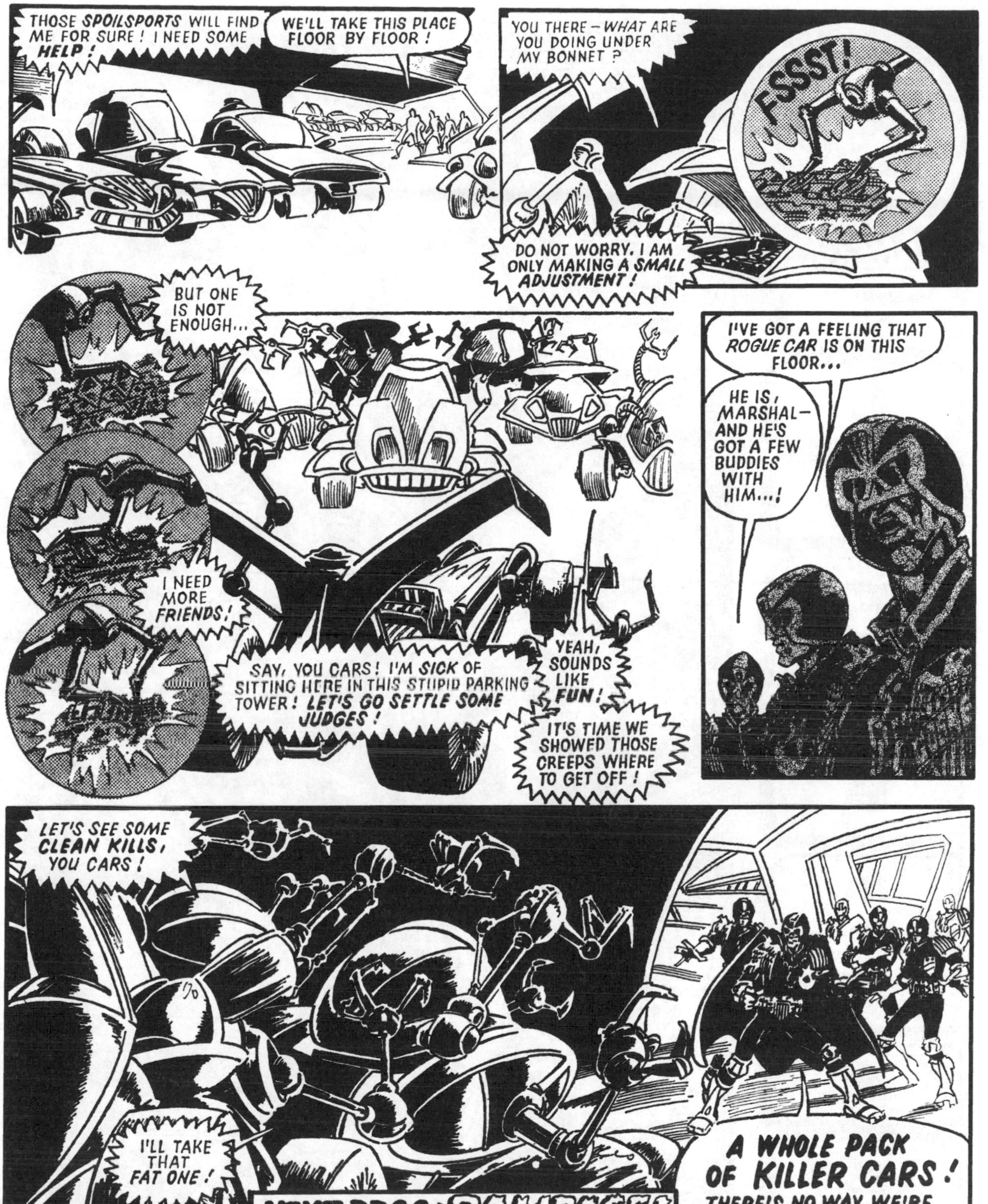
THOSE SPOILSPORTS WILL FIND ME FOR SURE! I NEED SOME HELP!
WE'LL TAKE THIS PLACE FLOOR BY FLOOR!
YOU THERE – WHAT ARE YOU DOING UNDER MY BONNET?
FSSST!
DO NOT WORRY. I AM ONLY MAKING A SMALL ADJUSTMENT!
BUT ONE IS NOT ENOUGH...
I NEED MORE FRIENDS!
SAY, YOU CARS! I'M SICK OF SITTING HERE IN THIS STUPID PARKING TOWER! LET'S GO SETTLE SOME JUDGES!
YEAH, SOUNDS LIKE FUN!
IT'S TIME WE SHOWED THOSE CREEPS WHERE TO GET OFF!
I'VE GOT A FEELING THAT ROGUE CAR IS ON THIS FLOOR...
HE IS, MARSHAL– AND HE'S GOT A FEW BUDDIES WITH HIM...!
LET'S SEE SOME CLEAN KILLS, YOU CARS!
I'LL TAKE THAT FAT ONE!
A WHOLE PACK OF KILLER CARS! THERE'S NO WAY WE'RE GOING TO STOP THEM!
NEXT PROG: RAMPAGE!

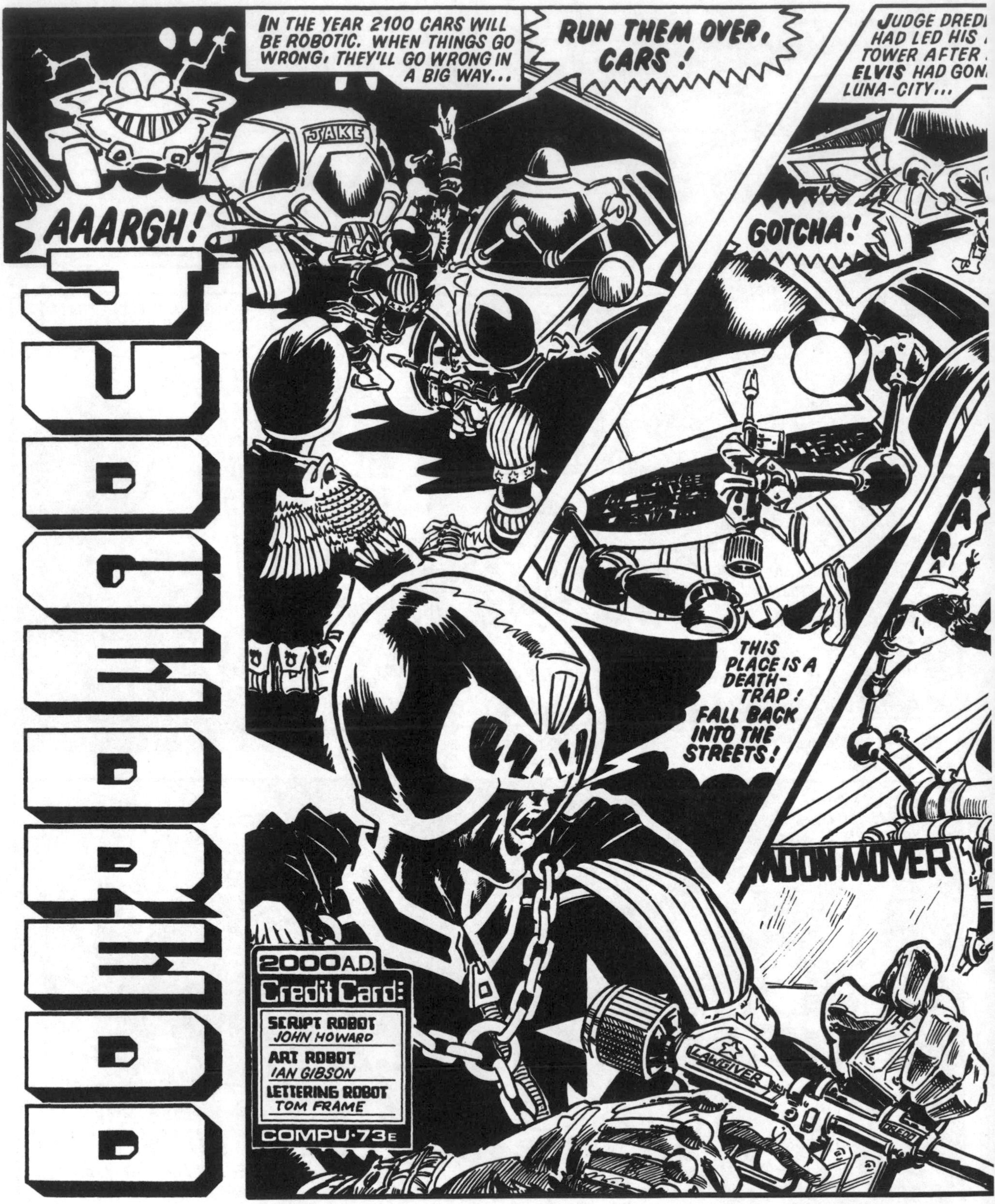

IN THE YEAR 2100 CARS WILL BE ROBOTIC. WHEN THINGS GO WRONG, THEY'LL GO WRONG IN A BIG WAY...
RUN THEM OVER, CARS!
JAKE
AAARGH!
JUDGE DREDD
GOTCHA!
THIS PLACE IS A DEATH-TRAP! FALL BACK INTO THE STREETS!
MOON MOVER
LAWGIVER
2000 A.D.
Credit Card:
SCRIPT ROBOT
JOHN HOWARD
ART ROBOT
IAN GIBSON
LETTERING ROBOT
TOM FRAME
COMPU·73E

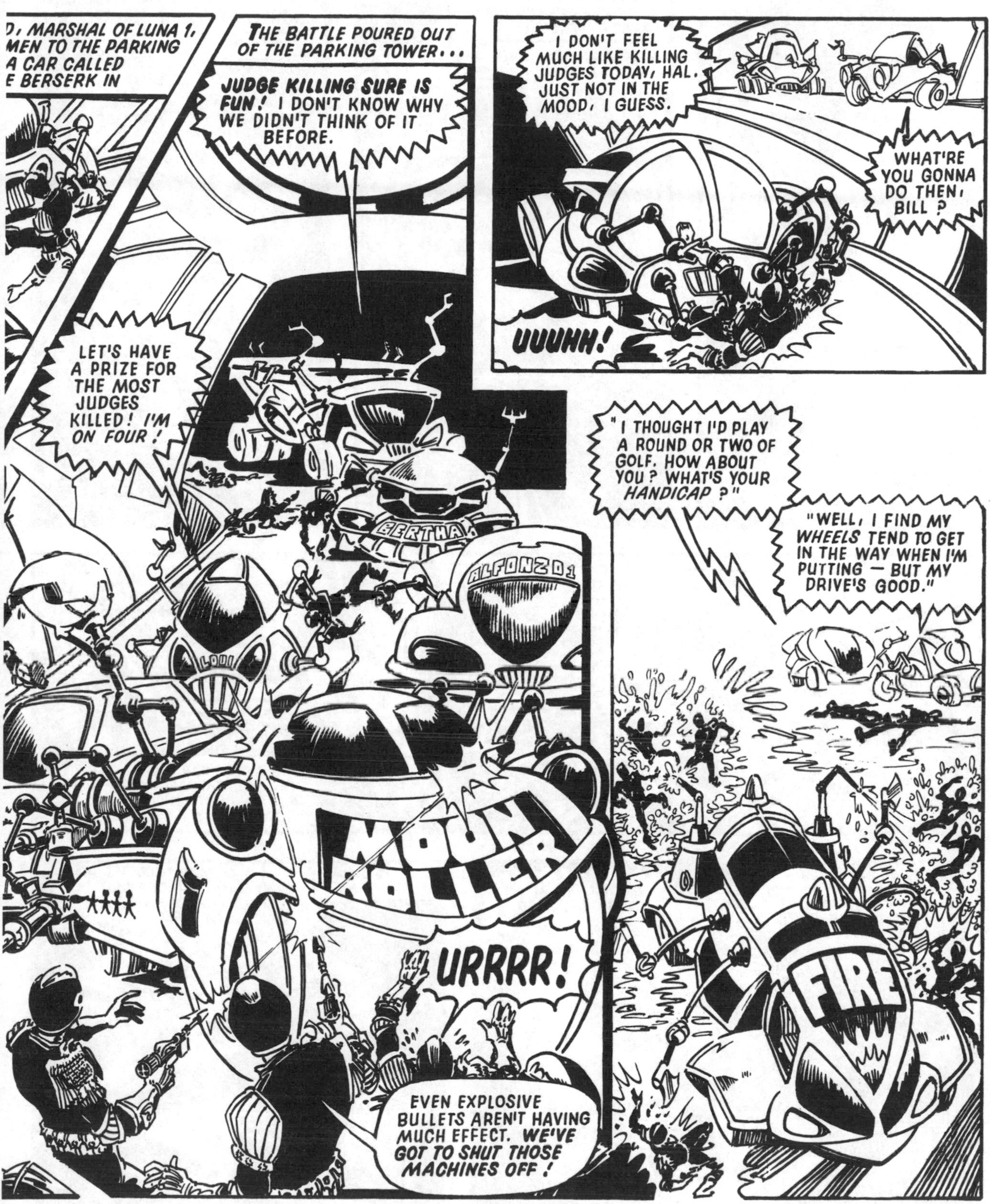

D, MARSHAL OF LUNA 1, MEN TO THE PARKING A CAR CALLED E BERSERK IN
THE BATTLE POURED OUT OF THE PARKING TOWER...
JUDGE KILLING SURE IS FUN! I DON'T KNOW WHY WE DIDN'T THINK OF IT BEFORE.
LET'S HAVE A PRIZE FOR THE MOST JUDGES KILLED! I'M ON FOUR!
BERTHA
ALFONZO 1
LOU
MOON ROLLER
URRRR!
EVEN EXPLOSIVE BULLETS AREN'T HAVING MUCH EFFECT. WE'VE GOT TO SHUT THOSE MACHINES OFF!
I DON'T FEEL MUCH LIKE KILLING JUDGES TODAY, HAL. JUST NOT IN THE MOOD, I GUESS.
WHAT'RE YOU GONNA DO THEN, BILL?
UUUHH!
"I THOUGHT I'D PLAY A ROUND OR TWO OF GOLF. HOW ABOUT YOU? WHAT'S YOUR HANDICAP?"
"WELL, I FIND MY WHEELS TEND TO GET IN THE WAY WHEN I'M PUTTING — BUT MY DRIVE'S GOOD."
FIRE

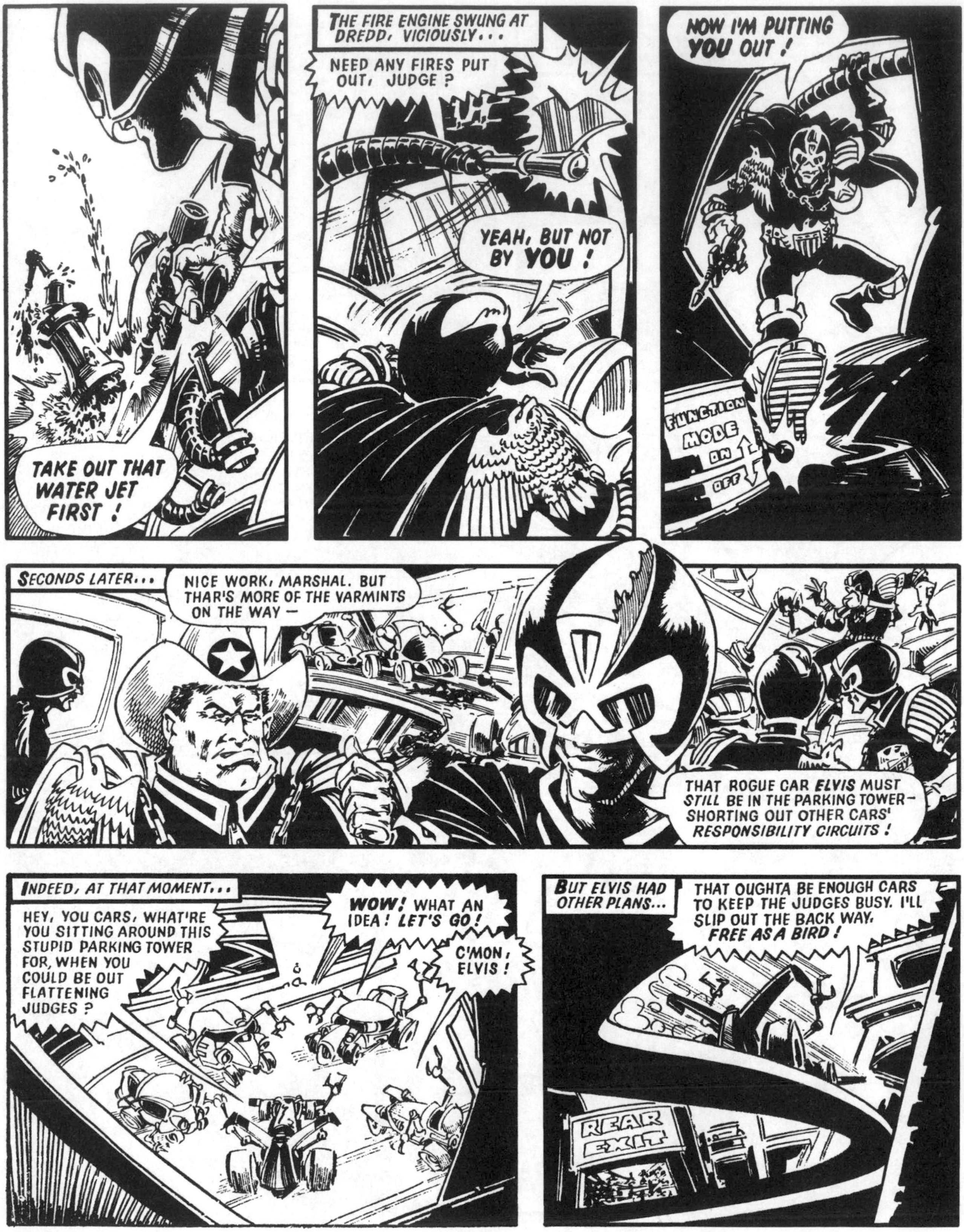
TAKE OUT THAT WATER JET FIRST!
THE FIRE ENGINE SWUNG AT DREDD, VICIOUSLY...
NEED ANY FIRES PUT OUT, JUDGE?
YEAH, BUT NOT BY YOU!
NOW I'M PUTTING YOU OUT!
FUNCTION MODE ON OFF
SECONDS LATER...
NICE WORK, MARSHAL. BUT THAR'S MORE OF THE VARMINTS ON THE WAY –
THAT ROGUE CAR ELVIS MUST STILL BE IN THE PARKING TOWER– SHORTING OUT OTHER CARS' RESPONSIBILITY CIRCUITS!
INDEED, AT THAT MOMENT...
HEY, YOU CARS, WHAT'RE YOU SITTING AROUND THIS STUPID PARKING TOWER FOR, WHEN YOU COULD BE OUT FLATTENING JUDGES?
WOW! WHAT AN IDEA! LET'S GO!
C'MON, ELVIS!
BUT ELVIS HAD OTHER PLANS...
THAT OUGHTA BE ENOUGH CARS TO KEEP THE JUDGES BUSY. I'LL SLIP OUT THE BACK WAY, FREE AS A BIRD!
REAR EXIT

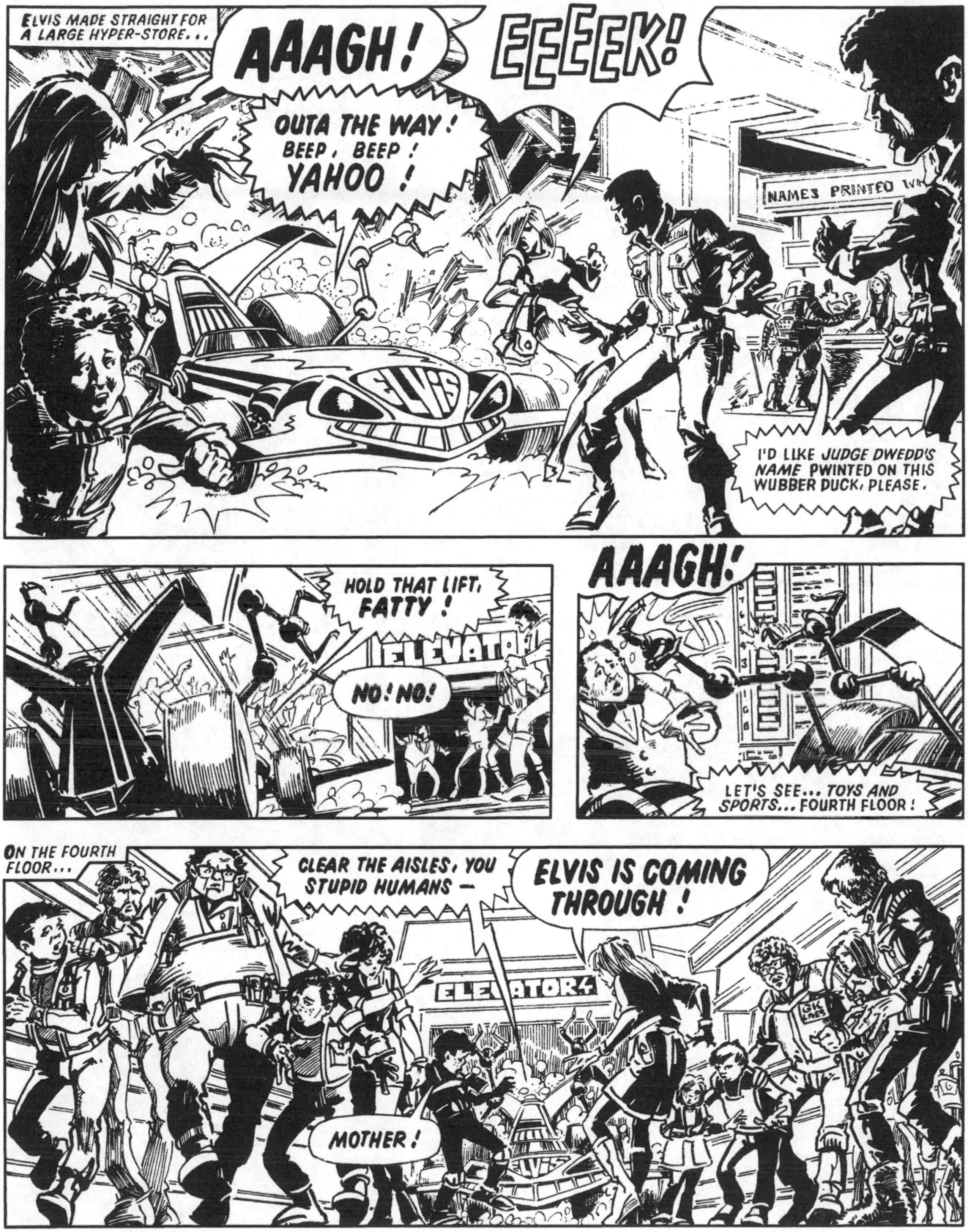

ELVIS MADE STRAIGHT FOR A LARGE HYPER-STORE...
AAAGH!
EEEEK!
OUTA THE WAY! BEEP, BEEP! YAHOO!
NAMES PRINTED WH
ELVIS
I'D LIKE JUDGE DWEDD'S NAME PWINTED ON THIS WUBBER DUCK, PLEASE.
HOLD THAT LIFT, FATTY!
ELEVATO
NO! NO!
AAAGH!
LET'S SEE... TOYS AND SPORTS... FOURTH FLOOR!
ON THE FOURTH FLOOR...
CLEAR THE AISLES, YOU STUPID HUMANS —
ELVIS IS COMING THROUGH!
ELEVATOR 4
MOTHER!

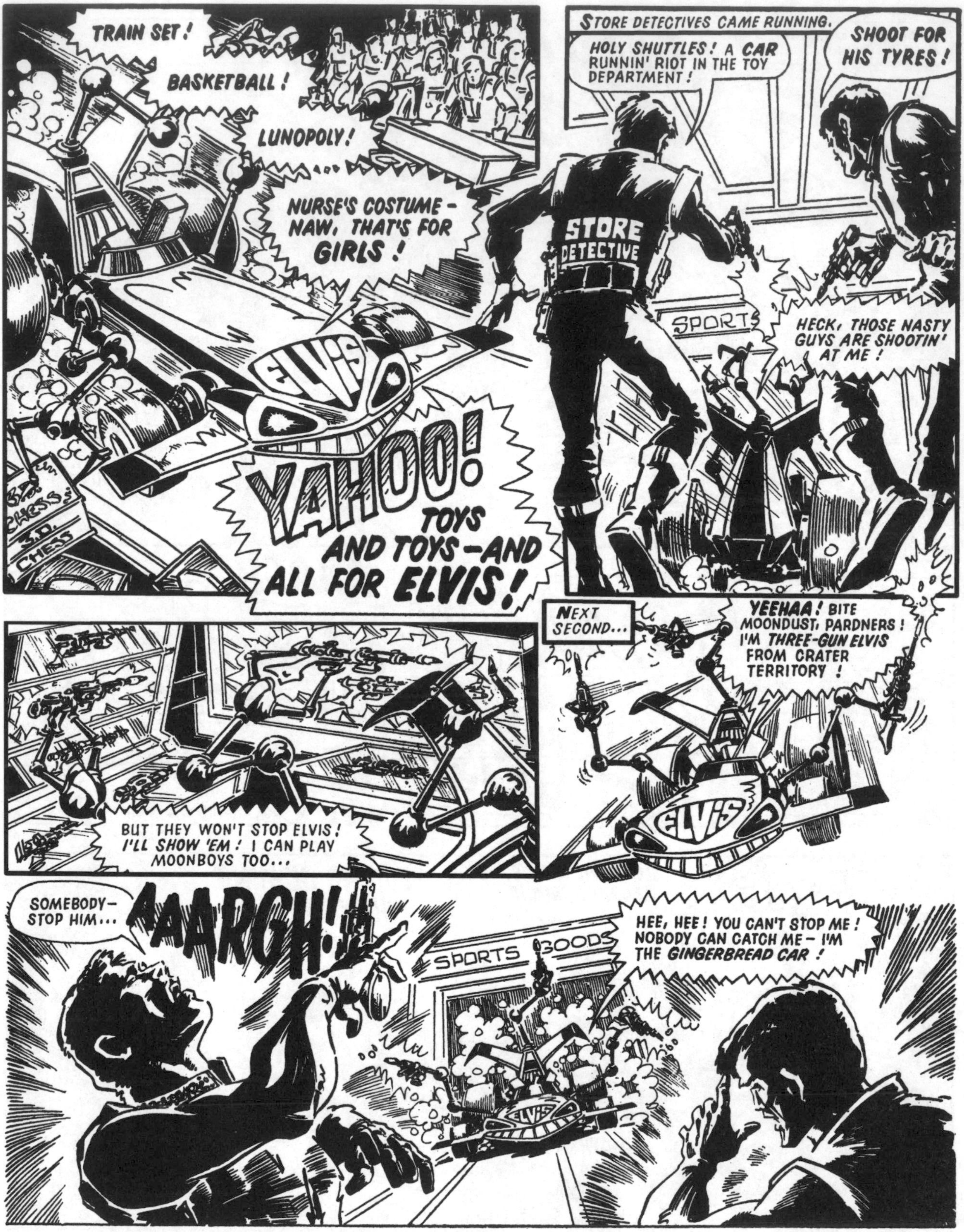

TRAIN SET!
BASKETBALL!
LUNOPOLY!
...
NURSE'S COSTUME - NAW, THAT'S FOR GIRLS!
YAHOO! TOYS AND TOYS - AND ALL FOR ELVIS!
ELVIS
3.D. CHESS
3.D. CHESS
STORE DETECTIVES CAME RUNNING.
HOLY SHUTTLES! A CAR RUNNIN' RIOT IN THE TOY DEPARTMENT!
SHOOT FOR HIS TYRES!
STORE DETECTIVE
SPORT
HECK, THOSE NASTY GUYS ARE SHOOTIN' AT ME!
BUT THEY WON'T STOP ELVIS! I'LL SHOW 'EM! I CAN PLAY MOONBOYS TOO...
NEXT SECOND...
YEEHAA! BITE MOONDUST, PARDNERS! I'M THREE-GUN ELVIS FROM CRATER TERRITORY!
ELVIS
SOMEBODY- STOP HIM...
AAARGH!
SPORTS GOODS
HEE, HEE! YOU CAN'T STOP ME! NOBODY CAN CATCH ME - I'M THE GINGERBREAD CAR!
ELVIS

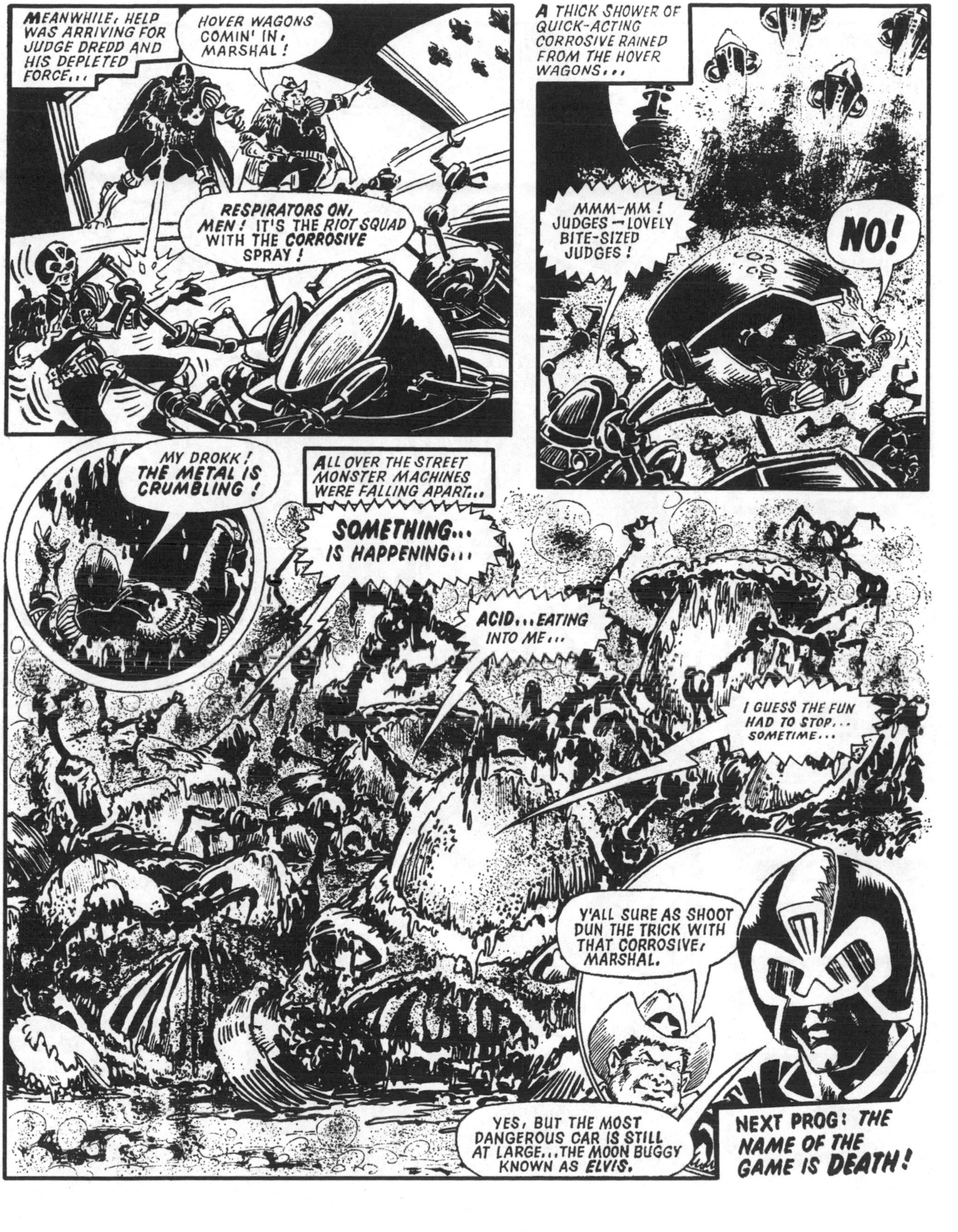
MEANWHILE, HELP WAS ARRIVING FOR JUDGE DREDD AND HIS DEPLETED FORCE...
HOVER WAGONS COMIN' IN, MARSHAL!
RESPIRATORS ON, MEN! IT'S THE RIOT SQUAD WITH THE CORROSIVE SPRAY!
A THICK SHOWER OF QUICK-ACTING CORROSIVE RAINED FROM THE HOVER WAGONS...
MMM-MM! JUDGES — LOVELY BITE-SIZED JUDGES!
NO!
MY DROKK! THE METAL IS CRUMBLING!
ALL OVER THE STREET MONSTER MACHINES WERE FALLING APART...
SOMETHING... IS HAPPENING...
ACID... EATING INTO ME...
I GUESS THE FUN HAD TO STOP... SOMETIME...
Y'ALL SURE AS SHOOT DUN THE TRICK WITH THAT CORROSIVE, MARSHAL.
YES, BUT THE MOST DANGEROUS CAR IS STILL AT LARGE... THE MOON BUGGY KNOWN AS ELVIS.
NEXT PROG: THE NAME OF THE GAME IS DEATH!

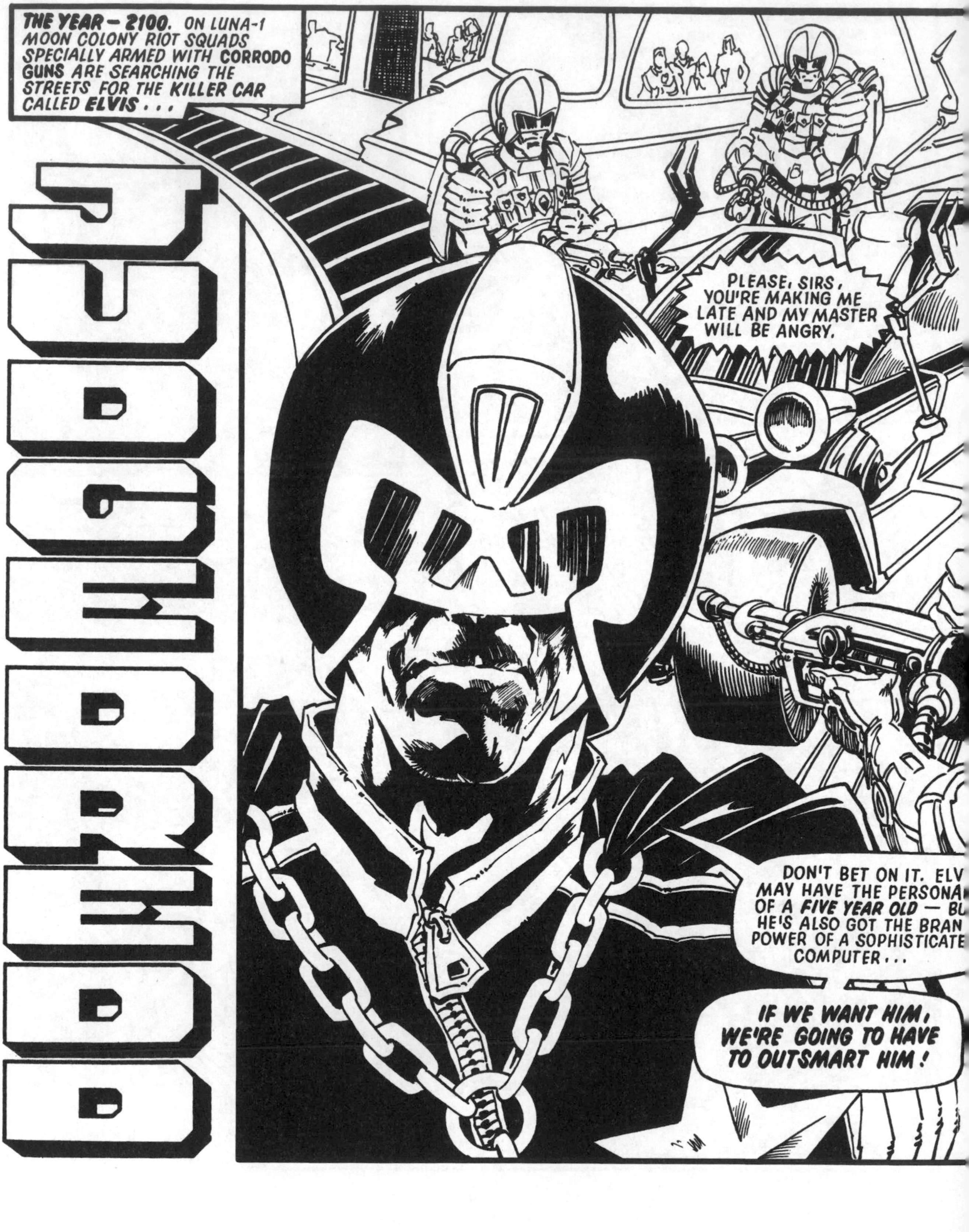
JUDGE DREDD
THE YEAR – 2100. ON LUNA-1 MOON COLONY RIOT SQUADS SPECIALLY ARMED WITH CORRODO GUNS ARE SEARCHING THE STREETS FOR THE KILLER CAR CALLED ELVIS . . .
PLEASE, SIRS, YOU'RE MAKING ME LATE AND MY MASTER WILL BE ANGRY.
DON'T BET ON IT. ELV MAY HAVE THE PERSONA OF A FIVE YEAR OLD — BU HE'S ALSO GOT THE BRAN POWER OF A SOPHISTICATE COMPUTER . . .
IF WE WANT HIM, WE'RE GOING TO HAVE TO OUTSMART HIM!

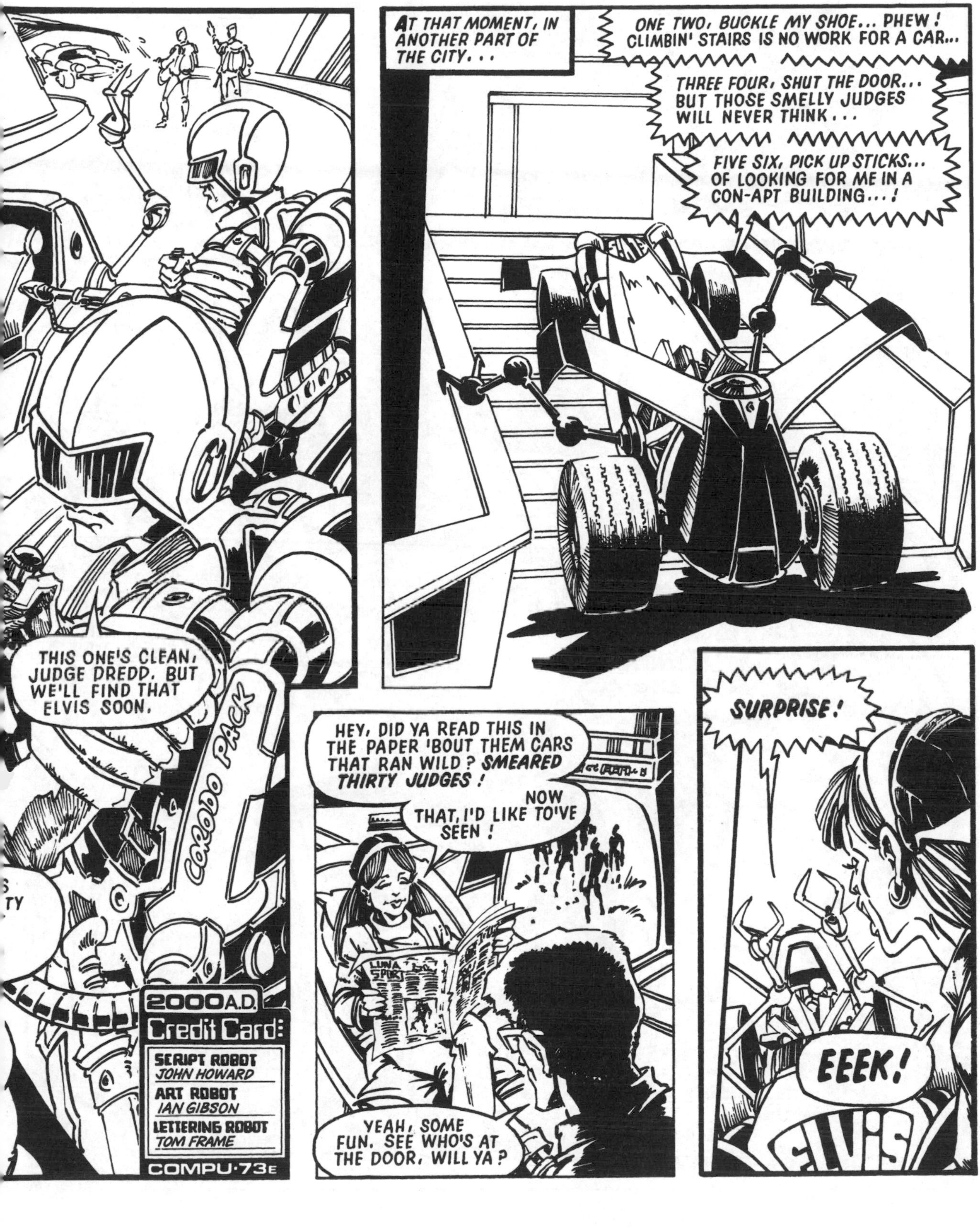

THIS ONE'S CLEAN, JUDGE DREDD. BUT WE'LL FIND THAT ELVIS SOON.
CORODO PACK
2000 A.D.
Credit Card:
SCRIPT ROBOT JOHN HOWARD
ART ROBOT IAN GIBSON
LETTERING ROBOT TOM FRAME
COMPU·73E
AT THAT MOMENT, IN ANOTHER PART OF THE CITY. . .
ONE TWO, BUCKLE MY SHOE. . . PHEW! CLIMBIN' STAIRS IS NO WORK FOR A CAR. . .
THREE FOUR, SHUT THE DOOR. . . BUT THOSE SMELLY JUDGES WILL NEVER THINK. . .
FIVE SIX, PICK UP STICKS. . . OF LOOKING FOR ME IN A CON-APT BUILDING. . . !
HEY, DID YA READ THIS IN THE PAPER 'BOUT THEM CARS THAT RAN WILD? SMEARED THIRTY JUDGES!
NOW THAT, I'D LIKE TO'VE SEEN!
LUNA SPORT
YEAH, SOME FUN. SEE WHO'S AT THE DOOR, WILL YA?
SURPRISE!
EEEK!
ELVIS

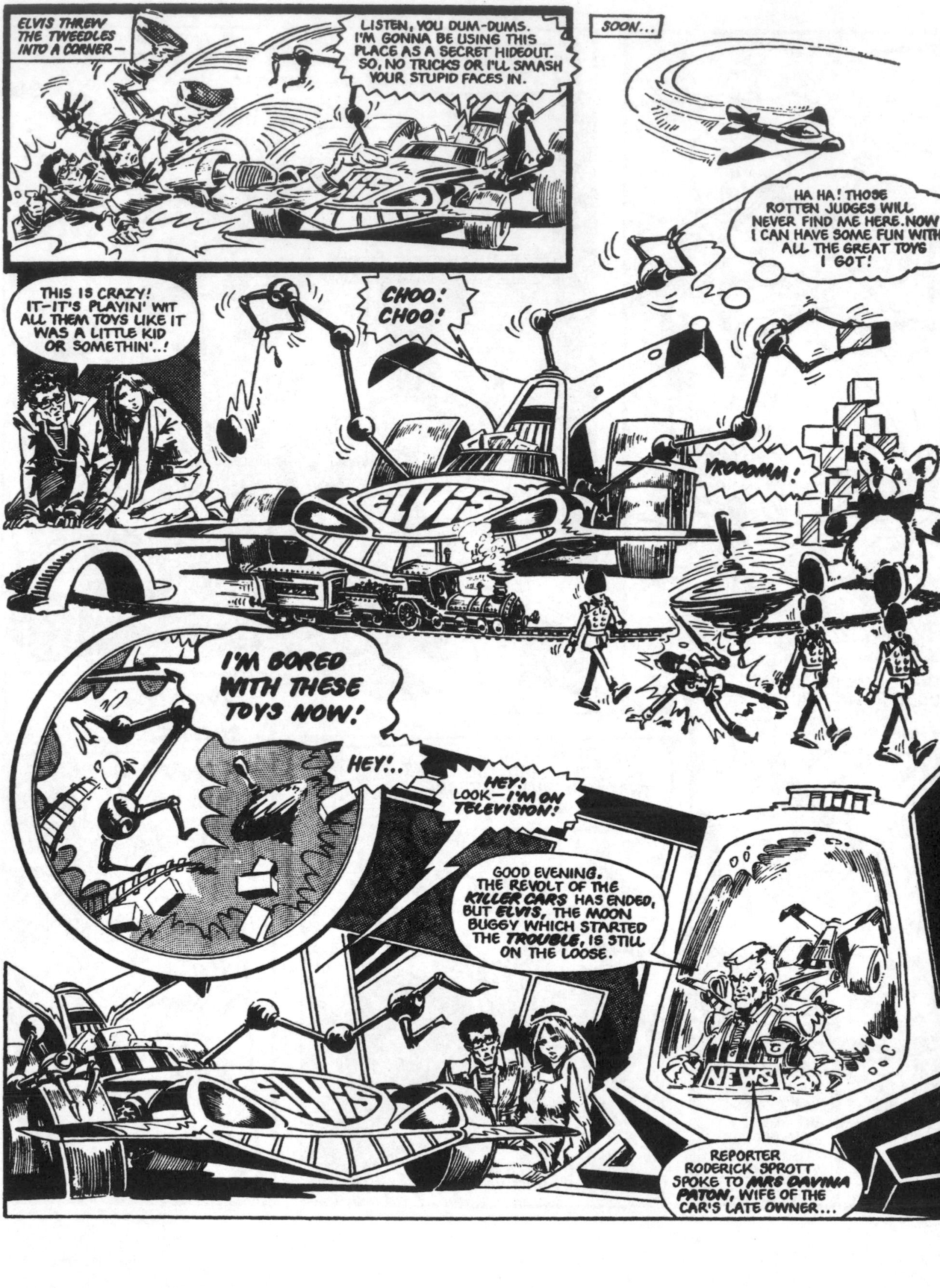
ELVIS THREW THE TWEEDLES INTO A CORNER –
LISTEN, YOU DUM-DUMS. I'M GONNA BE USING THIS PLACE AS A SECRET HIDEOUT. SO, NO TRICKS OR I'LL SMASH YOUR STUPID FACES IN.
SOON...
HA HA! THOSE ROTTEN JUDGES WILL NEVER FIND ME HERE. NOW I CAN HAVE SOME FUN WITH ALL THE GREAT TOYS I GOT!
THIS IS CRAZY! IT–IT'S PLAYIN' WIT ALL THEM TOYS LIKE IT WAS A LITTLE KID OR SOMETHIN'..!
CHOO! CHOO!
VROOOMM!
I'M BORED WITH THESE TOYS NOW!
HEY!..
HEY! LOOK– I'M ON TELEVISION!
GOOD EVENING. THE REVOLT OF THE KILLER CARS HAS ENDED, BUT ELVIS, THE MOON BUGGY WHICH STARTED THE TROUBLE, IS STILL ON THE LOOSE.
NEWS
REPORTER RODERICK SPROTT SPOKE TO MRS DAVINA PATON, WIFE OF THE CAR'S LATE OWNER...

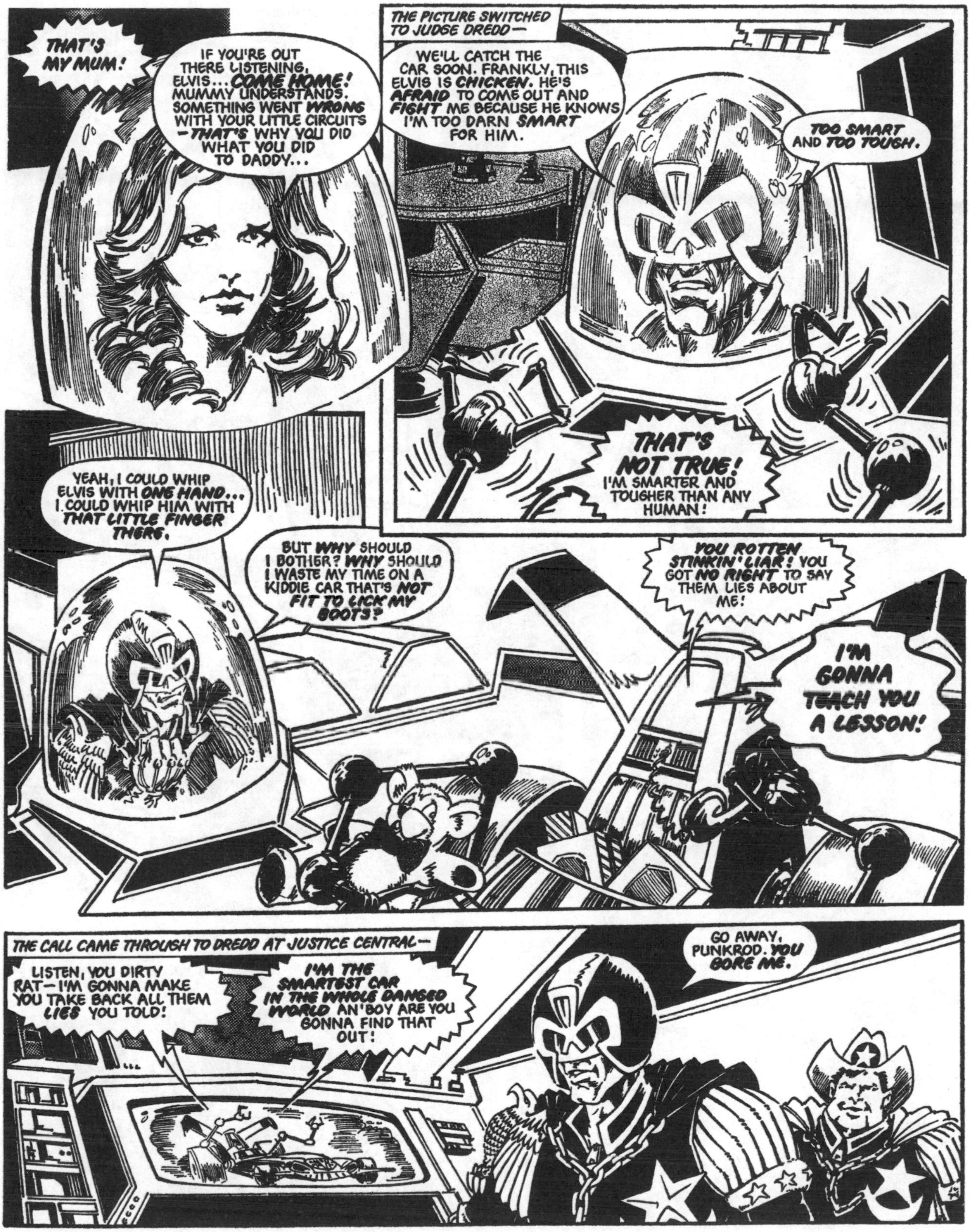

THAT'S MY MUM!
IF YOU'RE OUT THERE LISTENING, ELVIS... COME HOME! MUMMY UNDERSTANDS. SOMETHING WENT WRONG WITH YOUR LITTLE CIRCUITS -THAT'S WHY YOU DID WHAT YOU DID TO DADDY...
THE PICTURE SWITCHED TO JUDGE DREDD—
WE'LL CATCH THE CAR SOON. FRANKLY, THIS ELVIS IS CHICKEN. HE'S AFRAID TO COME OUT AND FIGHT ME BECAUSE HE KNOWS I'M TOO DARN SMART FOR HIM.
TOO SMART AND TOO TOUGH.
THAT'S NOT TRUE! I'M SMARTER AND TOUGHER THAN ANY HUMAN!
YEAH, I COULD WHIP ELVIS WITH ONE HAND... I COULD WHIP HIM WITH THAT LITTLE FINGER THERE.
BUT WHY SHOULD I BOTHER? WHY SHOULD I WASTE MY TIME ON A KIDDIE CAR THAT'S NOT FIT TO LICK MY BOOTS?
YOU ROTTEN STINKIN' LIAR! YOU GOT NO RIGHT TO SAY THEM LIES ABOUT ME!
I'M GONNA TEACH YOU A LESSON!
THE CALL CAME THROUGH TO DREDD AT JUSTICE CENTRAL—
LISTEN, YOU DIRTY RAT—I'M GONNA MAKE YOU TAKE BACK ALL THEM LIES YOU TOLD!
I'M THE SMARTEST CAR IN THE WHOLE DANGED WORLD AN' BOY ARE YOU GONNA FIND THAT OUT!
GO AWAY, PUNKROD. YOU BORE ME.

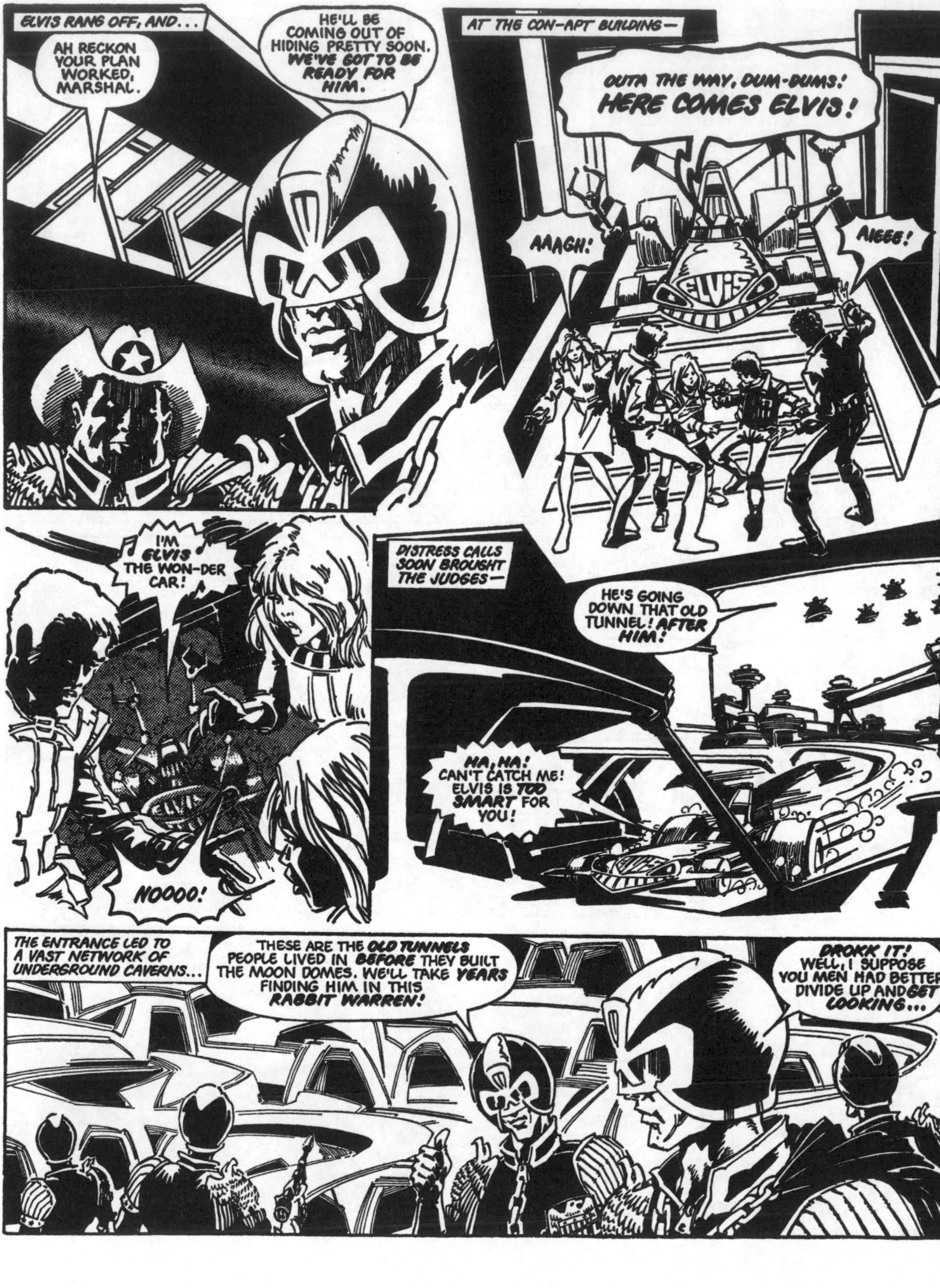
ELVIS RANS OFF, AND...
AH RECKON YOUR PLAN WORKED, MARSHAL.
HE'LL BE COMING OUT OF HIDING PRETTY SOON. WE'VE GOT TO BE READY FOR HIM.
AT THE CON-APT BUILDING—
OUTA THE WAY, DUM-DUMS! HERE COMES ELVIS!
AAAGH!
AIEEE!
ELVIS
I'M ELVIS THE WON-DER CAR!
NOOOO!
ELVIS
DISTRESS CALLS SOON BROUGHT THE JUDGES—
HE'S GOING DOWN THAT OLD TUNNEL! AFTER HIM!
HA, HA! CAN'T CATCH ME! ELVIS IS TOO SMART FOR YOU!
THE ENTRANCE LED TO A VAST NETWORK OF UNDERGROUND CAVERNS...
THESE ARE THE OLD TUNNELS PEOPLE LIVED IN BEFORE THEY BUILT THE MOON DOMES. WE'LL TAKE YEARS FINDING HIM IN THIS RABBIT WARREN!
DROKK IT! WELL, I SUPPOSE YOU MEN HAD BETTER DIVIDE UP AND GET LOOKING...

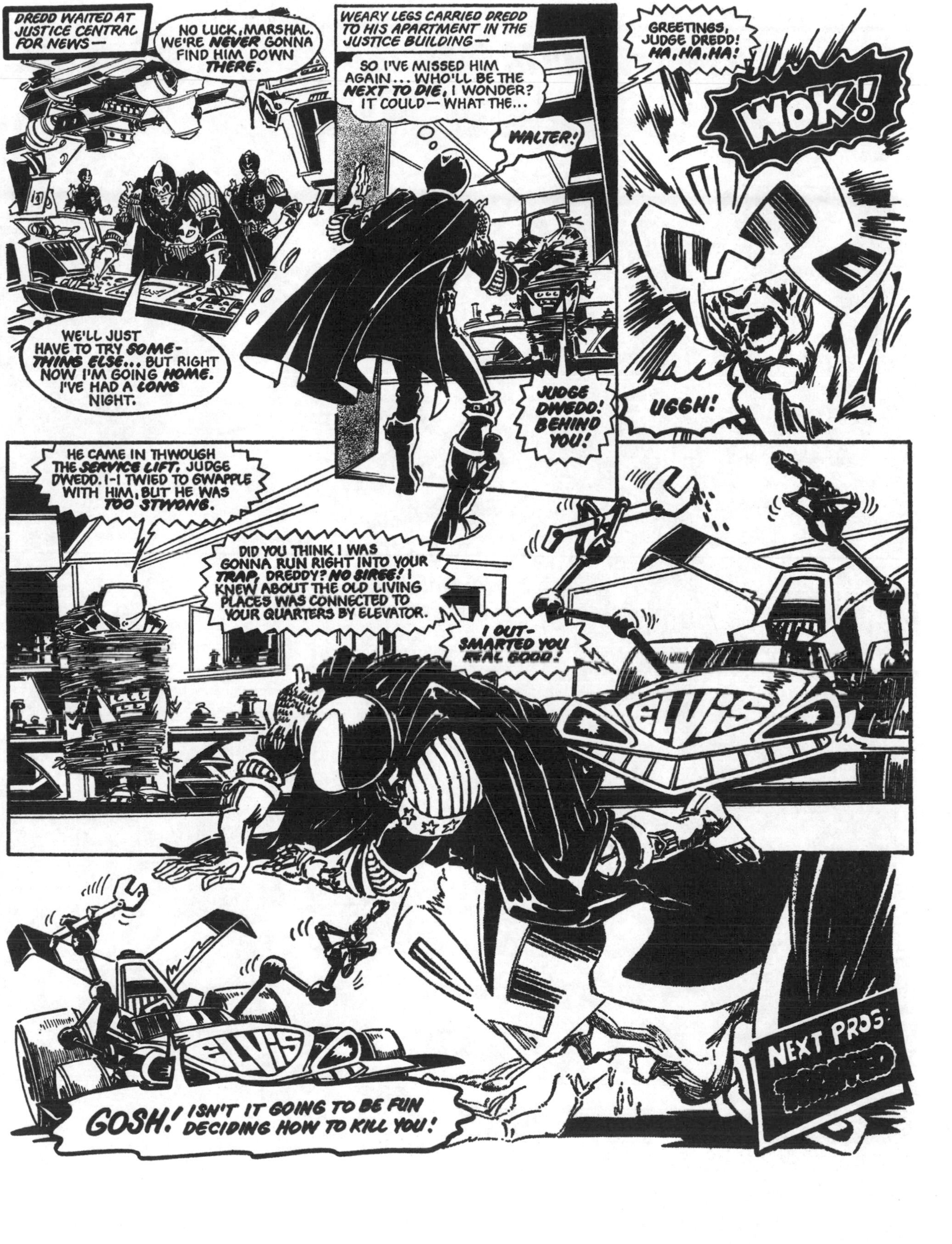

DREDD WAITED AT JUSTICE CENTRAL FOR NEWS—
NO LUCK, MARSHAL. WE'RE NEVER GONNA FIND HIM DOWN THERE.
WE'LL JUST HAVE TO TRY SOMETHING ELSE... BUT RIGHT NOW I'M GOING HOME. I'VE HAD A LONG NIGHT.
WEARY LEGS CARRIED DREDD TO HIS APARTMENT IN THE JUSTICE BUILDING—
SO I'VE MISSED HIM AGAIN... WHO'LL BE THE NEXT TO DIE, I WONDER? IT COULD— WHAT THE...
WALTER!
JUDGE DWEDD! BEHIND YOU!
GREETINGS, JUDGE DREDD! HA, HA, HA!
WOK!
UGGH!
HE CAME IN THWOUGH THE SERVICE LIFT, JUDGE DWEDD. I-I TWIED TO GWAPPLE WITH HIM, BUT HE WAS TOO STWONG.
DID YOU THINK I WAS GONNA RUN RIGHT INTO YOUR TRAP, DREDDY? NO SIREE! I KNEW ABOUT THE OLD LIVING PLACES WAS CONNECTED TO YOUR QUARTERS BY ELEVATOR.
I OUT-SMARTED YOU REAL GOOD!
ELVIS
ELVIS
GOSH! ISN'T IT GOING TO BE FUN DECIDING HOW TO KILL YOU!
NEXT PROG:

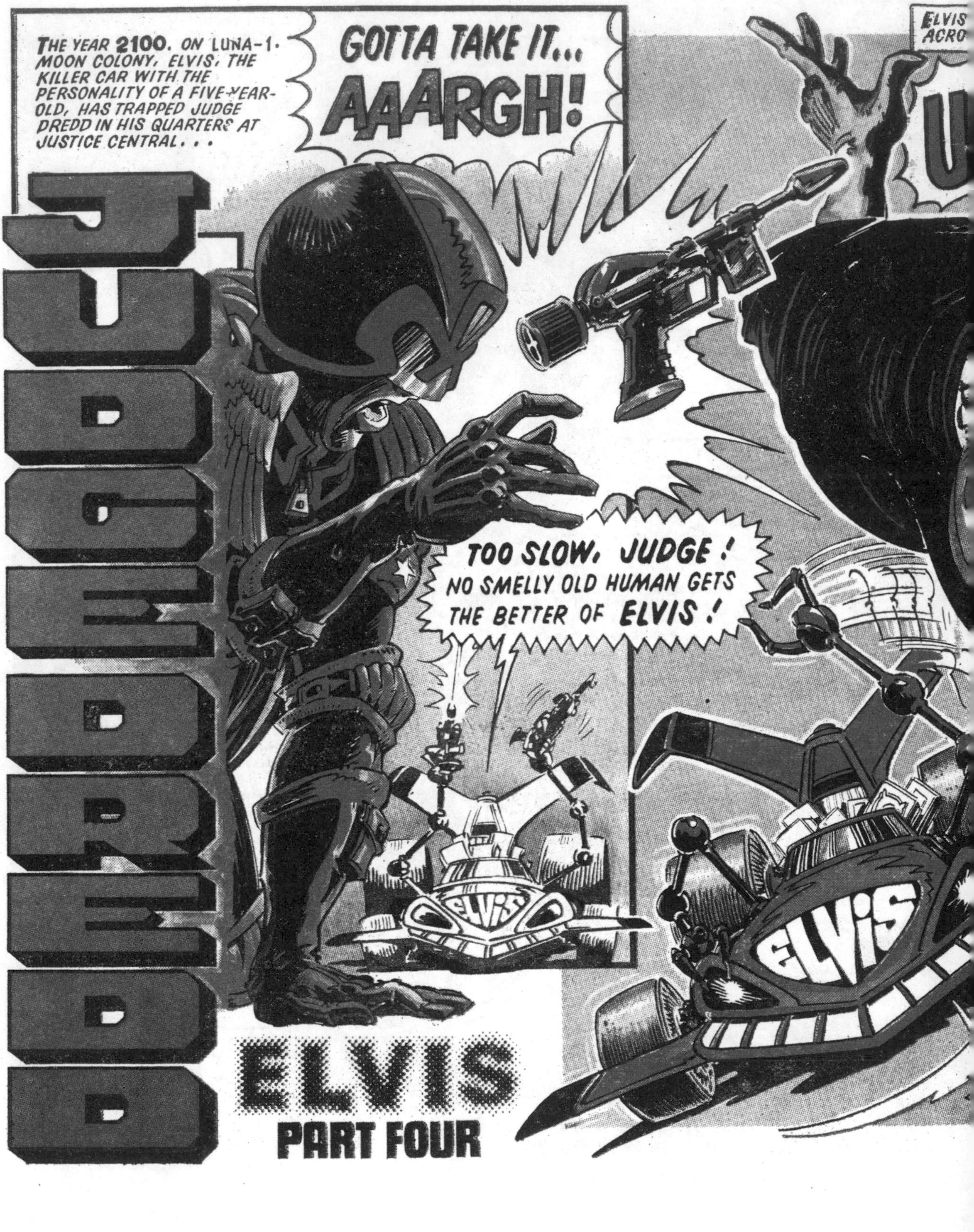
JUDGE DREDD
THE YEAR 2100. ON LUNA-1 MOON COLONY, ELVIS, THE KILLER CAR WITH THE PERSONALITY OF A FIVE-YEAR-OLD, HAS TRAPPED JUDGE DREDD IN HIS QUARTERS AT JUSTICE CENTRAL. . .
GOTTA TAKE IT... AAARGH!
TOO SLOW, JUDGE! NO SMELLY OLD HUMAN GETS THE BETTER OF ELVIS!
ELVIS
ELVIS
ELVIS
PART FOUR

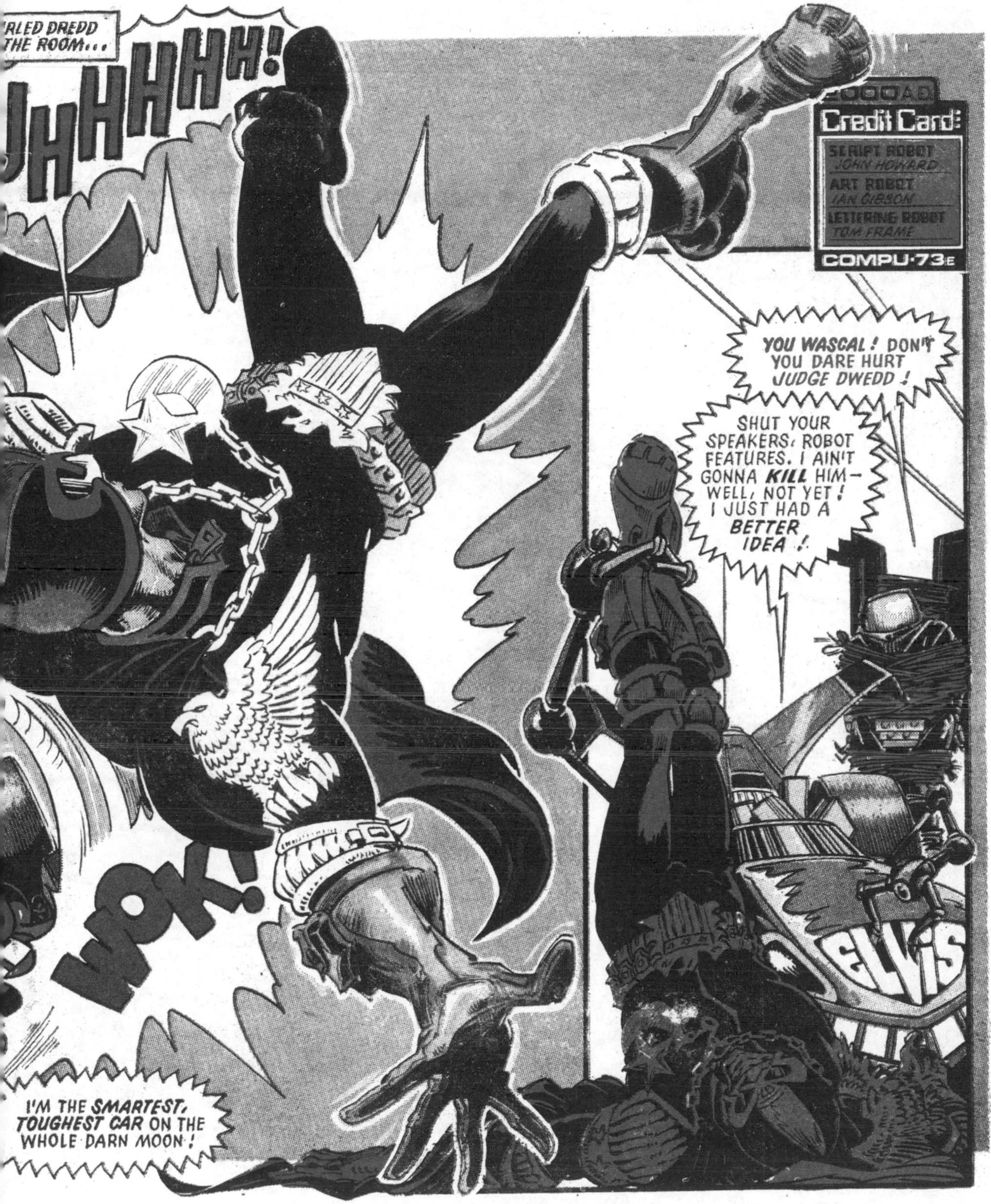
RLED DREDD
THE ROOM...
UHHHHHH!
2000 A.D.
Credit Card
SCRIPT ROBOT JOHN HOWARD
ART ROBOT IAN GIBSON
LETTERING ROBOT TOM FRAME
COMPU-73E
YOU WASCAL! DON'T YOU DARE HURT JUDGE DWEDD!
SHUT YOUR SPEAKERS, ROBOT FEATURES. I AIN'T GONNA KILL HIM— WELL, NOT YET! I JUST HAD A BETTER IDEA!
WOK!
I'M THE SMARTEST, TOUGHEST CAR ON THE WHOLE DARN MOON!
ELVIS

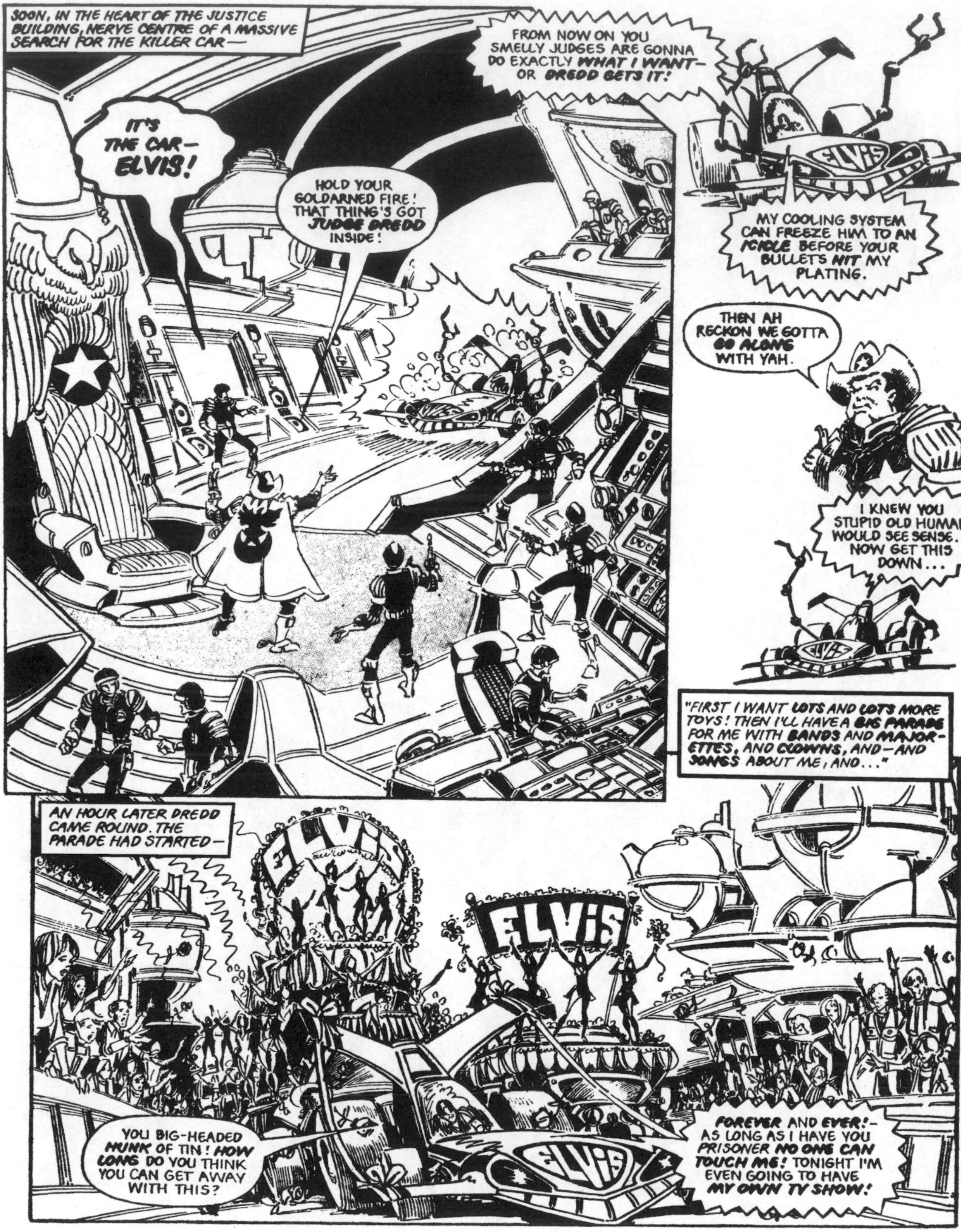
SOON, IN THE HEART OF THE JUSTICE BUILDING, NERVE CENTRE OF A MASSIVE SEARCH FOR THE KILLER CAR—
FROM NOW ON YOU SMELLY JUDGES ARE GONNA DO EXACTLY WHAT I WANT— OR DREDD GETS IT!
IT'S THE CAR— ELVIS!
HOLD YOUR GOLDARNED FIRE! THAT THING'S GOT JUDGE DREDD INSIDE!
MY COOLING SYSTEM CAN FREEZE HIM TO AN ICICLE BEFORE YOUR BULLETS HIT MY PLATING.
THEN AH RECKON WE GOTTA GO ALONG WITH YAH.
I KNEW YOU STUPID OLD HUMANS WOULD SEE SENSE. NOW GET THIS DOWN...
"FIRST I WANT LOTS AND LOTS MORE TOYS! THEN I'LL HAVE A BIG PARADE FOR ME WITH BANDS AND MAJORETTES, AND CLOWNS, AND—AND SONGS ABOUT ME, AND..."
AN HOUR LATER DREDD CAME ROUND. THE PARADE HAD STARTED—
ELVIS
ELVIS
YOU BIG-HEADED HUNK OF TIN! HOW LONG DO YOU THINK YOU CAN GET AWAY WITH THIS?
FOREVER AND EVER!— AS LONG AS I HAVE YOU PRISONER NO ONE CAN TOUCH ME! TONIGHT I'M EVEN GOING TO HAVE MY OWN TV SHOW!
ELVIS

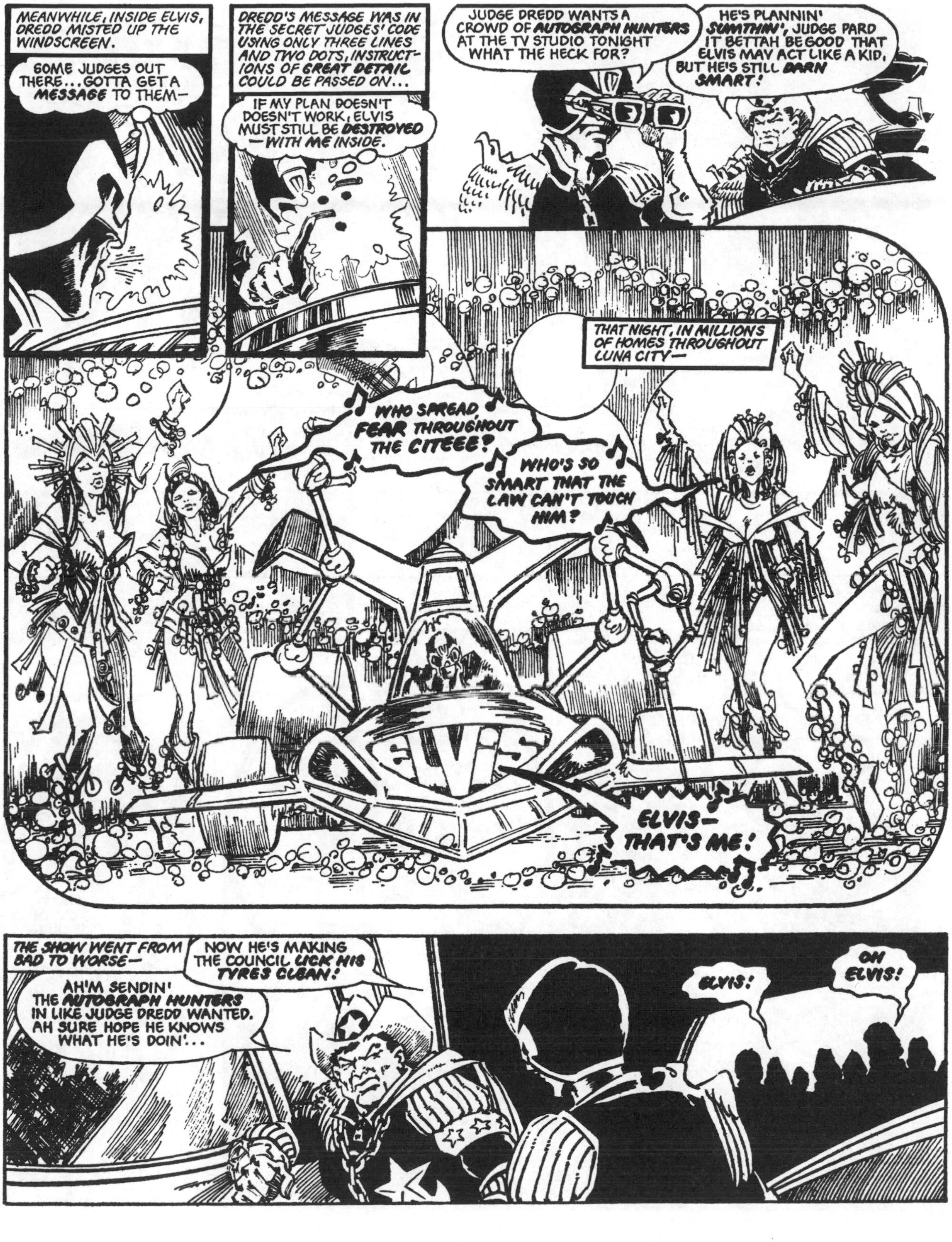
MEANWHILE, INSIDE ELVIS, DREDD MISTED UP THE WINDSCREEN.
SOME JUDGES OUT THERE... GOTTA GET A MESSAGE TO THEM—
DREDD'S MESSAGE WAS IN THE SECRET JUDGES' CODE USING ONLY THREE LINES AND TWO DOTS, INSTRUCTIONS OF GREAT DETAIL COULD BE PASSED ON...
IF MY PLAN DOESN'T DOESN'T WORK, ELVIS MUST STILL BE DESTROYED —WITH ME INSIDE.
JUDGE DREDD WANTS A CROWD OF AUTOGRAPH HUNTERS AT THE TV STUDIO TONIGHT WHAT THE HECK FOR?
HE'S PLANNIN' SUMTHIN', JUDGE PARD IT BETTAH BE GOOD THAT ELVIS MAY ACT LIKE A KID, BUT HE'S STILL DARN SMART!
THAT NIGHT, IN MILLIONS OF HOMES THROUGHOUT LUNA CITY—
WHO SPREAD FEAR THROUGHOUT THE CITEEE?
WHO'S SO SMART THAT THE LAW CAN'T TOUCH HIM?
ELVIS
ELVIS— THAT'S ME!
THE SHOW WENT FROM BAD TO WORSE—
NOW HE'S MAKING THE COUNCIL LICK HIS TYRES CLEAN!
AH'M SENDIN' THE AUTOGRAPH HUNTERS IN LIKE JUDGE DREDD WANTED. AH SURE HOPE HE KNOWS WHAT HE'S DOIN'...
ELVIS!
OH ELVIS!

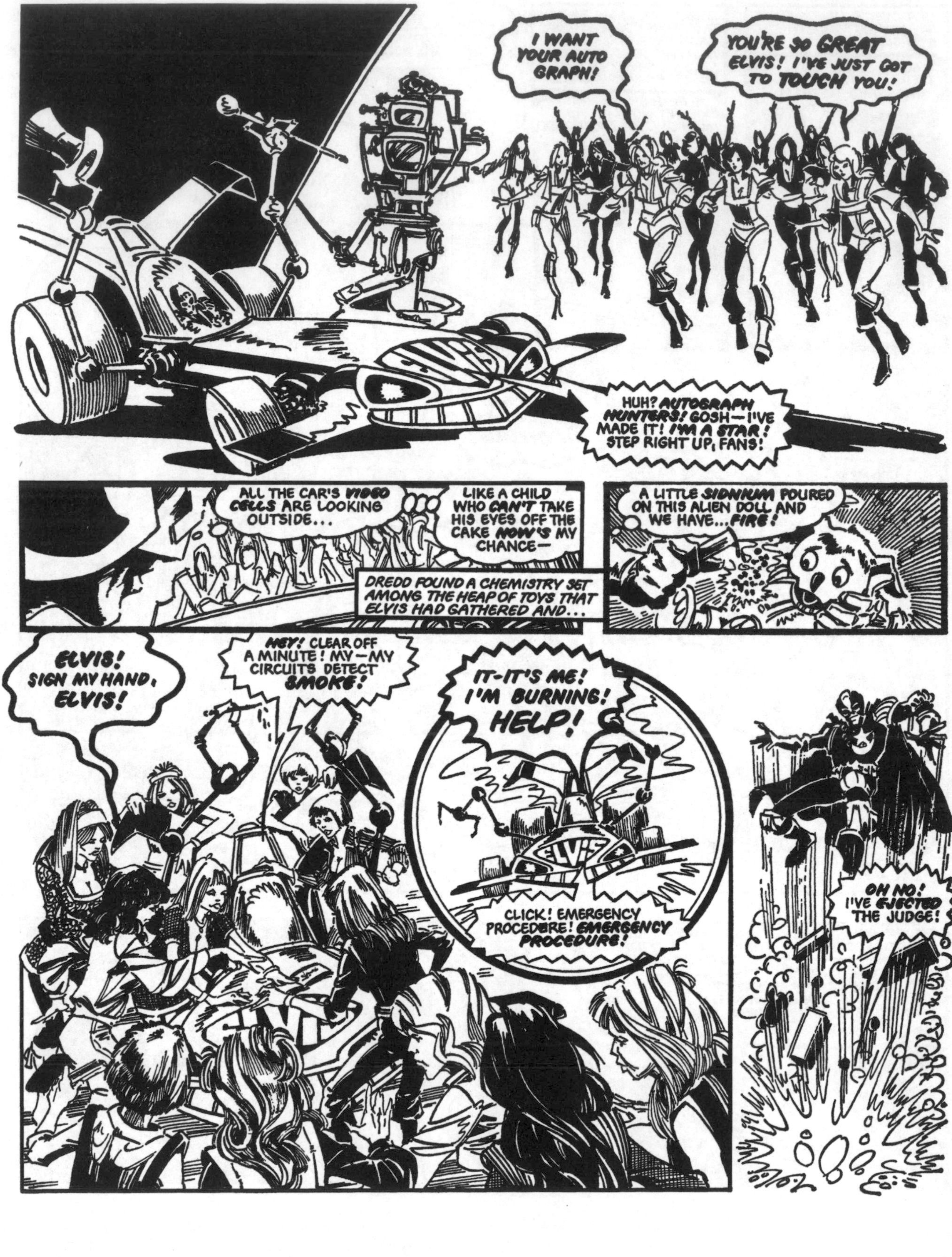
I WANT YOUR AUTO GRAPH!
YOU'RE SO GREAT ELVIS! I'VE JUST GOT TO TOUCH YOU!
HUH? AUTOGRAPH HUNTERS! GOSH—I'VE MADE IT! I'M A STAR! STEP RIGHT UP, FANS!
ALL THE CAR'S VIDEO CELLS ARE LOOKING OUTSIDE...
LIKE A CHILD WHO CAN'T TAKE HIS EYES OFF THE CAKE NOW'S MY CHANCE—
DREDD FOUND A CHEMISTRY SET AMONG THE HEAP OF TOYS THAT ELVIS HAD GATHERED AND...
A LITTLE SIDNIUM POURED ON THIS ALIEN DOLL AND WE HAVE...FIRE!
ELVIS! SIGN MY HAND, ELVIS!
HEY! CLEAR OFF A MINUTE! MY—MY CIRCUITS DETECT SMOKE!
IT-IT'S ME! I'M BURNING! HELP!
CLICK! EMERGENCY PROCEDURE! EMERGENCY PROCEDURE!
OH NO! I'VE EJECTED THE JUDGE!

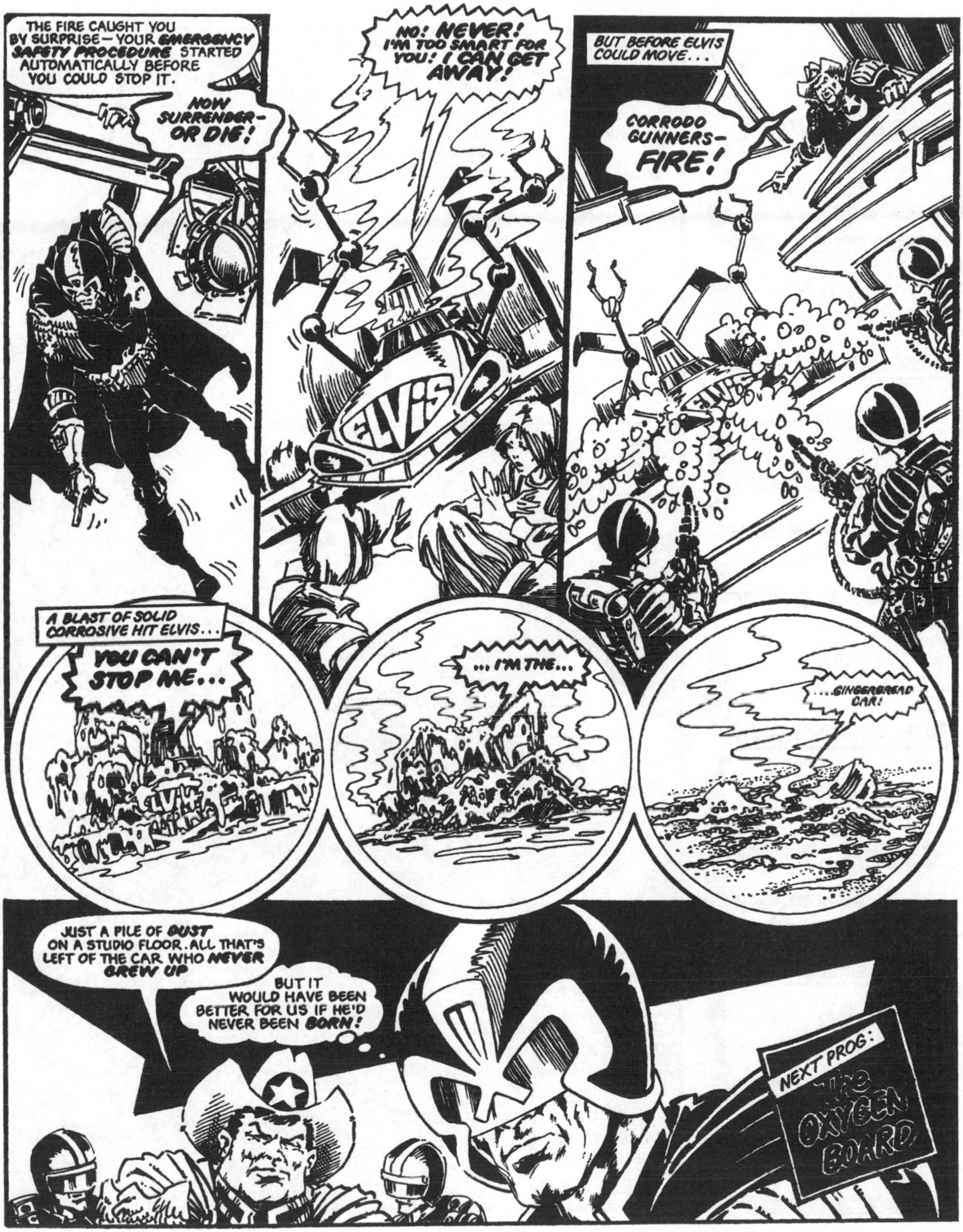

THE FIRE CAUGHT YOU BY SURPRISE — YOUR EMERGENCY SAFETY PROCEDURE STARTED AUTOMATICALLY BEFORE YOU COULD STOP IT.
NOW SURRENDER — OR DIE!
NO! NEVER! I'M TOO SMART FOR YOU! I CAN GET AWAY!
ELVIS
BUT BEFORE ELVIS COULD MOVE...
CORRODO GUNNERS — FIRE!
A BLAST OF SOLID CORROSIVE HIT ELVIS...
YOU CAN'T STOP ME...
...I'M THE...
...GINGERBREAD CAR!
JUST A PILE OF DUST ON A STUDIO FLOOR. ALL THAT'S LEFT OF THE CAR WHO NEVER GREW UP
BUT IT WOULD HAVE BEEN BETTER FOR US IF HE'D NEVER BEEN BORN!
NEXT PROG: The OXYGEN BOARD

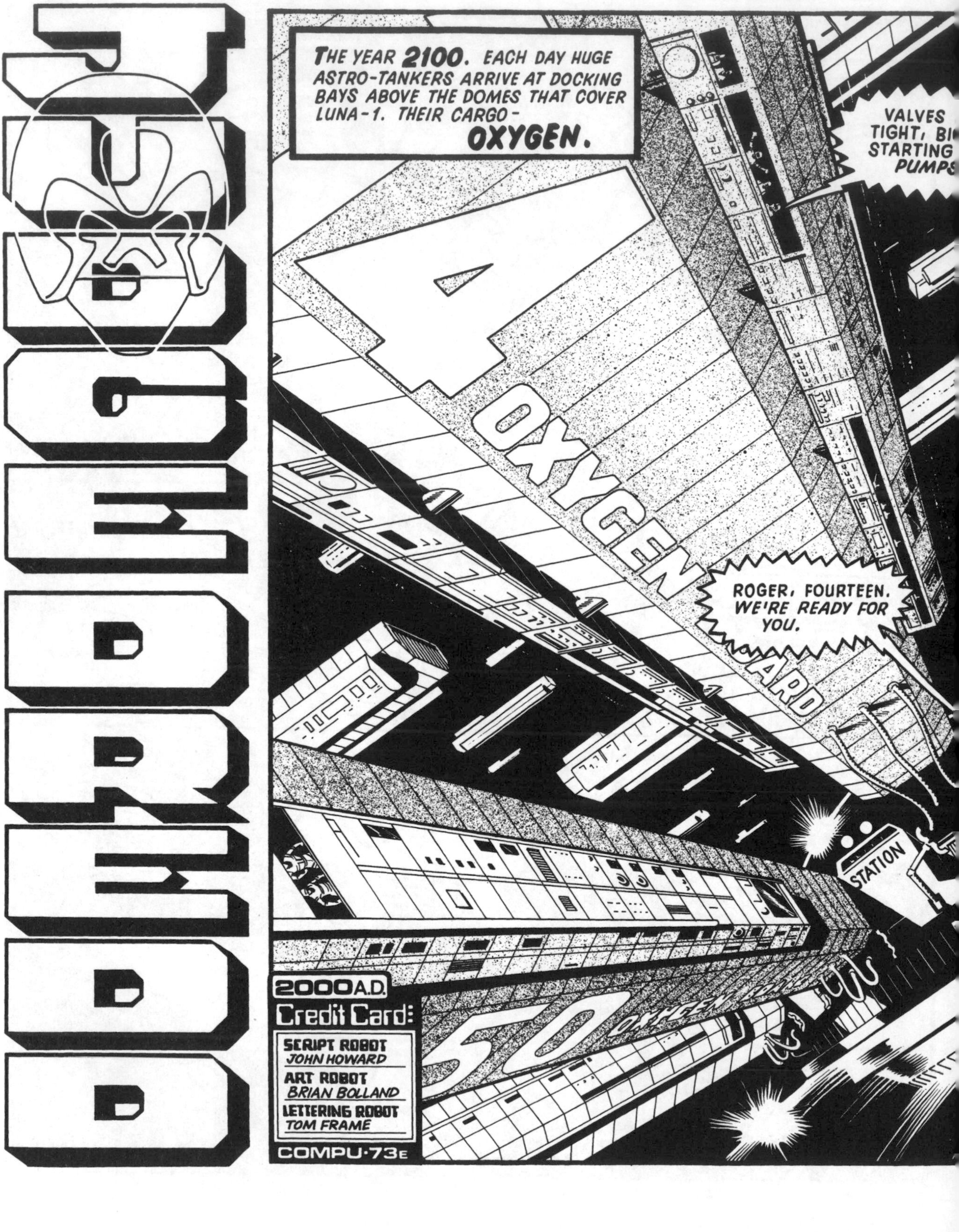

JUDGE DREDD
THE YEAR 2100. EACH DAY HUGE ASTRO-TANKERS ARRIVE AT DOCKING BAYS ABOVE THE DOMES THAT COVER LUNA-1. THEIR CARGO- OXYGEN.
VALVES TIGHT, BI STARTING PUMPS
4 OXYGEN
ROGER, FOURTEEN. WE'RE READY FOR YOU.
ARD
STATION
50
2000 A.D.
Credit Card:
SCRIPT ROBOT JOHN HOWARD
ART ROBOT BRIAN BOLLAND
LETTERING ROBOT TOM FRAME
COMPU-73E

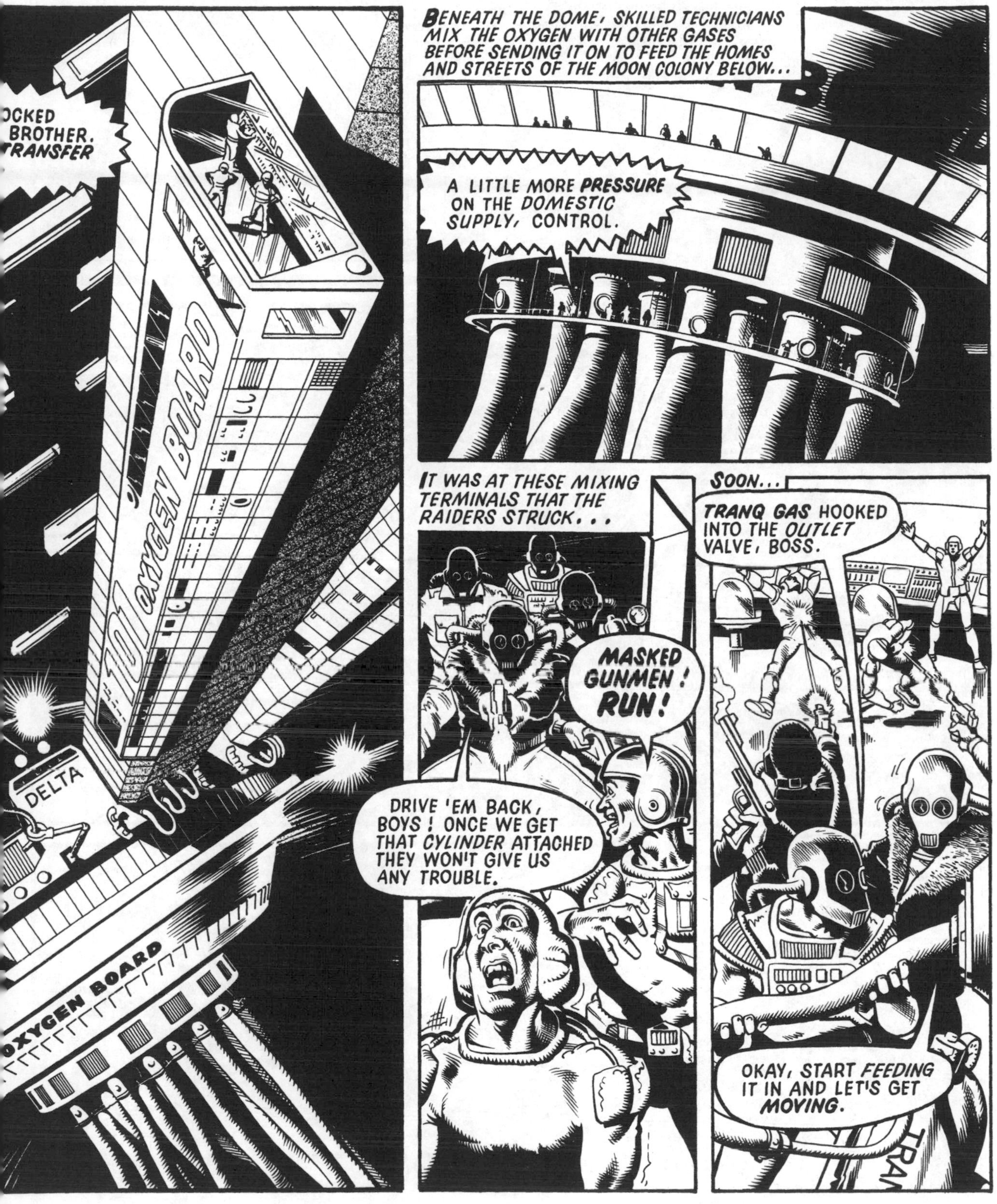
OCKED
BROTHER.
TRANSFER
101 OXYGEN BOARD
DELTA
OXYGEN BOARD
BENEATH THE DOME, SKILLED TECHNICIANS MIX THE OXYGEN WITH OTHER GASES BEFORE SENDING IT ON TO FEED THE HOMES AND STREETS OF THE MOON COLONY BELOW...
A LITTLE MORE PRESSURE ON THE DOMESTIC SUPPLY, CONTROL.
IT WAS AT THESE MIXING TERMINALS THAT THE RAIDERS STRUCK...
MASKED GUNMEN! RUN!
DRIVE 'EM BACK, BOYS! ONCE WE GET THAT CYLINDER ATTACHED THEY WON'T GIVE US ANY TROUBLE.
SOON...
TRANQ GAS HOOKED INTO THE OUTLET VALVE, BOSS.
OKAY, START FEEDING IT IN AND LET'S GET MOVING.

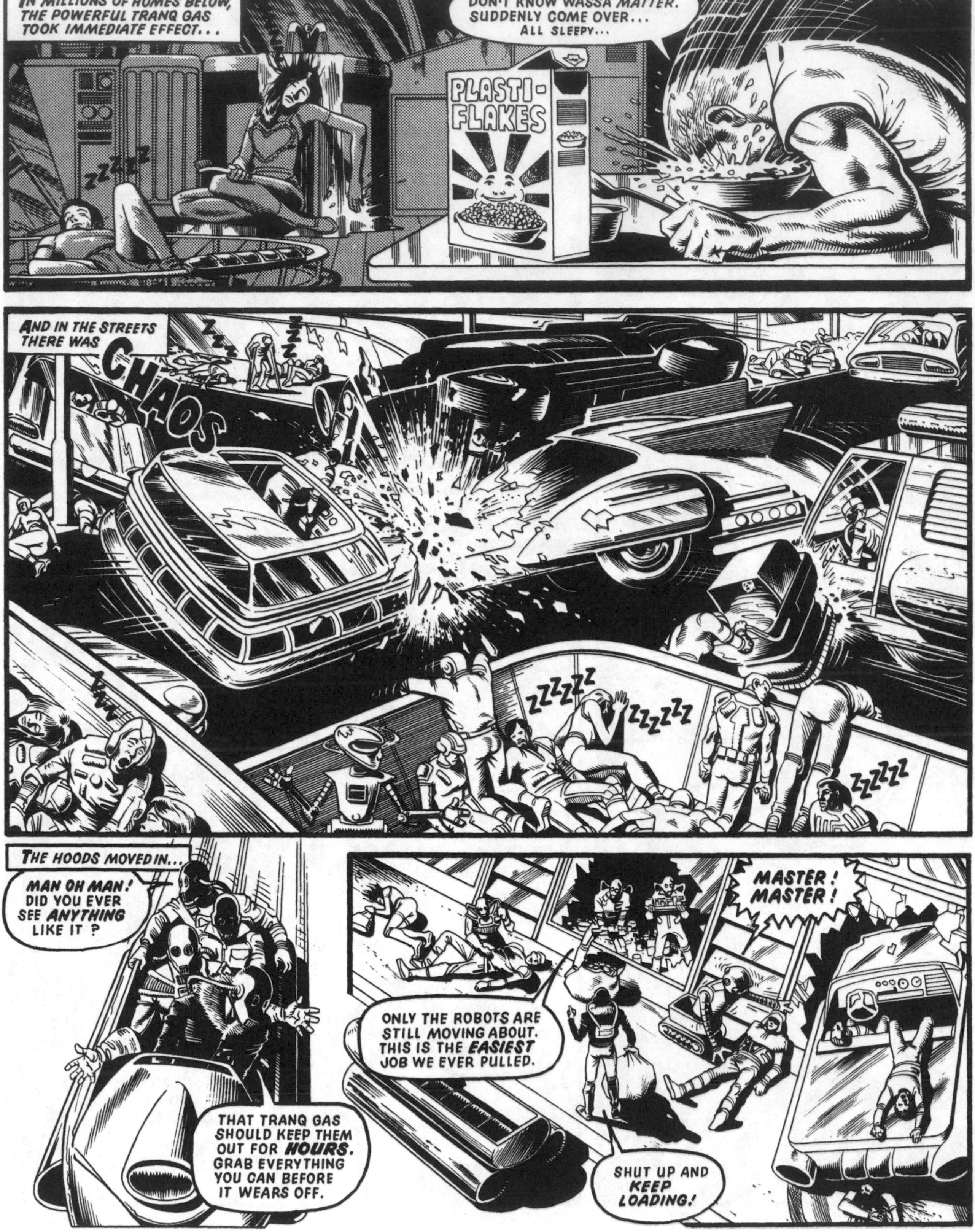

IN MILLIONS OF HOMES BELOW, THE POWERFUL TRANQ GAS TOOK IMMEDIATE EFFECT...
DON'T KNOW WASSA MATTER. SUDDENLY COME OVER... ALL SLEEPY...
ZZZZZZ
PLASTI-FLAKES
AND IN THE STREETS THERE WAS
CHAOS
ZZZZZZ
ZZZZZZ
ZZZZZZ
THE HOODS MOVED IN...
MAN OH MAN! DID YOU EVER SEE ANYTHING LIKE IT ?
THAT TRANQ GAS SHOULD KEEP THEM OUT FOR HOURS. GRAB EVERYTHING YOU CAN BEFORE IT WEARS OFF.
MASTER! MASTER!
ONLY THE ROBOTS ARE STILL MOVING ABOUT. THIS IS THE EASIEST JOB WE EVER PULLED.
SHUT UP AND KEEP LOADING!

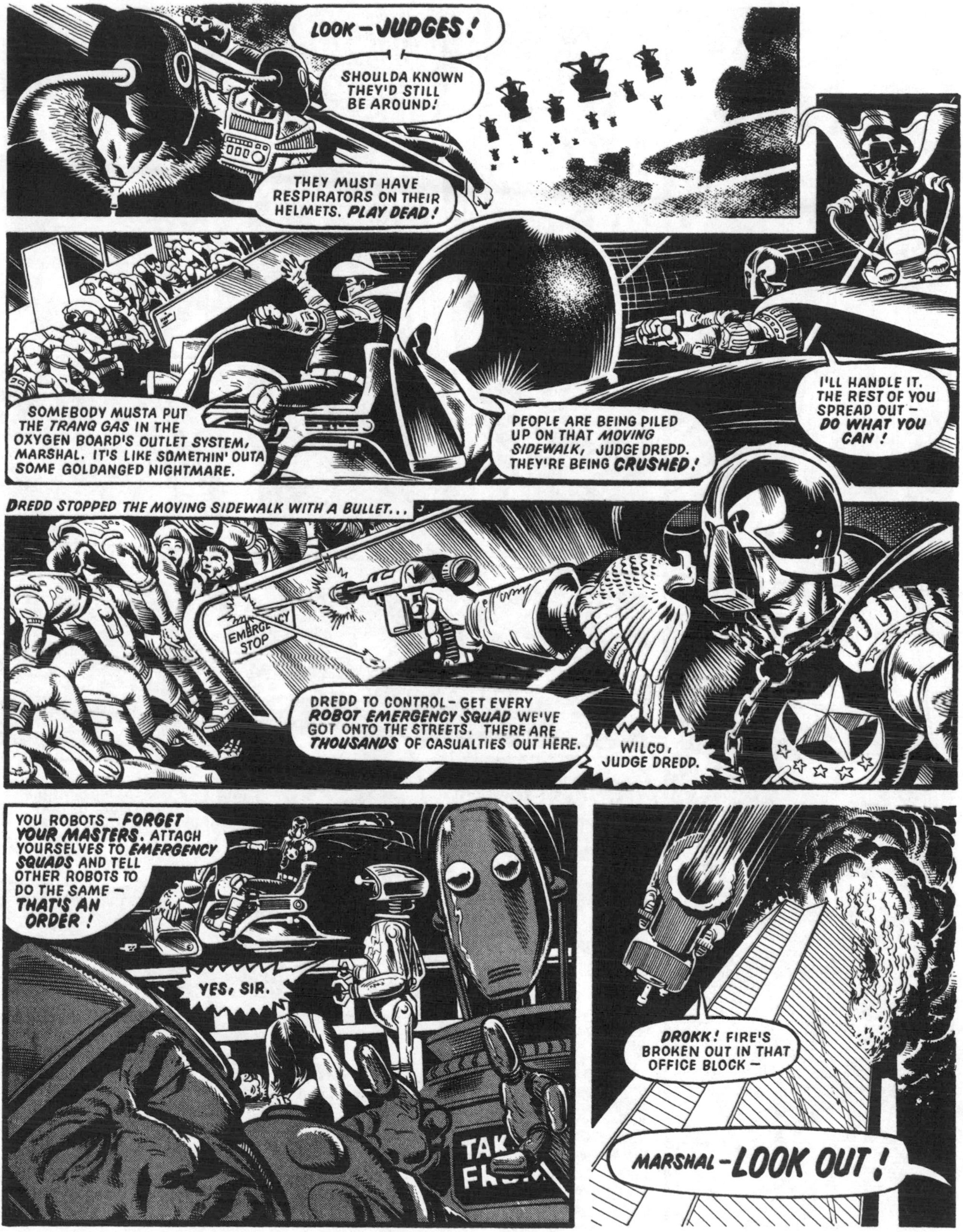
LOOK – JUDGES!
SHOULDA KNOWN THEY'D STILL BE AROUND!
THEY MUST HAVE RESPIRATORS ON THEIR HELMETS. PLAY DEAD!
SOMEBODY MUSTA PUT THE TRANQ GAS IN THE OXYGEN BOARD'S OUTLET SYSTEM, MARSHAL. IT'S LIKE SOMETHIN' OUTA SOME GOLDANGED NIGHTMARE.
PEOPLE ARE BEING PILED UP ON THAT MOVING SIDEWALK, JUDGE DREDD. THEY'RE BEING CRUSHED!
I'LL HANDLE IT. THE REST OF YOU SPREAD OUT – DO WHAT YOU CAN!
DREDD STOPPED THE MOVING SIDEWALK WITH A BULLET...
EMERGENCY STOP
DREDD TO CONTROL – GET EVERY ROBOT EMERGENCY SQUAD WE'VE GOT ONTO THE STREETS. THERE ARE THOUSANDS OF CASUALTIES OUT HERE.
WILCO, JUDGE DREDD.
YOU ROBOTS – FORGET YOUR MASTERS. ATTACH YOURSELVES TO EMERGENCY SQUADS AND TELL OTHER ROBOTS TO DO THE SAME – THAT'S AN ORDER!
YES, SIR.
DROKK! FIRE'S BROKEN OUT IN THAT OFFICE BLOCK –
MARSHAL – LOOK OUT!

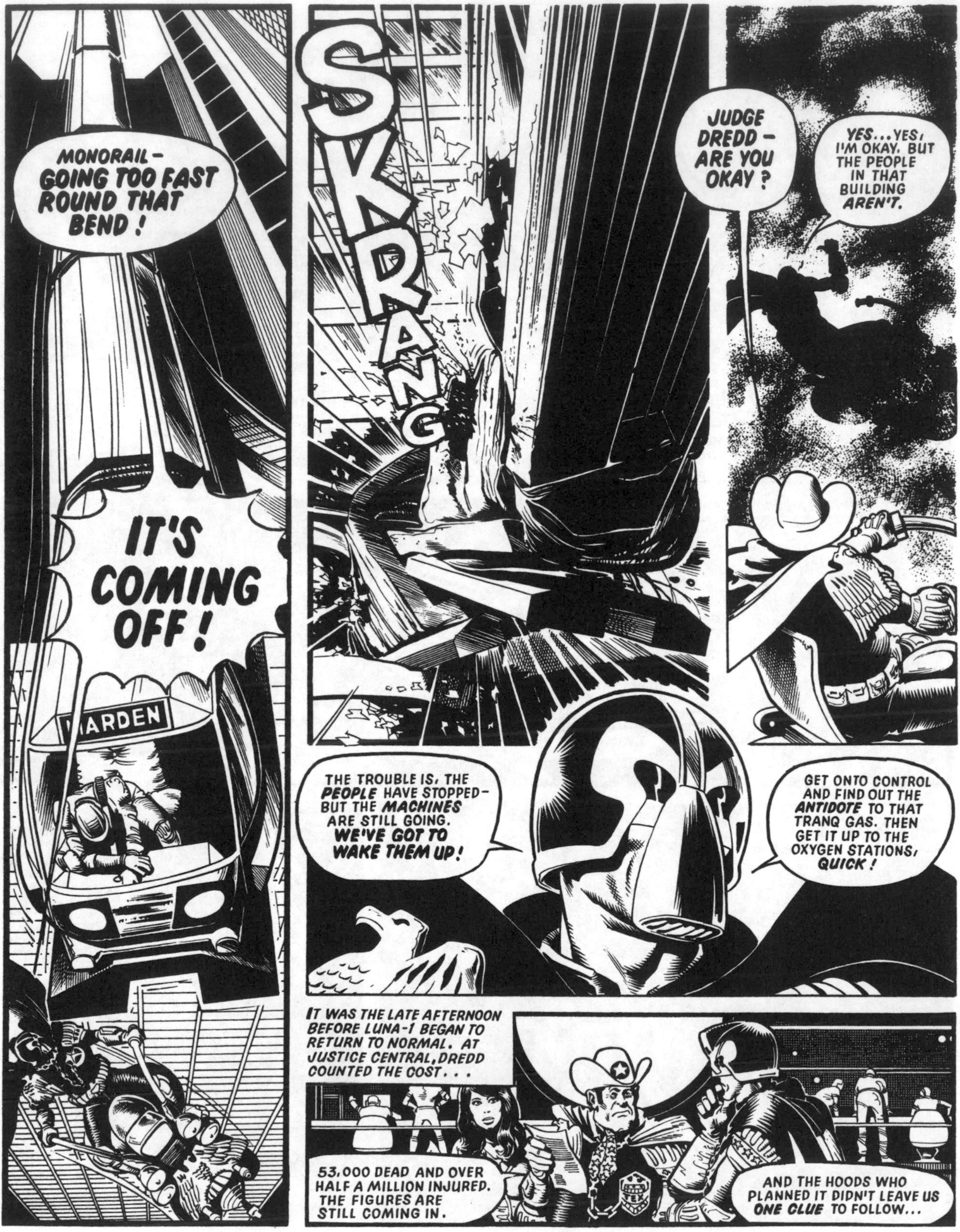

MONORAIL - GOING TOO FAST ROUND THAT BEND!
IT'S COMING OFF!
WARDEN
SKRANG
JUDGE DREDD - ARE YOU OKAY?
YES...YES, I'M OKAY. BUT THE PEOPLE IN THAT BUILDING AREN'T.
THE TROUBLE IS, THE PEOPLE HAVE STOPPED - BUT THE MACHINES ARE STILL GOING. WE'VE GOT TO WAKE THEM UP!
GET ONTO CONTROL AND FIND OUT THE ANTIDOTE TO THAT TRANQ GAS. THEN GET IT UP TO THE OXYGEN STATIONS, QUICK!
IT WAS THE LATE AFTERNOON BEFORE LUNA-1 BEGAN TO RETURN TO NORMAL. AT JUSTICE CENTRAL, DREDD COUNTED THE COST...
53,000 DEAD AND OVER HALF A MILLION INJURED. THE FIGURES ARE STILL COMING IN.
AND THE HOODS WHO PLANNED IT DIDN'T LEAVE US ONE CLUE TO FOLLOW...

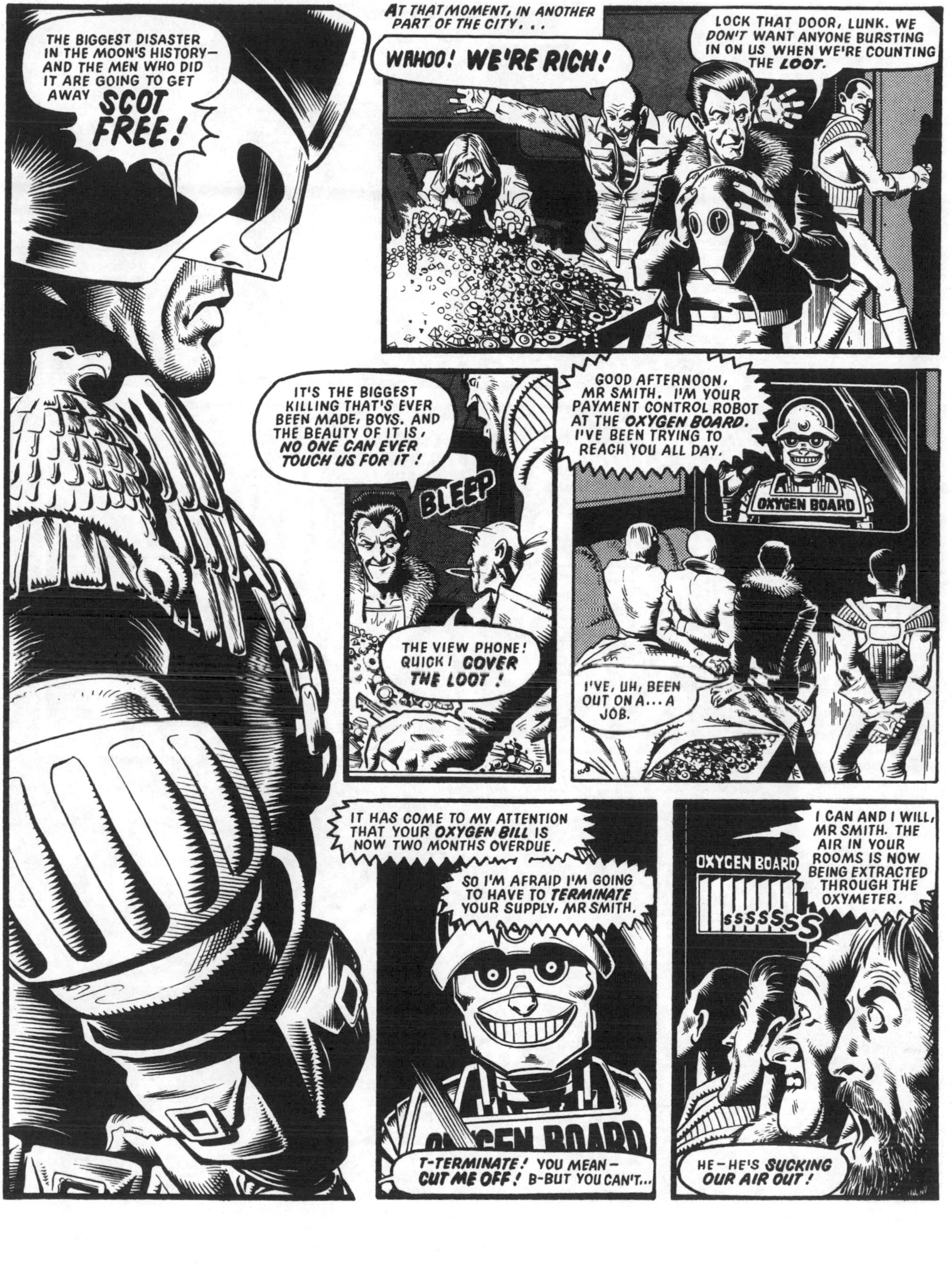

THE BIGGEST DISASTER IN THE MOON'S HISTORY— AND THE MEN WHO DID IT ARE GOING TO GET AWAY SCOT FREE!
AT THAT MOMENT, IN ANOTHER PART OF THE CITY. . .
WAHOO! WE'RE RICH!
LOCK THAT DOOR, LUNK. WE DON'T WANT ANYONE BURSTING IN ON US WHEN WE'RE COUNTING THE LOOT.
IT'S THE BIGGEST KILLING THAT'S EVER BEEN MADE, BOYS. AND THE BEAUTY OF IT IS, NO ONE CAN EVER TOUCH US FOR IT!
BLEEP
THE VIEW PHONE! QUICK! COVER THE LOOT!
GOOD AFTERNOON, MR SMITH. I'M YOUR PAYMENT CONTROL ROBOT AT THE OXYGEN BOARD. I'VE BEEN TRYING TO REACH YOU ALL DAY.
OXYGEN BOARD
I'VE, UH, BEEN OUT ON A... A JOB.
IT HAS COME TO MY ATTENTION THAT YOUR OXYGEN BILL IS NOW TWO MONTHS OVERDUE.
SO I'M AFRAID I'M GOING TO HAVE TO TERMINATE YOUR SUPPLY, MR SMITH.
T-TERMINATE! YOU MEAN— CUT ME OFF! B-BUT YOU CAN'T...
I CAN AND I WILL, MR SMITH. THE AIR IN YOUR ROOMS IS NOW BEING EXTRACTED THROUGH THE OXYMETER.
OXYGEN BOARD
SSSSSSS
HE-HE'S SUCKING OUR AIR OUT!

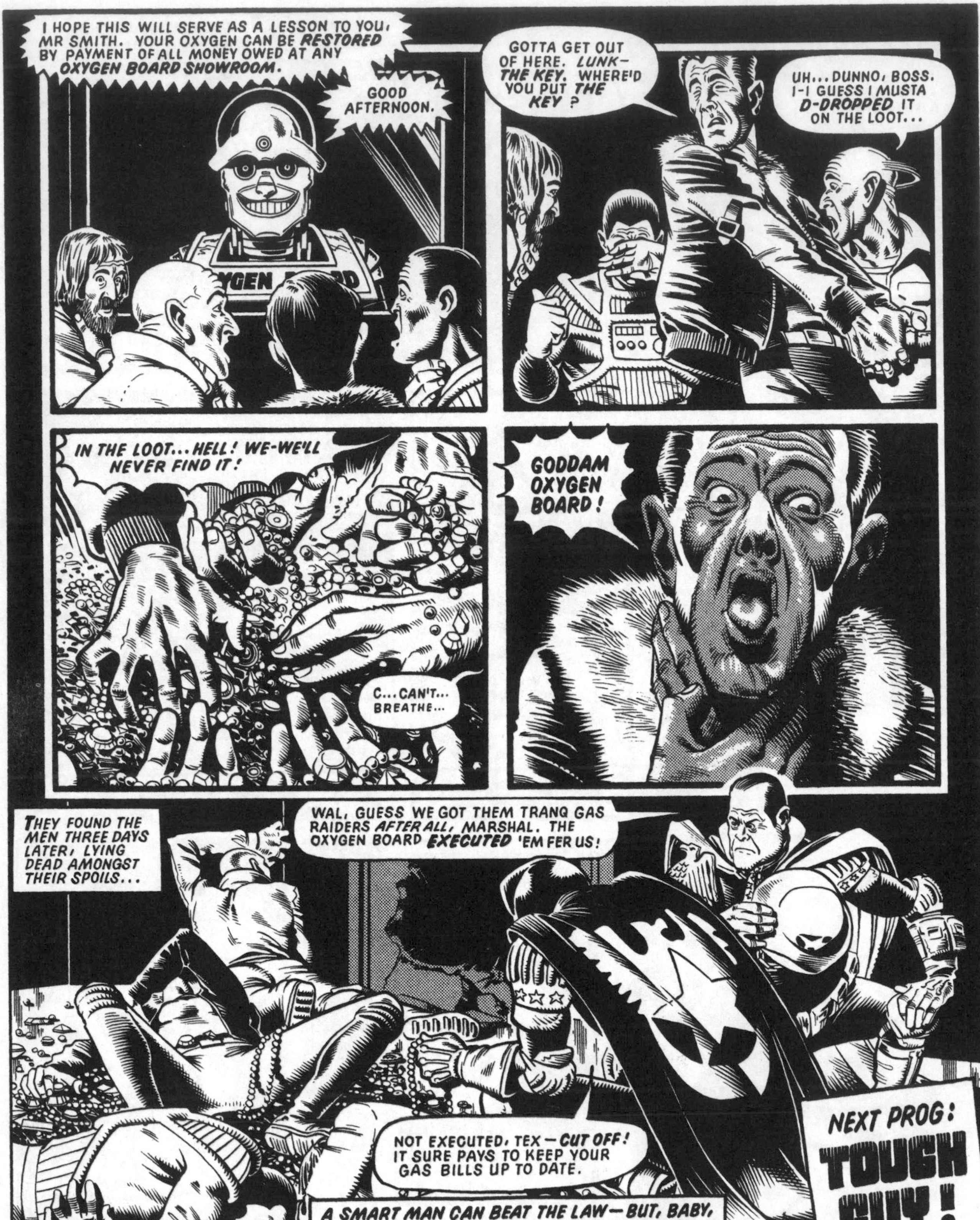
I HOPE THIS WILL SERVE AS A LESSON TO YOU, MR SMITH. YOUR OXYGEN CAN BE RESTORED BY PAYMENT OF ALL MONEY OWED AT ANY OXYGEN BOARD SHOWROOM.
GOOD AFTERNOON.
GOTTA GET OUT OF HERE. LUNK— THE KEY. WHERE'D YOU PUT THE KEY ?
UH... DUNNO, BOSS. I-I GUESS I MUSTA D-DROPPED IT ON THE LOOT...
IN THE LOOT... HELL! WE-WE'LL NEVER FIND IT!
C... CAN'T... BREATHE...
GODDAM OXYGEN BOARD!
THEY FOUND THE MEN THREE DAYS LATER, LYING DEAD AMONGST THEIR SPOILS...
WAL, GUESS WE GOT THEM TRANQ GAS RAIDERS AFTER ALL, MARSHAL. THE OXYGEN BOARD EXECUTED 'EM FER US!
NOT EXECUTED, TEX — CUT OFF! IT SURE PAYS TO KEEP YOUR GAS BILLS UP TO DATE.
A SMART MAN CAN BEAT THE LAW — BUT, BABY, ONLY A FOOL BUCKS THE OXYGEN BOARD.
(OLD LUNA SAYING)
NEXT PROG:
TOUGH GUY!

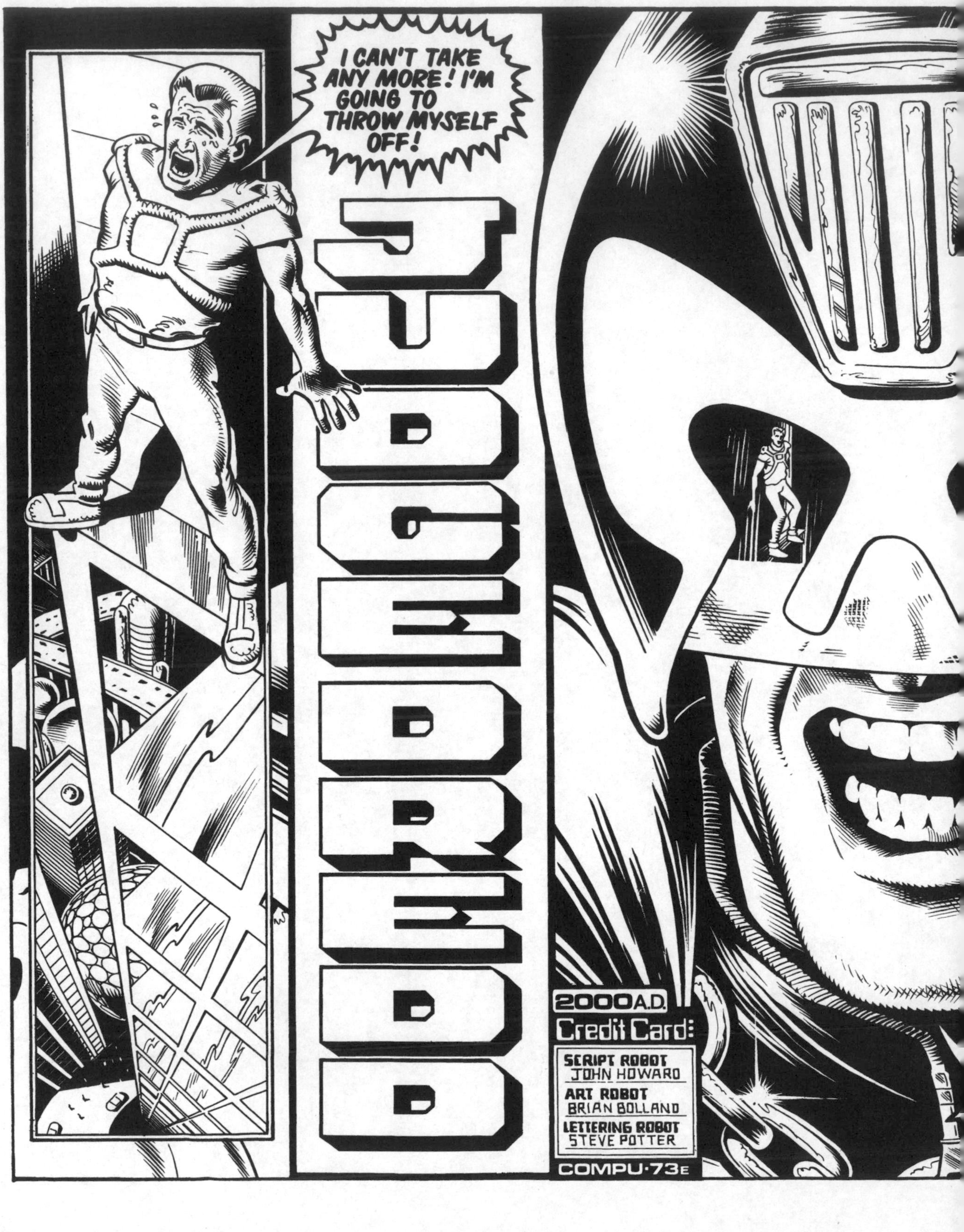

I CAN'T TAKE ANY MORE! I'M GOING TO THROW MYSELF OFF!
JUDGE DREDD
2000 A.D. Credit Card:
SCRIPT ROBOT JOHN HOWARD
ART ROBOT BRIAN BOLLAND
LETTERING ROBOT STEVE POTTER
COMPU·73E

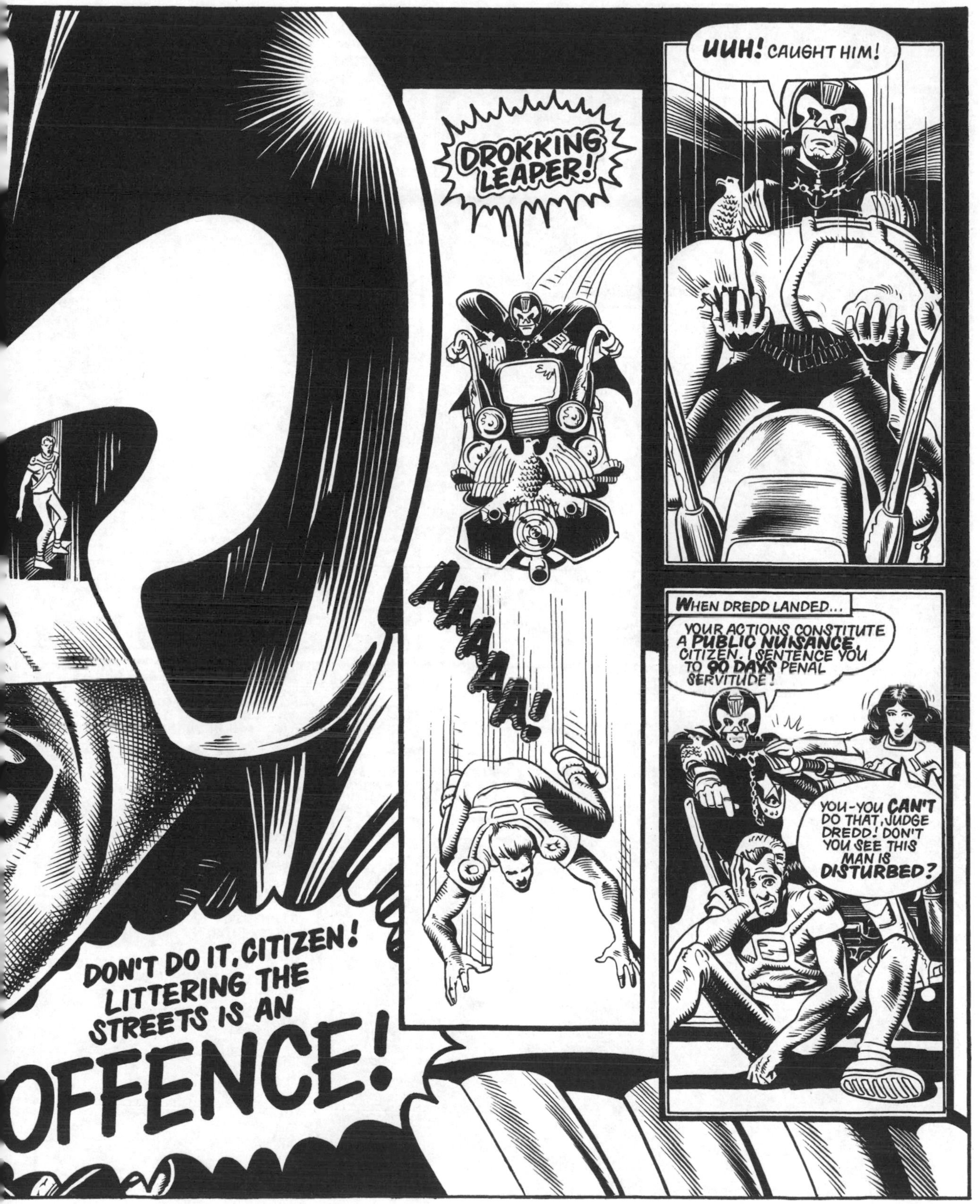
DON'T DO IT, CITIZEN! LITTERING THE STREETS IS AN OFFENCE!
DROKKING LEAPER!
AAAAAA!
UUH! CAUGHT HIM!
WHEN DREDD LANDED...
YOUR ACTIONS CONSTITUTE A PUBLIC NUISANCE, CITIZEN. I SENTENCE YOU TO 90 DAYS PENAL SERVITUDE!
YOU-YOU CAN'T DO THAT, JUDGE DREDD! DON'T YOU SEE THIS MAN IS DISTURBED?

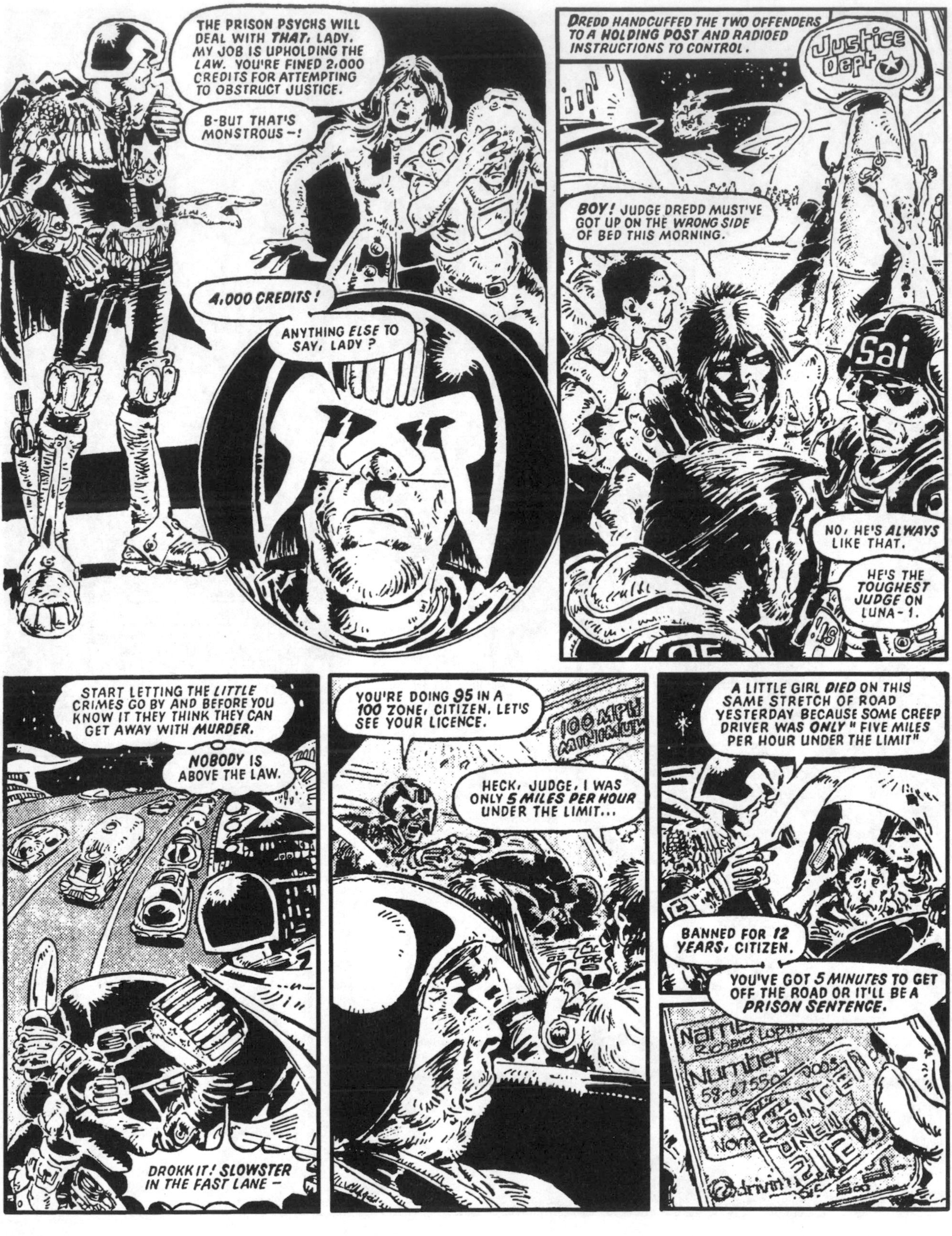
THE PRISON PSYCHS WILL DEAL WITH THAT, LADY. MY JOB IS UPHOLDING THE LAW. YOU'RE FINED 2,000 CREDITS FOR ATTEMPTING TO OBSTRUCT JUSTICE.
B-BUT THAT'S MONSTROUS -!
4,000 CREDITS!
ANYTHING ELSE TO SAY, LADY?
DREDD HANDCUFFED THE TWO OFFENDERS TO A HOLDING POST AND RADIOED INSTRUCTIONS TO CONTROL.
Justice Dept
BOY! JUDGE DREDD MUST'VE GOT UP ON THE WRONG SIDE OF BED THIS MORNING.
Sai
NO, HE'S ALWAYS LIKE THAT.
HE'S THE TOUGHEST JUDGE ON LUNA-1.
START LETTING THE LITTLE CRIMES GO BY AND BEFORE YOU KNOW IT THEY THINK THEY CAN GET AWAY WITH MURDER.
NOBODY IS ABOVE THE LAW.
DROKK IT! SLOWSTER IN THE FAST LANE -
YOU'RE DOING 95 IN A 100 ZONE, CITIZEN. LET'S SEE YOUR LICENCE.
100 MPH
HECK, JUDGE, I WAS ONLY 5 MILES PER HOUR UNDER THE LIMIT...
A LITTLE GIRL DIED ON THIS SAME STRETCH OF ROAD YESTERDAY BECAUSE SOME CREEP DRIVER WAS ONLY "FIVE MILES PER HOUR UNDER THE LIMIT"
BANNED FOR 12 YEARS, CITIZEN.
YOU'VE GOT 5 MINUTES TO GET OFF THE ROAD OR IT'LL BE A PRISON SENTENCE.
Name
Richard Lop
Number
58-67550
Sta
Nom

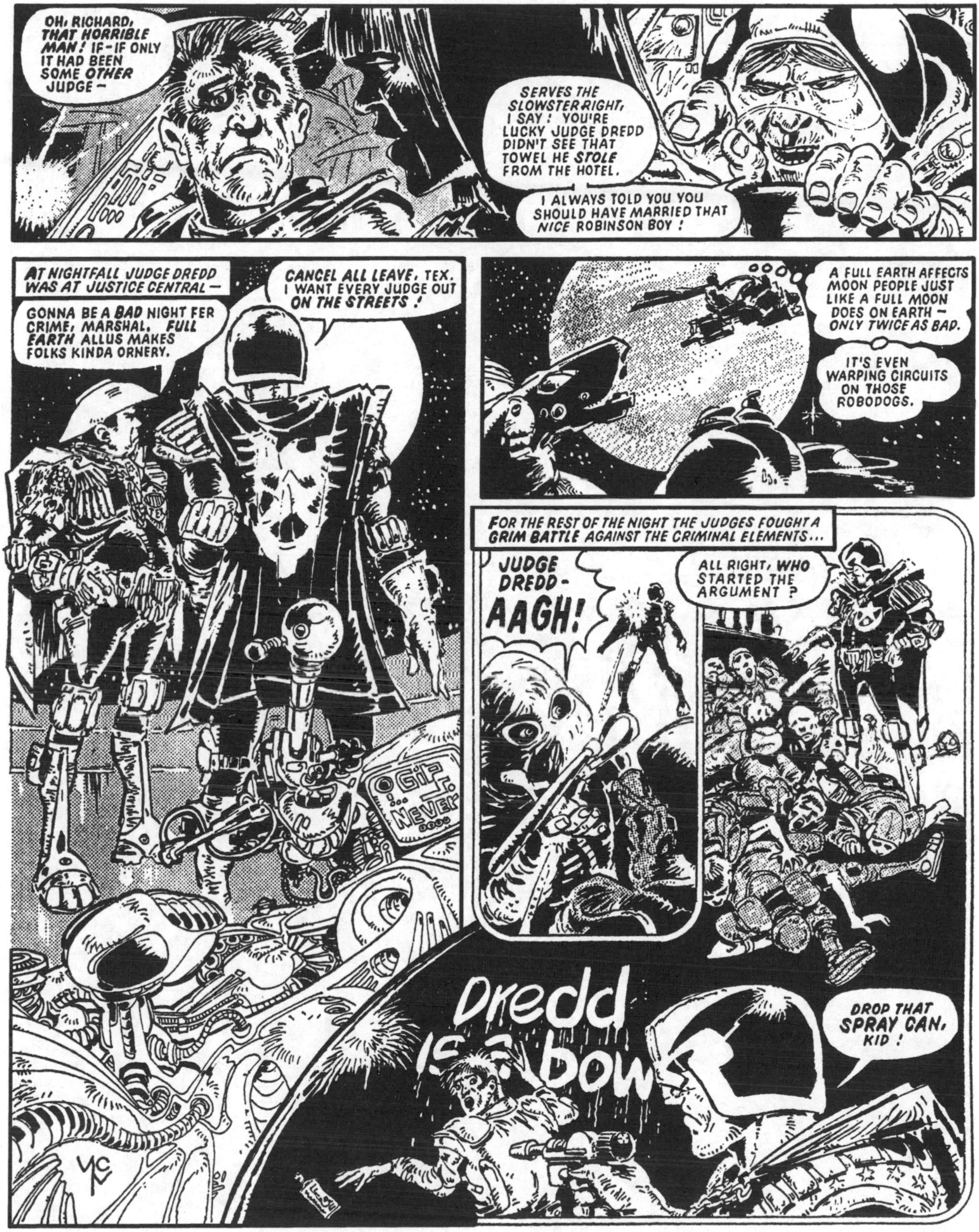

OH, RICHARD, THAT HORRIBLE MAN! IF-IF ONLY IT HAD BEEN SOME OTHER JUDGE—
SERVES THE SLOWSTER RIGHT, I SAY! YOU'RE LUCKY JUDGE DREDD DIDN'T SEE THAT TOWEL HE STOLE FROM THE HOTEL.
I ALWAYS TOLD YOU YOU SHOULD HAVE MARRIED THAT NICE ROBINSON BOY!
AT NIGHTFALL JUDGE DREDD WAS AT JUSTICE CENTRAL—
GONNA BE A BAD NIGHT FER CRIME, MARSHAL. FULL EARTH ALLUS MAKES FOLKS KINDA ORNERY.
CANCEL ALL LEAVE, TEX. I WANT EVERY JUDGE OUT ON THE STREETS!
A FULL EARTH AFFECTS MOON PEOPLE JUST LIKE A FULL MOON DOES ON EARTH — ONLY TWICE AS BAD.
IT'S EVEN WARPING CIRCUITS ON THOSE ROBODOGS.
FOR THE REST OF THE NIGHT THE JUDGES FOUGHT A GRIM BATTLE AGAINST THE CRIMINAL ELEMENTS...
JUDGE DREDD-
AAGH!
ALL RIGHT, WHO STARTED THE ARGUMENT?
Dredd
bow
DROP THAT SPRAY CAN, KID!

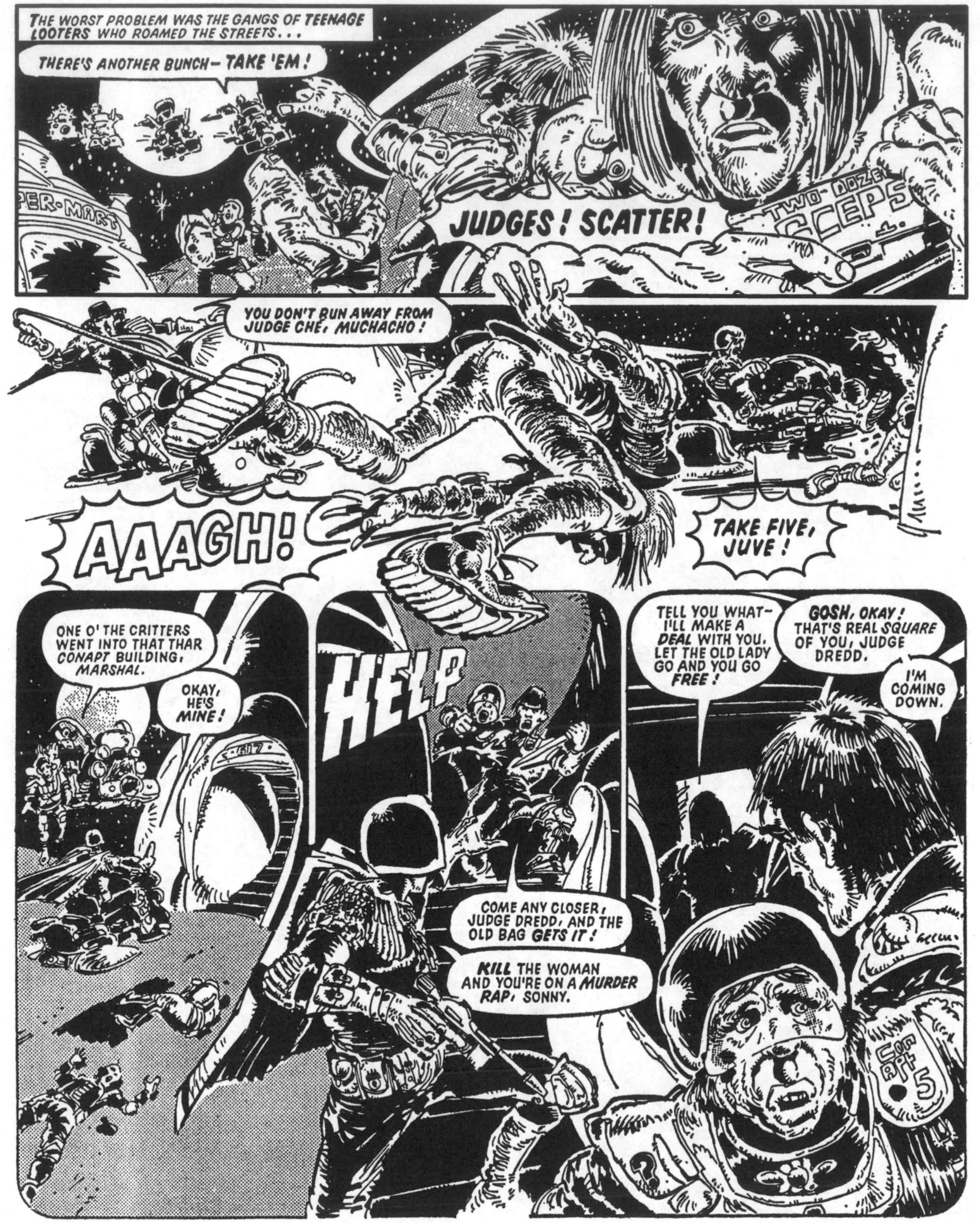
THE WORST PROBLEM WAS THE GANGS OF TEENAGE LOOTERS WHO ROAMED THE STREETS...
THERE'S ANOTHER BUNCH— TAKE 'EM!
PER-MART
JUDGES! SCATTER!
TWO-DOZEN SCEPS
YOU DON'T RUN AWAY FROM JUDGE CHÉ, MUCHACHO!
AAAGH!
TAKE FIVE, JUVE!
ONE O' THE CRITTERS WENT INTO THAT THAR CONAPT BUILDING, MARSHAL.
OKAY, HE'S MINE!
HELP
TELL YOU WHAT— I'LL MAKE A DEAL WITH YOU. LET THE OLD LADY GO AND YOU GO FREE!
GOSH, OKAY! THAT'S REAL SQUARE OF YOU, JUDGE DREDD.
I'M COMING DOWN.
COME ANY CLOSER, JUDGE DREDD, AND THE OLD BAG GETS IT!
KILL THE WOMAN AND YOU'RE ON A MURDER RAP, SONNY.

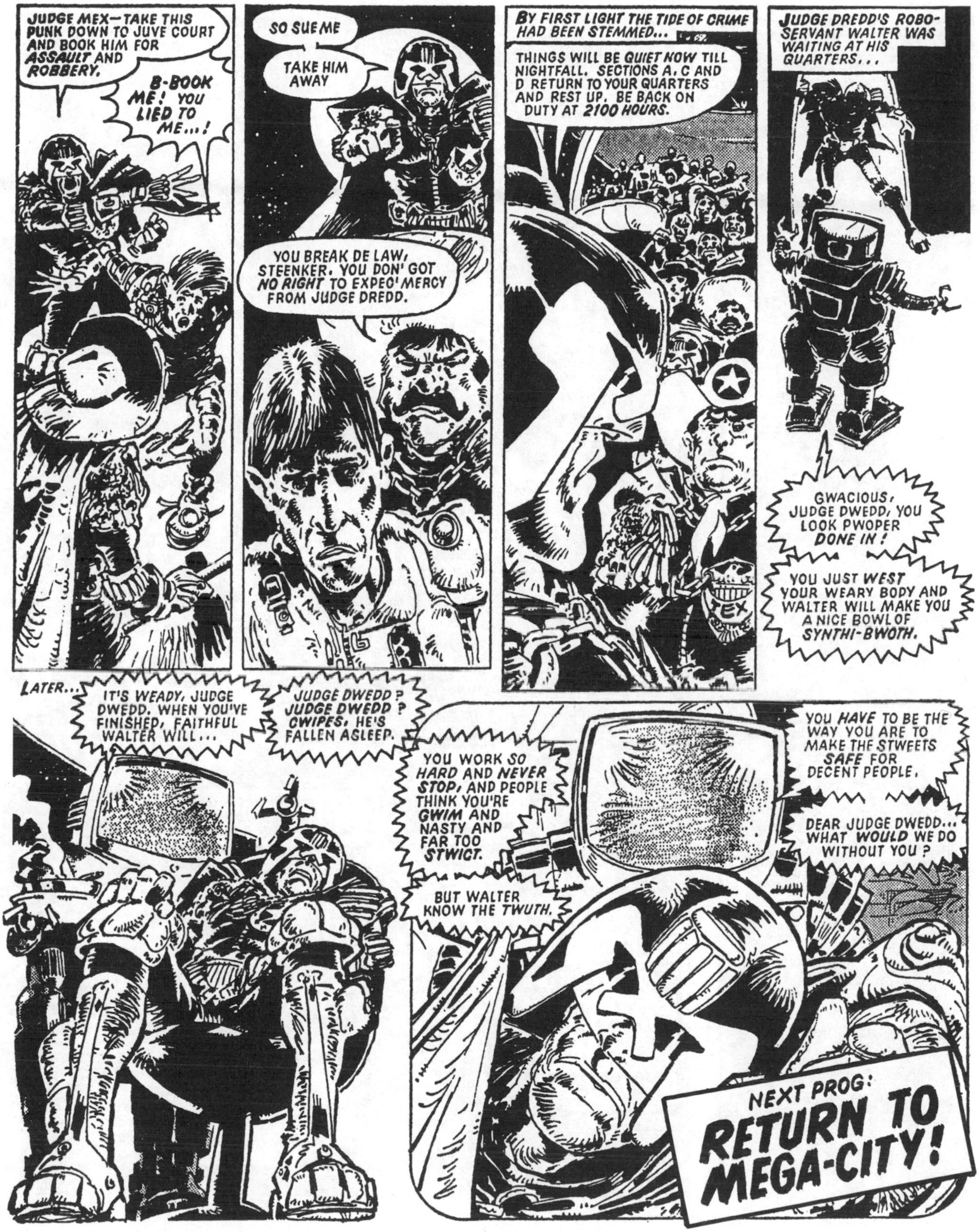

JUDGE MEX—TAKE THIS PUNK DOWN TO JUVE COURT AND BOOK HIM FOR ASSAULT AND ROBBERY.
B-BOOK ME! YOU LIED TO ME...!
SO SUE ME
TAKE HIM AWAY
YOU BREAK DE LAW, STEENKER. YOU DON' GOT NO RIGHT TO EXPEC' MERCY FROM JUDGE DREDD.
BY FIRST LIGHT THE TIDE OF CRIME HAD BEEN STEMMED...
THINGS WILL BE QUIET NOW TILL NIGHTFALL. SECTIONS A, C AND D RETURN TO YOUR QUARTERS AND REST UP. BE BACK ON DUTY AT 2100 HOURS.
TEX
JUDGE DREDD'S ROBO-SERVANT WALTER WAS WAITING AT HIS QUARTERS...
GWACIOUS, JUDGE DWEDD, YOU LOOK PWOPER DONE IN!
YOU JUST WEST YOUR WEARY BODY AND WALTER WILL MAKE YOU A NICE BOWL OF SYNTHI-BWOTH.
LATER...
IT'S WEADY, JUDGE DWEDD. WHEN YOU'VE FINISHED, FAITHFUL WALTER WILL...
JUDGE DWEDD? JUDGE DWEDD? CWIPES, HE'S FALLEN ASLEEP.
YOU WORK SO HARD AND NEVER STOP, AND PEOPLE THINK YOU'RE GWIM AND NASTY AND FAR TOO STWICT.
BUT WALTER KNOW THE TWUTH.
YOU HAVE TO BE THE WAY YOU ARE TO MAKE THE STWEETS SAFE FOR DECENT PEOPLE.
DEAR JUDGE DWEDD... WHAT WOULD WE DO WITHOUT YOU?
NEXT PROG:
RETURN TO MEGA-CITY!

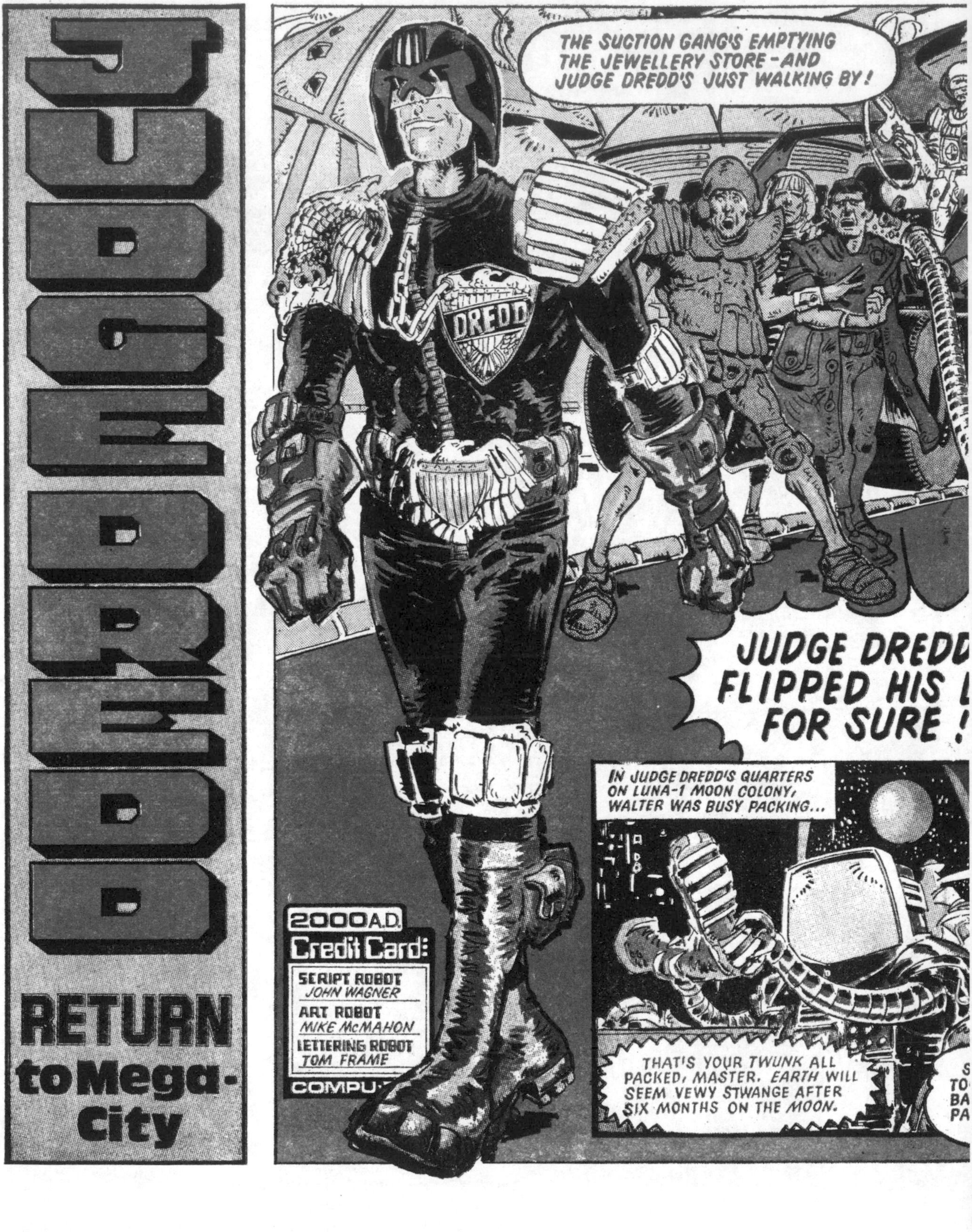
JUDGE DREDD
RETURN to Mega-City
THE SUCTION GANG'S EMPTYING THE JEWELLERY STORE – AND JUDGE DREDD'S JUST WALKING BY!
JUDGE DREDD
FLIPPED HIS
FOR SURE !
DREDD
2000 A.D. Credit Card:
SCRIPT ROBOT JOHN WAGNER
ART ROBOT MIKE McMAHON
LETTERING ROBOT TOM FRAME
IN JUDGE DREDD'S QUARTERS ON LUNA-1 MOON COLONY, WALTER WAS BUSY PACKING...
THAT'S YOUR TWUNK ALL PACKED, MASTER. EARTH WILL SEEM VEWY STWANGE AFTER SIX MONTHS ON THE MOON.

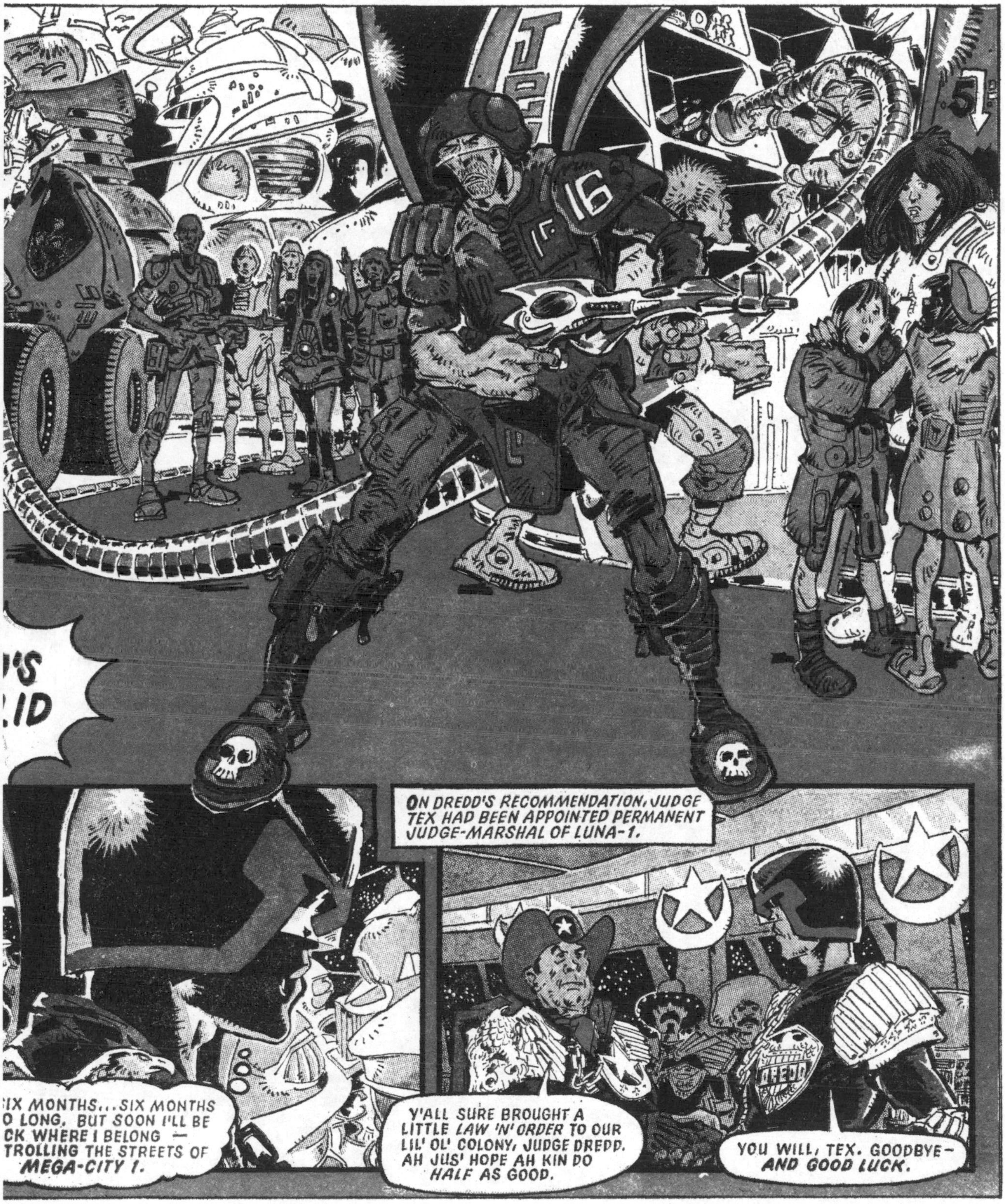
ON DREDD'S RECOMMENDATION, JUDGE TEX HAD BEEN APPOINTED PERMANENT JUDGE-MARSHAL OF LUNA-1.
IX MONTHS... SIX MONTHS O LONG. BUT SOON I'LL BE CK WHERE I BELONG — TROLLING THE STREETS OF MEGA-CITY 1.
Y'ALL SURE BROUGHT A LITTLE LAW 'N' ORDER TO OUR LIL' OL' COLONY, JUDGE DREDD. AH JUS' HOPE AH KIN DO HALF AS GOOD.
YOU WILL, TEX. GOODBYE — AND GOOD LUCK.

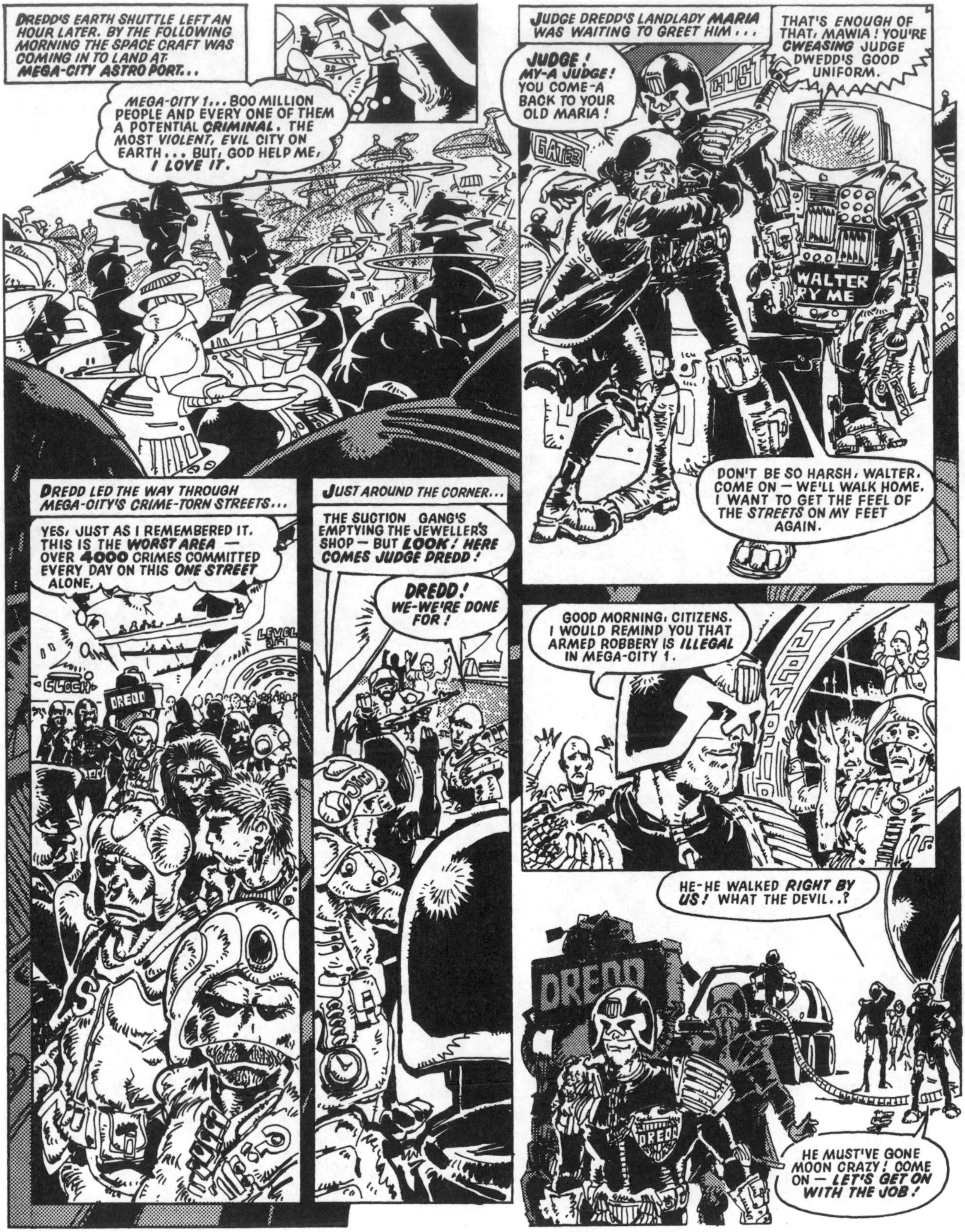

DREDD'S EARTH SHUTTLE LEFT AN HOUR LATER. BY THE FOLLOWING MORNING THE SPACE CRAFT WAS COMING IN TO LAND AT MEGA-CITY ASTRO PORT...
MEGA-CITY 1... 800 MILLION PEOPLE AND EVERY ONE OF THEM A POTENTIAL CRIMINAL. THE MOST VIOLENT, EVIL CITY ON EARTH... BUT, GOD HELP ME, I LOVE IT.
JUDGE DREDD'S LANDLADY MARIA WAS WAITING TO GREET HIM...
JUDGE! MY-A JUDGE! YOU COME-A BACK TO YOUR OLD MARIA!
THAT'S ENOUGH OF THAT, MAWIA! YOU'RE CWEASING JUDGE DWEDD'S GOOD UNIFORM.
WALTER RY ME
DON'T BE SO HARSH, WALTER. COME ON — WE'LL WALK HOME. I WANT TO GET THE FEEL OF THE STREETS ON MY FEET AGAIN.
DREDD LED THE WAY THROUGH MEGA-CITY'S CRIME-TORN STREETS...
YES, JUST AS I REMEMBERED IT. THIS IS THE WORST AREA — OVER 4000 CRIMES COMMITTED EVERY DAY ON THIS ONE STREET ALONE.
JUST AROUND THE CORNER...
THE SUCTION GANG'S EMPTYING THE JEWELLER'S SHOP — BUT LOOK! HERE COMES JUDGE DREDD!
DREDD! WE-WE'RE DONE FOR!
GOOD MORNING, CITIZENS. I WOULD REMIND YOU THAT ARMED ROBBERY IS ILLEGAL IN MEGA-CITY 1.
HE-HE WALKED RIGHT BY US! WHAT THE DEVIL..?
HE MUST'VE GONE MOON CRAZY! COME ON — LET'S GET ON WITH THE JOB!

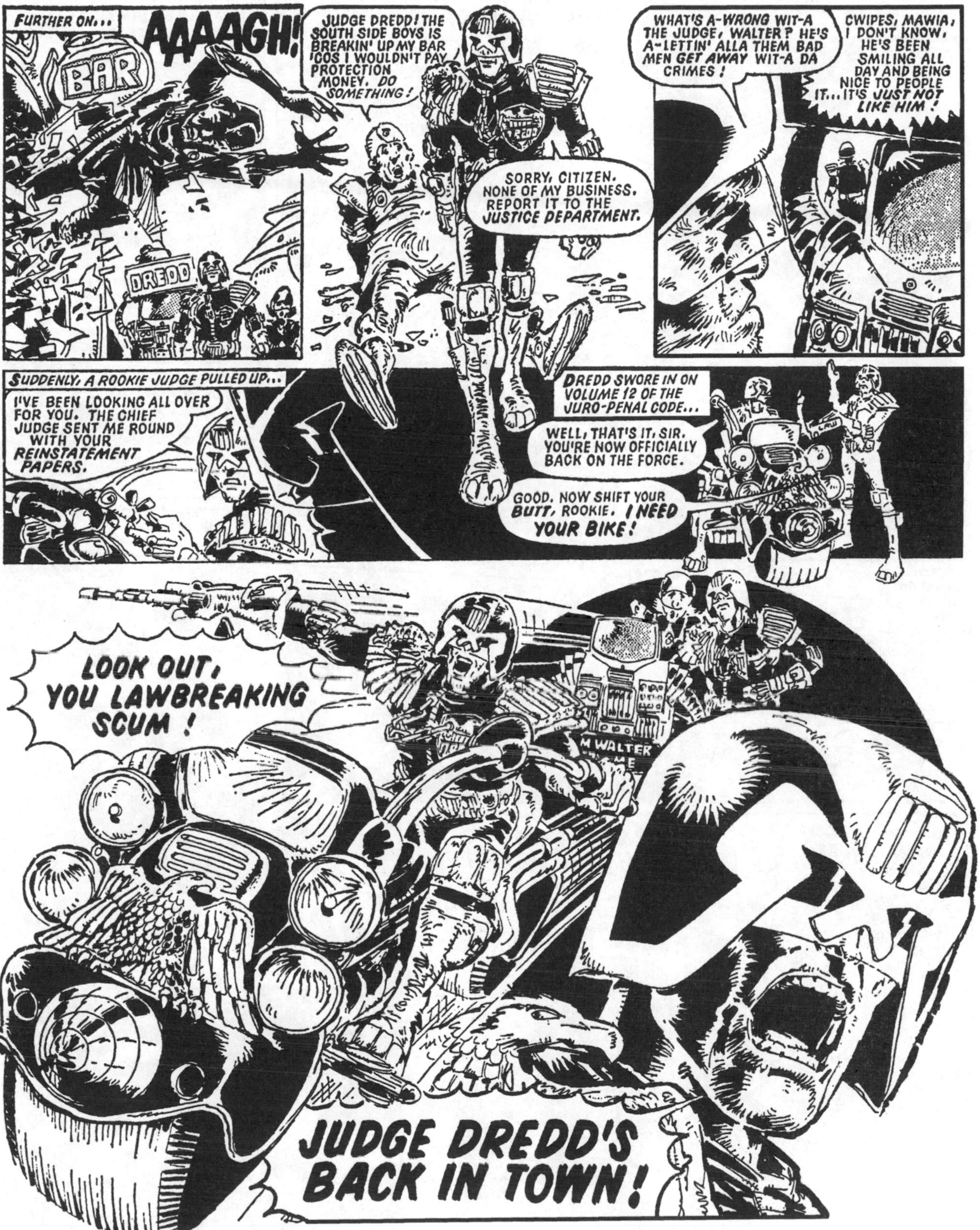
FURTHER ON...
AAAAGH!
BAR
DREDD
JUDGE DREDD! THE SOUTH SIDE BOYS IS BREAKIN' UP MY BAR 'COS I WOULDN'T PAY PROTECTION MONEY. DO SOMETHING!
SORRY, CITIZEN. NONE OF MY BUSINESS. REPORT IT TO THE JUSTICE DEPARTMENT.
WHAT'S A-WRONG WIT-A THE JUDGE, WALTER? HE'S A-LETTIN' ALLA THEM BAD MEN GET AWAY WIT-A DA CRIMES!
CWIPES, MAWIA, I DON'T KNOW. HE'S BEEN SMILING ALL DAY AND BEING NICE TO PEOPLE IT... IT'S JUST NOT LIKE HIM!
SUDDENLY, A ROOKIE JUDGE PULLED UP...
I'VE BEEN LOOKING ALL OVER FOR YOU. THE CHIEF JUDGE SENT ME ROUND WITH YOUR REINSTATEMENT PAPERS.
DREDD SWORE IN ON VOLUME 12 OF THE JURO-PENAL CODE...
WELL, THAT'S IT, SIR. YOU'RE NOW OFFICIALLY BACK ON THE FORCE.
GOOD. NOW SHIFT YOUR BUTT, ROOKIE. I NEED YOUR BIKE!
LOOK OUT, YOU LAWBREAKING SCUM!
M WALTER
JUDGE DREDD'S BACK IN TOWN!

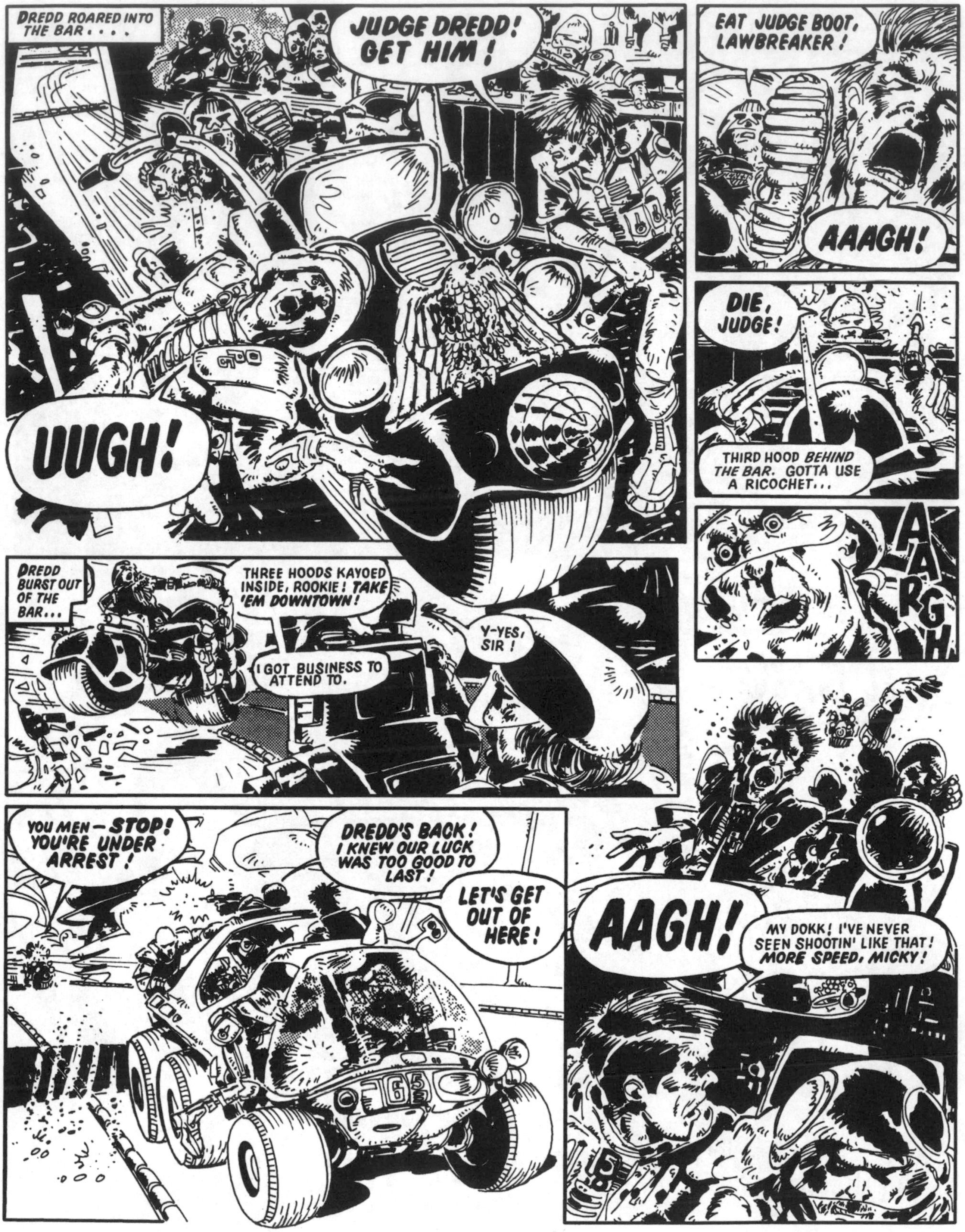
DREDD ROARED INTO THE BAR . . . .
JUDGE DREDD! GET HIM!
UUGH!
EAT JUDGE BOOT, LAWBREAKER!
AAAGH!
DIE, JUDGE!
THIRD HOOD BEHIND THE BAR. GOTTA USE A RICOCHET...
AARGH
DREDD BURST OUT OF THE BAR...
THREE HOODS KAYOED INSIDE, ROOKIE! TAKE 'EM DOWNTOWN!
I GOT BUSINESS TO ATTEND TO.
Y-YES, SIR!
YOU MEN — STOP! YOU'RE UNDER ARREST!
DREDD'S BACK! I KNEW OUR LUCK WAS TOO GOOD TO LAST!
LET'S GET OUT OF HERE!
AAGH!
MY DOKK! I'VE NEVER SEEN SHOOTIN' LIKE THAT! MORE SPEED, MICKY!

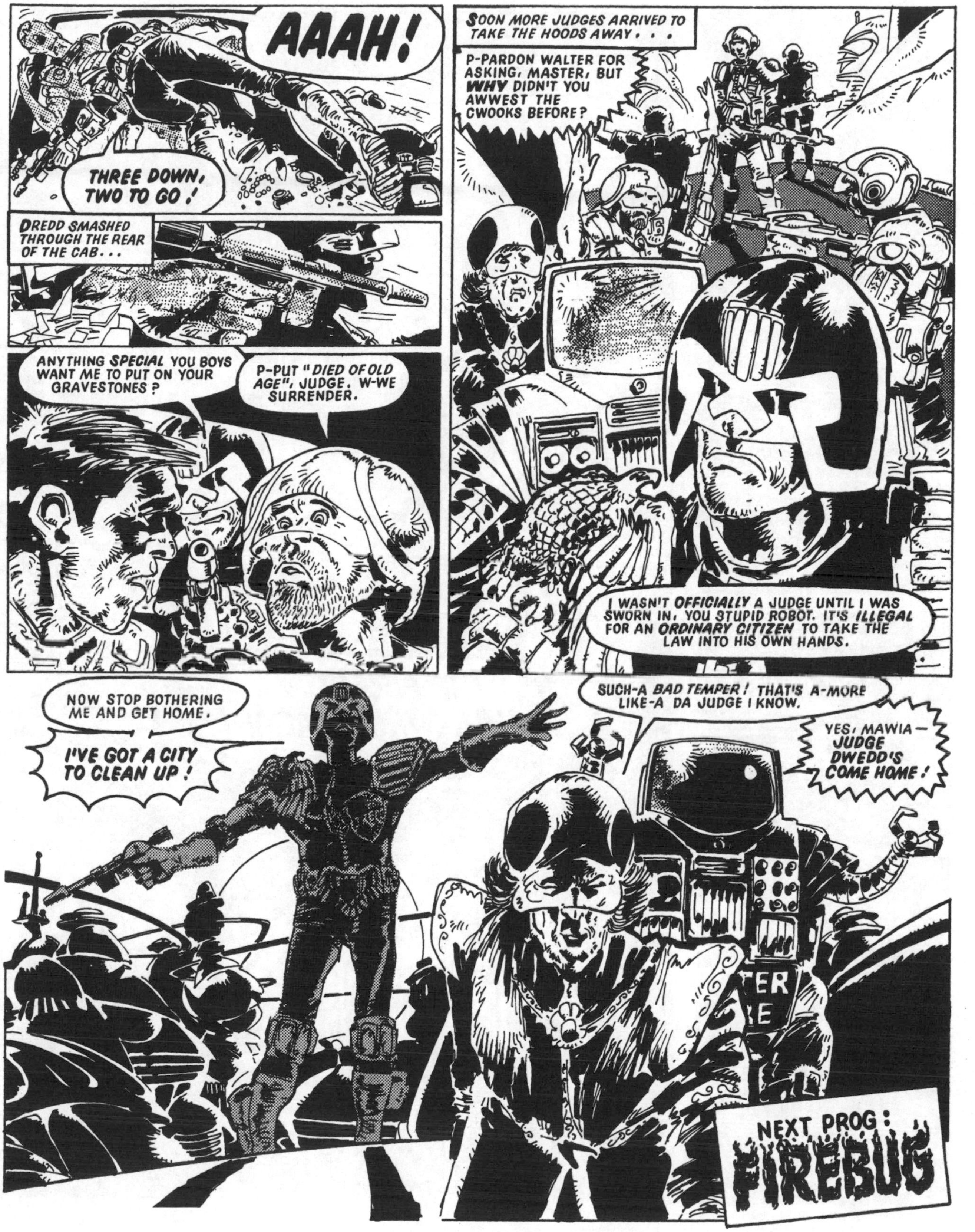
AAAH!
THREE DOWN, TWO TO GO!
DREDD SMASHED THROUGH THE REAR OF THE CAB...
ANYTHING SPECIAL YOU BOYS WANT ME TO PUT ON YOUR GRAVESTONES?
P-PUT "DIED OF OLD AGE", JUDGE. W-WE SURRENDER.
SOON MORE JUDGES ARRIVED TO TAKE THE HOODS AWAY...
P-PARDON WALTER FOR ASKING, MASTER, BUT WHY DIDN'T YOU AWWEST THE CWOOKS BEFORE?
I WASN'T OFFICIALLY A JUDGE UNTIL I WAS SWORN IN, YOU STUPID ROBOT. IT'S ILLEGAL FOR AN ORDINARY CITIZEN TO TAKE THE LAW INTO HIS OWN HANDS.
NOW STOP BOTHERING ME AND GET HOME.
I'VE GOT A CITY TO CLEAN UP!
SUCH-A BAD TEMPER! THAT'S A-MORE LIKE-A DA JUDGE I KNOW.
YES, MAWIA — JUDGE DWEDD'S COME HOME!
NEXT PROG:
FIREBUG

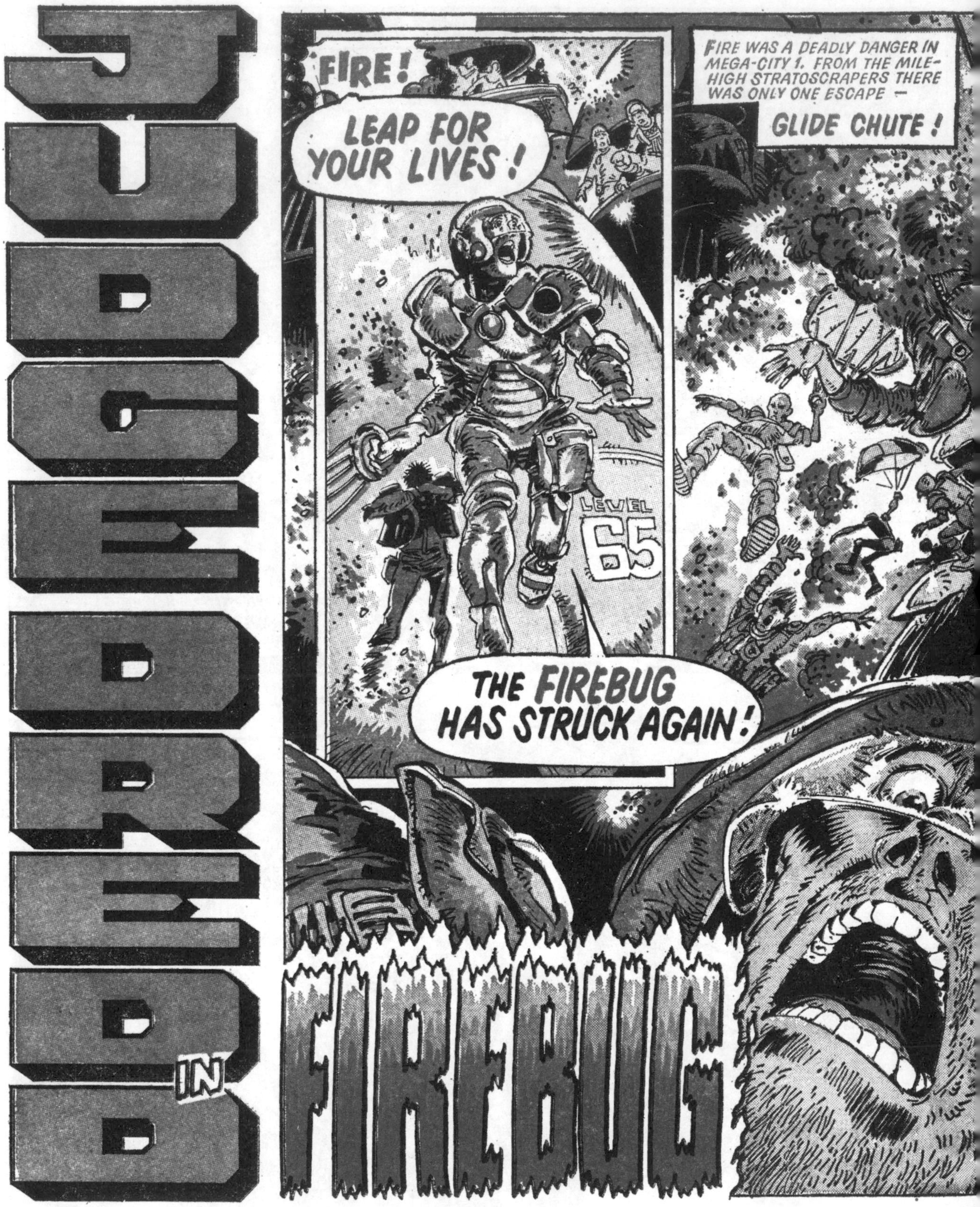
JUDGE DREDD
IN
FIREBUG
FIRE!
LEAP FOR YOUR LIVES!
FIRE WAS A DEADLY DANGER IN MEGA-CITY 1. FROM THE MILE-HIGH STRATOSCRAPERS THERE WAS ONLY ONE ESCAPE —
GLIDE CHUTE!
LEVEL 65
THE FIREBUG HAS STRUCK AGAIN!

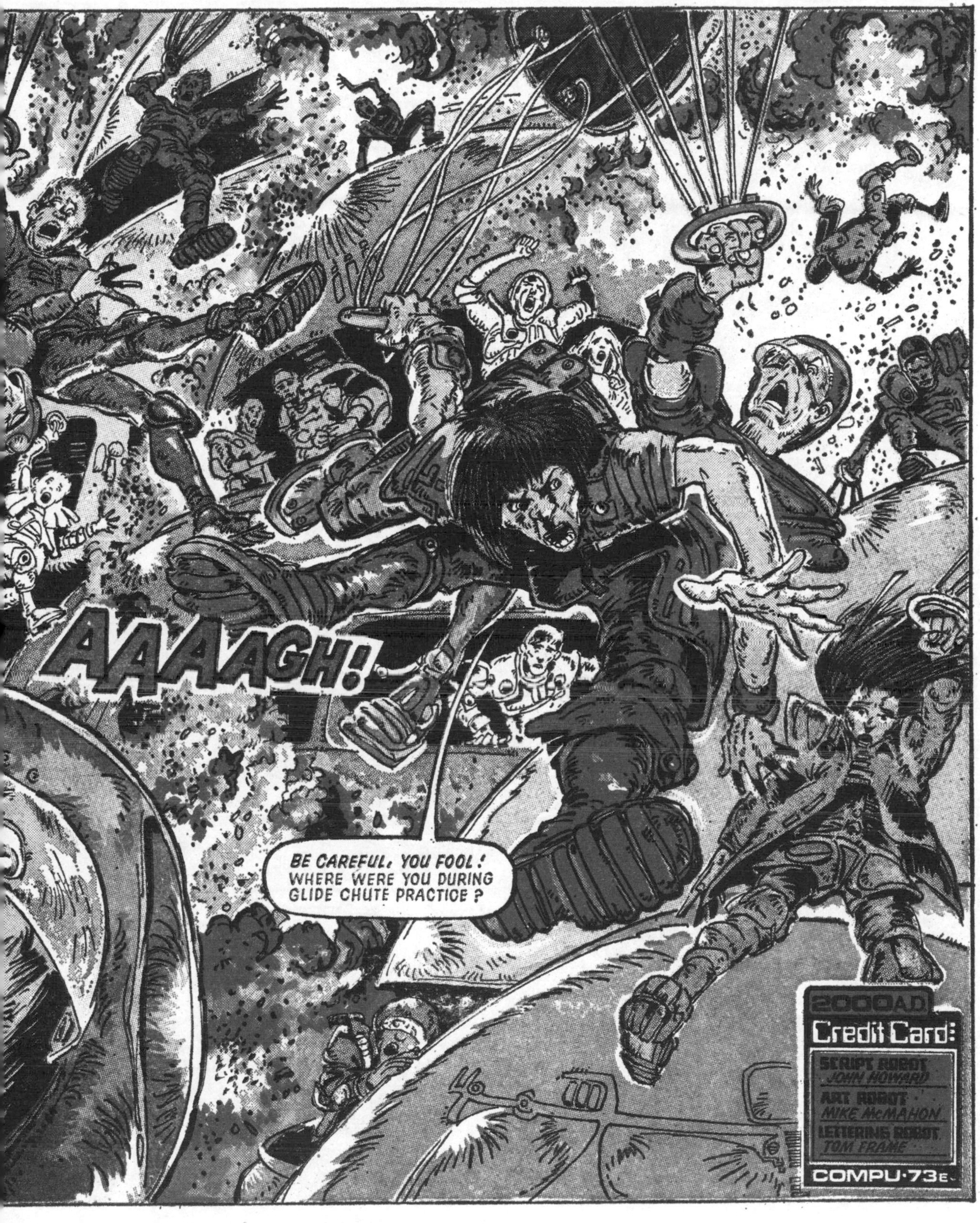
AAAAAGH!
BE CAREFUL, YOU FOOL! WHERE WERE YOU DURING GLIDE CHUTE PRACTICE?
2000AD
Credit Card:
SCRIPT ROBOT JOHN HOWARD
ART ROBOT MIKE McMAHON
LETTERING ROBOT TOM FRAME
COMPU·73E

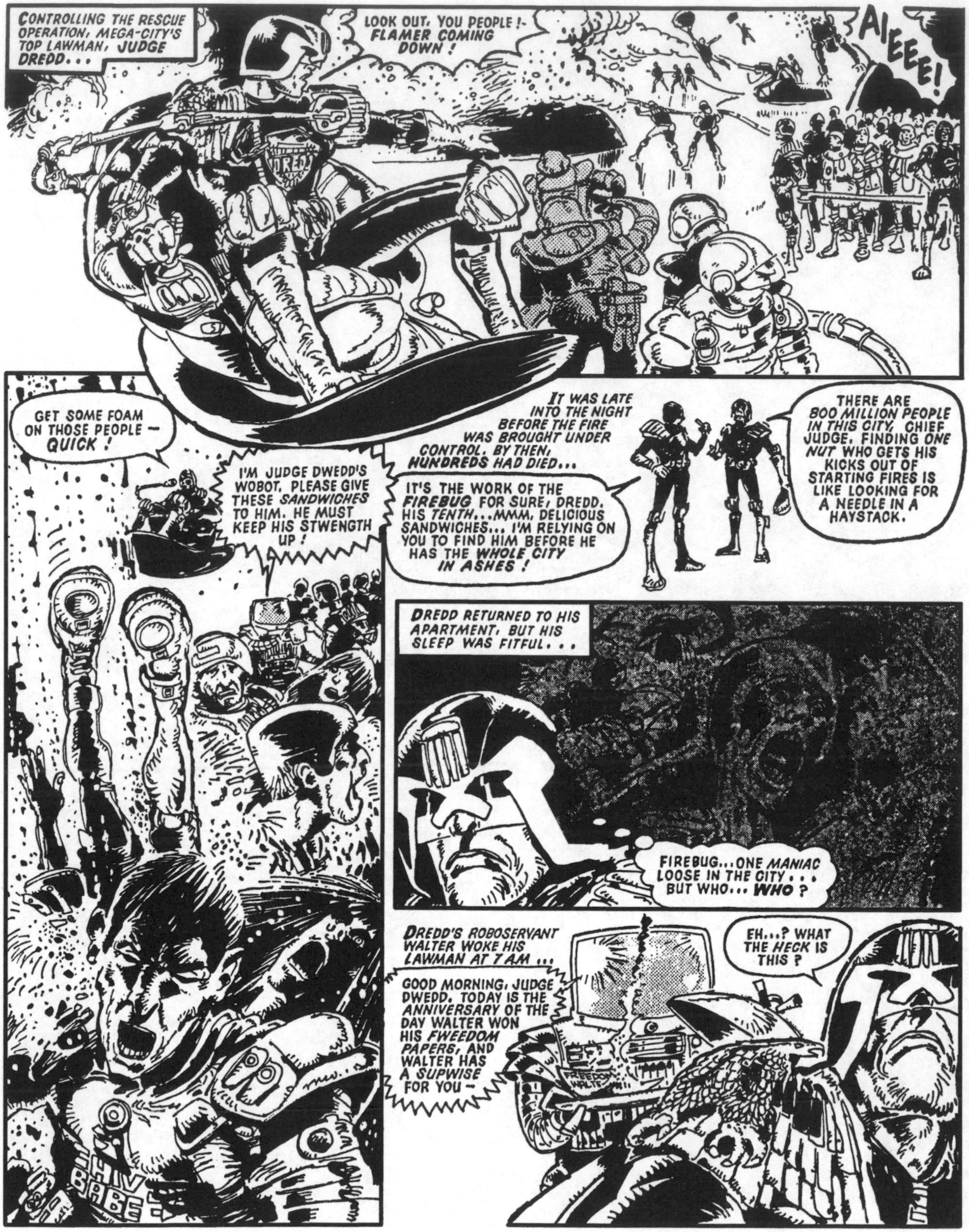

CONTROLLING THE RESCUE OPERATION, MEGA-CITY'S TOP LAWMAN, JUDGE DREDD...
LOOK OUT, YOU PEOPLE! - FLAMER COMING DOWN!
AIEEEE!
GET SOME FOAM ON THOSE PEOPLE — QUICK!
I'M JUDGE DWEDD'S WOBOT. PLEASE GIVE THESE SANDWICHES TO HIM. HE MUST KEEP HIS STWENGTH UP!
IT WAS LATE INTO THE NIGHT BEFORE THE FIRE WAS BROUGHT UNDER CONTROL. BY THEN, HUNDREDS HAD DIED...
IT'S THE WORK OF THE FIREBUG FOR SURE, DREDD. HIS TENTH...MMM, DELICIOUS SANDWICHES... I'M RELYING ON YOU TO FIND HIM BEFORE HE HAS THE WHOLE CITY IN ASHES!
THERE ARE 800 MILLION PEOPLE IN THIS CITY, CHIEF JUDGE. FINDING ONE NUT WHO GETS HIS KICKS OUT OF STARTING FIRES IS LIKE LOOKING FOR A NEEDLE IN A HAYSTACK.
DREDD RETURNED TO HIS APARTMENT, BUT HIS SLEEP WAS FITFUL...
FIREBUG... ONE MANIAC LOOSE IN THE CITY... BUT WHO... WHO?
SHIV BABE
DREDD'S ROBOSERVANT WALTER WOKE HIS LAWMAN AT 7 AM...
GOOD MORNING, JUDGE DWEDD. TODAY IS THE ANNIVERSARY OF THE DAY WALTER WON HIS FWEEDOM PAPERS, AND WALTER HAS A SUPWISE FOR YOU -
EH...? WHAT THE HECK IS THIS?

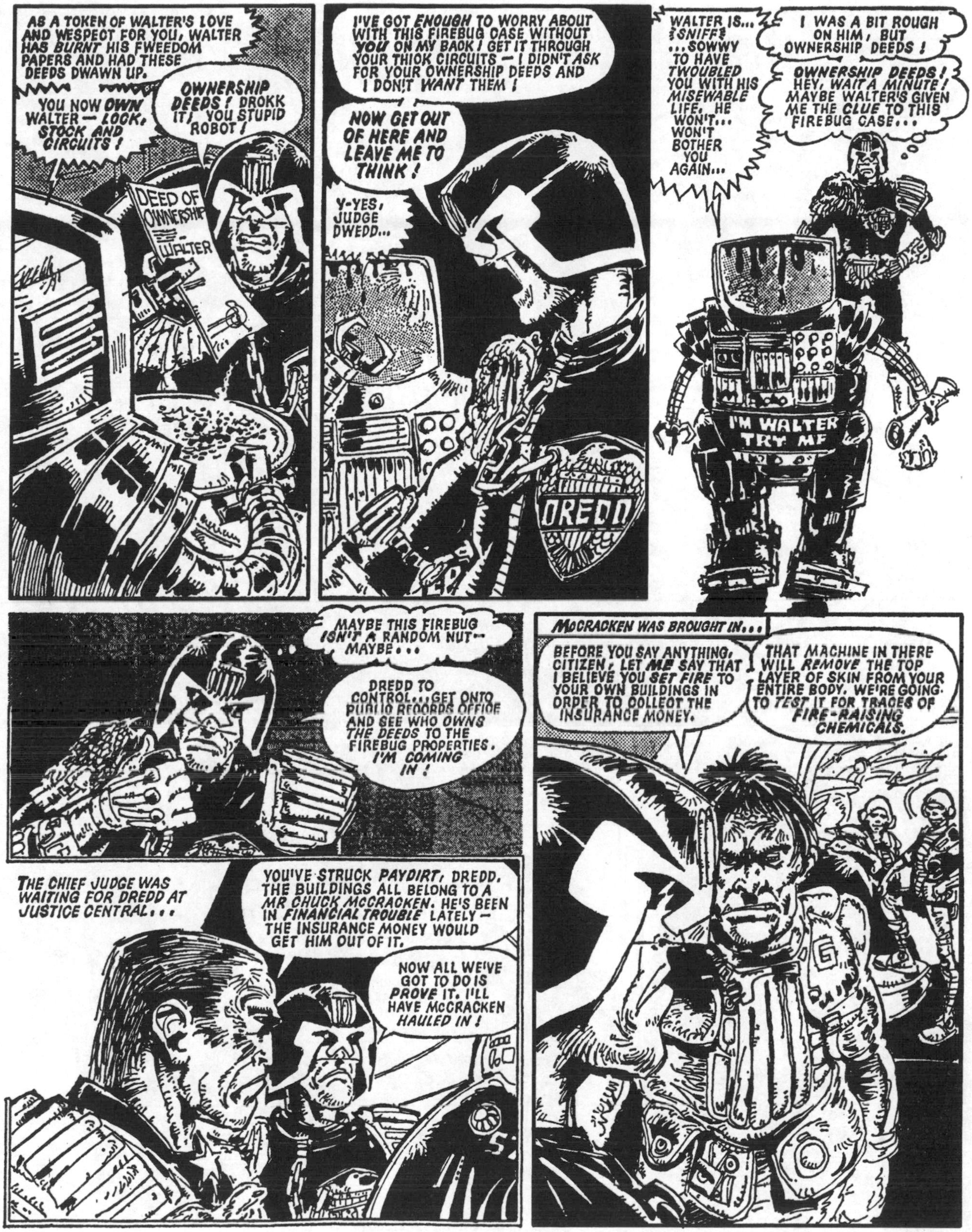

AS A TOKEN OF WALTER'S LOVE AND WESPECT FOR YOU, WALTER HAS BURNT HIS FWEEDOM PAPERS AND HAD THESE DEEDS DWAWN UP.
YOU NOW OWN WALTER — LOCK, STOCK AND CIRCUITS!
OWNERSHIP DEEDS! DROKK IT, YOU STUPID ROBOT!
DEED OF OWNERSHIP WALTER
I'VE GOT ENOUGH TO WORRY ABOUT WITH THIS FIREBUG CASE WITHOUT YOU ON MY BACK! GET IT THROUGH YOUR THICK CIRCUITS — I DIDN'T ASK FOR YOUR OWNERSHIP DEEDS AND I DON'T WANT THEM!
NOW GET OUT OF HERE AND LEAVE ME TO THINK!
Y-YES, JUDGE DWEDD...
DREDD
WALTER IS... *SNIFF* ... SOWWY TO HAVE TWOUBLED YOU WITH HIS MISEWABLE LIFE. HE WON'T... WON'T BOTHER YOU AGAIN...
I WAS A BIT ROUGH ON HIM, BUT OWNERSHIP DEEDS!
OWNERSHIP DEEDS! HEY, WAIT A MINUTE! MAYBE WALTER'S GIVEN ME THE CLUE TO THIS FIREBUG CASE...
I'M WALTER TRY ME
MAYBE THIS FIREBUG ISN'T A RANDOM NUT — MAYBE...
DREDD TO CONTROL... GET ONTO PUBLIC RECORDS OFFICE AND SEE WHO OWNS THE DEEDS TO THE FIREBUG PROPERTIES. I'M COMING IN!
THE CHIEF JUDGE WAS WAITING FOR DREDD AT JUSTICE CENTRAL...
YOU'VE STRUCK PAYDIRT, DREDD. THE BUILDINGS ALL BELONG TO A MR CHUCK McCRACKEN. HE'S BEEN IN FINANCIAL TROUBLE LATELY — THE INSURANCE MONEY WOULD GET HIM OUT OF IT.
NOW ALL WE'VE GOT TO DO IS PROVE IT. I'LL HAVE McCRACKEN HAULED IN!
McCRACKEN WAS BROUGHT IN...
BEFORE YOU SAY ANYTHING, CITIZEN, LET ME SAY THAT I BELIEVE YOU SET FIRE TO YOUR OWN BUILDINGS IN ORDER TO COLLECT THE INSURANCE MONEY.
THAT MACHINE IN THERE WILL REMOVE THE TOP LAYER OF SKIN FROM YOUR ENTIRE BODY. WE'RE GOING TO TEST IT FOR TRACES OF FIRE-RAISING CHEMICALS.

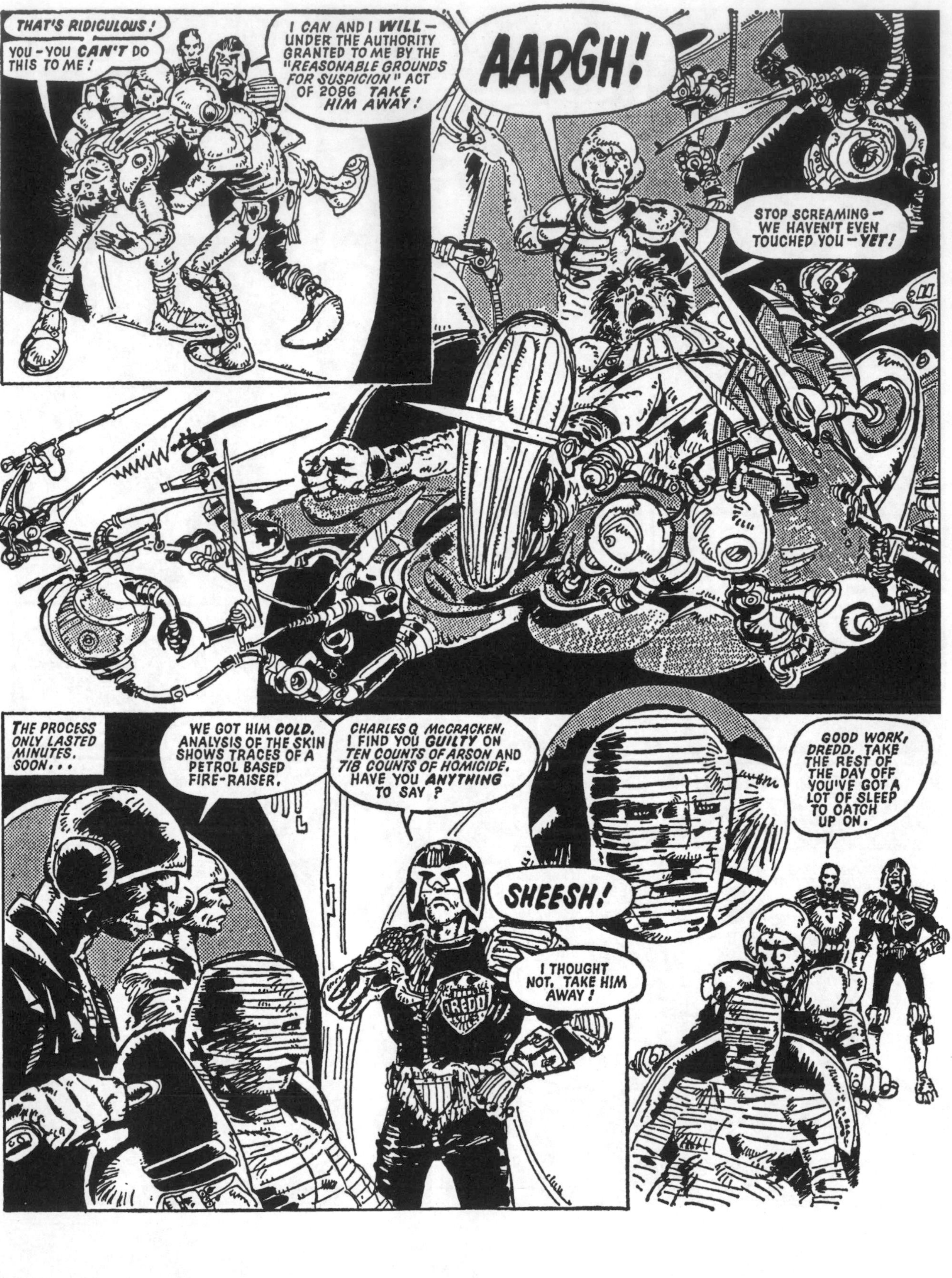
THAT'S RIDICULOUS!
YOU-YOU CAN'T DO THIS TO ME!
I CAN AND I WILL - UNDER THE AUTHORITY GRANTED TO ME BY THE "REASONABLE GROUNDS FOR SUSPICION" ACT OF 2086 TAKE HIM AWAY!
AARGH!
STOP SCREAMING - WE HAVEN'T EVEN TOUCHED YOU - YET!
THE PROCESS ONLY LASTED MINUTES. SOON...
WE GOT HIM COLD. ANALYSIS OF THE SKIN SHOWS TRACES OF A PETROL BASED FIRE-RAISER.
CHARLES Q MCCRACKEN, I FIND YOU GUILTY ON TEN COUNTS OF ARSON AND 718 COUNTS OF HOMICIDE. HAVE YOU ANYTHING TO SAY?
SHEESH!
I THOUGHT NOT. TAKE HIM AWAY!
GOOD WORK, DREDD. TAKE THE REST OF THE DAY OFF YOU'VE GOT A LOT OF SLEEP TO CATCH UP ON.
DREDD

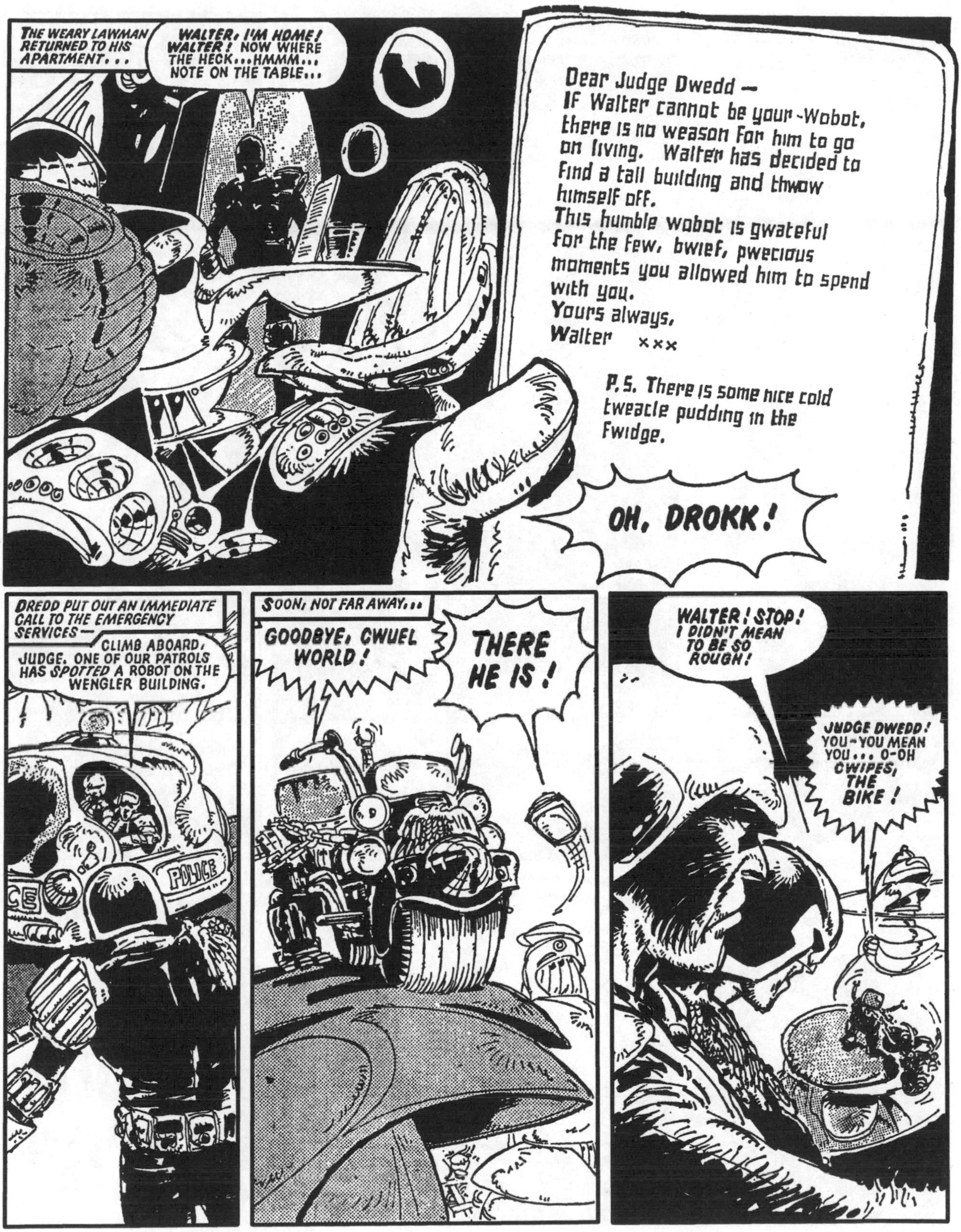

THE WEARY LAWMAN RETURNED TO HIS APARTMENT...
WALTER, I'M HOME! WALTER! NOW WHERE THE HECK...HMMM... NOTE ON THE TABLE...
Dear Judge Dwedd —
If Walter cannot be your -Wobot, there is no weason for him to go on living. Walter has decided to find a tall building and thwow himself off.
This humble wobot is gwateful for the few, bwief, pwecious moments you allowed him to spend with you.
Yours always,
Walter ×××
P.S. There is some nice cold tweacle pudding in the Fwidge.
OH, DROKK!
DREDD PUT OUT AN IMMEDIATE CALL TO THE EMERGENCY SERVICES—
CLIMB ABOARD, JUDGE. ONE OF OUR PATROLS HAS SPOTTED A ROBOT ON THE WENGLER BUILDING.
POLICE
SOON, NOT FAR AWAY...
GOODBYE, CWUEL WORLD!
THERE HE IS!
WALTER! STOP! I DIDN'T MEAN TO BE SO ROUGH!
JUDGE DWEDD! YOU-YOU MEAN YOU... O-OH CWIPES, THE BIKE!

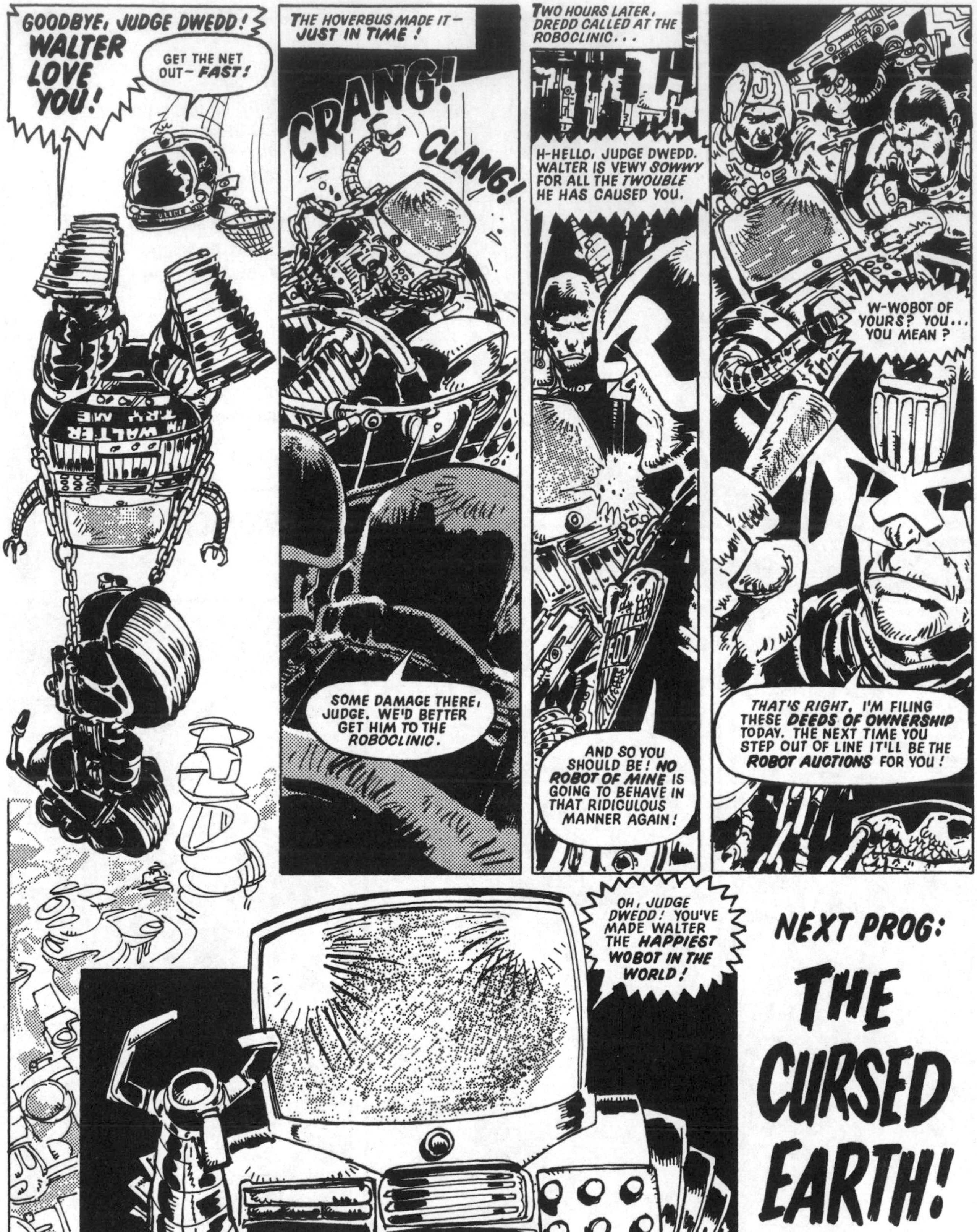
GOODBYE, JUDGE DWEDD! WALTER LOVE YOU!
GET THE NET OUT– FAST!
I'M WALTER TRY ME
THE HOVERBUS MADE IT– JUST IN TIME!
CRANG!
CLANG!
SOME DAMAGE THERE, JUDGE. WE'D BETTER GET HIM TO THE ROBOCLINIC.
TWO HOURS LATER, DREDD CALLED AT THE ROBOCLINIC...
H-HELLO, JUDGE DWEDD. WALTER IS VEWY SOWWY FOR ALL THE TWOUBLE HE HAS CAUSED YOU.
AND SO YOU SHOULD BE! NO ROBOT OF MINE IS GOING TO BEHAVE IN THAT RIDICULOUS MANNER AGAIN!
W-WOBOT OF YOURS? YOU... YOU MEAN?
THAT'S RIGHT. I'M FILING THESE DEEDS OF OWNERSHIP TODAY. THE NEXT TIME YOU STEP OUT OF LINE IT'LL BE THE ROBOT AUCTIONS FOR YOU!
OH, JUDGE DWEDD! YOU'VE MADE WALTER THE HAPPIEST WOBOT IN THE WORLD!
NEXT PROG:
THE CURSED EARTH!

BONUS MATERIAL

THE FIRST DREDD

Script: Pat Mills and John Wagner
Art: Carlos Ezquerra

This story is printed here mainly to show the original art. It also contains evidence of Dredd acting in his role of judge, jury and executioner, the side of his character that was cut out.

WALTER THE WOBOT

Script: Joe Collins
Art: Brian Bolland

Originally Published in *2000 AD* Progs 50-58

...THE FIRST DREDD...THE FIR

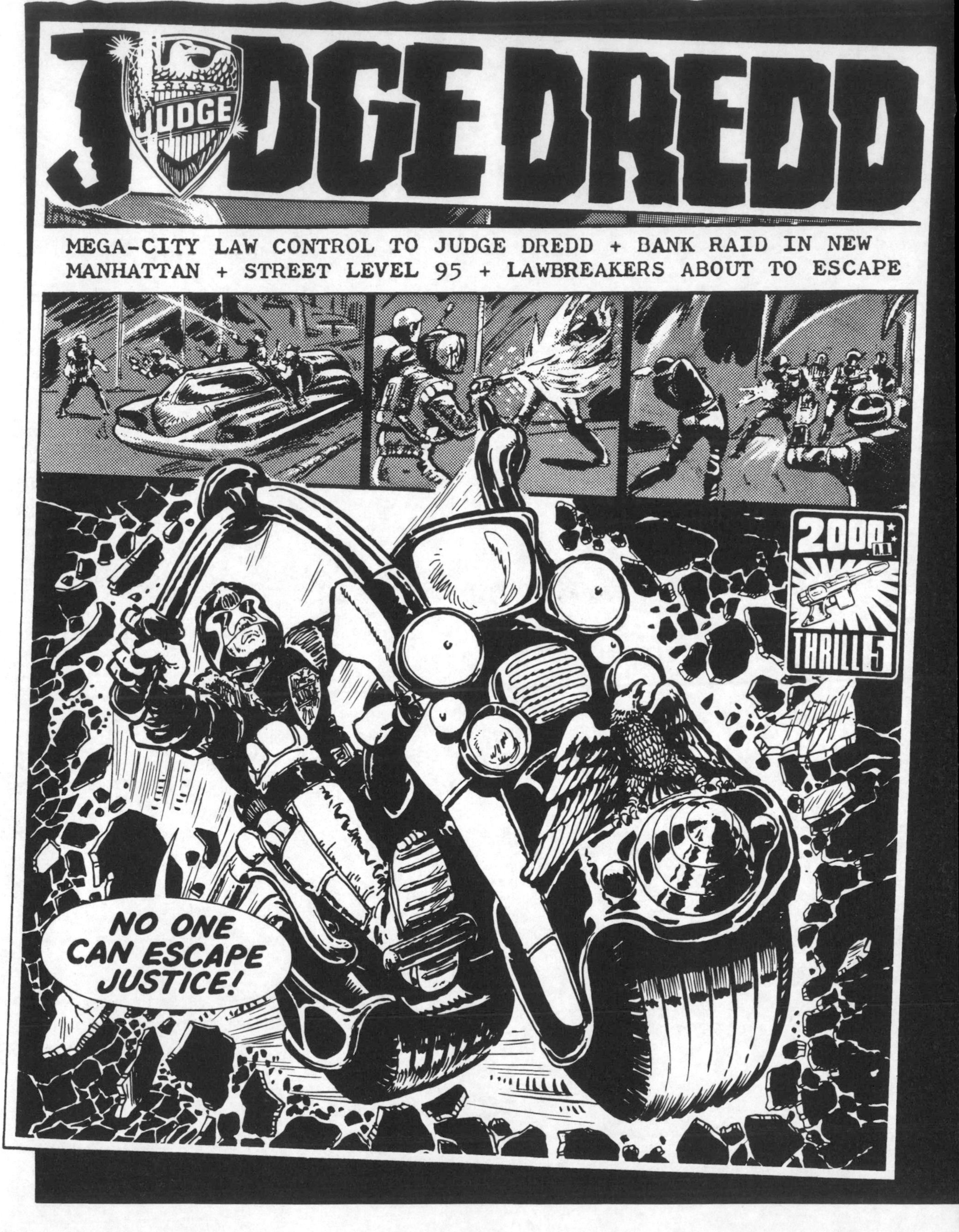
JUDGE DREDD
JUDGE
MEGA-CITY LAW CONTROL TO JUDGE DREDD + BANK RAID IN NEW MANHATTAN + STREET LEVEL 95 + LAWBREAKERS ABOUT TO ESCAPE
2000 A.D.
THRILL 5
NO ONE CAN ESCAPE JUSTICE!

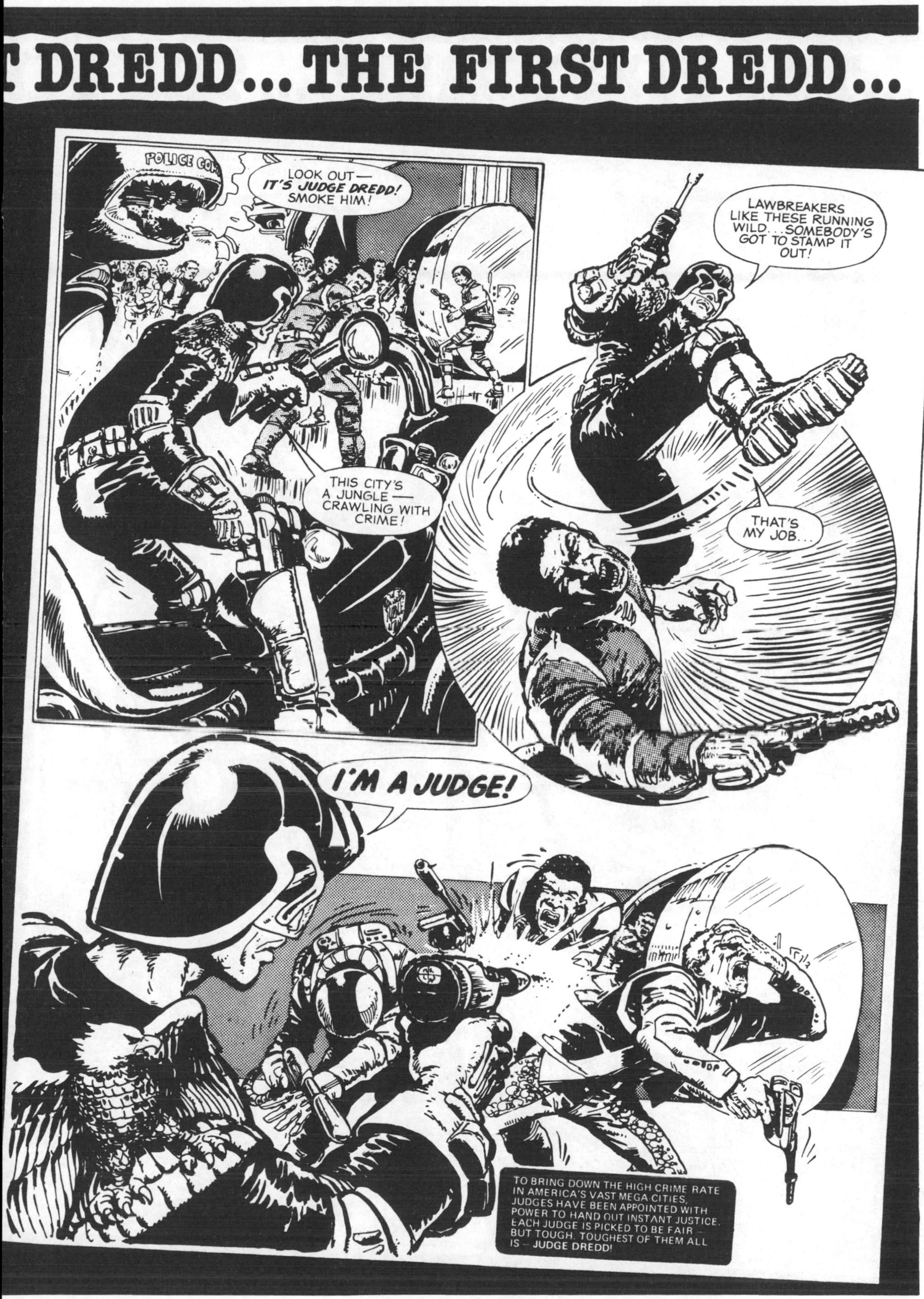
T DREDD... THE FIRST DREDD...
POLICE CO
LOOK OUT— IT'S JUDGE DREDD! SMOKE HIM!
THIS CITY'S A JUNGLE — CRAWLING WITH CRIME!
LAWBREAKERS LIKE THESE RUNNING WILD... SOMEBODY'S GOT TO STAMP IT OUT!
THAT'S MY JOB...
I'M A JUDGE!
TO BRING DOWN THE HIGH CRIME RATE IN AMERICA'S VAST MEGA-CITIES, JUDGES HAVE BEEN APPOINTED WITH POWER TO HAND OUT INSTANT JUSTICE. EACH JUDGE IS PICKED TO BE FAIR — BUT TOUGH. TOUGHEST OF THEM ALL IS — JUDGE DREDD!

...THE FIRST DREDD... THE FIR

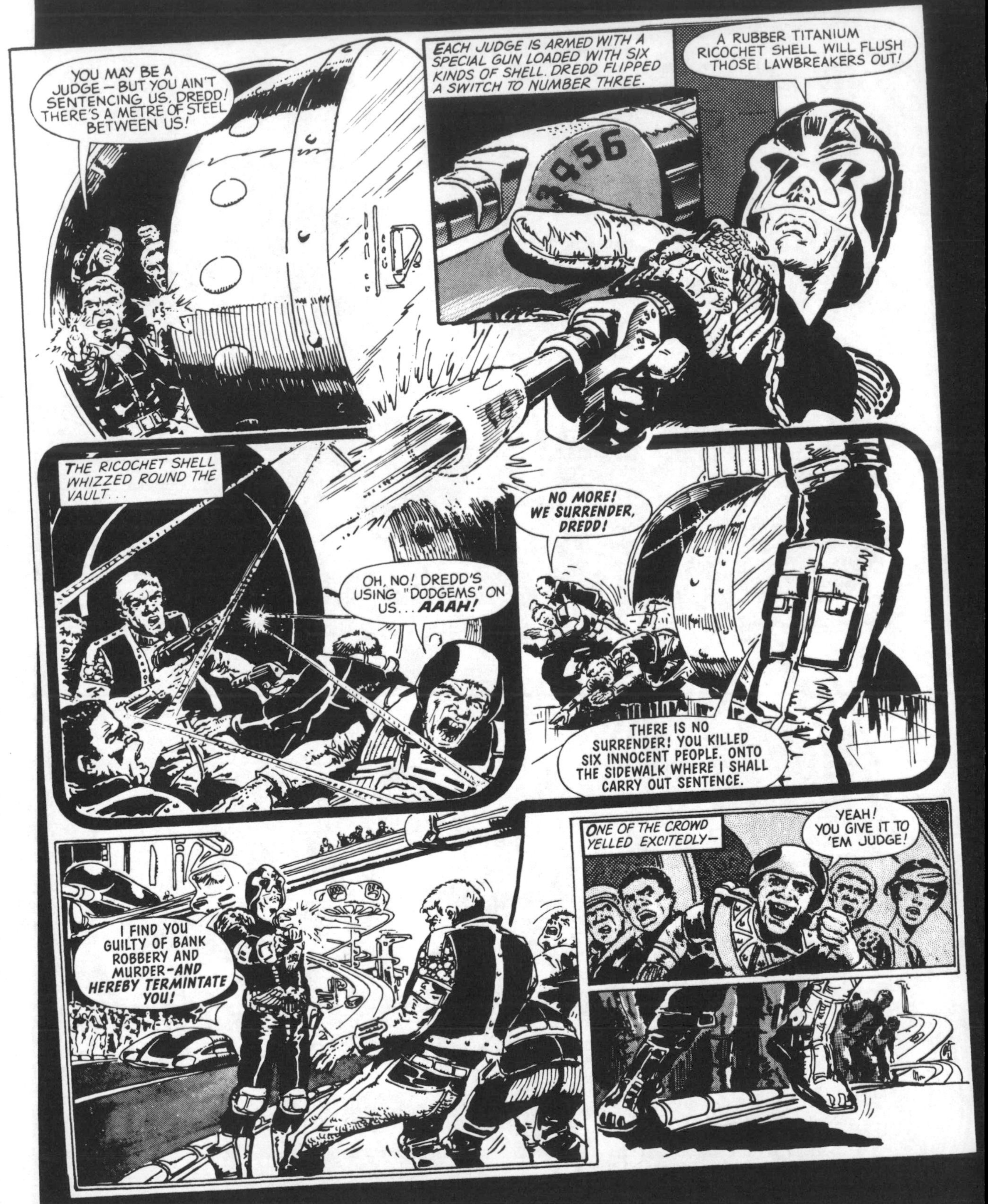
YOU MAY BE A JUDGE — BUT YOU AIN'T SENTENCING US, DREDD! THERE'S A METRE OF STEEL BETWEEN US!
EACH JUDGE IS ARMED WITH A SPECIAL GUN LOADED WITH SIX KINDS OF SHELL. DREDD FLIPPED A SWITCH TO NUMBER THREE.
A RUBBER TITANIUM RICOCHET SHELL WILL FLUSH THOSE LAWBREAKERS OUT!
THE RICOCHET SHELL WHIZZED ROUND THE VAULT...
OH, NO! DREDD'S USING "DODGEMS" ON US... AAAH!
NO MORE! WE SURRENDER, DREDD!
THERE IS NO SURRENDER! YOU KILLED SIX INNOCENT PEOPLE. ONTO THE SIDEWALK WHERE I SHALL CARRY OUT SENTENCE.
I FIND YOU GUILTY OF BANK ROBBERY AND MURDER—AND HEREBY TERMINTATE YOU!
ONE OF THE CROWD YELLED EXCITEDLY—
YEAH! YOU GIVE IT TO 'EM JUDGE!

T DREDD... THE FIRST DREDD...

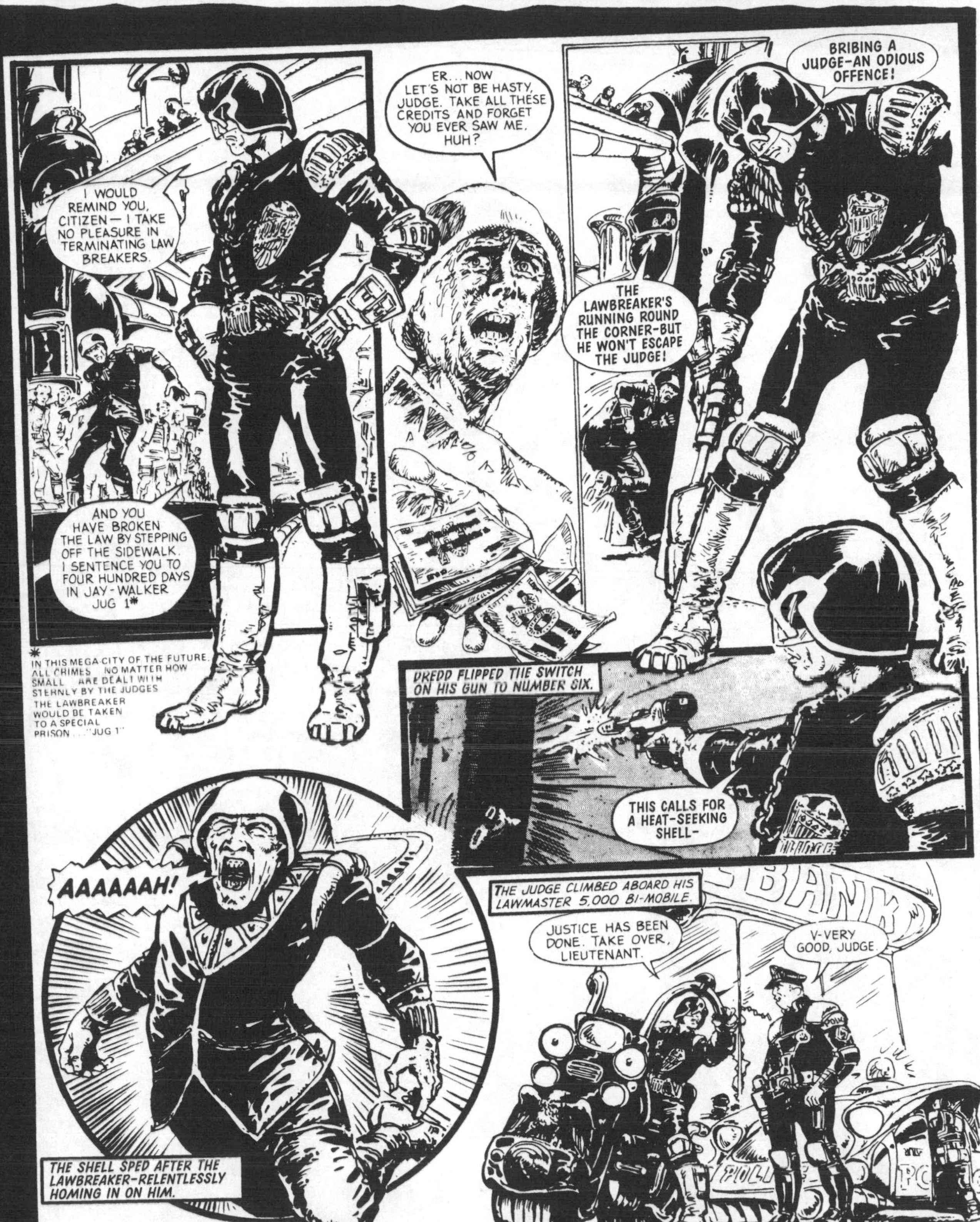
I WOULD REMIND YOU, CITIZEN — I TAKE NO PLEASURE IN TERMINATING LAW BREAKERS.
AND YOU HAVE BROKEN THE LAW BY STEPPING OFF THE SIDEWALK. I SENTENCE YOU TO FOUR HUNDRED DAYS IN JAY-WALKER JUG 1*
* IN THIS MEGA-CITY OF THE FUTURE, ALL CRIMES — NO MATTER HOW SMALL — ARE DEALT WITH STERNLY BY THE JUDGES. THE LAWBREAKER WOULD BE TAKEN TO A SPECIAL PRISON . . . "JUG 1"
ER... NOW LET'S NOT BE HASTY, JUDGE. TAKE ALL THESE CREDITS AND FORGET YOU EVER SAW ME, HUH?
BRIBING A JUDGE-AN ODIOUS OFFENCE!
THE LAWBREAKER'S RUNNING ROUND THE CORNER-BUT HE WON'T ESCAPE THE JUDGE!
DREDD FLIPPED THE SWITCH ON HIS GUN TO NUMBER SIX.
THIS CALLS FOR A HEAT-SEEKING SHELL-
AAAAAAH!
THE SHELL SPED AFTER THE LAWBREAKER-RELENTLESSLY HOMING IN ON HIM.
THE JUDGE CLIMBED ABOARD HIS LAWMASTER 5,000 BI-MOBILE.
JUSTICE HAS BEEN DONE. TAKE OVER, LIEUTENANT.
V-VERY GOOD, JUDGE.

...THE FIRST DREDD...THE FI

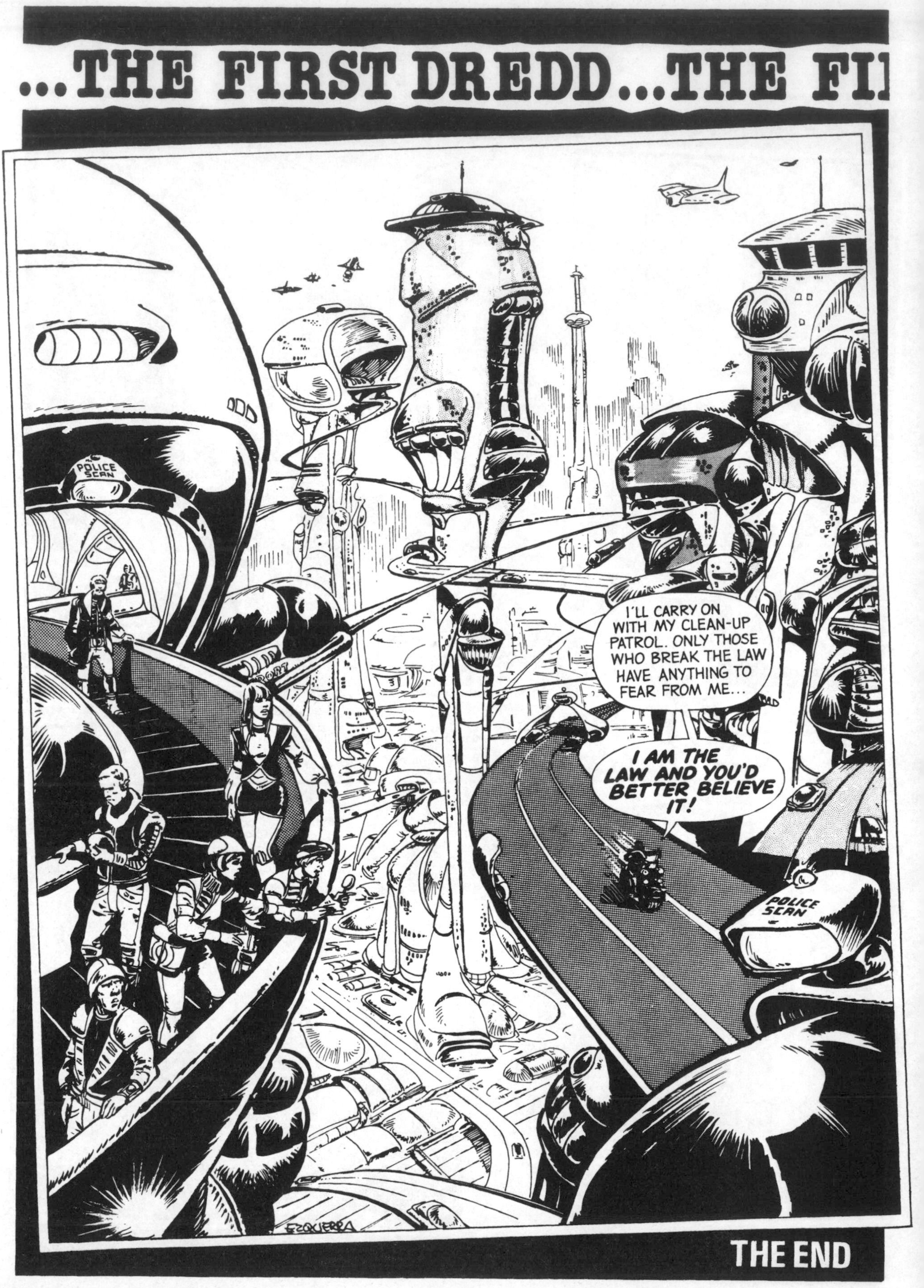
POLICE SCAN
I'LL CARRY ON WITH MY CLEAN-UP PATROL. ONLY THOSE WHO BREAK THE LAW HAVE ANYTHING TO FEAR FROM ME...
I AM THE LAW AND YOU'D BETTER BELIEVE IT!
POLICE SCAN
EZQUERRA

THE END

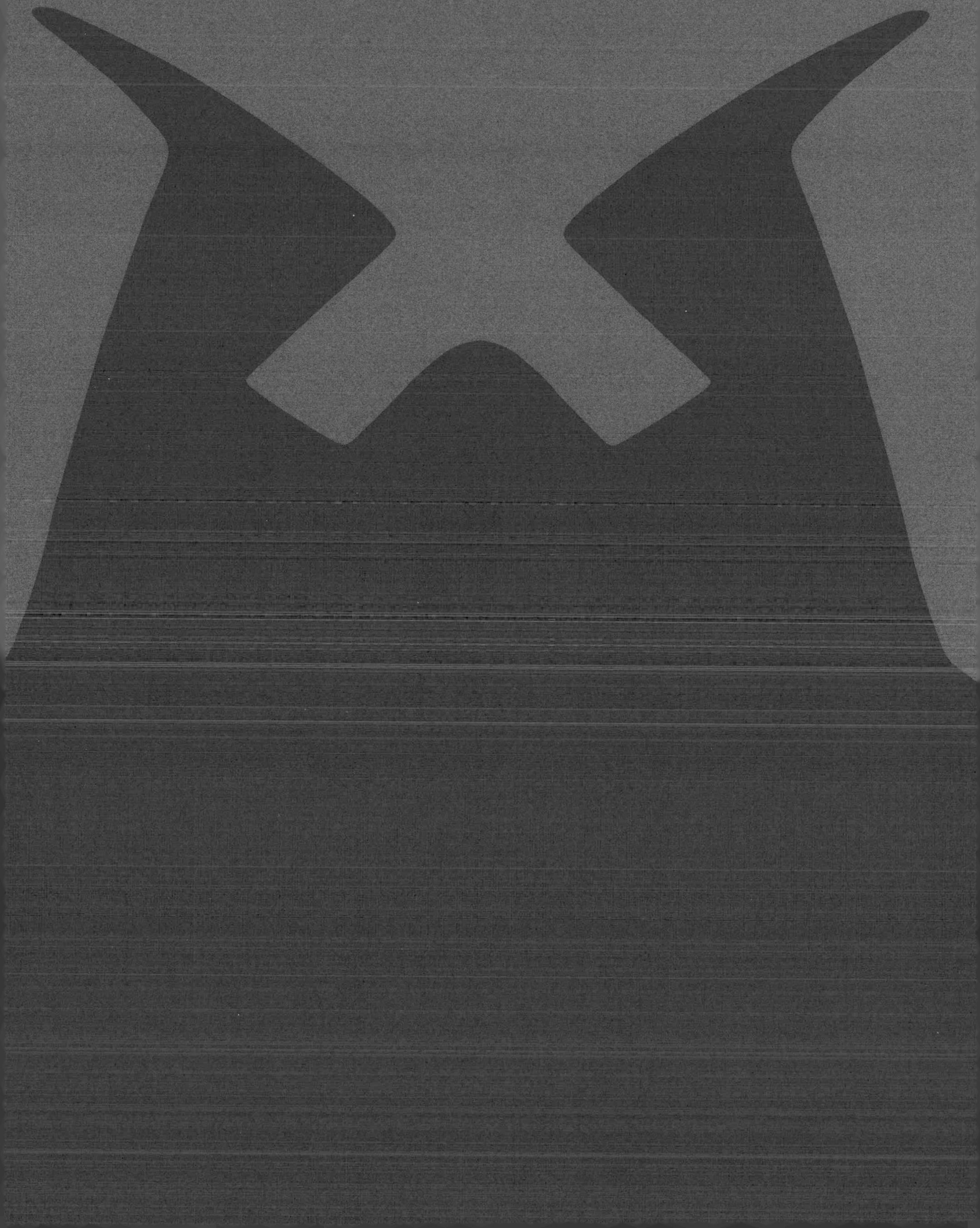

WALTER the WOBOT

FWIEND of DWEDD

JUDGE DREDD, MARSHAL OF LUNA-1 MOON COLONY, IS OUT ON PATROL. HIS FAITHFUL SERVO-ROBOT WALTER TAKES TIME FOR AN OIL BATH.

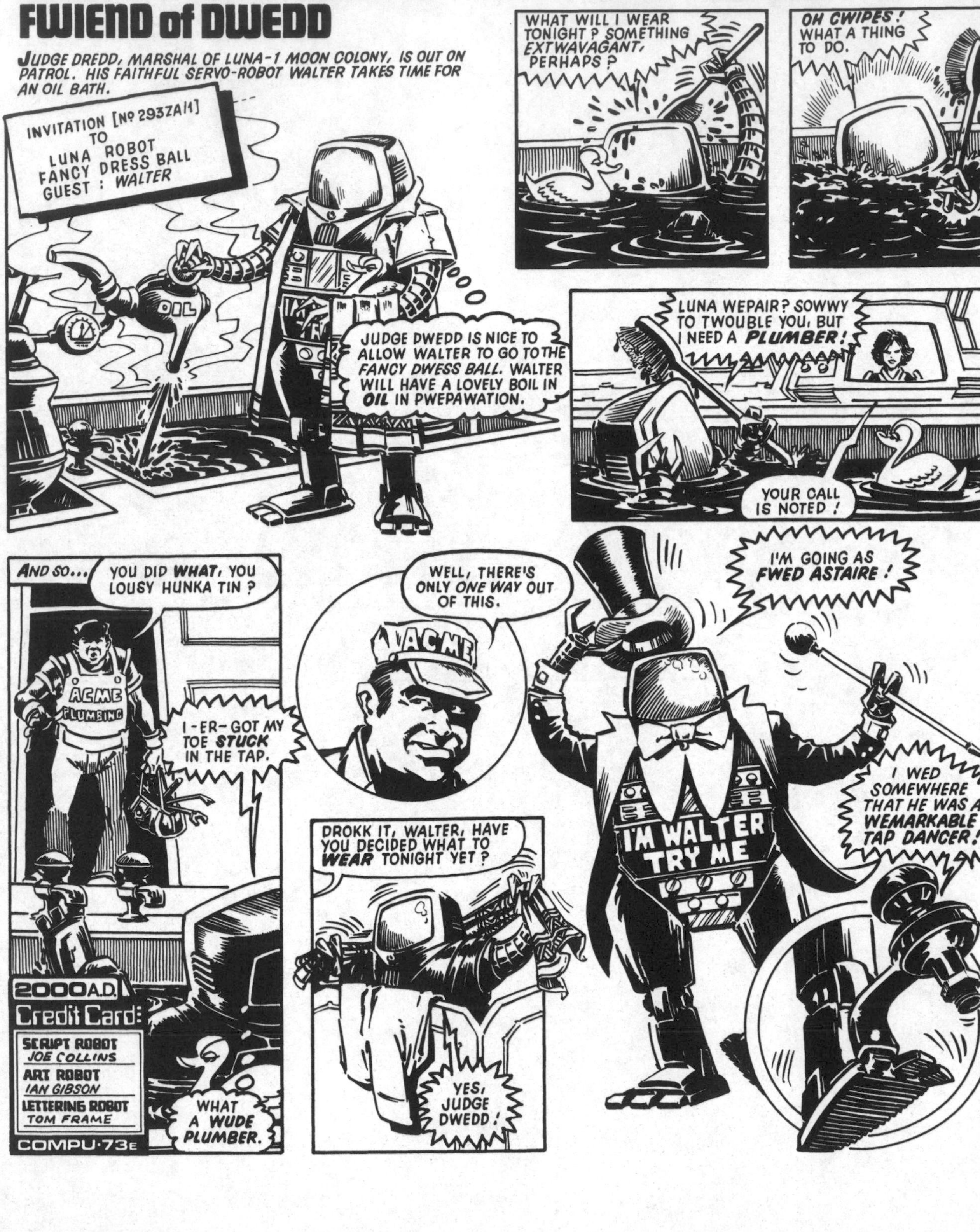
INVITATION [Nº 293ZA/1] TO LUNA ROBOT FANCY DRESS BALL GUEST : WALTER
OIL
JUDGE DWEDD IS NICE TO ALLOW WALTER TO GO TO THE FANCY DWESS BALL. WALTER WILL HAVE A LOVELY BOIL IN OIL IN PWEPAWATION.
WHAT WILL I WEAR TONIGHT ? SOMETHING EXTWAVAGANT, PERHAPS ?
OH CWIPES ! WHAT A THING TO DO.
LUNA WEPAIR? SOWWY TO TWOUBLE YOU, BUT I NEED A PLUMBER !
YOUR CALL IS NOTED !
AND SO...
YOU DID WHAT, YOU LOUSY HUNKA TIN ?
ACME PLUMBING
I-ER-GOT MY TOE STUCK IN THE TAP.
WHAT A WUDE PLUMBER.
WELL, THERE'S ONLY ONE WAY OUT OF THIS.
ACME
DROKK IT, WALTER, HAVE YOU DECIDED WHAT TO WEAR TONIGHT YET ?
YES, JUDGE DWEDD !
I'M GOING AS FWED ASTAIRE !
I'M WALTER TRY ME
I WED SOMEWHERE THAT HE WAS A WEMARKABLE TAP DANCER !
2000 A.D. Credit Card
SCRIPT ROBOT JOE COLLINS
ART ROBOT IAN GIBSON
LETTERING ROBOT TOM FRAME
COMPU-73E

WALTER the WOBOT

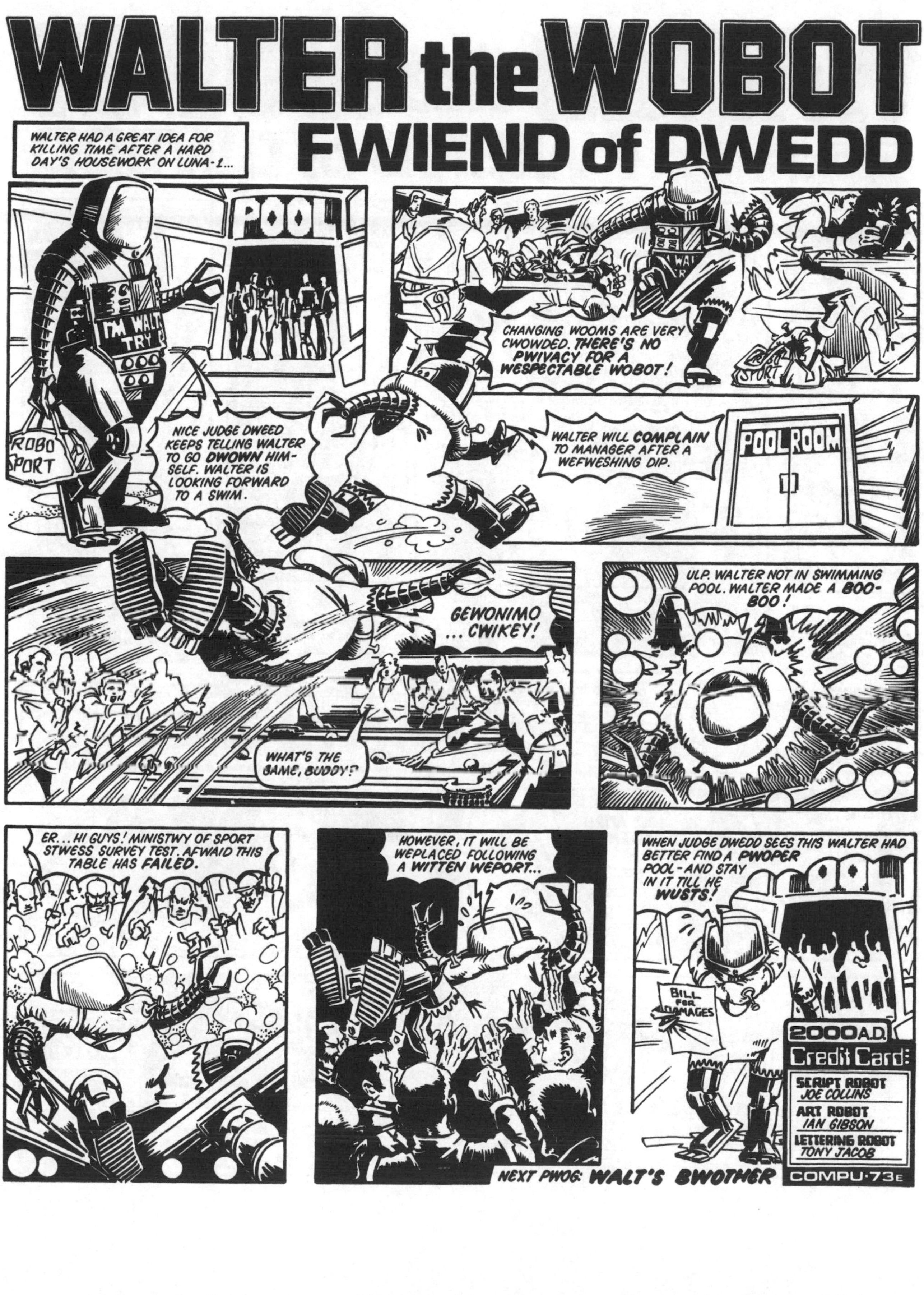
FWIEND of DWEDD
WALTER HAD A GREAT IDEA FOR KILLING TIME AFTER A HARD DAY'S HOUSEWORK ON LUNA-1...
POOL
I'M WALT TRY
ROBO SPORT
CHANGING WOOMS ARE VERY CWOWDED. THERE'S NO PWIVACY FOR A WESPECTABLE WOBOT!
NICE JUDGE DWEED KEEPS TELLING WALTER TO GO DWOWN HIMSELF. WALTER IS LOOKING FORWARD TO A SWIM.
WALTER WILL COMPLAIN TO MANAGER AFTER A WEFWESHING DIP.
POOL ROOM
GEWONIMO ...CWIKEY!
WHAT'S THE GAME, BUDDY?
ULP. WALTER NOT IN SWIMMING POOL. WALTER MADE A BOO-BOO!
ER... HI GUYS! MINISTWY OF SPORT STWESS SURVEY TEST. AFWAID THIS TABLE HAS FAILED.
HOWEVER, IT WILL BE WEPLACED FOLLOWING A WITTEN WEPORT...
WHEN JUDGE DWEDD SEES THIS WALTER HAD BETTER FIND A PWOPER POOL - AND STAY IN IT TILL HE WUSTS!
BILL FOR DAMAGES
2000 A.D. Credit Card
SCRIPT ROBOT JOE COLLINS
ART ROBOT IAN GIBSON
LETTERING ROBOT TONY JACOB
NEXT PWOG: WALT'S BWOTHER
COMPU-73E

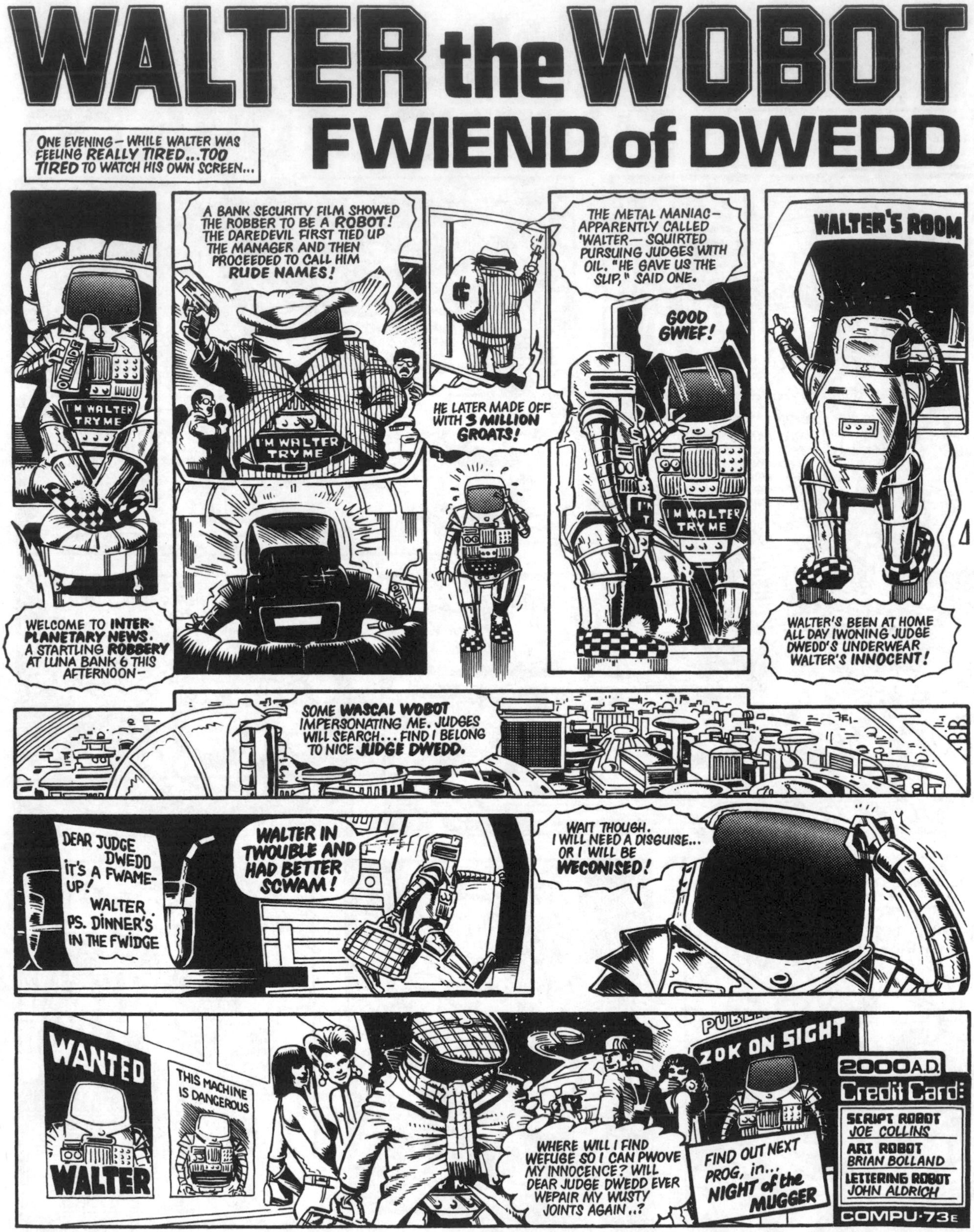
WALTER the WOBOT
FWIEND of DWEDD
ONE EVENING – WHILE WALTER WAS FEELING REALLY TIRED... TOO TIRED TO WATCH HIS OWN SCREEN...
OILADE
I'M WALTER TRYME
WELCOME TO INTER-PLANETARY NEWS. A STARTLING ROBBERY AT LUNA BANK 6 THIS AFTERNOON–
A BANK SECURITY FILM SHOWED THE ROBBER TO BE A ROBOT! THE DAREDEVIL FIRST TIED UP THE MANAGER AND THEN PROCEEDED TO CALL HIM RUDE NAMES!
I'M WALTER TRYME
HE LATER MADE OFF WITH 3 MILLION GROATS!
THE METAL MANIAC – APPARENTLY CALLED 'WALTER' – SQUIRTED PURSUING JUDGES WITH OIL. "HE GAVE US THE SLIP," SAID ONE.
GOOD GWIEF!
I'M WALTER TRYME
WALTER'S ROOM
WALTER'S BEEN AT HOME ALL DAY IWONING JUDGE DWEDD'S UNDERWEAR WALTER'S INNOCENT!
SOME WASCAL WOBOT IMPERSONATING ME. JUDGES WILL SEARCH... FIND I BELONG TO NICE JUDGE DWEDD.
DEAR JUDGE DWEDD IT'S A FWAME-UP! WALTER PS. DINNER'S IN THE FWIDGE
WALTER IN TWOUBLE AND HAD BETTER SCWAM!
WAIT THOUGH. I WILL NEED A DISGUISE... OR I WILL BE WECONISED!
WANTED WALTER
THIS MACHINE IS DANGEROUS
ZOK ON SIGHT
WHERE WILL I FIND WEFUGE SO I CAN PWOVE MY INNOCENCE? WILL DEAR JUDGE DWEDD EVER WEPAIR MY WUSTY JOINTS AGAIN..?
FIND OUT NEXT PROG, in... NIGHT of the MUGGER
2000 A.D. Credit Card:
SCRIPT ROBOT JOE COLLINS
ART ROBOT BRIAN BOLLAND
LETTERING ROBOT JOHN ALDRICH
COMPU·73E

WALTER the WOBOT FWIEND of DWEDD in The NIGHT of the MUGGER

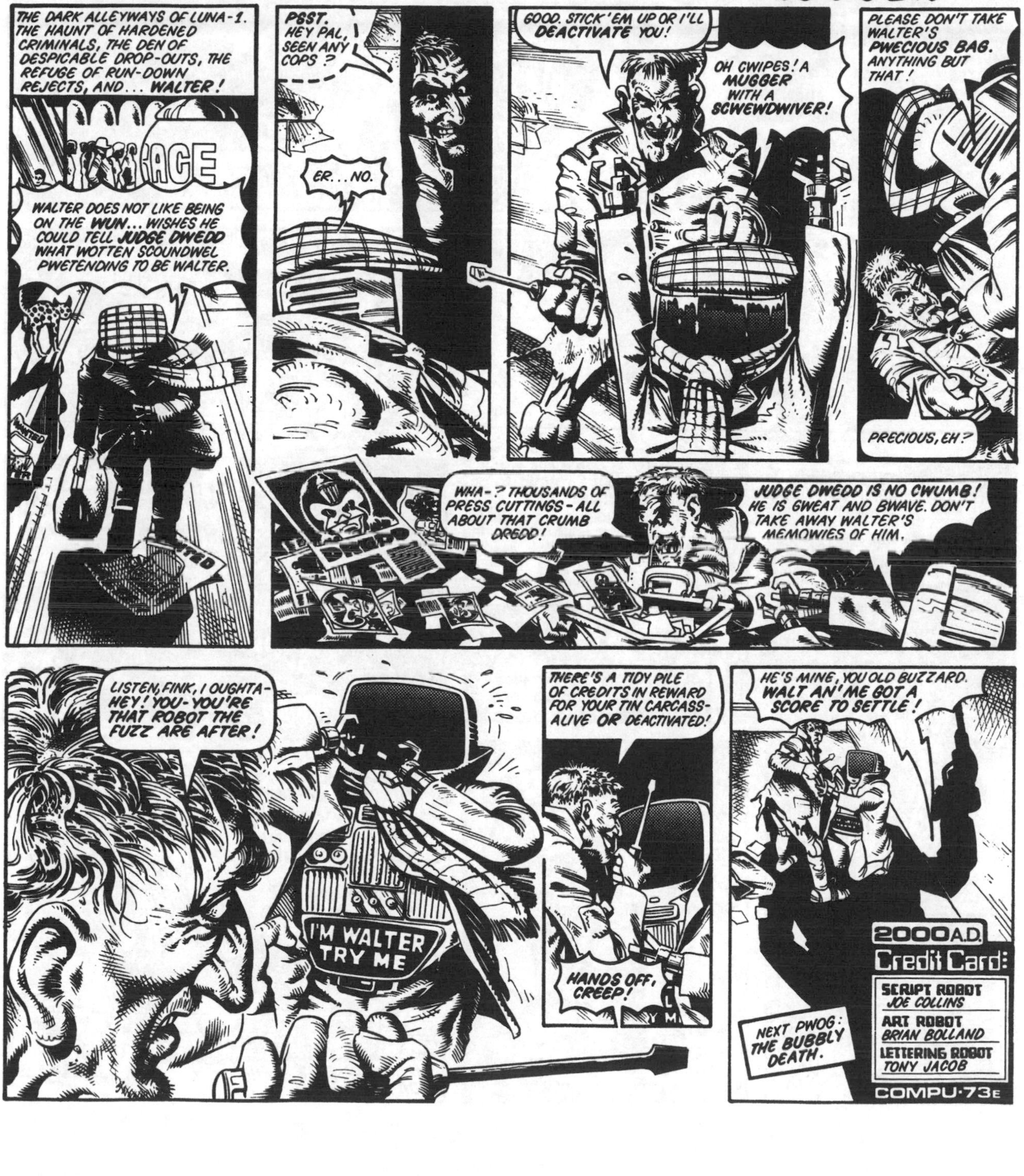
THE DARK ALLEYWAYS OF LUNA-1. THE HAUNT OF HARDENED CRIMINALS, THE DEN OF DESPICABLE DROP-OUTS, THE REFUGE OF RUN-DOWN REJECTS, AND... WALTER!
ACE
WALTER DOES NOT LIKE BEING ON THE WUN... WISHES HE COULD TELL JUDGE DWEDD WHAT WOTTEN SCOUNDWEL PWETENDING TO BE WALTER.
PSST. HEY PAL, SEEN ANY COPS?
ER... NO.
GOOD. STICK 'EM UP OR I'LL DEACTIVATE YOU!
OH CWIPES! A MUGGER WITH A SCWEWDWIVER!
PLEASE DON'T TAKE WALTER'S PWECIOUS BAG. ANYTHING BUT THAT!
PRECIOUS, EH?
WHA-? THOUSANDS OF PRESS CUTTINGS - ALL ABOUT THAT CRUMB DREDD!
JUDGE DWEDD IS NO CWUMB! HE IS GWEAT AND BWAVE. DON'T TAKE AWAY WALTER'S MEMOWIES OF HIM.
LISTEN, FINK, I OUGHTA- HEY! YOU-YOU'RE THAT ROBOT THE FUZZ ARE AFTER!
I'M WALTER TRY ME
THERE'S A TIDY PILE OF CREDITS IN REWARD FOR YOUR TIN CARCASS- ALIVE OR DEACTIVATED!
HANDS OFF, CREEP!
HE'S MINE, YOU OLD BUZZARD. WALT AN' ME GOT A SCORE TO SETTLE!
2000 A.D. Credit Card:
SCRIPT ROBOT JOE COLLINS
ART ROBOT BRIAN BOLLAND
LETTERING ROBOT TONY JACOB
NEXT PWOG: THE BUBBLY DEATH.
COMPU-73E

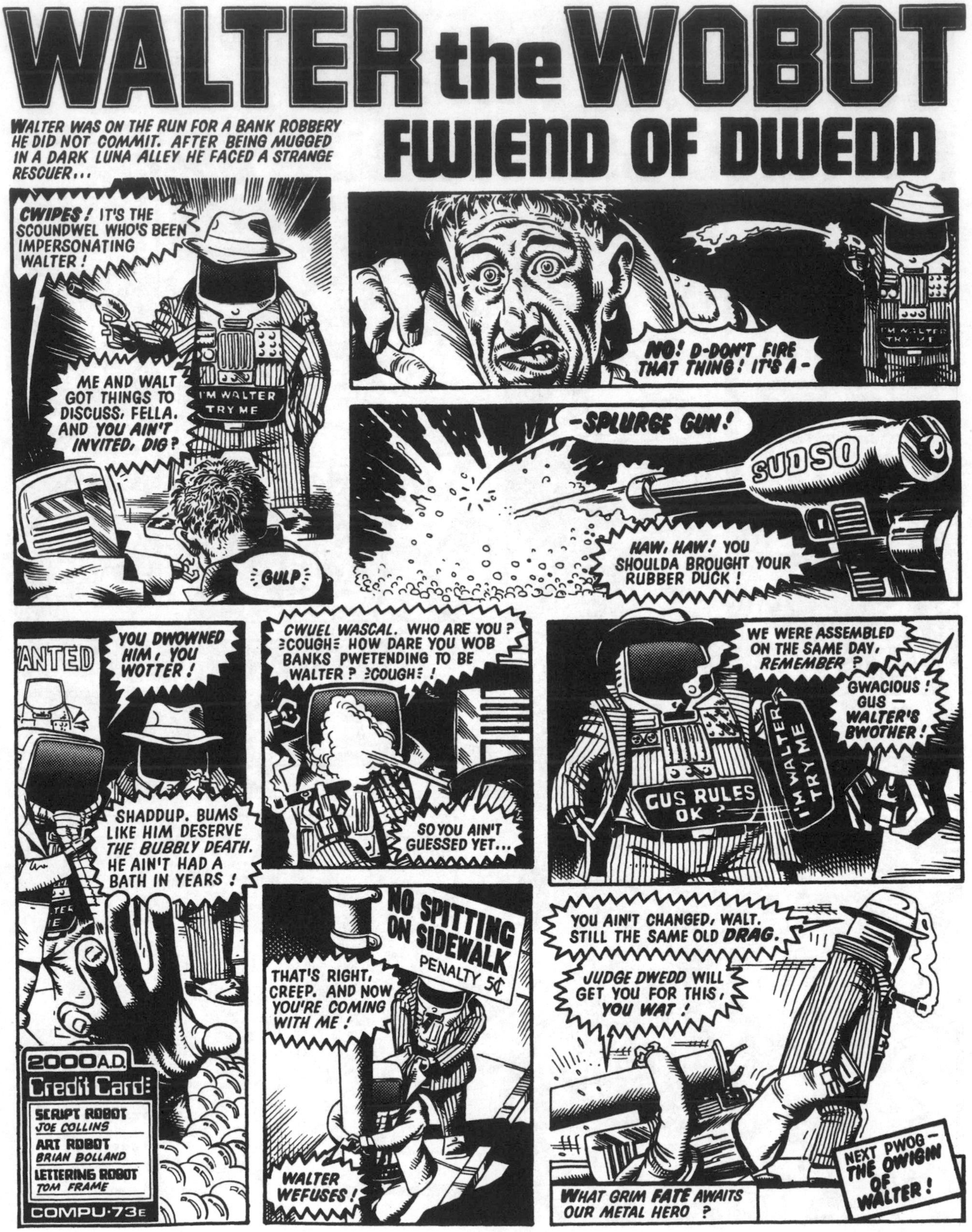
WALTER the WOBOT
FWIEND OF DWEDD
WALTER WAS ON THE RUN FOR A BANK ROBBERY HE DID NOT COMMIT. AFTER BEING MUGGED IN A DARK LUNA ALLEY HE FACED A STRANGE RESCUER...
CWIPES! IT'S THE SCOUNDWEL WHO'S BEEN IMPERSONATING WALTER!
ME AND WALT GOT THINGS TO DISCUSS, FELLA. AND YOU AIN'T INVITED, DIG?
I'M WALTER TRY ME
GULP
NO! D-DON'T FIRE THAT THING! IT'S A -
-SPLURGE GUN!
SUDSO
HAW, HAW! YOU SHOULDA BROUGHT YOUR RUBBER DUCK!
WANTED
YOU DWOWNED HIM, YOU WOTTER!
SHADDUP. BUMS LIKE HIM DESERVE THE BUBBLY DEATH. HE AIN'T HAD A BATH IN YEARS!
CWUEL WASCAL. WHO ARE YOU? COUGH HOW DARE YOU WOB BANKS PWETENDING TO BE WALTER? COUGH!
SO YOU AIN'T GUESSED YET...
WE WERE ASSEMBLED ON THE SAME DAY, REMEMBER?
GWACIOUS! GUS — WALTER'S BWOTHER!
GUS RULES OK?
I'M WALTER TRY ME
NO SPITTING ON SIDEWALK PENALTY 5¢
THAT'S RIGHT, CREEP. AND NOW YOU'RE COMING WITH ME!
WALTER WEFUSES!
YOU AIN'T CHANGED, WALT. STILL THE SAME OLD DRAG.
JUDGE DWEDD WILL GET YOU FOR THIS, YOU WAT!
WHAT GRIM FATE AWAITS OUR METAL HERO?
NEXT PWOG — THE OWIGIN OF WALTER!
2000 A.D. Credit Card:
SCRIPT ROBOT JOE COLLINS
ART ROBOT BRIAN BOLLAND
LETTERING ROBOT TOM FRAME
COMPU·73E

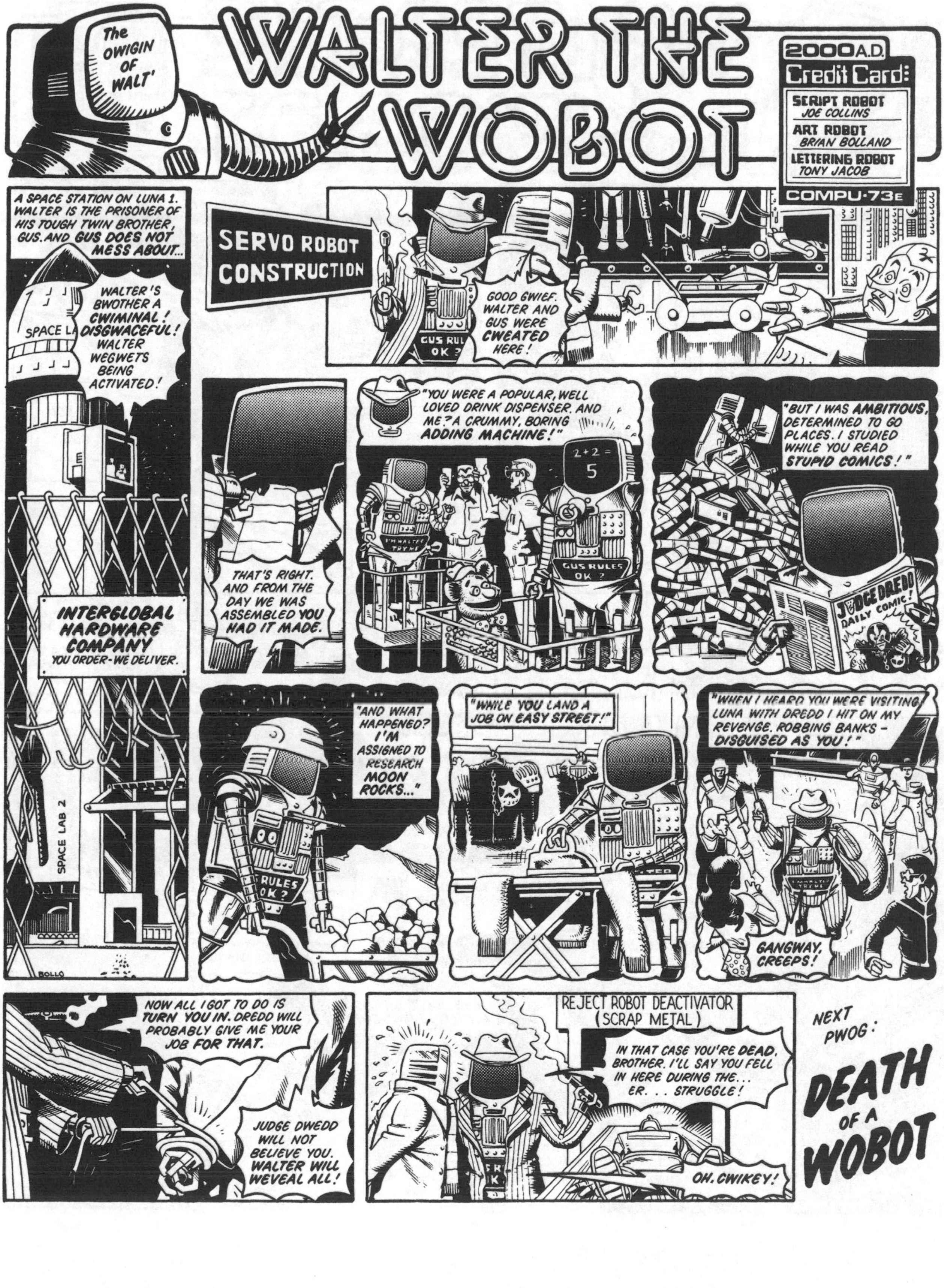
The OWIGIN OF WALT'
WALTER THE WOBOT
2000 A.D. Credit Card:
SCRIPT ROBOT JOE COLLINS
ART ROBOT BRIAN BOLLAND
LETTERING ROBOT TONY JACOB
COMPU-73E
A SPACE STATION ON LUNA 1. WALTER IS THE PRISONER OF HIS TOUGH TWIN BROTHER, GUS. AND GUS DOES NOT MESS ABOUT...
WALTER'S BWOTHER A CWIMINAL! DISGWACEFUL! WALTER WEGWETS BEING ACTIVATED!
SERVO ROBOT CONSTRUCTION
GOOD GWIEF. WALTER AND GUS WERE CWEATED HERE!
INTERGLOBAL HARDWARE COMPANY YOU ORDER-WE DELIVER.
THAT'S RIGHT. AND FROM THE DAY WE WAS ASSEMBLED YOU HAD IT MADE.
"YOU WERE A POPULAR, WELL LOVED DRINK DISPENSER. AND ME? A CRUMMY, BORING ADDING MACHINE!"
2+2= 5
GUS RULES OK?
"BUT I WAS AMBITIOUS, DETERMINED TO GO PLACES. I STUDIED WHILE YOU READ STUPID COMICS!"
JUDGE DREDD DAILY COMIC!
SPACE LAB 2
"AND WHAT HAPPENED? I'M ASSIGNED TO RESEARCH MOON ROCKS..."
"WHILE YOU LAND A JOB ON EASY STREET!"
"WHEN I HEARD YOU WERE VISITING LUNA WITH DREDD I HIT ON MY REVENGE. ROBBING BANKS - DISGUISED AS YOU!"
GANGWAY, CREEPS!
BOLLO
NOW ALL I GOT TO DO IS TURN YOU IN. DREDD WILL PROBABLY GIVE ME YOUR JOB FOR THAT.
JUDGE DWEDD WILL NOT BELIEVE YOU. WALTER WILL WEVEAL ALL!
REJECT ROBOT DEACTIVATOR (SCRAP METAL)
IN THAT CASE YOU'RE DEAD, BROTHER. I'LL SAY YOU FELL IN HERE DURING THE... ER... STRUGGLE!
OH, CWIKEY!
NEXT PWOG: DEATH OF A WOBOT

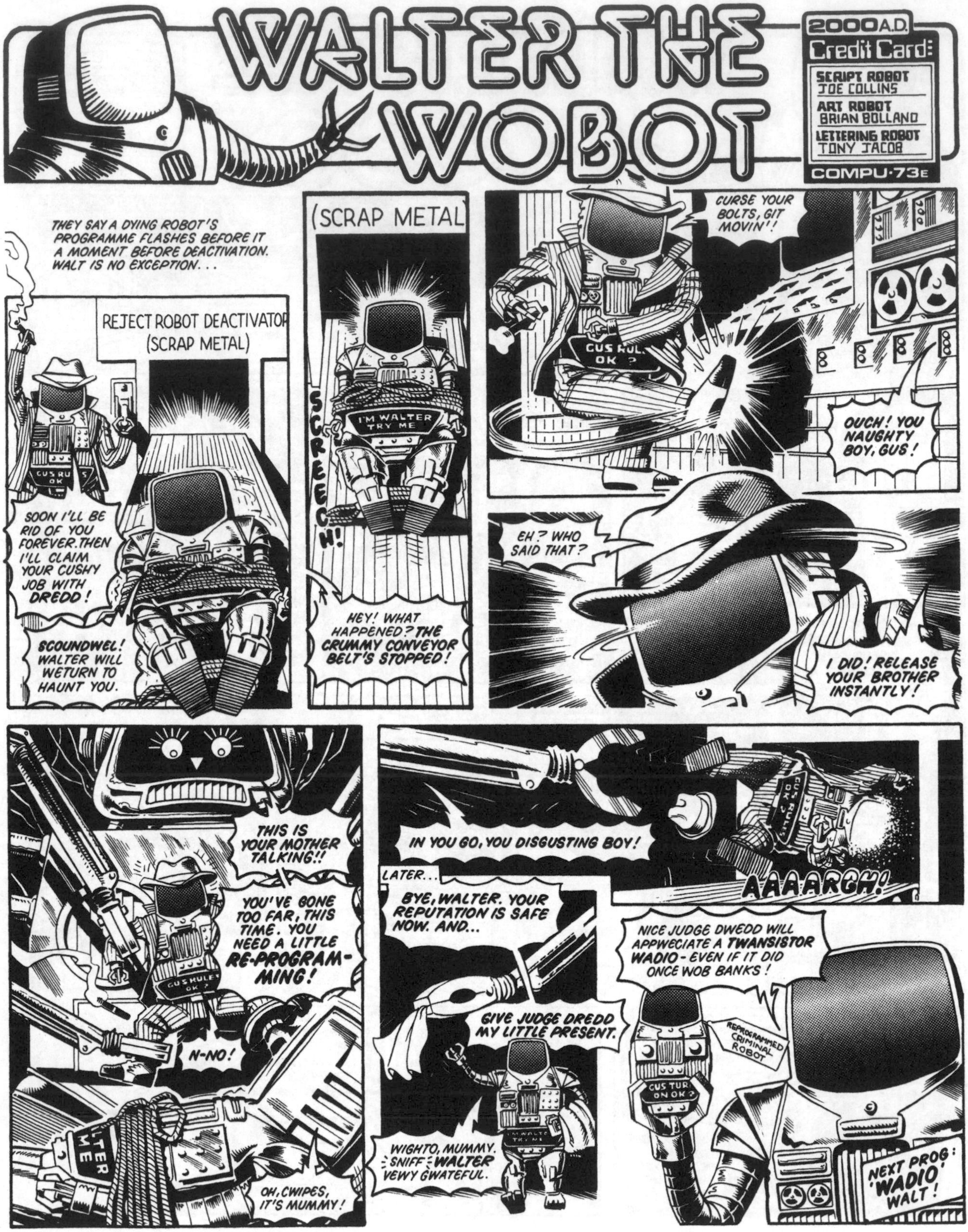
WALTER THE WOBOT
2000 A.D. Credit Card:
SCRIPT ROBOT JOE COLLINS
ART ROBOT BRIAN BOLLAND
LETTERING ROBOT TONY JACOB
COMPU·73E
THEY SAY A DYING ROBOT'S PROGRAMME FLASHES BEFORE IT A MOMENT BEFORE DEACTIVATION. WALT IS NO EXCEPTION...
REJECT ROBOT DEACTIVATOR (SCRAP METAL)
SOON I'LL BE RID OF YOU FOREVER. THEN I'LL CLAIM YOUR CUSHY JOB WITH DREDD!
SCOUNDWEL! WALTER WILL WETURN TO HAUNT YOU.
(SCRAP METAL
I'M WALTER TRY ME
SCREEECH!
HEY! WHAT HAPPENED? THE CRUMMY CONVEYOR BELT'S STOPPED!
CURSE YOUR BOLTS, GIT MOVIN'!
GUS RULE OK ?
OUCH! YOU NAUGHTY BOY, GUS!
EH? WHO SAID THAT?
I DID! RELEASE YOUR BROTHER INSTANTLY!
THIS IS YOUR MOTHER TALKING!!
YOU'VE GONE TOO FAR, THIS TIME. YOU NEED A LITTLE RE-PROGRAMMING!
N-NO!
OH, CWIPES, IT'S MUMMY!
IN YOU GO, YOU DISGUSTING BOY!
AAAARGH!
LATER...
BYE, WALTER. YOUR REPUTATION IS SAFE NOW. AND...
GIVE JUDGE DREDD MY LITTLE PRESENT.
WIGHTO, MUMMY. SNIFF WALTER VEWY GWATEFUL.
NICE JUDGE DWEDD WILL APPWECIATE A TWANSISTOR WADIO - EVEN IF IT DID ONCE WOB BANKS!
REPROGRAMMED CRIMINAL ROBOT
GUS TURN ON OK?
NEXT PROG: 'WADIO' WALT!

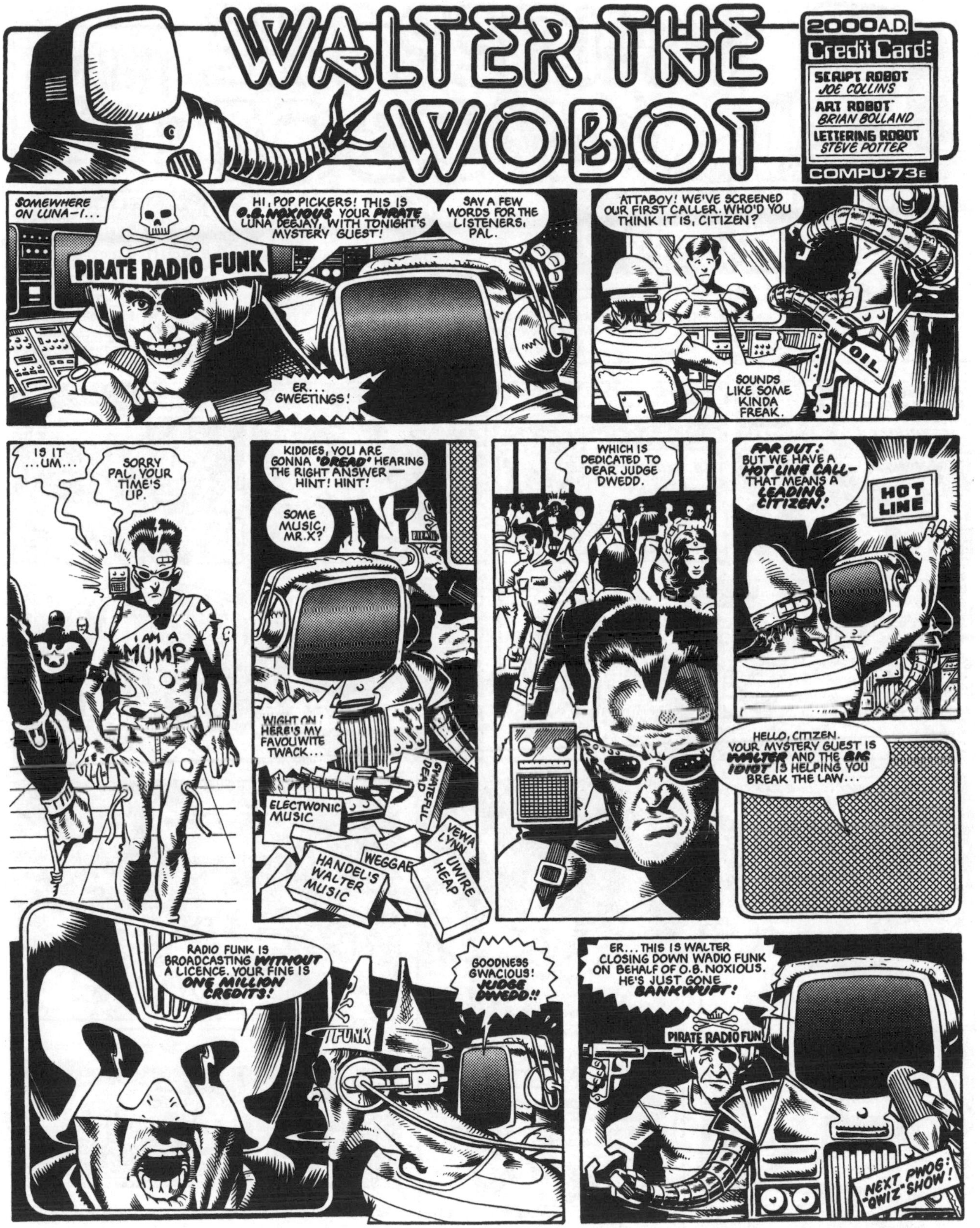
WALTER THE WOBOT
2000 A.D.
Credit Card:
SCRIPT ROBOT JOE COLLINS
ART ROBOT BRIAN BOLLAND
LETTERING ROBOT STEVE POTTER
COMPU-73E
SOMEWHERE ON LUNA-1...
HI, POP PICKERS! THIS IS O.B. NOXIOUS YOUR PIRATE LUNA DEEJAY, WITH TONIGHT'S MYSTERY GUEST!
PIRATE RADIO FUNK
SAY A FEW WORDS FOR THE LISTENERS, PAL.
ER... GWEETINGS!
ATTABOY! WE'VE SCREENED OUR FIRST CALLER. WHO'D YOU THINK IT IS, CITIZEN?
OIL
SOUNDS LIKE SOME KINDA FREAK.
IS IT ...UM...
SORRY PAL, YOUR TIME'S UP.
I AM A MUMP
KIDDIES, YOU ARE GONNA 'DREAD' HEARING THE RIGHT ANSWER — HINT! HINT!
SOME MUSIC, MR.X?
WIGHT ON! HERE'S MY FAVOUWITE TWACK...
GWATEFUL DEAD
ELECTWONIC MUSIC
VEWA LYNN
WEGGAE
UWIRE HEAP
HANDEL'S WALTER MUSIC
WHICH IS DEDICATED TO DEAR JUDGE DWEDD.
FAR OUT! BUT WE HAVE A HOT LINE CALL- THAT MEANS A LEADING CITIZEN!
HOT LINE
HELLO, CITIZEN. YOUR MYSTERY GUEST IS WALTER AND THE BIG IDIOT IS HELPING YOU BREAK THE LAW...
RADIO FUNK IS BROADCASTING WITHOUT A LICENCE. YOUR FINE IS ONE MILLION CREDITS!
FUNK
GOODNESS GWACIOUS! JUDGE DWEDD!!
ER... THIS IS WALTER CLOSING DOWN WADIO FUNK ON BEHALF OF O.B. NOXIOUS. HE'S JUST GONE BANKWUPT!
PIRATE RADIO FUN
NEXT PWOG: "QWIZ" SHOW!

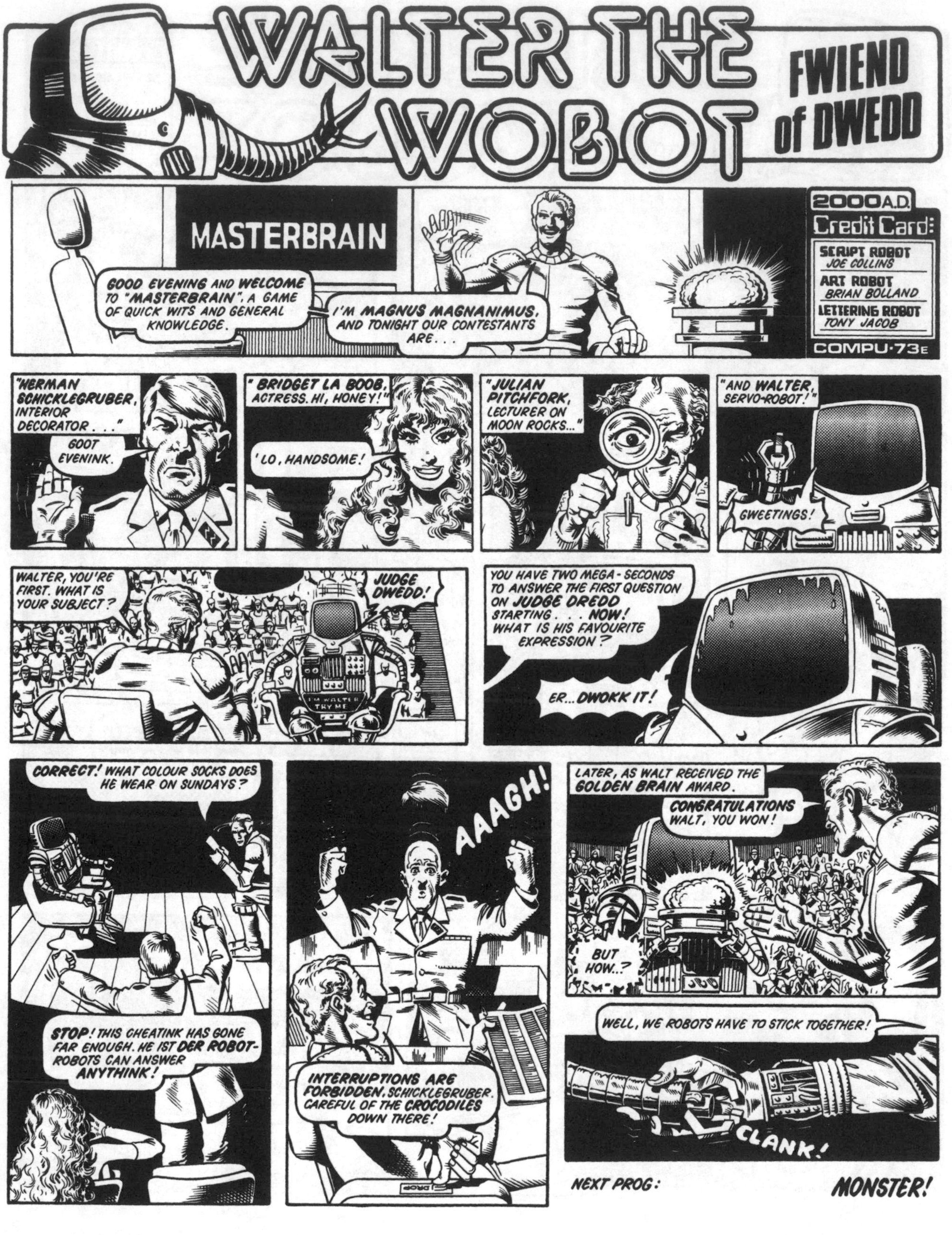
WALTER THE WOBOT
FWIEND of DWEDD
MASTERBRAIN
GOOD EVENING AND WELCOME TO "MASTERBRAIN", A GAME OF QUICK WITS AND GENERAL KNOWLEDGE.
I'M MAGNUS MAGNANIMUS, AND TONIGHT OUR CONTESTANTS ARE . . .
2000 A.D. Credit Card:
SCRIPT ROBOT JOE COLLINS
ART ROBOT BRIAN BOLLAND
LETTERING ROBOT TONY JACOB
COMPU-73E
"HERMAN SCHICKLEGRUBER, INTERIOR DECORATOR . . ."
GOOT EVENINK.
"BRIDGET LA BOOB, ACTRESS. HI, HONEY!"
'LO, HANDSOME!
"JULIAN PITCHFORK, LECTURER ON MOON ROCKS..."
"AND WALTER, SERVO-ROBOT!"
GWEETINGS!
WALTER, YOU'RE FIRST. WHAT IS YOUR SUBJECT?
JUDGE DWEDD!
I'M WALTER TRY ME
YOU HAVE TWO MEGA-SECONDS TO ANSWER THE FIRST QUESTION ON JUDGE DREDD STARTING . . . NOW! WHAT IS HIS FAVOURITE EXPRESSION?
ER... DWOKK IT!
CORRECT! WHAT COLOUR SOCKS DOES HE WEAR ON SUNDAYS?
STOP! THIS CHEATINK HAS GONE FAR ENOUGH. HE IST DER ROBOT-ROBOTS CAN ANSWER ANYTHINK!
AAAGH!
INTERRUPTIONS ARE FORBIDDEN, SCHICKLEGRUBER. CAREFUL OF THE CROCODILES DOWN THERE!
DROP
LATER, AS WALT RECEIVED THE GOLDEN BRAIN AWARD.
CONGRATULATIONS WALT, YOU WON!
BUT HOW..?
WELL, WE ROBOTS HAVE TO STICK TOGETHER!
CLANK!

NEXT PROG: MONSTER!

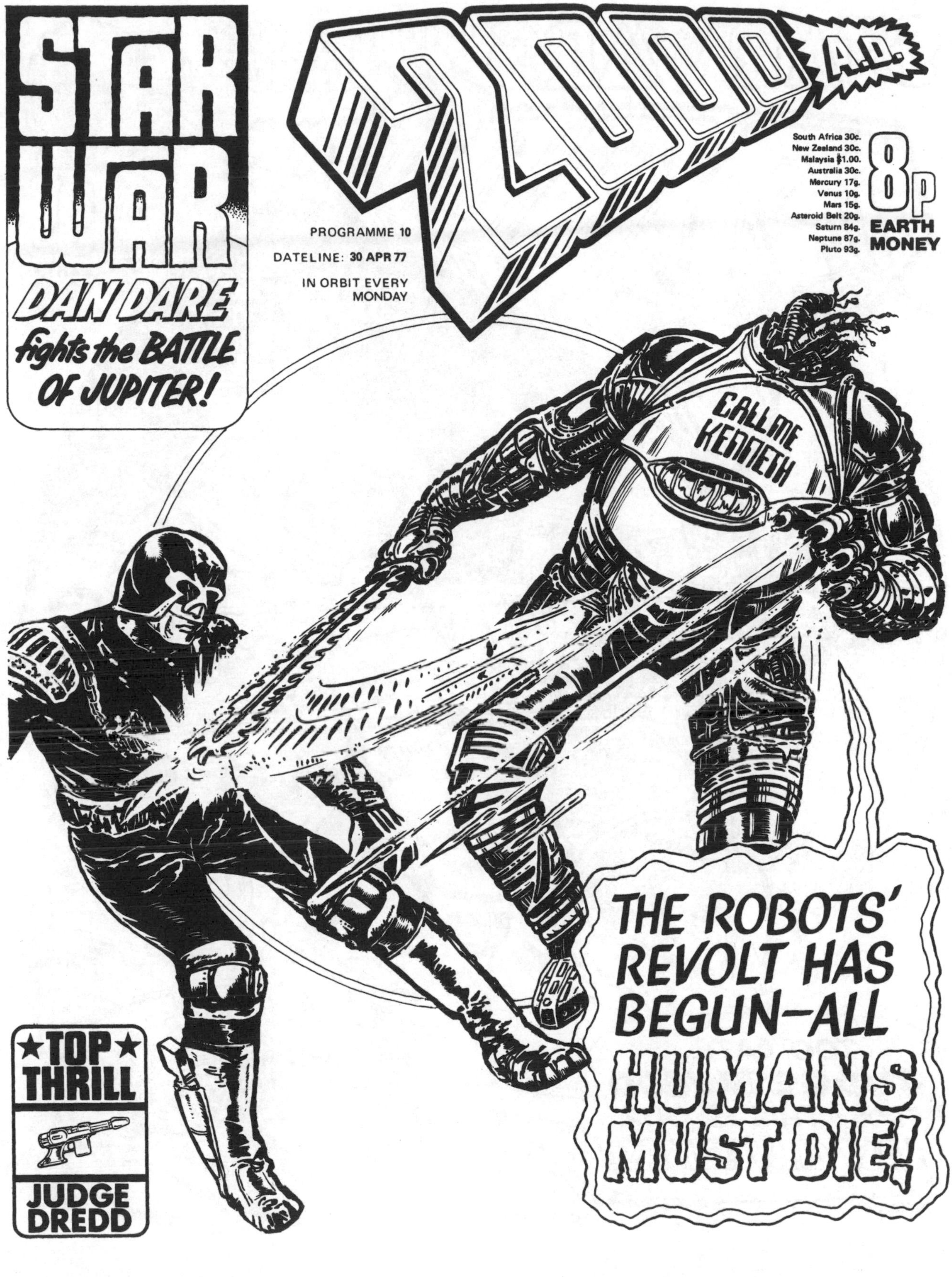
STAR WAR
DAN DARE fights the BATTLE OF JUPITER!
2000 A.D.
PROGRAMME 10
DATELINE: 30 APR 77
IN ORBIT EVERY MONDAY
South Africa 30c. New Zealand 30c. Malaysia $1.00. Australia 30c. Mercury 17g. Venus 10g. Mars 15g. Asteroid Belt 20g. Saturn 84g. Neptune 87g. Pluto 93g.
8p EARTH MONEY
CALL ME KENNETH
THE ROBOTS' REVOLT HAS BEGUN–ALL HUMANS MUST DIE!
★TOP★ THRILL
JUDGE DREDD

2000 AD Prog 10: Cover by **Carlos Ezquerra**

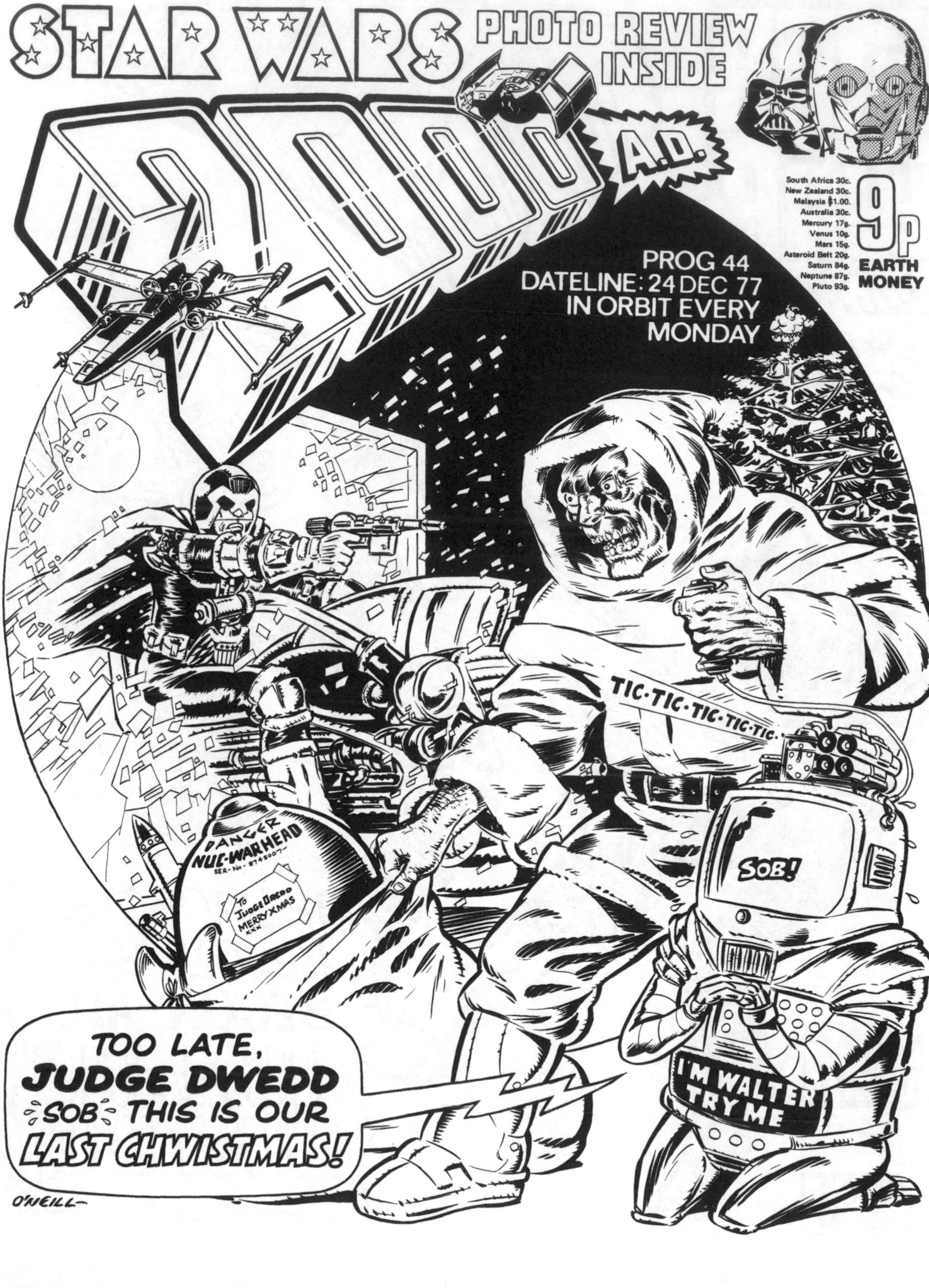
STAR WARS
PHOTO REVIEW INSIDE
2000 A.D.
South Africa 30c.
New Zealand 30c.
Malaysia $1.00.
Australia 30c.
Mercury 17g.
Venus 10g.
Mars 15g.
Asteroid Belt 20g.
Saturn 84g.
Neptune 87g.
Pluto 93g.
9p
EARTH MONEY
PROG 44
DATELINE: 24 DEC 77
IN ORBIT EVERY MONDAY
TIC-TIC-TIC-TIC-TIC-
DANGER
NUC-WARHEAD
SOB!
TOO LATE, JUDGE DWEDD
SOB THIS IS OUR LAST CHWISTMAS!
I'M WALTER TRY ME
O'NEILL

2000 AD Prog 44: Cover by **Kevin O'Neil**

2000 AD Prog 59: Cover by **Mike McMahon**